THE REPUBLIC

By

Plato

Translated by Benjamin Jowett

THE REPUBLIC

Contents

INTRODUCTION AND ANALYSIS.

The Republic of Plato is the longest of his works with the exception of the Laws, and is certainly the greatest of them. There are nearer approaches to modern metaphysics in the Philebus and in the Sophist; the Politicus or Statesman is more ideal; the form and institutions of the State are more clearly drawn out in the Laws; as works of art, the Symposium and the Protagoras are of higher excellence. But no other Dialogue of Plato has the same largeness of view and the same perfection of style; no other shows an equal knowledge of the world, or contains more of those thoughts which are new as well as old, and not of one age only but of all. Nowhere in Plato is there a deeper irony or a greater wealth of humour or imagery, or more dramatic power. Nor in any other of his writings is the attempt made to interweave life and speculation, or to connect politics with philosophy. The Republic is the centre around which the other Dialogues may be grouped; here philosophy reaches the highest point (cp, especially in Books V, VI, VII) to which ancient thinkers ever attained. Plato among the Greeks, like Bacon among the moderns, was the first who conceived a method of knowledge, although neither of them always distinguished the bare outline or form from the substance of truth; and both of them had to be content with an abstraction of science which was not yet realized. He was the greatest metaphysical genius whom the world has seen; and in him, more than in any other ancient thinker, the germs of future knowledge are contained. The sciences of logic and psychology, which have supplied so many instruments of thought to after-ages, are based upon the analyses of Socrates and Plato. The principles of definition, the law of contradiction, the fallacy of arguing in a circle, the distinction between the essence and accidents of a thing or notion, between means and ends, between causes and conditions; also the division of the mind into the rational, concupiscent, and irascible elements, or of pleasures and desires into necessary and unnecessary – these and other great forms of thought are all of them to be found in the Republic, and were probably first invented by Plato. The greatest of all logical truths, and the one of which writers on philosophy are most apt to lose sight, the difference between words and things, has been most strenuously insisted on by him (cp. Rep.; Polit.; Cratyl), although he has not always avoided the confusion of them in his own writings (e.g. Rep.). But he does not bind up truth in logical formulae, – logic is still veiled in metaphysics; and the science which he imagines to 'contemplate all truth and all existence' is very unlike the doctrine of the syllogism which Aristotle claims to have discovered (Soph. Elenchi).

Neither must we forget that the Republic is but the third part of a still larger design which was to have included an ideal history of Athens, as well as a political and physical philosophy. The fragment of the Critias has given birth to a world-famous fiction, second only in importance to the tale of Troy and the legend of Arthur; and is said as a fact to have inspired some of the early navigators of the sixteenth century. This mythical tale, of which the subject was a history of the wars of the Athenians against the Island of Atlantis, is supposed to be founded upon an unfinished poem of Solon, to which it would have stood in the same relation as the writings of the logographers to the poems of Homer. It would have told of a struggle for Liberty (cp. Tim.), intended to represent the conflict of Persia and Hellas. We may judge from the noble commencement of the Timaeus, from the fragment of the Critias itself, and from the third book of the Laws, in what manner Plato would have treated this high argument. We can only guess why the great design was abandoned; perhaps because Plato became sensible of some incongruity in a fictitious history, or because he had lost his interest in it, or because advancing years forbade the completion of it; and we may please ourselves with the fancy that had this imaginary narrative ever been finished, we should have found Plato himself sympathising with the struggle for Hellenic independence (cp. Laws), singing a hymn of triumph over Marathon and Salamis, perhaps making the reflection of Herodotus where he contemplates the growth of the Athenian empire – 'How brave a thing is freedom of speech, which has made the Athenians so far exceed every other state of Hellas in greatness!' or, more probably, attributing the victory to the ancient good order of Athens and to the favor of Apollo and Athene (cp. Introd. to Critias).

Again, Plato may be regarded as the 'captain' ('arhchegoz') or leader of a goodly band of followers; for in the Republic is to be found the original of Cicero's De Republica, of St. Augustine's City of God, of the Utopia of Sir Thomas More, and of the numerous other imaginary States which are framed upon the same model. The extent to which Aristotle or the Aristotelian school were indebted to him in the Politics has been little recognised, and the recognition is the more necessary because it is not made by Aristotle himself. The two philosophers had more in common than they were conscious of; and probably some elements of Plato remain still undetected in Aristotle. In English philosophy too, many affinities may be traced, not only in the works of the Cambridge Platonists, but in great original writers like Berkeley or Coleridge, to Plato and his ideas. That there is a truth higher than experience, of which the mind bears witness to herself, is a conviction which in our own generation has been enthusiastically asserted, and is perhaps gaining ground. Of the Greek authors who at the Renaissance brought a new life into the world Plato has had the greatest influence. The Republic of Plato is also the first treatise upon education, of which the writings of Milton and Locke, Rousseau, Jean Paul, and Goethe are the legitimate descendants. Like Dante or Bunyan, he has a revelation of another life; like Bacon, he is profoundly impressed with the unity of knowledge; in the early Church he exercised a real influence on theology, and at the Revival of Literature on politics. Even the fragments of his words when 'repeated at second-hand' (Symp.) have in all ages ravished the hearts of men, who have seen reflected in them their own higher nature. He is the father of idealism in philosophy, in politics, in literature. And many of the latest conceptions of modern thinkers and statesmen, such as the unity of knowledge, the reign of law, and the equality of the sexes, have been anticipated in a dream by him.

The argument of the Republic is the search after Justice, the nature of which is first hinted at by Cephalus, the just and blameless old man – then discussed on the basis of proverbial morality by Socrates and Polemarchus – then caricatured by Thrasymachus and partially explained by Socrates – reduced to an abstraction by Glaucon and Adeimantus, and having become invisible in the individual reappears at length in the ideal State which is constructed by Socrates. The first care of the rulers is to be education, of which an outline is drawn after the old Hellenic model, providing only for an improved religion and morality, and more simplicity in music and gymnastic, a manlier strain of poetry, and greater harmony of the individual and the State. We are thus led on to the conception of a higher State, in which 'no man calls anything his own,' and in which there is neither 'marrying nor giving in marriage,' and 'kings are philosophers' and 'philosophers are kings;' and there is another and higher education, intellectual as well as moral and religious, of science as well as of art, and not of youth only but of the whole of life. Such a State is hardly to be realized in this world and quickly degenerates. To the perfect ideal succeeds the government of the soldier and the lover of honour, this again declining into democracy, and democracy into tyranny, in an imaginary but regular order having not much resemblance to the actual facts. When 'the wheel has come full circle' we do not begin again with a new period of human life; but we have passed from the best to the worst, and there we end. The subject is then changed and the old quarrel of poetry and philosophy which had been more lightly treated in the earlier books of the Republic is now resumed and fought out to a conclusion. Poetry is discovered to be an imitation thrice removed from the truth, and Homer, as well as the dramatic poets, having been condemned as an imitator, is sent into banishment along with them. And the idea of the State is supplemented by the revelation of a future life.

The division into books, like all similar divisions (Cp. Sir G.C. Lewis in the Classical Museum.), is probably later than the age of Plato. The natural divisions are five in number; – (1) Book I and the first half of Book II down to the paragraph beginning, 'I had always admired the genius of Glaucon and Adeimantus,' which is introductory; the first book containing a refutation of the popular and sophistical notions of justice, and concluding, like some of the earlier Dialogues, without arriving at any definite result. To this is appended a restatement of the nature of justice according to common opinion, and an answer is demanded to the question – What is justice, stripped of appearances? The second division (2) includes the remainder of the second and the whole of the third and fourth books, which are mainly occupied with the construction of the first State and the first education. The third division (3) consists of the fifth, sixth, and seventh books, in which philosophy rather than justice is the subject of enquiry, and the second State is constructed on principles of communism and ruled by philosophers, and the contemplation of the idea of good takes the place of the social and political virtues. In the eighth and ninth books (4) the perversions of States and of the individuals who correspond to them are reviewed in succession; and the nature of pleasure and the principle of tyranny are further analysed in the individual man. The tenth book (5) is the conclusion of the whole, in which the relations of philosophy to poetry are finally determined, and the happiness of the citizens in this life, which has now been assured, is crowned by the vision of another.

Or a more general division into two parts may be adopted; the first (Books I - IV) containing the description of a State framed generally in accordance with Hellenic notions of religion and morality, while in the second (Books V - X) the Hellenic State is transformed into an ideal kingdom of philosophy, of which all other governments are the perversions. These two points of view are really opposed, and the opposition is only veiled by the genius of Plato. The Republic, like the Phaedrus (see Introduction to Phaedrus), is an imperfect whole; the higher light of philosophy breaks through the regularity of the Hellenic temple, which at last fades away into the heavens. Whether this imperfection of structure arises from an enlargement of the plan; or from the imperfect reconcilement in the writer's own mind of the struggling elements of thought which are now first brought together by him; or, perhaps, from the composition of the work at different times – are questions, like the similar question about the Iliad and the Odyssey, which are worth asking, but which cannot have a distinct answer. In the age of Plato there was no regular mode of publication, and an author would have the less scruple in altering or adding to a work which was known only to a few of his friends. There is no absurdity in supposing that he may have laid his labours aside for a time, or turned from one work to another; and such interruptions would be more likely to occur in the case of a long than of a short writing. In all attempts to determine the chronological order of the Platonic writings on internal evidence, this uncertainty about any single Dialogue being composed at one time is a disturbing element, which must be admitted to affect longer works, such as the Republic and the Laws, more than shorter ones. But, on the other hand, the seeming discrepancies of the Republic may only arise out of the discordant elements which the philosopher has attempted to unite in a single whole, perhaps without being himself able to recognise the inconsistency which is obvious to us. For there is a judgment of after ages which few great writers have ever been able to anticipate for themselves. They do not perceive the want of connexion in their own writings, or the gaps in their systems which are visible enough to those who come after them. In the beginnings of literature and philosophy, amid the first efforts of thought and language, more inconsistencies occur than now, when the paths of speculation are well worn and the meaning of words precisely defined. For consistency, too, is the growth of time; and some of the greatest creations of the human mind have been wanting in unity. Tried by this test, several of the Platonic Dialogues, according to our modern ideas, appear to be defective, but the deficiency is no proof that they were composed at different times or by different hands. And the supposition that the Republic was written uninterruptedly and by a continuous effort is in some degree confirmed by the numerous references from one part of the work to another.

The second title, 'Concerning Justice,' is not the one by which the Republic is quoted, either by Aristotle or generally in antiquity, and, like the other second titles of the Platonic Dialogues, may therefore be assumed to be of later date. Morgenstern and others have asked whether the definition of justice, which is the professed aim, or the construction of the State is the principal argument of the work. The answer is, that the two blend in one, and are two faces of the same truth; for justice is the order of the State, and the State is the visible embodiment of justice under the conditions of human society. The one is the soul and the other is the body, and the Greek ideal of the State, as of the individual, is a fair mind in a fair body. In Hegelian phraseology the state is the reality of which justice is the idea. Or, described in Christian language, the kingdom of God is within, and yet developes into a Church or external kingdom; 'the house not made with hands, eternal in the heavens,' is reduced to the proportions of an earthly building. Or, to use a Platonic image, justice and the State are the warp and the woof which run through the whole texture. And when the constitution of the State is completed, the conception of justice is not dismissed, but reappears under the same or different names throughout the work, both as the inner law of the individual soul, and finally as the principle of rewards and punishments in another life. The virtues are based on justice, of which common honesty in buying and selling is the shadow, and justice is based on the idea of good, which is the harmony of the world, and is reflected both in the institutions of states and in motions of the heavenly bodies (cp. Tim.). The Timaeus, which takes up the political rather than the ethical side of the Republic, and is chiefly occupied with hypotheses concerning the outward world, yet contains many indications that the same law is supposed to reign over the State, over nature, and over man.

Too much, however, has been made of this question both in ancient and modern times. There is a stage of criticism in which all works, whether of nature or of art, are referred to design. Now in ancient writings, and indeed in literature generally, there remains often a large element which was not comprehended in the original design. For the plan grows under the author's hand; new thoughts occur to him in the act of writing; he has not worked out the argument to the end before he begins. The reader who seeks to find some one idea under which the whole may be conceived, must necessarily seize on the vaguest and most general. Thus Stallbaum, who is dissatisfied with the ordinary explanations of the argument of the Republic, imagines himself to have found the true argument 'in the representation of human life in a State perfected by justice, and governed according to the idea of good.' There may be some use in such general descriptions, but they can hardly be said to express the design of the writer. The truth is, that we may as well speak of many designs as of one; nor need anything be excluded from the plan of a great work to which the mind is naturally led by the association of ideas, and which does not interfere with the general purpose. What kind or degree of unity is to be sought after in a building, in the plastic arts, in poetry, in prose, is a problem which has to be determined relatively to the subject-matter. To Plato himself, the enquiry 'what was the intention of the writer,' or 'what was the principal argument of the Republic' would have been hardly intelligible, and therefore had better be at once dismissed (cp. the Introduction to the Phaedrus).

Is not the Republic the vehicle of three or four great truths which, to Plato's own mind, are most naturally represented in the form of the State? Just as in the Jewish prophets the reign of Messiah, or 'the day of the Lord,' or the suffering Servant or people of God, or the 'Sun of righteousness with healing in his wings' only convey, to us at least, their great spiritual ideals, so through the Greek State Plato reveals to us his own thoughts about divine perfection, which is the idea of good – like the sun in the visible world; – about human perfection, which is justice – about education beginning in youth and continuing in later years – about poets and sophists and tyrants who are the false teachers and evil rulers of mankind – about 'the world' which is the embodiment of them – about a kingdom which exists nowhere upon earth but is laid up in heaven to be the pattern and rule of human life. No such inspired creation is at unity with itself, any more than the clouds of heaven when the sun pierces through them. Every shade of light and dark, of truth, and of fiction which is the veil of truth, is allowable in a work of philosophical imagination. It is not all on the same plane; it easily passes from ideas to myths and fancies, from facts to figures of speech. It is not prose but poetry, at least a great part of it, and ought not to be judged by the rules of logic or the probabilities of history. The writer is not fashioning his ideas into an artistic whole; they take possession of him and are too much for him. We have no need therefore to discuss whether a State such as Plato has conceived is practicable or not, or whether the outward form or the inward life came first into the mind of the writer. For the practicability of his ideas has nothing to do with their truth; and the highest thoughts to which he attains may be truly said to bear the greatest 'marks of design' – justice more than the external frame-work of the State, the idea of good more than justice. The great science of dialectic or the organisation of ideas has no real content; but is only a type of the method or spirit in which the higher knowledge is to be pursued by the spectator of all time and all existence. It is in the fifth, sixth, and seventh books that Plato reaches the 'summit of speculation,' and these, although they fail to satisfy the requirements of a modern thinker, may therefore be regarded as the most important, as they are also the most original, portions of the work.

It is not necessary to discuss at length a minor question which has been raised by Boeckh, respecting the imaginary date at which the conversation was held (the year 411 B.C. which is proposed by him will do as well as any other); for a writer of fiction, and especially a writer who, like Plato, is notoriously careless of chronology (cp. Rep., Symp., etc.), only aims at general probability. Whether all the persons mentioned in the Republic could ever have met at any one time is not a difficulty which would have occurred to an Athenian reading the work forty years later, or to Plato himself at the time of writing (any more than to Shakespeare respecting one of his own dramas); and need not greatly trouble us now. Yet this may be a question having no answer 'which is still worth asking,' because the investigation shows that we cannot argue historically from the dates in Plato; it would be useless therefore to waste time in inventing far-fetched reconcilements of them in order to avoid chronological difficulties, such, for example, as the conjecture of C.F. Hermann, that Glaucon and Adeimantus are not the brothers but the uncles of Plato (cp. Apol.), or the fancy of Stallbaum that Plato intentionally left anachronisms indicating the dates at which some of his Dialogues were written.

The principal characters in the Republic are Cephalus, Polemarchus, Thrasymachus, Socrates, Glaucon, and Adeimantus. Cephalus appears in the introduction only, Polemarchus drops at the end of the first argument, and Thrasymachus is reduced to silence at the close of the first book. The main discussion is carried on by Socrates, Glaucon, and Adeimantus. Among the company are Lysias (the orator) and Euthydemus, the sons of Cephalus and brothers of Polemarchus, an unknown Charmantides – these are mute auditors; also there is Cleitophon, who once interrupts, where, as in the Dialogue which bears his name, he appears as the friend and ally of Thrasymachus.

Cephalus, the patriarch of the house, has been appropriately engaged in offering a sacrifice. He is the pattern of an old man who has almost done with life, and is at peace with himself and with all mankind. He feels that he is drawing nearer to the world below, and seems to linger around the memory of the past. He is eager that Socrates should come to visit him, fond of the poetry of the last generation, happy in the consciousness of a well-spent life, glad at having escaped from the tyranny of youthful lusts. His love of conversation, his affection, his indifference to riches, even his garrulity, are interesting traits of character. He is not one of those who have nothing to say, because their whole mind has been absorbed in making money. Yet he acknowledges that riches have the advantage of placing men above the temptation to dishonesty or falsehood. The respectful attention shown to him by Socrates, whose love of conversation, no less than the mission imposed upon him by the Oracle, leads him to ask questions of all men, young and old alike, should also be noted. Who better suited to raise the question of justice than Cephalus, whose life might seem to be the expression of it? The moderation with which old age is pictured by Cephalus as a very tolerable portion of existence is characteristic, not only of him, but of Greek feeling generally, and contrasts with the exaggeration of Cicero in the De Senectute. The evening of life is described by Plato in the most expressive manner, yet with the fewest possible touches. As Cicero remarks (Ep. ad Attic.), the aged Cephalus would have been out of place in the discussion which follows, and which he could neither have understood nor taken part in without a violation of dramatic propriety (cp. Lysimachus in the Laches).

His 'son and heir' Polemarchus has the frankness and impetuousness of youth; he is for detaining Socrates by force in the opening scene, and will not 'let him off' on the subject of women and children. Like Cephalus, he is limited in his point of view, and represents the proverbial stage of morality which has rules of life rather than principles; and he quotes Simonides (cp. Aristoph. Clouds) as his father had quoted Pindar. But after this he has no more to say; the answers which he makes are only elicited from him by the dialectic of Socrates. He has not yet experienced the influence of the Sophists like Glaucon and Adeimantus, nor is he sensible of the necessity of refuting them; he belongs to the pre-Socratic or pre-dialectical age. He is incapable of arguing, and is bewildered by Socrates to such a degree that he does not know what he is saying. He is made to admit that justice is a thief, and that the virtues follow the analogy of the arts. From his brother Lysias (contra Eratosth.) we learn that he fell a victim to the Thirty Tyrants, but no allusion is here made to his fate, nor to the circumstance that Cephalus and his family were of Syracusan origin, and had migrated from Thurii to Athens.

The 'Chalcedonian giant,' Thrasymachus, of whom we have already heard in the Phaedrus, is the personification of the Sophists, according to Plato's conception of them, in some of their worst characteristics. He is vain and blustering, refusing to discourse unless he is paid, fond of making an oration, and hoping thereby to escape the inevitable Socrates; but a mere child in argument, and unable to foresee that the next 'move' (to use a Platonic expression) will 'shut him up.' He has reached the stage of framing general notions, and in this respect is in advance of Cephalus and Polemarchus. But he is incapable of defending them in a discussion, and vainly tries to cover his confusion with banter and insolence. Whether such doctrines as are attributed to him by Plato were really held either by him or by any other Sophist is uncertain; in the infancy of philosophy serious errors about morality might easily grow up – they are certainly put into the mouths of speakers in Thucydides; but we are concerned at present with Plato's description of him, and not with the historical reality. The inequality of the contest adds greatly to the humour of the scene. The pompous and empty Sophist is utterly helpless in the hands of the great master of dialectic, who knows how to touch all the springs of vanity and weakness in him. He is greatly irritated by the irony of Socrates, but his noisy and imbecile rage only lays him more and more open to the thrusts of his assailant. His determination to cram down their throats, or put 'bodily into their souls' his own words, elicits a cry of horror from Socrates. The state of his temper is quite as worthy of remark as the process of the argument. Nothing is more amusing than his complete submission when he has been once thoroughly beaten. At first he seems to continue the discussion with reluctance, but soon with apparent good-will, and he even testifies his interest at a later stage by one or two occasional remarks. When attacked by Glaucon he is humorously protected by Socrates 'as one who has never been his enemy and is now his friend.' From Cicero and Quintilian and from Aristotle's Rhetoric we learn that the Sophist whom Plato has made so ridiculous was a man of note whose writings were preserved in later ages. The play on his name which was made by his contemporary Herodicus (Aris. Rhet.), 'thou wast ever bold in battle,' seems to show that the description of him is not devoid of verisimilitude.

When Thrasymachus has been silenced, the two principal respondents, Glaucon and Adeimantus, appear on the scene: here, as in Greek tragedy (cp. Introd. to Phaedo), three actors are introduced. At first sight the two sons of Ariston may seem to wear a family likeness, like the two friends Simmias and Cebes in the Phaedo. But on a nearer examination of them the similarity vanishes, and they are seen to be distinct characters. Glaucon is the impetuous youth who can 'just never have enough of fechting' (cp. the character of him in Xen. Mem. iii. 6); the man of pleasure who is acquainted with the mysteries of love; the 'juvenis qui gaudet canibus,' and who improves the breed of animals; the lover of art and music who has all the experiences of youthful life. He is full of quickness and penetration, piercing easily below the clumsy platitudes of Thrasymachus to the real difficulty; he turns out to the light the seamy side of human life, and yet does not lose faith in the just and true. It is Glaucon who seizes what may be termed the ludicrous relation of the philosopher to the world, to whom a state of simplicity is 'a city of pigs,' who is always prepared with a jest when the argument offers him an opportunity, and who is ever ready to second the humour of Socrates and to appreciate the ridiculous, whether in the connoisseurs of music, or in the lovers of theatricals, or in the fantastic behaviour of the citizens of democracy. His weaknesses are several times alluded to by Socrates, who, however, will not allow him to be attacked by his brother Adeimantus. He is a soldier, and, like Adeimantus, has been distinguished at the battle of Megara (anno 456?)...The character of Adeimantus is deeper and graver, and the profounder objections are commonly put into his mouth. Glaucon is more demonstrative, and generally opens the game. Adeimantus pursues the argument further. Glaucon has more of the liveliness and quick sympathy of youth; Adeimantus has the maturer judgment of a grown-up man of the world. In the second book, when Glaucon insists that justice and injustice shall be considered without regard to their consequences, Adeimantus remarks that they are regarded by mankind in general only for the sake of their consequences; and in a similar vein of reflection he urges at the beginning of the fourth book that Socrates fails in making his citizens happy, and is answered that happiness is not the first but the second thing, not the direct aim but the indirect consequence of the good government of a State. In the discussion about religion and mythology, Adeimantus is the respondent, but Glaucon breaks in with a slight jest, and carries on the conversation in a lighter tone about music and gymnastic to the end of the book. It is Adeimantus again who volunteers the criticism of common sense on the Socratic method of argument, and who refuses to let Socrates pass lightly over the question of women and children. It is Adeimantus who is the respondent in the more argumentative, as Glaucon in the lighter and more imaginative portions of the Dialogue. For example, throughout the greater part of the sixth book, the causes of the corruption of philosophy and the conception of the idea of good are discussed with Adeimantus. Glaucon resumes his place of principal respondent; but he has a difficulty in apprehending the higher education of Socrates, and makes some false hits in the course of the discussion. Once more Adeimantus returns with the allusion to his brother Glaucon whom he compares to the contentious State; in the next book he is again superseded, and Glaucon continues to the end.

Thus in a succession of characters Plato represents the successive stages of morality, beginning with the Athenian gentleman of the olden time, who is followed by the practical man of that day regulating his life by proverbs and saws; to him succeeds the wild generalization of the Sophists, and lastly come the young disciples of the great teacher, who know the sophistical arguments but will not be convinced by them, and desire to go deeper into the nature of things. These too, like Cephalus, Polemarchus, Thrasymachus, are clearly distinguished from one another. Neither in the Republic, nor in any other Dialogue of Plato, is a single character repeated.

The delineation of Socrates in the Republic is not wholly consistent. In the first book we have more of the real Socrates, such as he is depicted in the Memorabilia of Xenophon, in the earliest Dialogues of Plato, and in the Apology. He is ironical, provoking, questioning, the old enemy of the Sophists, ready to put on the mask of Silenus as well as to argue seriously. But in the sixth book his enmity towards the Sophists abates; he acknowledges that they are the representatives rather than the corrupters of the world. He also becomes more dogmatic and constructive, passing beyond the range either of the political or the speculative ideas of the real Socrates. In one passage Plato himself seems to intimate that the time had now come for Socrates, who had passed his whole life in philosophy, to give his own opinion and not to be always repeating the notions of other men. There is no evidence that either the idea of good or the conception of a perfect state were comprehended in the Socratic teaching, though he certainly dwelt on the nature of the universal and of final causes (cp. Xen. Mem.; Phaedo); and a deep thinker like him, in his thirty or forty years of public teaching, could hardly have failed to touch on the nature of family relations, for which there is also some positive evidence in the Memorabilia (Mem.) The Socratic method is nominally retained; and every inference is either put into the mouth of the respondent or represented as the common discovery of him and Socrates. But any one can see that this is a mere form, of which the affectation grows wearisome as the work advances. The method of enquiry has passed into a method of teaching in which by the help of interlocutors the same thesis is looked at from various points of view. The nature of the process is truly characterized by Glaucon, when he describes himself as a companion who is not good for much in an investigation, but can see what he is shown, and may, perhaps, give the answer to a question more fluently than another.

Neither can we be absolutely certain that Socrates himself taught the immortality of the soul, which is unknown to his disciple Glaucon in the Republic (cp. Apol.); nor is there any reason to suppose that he used myths or revelations of another world as a vehicle of instruction, or that he would have banished poetry or have denounced the Greek mythology. His favorite oath is retained, and a slight mention is made of the daemonium, or internal sign, which is alluded to by Socrates as a phenomenon peculiar to himself. A real element of Socratic teaching, which is more prominent in the Republic than in any of the other Dialogues of Plato, is the use of example and illustration (Greek): 'Let us apply the test of common instances.' 'You,' says Adeimantus, ironically, in the sixth book, 'are so unaccustomed to speak in images.' And this use of examples or images, though truly Socratic in origin, is enlarged by the genius of Plato into the form of an allegory or parable, which embodies in the concrete what has been already described, or is about to be described, in the abstract. Thus the figure of the cave in Book VII is a recapitulation of the divisions of knowledge in Book VI. The composite animal in Book IX is an allegory of the parts of the soul. The noble captain and the ship and the true pilot in Book VI are a figure of the relation of the people to the philosophers in the State which has been described. Other figures, such as the dog, or the marriage of the portionless maiden, or the drones and wasps in the eighth and ninth books, also form links of connexion in long passages, or are used to recall previous discussions.

Plato is most true to the character of his master when he describes him as 'not of this world.' And with this representation of him the ideal state and the other paradoxes of the Republic are quite in accordance, though they cannot be shown to have been speculations of Socrates. To him, as to other great teachers both philosophical and religious, when they looked upward, the world seemed to be the embodiment of error and evil. The common sense of mankind has revolted against this view, or has only partially admitted it. And even in Socrates himself the sterner judgement of the multitude at times passes into a sort of ironical pity or love. Men in general are incapable of philosophy, and are therefore at enmity with the philosopher; but their misunderstanding of him is unavoidable: for they have never seen him as he truly is in his own image; they are only acquainted with artificial systems possessing no native force of truth – words which admit of many applications. Their leaders have nothing to measure with, and are therefore ignorant of their own stature. But they are to be pitied or laughed at, not to be quarrelled with; they mean well with their nostrums, if they could only learn that they are cutting off a Hydra's head. This moderation towards those who are in error is one of the most characteristic features of Socrates in the Republic. In all the different representations of Socrates, whether of Xenophon or Plato, and amid the differences of the earlier or later Dialogues, he always retains the character of the unwearied and disinterested seeker after truth, without which he would have ceased to be Socrates.

Leaving the characters we may now analyse the contents of the Republic, and then proceed to consider (1) The general aspects of this Hellenic ideal of the State, (2) The modern lights in which the thoughts of Plato may be read.

BOOK I.

The Republic opens with a truly Greek scene – a festival in honour of the goddess Bendis which is held in the Piraeus; to this is added the promise of an equestrian torch-race in the evening. The whole work is supposed to be recited by Socrates on the day after the festival to a small party, consisting of Critias, Timaeus, Hermocrates, and another; this we learn from the first words of the Timaeus.

When the rhetorical advantage of reciting the Dialogue has been gained, the attention is not distracted by any reference to the audience; nor is the reader further reminded of the extraordinary length of the narrative. Of the numerous company, three only take any serious part in the discussion; nor are we informed whether in the evening they went to the torch-race, or talked, as in the Symposium, through the night. The manner in which the conversation has arisen is described as follows: – Socrates and his companion Glaucon are about to leave the festival when they are detained by a message from Polemarchus, who speedily appears accompanied by Adeimantus, the brother of Glaucon, and with playful violence compels them to remain, promising them not only the torch-race, but the pleasure of conversation with the young, which to Socrates is a far greater attraction. They return to the house of Cephalus, Polemarchus' father, now in extreme old age, who is found sitting upon a cushioned seat crowned for a sacrifice. 'You should come to me oftener, Socrates, for I am too old to go to you; and at my time of life, having lost other pleasures, I care the more for conversation.' Socrates asks him what he thinks of age, to which the old man replies, that the sorrows and discontents of age are to be attributed to the tempers of men, and that age is a time of peace in which the tyranny of the passions is no longer felt. Yes, replies Socrates, but the world will say, Cephalus, that you are happy in old age because you are rich. 'And there is something in what they say, Socrates, but not so much as they imagine – as Themistocles replied to the Seriphian, "Neither you, if you had been an Athenian, nor I, if I had been a Seriphian, would ever have been famous," I might in like manner reply to you, Neither a good poor man can be happy in age, nor yet a bad rich man.' Socrates remarks that Cephalus appears not to care about riches, a quality which he ascribes to his having inherited, not acquired them, and would like to know what he considers to be the chief advantage of them. Cephalus answers that when you are old the belief in the world below grows upon you, and then to have done justice and never to have been compelled to do injustice through poverty, and never to have deceived anyone, are felt to be unspeakable blessings. Socrates, who is evidently preparing for an argument, next asks, What is the meaning of the word justice? To tell the truth and pay your debts? No more than this? Or must we admit exceptions? Ought I, for example, to put back into the hands of my friend, who has gone mad, the sword which I borrowed of him when he was in his right mind? 'There must be exceptions.' 'And yet,' says Polemarchus, 'the definition which has been given has the authority of Simonides.' Here Cephalus retires to look after the sacrifices, and bequeaths, as Socrates facetiously remarks, the possession of the argument to his heir, Polemarchus...

The description of old age is finished, and Plato, as his manner is, has touched the key-note of the whole work in asking for the definition of justice, first suggesting the question which Glaucon afterwards pursues respecting external goods, and preparing for the concluding mythus of the world below in the slight allusion of Cephalus. The portrait of the just man is a natural frontispiece or introduction to the long discourse which follows, and may perhaps imply that in all our perplexity about the nature of justice, there is no difficulty in discerning 'who is a just man.' The first explanation has been supported by a saying of Simonides; and now Socrates has a mind to show that the resolution of justice into two unconnected precepts, which have no common principle, fails to satisfy the demands of dialectic.

...He proceeds: What did Simonides mean by this saying of his? Did he mean that I was to give back arms to a madman? 'No, not in that case, not if the parties are friends, and evil would result. He meant that you were to do what was proper, good to friends and harm to enemies.' Every act does something to somebody; and following this analogy, Socrates asks, What is this due and proper thing which justice does, and to whom? He is answered that justice does good to friends and harm to enemies. But in what way good or harm? 'In making alliances with the one, and going to war with the other.' Then in time of peace what is the good of justice? The answer is that justice is of use in contracts, and contracts are money partnerships. Yes; but how in such partnerships is the just man of more use than any other man? 'When you want to have money safely kept and not used.' Then justice will be useful when money is useless. And there is another difficulty: justice, like the art of war or any other art, must be of opposites, good at attack as well as at defence, at stealing as well as at guarding. But then justice is a thief, though a hero notwithstanding, like Autolycus, the

Homeric hero, who was 'excellent above all men in theft and perjury' – to such a pass have you and Homer and Simonides brought us; though I do not forget that the thieving must be for the good of friends and the harm of enemies. And still there arises another question: Are friends to be interpreted as real or seeming; enemies as real or seeming? And are our friends to be only the good, and our enemies to be the evil? The answer is, that we must do good to our seeming and real good friends, and evil to our seeming and real evil enemies – good to the good, evil to the evil. But ought we to render evil for evil at all, when to do so will only make men more evil? Can justice produce injustice any more than the art of horsemanship can make bad horsemen, or heat produce cold? The final conclusion is, that no sage or poet ever said that the just return evil for evil; this was a maxim of some rich and mighty man, Periander, Perdiccas, or Ismenias the Theban (about B.C. 398-381)...

Thus the first stage of aphoristic or unconscious morality is shown to be inadequate to the wants of the age; the authority of the poets is set aside, and through the winding mazes of dialectic we make an approach to the Christian precept of forgiveness of injuries. Similar words are applied by the Persian mystic poet to the Divine being when the questioning spirit is stirred within him: – 'If because I do evil, Thou punishest me by evil, what is the difference between Thee and me?' In this both Plato and Kheyam rise above the level of many Christian (?) theologians. The first definition of justice easily passes into the second; for the simple words 'to speak the truth and pay your debts' is substituted the more abstract 'to do good to your friends and harm to your enemies.' Either of these explanations gives a sufficient rule of life for plain men, but they both fall short of the precision of philosophy. We may note in passing the antiquity of casuistry, which not only arises out of the conflict of established principles in particular cases, but also out of the effort to attain them, and is prior as well as posterior to our fundamental notions of morality. The 'interrogation' of moral ideas; the appeal to the authority of Homer; the conclusion that the maxim, 'Do good to your friends and harm to your enemies,' being erroneous, could not have been the word of any great man, are all of them very characteristic of the Platonic Socrates.

...Here Thrasymachus, who has made several attempts to interrupt, but has hitherto been kept in order by the company, takes advantage of a pause and rushes into the arena, beginning, like a savage animal, with a roar. 'Socrates,' he says, 'what folly is this? – Why do you agree to be vanquished by one another in a pretended argument?' He then prohibits all the ordinary definitions of justice; to which Socrates replies that he cannot tell how many twelve is, if he is forbidden to say 2 x 6, or 3 x 4, or 6 x 2, or 4 x 3. At first Thrasymachus is reluctant to argue; but at length, with a promise of payment on the part of the company and of praise from Socrates, he is induced to open the game. 'Listen,' he says, 'my answer is that might is right, justice the interest of the stronger: now praise me.' Let me understand you first. Do you mean that because Polydamas the wrestler, who is stronger than we are, finds the eating of beef for his interest, the eating of beef is also for our interest, who are not so strong? Thrasymachus is indignant at the illustration, and in pompous words, apparently intended to restore dignity to the argument, he explains his meaning to be that the rulers make laws for their own interests. But suppose, says Socrates, that the ruler or stronger makes a mistake – then the interest of the stronger is not his interest. Thrasymachus is saved from this speedy downfall by his disciple Cleitophon, who introduces the word 'thinks;' – not the actual interest of the ruler, but what he thinks or what seems to be his interest, is justice. The contradiction is escaped by the unmeaning evasion: for though his real and apparent interests may differ, what the ruler thinks to be his interest will always remain what he thinks to be his interest.

Of course this was not the original assertion, nor is the new interpretation accepted by Thrasymachus himself. But Socrates is not disposed to quarrel about words, if, as he significantly insinuates, his adversary has changed his mind. In what follows Thrasymachus does in fact withdraw his admission that the ruler may make a mistake, for he affirms that the ruler as a ruler is infallible. Socrates is quite ready to accept the new position, which he equally turns against Thrasymachus by the help of the analogy of the arts. Every art or science has an interest, but this interest is to be distinguished from the accidental interest of the artist, and is only concerned with the good of the things or persons which come under the art. And justice has an interest which is the interest not of the ruler or judge, but of those who come under his sway.

Thrasymachus is on the brink of the inevitable conclusion, when he makes a bold diversion. 'Tell me, Socrates,' he says, 'have you a nurse?' What a question! Why do you ask? 'Because, if you have, she neglects you and lets you go about drivelling, and has not even taught you to know the shepherd from the sheep. For you fancy that shepherds and rulers never think of their own interest, but only of their sheep or subjects, whereas the truth is that they fatten them for their use, sheep and subjects alike. And experience proves that in every relation of life the just man is the loser and the unjust the gainer, especially where injustice is on the grand scale, which is quite another thing from the petty rogueries of swindlers and burglars and robbers of temples. The language of men proves this – our 'gracious' and 'blessed' tyrant and the like – all which tends to show (1) that justice is the interest of the stronger; and (2) that injustice is more profitable and also stronger than justice.'

Thrasymachus, who is better at a speech than at a close argument, having deluged the company with words, has a mind to escape. But the others will not let him go, and Socrates adds a humble but earnest request that he will not desert them at such a crisis of their fate. 'And what can I do more for you?' he says; 'would you have me put the words bodily into your souls?' God forbid! replies Socrates; but we want you to be consistent in the use of terms, and not to employ 'physician' in an exact sense, and then again 'shepherd' or 'ruler' in an inexact, – if the words are strictly taken, the ruler and the shepherd look only to the good of their people or flocks and not to their own: whereas you insist that rulers are solely actuated by love of office. 'No doubt about it,' replies Thrasymachus. Then why are they paid? Is not the reason, that their interest is not comprehended in their art, and is therefore the concern of another art, the art of pay, which is common to the arts in general, and therefore not identical with any one of them? Nor would any man be a ruler unless he were induced by the hope of reward or the fear of punishment; – the reward is money or honour, the punishment is the necessity of being ruled by a man worse than himself. And if a State (or Church) were composed entirely of good men, they would be affected by the last motive only; and there would be as much 'nolo episcopari' as there is at present of the opposite...

The satire on existing governments is heightened by the simple and apparently incidental manner in which the last remark is introduced. There is a similar irony in the argument that the governors of mankind do not like being in office, and that therefore they demand pay.

...Enough of this: the other assertion of Thrasymachus is far more important – that the unjust life is more gainful than the just. Now, as you and I, Glaucon, are not convinced by him, we must reply to him; but if we try to compare their respective gains we shall want a judge to decide for us; we had better therefore proceed by making mutual admissions of the truth to one another.

Thrasymachus had asserted that perfect injustice was more gainful than perfect justice, and after a little hesitation he is induced by Socrates to admit the still greater paradox that injustice is virtue and justice vice. Socrates praises his frankness, and assumes the attitude of one whose only wish is to understand the meaning of his opponents. At the same time he is weaving a net in which Thrasymachus is finally enclosed. The admission is elicited from him that the just man seeks to gain an advantage over the unjust only, but not over the just, while the unjust would gain an advantage over either. Socrates, in order to test this statement, employs once more the favourite analogy of the arts. The musician, doctor, skilled artist of any sort, does not seek to gain more than the skilled, but only more than the unskilled (that is to say, he works up to a rule, standard, law, and does not exceed it), whereas the unskilled makes random efforts at excess. Thus the skilled falls on the side of the good, and the unskilled on the side of the evil, and the just is the skilled, and the unjust is the unskilled.

There was great difficulty in bringing Thrasymachus to the point; the day was hot and he was streaming with perspiration, and for the first time in his life he was seen to blush. But his other thesis that injustice was stronger than justice has not yet been refuted, and Socrates now proceeds to the consideration of this, which, with the assistance of Thrasymachus, he hopes to clear up; the latter is at first churlish, but in the judicious hands of Socrates is soon restored to good-humour: Is there not honour among thieves? Is not the strength of injustice only a remnant of justice? Is not absolute injustice absolute weakness also? A house that is divided against itself cannot stand; two men who quarrel detract from one another's strength, and he who is at war with himself is the enemy of himself and the gods. Not wickedness therefore, but semi-wickedness flourishes in states, – a remnant of good is needed in order to make union in action possible, – there is no kingdom of evil in this world.

Another question has not been answered: Is the just or the unjust the happier? To this we reply, that every art has an end and an excellence or virtue by which the end is accomplished. And is not the end of the soul happiness, and justice the excellence of the soul by which happiness is attained? Justice and happiness being thus shown to be inseparable, the question whether the just or the unjust is the happier has disappeared.

Thrasymachus replies: 'Let this be your entertainment, Socrates, at the festival of Bendis.' Yes; and a very good entertainment with which your kindness has supplied me, now that you have left off scolding. And yet not a good entertainment – but that was my own fault, for I tasted of too many things. First of all the nature of justice was the subject of our enquiry, and then whether justice is virtue and wisdom, or evil and folly; and then the comparative advantages of just and unjust: and the sum of all is that I know not what justice is; how then shall I know whether the just is happy or not?...

Thus the sophistical fabric has been demolished, chiefly by appealing to the analogy of the arts. 'Justice is like the arts (1) in having no external interest, and (2) in not aiming at excess, and (3) justice is to happiness what the implement of the workman is to his work.' At this the modern reader is apt to stumble, because he forgets that Plato is writing in an age when the arts and the virtues, like the moral and intellectual faculties, were still undistinguished. Among early enquirers into the nature of human action the arts helped to fill up the void of speculation; and at first the comparison of the arts and the virtues was not perceived by them to be fallacious. They only saw the points of agreement in them and not the points of difference. Virtue, like art, must take means to an end; good manners are both an art and a virtue; character is naturally described under the image of a statue; and there are many other figures of speech which are readily transferred from art to morals. The next generation cleared up these perplexities; or at least supplied after ages with a further analysis of them. The contemporaries of Plato were in a state of transition, and had not yet fully realized the common-sense distinction of Aristotle, that 'virtue is concerned with action, art with production' (Nic. Eth.), or that 'virtue implies intention and constancy of purpose,' whereas 'art requires knowledge only'. And yet in the absurdities which follow from some uses of the analogy, there seems to be an intimation conveyed that virtue is more than art. This is implied in the reductio ad absurdum that 'justice is a thief,' and in the dissatisfaction which Socrates expresses at the final result.

The expression 'an art of pay' which is described as 'common to all the arts' is not in accordance with the ordinary use of language. Nor is it employed elsewhere either by Plato or by any other Greek writer. It is suggested by the argument, and seems to extend the conception of art to doing as well as making. Another flaw or inaccuracy of language may be noted in the words 'men who are injured are made more unjust.' For those who are injured are not necessarily made worse, but only harmed or ill-treated.

The second of the three arguments, 'that the just does not aim at excess,' has a real meaning, though wrapped up in an enigmatical form. That the good is of the nature of the finite is a peculiarly Hellenic sentiment, which may be compared with the language of those modern writers who speak of virtue as fitness, and of freedom as obedience to law. The mathematical or logical notion of limit easily passes into an ethical one, and even finds a mythological expression in the conception of envy (Greek). Ideas of measure, equality, order, unity, proportion, still linger in the writings of moralists; and the true spirit of the fine arts is better conveyed by such terms than by superlatives.

'When workmen strive to do better than well, They do confound their skill in covetousness.' (King John.)

The harmony of the soul and body, and of the parts of the soul with one another, a harmony 'fairer than that of musical notes,' is the true Hellenic mode of conceiving the perfection of human nature.

In what may be called the epilogue of the discussion with Thrasymachus, Plato argues that evil is not a principle of strength, but of discord and dissolution, just touching the question which has been often treated in modern times by theologians and philosophers, of the negative nature of evil. In the last argument we trace the germ of the Aristotelian doctrine of an end and a virtue directed towards the end, which again is suggested by the arts. The final reconcilement of justice and happiness and the identity of the individual and the State are also intimated. Socrates reassumes the character of a 'know-nothing;' at the same time he appears to be not wholly satisfied with the manner in which the argument has been conducted. Nothing is concluded; but the tendency of the dialectical process, here as always, is to enlarge our conception of ideas, and to widen their application to human life.

BOOK II.

Thrasymachus is pacified, but the intrepid Glaucon insists on continuing the argument. He is not satisfied with the indirect manner in which, at the end of the last book, Socrates had disposed of the question 'Whether the just or the unjust is the happier.' He begins by dividing goods into three classes: – first, goods desirable in themselves; secondly, goods desirable in themselves and for their results; thirdly, goods desirable for their results only. He then asks Socrates in which of the three classes he would place justice. In the second class, replies Socrates, among goods desirable for themselves and also for their results. 'Then the world in general are of another mind, for they say that justice belongs to the troublesome class of goods which are desirable for their results only. Socrates answers that this is the doctrine of Thrasymachus which he rejects. Glaucon thinks that Thrasymachus was too ready to listen to the voice of the charmer, and proposes to consider the nature of justice and injustice in themselves and apart from the results and rewards of them which the world is always dinning in his ears. He will first of all speak of the nature and origin of justice; secondly, of the manner in which men view justice as a necessity and not a good; and thirdly, he will prove the reasonableness of this view.

'To do injustice is said to be a good; to suffer injustice an evil. As the evil is discovered by experience to be greater than the good, the sufferers, who cannot also be doers, make a compact that they will have neither, and this compact or mean is called justice, but is really the impossibility of doing injustice. No one would observe such a compact if he were not obliged. Let us suppose that the just and unjust have two rings, like that of Gyges in the well-known story, which make them invisible, and then no difference will appear in them, for every one will do evil if he can. And he who abstains will be regarded by the world as a fool for his pains. Men may praise him in public out of fear for themselves, but they will laugh at him in their hearts (Cp. Gorgias.)

'And now let us frame an ideal of the just and unjust. Imagine the unjust man to be master of his craft, seldom making mistakes and easily correcting them; having gifts of money, speech, strength – the greatest villain bearing the highest character: and at his side let us place the just in his nobleness and simplicity – being, not seeming – without name or reward – clothed in his justice only – the best of men who is thought to be the worst, and let him die as he has lived. I might add (but I would rather put the rest into the mouth of the panegyrists of injustice – they will tell you) that the just man will be scourged, racked, bound, will have his eyes put out, and will at last be crucified (literally impaled) – and all this because he ought to have preferred seeming to being. How different is the case of the unjust who clings to appearance as the true reality! His high character makes him a ruler; he can marry where he likes, trade where he likes, help his friends and hurt his enemies; having got rich by dishonesty he can worship the gods better, and will therefore be more loved by them than the just.'

I was thinking what to answer, when Adeimantus joined in the already unequal fray. He considered that the most important point of all had been omitted: – 'Men are taught to be just for the sake of rewards; parents and guardians make reputation the incentive to virtue. And other advantages are promised by them of a more solid kind, such as wealthy marriages and high offices. There are the pictures in Homer and Hesiod of fat sheep and heavy fleeces, rich corn-fields and trees toppling with fruit, which the gods provide in this life for the just. And the Orphic poets add a similar picture of another. The heroes of Musaeus and Eumolpus lie on couches at a festival, with garlands on their heads, enjoying as the meed of virtue a paradise of immortal drunkenness. Some go further, and speak of a fair posterity in the third and fourth generation. But the wicked they bury in a slough and make them carry water in a sieve: and in this life they attribute to them the infamy which Glaucon was assuming to be the lot of the just who are supposed to be unjust.

'Take another kind of argument which is found both in poetry and prose: – "Virtue," as Hesiod says, "is honourable but difficult, vice is easy and profitable." You may often see the wicked in great prosperity and the righteous afflicted by the will of heaven. And mendicant prophets knock at rich men's doors, promising to atone for the sins of themselves or their fathers in an easy fashion with sacrifices and festive games, or with charms and invocations to get rid of an enemy good or bad by divine help and at a small charge; – they appeal to books professing to be written by Musaeus and Orpheus, and carry away the minds of whole cities, and promise to "get souls out of purgatory;" and if we refuse to listen to them, no one knows what will happen to us.

'When a lively-minded ingenuous youth hears all this, what will be his conclusion? "Will he," in the language of Pindar, "make justice his high tower, or fortify himself with crooked deceit?" Justice, he reflects, without the appearance of justice, is misery and ruin; injustice has the promise of a glorious life. Appearance is master of truth and lord of happiness. To appearance then I will turn, – I will put on the show of virtue and trail behind me the fox of Archilochus. I hear some one saying that "wickedness is not easily concealed," to which I reply that "nothing great is easy." Union and force and rhetoric will do much; and if men say that they cannot prevail over the gods, still how do we know that there are gods? Only from the poets, who acknowledge that they may be appeased by sacrifices. Then why not sin and pay for indulgences out of your sin? For if the righteous are only unpunished, still they have no further reward, while the wicked may be unpunished and have the pleasure of sinning too. But what of the world below? Nay, says the argument, there are atoning powers who will set that matter right, as the poets, who are the sons of the gods, tell us; and this is confirmed by the authority of the State.

'How can we resist such arguments in favour of injustice? Add good manners, and, as the wise tell us, we shall make the best of both worlds. Who that is not a miserable caitiff will refrain from smiling at the praises of justice? Even if a man knows the better part he will not be angry with others; for he knows also that more than human virtue is needed to save a man, and that he only praises justice who is incapable of injustice.

'The origin of the evil is that all men from the beginning, heroes, poets, instructors of youth, have always asserted "the temporal dispensation," the honours and profits of justice. Had we been taught in early youth the power of justice and injustice inherent in the soul, and unseen by any human or divine eye, we should not have needed others to be our guardians, but every one would have been the guardian of himself. This is what I want you to show, Socrates; – other men use arguments which rather tend to strengthen the position of Thrasymachus that "might is right;" but from you I expect better things. And please, as Glaucon said, to exclude reputation; let the just be thought unjust and the unjust just, and do you still prove to us the superiority of justice'...

The thesis, which for the sake of argument has been maintained by Glaucon, is the converse of that of Thrasymachus – not right is the interest of the stronger, but right is the necessity of the weaker. Starting from the same premises he carries the analysis of society a step further back; – might is still right, but the might is the weakness of the many combined against the strength of the few.

There have been theories in modern as well as in ancient times which have a family likeness to the speculations of Glaucon; e.g. that power is the foundation of right; or that a monarch has a divine right to govern well or ill; or that virtue is self-love or the love of power; or that war is the natural state of man; or that private vices are public benefits. All such theories have a kind of plausibility from their partial agreement with experience. For human nature oscillates between good and evil, and the motives of actions and the origin of institutions may be explained to a certain extent on either hypothesis according to the character or point of view of a particular thinker. The obligation of maintaining authority under all circumstances and sometimes by rather questionable means is felt strongly and has become a sort of instinct among civilized men. The divine right of kings, or more generally of governments, is one of the forms under which this natural feeling is expressed. Nor again is there any evil which has not some accompaniment of good or pleasure; nor any good which is free from some alloy of evil; nor any noble or generous thought which may not be attended by a shadow or the ghost of a shadow of self-interest or of self-love. We know that all human actions are imperfect; but we do not therefore attribute them to the worse rather than to the better motive or principle. Such a philosophy is both foolish and false, like that opinion of the clever rogue who assumes all other men to be like himself. And theories of this sort do not represent the real nature of the State, which is based on a vague sense of right gradually corrected and enlarged by custom and law (although capable also of perversion), any more than they describe the origin of society, which is to be sought in the family and in the social and religious feelings of man. Nor do they represent the average character of individuals, which cannot be explained simply on a theory of evil, but has always a counteracting element of good. And as men become better such theories appear more and more untruthful to them, because they are more conscious of their own disinterestedness. A little experience may make a man a cynic; a great deal will bring him back to a truer and kindlier view of the mixed nature of himself and his fellow men.

The two brothers ask Socrates to prove to them that the just is happy when they have taken from him all that in which happiness is ordinarily supposed to consist. Not that there is (1) any absurdity in the attempt to frame a notion of justice apart from circumstances. For the ideal must always be a paradox when compared with the ordinary conditions of human life. Neither the Stoical ideal nor the Christian ideal is true as a fact, but they may serve as a basis of education, and may exercise an ennobling influence. An ideal is none the worse because 'some one has made the discovery' that no such ideal was ever realized. And in a few exceptional individuals who are raised above the ordinary level of humanity, the ideal of happiness may be realized in death and misery. This may be the state which the reason deliberately approves, and which the utilitarian as well as every other moralist may be bound in certain cases to prefer.

Nor again, (2) must we forget that Plato, though he agrees generally with the view implied in the argument of the two brothers, is not expressing his own final conclusion, but rather seeking to dramatize one of the aspects of ethical truth. He is developing his idea gradually in a series of positions or situations. He is exhibiting Socrates for the first time undergoing the Socratic interrogation. Lastly, (3) the word 'happiness' involves some degree of confusion because associated in the language of modern philosophy with conscious pleasure or satisfaction, which was not equally present to his mind.

Glaucon has been drawing a picture of the misery of the just and the happiness of the unjust, to which the misery of the tyrant in Book IX is the answer and parallel. And still the unjust must appear just; that is 'the homage which vice pays to virtue.' But now Adeimantus, taking up the hint which had been already given by Glaucon, proceeds to show that in the opinion of mankind justice is regarded only for the sake of rewards and reputation, and points out the advantage which is given to such arguments as those of Thrasymachus and Glaucon by the conventional morality of mankind. He seems to feel the difficulty of 'justifying the ways of God to man.' Both the brothers touch upon the question, whether the morality of actions is determined by their consequences; and both of them go beyond the position of Socrates, that justice belongs to the class of goods not desirable for themselves only, but desirable for themselves and for their results, to which he recalls them. In their attempt to view justice as an internal principle, and in their condemnation of the poets, they anticipate him. The common life of Greece is not enough for them; they must penetrate deeper into the nature of things.

It has been objected that justice is honesty in the sense of Glaucon and Adeimantus, but is taken by Socrates to mean all virtue. May we not more truly say that the old-fashioned notion of justice is enlarged by Socrates, and becomes equivalent to universal order or well-being, first in the State, and secondly in the individual? He has found a new answer to his old question (Protag.), 'whether the virtues are one or many,' viz. that one is the ordering principle of the three others. In seeking to establish the purely internal nature of justice, he is met by the fact that man is a social being, and he tries to harmonise the two opposite theses as well as he can. There is no more inconsistency in this than was inevitable in his age and country; there is no use in turning upon him the cross lights of modern philosophy, which, from some other point of view, would appear equally inconsistent. Plato does not give the final solution of philosophical questions for us; nor can he be judged of by our standard.

The remainder of the Republic is developed out of the question of the sons of Ariston. Three points are deserving of remark in what immediately follows: – First, that the answer of Socrates is altogether indirect. He does not say that happiness consists in the contemplation of the idea of justice, and still less will he be tempted to affirm the Stoical paradox that the just man can be happy on the rack. But first he dwells on the difficulty of the problem and insists on restoring man to his natural condition, before he will answer the question at all. He too will frame an ideal, but his ideal comprehends not only abstract justice, but the whole relations of man. Under the fanciful illustration of the large letters he implies that he will only look for justice in society, and that from the State he will proceed to the individual. His answer in substance amounts to this, – that under favourable conditions, i.e. in the perfect State, justice and happiness will coincide, and that when justice has been once found, happiness may be left to take care of itself. That he falls into some degree of inconsistency, when in the tenth book he claims to have got rid of the rewards and honours of justice, may be admitted; for he has left those which exist in the perfect State. And the philosopher 'who retires under the shelter of a wall' can hardly have been esteemed happy by him, at least not in this world. Still he maintains the true attitude of moral action. Let a man do his duty first, without asking whether he will be happy or not, and happiness will be the inseparable accident which attends him. 'Seek ye first the kingdom of God and his righteousness, and all these things shall be added unto you.'

Secondly, it may be remarked that Plato preserves the genuine character of Greek thought in beginning with the State and in going on to the individual. First ethics, then politics – this is the order of ideas to us; the reverse is the order of history. Only after many struggles of thought does the individual assert his right as a moral being. In early ages he is not ONE, but one of many, the citizen of a State which is prior to him; and he has no notion of good or evil apart from the law of his country or the creed of his church. And to this type he is constantly tending to revert, whenever the influence of custom, or of party spirit, or the recollection of the past becomes too strong for him.

Thirdly, we may observe the confusion or identification of the individual and the State, of ethics and politics, which pervades early Greek speculation, and even in modern times retains a certain degree of influence. The subtle difference between the collective and individual action of mankind seems to have escaped early thinkers, and we too are sometimes in danger of forgetting the conditions of united human action, whenever we either elevate politics into ethics, or lower ethics to the standard of politics. The good man and the good citizen only coincide in the perfect State; and this perfection cannot be attained by legislation acting upon them from without, but, if at all, by education fashioning them from within.

...Socrates praises the sons of Ariston, 'inspired offspring of the renowned hero,' as the elegiac poet terms them; but he does not understand how they can argue so eloquently on behalf of injustice while their character shows that they are uninfluenced by their own arguments. He knows not how to answer them, although he is afraid of deserting justice in the hour of need. He therefore makes a condition, that having weak eyes he shall be allowed to read the large letters first and then go on to the smaller, that is, he must look for justice in the State first, and will then proceed to the individual. Accordingly he begins to construct the State.

Society arises out of the wants of man. His first want is food; his second a house; his third a coat. The sense of these needs and the possibility of satisfying them by exchange, draw individuals together on the same spot; and this is the beginning of a State, which we take the liberty to invent, although necessity is the real inventor. There must be first a husbandman, secondly a builder, thirdly a weaver, to which may be added a cobbler. Four or five citizens at least are required to make a city. Now men have different natures, and one man will do one thing better than many; and business waits for no man. Hence there must be a division of labour into different employments; into wholesale and retail trade; into workers, and makers of workmen's tools; into shepherds and husbandmen. A city which includes all this will have far exceeded the limit of four or five, and yet not be very large. But then again imports will be required, and imports necessitate exports, and this implies variety of produce in order to attract the taste of purchasers; also merchants and ships. In the city too we must have a market and money and retail trades; otherwise buyers and sellers will never meet, and the valuable time of the producers will be wasted in vain efforts at exchange. If we add hired servants the State will be complete. And we may guess that somewhere in the intercourse of the citizens with one another justice and injustice will appear.

Here follows a rustic picture of their way of life. They spend their days in houses which they have built for themselves; they make their own clothes and produce their own corn and wine. Their principal food is meal and flour, and they drink in moderation. They live on the best of terms with each other, and take care not to have too many children. 'But,' said Glaucon, interposing, 'are they not to have a relish?' Certainly; they will have salt and olives and cheese, vegetables and fruits, and chestnuts to roast at the fire. ''Tis a city of pigs, Socrates.' Why, I replied, what do you want more? 'Only the comforts of life, – sofas and tables, also sauces and sweets.' I see; you want not only a State, but a luxurious State; and possibly in the more complex frame we may sooner find justice and injustice. Then the fine arts must go to work – every conceivable instrument and ornament of luxury will be wanted. There will be dancers, painters, sculptors, musicians, cooks, barbers, tire-women, nurses, artists; swineherds and neatherds too for the animals, and physicians to cure the disorders of which luxury is the source. To feed all these superfluous mouths we shall need a part of our neighbour's land, and they will want a part of ours. And this is the origin of war, which may be traced to the same causes as other political evils. Our city will now require the slight addition of a camp, and the citizen will be converted into a soldier. But then again our old doctrine of the division of labour must not be forgotten. The art of war cannot be learned in a day, and there must be a natural aptitude for military duties. There will be some warlike natures who have this aptitude – dogs keen of scent, swift of foot to pursue, and strong of limb to fight. And as spirit is the foundation of courage, such natures, whether of men or animals, will be full of spirit. But these spirited natures are apt to bite and devour one another; the union of gentleness to friends and fierceness against enemies appears to be an impossibility, and the guardian of a State requires both qualities. Who then can be a guardian? The image of the dog suggests an answer. For dogs are gentle to friends and fierce to strangers. Your dog is a philosopher who judges by the rule of knowing or not knowing; and philosophy, whether in man or beast, is the parent of gentleness. The human watchdogs must be philosophers or lovers of learning which will make them gentle. And how are they to be learned without education?

But what shall their education be? Is any better than the old-fashioned sort which is comprehended under the name of music and gymnastic? Music includes literature, and literature is of two kinds, true and false. 'What do you mean?' he said. I mean that children hear stories before they learn gymnastics, and that the stories are either untrue, or have at most one or two grains of truth in a bushel of falsehood. Now early life is very impressible, and children ought not to learn what they will have to unlearn when they grow up; we must therefore have a censorship of nursery tales, banishing some and keeping others. Some of them are very improper, as we may see in the great instances of Homer and Hesiod, who not only tell lies but bad lies; stories about Uranus and Saturn, which are immoral as well as false, and which should never be spoken of to young persons, or indeed at all; or, if at all, then in a mystery, after the sacrifice, not of an Eleusinian pig, but of some unprocurable animal. Shall our youth be encouraged to beat their fathers by the example of Zeus, or our citizens be incited to quarrel by hearing or seeing representations of strife among the gods? Shall they listen to the narrative of Hephaestus binding his mother, and of Zeus sending him flying for helping her when she was beaten? Such tales may possibly have a mystical interpretation, but the young are incapable of understanding allegory. If any one asks what tales are to be allowed, we will answer that we are legislators and not book-makers; we only lay down the principles according to which books are to be written; to write them is the duty of others.

And our first principle is, that God must be represented as he is; not as the author of all things, but of good only. We will not suffer the poets to say that he is the steward of good and evil, or that he has two casks full of destinies; – or that Athene and Zeus incited Pandarus to break the treaty; or that God caused the sufferings of Niobe, or of Pelops, or the Trojan war; or that he makes men sin when he wishes to destroy them. Either these were not the actions of the gods, or God was just, and men were the better for being punished. But that the deed was evil, and God the author, is a wicked, suicidal fiction which we will allow no one, old or young, to utter. This is our first and great principle – God is the author of good only.

And the second principle is like unto it: – With God is no variableness or change of form. Reason teaches us this; for if we suppose a change in God, he must be changed either by another or by himself. By another? – but the best works of nature and art and the noblest qualities of mind are least liable to be changed by any external force. By himself? – but he cannot change for the better; he will hardly change for the worse. He remains for ever fairest and best in his own image. Therefore we refuse to listen to the poets who tell us of Here begging in the likeness of a priestess or of other deities who prowl about at night in strange disguises; all that blasphemous nonsense with which mothers fool the manhood out of their children must be suppressed. But some one will say that God, who is himself unchangeable, may take a form in relation to us. Why should he? For gods as well as men hate the lie in the soul, or principle of falsehood; and as for any other form of lying which is used for a purpose and is regarded as innocent in certain exceptional cases – what need have the gods of this? For they are not ignorant of antiquity like the poets, nor are they afraid of their enemies, nor is any madman a friend of theirs. God then is true, he is absolutely true; he changes not, he deceives not, by day or night, by word or sign. This is our second great principle – God is true. Away with the lying dream of Agamemnon in Homer, and the accusation of Thetis against Apollo in Aeschylus...

In order to give clearness to his conception of the State, Plato proceeds to trace the first principles of mutual need and of division of labour in an imaginary community of four or five citizens. Gradually this community increases; the division of labour extends to countries; imports necessitate exports; a medium of exchange is required, and retailers sit in the market-place to save the time of the producers. These are the steps by which Plato constructs the first or primitive State, introducing the elements of political economy by the way. As he is going to frame a second or civilized State, the simple naturally comes before the complex. He indulges, like Rousseau, in a picture of primitive life – an idea which has indeed often had a powerful influence on the imagination of mankind, but he does not seriously mean to say that one is better than the other (Politicus); nor can any inference be drawn from the description of the first state taken apart from the second, such as Aristotle appears to draw in the Politics. We should not interpret a Platonic dialogue any more than a poem or a parable in too literal or matter-of-fact a style. On the other hand, when we compare the lively fancy of Plato with the dried-up abstractions of modern treatises on philosophy, we are compelled to say with Protagoras, that the 'mythus is more interesting' (Protag.)

Several interesting remarks which in modern times would have a place in a treatise on Political Economy are scattered up and down the writings of Plato: especially Laws, Population; Free Trade; Adulteration; Wills and Bequests; Begging; Eryxias, (though not Plato's), Value and Demand; Republic, Division of Labour. The last subject, and also the origin of Retail

Trade, is treated with admirable lucidity in the second book of the Republic. But Plato never combined his economic ideas into a system, and never seems to have recognized that Trade is one of the great motive powers of the State and of the world. He would make retail traders only of the inferior sort of citizens (Rep., Laws), though he remarks, quaintly enough (Laws), that 'if only the best men and the best women everywhere were compelled to keep taverns for a time or to carry on retail trade, etc., then we should knew how pleasant and agreeable all these things are.'

The disappointment of Glaucon at the 'city of pigs,' the ludicrous description of the ministers of luxury in the more refined State, and the afterthought of the necessity of doctors, the illustration of the nature of the guardian taken from the dog, the desirableness of offering some almost unprocurable victim when impure mysteries are to be celebrated, the behaviour of Zeus to his father and of Hephaestus to his mother, are touches of humour which have also a serious meaning. In speaking of education Plato rather startles us by affirming that a child must be trained in falsehood first and in truth afterwards. Yet this is not very different from saying that children must be taught through the medium of imagination as well as reason; that their minds can only develope gradually, and that there is much which they must learn without understanding. This is also the substance of Plato's view, though he must be acknowledged to have drawn the line somewhat differently from modern ethical writers, respecting truth and falsehood. To us, economies or accommodations would not be allowable unless they were required by the human faculties or necessary for the communication of knowledge to the simple and ignorant. We should insist that the word was inseparable from the intention, and that we must not be 'falsely true,' i.e. speak or act falsely in support of what was right or true. But Plato would limit the use of fictions only by requiring that they should have a good moral effect, and that such a dangerous weapon as falsehood should be employed by the rulers alone and for great objects.

A Greek in the age of Plato attached no importance to the question whether his religion was an historical fact. He was just beginning to be conscious that the past had a history; but he could see nothing beyond Homer and Hesiod. Whether their narratives were true or false did not seriously affect the political or social life of Hellas. Men only began to suspect that they were fictions when they recognised them to be immoral. And so in all religions: the consideration of their morality comes first, afterwards the truth of the documents in which they are recorded, or of the events natural or supernatural which are told of them. But in modern times, and in Protestant countries perhaps more than in Catholic, we have been too much inclined to identify the historical with the moral; and some have refused to believe in religion at all, unless a superhuman accuracy was discernible in every part of the record. The facts of an ancient or religious history are amongst the most important of all facts; but they are frequently uncertain, and we only learn the true lesson which is to be gathered from them when we place ourselves above them. These reflections tend to show that the difference between Plato and ourselves, though not unimportant, is not so great as might at first sight appear. For we should agree with him in placing the moral before the historical truth of religion; and, generally, in disregarding those errors or misstatements of fact which necessarily occur in the early stages of all religions. We know also that changes in the traditions of a country cannot be made in a day; and are therefore tolerant of many things which science and criticism would condemn.

We note in passing that the allegorical interpretation of mythology, said to have been first introduced as early as the sixth century before Christ by Theagenes of Rhegium, was well established in the age of Plato, and here, as in the Phaedrus, though for a different reason, was rejected by him. That anachronisms whether of religion or law, when men have reached another stage of civilization, should be got rid of by fictions is in accordance with universal experience. Great is the art of interpretation; and by a natural process, which when once discovered was always going on, what could not be altered was explained away. And so without any palpable inconsistency there existed side by side two forms of religion, the tradition inherited or invented by the poets and the customary worship of the temple; on the other hand, there was the religion of the philosopher, who was dwelling in the heaven of ideas, but did not therefore refuse to offer a cock to Aesculapius, or to be seen saying his prayers at the rising of the sun. At length the antagonism between the popular and philosophical religion, never so great among the Greeks as in our own age, disappeared, and was only felt like the difference between the religion of the educated and uneducated among ourselves. The Zeus of Homer and Hesiod easily passed into the 'royal mind' of Plato (Philebus); the giant Heracles became the knight-errant and benefactor of mankind. These and still more wonderful transformations were readily effected by the ingenuity of Stoics and neo-Platonists in the two or three centuries before and after Christ. The Greek and Roman religions were gradually permeated by the spirit of philosophy; having lost their ancient meaning, they were resolved into poetry and morality; and probably were never purer than at the time of their decay, when their influence over the world was waning.

A singular conception which occurs towards the end of the book is the lie in the soul; this is connected with the Platonic and Socratic doctrine that involuntary ignorance is worse than voluntary. The lie in the soul is a true lie, the corruption of the highest truth, the deception of the highest part of the soul, from which he who is deceived has no power of delivering himself. For example, to represent God as false or immoral, or, according to Plato, as deluding men with appearances or as the author of evil; or again, to affirm with Protagoras that 'knowledge is sensation,' or that 'being is becoming,' or with Thrasymachus 'that might is right,' would have been regarded by Plato as a lie of this hateful sort. The greatest unconsciousness of the greatest untruth, e.g. if, in the language of the Gospels (John), 'he who was blind' were to say 'I see,' is another aspect of the state of mind which Plato is describing. The lie in the soul may be further compared with the sin against the Holy Ghost (Luke), allowing for the difference between Greek and Christian modes of speaking. To this is opposed the lie in words, which is only such a deception as may occur in a play or poem, or allegory or figure of speech, or in any sort of accommodation, – which though useless to the gods may be useful to men in certain cases. Socrates is here answering the question which he had himself raised about the propriety of deceiving a madman; and he is also contrasting the nature of God and man. For God is Truth, but mankind can only be true by appearing sometimes to be partial, or false. Reserving for another place the greater questions of religion or education, we may note further, (1) the approval of the old traditional education of Greece; (2) the preparation which Plato is making for the attack on Homer and the poets; (3) the preparation which he is also making for the use of economies in the State; (4) the contemptuous and at the same time euphemistic manner in which here as below he alludes to the 'Chronique Scandaleuse' of the gods.

BOOK III.

There is another motive in purifying religion, which is to banish fear; for no man can be courageous who is afraid of death, or who believes the tales which are repeated by the poets concerning the world below. They must be gently requested not to abuse hell; they may be reminded that their stories are both untrue and discouraging. Nor must they be angry if we expunge obnoxious passages, such as the depressing words of Achilles – 'I would rather be a serving-man than rule over all the dead;' and the verses which tell of the squalid mansions, the senseless shadows, the flitting soul mourning over lost strength and youth, the soul with a gibber going beneath the earth like smoke, or the souls of the suitors which flutter about like bats. The terrors and horrors of Cocytus and Styx, ghosts and sapless shades, and the rest of their Tartarean nomenclature, must vanish. Such tales may have their use; but they are not the proper food for soldiers. As little can we admit the sorrows and sympathies of the Homeric heroes: – Achilles, the son of Thetis, in tears, throwing ashes on his head, or pacing up and down the sea-shore in distraction; or Priam, the cousin of the gods, crying aloud, rolling in the mire. A good man is not prostrated at the loss of children or fortune. Neither is death terrible to him; and therefore lamentations over the dead should not be practised by men of note; they should be the concern of inferior persons only, whether women or men. Still worse is the attribution of such weakness to the gods; as when the goddesses say, 'Alas! my travail!' and worst of all, when the king of heaven himself laments his inability to save Hector, or sorrows over the impending doom of his dear Sarpedon. Such a character of God, if not ridiculed by our young men, is likely to be imitated by them. Nor should our citizens be given to excess of laughter – 'Such violent delights' are followed by a violent re-action. The description in the Iliad of the gods shaking their sides at the clumsiness of Hephaestus will not be admitted by us. 'Certainly not.'

Truth should have a high place among the virtues, for falsehood, as we were saying, is useless to the gods, and only useful to men as a medicine. But this employment of falsehood must remain a privilege of state; the common man must not in return tell a lie to the ruler; any more than the patient would tell a lie to his physician, or the sailor to his captain.

In the next place our youth must be temperate, and temperance consists in self-control and obedience to authority. That is a lesson which Homer teaches in some places: 'The Achaeans marched on breathing prowess, in silent awe of their leaders;' – but a very different one in other places: 'O heavy with wine, who hast the eyes of a dog, but the heart of a stag.' Language of the latter kind will not impress self-control on the minds of youth. The same may be said about his praises of eating and drinking and his dread of starvation; also about the verses in which he tells of the rapturous loves of Zeus and Here, or of how Hephaestus once detained Ares and Aphrodite in a net on a similar occasion. There is a nobler strain heard in the words: – 'Endure, my soul, thou hast endured worse.' Nor must we allow our citizens to receive bribes, or to say, 'Gifts persuade the gods, gifts reverend kings;' or to applaud the ignoble advice of Phoenix to Achilles that he should get money out of the Greeks before he assisted them; or the meanness of Achilles himself in taking gifts from Agamemnon; or his requiring a ransom for the body of Hector; or his cursing of Apollo; or his insolence to the river-god Scamander; or his dedication to the dead Patroclus of his own hair which had been already dedicated to the other river-god Spercheius; or his cruelty in dragging the body of Hector round the walls, and slaying the captives at the pyre: such a combination of meanness and cruelty in Cheiron's pupil is inconceivable. The amatory exploits of Peirithous and Theseus are equally unworthy. Either these so-called sons of gods were not the sons of gods, or they were not such as the poets imagine them, any more than the gods themselves are the authors of evil. The youth who believes that such things are done by those who have the blood of heaven flowing in their veins will be too ready to imitate their example.

Enough of gods and heroes; – what shall we say about men? What the poets and story-tellers say – that the wicked prosper and the righteous are afflicted, or that justice is another's gain? Such misrepresentations cannot be allowed by us. But in this we are anticipating the definition of justice, and had therefore better defer the enquiry.

The subjects of poetry have been sufficiently treated; next follows style. Now all poetry is a narrative of events past, present, or to come; and narrative is of three kinds, the simple, the imitative, and a composition of the two. An instance will make my meaning clear. The first scene in Homer is of the last or mixed kind, being partly description and partly dialogue. But if you throw the dialogue into the 'oratio obliqua,' the passage will run thus: The priest came and prayed Apollo that the Achaeans might take Troy and have a safe return if Agamemnon would only give him back his daughter; and the other Greeks assented, but Agamemnon was wroth, and so on – The whole then becomes descriptive, and the poet is the only speaker left; or, if you omit the narrative, the whole becomes dialogue. These are the three styles – which of them is to be admitted into our State? 'Do you ask whether tragedy and comedy are to be admitted?' Yes, but also something more – Is it not doubtful whether our guardians are to be imitators at all? Or rather, has not the question been already answered, for we have decided that one man cannot in his life play many parts, any more than he can act both tragedy and comedy, or be rhapsodist and actor at once? Human nature is coined into very small pieces, and as our guardians have their own business already, which is the care of freedom, they will have enough to do without imitating. If they imitate they should imitate, not any meanness or baseness, but the good only; for the mask which the actor wears is apt to become his face. We cannot allow men to play the parts of women, quarrelling, weeping, scolding, or boasting against the gods, – least of all when making love or in labour. They must not represent slaves, or bullies, or cowards, drunkards, or madmen, or blacksmiths, or neighing horses, or bellowing bulls, or sounding rivers, or a raging sea. A good or wise man will be willing to perform good and wise actions, but he will be ashamed to play an inferior part which he has never practised; and he will prefer to employ the descriptive style with as little imitation as possible. The man who has no self-respect, on the contrary, will imitate anybody and anything; sounds of nature and cries of animals alike; his whole performance will be imitation of gesture and voice. Now in the descriptive style there are few changes, but in the dramatic there are a great many. Poets and musicians use either, or a compound of both, and this compound is very attractive to youth and their teachers as well as to the vulgar. But our State in which one man plays one part only is not adapted for complexity. And when one of these polyphonous pantomimic gentlemen offers to exhibit himself and his poetry we will show him every observance of respect, but at the same time tell him that there is no room for his kind in our State; we prefer the rough, honest poet, and will not depart from our original models (Laws).

Next as to the music. A song or ode has three parts, – the subject, the harmony, and the rhythm; of which the two last are dependent upon the first. As we banished strains of lamentation, so we may now banish the mixed Lydian harmonies, which are the harmonies of lamentation; and as our citizens are to be temperate, we may also banish convivial harmonies, such as the Ionian and pure Lydian. Two remain – the Dorian and Phrygian, the first for war, the second for peace; the one expressive of courage, the other of obedience or instruction or religious feeling. And as we reject varieties of harmony, we shall also reject the many-stringed, variously-shaped instruments which give utterance to them, and in particular the flute, which is more complex than any of them. The lyre and the harp may be permitted in the town, and the Pan's-pipe in the fields. Thus we have made a purgation of music, and will now make a purgation of metres. These should be like the harmonies, simple and suitable to the occasion. There are four notes of the tetrachord, and there are three ratios of metre, 3/2, 2/2, 2/1, which have all their characteristics, and the feet have different characteristics as well as the rhythms. But about this you and I must ask Damon, the great musician, who speaks, if I remember rightly, of a martial measure as well as of dactylic, trochaic, and iambic rhythms, which he arranges so as to equalize the syllables with one another, assigning to each the proper quantity. We only venture to affirm the general principle that the style is to conform to the subject and the metre to the style; and that the simplicity and harmony of the soul should be reflected in them all. This principle of simplicity has to be learnt by every one in the days of his youth, and may be gathered anywhere, from the creative and constructive arts, as well as from the forms of plants and animals.

Other artists as well as poets should be warned against meanness or unseemliness. Sculpture and painting equally with music must conform to the law of simplicity. He who violates it cannot be allowed to work in our city, and to corrupt the taste of our citizens. For our guardians must grow up, not amid images of deformity which will gradually poison and corrupt their souls, but in a land of health and beauty where they will drink in from every object sweet and harmonious influences. And of all these influences the greatest is the education given by music, which finds a way into the innermost soul and imparts to it the sense of beauty and of deformity. At first the effect is unconscious; but when reason arrives, then he who has been thus trained welcomes her as the friend whom he always knew. As in learning to read, first we acquire the elements or letters separately, and afterwards their combinations, and cannot recognize reflections of them until we know the letters themselves; – in like manner we must first attain the elements or essential forms of the virtues, and then trace their combinations in life and experience. There is a music of the soul which answers to the harmony of the world; and the fairest object of a musical soul is the fair mind in the fair body. Some defect in the latter may be excused, but not in the former. True love is the daughter of temperance, and temperance is utterly opposed to the madness of bodily pleasure. Enough has been said of music, which makes a fair ending with love.

Next we pass on to gymnastics; about which I would remark, that the soul is related to the body as a cause to an effect, and therefore if we educate the mind we may leave the education of the body in her charge, and need only give a general outline of the course to be pursued. In the first place the guardians must abstain from strong drink, for they should be the last persons to lose their wits. Whether the habits of the palaestra are suitable to them is more doubtful, for the ordinary gymnastic is a sleepy sort of thing, and if left off suddenly is apt to endanger health. But our warrior athletes must be wide-awake dogs, and must also be inured to all changes of food and climate. Hence they will require a simpler kind of gymnastic, akin to their simple music; and for their diet a rule may be found in Homer, who feeds his heroes on roast meat only, and gives them no fish although they are living at the sea-side, nor boiled meats which involve an apparatus of pots and pans; and, if I am not mistaken, he nowhere mentions sweet sauces. Sicilian cookery and Attic confections and Corinthian courtezans, which are to gymnastic what Lydian and Ionian melodies are to music, must be forbidden. Where gluttony and intemperance prevail the town quickly fills with doctors and pleaders; and law and medicine give themselves airs as soon as the freemen of a State take an interest in them. But what can show a more disgraceful state of education than to have to go abroad for justice because you have none of your own at home? And yet there IS a worse stage of the same disease – when men have learned to take a pleasure and pride in the twists and turns of the law; not considering how much better it would be for them so to order their lives as to have no need of a nodding justice. And there is a like disgrace in employing a physician, not for the cure of wounds or epidemic disorders, but because a man has by laziness and luxury contracted diseases which were unknown in the days of Asclepius. How simple is the Homeric practice of medicine. Eurypylus after he has been wounded drinks a posset of Pramnian wine, which is of a heating nature; and yet the sons of Asclepius blame neither the damsel who gives him the drink, nor Patroclus who is attending on him. The truth is that this modern system of nursing diseases was introduced by Herodicus the trainer; who, being of a sickly constitution, by a compound of training and medicine tortured first himself and then a good many other people, and lived a great deal longer than he had any right. But Asclepius would not practise this art, because he knew that the citizens of a well-ordered State have no leisure to be ill, and therefore he adopted the 'kill or cure' method, which artisans and labourers employ. 'They must be at their business,' they say, 'and have no time for coddling: if they recover, well; if they don't, there is an end of them.' Whereas the rich man is supposed to be a gentleman who can afford to be ill. Do you know a maxim of Phocylides – that 'when a man begins to be rich' (or, perhaps, a little sooner) 'he should practise virtue'? But how can excessive care of health be inconsistent with an ordinary occupation, and yet consistent with that practice of virtue which Phocylides inculcates? When a student imagines that philosophy gives him a headache, he never does anything; he is always unwell. This was the reason why Asclepius and his sons practised no such art. They were acting in the interest of the public, and did not wish to preserve useless lives, or raise up a puny offspring to wretched sires. Honest diseases they honestly cured; and if a man was wounded, they applied the proper remedies, and then let him eat and drink what he liked. But they declined to treat intemperate and worthless subjects, even though they might have made large fortunes out of them. As to the story of Pindar, that Asclepius was slain by a thunderbolt for restoring a rich man to life, that is a lie – following our old rule we must say either that he did not take bribes, or that he was not the son of a god.

Glaucon then asks Socrates whether the best physicians and the best judges will not be those who have had severally the greatest experience of diseases and of crimes. Socrates draws a distinction between the two professions. The physician should have had experience of disease in his own body, for he cures with his mind and not with his body. But the judge controls mind by mind; and therefore his mind should not be corrupted by crime. Where then is he to gain experience? How is he to be wise and also innocent? When young a good man is apt to be deceived by evil-doers, because he has no pattern of evil in himself; and therefore the judge should be of a certain age; his youth should have been innocent, and he should have acquired insight into evil not by the practice of it, but by the observation of it in others. This is the ideal of a judge; the criminal turned detective is wonderfully suspicious, but when in company with good men who have experience, he is at fault, for he foolishly imagines that every one is as bad as himself. Vice may be known of virtue, but cannot know virtue. This is the sort of medicine and this the sort of law which will prevail in our State; they will be healing arts to better natures; but the evil body will be left to die by the one, and the evil soul will be put to death by the other. And the need of either will be greatly diminished by good music which will give harmony to the soul, and good gymnastic which will give health to the body. Not that this division of music and gymnastic really corresponds to soul and body; for they are both equally concerned with the soul, which is tamed by the one and aroused and sustained by the other. The two together supply our guardians with their twofold nature. The passionate disposition when it has too much gymnastic is hardened and brutalized, the gentle or philosophic temper which has too much music becomes enervated. While a man is allowing music to pour like water through the funnel of his ears, the edge of his soul gradually wears away, and the passionate or spirited element is melted out of him. Too little spirit is easily exhausted; too much quickly passes into nervous irritability. So, again, the athlete by feeding and training has his courage doubled, but he soon grows stupid; he is like a wild beast, ready to do everything by blows and nothing by counsel or policy. There are two principles in man, reason and passion, and to these, not to the soul and body, the two arts of music and gymnastic correspond. He who mingles them in harmonious concord is the true musician, – he shall be the presiding genius of our State.

The next question is, Who are to be our rulers? First, the elder must rule the younger; and the best of the elders will be the best guardians. Now they will be the best who love their subjects most, and think that they have a common interest with them in the welfare of the state. These we must select; but they must be watched at every epoch of life to see whether they have retained the same opinions and held out against force and enchantment. For time and persuasion and the love of pleasure may enchant a man into a change of purpose, and the force of grief and pain may compel him. And therefore our guardians must be men who have been tried by many tests, like gold in the refiner's fire, and have been passed first through danger, then through pleasure, and at every age have come out of such trials victorious and without stain, in full command of themselves and their principles; having all their faculties in harmonious exercise for their country's good. These shall receive the highest honours both in life and death. (It would perhaps be better to confine the term 'guardians' to this select class: the younger men may be called 'auxiliaries.')

And now for one magnificent lie, in the belief of which, Oh that we could train our rulers! – at any rate let us make the attempt with the rest of the world. What I am going to tell is only another version of the legend of Cadmus; but our unbelieving generation will be slow to accept such a story. The tale must be imparted, first to the rulers, then to the soldiers, lastly to the people. We will inform them that their youth was a dream, and that during the time when they seemed to be undergoing their education they were really being fashioned in the earth, who sent them up when they were ready; and that they must protect and cherish her whose children they are, and regard each other as brothers and sisters. 'I do not wonder at your being ashamed to propound such a fiction.' There is more behind. These brothers and sisters have different natures, and some of them God framed to rule, whom he fashioned of gold; others he made of silver, to be auxiliaries; others again to be husbandmen and craftsmen, and these were formed by him of brass and iron. But as they are all sprung from a common stock, a golden parent may have a silver son, or a silver parent a golden son, and then there must be a change of rank; the son of the rich must descend, and the child of the artisan rise, in the social scale; for an oracle says 'that the State will come to an end if governed by a man of brass or iron.' Will our citizens ever believe all this? 'Not in the present generation, but in the next, perhaps, Yes.'

Now let the earthborn men go forth under the command of their rulers, and look about and pitch their camp in a high place, which will be safe against enemies from without, and likewise against insurrections from within. There let them sacrifice and set up their tents; for soldiers they are to be and not shopkeepers, the watchdogs and guardians of the sheep; and luxury and avarice will turn them into wolves and tyrants. Their habits and their dwellings should correspond to their education. They should have no property; their pay should only meet their expenses; and they should have common meals. Gold and silver we will tell them that they have from God, and this divine gift in their souls they must not alloy with that earthly dross which passes under the name of gold. They only of the citizens may not touch it, or be under the same roof with it, or drink from it; it is the accursed thing. Should they ever acquire houses or lands or money of their own, they will become householders and tradesmen instead of guardians, enemies and tyrants instead of helpers, and the hour of ruin, both to themselves and the rest of the State, will be at hand.

The religious and ethical aspect of Plato's education will hereafter be considered under a separate head. Some lesser points may be more conveniently noticed in this place.

1. The constant appeal to the authority of Homer, whom, with grave irony, Plato, after the manner of his age, summons as a witness about ethics and psychology, as well as about diet and medicine; attempting to distinguish the better lesson from the worse, sometimes altering the text from design; more than once quoting or alluding to Homer inaccurately, after the manner of the early logographers turning the Iliad into prose, and delighting to draw far-fetched inferences from his words, or to make ludicrous applications of them. He does not, like Heracleitus, get into a rage with Homer and Archilochus (Heracl.), but uses their words and

expressions as vehicles of a higher truth; not on a system like Theagenes of Rhegium or Metrodorus, or in later times the Stoics, but as fancy may dictate. And the conclusions drawn from them are sound, although the premises are fictitious. These fanciful appeals to Homer add a charm to Plato's style, and at the same time they have the effect of a satire on the follies of Homeric interpretation. To us (and probably to himself), although they take the form of arguments, they are really figures of speech. They may be compared with modern citations from Scripture, which have often a great rhetorical power even when the original meaning of the words is entirely lost sight of. The real, like the Platonic Socrates, as we gather from the Memorabilia of Xenophon, was fond of making similar adaptations. Great in all ages and countries, in religion as well as in law and literature, has been the art of interpretation.

2. 'The style is to conform to the subject and the metre to the style.' Notwithstanding the fascination which the word 'classical' exercises over us, we can hardly maintain that this rule is observed in all the Greek poetry which has come down to us. We cannot deny that the thought often exceeds the power of lucid expression in Aeschylus and Pindar; or that rhetoric gets the better of the thought in the Sophist-poet Euripides. Only perhaps in Sophocles is there a perfect harmony of the two; in him alone do we find a grace of language like the beauty of a Greek statue, in which there is nothing to add or to take away; at least this is true of single plays or of large portions of them. The connection in the Tragic Choruses and in the Greek lyric poets is not unfrequently a tangled thread which in an age before logic the poet was unable to draw out. Many thoughts and feelings mingled in his mind, and he had no power of disengaging or arranging them. For there is a subtle influence of logic which requires to be transferred from prose to poetry, just as the music and perfection of language are infused by poetry into prose. In all ages the poet has been a bad judge of his own meaning (Apol.); for he does not see that the word which is full of associations to his own mind is difficult and unmeaning to that of another; or that the sequence which is clear to himself is puzzling to others. There are many passages in some of our greatest modern poets which are far too obscure; in which there is no proportion between style and subject, in which any half-expressed figure, any harsh construction, any distorted collocation of words, any remote sequence of ideas is admitted; and there is no voice 'coming sweetly from nature,' or music adding the expression of feeling to thought. As if there could be poetry without beauty, or beauty without ease and clearness. The obscurities of early Greek poets arose necessarily out of the state of language and logic which existed in their age. They are not

examples to be followed by us; for the use of language ought in every generation to become clearer and clearer. Like Shakespere, they were great in spite, not in consequence, of their imperfections of expression. But there is no reason for returning to the necessary obscurity which prevailed in the infancy of literature. The English poets of the last century were certainly not obscure; and we have no excuse for losing what they had gained, or for going back to the earlier or transitional age which preceded them. The thought of our own times has not out-stripped language; a want of Plato's 'art of measuring' is the rule cause of the disproportion between them.

3. In the third book of the Republic a nearer approach is made to a theory of art than anywhere else in Plato. His views may be summed up as follows: − True art is not fanciful and imitative, but simple and ideal, − the expression of the highest moral energy, whether in action or repose. To live among works of plastic art which are of this noble and simple character, or to listen to such strains, is the best of influences, − the true Greek atmosphere, in which youth should be brought up. That is the way to create in them a natural good taste, which will have a feeling of truth and beauty in all things. For though the poets are to be expelled, still art is recognized as another aspect of reason − like love in the Symposium, extending over the same sphere, but confined to the preliminary education, and acting through the power of habit; and this conception of art is not limited to strains of music or the forms of plastic art, but pervades all nature and has a wide kindred in the world. The Republic of Plato, like the Athens of Pericles, has an artistic as well as a political side.

There is hardly any mention in Plato of the creative arts; only in two or three passages does he even allude to them (Rep.; Soph.). He is not lost in rapture at the great works of Phidias, the Parthenon, the Propylea, the statues of Zeus or Athene. He would probably have regarded any abstract truth of number or figure as higher than the greatest of them. Yet it is hard to suppose that some influence, such as he hopes to inspire in youth, did not pass into his own mind from the works of art which he saw around him. We are living upon the fragments of them, and find in a few broken stones the standard of truth and beauty. But in Plato this feeling has no expression; he nowhere says that beauty is the object of art; he seems to deny that wisdom can take an external form (Phaedrus); he does not distinguish the fine from the mechanical arts. Whether or no, like some writers, he felt more than he expressed, it is at any rate remarkable that the greatest perfection of the fine arts should coincide with an almost entire silence about them. In one very striking passage he tells us that a work of art, like the State, is a whole; and this conception of a whole and the love of the newly-born mathematical sciences may be regarded, if not as the inspiring, at any rate as the regulating principles of Greek art (Xen. Mem.; and Sophist).

4. Plato makes the true and subtle remark that the physician had better not be in robust health; and should have known what illness is in his own person. But the judge ought to have had no similar experience of evil; he is to be a good man who, having passed his youth in innocence, became acquainted late in life with the vices of others. And therefore, according to Plato, a judge should not be young, just as a young man according to Aristotle is not fit to be a hearer of moral philosophy. The bad, on the other hand, have a knowledge of vice, but no knowledge of virtue. It may be doubted, however, whether this train of reflection is well founded. In a remarkable passage of the Laws it is acknowledged that the evil may form a correct estimate of the good. The union of gentleness and courage in Book ii. at first seemed to be a paradox, yet was afterwards ascertained to be a truth. And Plato might also have found that the intuition of evil may be consistent with the abhorrence of it. There is a directness of aim in virtue which gives an insight into vice. And the knowledge of character is in some degree a natural sense independent of any special experience of good or evil.

5. One of the most remarkable conceptions of Plato, because un-Greek and also very different from anything which existed at all in his age of the world, is the transposition of ranks. In the Spartan state there had been enfranchisement of Helots and degradation of citizens under special circumstances. And in the ancient Greek aristocracies, merit was certainly recognized as one of the elements on which government was based. The founders of states were supposed to be their benefactors, who were raised by their great actions above the ordinary level of humanity; at a later period, the services of warriors and legislators were held to entitle them and their descendants to the privileges of citizenship and to the first rank in the state. And although the existence of an ideal aristocracy is slenderly proven from the remains of early Greek history, and we have a difficulty in ascribing such a character, however the idea may be defined, to any actual Hellenic state – or indeed to any state which has ever existed in the world – still the rule of the best was certainly the aspiration of philosophers, who probably accommodated a good deal their views of primitive history to their own notions of good government. Plato further insists on applying to the guardians of his state a series of tests by which all those who fell short

of a fixed standard were either removed from the governing body, or not admitted to it; and this 'academic' discipline did to a certain extent prevail in Greek states, especially in Sparta. He also indicates that the system of caste, which existed in a great part of the ancient, and is by no means extinct in the modern European world, should be set aside from time to time in favour of merit. He is aware how deeply the greater part of mankind resent any interference with the order of society, and therefore he proposes his novel idea in the form of what he himself calls a 'monstrous fiction.' (Compare the ceremony of preparation for the two 'great waves' in Book v.) Two principles are indicated by him: first, that there is a distinction of ranks dependent on circumstances prior to the individual: second, that this distinction is and ought to be broken through by personal qualities. He adapts mythology like the Homeric poems to the wants of the state, making 'the Phoenician tale' the vehicle of his ideas. Every Greek state had a myth respecting its own origin; the Platonic republic may also have a tale of earthborn men. The gravity and verisimilitude with which the tale is told, and the analogy of Greek tradition, are a sufficient verification of the 'monstrous falsehood.' Ancient poetry had spoken of a gold and silver and brass and iron age succeeding one another, but Plato supposes these differences in the natures of men to exist together in a single state. Mythology supplies a figure under which the lesson may be taught (as Protagoras says, 'the myth is more interesting'), and also enables Plato to touch lightly on new principles without going into details. In this passage he shadows forth a general truth, but he does not tell us by what steps the transposition of ranks is to be effected. Indeed throughout the Republic he allows the lower ranks to fade into the distance. We do not know whether they are to carry arms, and whether in the fifth book they are or are not included in the communistic regulations respecting property and marriage. Nor is there any use in arguing strictly either from a few chance words, or from the silence of Plato, or in drawing inferences which were beyond his vision. Aristotle, in his criticism on the position of the lower classes, does not perceive that the poetical creation is 'like the air, invulnerable,' and cannot be penetrated by the shafts of his logic (Pol.).

6. Two paradoxes which strike the modern reader as in the highest degree fanciful and ideal, and which suggest to him many reflections, are to be found in the third book of the Republic: first, the great power of music, so much beyond any influence which is experienced by us in modern times, when the art or science has been far more developed, and has found the secret of harmony, as well as of melody; secondly, the indefinite and almost

absolute control which the soul is supposed to exercise over the body.

In the first we suspect some degree of exaggeration, such as we may also observe among certain masters of the art, not unknown to us, at the present day. With this natural enthusiasm, which is felt by a few only, there seems to mingle in Plato a sort of Pythagorean reverence for numbers and numerical proportion to which Aristotle is a stranger. Intervals of sound and number are to him sacred things which have a law of their own, not dependent on the variations of sense. They rise above sense, and become a connecting link with the world of ideas. But it is evident that Plato is describing what to him appears to be also a fact. The power of a simple and characteristic melody on the impressible mind of the Greek is more than we can easily appreciate. The effect of national airs may bear some comparison with it. And, besides all this, there is a confusion between the harmony of musical notes and the harmony of soul and body, which is so potently inspired by them.

The second paradox leads up to some curious and interesting questions – How far can the mind control the body? Is the relation between them one of mutual antagonism or of mutual harmony? Are they two or one, and is either of them the cause of the other? May we not at times drop the opposition between them, and the mode of describing them, which is so familiar to us, and yet hardly conveys any precise meaning, and try to view this composite creature, man, in a more simple manner? Must we not at any rate admit that there is in human nature a higher and a lower principle, divided by no distinct line, which at times break asunder and take up arms against one another? Or again, they are reconciled and move together, either unconsciously in the ordinary work of life, or consciously in the pursuit of some noble aim, to be attained not without an effort, and for which every thought and nerve are strained. And then the body becomes the good friend or ally, or servant or instrument of the mind. And the mind has often a wonderful and almost superhuman power of banishing disease and weakness and calling out a hidden strength. Reason and the desires, the intellect and the senses are brought into harmony and obedience so as to form a single human being. They are ever parting, ever meeting; and the identity or diversity of their tendencies or operations is for the most part unnoticed by us. When the mind touches the body through the appetites, we acknowledge the responsibility of the one to the other. There is a tendency in us which says 'Drink.' There is another which says, 'Do not drink; it is not good for you.' And we all of us know which is the rightful superior. We are also responsible for our health, although into this sphere there enter some elements of necessity which may be beyond our control. Still even in the management of health, care and thought, continued over many years, may make us almost free agents, if we do not exact too much of ourselves, and if we acknowledge that all human freedom is limited by the laws of nature and of mind.

We are disappointed to find that Plato, in the general condemnation which he passes on the practice of medicine prevailing in his own day, depreciates the effects of diet. He would like to have diseases of a definite character and capable of receiving a definite treatment. He is afraid of invalidism interfering with the business of life. He does not recognize that time is the great healer both of mental and bodily disorders; and that remedies which are gradual and proceed little by little are safer than those which produce a sudden catastrophe. Neither does he see that there is no way in which the mind can more surely influence the body than by the control of eating and drinking; or any other action or occasion of human life on which the higher freedom of the will can be more simple or truly asserted.

7. Lesser matters of style may be remarked.

(1) The affected ignorance of music, which is Plato's way of expressing that he is passing lightly over the subject.

(2) The tentative manner in which here, as in the second book, he proceeds with the construction of the State.

(3) The description of the State sometimes as a reality, and then again as a work of imagination only; these are the arts by which he sustains the reader's interest.

(4) Connecting links, or the preparation for the entire expulsion of the poets in Book X.

(5) The companion pictures of the lover of litigation and the valetudinarian, the satirical jest about the maxim of Phocylides, the manner in which the image of the gold and silver citizens is taken up into the subject, and the argument from the practice of Asclepius, should not escape notice.

BOOK IV.

Adeimantus said: 'Suppose a person to argue, Socrates, that you make your citizens miserable, and this by their own free-will; they are the lords of the city, and yet instead of having, like other men, lands and houses and money of their own, they live as mercenaries and are always mounting guard.' You may add, I replied, that they receive no pay but only their food, and have no money to spend on a journey or a mistress. 'Well, and what answer do you give?' My answer is, that our guardians may or may not be the happiest of men, – I should not be surprised to find in the long-run that they were, – but this is not the aim of our constitution, which was designed for the good of the whole and not of any one part. If I went to a sculptor and blamed him for having painted the eye, which is the noblest feature of the face, not purple but black, he would reply: 'The eye must be an eye, and you should look at the statue as a whole.' 'Now I can well imagine a fool's paradise, in which everybody is eating and drinking, clothed in purple and fine linen, and potters lie on sofas and have their wheel at hand, that they may work a little when they please; and cobblers and all the other classes of a State lose their distinctive character. And a State may get on without cobblers; but when the guardians degenerate into boon companions, then the ruin is complete. Remember that we are not talking of peasants keeping holiday, but of a State in which every man is expected to do his own work. The happiness resides not in this or that class, but in the State as a whole. I have another remark to make: – A middle condition is best for artisans; they should have money enough to buy tools, and not enough to be independent of business. And will not the same condition be best for our citizens? If they are poor, they will be mean; if rich, luxurious and lazy; and in neither case contented. 'But then how will our poor city be able to go to war against an enemy who has money?' There may be a difficulty in fighting against one enemy; against two there will be none. In the first place, the contest will be carried on by trained warriors against well-to-do citizens: and is not a regular athlete an easy match for two stout opponents at least? Suppose also, that before engaging we send ambassadors to one of the two cities, saying, 'Silver and gold we have not; do you help us and take our share of the spoil;' – who would fight against the lean, wiry dogs, when they might join with them in preying upon the fatted sheep? 'But if many states join their resources, shall we not be in danger?' I am amused to hear you use the word 'state' of any but our own State. They are 'states,' but not 'a state' – many in one. For in every state there are two hostile nations, rich and poor, which you may set one against the other. But our State, while she remains true to her principles, will be in very deed the mightiest of Hellenic states.

To the size of the state there is no limit but the necessity of unity; it must be neither too large nor too small to be one. This is a matter of secondary importance, like the principle of transposition which was intimated in the parable of the earthborn men. The meaning there implied was that every man should do that for which he was fitted, and be at one with himself, and then the whole city would be united. But all these things are secondary, if education, which is the great matter, be duly regarded. When the wheel has once been set in motion, the speed is always increasing; and each generation improves upon the preceding, both in physical and moral qualities. The care of the governors should be directed to preserve music and gymnastic from innovation; alter the songs of a country, Damon says, and you will soon end by altering its laws. The change appears innocent at first, and begins in play; but the evil soon becomes serious, working secretly upon the characters of individuals, then upon social and commercial relations, and lastly upon the institutions of a state; and there is ruin and confusion everywhere. But if education remains in the established form, there will be no danger. A restorative process will be always going on; the spirit of law and order will raise up what has fallen down. Nor will any regulations be needed for the lesser matters of life – rules of deportment or fashions of dress. Like invites like for good or for evil. Education will correct deficiencies and supply the power of self-government. Far be it from us to enter into the particulars of legislation; let the guardians take care of education, and education will take care of all other things.

But without education they may patch and mend as they please; they will make no progress, any more than a patient who thinks to cure himself by some favourite remedy and will not give up his luxurious mode of living. If you tell such persons that they must first alter their habits, then they grow angry; they are charming people. 'Charming, – nay, the very reverse.' Evidently these gentlemen are not in your good graces, nor the state which is like them. And such states there are which first ordain under penalty of death that no one shall alter the constitution, and then suffer themselves to be flattered into and out of anything; and he who indulges them and fawns upon them, is their leader and saviour. 'Yes, the men are as bad as the states.' But do you not admire their cleverness? 'Nay, some of them are stupid enough to believe what the people tell them.' And when all the world is telling a man that he is six feet high, and he has no measure, how can he believe anything else? But don't get into a passion: to see our statesmen trying their nostrums, and fancying that they can cut off at a blow the Hydra-like rogueries of mankind, is as good as a play. Minute enactments are superfluous in good states, and are useless in bad ones.

And now what remains of the work of legislation? Nothing for us; but to Apollo the god of Delphi we leave the ordering of the greatest of all things – that is to say, religion. Only our ancestral deity sitting upon the centre and navel of the earth will be trusted by us if we have any sense, in an affair of such magnitude. No foreign god shall be supreme in our realms...

Here, as Socrates would say, let us 'reflect on' (Greek) what has preceded: thus far we have spoken not of the happiness of the citizens, but only of the well-being of the State. They may be the happiest of men, but our principal aim in founding the State was not to make them happy. They were to be guardians, not holiday-makers. In this pleasant manner is presented to us the famous question both of ancient and modern philosophy, touching the relation of duty to happiness, of right to utility.

First duty, then happiness, is the natural order of our moral ideas. The utilitarian principle is valuable as a corrective of error, and shows to us a side of ethics which is apt to be neglected. It may be admitted further that right and utility are co-extensive, and that he who makes the happiness of mankind his object has one of the highest and noblest motives of human action. But utility is not the historical basis of morality; nor the aspect in which moral and religious ideas commonly occur to the mind. The greatest happiness of all is, as we believe, the far-off result of the divine government of the universe. The greatest happiness of the individual is certainly to be found in a life of virtue and goodness. But we seem to be more assured of a law of right than we can be of a divine purpose, that 'all mankind should be saved;' and we infer the one from the other. And the greatest happiness of the individual may be the reverse of the greatest happiness in the ordinary sense of the term, and may be realised in a life of pain, or in a voluntary death. Further, the word 'happiness' has several ambiguities; it may mean either pleasure or an ideal life, happiness subjective or objective, in this world or in another, of ourselves only or of our neighbours and of all men everywhere. By the modern founder of Utilitarianism the self-regarding and disinterested motives of action are included under the same term, although they are commonly opposed by us as benevolence and self-love. The word happiness has not the definiteness or the sacredness of 'truth' and 'right'; it does not equally appeal to our higher nature, and has not sunk into the conscience of mankind. It is associated too much with the comforts and conveniences of life; too little with 'the goods of the soul which we desire for their own sake.' In a great trial, or danger, or temptation, or in any great and heroic action, it is scarcely thought of. For these reasons 'the greatest happiness' principle is not the true foundation of ethics. But though not the first principle, it is the second, which is like unto it, and is often of easier application. For the larger part of human actions are neither right nor wrong, except in so far as they tend to the happiness of mankind (Introd. to Gorgias and Philebus).

The same question reappears in politics, where the useful or expedient seems to claim a larger sphere and to have a greater authority. For concerning political measures, we chiefly ask: How will they affect the happiness of mankind? Yet here too we may observe that what we term expediency is merely the law of right limited by the conditions of human society. Right and truth are the highest aims of government as well as of individuals; and we ought not to lose sight of them because we cannot directly enforce them. They appeal to the better mind of nations; and sometimes they are too much for merely temporal interests to resist. They are the watchwords which all men use in matters of public policy, as well as in their private dealings; the peace of Europe may be said to depend upon them. In the most commercial and utilitarian states of society the power of ideas remains. And all the higher class of statesmen have in them something of that idealism which Pericles is said to have gathered from the teaching of Anaxagoras. They recognise that the true leader of men must be above the motives of ambition, and that national character is of greater value than material comfort and prosperity. And this is the order of thought in Plato; first, he expects his citizens to do their duty, and then under favourable circumstances, that is to say, in a well-ordered State, their happiness is assured. That he was far from excluding the modern principle of utility in politics is sufficiently evident from other passages; in which 'the most beneficial is affirmed to be the most honourable', and also 'the most sacred'.

We may note

(1) The manner in which the objection of Adeimantus here, is designed to draw out and deepen the argument of Socrates.

(2) The conception of a whole as lying at the foundation both of politics and of art, in the latter supplying the only principle of criticism, which, under the various names of harmony, symmetry, measure, proportion, unity, the Greek seems to have applied to works of art.

(3) The requirement that the State should be limited in size, after the traditional model of a Greek state; as in the Politics of Aristotle, the fact that the cities of Hellas were small is converted into a principle.

(4) The humorous pictures of the lean dogs and the fatted sheep, of the light active boxer upsetting two stout gentlemen at least, of the 'charming' patients who are always making themselves worse; or again, the playful assumption that there is no State but our own; or the grave irony with which the statesman is excused who believes that he is six feet high because he is told so, and having nothing to measure with is to be pardoned for his ignorance – he is too amusing for us to be seriously angry with him.

(5) The light and superficial manner in which religion is passed over when provision has been made for two great principles, – first, that religion shall be based on the highest conception of the gods, secondly, that the true national or Hellenic type shall be maintained...

Socrates proceeds: But where amid all this is justice? Son of Ariston, tell me where. Light a candle and search the city, and get your brother and the rest of our friends to help in seeking for her. 'That won't do,' replied Glaucon, 'you yourself promised to make the search and talked about the impiety of deserting justice.' Well, I said, I will lead the way, but do you follow. My notion is, that our State being perfect will contain all the four virtues – wisdom, courage, temperance, justice. If we eliminate the three first, the unknown remainder will be justice.

First then, of wisdom: the State which we have called into being will be wise because politic. And policy is one among many kinds of skill, – not the skill of the carpenter, or of the worker in metal, or of the husbandman, but the skill of him who advises about the interests of the whole State. Of such a kind is the skill of the guardians, who are a small class in number, far smaller than the blacksmiths; but in them is concentrated the wisdom of the State. And if this small ruling class have wisdom, then the whole State will be wise.

Our second virtue is courage, which we have no difficulty in finding in another class – that of soldiers. Courage may be defined as a sort of salvation – the never-failing salvation of the opinions which law and education have prescribed concerning dangers. You know the way in which dyers first prepare the white ground and then lay on the dye of purple or of any other colour. Colours dyed in this way become fixed, and no soap or lye will ever wash them out. Now the ground is education, and the laws are the colours; and if the ground is properly laid, neither the soap of pleasure nor the lye of pain or fear will ever wash them out. This power which preserves right opinion about danger I would ask you to call 'courage,' adding the epithet 'political' or 'civilized' in order to distinguish it from mere animal courage and from a higher courage which may hereafter be discussed.

Two virtues remain; temperance and justice. More than the preceding virtues temperance suggests the idea of harmony. Some light is thrown upon the nature of this virtue by the popular description of a man as 'master of himself' – which has an absurd sound, because the master is also the servant. The expression really means that the better principle in a man masters the worse. There are in cities whole classes – women, slaves and the like – who correspond to the worse, and a few only to the better; and in our State the former class are held under control by the latter. Now to which of these classes does temperance belong? 'To both of them.' And our State if any will be the abode of temperance; and we were right in describing this virtue as a harmony which is diffused through the whole, making the dwellers in the city to be of one mind, and attuning the upper and middle and lower classes like the strings of an instrument, whether you suppose them to differ in wisdom, strength or wealth.

And now we are near the spot; let us draw in and surround the cover and watch with all our eyes, lest justice should slip away and escape. Tell me, if you see the thicket move first. 'Nay, I would have you lead.' Well then, offer up a prayer and follow. The way is dark and difficult; but we must push on. I begin to see a track. 'Good news.' Why, Glaucon, our dulness of scent is quite ludicrous! While we are straining our eyes into the distance, justice is tumbling out at our feet. We are as bad as people looking for a thing which they have in their hands. Have you forgotten our old principle of the division of labour, or of every man doing his own business, concerning which we spoke at the foundation of the State – what but this was justice? Is there any other virtue remaining which can compete with wisdom and temperance and courage in the scale of political virtue? For 'every one having his own' is the great object of government; and the great object of trade is that every man should do his own business. Not that there is much harm in a carpenter trying to be a cobbler, or a cobbler transforming himself into a carpenter; but great evil may arise from the cobbler leaving his last and turning into a guardian or legislator, or when a single individual is trainer, warrior, legislator, all in one. And this evil is injustice, or every man doing another's business. I do not say that as yet we are in a condition to arrive at a final conclusion. For the definition which we believe to hold good in states has still to be tested by the individual. Having read the large letters we will now come back to the small. From the two together a brilliant light may be struck out...

Socrates proceeds to discover the nature of justice by a method of residues. Each of the first three virtues corresponds to one of the three parts of the soul and one of the three classes in the State, although the third, temperance, has more of the nature of a harmony than the first two. If there be a fourth virtue, that can only be sought for in the relation of the three parts in the soul or classes in the State to one another. It is obvious and simple, and for that very reason has not been found out. The modern logician will be inclined to object that ideas cannot be separated like chemical substances, but that they run into one another and may be only different aspects or names of the same thing, and such in this instance appears to be the case. For the definition here given of justice is verbally the same as one of the definitions of temperance given by Socrates in the Charmides, which however is only provisional, and is afterwards rejected. And so far from justice remaining over when the other virtues are eliminated, the justice and temperance of the Republic can with difficulty be distinguished. Temperance appears to be the virtue of a part only, and one of three, whereas justice is a universal virtue of the whole soul. Yet on the other hand temperance is also described as a sort of harmony, and in this respect is akin to justice. Justice seems to differ from temperance in degree rather than in kind; whereas temperance is the harmony of discordant elements, justice is the perfect order by which all natures and classes do their own business, the right man in the right place, the division and co-operation of all the citizens. Justice, again, is a more abstract notion than the other virtues, and therefore, from Plato's point of view, the foundation of them, to which they are referred and which in idea precedes them. The proposal to omit temperance is a mere trick of style intended to avoid monotony.

There is a famous question discussed in one of the earlier Dialogues of Plato (Protagoras; Arist. Nic. Ethics), 'Whether the virtues are one or many?' This receives an answer which is to the effect that there are four cardinal virtues (now for the first time brought together in ethical philosophy), and one supreme over the rest, which is not like Aristotle's conception of universal justice, virtue relative to others, but the whole of virtue relative to the parts. To this universal conception of justice or order in the first education and in the moral nature of man, the still more universal conception of the good in the second education and in the sphere of speculative knowledge seems to succeed. Both might be equally described by the terms 'law,' 'order,' 'harmony;' but while the idea of good embraces 'all time and all existence,' the conception of justice is not extended beyond man.

...Socrates is now going to identify the individual and the State. But first he must prove that there are three parts of the individual soul. His argument is as follows: – Quantity makes no difference in quality. The word 'just,' whether applied to the individual or to the State, has the same meaning. And the term 'justice' implied that the same three principles in the State and in the individual were doing their own business. But are they really three or one? The question is difficult, and one which can hardly be solved by the methods which we are now using; but the truer and longer way would take up too much of our time. 'The shorter will satisfy me.' Well then, you would admit that the qualities of states mean the qualities of the individuals who compose them? The Scythians and Thracians are passionate, our own race intellectual, and the Egyptians and Phoenicians covetous, because the individual members of each have such and such a character; the difficulty is to determine whether the several principles are one or three; whether, that is to say, we reason with one part of our nature, desire with another, are angry with another, or whether the whole soul comes into play in each sort of action. This enquiry, however, requires a very exact definition of terms. The same thing in the same relation cannot be affected in two opposite ways. But there is no impossibility in a man standing still, yet moving his arms, or in a top which is fixed on one spot going round upon its axis. There is no necessity to mention all the possible exceptions; let us provisionally assume that opposites cannot do or be or suffer opposites in the same relation. And to the class of opposites belong assent and dissent, desire and avoidance. And one form of desire is thirst and hunger: and here arises a new point – thirst is thirst of drink, hunger is hunger of food; not of warm drink or of a particular kind of food, with the single exception of course that the very fact of our desiring anything implies that it is good. When relative terms have no attributes, their correlatives have no attributes; when they have attributes, their correlatives also have them. For example, the term 'greater' is simply relative to 'less,' and knowledge refers to a subject of knowledge. But on the other hand, a particular knowledge is of a particular subject. Again, every science has a distinct character, which is defined by an object; medicine, for example, is the science of health, although not to be confounded with health. Having cleared our ideas thus far, let us return to the original instance of thirst, which has a definite object – drink. Now the thirsty soul may feel two distinct impulses; the animal one saying 'Drink;' the rational one, which says 'Do not drink.' The two impulses are contradictory; and therefore we may assume that they spring from distinct principles in the soul. But is passion a third principle, or akin to desire? There is a story of a certain Leontius which throws some light on this question. He was coming up from the Piraeus outside the north wall, and he passed a spot where there were dead bodies lying by the executioner. He felt a longing desire to see them and also an abhorrence of them; at first he turned away and shut his eyes, then, suddenly tearing them open, he said, – 'Take your fill, ye wretches, of the fair sight.' Now is there not here a third principle which is often found to come to the assistance of reason against desire, but never of desire against reason? This is passion or spirit, of the separate existence of which we may further convince ourselves by putting the following case: – When a man suffers justly, if he be of a generous nature he is not indignant at the hardships which he undergoes: but when he suffers unjustly, his indignation is his great support; hunger and thirst cannot tame him; the spirit within him must do or die, until the voice of the shepherd, that is, of reason, bidding his dog bark no more, is heard within. This shows that passion is the ally of reason. Is passion then the same with reason? No, for the former exists in children and brutes; and Homer affords a proof of the distinction between them when he says, 'He smote his breast, and thus rebuked his soul.'

And now, at last, we have reached firm ground, and are able to infer that the virtues of the State and of the individual are the same. For wisdom and courage and justice in the State are severally the wisdom and courage and justice in the individuals who form the State. Each of the three classes will do the work of its own class in the State, and each part in the individual soul; reason, the superior, and passion, the inferior, will be harmonized by the influence of music and gymnastic. The counsellor and the warrior, the head and the arm, will act together in the town of Mansoul, and keep the desires in proper subjection. The courage of the warrior is that quality which preserves a right opinion about dangers in spite of pleasures and pains. The wisdom of the counsellor is that small part of the soul which has authority and reason. The virtue of temperance is the friendship of the ruling and the subject principles, both in the State and in the individual. Of justice we have already spoken; and the notion already given of it may be confirmed by common instances. Will the just state or the just individual steal, lie, commit adultery, or be guilty of impiety to gods and men? 'No.' And is not the reason of this that the several principles, whether in the state or in the individual, do their own business? And justice is the quality which makes just men and just states. Moreover, our old division of labour, which required that there should be one man for one use, was a dream or anticipation of what was to follow; and that dream has now been realized in justice, which begins by binding together the three chords of the soul, and then acts harmoniously in every relation of life. And injustice, which is the insubordination and disobedience of the inferior elements in the soul, is the opposite of justice, and is inharmonious and unnatural, being to the soul what disease is to the body; for in the soul as well as in the body, good or bad actions produce good or bad habits. And virtue is the health and beauty and well-being of the soul, and vice is the disease and weakness and deformity of the soul.

Again the old question returns upon us: Is justice or injustice the more profitable? The question has become ridiculous. For injustice, like mortal disease, makes life not worth having. Come up with me to the hill which overhangs the city and look down upon the single form of virtue, and the infinite forms of vice, among which are four special ones, characteristic both of states and of individuals. And the state which corresponds to the single form of virtue is that which we have been describing, wherein reason rules under one of two names – monarchy and aristocracy. Thus there are five forms in all, both of states and of souls...

In attempting to prove that the soul has three separate faculties, Plato takes occasion to discuss what makes difference of faculties. And the criterion which he proposes is difference in the working of the faculties. The same faculty cannot produce contradictory effects. But the path of early reasoners is beset by thorny entanglements, and he will not proceed a step without first clearing the ground. This leads him into a tiresome digression, which is intended to explain the nature of contradiction. First, the contradiction must be at the same time and in the same relation. Secondly, no extraneous word must be introduced into either of the terms in which the contradictory proposition is expressed: for example, thirst is of drink, not of warm drink. He implies, what he does not say, that if, by the advice of reason, or by the impulse of anger, a man is restrained from drinking, this proves that thirst, or desire under which thirst is included, is distinct from anger and reason. But suppose that we allow the term 'thirst' or 'desire' to be modified, and say an 'angry thirst,' or a 'revengeful desire,' then the two spheres of desire and anger overlap and become confused. This case therefore has to be excluded. And still there remains an exception to the rule in the use of the term 'good,' which is always implied in the object of desire. These are the discussions of an age before logic; and any one who is wearied by them should remember that they are necessary to the clearing up of ideas in the first development of the human faculties.

 The psychology of Plato extends no further than the division of the soul into the rational, irascible, and concupiscent elements, which, as far as we know, was first made by him, and has been retained by Aristotle and succeeding ethical writers. The chief difficulty in this early analysis of the mind is to define exactly the place of the irascible faculty (Greek), which may be variously described under the terms righteous indignation, spirit, passion. It is the foundation of courage, which includes in Plato moral courage, the courage of enduring pain, and of surmounting intellectual difficulties, as well as of meeting dangers in war. Though irrational, it inclines to side with the rational: it cannot be aroused by punishment when justly inflicted: it sometimes takes the form of an enthusiasm which sustains a man in the performance of great actions. It is the 'lion heart' with which the reason makes a treaty. On the other hand it is negative rather than positive; it is indignant at wrong or falsehood, but does not, like Love in the Symposium and Phaedrus, aspire to the vision of Truth or Good. It is the peremptory military spirit which prevails in the government of honour. It differs from anger (Greek), this latter term having no accessory notion of righteous indignation. Although Aristotle has retained the word, yet we may observe that 'passion' (Greek) has with him lost its affinity to the rational and has become indistinguishable from 'anger' (Greek). And to this vernacular use Plato himself in the Laws seems to revert, though not always. By modern philosophy too, as well as in our ordinary conversation, the words anger or passion are employed almost exclusively in a bad sense; there is no connotation of a just or reasonable cause by which they are aroused. The feeling of 'righteous indignation' is too partial and accidental to admit of our regarding it as a separate virtue or habit. We are tempted also to doubt whether Plato is right in supposing that an offender, however justly condemned, could be expected to acknowledge the justice of his sentence; this is the spirit of a philosopher or martyr rather than of a criminal.

We may observe how nearly Plato approaches Aristotle's famous thesis, that 'good actions produce good habits.' The words 'as healthy practices (Greek) produce health, so do just practices produce justice,' have a sound very like the Nicomachean Ethics. But we note also that an incidental remark in Plato has become a far-reaching principle in Aristotle, and an inseparable part of a great Ethical system.

There is a difficulty in understanding what Plato meant by 'the longer way': he seems to intimate some metaphysic of the future which will not be satisfied with arguing from the principle of contradiction. In the sixth and seventh books (compare Sophist and Parmenides) he has given us a sketch of such a metaphysic; but when Glaucon asks for the final revelation of the idea of good, he is put off with the declaration that he has not yet studied the preliminary sciences. How he would have filled up the sketch, or argued about such questions from a higher point of view, we can only conjecture. Perhaps he hoped to find some a priori method of developing the parts out of the whole; or he might have asked which of the ideas contains the other ideas, and possibly have stumbled on the Hegelian identity of the 'ego' and the 'universal.' Or he may have imagined that ideas might be constructed in some manner analogous to the construction of figures and numbers in the mathematical sciences. The most certain and necessary truth was to Plato the universal; and to this he was always seeking to refer all knowledge or opinion, just as in modern times we seek to rest them on the opposite pole of induction and experience. The aspirations of metaphysicians have always tended to pass beyond the limits of human thought and language: they seem to have reached a height at which they are 'moving about in worlds unrealized,' and their conceptions, although profoundly affecting their own minds, become invisible or unintelligible to others. We are not therefore surprized to find that Plato himself has nowhere clearly explained his doctrine of ideas; or that his school in a later generation, like his contemporaries Glaucon and Adeimantus, were unable to follow him in this region of speculation. In the Sophist, where he is refuting the scepticism which maintained either that there was no such thing as predication, or that all might be predicated of all, he arrives at the conclusion that some ideas combine with some, but not all with all. But he makes only one or two steps forward on this path; he nowhere attains to any connected system of ideas, or even to a knowledge of the most elementary relations of the sciences to one another.

BOOK V.

I was going to enumerate the four forms of vice or decline in states, when Polemarchus – he was sitting a little farther from me than Adeimantus – taking him by the coat and leaning towards him, said something in an undertone, of which I only caught the words, 'Shall we let him off?' 'Certainly not,' said Adeimantus, raising his voice. Whom, I said, are you not going to let off? 'You,' he said. Why? 'Because we think that you are not dealing fairly with us in omitting women and children, of whom you have slily disposed under the general formula that friends have all things in common.' And was I not right? 'Yes,' he replied, 'but there are many sorts of communism or community, and we want to know which of them is right. The company, as you have just heard, are resolved to have a further explanation.' Thrasymachus said, 'Do you think that we have come hither to dig for gold, or to hear you discourse?' Yes, I said; but the discourse should be of a reasonable length. Glaucon added, 'Yes, Socrates, and there is reason in spending the whole of life in such discussions; but pray, without more ado, tell us how this community is to be carried out, and how the interval between birth and education is to be filled up.' Well, I said, the subject has several difficulties – What is possible? is the first question. What is desirable? is the second. 'Fear not,' he replied, 'for you are speaking among friends.' That, I replied, is a sorry consolation; I shall destroy my friends as well as myself. Not that I mind a little innocent laughter; but he who kills the truth is a murderer. 'Then,' said Glaucon, laughing, 'in case you should murder us we will acquit you beforehand, and you shall be held free from the guilt of deceiving us.'

Socrates proceeds: – The guardians of our state are to be watch-dogs, as we have already said. Now dogs are not divided into hes and shes – we do not take the masculine gender out to hunt and leave the females at home to look after their puppies. They have the same employments – the only difference between them is that the one sex is stronger and the other weaker. But if women are to have the same employments as men, they must have the same education – they must be taught music and gymnastics, and the art of war. I know that a great joke will be made of their riding on horseback and carrying weapons; the sight of the naked old wrinkled women showing their agility in the palaestra will certainly not be a vision of beauty, and may be expected to become a famous jest. But we must not mind the wits; there was a time when they might have laughed at our present gymnastics. All is habit: people have at last found out that the exposure is better than the concealment of the person, and now they laugh no more. Evil only should be the subject of ridicule.

The first question is, whether women are able either wholly or partially to share in the employments of men. And here we may be charged with inconsistency in making the proposal at all. For we started originally with the division of labour; and the diversity of employments was based on the difference of natures. But is there no difference between men and women? Nay, are they not wholly different? THERE was the difficulty, Glaucon, which made me unwilling to speak of family relations. However, when a man is out of his depth, whether in a pool or in an ocean, he can only swim for his life; and we must try to find a way of escape, if we can.

The argument is, that different natures have different uses, and the natures of men and women are said to differ. But this is only a verbal opposition. We do not consider that the difference may be purely nominal and accidental; for example, a bald man and a hairy man are opposed in a single point of view, but you cannot infer that because a bald man is a cobbler a hairy man ought not to be a cobbler. Now why is such an inference erroneous? Simply because the opposition between them is partial only, like the difference between a male physician and a female physician, not running through the whole nature, like the difference between a physician and a carpenter. And if the difference of the sexes is only that the one beget and the other bear children, this does not prove that they ought to have distinct educations. Admitting that women differ from men in capacity, do not men equally differ from one another? Has not nature scattered all the qualities which our citizens require indifferently up and down among the two sexes? and even in their peculiar pursuits, are not women often, though in some cases superior to men, ridiculously enough surpassed by them? Women are the same in kind as men, and have the same aptitude or want of aptitude for medicine or gymnastic or war, but in a less degree. One woman will be a good guardian, another not; and the good must be chosen to be the colleagues of our guardians. If however their natures are the same, the inference is that their education must also be the same; there is no longer anything unnatural or impossible in a woman learning music and gymnastic. And the education which we give them will be the very best, far superior to that of cobblers, and will train up the very best women, and nothing can be more advantageous to the State than this. Therefore let them strip, clothed in their chastity, and share in the toils of war and in the defence of their country; he who laughs at them is a fool for his pains.

The first wave is past, and the argument is compelled to admit that men and women have common duties and pursuits. A second and greater wave is rolling in – community of wives and children; is this either expedient or possible? The expediency I do not doubt; I am not so sure of the possibility. 'Nay, I think that a considerable doubt will be entertained on both points.' I meant to have escaped the trouble of proving the first, but as you have detected the little stratagem I must even submit. Only allow me to feed my fancy like the solitary in his walks, with a dream of what might be, and then I will return to the question of what can be.

In the first place our rulers will enforce the laws and make new ones where they are wanted, and their allies or ministers will obey. You, as legislator, have already selected the men; and now you shall select the women. After the selection has been made, they will dwell in common houses and have their meals in common, and will be brought together by a necessity more certain than that of mathematics. But they cannot be allowed to live in licentiousness; that is an unholy thing, which the rulers are determined to prevent. For the avoidance of this, holy marriage festivals will be instituted, and their holiness will be in proportion to their usefulness. And here, Glaucon, I should like to ask (as I know that you are a breeder of birds and animals), Do you not take the greatest care in the mating? 'Certainly.' And there is no reason to suppose that less care is required in the marriage of human beings. But then our rulers must be skilful physicians of the State, for they will often need a strong dose of falsehood in order to bring about desirable unions between their subjects. The good must be paired with the good, and the bad with the bad, and the offspring of the one must be reared, and of the other destroyed; in this way the flock will be preserved in prime condition. Hymeneal festivals will be celebrated at times fixed with an eye to population, and the brides and bridegrooms will meet at them; and by an ingenious system of lots the rulers will contrive that the brave and the fair come together, and that those of inferior breed are paired with inferiors – the latter will ascribe to chance what is really the invention of the rulers. And when children are born, the offspring of the brave and fair will be carried to an enclosure in a certain part of the city, and there attended by suitable nurses; the rest will be hurried away to places unknown. The mothers will be brought to the fold and will suckle the children; care however must be taken that none of them recognise their own offspring; and if necessary other nurses may also be hired. The trouble of watching and getting up at night will be transferred to attendants. 'Then the wives of our guardians will have a fine easy time when they are having children.' And quite right too, I said, that they should.

The parents ought to be in the prime of life, which for a man may be reckoned at thirty years – from twenty-five, when he has 'passed the point at which the speed of life is greatest,' to fifty-five; and at twenty years for a woman – from twenty to forty. Any one above or below those ages who partakes in the hymeneals shall be guilty of impiety; also every one who forms a marriage connexion at other times without the consent of the rulers. This latter regulation applies to those who are within the specified ages, after which they may range at will, provided they avoid the prohibited degrees of parents and children, or of brothers and sisters, which last, however, are not absolutely prohibited, if a dispensation be procured. 'But how shall we know the degrees of affinity, when all things are common?' The answer is, that brothers and sisters are all such as are born seven or nine months after the espousals, and their parents those who are then espoused, and every one will have many children and every child many parents.

Socrates proceeds: I have now to prove that this scheme is advantageous and also consistent with our entire polity. The greatest good of a State is unity; the greatest evil, discord and distraction. And there will be unity where there are no private pleasures or pains or interests – where if one member suffers all the members suffer, if one citizen is touched all are quickly sensitive; and the least hurt to the little finger of the State runs through the whole body and vibrates to the soul. For the true State, like an individual, is injured as a whole when any part is affected. Every State has subjects and rulers, who in a democracy are called rulers, and in other States masters: but in our State they are called saviours and allies; and the subjects who in other States are termed slaves, are by us termed nurturers and paymasters, and those who are termed comrades and colleagues in other places, are by us called fathers and brothers. And whereas in other States members of the same government regard one of their colleagues as a friend and another as an enemy, in our State no man is a stranger to another; for every citizen is connected with every other by ties of blood, and these names and this way of speaking will have a corresponding reality – brother, father, sister, mother, repeated from infancy in the ears of children, will not be mere words. Then again the citizens will have all things in common, in having common property they will have common pleasures and pains.

Can there be strife and contention among those who are of one mind; or lawsuits about property when men have nothing but their bodies which they call their own; or suits about violence when every one is bound to defend himself? The permission to strike when insulted will be an 'antidote' to the knife and will prevent disturbances in the State. But no younger man will strike an elder; reverence will prevent him from laying hands on his kindred, and he will fear that the rest of the family may retaliate. Moreover, our citizens will be rid of the lesser evils of life; there will be no flattery of the rich, no sordid household cares, no borrowing and not paying. Compared with the citizens of other States, ours will be Olympic victors, and crowned with blessings greater still – they and their children having a better maintenance during life, and after death an honourable burial. Nor has the happiness of the individual been sacrificed to the happiness of the State; our Olympic victor has not been turned into a cobbler, but he has a happiness beyond that of any cobbler. At the same time, if any conceited youth begins to dream of appropriating the State to himself, he must be reminded that 'half is better than the whole.' 'I should certainly advise him to stay where he is when he has the promise of such a brave life.'

But is such a community possible? – as among the animals, so also among men; and if possible, in what way possible? About war there is no difficulty; the principle of communism is adapted to military service. Parents will take their children to look on at a battle, just as potters' boys are trained to the business by looking on at the wheel. And to the parents themselves, as to other animals, the sight of their young ones will prove a great incentive to bravery. Young warriors must learn, but they must not run into danger, although a certain degree of risk is worth incurring when the benefit is great. The young creatures should be placed under the care of experienced veterans, and they should have wings – that is to say, swift and tractable steeds on which they may fly away and escape. One of the first things to be done is to teach a youth to ride.

Cowards and deserters shall be degraded to the class of husbandmen; gentlemen who allow themselves to be taken prisoners, may be presented to the enemy. But what shall be done to the hero? First of all he shall be crowned by all the youths in the army; secondly, he shall receive the right hand of fellowship; and thirdly, do you think that there is any harm in his being kissed? We have already determined that he shall have more wives than others, in order that he may have as many children as possible. And at a feast he shall have more to eat; we have the authority of Homer for honouring brave men with 'long chines,' which is an appropriate compliment, because meat is a very strengthening thing. Fill the bowl then, and give the best seats and meats to the brave – may they do them good! And he who dies in battle will be at once declared to be of the golden race, and will, as we believe, become one of Hesiod's guardian angels. He shall be worshipped after death in the manner prescribed by the oracle; and not only he, but all other benefactors of the State who die in any other way, shall be admitted to the same honours.

The next question is, How shall we treat our enemies? Shall Hellenes be enslaved? No; for there is too great a risk of the whole race passing under the yoke of the barbarians. Or shall the dead be despoiled? Certainly not; for that sort of thing is an excuse for skulking, and has been the ruin of many an army. There is meanness and feminine malice in making an enemy of the dead body, when the soul which was the owner has fled – like a dog who cannot reach his assailants, and quarrels with the stones which are thrown at him instead. Again, the arms of Hellenes should not be offered up in the temples of the Gods; they are a pollution, for they are taken from brethren. And on similar grounds there should be a limit to the devastation of Hellenic territory – the houses should not be burnt, nor more than the annual produce carried off. For war is of two kinds, civil and foreign; the first of which is properly termed 'discord,' and only the second 'war;' and war between Hellenes is in reality civil war – a quarrel in a family, which is ever to be regarded as unpatriotic and unnatural, and ought to be prosecuted with a view to reconciliation in a true phil-Hellenic spirit, as of those who would chasten but not utterly enslave. The war is not against a whole nation who are a friendly multitude of men, women, and children, but only against a few guilty persons; when they are punished peace will be restored. That is the way in which Hellenes should war against one another – and against barbarians, as they war against one another now.

'But, my dear Socrates, you are forgetting the main question: Is such a State possible? I grant all and more than you say about the blessedness of being one family – fathers, brothers, mothers, daughters, going out to war together; but I want to ascertain the possibility of this ideal State.' You are too unmerciful. The first wave and the second wave I have hardly escaped, and now you will certainly drown me with the third. When you see the towering crest of the wave, I expect you to take pity. 'Not a whit.'

Well, then, we were led to form our ideal polity in the search after justice, and the just man answered to the just State. Is this ideal at all the worse for being impracticable? Would the picture of a perfectly beautiful man be any the worse because no such man ever lived? Can any reality come up to the idea? Nature will not allow words to be fully realized; but if I am to try and realize the ideal of the State in a measure, I think that an approach may be made to the perfection of which I dream by one or two, I do not say slight, but possible changes in the present constitution of States. I would reduce them to a single one – the great wave, as I call it. Until, then, kings are philosophers, or philosophers are kings, cities will never cease from ill: no, nor the human race; nor will our ideal polity ever come into being. I know that this is a hard saying, which few will be able to receive. 'Socrates, all the world will take off his coat and rush upon you with sticks and stones, and therefore I would advise you to prepare an answer.' You got me into the scrape, I said. 'And I was right,' he replied; 'however, I will stand by you as a sort of do-nothing, well-meaning ally.' Having the help of such a champion, I will do my best to maintain my position. And first, I must explain of whom I speak and what sort of natures these are who are to be philosophers and rulers. As you are a man of pleasure, you will not have forgotten how indiscriminate lovers are in their attachments; they love all, and turn blemishes into beauties. The snub-nosed youth is said to have a winning grace; the beak of another has a royal look; the featureless are faultless; the dark are manly, the fair angels; the sickly have a new term of endearment invented expressly for them, which is 'honey-pale.' Lovers of wine and lovers of ambition also desire the objects of their affection in every form. Now here comes the point: – The philosopher too is a lover of knowledge in every form; he has an insatiable curiosity. 'But will curiosity make a philosopher? Are the lovers of sights and sounds, who let out their ears to every chorus at the Dionysiac festivals, to be called philosophers?' They are not true philosophers, but only an imitation. 'Then how are we to describe the true?'

You would acknowledge the existence of abstract ideas, such as justice, beauty, good, evil, which are severally one, yet in their various combinations appear to be many. Those who recognize these realities are philosophers; whereas the other class hear sounds and see colours, and understand their use in the arts, but cannot attain to the true or waking vision of absolute justice or beauty or truth; they have not the light of knowledge, but of opinion, and what they see is a dream only. Perhaps he of whom we say the last will be angry with us; can we pacify him without revealing the disorder of his mind? Suppose we say that, if he has knowledge we rejoice to hear it, but knowledge must be of something which is, as ignorance is of something which is not; and there is a third thing, which both is and is not, and is matter of opinion only. Opinion and knowledge, then, having distinct objects, must also be distinct faculties. And by faculties I mean powers unseen and distinguishable only by the difference in their objects, as opinion and knowledge differ, since the one is liable to err, but the other is unerring and is the mightiest of all our faculties. If being is the object of knowledge, and not-being of ignorance, and these are the extremes, opinion must lie between them, and may be called darker than the one and brighter than the other. This intermediate or contingent matter is and is not at the same time, and partakes both of existence and of non-existence. Now I would ask my good friend, who denies abstract beauty and justice, and affirms a many beautiful and a many just, whether everything he sees is not in some point of view different – the beautiful ugly, the pious impious, the just unjust? Is not the double also the half, and are not heavy and light relative terms which pass into one another? Everything is and is not, as in the old riddle – 'A man and not a man shot and did not shoot a bird and not a bird with a stone and not a stone.' The mind cannot be fixed on either alternative; and these ambiguous, intermediate, erring, half-lighted objects, which have a disorderly movement in the region between being and not-being, are the proper matter of opinion, as the immutable objects are the proper matter of knowledge. And he who grovels in the world of sense, and has only this uncertain perception of things, is not a philosopher, but a lover of opinion only...

The fifth book is the new beginning of the Republic, in which the community of property and of family are first maintained, and the transition is made to the kingdom of philosophers. For both of these Plato, after his manner, has been preparing in some chance words of Book IV, which fall unperceived on the reader's mind, as they are supposed at first to have fallen on the ear of Glaucon and Adeimantus. The 'paradoxes,' as Morgenstern terms them, of this book of the Republic will be reserved for another place; a few remarks on the style, and some explanations of difficulties, may be briefly added.

First, there is the image of the waves, which serves for a sort of scheme or plan of the book. The first wave, the second wave, the third and greatest wave come rolling in, and we hear the roar of them. All that can be said of the extravagance of Plato's proposals is anticipated by himself. Nothing is more admirable than the hesitation with which he proposes the solemn text, 'Until kings are philosophers,' etc.; or the reaction from the sublime to the ridiculous, when Glaucon describes the manner in which the new truth will be received by mankind.

Some defects and difficulties may be noted in the execution of the communistic plan. Nothing is told us of the application of communism to the lower classes; nor is the table of prohibited degrees capable of being made out. It is quite possible that a child born at one hymeneal festival may marry one of its own brothers or sisters, or even one of its parents, at another. Plato is afraid of incestuous unions, but at the same time he does not wish to bring before us the fact that the city would be divided into families of those born seven and nine months after each hymeneal festival. If it were worth while to argue seriously about such fancies, we might remark that while all the old affinities are abolished, the newly prohibited affinity rests not on any natural or rational principle, but only upon the accident of children having been born in the same month and year. Nor does he explain how the lots could be so manipulated by the legislature as to bring together the fairest and best. The singular expression which is employed to describe the age of five-and-twenty may perhaps be taken from some poet.

In the delineation of the philosopher, the illustrations of the nature of philosophy derived from love are more suited to the apprehension of Glaucon, the Athenian man of pleasure, than to modern tastes or feelings. They are partly facetious, but also contain a germ of truth. That science is a whole, remains a true principle of inductive as well as of metaphysical philosophy; and the love of universal knowledge is still the characteristic of the philosopher in modern as well as in ancient times.

At the end of the fifth book Plato introduces the figment of contingent matter, which has exercised so great an influence both on the Ethics and Theology of the modern world, and which occurs here for the first time in the history of philosophy. He did not remark that the degrees of knowledge in the subject have nothing corresponding to them in the object. With him a word must answer to an idea; and he could not conceive of an opinion which was an opinion about nothing. The influence of analogy led him to invent 'parallels and conjugates' and to overlook facts. To us some of his difficulties are puzzling only from their simplicity: we do not perceive that the answer to them 'is tumbling out at our feet.' To the mind of early thinkers, the conception of not-being was dark and mysterious; they did not see that this terrible apparition which threatened destruction to all knowledge was only a logical determination. The common term under which, through the accidental use of language, two entirely different ideas were included was another source of confusion. Thus through the ambiguity of (Greek) Plato, attempting to introduce order into the first chaos of human thought, seems to have confused perception and opinion, and to have failed to distinguish the contingent from the relative. In the Theaetetus the first of these difficulties begins to clear up; in the Sophist the second; and for this, as well as for other reasons, both these dialogues are probably to be regarded as later than the Republic.

BOOK VI.

Having determined that the many have no knowledge of true being, and have no clear patterns in their minds of justice, beauty, truth, and that philosophers have such patterns, we have now to ask whether they or the many shall be rulers in our State. But who can doubt that philosophers should be chosen, if they have the other qualities which are required in a ruler? For they are lovers of the knowledge of the eternal and of all truth; they are haters of falsehood; their meaner desires are absorbed in the interests of knowledge; they are spectators of all time and all existence; and in the magnificence of their contemplation the life of man is as nothing to them, nor is death fearful. Also they are of a social, gracious disposition, equally free from cowardice and arrogance. They learn and remember easily; they have harmonious, well-regulated minds; truth flows to them sweetly by nature. Can the god of Jealousy himself find any fault with such an assemblage of good qualities?

Here Adeimantus interposes: − 'No man can answer you, Socrates; but every man feels that this is owing to his own deficiency in argument. He is driven from one position to another, until he has nothing more to say, just as an unskilful player at draughts is reduced to his last move by a more skilled opponent. And yet all the time he may be right. He may know, in this very instance, that those who make philosophy the business of their lives, generally turn out rogues if they are bad men, and fools if they are good. What do you say?' I should say that he is quite right. 'Then how is such an admission reconcileable with the doctrine that philosophers should be kings?'

I shall answer you in a parable which will also let you see how poor a hand I am at the invention of allegories. The relation of good men to their governments is so peculiar, that in order to defend them I must take an illustration from the world of fiction. Conceive the captain of a ship, taller by a head and shoulders than any of the crew, yet a little deaf, a little blind, and rather ignorant of the seaman's art. The sailors want to steer, although they know nothing of the art; and they have a theory that it cannot be learned. If the helm is refused them, they drug the captain's posset, bind him hand and foot, and take possession of the ship. He who joins in the mutiny is termed a good pilot and what not; they have no conception that the true pilot must observe the winds and the stars, and must be their master, whether they like it or not; − such an one would be called by them fool, prater, star-gazer. This is my parable; which I will beg you to interpret for me to those gentlemen who ask why the philosopher has such an evil name, and to explain to them that not he, but those who will not use him, are to blame for his uselessness. The philosopher should not beg of mankind to be put in authority over them. The wise man should not seek the rich, as the proverb bids, but every man, whether rich or poor, must knock at the door of the physician when he has need of him. Now the pilot is the philosopher – he whom in the parable they call star-gazer, and the mutinous sailors are the mob of politicians by whom he is rendered useless. Not that these are the worst enemies of philosophy, who is far more dishonoured by her own professing sons when they are corrupted by the world. Need I recall the original image of the philosopher? Did we not say of him just now, that he loved truth and hated falsehood, and that he could not rest in the multiplicity of phenomena, but was led by a sympathy in his own nature to the contemplation of the absolute? All the virtues as well as truth, who is the leader of them, took up their abode in his soul. But as you were observing, if we turn aside to view the reality, we see that the persons who were thus described, with the exception of a small and useless class, are utter rogues.

 The point which has to be considered, is the origin of this corruption in nature. Every one will admit that the philosopher, in our description of him, is a rare being. But what numberless causes tend to destroy these rare beings! There is no good thing which may not be a cause of evil – health, wealth, strength, rank, and the virtues themselves, when placed under unfavourable circumstances. For as in the animal or vegetable world the strongest seeds most need the accompaniment of good air and soil, so the best of human characters turn out the worst when they fall upon an unsuitable soil; whereas weak natures hardly ever do any considerable good or harm; they are not the stuff out of which either great criminals or great heroes are made. The philosopher follows the same analogy: he is either the best or the worst of all men. Some persons say that the Sophists are the corrupters of youth; but is not public opinion the real Sophist who is everywhere present – in those very persons, in the assembly, in the courts, in the camp, in the applauses and hisses of the theatre re-echoed by the surrounding hills? Will not a young man's heart leap amid these discordant sounds? and will any education save him from being carried away by the torrent? Nor is this all. For if he will not yield to opinion, there follows the gentle compulsion of exile or death. What principle of rival Sophists or anybody else can overcome in such an unequal contest? Characters there may be more than human, who are exceptions – God may save a man, but not his own strength. Further, I would have you consider that the hireling Sophist only gives back to the world their own opinions; he is the keeper of the monster, who knows how to flatter or anger him, and observes the meaning of his inarticulate grunts. Good is what pleases him, evil what he dislikes; truth and beauty are determined only by the taste of the brute. Such is the Sophist's wisdom, and such is the condition of those who make public opinion the test of truth, whether in art or in morals. The curse is laid upon them of being and doing what it approves, and when they attempt first principles the failure is ludicrous. Think of all this and ask yourself whether the world is more likely to be a believer in the unity of the idea, or in the multiplicity of phenomena. And the world if not a believer in the idea cannot be a philosopher, and must therefore be a persecutor of philosophers. There is another evil: – the world does not like to lose the gifted nature, and so they flatter the young (Alcibiades) into a magnificent opinion of his own capacity; the tall, proper youth begins to expand, and is dreaming of kingdoms and empires. If at this instant a friend whispers to him, 'Now the gods lighten thee; thou art a great fool' and must be educated – do you think that he will listen? Or suppose a better sort of man who is attracted towards philosophy, will they not make Herculean efforts to spoil and corrupt him? Are we not right in saying that the love of knowledge, no less than riches, may divert him? Men of this class (Critias) often become politicians – they are the authors of great mischief in states, and sometimes also of great good. And thus philosophy is deserted by her natural protectors, and others enter in and dishonour her. Vulgar little minds see the land open and rush from the prisons of the arts into her temple. A clever mechanic having a soul coarse as his body, thinks that he will gain caste by becoming her suitor. For philosophy, even in her fallen estate, has a dignity of her own – and he, like a bald little blacksmith's apprentice as he is, having made some money and got out of durance, washes and dresses himself as a bridegroom and marries his master's daughter. What will be the issue of such marriages? Will they not be vile and bastard, devoid of truth and nature? 'They will.' Small, then, is the remnant of genuine philosophers; there may be a few who are citizens of small states, in which politics are not worth thinking of, or who have been detained by Theages' bridle of ill health; for my own case of the oracular sign is almost unique, and too rare to be worth mentioning. And these few when they have tasted the pleasures of philosophy, and have taken a look at that den of thieves and place of wild beasts, which is human life, will stand aside from the storm under the shelter of a wall, and try to preserve their own innocence and to depart in peace. 'A great work, too, will have been accomplished by them.' Great, yes, but not the greatest; for man is a social being, and can only attain his highest development in the society which is best suited to him.

Enough, then, of the causes why philosophy has such an evil name. Another question is, Which of existing states is suited to her? Not one of them; at present she is like some exotic seed which degenerates in a strange soil; only in her proper state will she be shown to be of heavenly growth. 'And is her proper state ours or some other?' Ours in all points but one, which was left undetermined. You may remember our saying that some living mind or witness of the legislator was needed in states. But we were afraid to enter upon a subject of such difficulty, and now the question recurs and has not grown easier: – How may philosophy be safely studied? Let us bring her into the light of day, and make an end of the inquiry.

In the first place, I say boldly that nothing can be worse than the present mode of study. Persons usually pick up a little philosophy in early youth, and in the intervals of business, but they never master the real difficulty, which is dialectic. Later, perhaps, they occasionally go to a lecture on philosophy. Years advance, and the sun of philosophy, unlike that of Heracleitus, sets never to rise again. This order of education should be reversed; it should begin with gymnastics in youth, and as the man strengthens, he should increase the gymnastics of his soul. Then, when active life is over, let him finally return to philosophy. 'You are in earnest, Socrates, but the world will be equally earnest in withstanding you – no more than Thrasymachus.' Do not make a quarrel between Thrasymachus and me, who were never enemies and are now good friends enough. And I shall do my best to convince him and all mankind of the truth of my words, or at any rate to prepare for the future when, in another life, we may again take part in similar discussions. 'That will be a long time hence.' Not long in comparison with eternity. The many will probably remain incredulous, for they have never seen the natural unity of ideas, but only artificial juxtapositions; not free and generous thoughts, but tricks of controversy and quips of law; – a perfect man ruling in a perfect state, even a single one they have not known. And we foresaw that there was no chance of perfection either in states or individuals until a necessity was laid upon philosophers – not the rogues, but those whom we called the useless class – of holding office; or until the sons of kings were inspired with a true love of philosophy. Whether in the infinity of past time there has been, or is in some distant land, or ever will be hereafter, an ideal such as we have described, we stoutly maintain that there has been, is, and will be such a state whenever the Muse of philosophy rules. Will you say that the world is of another mind? O, my friend, do not revile the world! They will soon change their opinion if they are gently entreated, and are taught the true nature of the philosopher. Who can hate a man who loves him? Or be jealous of one who has no jealousy? Consider, again, that the many hate not the true but the false philosophers – the pretenders who force their way in without invitation, and are always speaking of persons and not of principles, which is unlike the spirit of philosophy. For the true philosopher despises earthly strife; his eye is fixed on the eternal order in accordance with which he moulds himself into the Divine image (and not himself only, but other men), and is the creator of the virtues private as well as public. When mankind see that the happiness of states is only to be found in that image, will they be angry with us for attempting to delineate it? 'Certainly not. But what will be the process of delineation?' The artist will do nothing until he has made a tabula rasa; on this he will inscribe the constitution of a state, glancing often at the divine truth of nature, and from that deriving the godlike among men, mingling the two elements, rubbing out and painting in, until there is a perfect harmony or fusion of the divine and human. But perhaps the world will doubt the existence of such an artist. What will they doubt? That the philosopher is a lover of truth, having a nature akin to the best? – and if they admit this will they still quarrel with us for making philosophers our kings? 'They will be less disposed to quarrel.' Let us assume then that they are pacified. Still, a person may hesitate about the probability of the son of a king being a philosopher. And we do not deny that they are very liable to be corrupted; but yet surely in the course of ages there might be one exception – and one is enough. If one son of a king were a philosopher, and had obedient citizens, he might bring the ideal polity into being. Hence we conclude that our laws are not only the best, but that they are also possible, though not free from difficulty.

I gained nothing by evading the troublesome questions which arose concerning women and children. I will be wiser now and acknowledge that we must go to the bottom of another question: What is to be the education of our guardians? It was agreed that they were to be lovers of their country, and were to be tested in the refiner's fire of pleasures and pains, and those who came forth pure and remained fixed in their principles were to have honours and rewards in life and after death. But at this point, the argument put on her veil and turned into another path. I hesitated to make the assertion which I now hazard, – that our guardians must be philosophers. You remember all the contradictory elements, which met in the philosopher – how difficult to find them all in a single person! Intelligence and spirit are not often combined with steadiness; the stolid, fearless, nature is averse to intellectual toil. And yet these opposite elements are all necessary, and therefore, as we were saying before, the aspirant must be tested in pleasures and dangers; and also, as we must now further add, in the highest branches of knowledge. You will remember, that when we spoke of the virtues mention was made of a longer road, which you were satisfied to leave unexplored. 'Enough seemed to have been said.' Enough, my friend; but what is enough while anything remains wanting? Of all men the guardian must not faint in the search after truth; he must be prepared to take the longer road, or he will never reach that higher region which is above the four virtues; and of the virtues too he must not only get an outline, but a clear and distinct vision. (Strange that we should be so precise about trifles, so careless about the highest truths!) 'And what are the highest?' You to pretend unconsciousness, when you have so often heard me speak of the idea of good, about which we know so little, and without which though a man gain the world he has no profit of it! Some people imagine that the good is wisdom; but this involves a circle, – the good, they say, is wisdom, wisdom has to do with the good. According to others the good is pleasure; but then comes the absurdity that good is bad, for there are bad pleasures as well as good. Again, the good must have reality; a man may desire the appearance of virtue, but he will not desire the appearance of good. Ought our guardians then to be ignorant of this supreme principle, of which every man has a presentiment, and without which no man has any real knowledge of anything? 'But, Socrates, what is this supreme principle, knowledge or pleasure, or what? You may think me troublesome, but I say that you have no business to be always repeating the doctrines of others instead of giving us your own.' Can I say what I do not know? 'You may offer an opinion.' And will the blindness and crookedness of opinion content you when you might have the light and certainty of science? 'I will only ask you to give such an explanation of the good as you have given already of temperance and justice.' I wish that I could, but in my present mood I cannot reach to the height of the knowledge of the good. To the parent or principal I cannot introduce you, but to the child begotten in his image, which I may compare with the interest on the principal, I will. (Audit the account, and do not let me give you a false statement of the debt.) You remember our old distinction of the many beautiful and the one beautiful, the particular and the universal, the objects of sight and the objects of thought? Did you ever consider that the objects of sight imply a faculty of sight which is the most complex and costly of our senses, requiring not only objects of sense, but also a medium, which is light; without which the sight will not distinguish between colours and all will be a blank? For light is the noble bond between the perceiving faculty and the thing perceived, and the god who gives us light is the sun, who is the eye of the day, but is not to be confounded with the eye of man. This eye of the day or sun is what I call the child of the good, standing in the same relation to the visible world as the good to the intellectual. When the sun shines the eye sees, and in the intellectual world where truth is, there is sight and light. Now that which is the sun of intelligent natures, is the idea of good, the cause of knowledge and truth, yet other and fairer than they are, and standing in the same relation to them in which the sun stands to light. O inconceivable height of beauty, which is above knowledge and above truth! ('You cannot surely mean pleasure,' he said. Peace, I replied.) And this idea of good, like the sun, is also the cause of growth, and the author not of knowledge only, but of being, yet greater far than either in dignity and power. 'That is a reach of thought more than human; but, pray, go on with the image, for I suspect that there is more behind.' There is, I said; and bearing in mind our two suns or principles, imagine further their corresponding worlds – one of the visible, the other of the intelligible; you may assist your fancy by figuring the distinction under the image of a line divided into two unequal parts, and may again subdivide each part into two lesser segments representative of the stages of knowledge in either sphere. The lower portion of the lower or visible sphere will consist of shadows and reflections, and its upper and smaller portion will contain real objects in the world of nature or of art. The sphere of the intelligible will also have two divisions, – one of mathematics, in which there is no ascent but all is descent; no inquiring into premises, but only drawing of inferences. In this division the mind works with figures and numbers, the images of which are taken not from the shadows, but from the objects, although the truth of them is seen only with the mind's eye; and they are used as hypotheses without being analysed. Whereas in the other division reason uses the hypotheses as stages or steps in the ascent to the idea of good, to which she fastens them, and then again descends, walking firmly in the region of ideas, and of ideas only, in her ascent as well as descent, and finally resting in them. 'I partly understand,' he replied; 'you mean that the ideas of science are superior to the hypothetical, metaphorical conceptions of geometry and the other arts or sciences, whichever is to be the name of them; and the latter conceptions you refuse to make subjects of pure intellect, because they have no first principle, although when resting on a first principle, they pass into the higher sphere.' You understand me very well, I said. And now to those four divisions of knowledge you may assign four corresponding faculties – pure intelligence to the highest sphere; active intelligence to the second; to the third, faith; to the fourth, the perception of shadows – and the clearness of the several faculties will be in the same ratio as the truth of the objects to which they are related...

Like Socrates, we may recapitulate the virtues of the philosopher. In language which seems to reach beyond the horizon of that age and country, he is described as 'the spectator of all time and all existence.' He has the noblest gifts of nature, and makes the highest use of them. All his desires are absorbed in the love of wisdom, which is the love of truth. None of the graces of a beautiful soul are wanting in him; neither can he fear death, or think much of human life. The ideal of modern times hardly retains the simplicity of the antique; there is not the same originality either in truth or error which characterized the Greeks. The philosopher is no longer living in the unseen, nor is he sent by an oracle to convince mankind of ignorance; nor does he regard knowledge as a system of ideas leading upwards by regular stages to the idea of good. The eagerness of the pursuit has abated; there is more division of labour and less of comprehensive reflection upon nature and human life as a whole; more of exact observation and less of anticipation and inspiration. Still, in the altered conditions of knowledge, the parallel is not wholly lost; and there may be a use in translating the conception of Plato into the language of our own age. The philosopher in modern times is one who fixes his mind on the laws of nature in their sequence and connexion, not on fragments or pictures of nature; on history, not on controversy; on the truths which are acknowledged by the few, not on the opinions of the many. He is aware of the importance of 'classifying according to nature,' and will try to 'separate the limbs of science without breaking them' (Phaedr.). There is no part of truth, whether great or small, which he will dishonour; and in the least things he will discern the greatest (Parmen.). Like the ancient philosopher he sees the world pervaded by analogies, but he can also tell 'why in some cases a single instance is sufficient for an induction' (Mill's Logic), while in other cases a thousand examples would prove nothing. He inquires into a portion of knowledge only, because the whole has grown too vast to be embraced by a single mind or life. He has a clearer conception of the divisions of science and of their relation to the mind of man than was possible to the ancients. Like Plato, he has a vision of the unity of knowledge, not as the beginning of philosophy to be attained by a study of elementary mathematics, but as the far-off result of the working of many minds in many ages. He is aware that mathematical studies are preliminary to almost every other; at the same time, he will not reduce all varieties of knowledge to the type of mathematics. He too must have a nobility of character, without which genius loses the better half of greatness. Regarding the world as a point in immensity, and each individual as a link in a never-ending chain of existence, he will not think much of his own life, or be greatly afraid of death.

Adeimantus objects first of all to the form of the Socratic reasoning, thus showing that Plato is aware of the imperfection of his own method. He brings the accusation against himself which might be brought against him by a modern logician – that he extracts the answer because he knows how to put the question. In a long argument words are apt to change their meaning slightly, or premises may be assumed or conclusions inferred with rather too much certainty or universality; the variation at each step may be unobserved, and yet at last the divergence becomes considerable. Hence the failure of attempts to apply arithmetical or algebraic formulae to logic. The imperfection, or rather the higher and more elastic nature of language, does not allow words to have the precision of numbers or of symbols. And this quality in language impairs the force of an argument which has many steps.

The objection, though fairly met by Socrates in this particular instance, may be regarded as implying a reflection upon the Socratic mode of reasoning. And here, as elsewhere, Plato seems to intimate that the time had come when the negative and interrogative method of Socrates must be superseded by a positive and constructive one, of which examples are given in some of the later dialogues. Adeimantus further argues that the ideal is wholly at variance with facts; for experience proves philosophers to be either useless or rogues. Contrary to all expectation Socrates has no hesitation in admitting the truth of this, and explains the anomaly in an allegory, first characteristically depreciating his own inventive powers. In this allegory the people are distinguished from the professional politicians, and, as elsewhere, are spoken of in a tone of pity rather than of censure under the image of 'the noble captain who is not very quick in his perceptions.'

The uselessness of philosophers is explained by the circumstance that mankind will not use them. The world in all ages has been divided between contempt and fear of those who employ the power of ideas and know no other weapons. Concerning the false philosopher, Socrates argues that the best is most liable to corruption; and that the finer nature is more likely to suffer from alien conditions. We too observe that there are some kinds of excellence which spring from a peculiar delicacy of constitution; as is evidently true of the poetical and imaginative temperament, which often seems to depend on impressions, and hence can only breathe or live in a certain atmosphere. The man of genius has greater pains and greater pleasures, greater powers and greater weaknesses, and often a greater play of character than is to be found in ordinary men. He can assume the disguise of virtue or disinterestedness without having them, or veil personal enmity in the language of patriotism and philosophy, – he can say the word which all men are thinking, he has an insight which is terrible into the follies and weaknesses of his fellow-men. An Alcibiades, a Mirabeau, or a Napoleon the First, are born either to be the authors of great evils in states, or 'of great good, when they are drawn in that direction.'

Yet the thesis, 'corruptio optimi pessima,' cannot be maintained generally or without regard to the kind of excellence which is corrupted. The alien conditions which are corrupting to one nature, may be the elements of culture to another. In general a man can only receive his highest development in a congenial state or family, among friends or fellow-workers. But also he may sometimes be stirred by adverse circumstances to such a degree that he rises up against them and reforms them. And while weaker or coarser characters will extract good out of evil, say in a corrupt state of the church or of society, and live on happily, allowing the evil to remain, the finer or stronger natures may be crushed or spoiled by surrounding influences – may become misanthrope and philanthrope by turns; or in a few instances, like the founders of the monastic orders, or the Reformers, owing to some peculiarity in themselves or in their age, may break away entirely from the world and from the church, sometimes into great good, sometimes into great evil, sometimes into both. And the same holds in the lesser sphere of a convent, a school, a family.

Plato would have us consider how easily the best natures are overpowered by public opinion, and what efforts the rest of mankind will make to get possession of them. The world, the church, their own profession, any political or party organization, are always carrying them off their legs and teaching them to apply high and holy names to their own prejudices and interests. The 'monster' corporation to which they belong judges right and truth to be the pleasure of the community. The individual becomes one with his order; or, if he resists, the world is too much for him, and will sooner or later be revenged on him. This is, perhaps, a one-sided but not wholly untrue picture of the maxims and practice of mankind when they 'sit down together at an assembly,' either in ancient or modern times.

When the higher natures are corrupted by politics, the lower take possession of the vacant place of philosophy. This is described in one of those continuous images in which the argument, to use a Platonic expression, 'veils herself,' and which is dropped and reappears at intervals. The question is asked, – Why are the citizens of states so hostile to philosophy? The answer is, that they do not know her. And yet there is also a better mind of the many; they would believe if they were taught. But hitherto they have only known a conventional imitation of philosophy, words without thoughts, systems which have no life in them; a (divine) person uttering the words of beauty and freedom, the friend of man holding communion with the Eternal, and seeking to frame the state in that image, they have never known. The same double feeling respecting the mass of mankind has always existed among men. The first thought is that the people are the enemies of truth and right; the second, that this only arises out of an accidental error and confusion, and that they do not really hate those who love them, if they could be educated to know them.

In the latter part of the sixth book, three questions have to be considered: 1st, the nature of the longer and more circuitous way, which is contrasted with the shorter and more imperfect method of Book IV; 2nd, the heavenly pattern or idea of the state; 3rd, the relation of the divisions of knowledge to one another and to the corresponding faculties of the soul:

1. Of the higher method of knowledge in Plato we have only a glimpse. Neither here nor in the Phaedrus or Symposium, nor yet in the Philebus or Sophist, does he give any clear explanation of his meaning. He would probably have described his method as proceeding by regular steps to a system of universal knowledge, which inferred the parts from the whole rather than the whole from the parts. This ideal logic is not practised by him in the search after justice, or in the analysis of the parts of the soul; there, like Aristotle in the Nicomachean Ethics, he argues from experience and the common use of language. But at the end of the sixth book he conceives another and more perfect method, in which all ideas are only steps or grades or moments of thought, forming a connected whole which is self-supporting, and in which consistency is the test of truth. He does not explain to us in detail the nature of the process. Like many other thinkers both in ancient and modern times his mind seems to be filled with a vacant form which he is unable to realize. He supposes the sciences to have a

natural order and connexion in an age when they can hardly be said to exist. He is hastening on to the 'end of the intellectual world' without even making a beginning of them.

In modern times we hardly need to be reminded that the process of acquiring knowledge is here confused with the contemplation of absolute knowledge. In all science a priori and a posteriori truths mingle in various proportions. The a priori part is that which is derived from the most universal experience of men, or is universally accepted by them; the a posteriori is that which grows up around the more general principles and becomes imperceptibly one with them. But Plato erroneously imagines that the synthesis is separable from the analysis, and that the method of science can anticipate science. In entertaining such a vision of a priori knowledge he is sufficiently justified, or at least his meaning may be sufficiently explained by the similar attempts of Descartes, Kant, Hegel, and even of Bacon himself, in modern philosophy. Anticipations or divinations, or prophetic glimpses of truths whether concerning man or nature, seem to stand in the same relation to ancient philosophy which hypotheses bear to modern inductive science. These 'guesses at truth' were not made at random; they arose from a superficial impression of uniformities and first principles in nature which the genius of the Greek, contemplating the expanse of heaven and earth, seemed to recognize in the distance. Nor can we deny that in ancient times knowledge must have stood still, and the human mind been deprived of the very instruments of thought, if philosophy had been strictly confined to the results of experience.

2. Plato supposes that when the tablet has been made blank the artist will fill in the lineaments of the ideal state. Is this a pattern laid up in heaven, or mere vacancy on which he is supposed to gaze with wondering eye? The answer is, that such ideals are framed partly by the omission of particulars, partly by imagination perfecting the form which experience supplies (Phaedo). Plato represents these ideals in a figure as belonging to another world; and in modern times the idea will sometimes seem to precede, at other times to co-operate with the hand of the artist. As in science, so also in creative art, there is a synthetical as well as an analytical method. One man will have the whole in his mind before he begins; to another the processes of mind and hand will be simultaneous.

3. There is no difficulty in seeing that Plato's divisions of knowledge are based, first, on the fundamental antithesis of sensible and intellectual which pervades the whole pre-Socratic philosophy; in which is implied also

the opposition of the permanent and transient, of the universal and particular. But the age of philosophy in which he lived seemed to require a further distinction; – numbers and figures were beginning to separate from ideas. The world could no longer regard justice as a cube, and was learning to see, though imperfectly, that the abstractions of sense were distinct from the abstractions of mind. Between the Eleatic being or essence and the shadows of phenomena, the Pythagorean principle of number found a place, and was, as Aristotle remarks, a conducting medium from one to the other. Hence Plato is led to introduce a third term which had not hitherto entered into the scheme of his philosophy. He had observed the use of mathematics in education; they were the best preparation for higher studies. The subjective relation between them further suggested an objective one; although the passage from one to the other is really imaginary (Metaph.). For metaphysical and moral philosophy has no connexion with mathematics; number and figure are the abstractions of time and space, not the expressions of purely intellectual conceptions. When divested of metaphor, a straight line or a square has no more to do with right and justice than a crooked line with vice. The figurative association was mistaken for a real one; and thus the three latter divisions of the Platonic proportion were constructed.

There is more difficulty in comprehending how he arrived at the first term of the series, which is nowhere else mentioned, and has no reference to any other part of his system. Nor indeed does the relation of shadows to objects correspond to the relation of numbers to ideas. Probably Plato has been led by the love of analogy (Timaeus) to make four terms instead of three, although the objects perceived in both divisions of the lower sphere are equally objects of sense. He is also preparing the way, as his manner is, for the shadows of images at the beginning of the seventh book, and the imitation of an imitation in the tenth. The line may be regarded as reaching from unity to infinity, and is divided into two unequal parts, and subdivided into two more; each lower sphere is the multiplication of the preceding. Of the four faculties, faith in the lower division has an intermediate position (cp. for the use of the word faith or belief, (Greek), Timaeus), contrasting equally with the vagueness of the perception of shadows (Greek) and the higher certainty of understanding (Greek) and reason (Greek).

The difference between understanding and mind or reason (Greek) is analogous to the difference between acquiring knowledge in the parts and the contemplation of the whole. True knowledge is a whole, and is at rest;

consistency and universality are the tests of truth. To this self-evidencing knowledge of the whole the faculty of mind is supposed to correspond. But there is a knowledge of the understanding which is incomplete and in motion always, because unable to rest in the subordinate ideas. Those ideas are called both images and hypotheses – images because they are clothed in sense, hypotheses because they are assumptions only, until they are brought into connexion with the idea of good.

The general meaning of the passage, 'Noble, then, is the bond which links together sight...And of this kind I spoke as the intelligible...' so far as the thought contained in it admits of being translated into the terms of modern philosophy, may be described or explained as follows: – There is a truth, one and self-existent, to which by the help of a ladder let down from above, the human intelligence may ascend. This unity is like the sun in the heavens, the light by which all things are seen, the being by which they are created and sustained. It is the IDEA of good. And the steps of the ladder leading up to this highest or universal existence are the mathematical sciences, which also contain in themselves an element of the universal. These, too, we see in a new manner when we connect them with the idea of good. They then cease to be hypotheses or pictures, and become essential parts of a higher truth which is at once their first principle and their final cause.

We cannot give any more precise meaning to this remarkable passage, but we may trace in it several rudiments or vestiges of thought which are common to us and to Plato: such as (1) the unity and correlation of the sciences, or rather of science, for in Plato's time they were not yet parted off or distinguished; (2) the existence of a Divine Power, or life or idea or cause or reason, not yet conceived or no longer conceived as in the Timaeus and elsewhere under the form of a person; (3) the recognition of the hypothetical and conditional character of the mathematical sciences, and in a measure of every science when isolated from the rest; (4) the conviction of a truth which is invisible, and of a law, though hardly a law of nature, which permeates the intellectual rather than the visible world.

The method of Socrates is hesitating and tentative, awaiting the fuller explanation of the idea of good, and of the nature of dialectic in the seventh book. The imperfect intelligence of Glaucon, and the reluctance of Socrates to make a beginning, mark the difficulty of the subject. The allusion to Theages' bridle, and to the internal oracle, or demonic sign, of Socrates, which here, as always in Plato, is only prohibitory; the remark that the salvation of any remnant of good in the present evil state of the world is due to God only; the reference to a future state of existence, which is unknown to Glaucon in the tenth book, and in which the discussions of Socrates and his disciples would be resumed; the surprise in the answers; the fanciful irony of Socrates, where he pretends that he can only describe the strange position of the philosopher in a figure of speech; the original observation that the Sophists, after all, are only the representatives and not the leaders of public opinion; the picture of the philosopher standing aside in the shower of sleet under a wall; the figure of 'the great beast' followed by the expression of good-will towards the common people who would not have rejected the philosopher if they had known him; the 'right noble thought' that the highest truths demand the greatest exactness; the hesitation of Socrates in returning once more to his well-worn theme of the idea of good; the ludicrous earnestness of Glaucon; the comparison of philosophy to a deserted maiden who marries beneath her – are some of the most interesting characteristics of the sixth book.

Yet a few more words may be added, on the old theme, which was so oft discussed in the Socratic circle, of which we, like Glaucon and Adeimantus, would fain, if possible, have a clearer notion. Like them, we are dissatisfied when we are told that the idea of good can only be revealed to a student of the mathematical sciences, and we are inclined to think that neither we nor they could have been led along that path to any satisfactory goal. For we have learned that differences of quantity cannot pass into differences of quality, and that the mathematical sciences can never rise above themselves into the sphere of our higher thoughts, although they may sometimes furnish symbols and expressions of them, and may train the mind in habits of abstraction and self-concentration. The illusion which was natural to an ancient philosopher has ceased to be an illusion to us. But if the process by which we are supposed to arrive at the idea of good be really imaginary, may not the idea itself be also a mere abstraction? We remark, first, that in all ages, and especially in primitive philosophy, words such as being, essence, unity, good, have exerted an extraordinary influence over the minds of men. The meagreness or negativeness of their content has been in an inverse ratio to their power. They have become the forms under which all things were comprehended. There was a need or instinct in the human soul which they satisfied; they were not ideas, but gods, and to this new mythology the men of a later generation began to attach the powers and associations of the elder deities.

The idea of good is one of those sacred words or forms of thought, which were beginning to take the place of the old mythology. It meant unity, in which all time and all existence were gathered up. It was the truth of all things, and also the light in which they shone forth, and became evident to intelligences human and divine. It was the cause of all things, the power by which they were brought into being. It was the universal reason divested of a human personality. It was the life as well as the light of the world, all knowledge and all power were comprehended in it. The way to it was through the mathematical sciences, and these too were dependent on it. To ask whether God was the maker of it, or made by it, would be like asking whether God could be conceived apart from goodness, or goodness apart from God. The God of the Timaeus is not really at variance with the idea of good; they are aspects of the same, differing only as the personal from the impersonal, or the masculine from the neuter, the one being the expression or language of mythology, the other of philosophy.

This, or something like this, is the meaning of the idea of good as conceived by Plato. Ideas of number, order, harmony, development may also be said to enter into it. The paraphrase which has just been given of it goes beyond the actual words of Plato. We have perhaps arrived at the stage of philosophy which enables us to understand what he is aiming at, better than he did himself. We are beginning to realize what he saw darkly and at a distance. But if he could have been told that this, or some conception of the same kind, but higher than this, was the truth at which he was aiming, and the need which he sought to supply, he would gladly have recognized that more was contained in his own thoughts than he himself knew. As his words are few and his manner reticent and tentative, so must the style of his interpreter be. We should not approach his meaning more nearly by attempting to define it further. In translating him into the language of modern thought, we might insensibly lose the spirit of ancient philosophy. It is remarkable that although Plato speaks of the idea of good as the first principle of truth and being, it is nowhere mentioned in his writings except in this passage. Nor did it retain any hold upon the minds of his disciples in a later generation; it was probably unintelligible to them. Nor does the mention of it in Aristotle appear to have any reference to this or any other passage in his extant writings.

BOOK VII.

And now I will describe in a figure the enlightenment or unenlightenment of our nature: – Imagine human beings living in an underground den which is open towards the light; they have been there from childhood, having their necks and legs chained, and can only see into the den. At a distance there is a fire, and between the fire and the prisoners a raised way, and a low wall is built along the way, like the screen over which marionette players show their puppets. Behind the wall appear moving figures, who hold in their hands various works of art, and among them images of men and animals, wood and stone, and some of the passers-by are talking and others silent. 'A strange parable,' he said, 'and strange captives.' They are ourselves, I replied; and they see only the shadows of the images which the fire throws on the wall of the den; to these they give names, and if we add an echo which returns from the wall, the voices of the passengers will seem to proceed from the shadows. Suppose now that you suddenly turn them round and make them look with pain and grief to themselves at the real images; will they believe them to be real? Will not their eyes be dazzled, and will they not try to get away from the light to something which they are able to behold without blinking? And suppose further, that they are dragged up a steep and rugged ascent into the presence of the sun himself, will not their sight be darkened with the excess of light? Some time will pass before they get the habit of perceiving at all; and at first they will be able to perceive only shadows and reflections in the water; then they will recognize the moon and the stars, and will at length behold the sun in his own proper place as he is. Last of all they will conclude: – This is he who gives us the year and the seasons, and is the author of all that we see. How will they rejoice in passing from darkness to light! How worthless to them will seem the honours and glories of the den! But now imagine further, that they descend into their old habitations; – in that underground dwelling they will not see as well as their fellows, and will not be able to compete with them in the measurement of the shadows on the wall; there will be many jokes about the man who went on a visit to the sun and lost his eyes, and if they find anybody trying to set free and enlighten one of their number, they will put him to death, if they can catch him. Now the cave or den is the world of sight, the fire is the sun, the way upwards is the way to knowledge, and in the world of knowledge the idea of good is last seen and with difficulty, but when seen is inferred to be the author of good and right – parent of the lord of light in this world, and of truth and understanding in the other. He who attains to the beatific vision is always going upwards; he is unwilling to descend into political assemblies and courts of law; for his eyes are apt to blink at the images or shadows of images which they behold in them – he cannot enter into the ideas of those who have never in their lives understood the relation of the shadow to the substance. But blindness is of two kinds, and may be caused either by passing out of darkness into light or out of light into darkness, and a man of sense will distinguish between them, and will not laugh equally at both of them, but the blindness which arises from fulness of light he will deem blessed, and pity the other; or if he laugh at the puzzled soul looking at the sun, he will have more reason to laugh than the inhabitants of the den at those who descend from above. There is a further lesson taught by this parable of ours. Some persons fancy that instruction is like giving eyes to the blind, but we say that the faculty of sight was always there, and that the soul only requires to be turned round towards the light. And this is conversion; other virtues are almost like bodily habits, and may be acquired in the same manner, but intelligence has a diviner life, and is indestructible, turning either to good or evil according to the direction given. Did you never observe how the mind of a clever rogue peers out of his eyes, and the more clearly he sees, the more evil he does? Now if you take such an one, and cut away from him those leaden weights of pleasure and desire which bind his soul to earth, his intelligence will be turned round, and he will behold the truth as clearly as he now discerns his meaner ends. And have we not decided that our rulers must neither be so uneducated as to have no fixed rule of life, nor so over-educated as to be unwilling to leave their paradise for the business of the world? We must choose out therefore the natures who are most likely to ascend to the light and knowledge of the good; but we must not allow them to remain in the region of light; they must be forced down again among the captives in the den to partake of their labours and honours. 'Will they not think this a hardship?' You should remember that our purpose in framing the State was not that our citizens should do what they like, but that they should serve the State for the common good of all. May we not fairly say to our philosopher, – Friend, we do you no wrong; for in other States philosophy grows wild, and a wild plant owes nothing to the gardener, but you have been trained by us to be the rulers and kings of our hive, and therefore we must insist on your descending into the den. You must, each of you, take your turn, and become able to use your eyes in the dark, and with a little practice you will see far better than those who quarrel about the shadows, whose knowledge is a dream only, whilst yours is a waking reality. It may be that the saint or philosopher who is best fitted, may also be the least inclined to rule, but necessity is laid upon him, and he must no longer live in the heaven of ideas. And this will be the salvation of the State. For those who rule must not be those who are desirous to rule; and, if you can offer to our citizens a better life than that of rulers generally is, there will be a chance that the rich, not only in this world's goods, but in virtue and wisdom, may bear rule. And the only life which is better than the life of political ambition is that of philosophy, which is also the best preparation for the government of a State.

Then now comes the question, – How shall we create our rulers; what way is there from darkness to light? The change is effected by philosophy; it is not the turning over of an oyster-shell, but the conversion of a soul from night to day, from becoming to being. And what training will draw the soul upwards? Our former education had two branches, gymnastic, which was occupied with the body, and music, the sister art, which infused a natural harmony into mind and literature; but neither of these sciences gave any promise of doing what we want. Nothing remains to us but that universal or primary science of which all the arts and sciences are partakers, I mean number or calculation. 'Very true.' Including the art of war? 'Yes, certainly.' Then there is something ludicrous about Palamedes in the tragedy, coming in and saying that he had invented number, and had counted the ranks and set them in order. For if Agamemnon could not count his feet (and without number how could he?) he must have been a pretty sort of general indeed. No man should be a soldier who cannot count, and indeed he is hardly to be called a man. But I am not speaking of these practical applications of arithmetic, for number, in my view, is rather to be regarded as a conductor to thought and being. I will explain what I mean by the last expression: – Things sensible are of two kinds; the one class invite or stimulate the mind, while in the other the mind acquiesces. Now the stimulating class are the things which suggest contrast and relation. For example, suppose that I hold up to the eyes three fingers – a fore finger, a middle finger, a little finger – the sight equally recognizes all three fingers, but without number cannot further distinguish them. Or again, suppose two objects to be relatively great and small, these ideas of greatness and smallness are supplied not by the sense, but by the mind. And the perception of their contrast or relation quickens and sets in motion the mind, which is puzzled by the confused intimations of sense, and has recourse to number in order to find out whether the things indicated are one or more than one. Number replies that they are two and not one, and are to be distinguished from one another. Again, the sight beholds great and small, but only in a confused chaos, and not until they are distinguished does the question arise of their respective natures; we are thus led on to the distinction between the visible and intelligible. That was what I meant when I spoke of stimulants to the intellect; I was thinking of the contradictions which arise in perception. The idea of unity, for example, like that of a finger, does not arouse thought unless involving some conception of plurality; but when the one is also the opposite of one, the contradiction gives rise to reflection; an example of this is afforded by any object of sight. All number has also an elevating effect; it raises the mind out of the foam and flux of generation to the contemplation of being, having lesser military and retail uses also. The retail use is not required by us; but as our guardian is to be a soldier as well as a philosopher, the military one may be retained. And to our higher purpose no science can be better adapted; but it must be pursued in the spirit of a philosopher, not of a shopkeeper. It is concerned, not with visible objects, but with abstract truth; for numbers are pure abstractions – the true arithmetician indignantly denies that his unit is capable of division. When you divide, he insists that you are only multiplying; his 'one' is not material or resolvable into fractions, but an unvarying and absolute equality; and this proves the purely intellectual character of his study. Note also the great power which arithmetic has of sharpening the wits; no other discipline is equally severe, or an equal test of general ability, or equally improving to a stupid person.

Let our second branch of education be geometry. 'I can easily see,' replied Glaucon, 'that the skill of the general will be doubled by his knowledge of geometry.' That is a small matter; the use of geometry, to which I refer, is the assistance given by it in the contemplation of the idea of good, and the compelling the mind to look at true being, and not at generation only. Yet the present mode of pursuing these studies, as any one who is the least of a mathematician is aware, is mean and ridiculous; they are made to look downwards to the arts, and not upwards to eternal existence. The geometer is always talking of squaring, subtending, apposing, as if he had in view action; whereas knowledge is the real object of the study. It should elevate the soul, and create the mind of philosophy; it should raise up what has fallen down, not to speak of lesser uses in war and military tactics, and in the improvement of the faculties.

Shall we propose, as a third branch of our education, astronomy? 'Very good,' replied Glaucon; 'the knowledge of the heavens is necessary at once for husbandry, navigation, military tactics.' I like your way of giving useful reasons for everything in order to make friends of the world. And there is a difficulty in proving to mankind that education is not only useful information but a purification of the eye of the soul, which is better than the bodily eye, for by this alone is truth seen. Now, will you appeal to mankind in general or to the philosopher? or would you prefer to look to yourself only? 'Every man is his own best friend.' Then take a step backward, for we are out of order, and insert the third dimension which is of solids, after the second which is of planes, and then you may proceed to solids in motion. But solid geometry is not popular and has not the patronage of the State, nor is the use of it fully recognized; the difficulty is great, and the votaries of the study are conceited and impatient. Still the charm of the pursuit wins upon men, and, if government would lend a little assistance, there might be great progress made. 'Very true,' replied Glaucon; 'but do I understand you now to begin with plane geometry, and to place next geometry of solids, and thirdly, astronomy, or the motion of solids?' Yes, I said; my hastiness has only hindered us.

'Very good, and now let us proceed to astronomy, about which I am willing to speak in your lofty strain. No one can fail to see that the contemplation of the heavens draws the soul upwards.' I am an exception, then; astronomy as studied at present appears to me to draw the soul not upwards, but downwards. Star-gazing is just looking up at the ceiling – no better; a man may lie on his back on land or on water – he may look up or look down, but there is no science in that. The vision of knowledge of which I speak is seen not with the eyes, but with the mind. All the magnificence of the heavens is but the embroidery of a copy which falls far short of the divine Original, and teaches nothing about the absolute harmonies or motions of things. Their beauty is like the beauty of figures drawn by the hand of Daedalus or any other great artist, which may be used for illustration, but no mathematician would seek to obtain from them true conceptions of equality or numerical relations. How ridiculous then to look for these in the map of the heavens, in which the imperfection of matter comes in everywhere as a disturbing element, marring the symmetry of day and night, of months and years, of the sun and stars in their courses. Only by problems can we place astronomy on a truly scientific basis. Let the heavens alone, and exert the intellect.

Still, mathematics admit of other applications, as the Pythagoreans say, and we agree. There is a sister science of harmonical motion, adapted to the ear as astronomy is to the eye, and there may be other applications also. Let us inquire of the Pythagoreans about them, not forgetting that we have an aim higher than theirs, which is the relation of these sciences to the idea of good. The error which pervades astronomy also pervades harmonics.

THE REPUBLIC

The musicians put their ears in the place of their minds. 'Yes,' replied Glaucon, 'I like to see them laying their ears alongside of their neighbours' faces – some saying, "That's a new note," others declaring that the two notes are the same.' Yes, I said; but you mean the empirics who are always twisting and torturing the strings of the lyre, and quarrelling about the tempers of the strings; I am referring rather to the Pythagorean harmonists, who are almost equally in error. For they investigate only the numbers of the consonances which are heard, and ascend no higher, – of the true numerical harmony which is unheard, and is only to be found in problems, they have not even a conception. 'That last,' he said, 'must be a marvellous thing.' A thing, I replied, which is only useful if pursued with a view to the good.

All these sciences are the prelude of the strain, and are profitable if they are regarded in their natural relations to one another. 'I dare say, Socrates,' said Glaucon; 'but such a study will be an endless business.' What study do you mean – of the prelude, or what? For all these things are only the prelude, and you surely do not suppose that a mere mathematician is also a dialectician? 'Certainly not. I have hardly ever known a mathematician who could reason.' And yet, Glaucon, is not true reasoning that hymn of dialectic which is the music of the intellectual world, and which was by us compared to the effort of sight, when from beholding the shadows on the wall we arrived at last at the images which gave the shadows? Even so the dialectical faculty withdrawing from sense arrives by the pure intellect at the contemplation of the idea of good, and never rests but at the very end of the intellectual world. And the royal road out of the cave into the light, and the blinking of the eyes at the sun and turning to contemplate the shadows of reality, not the shadows of an image only – this progress and gradual acquisition of a new faculty of sight by the help of the mathematical sciences, is the elevation of the soul to the contemplation of the highest ideal of being.

'So far, I agree with you. But now, leaving the prelude, let us proceed to the hymn. What, then, is the nature of dialectic, and what are the paths which lead thither?' Dear Glaucon, you cannot follow me here. There can be no revelation of the absolute truth to one who has not been disciplined in the previous sciences. But that there is a science of absolute truth, which is attained in some way very different from those now practised, I am confident. For all other arts or sciences are relative to human needs and opinions; and the mathematical sciences are but a dream or hypothesis of true being, and never analyse their own principles. Dialectic alone rises to the principle which is above hypotheses, converting and gently leading the eye of the soul out of the barbarous slough of ignorance into the light of the upper world, with the help of the sciences which we have been describing – sciences, as they are often termed, although they require some other name, implying greater clearness than opinion and less clearness than science, and this in our previous sketch was understanding. And so we get four names – two for intellect, and two for opinion, – reason or mind, understanding, faith, perception of shadows – which make a proportion – being:becoming::intellect:opinion – and science:belief::understanding: perception of shadows. Dialectic may be further described as that science which defines and explains the essence or being of each nature, which distinguishes and abstracts the good, and is ready to do battle against all opponents in the cause of good. To him who is not a dialectician life is but a sleepy dream; and many a man is in his grave before his is well waked up. And would you have the future rulers of your ideal State intelligent beings, or stupid as posts? 'Certainly not the latter.' Then you must train them in dialectic, which will teach them to ask and answer questions, and is the coping-stone of the sciences.

I dare say that you have not forgotten how our rulers were chosen; and the process of selection may be carried a step further: – As before, they must be constant and valiant, good-looking, and of noble manners, but now they must also have natural ability which education will improve; that is to say, they must be quick at learning, capable of mental toil, retentive, solid, diligent natures, who combine intellectual with moral virtues; not lame and one-sided, diligent in bodily exercise and indolent in mind, or conversely; not a maimed soul, which hates falsehood and yet unintentionally is always wallowing in the mire of ignorance; not a bastard or feeble person, but sound in wind and limb, and in perfect condition for the great gymnastic trial of the mind. Justice herself can find no fault with natures such as these; and they will be the saviours of our State; disciples of another sort would only make philosophy more ridiculous than she is at present. Forgive my enthusiasm; I am becoming excited; but when I see her trampled underfoot, I am angry at the authors of her disgrace. 'I did not notice that you were more excited than you ought to have been.' But I felt that I was. Now do not let us forget another point in the selection of our disciples – that they must be young and not old. For Solon is mistaken in saying that an old man can be always learning; youth is the time of study, and here we must remember that the mind is free and dainty, and, unlike the body, must not be made to work against the grain. Learning should be at first a sort of play, in which the natural bent is detected. As in training them for war, the young dogs should at first only taste blood; but when the necessary gymnastics are over which during two or three years divide life between sleep and bodily exercise, then the education of the soul will become a more serious matter. At twenty years of age, a selection must be made of the more promising disciples, with whom a new epoch of education will begin. The sciences which they have hitherto learned in fragments will now be brought into relation with each other and with true being; for the power of combining them is the test of speculative and dialectical ability. And afterwards at thirty a further selection shall be made of those who are able to withdraw from the world of sense into the abstraction of ideas. But at this point, judging from present experience, there is a danger that dialectic may be the source of many evils. The danger may be illustrated by a parallel case: – Imagine a person who has been brought up in wealth and luxury amid a crowd of flatterers, and who is suddenly informed that he is a supposititious son. He has hitherto honoured his reputed parents and disregarded the flatterers, and now he does the reverse. This is just what happens with a man's principles. There are certain doctrines which he learnt at home and which exercised a parental authority over him. Presently he finds that imputations are cast upon them; a troublesome querist comes and asks, 'What is the just and good?' or proves that virtue is vice and vice virtue, and his mind becomes unsettled, and he ceases to love, honour, and obey them as he has hitherto done. He is seduced into the life of pleasure, and becomes a lawless person and a rogue. The case of such speculators is very pitiable, and, in order that our thirty years' old pupils may not require this pity, let us take every possible care that young persons do not study philosophy too early. For a young man is a sort of puppy who only plays with an argument; and is reasoned into and out of his opinions every day; he soon begins to believe nothing, and brings himself and philosophy into discredit. A man of thirty does not run on in this way; he will argue and not merely contradict, and adds new honour to philosophy by the sobriety of his conduct. What time shall we allow for this second gymnastic training of the soul? – say, twice the time required for the gymnastics of the body; six, or perhaps five years, to commence at thirty, and then for fifteen years let the student go down into the den, and command armies, and gain experience of life. At fifty let him return to the end of all things, and have his eyes uplifted to the idea of good, and order his life after that pattern; if necessary, taking his turn at the helm of State, and training up others to be his successors. When his time comes he shall depart in peace to the islands of the blest. He shall be honoured with sacrifices, and receive such worship as the Pythian oracle approves.

'You are a statuary, Socrates, and have made a perfect image of our governors.' Yes, and of our governesses, for the women will share in all things with the men. And you will admit that our State is not a mere aspiration, but may really come into being when there shall arise philosopher-kings, one or more, who will despise earthly vanities, and will be the servants of justice only. 'And how will they begin their work?' Their first act will be to send away into the country all those who are more than ten years of age, and to proceed with those who are left...

At the commencement of the sixth book, Plato anticipated his explanation of the relation of the philosopher to the world in an allegory, in this, as in other passages, following the order which he prescribes in education, and proceeding from the concrete to the abstract. At the commencement of Book VII, under the figure of a cave having an opening towards a fire and a way upwards to the true light, he returns to view the divisions of knowledge, exhibiting familiarly, as in a picture, the result which had been hardly won by a great effort of thought in the previous discussion; at the same time casting a glance onward at the dialectical process, which is represented by the way leading from darkness to light. The shadows, the images, the reflection of the sun and stars in the water, the stars and sun themselves, severally correspond, – the first, to the realm of fancy and poetry, – the second, to the world of sense, – the third, to the abstractions or universals of sense, of which the mathematical sciences furnish the type, – the fourth and last to the same abstractions, when seen in the unity of the idea, from which they derive a new meaning and power. The true dialectical process begins with the contemplation of the real stars, and not mere reflections of them, and ends with the recognition of the sun, or idea of good, as the parent not only of light but of warmth and growth. To the divisions of knowledge the stages of education partly answer: – first, there is the early education of childhood and youth in the fancies of the poets, and in the laws and customs of the State; – then there is the training of the body to be a warrior athlete, and a good servant of the mind; – and thirdly, after an interval follows the education of later life, which begins with mathematics and proceeds to philosophy in general.

There seem to be two great aims in the philosophy of Plato, – first, to realize abstractions; secondly, to connect them. According to him, the true education is that which draws men from becoming to being, and to a comprehensive survey of all being. He desires to develop in the human mind the faculty of seeing the universal in all things; until at last the particulars of sense drop away and the universal alone remains. He then seeks to combine the universals which he has disengaged from sense, not perceiving that the correlation of them has no other basis but the common use of language. He never understands that abstractions, as Hegel says, are 'mere abstractions' – of use when employed in the arrangement of facts, but adding nothing to the sum of knowledge when pursued apart from them, or with reference to an imaginary idea of good. Still the exercise of the faculty of abstraction apart from facts has enlarged the mind, and played a great part in the education of the human race. Plato appreciated the value of this faculty, and saw that it might be quickened by the study of number and relation. All things in which there is opposition or proportion are suggestive of reflection. The mere impression of sense evokes no power of thought or of mind, but when sensible objects ask to be compared and distinguished, then philosophy begins. The science of arithmetic first suggests such distinctions. The follow in order the other sciences of plain and solid geometry, and of solids in motion, one branch of which is astronomy or the harmony of the spheres, – to this is appended the sister science of the harmony of sounds. Plato seems also to hint at the possibility of other applications of arithmetical or mathematical proportions, such as we employ in chemistry and natural philosophy, such as the Pythagoreans and even Aristotle make use of in Ethics and Politics, e.g. his distinction between arithmetical and geometrical proportion in the Ethics (Book V), or between numerical and proportional equality in the Politics.

 The modern mathematician will readily sympathise with Plato's delight in the properties of pure mathematics. He will not be disinclined to say with him: – Let alone the heavens, and study the beauties of number and figure in themselves. He too will be apt to depreciate their application to the arts. He will observe that Plato has a conception of geometry, in which figures are to be dispensed with; thus in a distant and shadowy way seeming to anticipate the possibility of working geometrical problems by a more general mode of analysis. He will remark with interest on the backward state of solid geometry, which, alas! was not encouraged by the aid of the State in the age of Plato; and he will recognize the grasp of Plato's mind in his ability to conceive of one science of solids in motion including the earth as well as the heavens, – not forgetting to notice the intimation to which allusion has been already made, that besides astronomy and harmonics the science of solids in motion may have other applications. Still more will he be struck with the comprehensiveness of view which led Plato, at a time when these sciences hardly existed, to say that they must be studied in relation to one another, and to the idea of good, or common principle of truth and being. But he will also see (and perhaps without surprise) that in that stage of physical and mathematical knowledge, Plato has fallen into the error of supposing that he can construct the heavens a priori by mathematical problems, and determine the principles of harmony irrespective of the adaptation of sounds to the human ear. The illusion was a natural one in that age and country. The simplicity and certainty of astronomy and harmonics seemed to contrast with the variation and complexity of the world of sense; hence the circumstance that there was some elementary basis of fact, some measurement of distance or time or vibrations on which they must ultimately rest, was overlooked by him. The modern predecessors of Newton fell into errors equally great; and Plato can hardly be said to have been very far wrong, or may even claim a sort of prophetic insight into the subject, when we consider that the greater part of astronomy at the present day consists of abstract dynamics, by the help of which most astronomical discoveries have been made.

The metaphysical philosopher from his point of view recognizes mathematics as an instrument of education, – which strengthens the power of attention, developes the sense of order and the faculty of construction, and enables the mind to grasp under simple formulae the quantitative differences of physical phenomena. But while acknowledging their value in education, he sees also that they have no connexion with our higher moral and intellectual ideas. In the attempt which Plato makes to connect them, we easily trace the influences of ancient Pythagorean notions. There is no reason to suppose that he is speaking of the ideal numbers; but he is describing numbers which are pure abstractions, to which he assigns a real and separate existence, which, as 'the teachers of the art' (meaning probably the Pythagoreans) would have affirmed, repel all attempts at subdivision, and in which unity and every other number are conceived of as absolute. The truth and certainty of numbers, when thus disengaged from phenomena, gave them a kind of sacredness in the eyes of an ancient philosopher. Nor is it easy to say how far ideas of order and fixedness may have had a moral and elevating influence on the minds of men, 'who,' in the words of the Timaeus, 'might learn to regulate their erring lives according to them.' It is worthy of remark that the old Pythagorean ethical symbols still exist as figures of speech among ourselves. And those who in modern times see the world pervaded by universal law, may also see an anticipation of this last word of modern philosophy in the Platonic idea of good, which is the source and measure of all things, and yet only an abstraction (Philebus).

Two passages seem to require more particular explanations. First, that which relates to the analysis of vision. The difficulty in this passage may be explained, like many others, from differences in the modes of conception prevailing among ancient and modern thinkers. To us, the perceptions of sense are inseparable from the act of the mind which accompanies them. The consciousness of form, colour, distance, is indistinguishable from the simple sensation, which is the medium of them. Whereas to Plato sense is the Heraclitean flux of sense, not the vision of objects in the order in which they actually present themselves to the experienced sight, but as they may be imagined to appear confused and blurred to the half-awakened eye of the infant. The first action of the mind is aroused by the attempt to set in order this chaos, and the reason is required to frame distinct conceptions under which the confused impressions of sense may be arranged. Hence arises the question, 'What is great, what is small?' and thus begins the distinction of the visible and the intelligible.

The second difficulty relates to Plato's conception of harmonics. Three classes of harmonists are distinguished by him: – first, the Pythagoreans, whom he proposes to consult as in the previous discussion on music he was to consult Damon – they are acknowledged to be masters in the art, but are altogether deficient in the knowledge of its higher import and relation to the good; secondly, the mere empirics, whom Glaucon appears to confuse with them, and whom both he and Socrates ludicrously describe as experimenting by mere auscultation on the intervals of sounds. Both of these fall short in different degrees of the Platonic idea of harmony, which must be studied in a purely abstract way, first by the method of problems, and secondly as a part of universal knowledge in relation to the idea of good.

The allegory has a political as well as a philosophical meaning. The den or cave represents the narrow sphere of politics or law (compare the description of the philosopher and lawyer in the Theaetetus), and the light of the eternal ideas is supposed to exercise a disturbing influence on the minds of those who return to this lower world. In other words, their principles are too wide for practical application; they are looking far away into the past and future, when their business is with the present. The ideal is not easily reduced to the conditions of actual life, and may often be at variance with them. And at first, those who return are unable to compete with the inhabitants of the den in the measurement of the shadows, and are derided and persecuted by them; but after a while they see the things below in far truer proportions than those who have never ascended into the upper world. The difference between the politician turned into a philosopher and the philosopher turned into a politician, is symbolized by the two kinds of disordered eyesight, the one which is experienced by the captive who is transferred from darkness to day, the other, of the heavenly messenger who voluntarily for the good of his fellow-men descends into the den. In what way the brighter light is to dawn on the inhabitants of the lower world, or how the idea of good is to become the guiding principle of politics, is left unexplained by Plato. Like the nature and divisions of dialectic, of which Glaucon impatiently demands to be informed, perhaps he would have said that the explanation could not be given except to a disciple of the previous sciences. (Symposium.)

Many illustrations of this part of the Republic may be found in modern Politics and in daily life. For among ourselves, too, there have been two sorts of Politicians or Statesmen, whose eyesight has become disordered in two different ways. First, there have been great men who, in the language of Burke, 'have been too much given to general maxims,' who, like J.S. Mill or Burke himself, have been theorists or philosophers before they were politicians, or who, having been students of history, have allowed some great historical parallel, such as the English Revolution of 1688, or possibly Athenian democracy or Roman Imperialism, to be the medium through which they viewed contemporary events. Or perhaps the long projecting shadow of some existing institution may have darkened their vision. The Church of the future, the Commonwealth of the future, the Society of the future, have so absorbed their minds, that they are unable to see in their true proportions the Politics of to-day. They have been intoxicated with great ideas, such as liberty, or equality, or the greatest happiness of the greatest number, or the brotherhood of humanity, and they no longer care to consider how these ideas must be limited in practice or harmonized with the conditions of human life. They are full of light, but the light to them has become only a sort of luminous mist or blindness. Almost every one has known some enthusiastic half-educated person, who sees everything at false distances, and in erroneous proportions.

With this disorder of eyesight may be contrasted another – of those who see not far into the distance, but what is near only; who have been engaged all their lives in a trade or a profession; who are limited to a set or sect of their own. Men of this kind have no universal except their own interests or the interests of their class, no principle but the opinion of persons like themselves, no knowledge of affairs beyond what they pick up in the streets or at their club. Suppose them to be sent into a larger world, to undertake some higher calling, from being tradesmen to turn generals or politicians, from being schoolmasters to become philosophers: – or imagine them on a sudden to receive an inward light which reveals to them for the first time in their lives a higher idea of God and the existence of a spiritual world, by this sudden conversion or change is not their daily life likely to be upset; and on the other hand will not many of their old prejudices and narrownesses still adhere to them long after they have begun to take a more comprehensive view of human things? From familiar examples like these we may learn what Plato meant by the eyesight which is liable to two kinds of disorders.

Nor have we any difficulty in drawing a parallel between the young Athenian in the fifth century before Christ who became unsettled by new ideas, and the student of a modern University who has been the subject of a similar 'aufklarung.' We too observe that when young men begin to criticise customary beliefs, or to analyse the constitution of human nature, they are apt to lose hold of solid principle (Greek). They are like trees which have been frequently transplanted. The earth about them is loose, and they have no roots reaching far into the soil. They 'light upon every flower,' following their own wayward wills, or because the wind blows them. They catch opinions, as diseases are caught – when they are in the air. Borne hither and thither, 'they speedily fall into beliefs' the opposite of those in which they were brought up. They hardly retain the distinction of right and wrong; they seem to think one thing as good as another. They suppose themselves to be searching after truth when they are playing the game of 'follow my leader.' They fall in love 'at first sight' with paradoxes respecting morality, some fancy about art, some novelty or eccentricity in religion, and like lovers they are so absorbed for a time in their new notion that they can think of nothing else. The resolution of some philosophical or theological question seems to them more interesting and important than any substantial knowledge of literature or science or even than a good life. Like the youth in the Philebus, they are ready to discourse to any one about a new philosophy. They are generally the disciples of some eminent professor or sophist, whom they rather imitate than understand. They may be counted happy if in later years they retain some of the simple truths which they acquired in early education, and which they may, perhaps, find to be worth all the rest. Such is the picture which Plato draws and which we only reproduce, partly in his own words, of the dangers which beset youth in times of transition, when old opinions are fading away and the new are not yet firmly established. Their condition is ingeniously compared by him to that of a supposititious son, who has made the discovery that his reputed parents are not his real ones, and, in consequence, they have lost their authority over him.

The distinction between the mathematician and the dialectician is also noticeable. Plato is very well aware that the faculty of the mathematician is quite distinct from the higher philosophical sense which recognizes and combines first principles. The contempt which he expresses for distinctions of words, the danger of involuntary falsehood, the apology which Socrates makes for his earnestness of speech, are highly characteristic of the Platonic style and mode of thought. The quaint notion that if Palamedes was the inventor of number Agamemnon could not have counted his feet; the art by which we are made to believe that this State of ours is not a dream only; the gravity with which the first step is taken in the actual creation of the State, namely, the sending out of the city all who had arrived at ten years of age, in order to expedite the business of education by a generation, are also truly Platonic. (For the last, compare the passage at the end of the third book, in which he expects the lie about the earthborn men to be believed in the second generation.)

BOOK VIII.

And so we have arrived at the conclusion, that in the perfect State wives and children are to be in common; and the education and pursuits of men and women, both in war and peace, are to be common, and kings are to be philosophers and warriors, and the soldiers of the State are to live together, having all things in common; and they are to be warrior athletes, receiving no pay but only their food, from the other citizens. Now let us return to the point at which we digressed. 'That is easily done,' he replied: 'You were speaking of the State which you had constructed, and of the individual who answered to this, both of whom you affirmed to be good; and you said that of inferior States there were four forms and four individuals corresponding to them, which although deficient in various degrees, were all of them worth inspecting with a view to determining the relative happiness or misery of the best or worst man. Then Polemarchus and Adeimantus interrupted you, and this led to another argument, – and so here we are.' Suppose that we put ourselves again in the same position, and do you repeat your question. 'I should like to know of what constitutions you were speaking?' Besides the perfect State there are only four of any note in Hellas: – first, the famous Lacedaemonian or Cretan commonwealth; secondly, oligarchy, a State full of evils; thirdly, democracy, which follows next in order; fourthly, tyranny, which is the disease or death of all government. Now, States are not made of 'oak and rock,' but of flesh and blood; and therefore as there are five States there must be five human natures in individuals, which correspond to them. And first, there is the ambitious nature, which answers to the Lacedaemonian State; secondly, the oligarchical nature; thirdly, the democratical; and fourthly, the tyrannical. This last will have to be compared with the perfectly just, which is the fifth, that we may know which is the happier, and then we shall be able to determine whether the argument of Thrasymachus or our own is the more convincing. And as before we began with the State and went on to the individual, so now, beginning with timocracy, let us go on to the timocratical man, and then proceed to the other forms of government, and the individuals who answer to them.

But how did timocracy arise out of the perfect State? Plainly, like all changes of government, from division in the rulers. But whence came division? 'Sing, heavenly Muses,' as Homer says; – let them condescend to answer us, as if we were children, to whom they put on a solemn face in jest. 'And what will they say?' They will say that human things are fated to decay, and even the perfect State will not escape from this law of destiny, when 'the wheel comes full circle' in a period short or long. Plants or animals have times of fertility and sterility, which the intelligence of rulers because alloyed by sense will not enable them to ascertain, and children will be born out of season. For whereas divine creations are in a perfect cycle or number, the human creation is in a number which declines from perfection, and has four terms and three intervals of numbers, increasing, waning, assimilating, dissimilating, and yet perfectly commensurate with each other. The base of the number with a fourth added (or which is 3:4), multiplied by five and cubed, gives two harmonies: – the first a square number, which is a hundred times the base (or a hundred times a hundred); the second, an oblong, being a hundred squares of the rational diameter of a figure the side of which is five, subtracting one from each square or two perfect squares from all, and adding a hundred cubes of three. This entire number is geometrical and contains the rule or law of generation. When this law is neglected marriages will be unpropitious; the inferior offspring who are then born will in time become the rulers; the State will decline, and education fall into decay; gymnastic will be preferred to music, and the gold and silver and brass and iron will form a chaotic mass – thus division will arise. Such is the Muses' answer to our question. 'And a true answer, of course: – but what more have they to say?' They say that the two races, the iron and brass, and the silver and gold, will draw the State different ways; – the one will take to trade and moneymaking, and the others, having the true riches and not caring for money, will resist them: the contest will end in a compromise; they will agree to have private property, and will enslave their fellow-citizens who were once their friends and nurturers. But they will retain their warlike character, and will be chiefly occupied in fighting and exercising rule. Thus arises timocracy, which is intermediate between aristocracy and oligarchy.

The new form of government resembles the ideal in obedience to rulers and contempt for trade, and having common meals, and in devotion to warlike and gymnastic exercises. But corruption has crept into philosophy, and simplicity of character, which was once her note, is now looked for only in the military class. Arts of war begin to prevail over arts of peace; the ruler is no longer a philosopher; as in oligarchies, there springs up among them an extravagant love of gain – get another man's and save your own, is their principle; and they have dark places in which they hoard their gold and silver, for the use of their women and others; they take their pleasures by stealth, like boys who are running away from their father – the law; and

107 | P a g e

their education is not inspired by the Muse, but imposed by the strong arm of power. The leading characteristic of this State is party spirit and ambition.

And what manner of man answers to such a State? 'In love of contention,' replied Adeimantus, 'he will be like our friend Glaucon.' In that respect, perhaps, but not in others. He is self-asserting and ill-educated, yet fond of literature, although not himself a speaker, – fierce with slaves, but obedient to rulers, a lover of power and honour, which he hopes to gain by deeds of arms, – fond, too, of gymnastics and of hunting. As he advances in years he grows avaricious, for he has lost philosophy, which is the only saviour and guardian of men. His origin is as follows: – His father is a good man dwelling in an ill-ordered State, who has retired from politics in order that he may lead a quiet life. His mother is angry at her loss of precedence among other women; she is disgusted at her husband's selfishness, and she expatiates to her son on the unmanliness and indolence of his father. The old family servant takes up the tale, and says to the youth: – 'When you grow up you must be more of a man than your father.' All the world are agreed that he who minds his own business is an idiot, while a busybody is highly honoured and esteemed. The young man compares this spirit with his father's words and ways, and as he is naturally well disposed, although he has suffered from evil influences, he rests at a middle point and becomes ambitious and a lover of honour.

And now let us set another city over against another man. The next form of government is oligarchy, in which the rule is of the rich only; nor is it difficult to see how such a State arises. The decline begins with the possession of gold and silver; illegal modes of expenditure are invented; one draws another on, and the multitude are infected; riches outweigh virtue; lovers of money take the place of lovers of honour; misers of politicians; and, in time, political privileges are confined by law to the rich, who do not shrink from violence in order to effect their purposes.

Thus much of the origin, – let us next consider the evils of oligarchy. Would a man who wanted to be safe on a voyage take a bad pilot because he was rich, or refuse a good one because he was poor? And does not the analogy apply still more to the State? And there are yet greater evils: two nations are struggling together in one – the rich and the poor; and the rich dare not put arms into the hands of the poor, and are unwilling to pay for defenders out of their own money. And have we not already condemned that State in which the same persons are warriors as well as shopkeepers?

The greatest evil of all is that a man may sell his property and have no place in the State; while there is one class which has enormous wealth, the other is entirely destitute. But observe that these destitutes had not really any more of the governing nature in them when they were rich than now that they are poor; they were miserable spendthrifts always. They are the drones of the hive; only whereas the actual drone is unprovided by nature with a sting, the two-legged things whom we call drones are some of them without stings and some of them have dreadful stings; in other words, there are paupers and there are rogues. These are never far apart; and in oligarchical cities, where nearly everybody is a pauper who is not a ruler, you will find abundance of both. And this evil state of society originates in bad education and bad government.

Like State, like man, – the change in the latter begins with the representative of timocracy; he walks at first in the ways of his father, who may have been a statesman, or general, perhaps; and presently he sees him 'fallen from his high estate,' the victim of informers, dying in prison or exile, or by the hand of the executioner. The lesson which he thus receives, makes him cautious; he leaves politics, represses his pride, and saves pence. Avarice is enthroned as his bosom's lord, and assumes the style of the Great King; the rational and spirited elements sit humbly on the ground at either side, the one immersed in calculation, the other absorbed in the admiration of wealth. The love of honour turns to love of money; the conversion is instantaneous. The man is mean, saving, toiling, the slave of one passion which is the master of the rest: Is he not the very image of the State? IIe has had no education, or he would never have allowed the blind god of riches to lead the dance within him. And being uneducated he will have many slavish desires, some beggarly, some knavish, breeding in his soul. If he is the trustee of an orphan, and has the power to defraud, he will soon prove that he is not without the will, and that his passions are only restrained by fear and not by reason. Hence he leads a divided existence; in which the better desires mostly prevail. But when he is contending for prizes and other distinctions, he is afraid to incur a loss which is to be repaid only by barren honour; in time of war he fights with a small part of his resources, and usually keeps his money and loses the victory.

Next comes democracy and the democratic man, out of oligarchy and the oligarchical man. Insatiable avarice is the ruling passion of an oligarchy; and they encourage expensive habits in order that they may gain by the ruin of extravagant youth. Thus men of family often lose their property or rights of citizenship; but they remain in the city, full of hatred against the new owners of their estates and ripe for revolution. The usurer with stooping walk pretends not to see them; he passes by, and leaves his sting – that is, his money – in some other victim; and many a man has to pay the parent or principal sum multiplied into a family of children, and is reduced into a state of dronage by him. The only way of diminishing the evil is either to limit a man in his use of his property, or to insist that he shall lend at his own risk. But the ruling class do not want remedies; they care only for money, and are as careless of virtue as the poorest of the citizens. Now there are occasions on which the governors and the governed meet together, – at festivals, on a journey, voyaging or fighting. The sturdy pauper finds that in the hour of danger he is not despised; he sees the rich man puffing and panting, and draws the conclusion which he privately imparts to his companions, – 'that our people are not good for much;' and as a sickly frame is made ill by a mere touch from without, or sometimes without external impulse is ready to fall to pieces of itself, so from the least cause, or with none at all, the city falls ill and fights a battle for life or death. And democracy comes into power when the poor are the victors, killing some and exiling some, and giving equal shares in the government to all the rest.

The manner of life in such a State is that of democrats; there is freedom and plainness of speech, and every man does what is right in his own eyes, and has his own way of life. Hence arise the most various developments of character; the State is like a piece of embroidery of which the colours and figures are the manners of men, and there are many who, like women and children, prefer this variety to real beauty and excellence. The State is not one but many, like a bazaar at which you can buy anything. The great charm is, that you may do as you like; you may govern if you like, let it alone if you like; go to war and make peace if you feel disposed, and all quite irrespective of anybody else. When you condemn men to death they remain alive all the same; a gentleman is desired to go into exile, and he stalks about the streets like a hero; and nobody sees him or cares for him. Observe, too, how grandly Democracy sets her foot upon all our fine theories of education, – how little she cares for the training of her statesmen! The only qualification which she demands is the profession of patriotism. Such is democracy; – a pleasing, lawless, various sort of government, distributing equality to equals and unequals alike.

Let us now inspect the individual democrat; and first, as in the case of the State, we will trace his antecedents. He is the son of a miserly oligarch, and has been taught by him to restrain the love of unnecessary pleasures.

Perhaps I ought to explain this latter term: – Necessary pleasures are those which are good, and which we cannot do without; unnecessary pleasures are those which do no good, and of which the desire might be eradicated by early training. For example, the pleasures of eating and drinking are necessary and healthy, up to a certain point; beyond that point they are alike hurtful to body and mind, and the excess may be avoided. When in excess, they may be rightly called expensive pleasures, in opposition to the useful ones. And the drone, as we called him, is the slave of these unnecessary pleasures and desires, whereas the miserly oligarch is subject only to the necessary.

The oligarch changes into the democrat in the following manner: – The youth who has had a miserly bringing up, gets a taste of the drone's honey; he meets with wild companions, who introduce him to every new pleasure. As in the State, so in the individual, there are allies on both sides, temptations from without and passions from within; there is reason also and external influences of parents and friends in alliance with the oligarchical principle; and the two factions are in violent conflict with one another. Sometimes the party of order prevails, but then again new desires and new disorders arise, and the whole mob of passions gets possession of the Acropolis, that is to say, the soul, which they find void and unguarded by true words and works. Falsehoods and illusions ascend to take their place; the prodigal goes back into the country of the Lotophagi or drones, and openly dwells there. And if any offer of alliance or parley of individual elders comes from home, the false spirits shut the gates of the castle and permit no one to enter, – there is a battle, and they gain the victory; and straightway making alliance with the desires, they banish modesty, which they call folly, and send temperance over the border. When the house has been swept and garnished, they dress up the exiled vices, and, crowning them with garlands, bring them back under new names. Insolence they call good breeding, anarchy freedom, waste magnificence, impudence courage. Such is the process by which the youth passes from the necessary pleasures to the unnecessary. After a while he divides his time impartially between them; and perhaps, when he gets older and the violence of passion has abated, he restores some of the exiles and lives in a sort of equilibrium, indulging first one pleasure and then another; and if reason comes and tells him that some pleasures are good and honourable, and others bad and vile, he shakes his head and says that he can make no distinction between them. Thus he lives in the fancy of the hour; sometimes he takes to drink, and then he turns abstainer; he practises in the gymnasium or he does nothing at all; then again he would be a philosopher or a politician; or again, he would be a warrior or a man of business; he is

'Every thing by starts and nothing long.'

There remains still the finest and fairest of all men and all States – tyranny and the tyrant. Tyranny springs from democracy much as democracy springs from oligarchy. Both arise from excess; the one from excess of wealth, the other from excess of freedom. 'The great natural good of life,' says the democrat, 'is freedom.' And this exclusive love of freedom and regardlessness of everything else, is the cause of the change from democracy to tyranny. The State demands the strong wine of freedom, and unless her rulers give her a plentiful draught, punishes and insults them; equality and fraternity of governors and governed is the approved principle. Anarchy is the law, not of the State only, but of private houses, and extends even to the animals. Father and son, citizen and foreigner, teacher and pupil, old and young, are all on a level; fathers and teachers fear their sons and pupils, and the wisdom of the young man is a match for the elder, and the old imitate the jaunty manners of the young because they are afraid of being thought morose. Slaves are on a level with their masters and mistresses, and there is no difference between men and women. Nay, the very animals in a democratic State have a freedom which is unknown in other places. The she-dogs are as good as their she-mistresses, and horses and asses march along with dignity and run their noses against anybody who comes in their way. 'That has often been my experience.' At last the citizens become so sensitive that they cannot endure the yoke of laws, written or unwritten; they would have no man call himself their master. Such is the glorious beginning of things out of which tyranny springs. 'Glorious, indeed; but what is to follow?' The ruin of oligarchy is the ruin of democracy; for there is a law of contraries; the excess of freedom passes into the excess of slavery, and the greater the freedom the greater the slavery. You will remember that in the oligarchy were found two classes – rogues and paupers, whom we compared to drones with and without stings. These two classes are to the State what phlegm and bile are to the human body; and the State-physician, or legislator, must get rid of them, just as the bee-master keeps the drones out of the hive. Now in a democracy, too, there are drones, but they are more numerous and more dangerous than in the oligarchy; there they are inert and unpractised, here they are full of life and animation; and the keener sort speak and act, while the others buzz about the bema and prevent their opponents from being heard. And there is another class in democratic States, of respectable,

THE REPUBLIC

thriving individuals, who can be squeezed when the drones have need of their possessions; there is moreover a third class, who are the labourers and the artisans, and they make up the mass of the people. When the people meet, they are omnipotent, but they cannot be brought together unless they are attracted by a little honey; and the rich are made to supply the honey, of which the demagogues keep the greater part themselves, giving a taste only to the mob. Their victims attempt to resist; they are driven mad by the stings of the drones, and so become downright oligarchs in self-defence. Then follow informations and convictions for treason. The people have some protector whom they nurse into greatness, and from this root the tree of tyranny springs. The nature of the change is indicated in the old fable of the temple of Zeus Lycaeus, which tells how he who tastes human flesh mixed up with the flesh of other victims will turn into a wolf. Even so the protector, who tastes human blood, and slays some and exiles others with or without law, who hints at abolition of debts and division of lands, must either perish or become a wolf – that is, a tyrant. Perhaps he is driven out, but he soon comes back from exile; and then if his enemies cannot get rid of him by lawful means, they plot his assassination. Thereupon the friend of the people makes his well-known request to them for a body-guard, which they readily grant, thinking only of his danger and not of their own. Now let the rich man make to himself wings, for he will never run away again if he does not do so then. And the Great Protector, having crushed all his rivals, stands proudly erect in the chariot of State, a full-blown tyrant: Let us enquire into the nature of his happiness.

In the early days of his tyranny he smiles and beams upon everybody; he is not a 'dominus,' no, not he: he has only come to put an end to debt and the monopoly of land. Having got rid of foreign enemies, he makes himself necessary to the State by always going to war. He is thus enabled to depress the poor by heavy taxes, and so keep them at work; and he can get rid of bolder spirits by handing them over to the enemy. Then comes unpopularity; some of his old associates have the courage to oppose him. The consequence is, that he has to make a purgation of the State; but, unlike the physician who purges away the bad, he must get rid of the high-spirited, the wise and the wealthy; for he has no choice between death and a life of shame and dishonour. And the more hated he is, the more he will require trusty guards; but how will he obtain them? 'They will come flocking like birds – for pay.' Will he not rather obtain them on the spot? He will take the slaves from their owners and make them his body-guard; these are his trusted friends, who admire and look up to him. Are not the tragic poets wise who magnify and exalt the tyrant, and say that he is wise by association with the wise? And are not their praises of tyranny alone a sufficient reason why we should exclude them from our State? They may go to other cities, and gather the mob about them with fine words, and change commonwealths into tyrannies and democracies, receiving honours and rewards for their services; but the higher they and their friends ascend constitution hill, the more their honour will fail and become 'too asthmatic to mount.' To return to the tyrant – How will he support that rare army of his? First, by robbing the temples of their treasures, which will enable him to lighten the taxes; then he will take all his father's property, and spend it on his companions, male or female. Now his father is the demus, and if the demus gets angry, and says that a great hulking son ought not to be a burden on his parents, and bids him and his riotous crew begone, then will the parent know what a monster he has been nurturing, and that the son whom he would fain expel is too strong for him. 'You do not mean to say that he will beat his father?' Yes, he will, after having taken away his arms. 'Then he is a parricide and a cruel, unnatural son.' And the people have jumped from the fear of slavery into slavery, out of the smoke into the fire. Thus liberty, when out of all order and reason, passes into the worst form of servitude...

In the previous books Plato has described the ideal State; now he returns to the perverted or declining forms, on which he had lightly touched at the end of Book IV. These he describes in a succession of parallels between the individuals and the States, tracing the origin of either in the State or individual which has preceded them. He begins by asking the point at which he digressed; and is thus led shortly to recapitulate the substance of the three former books, which also contain a parallel of the philosopher and the State.

Of the first decline he gives no intelligible account; he would not have liked to admit the most probable causes of the fall of his ideal State, which to us would appear to be the impracticability of communism or the natural antagonism of the ruling and subject classes. He throws a veil of mystery over the origin of the decline, which he attributes to ignorance of the law of population. Of this law the famous geometrical figure or number is the expression. Like the ancients in general, he had no idea of the gradual perfectibility of man or of the education of the human race. His ideal was not to be attained in the course of ages, but was to spring in full armour from the head of the legislator. When good laws had been given, he thought only of the manner in which they were likely to be corrupted, or of how they might be filled up in detail or restored in accordance with their original spirit. He appears not to have reflected upon the full meaning of his own words, 'In the brief space of human life, nothing great can be accomplished'; or again, as he afterwards says in the Laws, 'Infinite time is the maker of cities.' The order of constitutions which is adopted by him represents an order of thought rather than a succession of time, and may be considered as the first attempt to frame a philosophy of history.

The first of these declining States is timocracy, or the government of soldiers and lovers of honour, which answers to the Spartan State; this is a government of force, in which education is not inspired by the Muses, but imposed by the law, and in which all the finer elements of organization have disappeared. The philosopher himself has lost the love of truth, and the soldier, who is of a simpler and honester nature, rules in his stead. The individual who answers to timocracy has some noticeable qualities. He is described as ill educated, but, like the Spartan, a lover of literature; and although he is a harsh master to his servants he has no natural superiority over them. His character is based upon a reaction against the circumstances of his father, who in a troubled city has retired from politics; and his mother, who is dissatisfied at her own position, is always urging him towards the life of political ambition. Such a character may have had this origin, and indeed Livy attributes the Licinian laws to a feminine jealousy of a similar kind. But there is obviously no connection between the manner in which the timocratic State springs out of the ideal, and the mere accident by which the timocratic man is the son of a retired statesman.

The two next stages in the decline of constitutions have even less historical foundation. For there is no trace in Greek history of a polity like the Spartan or Cretan passing into an oligarchy of wealth, or of the oligarchy of wealth passing into a democracy. The order of history appears to be different; first, in the Homeric times there is the royal or patriarchal form of government, which a century or two later was succeeded by an oligarchy of birth rather than of wealth, and in which wealth was only the accident of the hereditary possession of land and power. Sometimes this oligarchical government gave way to a government based upon a qualification of property, which, according to Aristotle's mode of using words, would have been called a timocracy; and this in some cities, as at Athens, became the conducting medium to democracy. But such was not the necessary order of succession in States; nor, indeed, can any order be discerned in the endless fluctuation of Greek history (like the tides in the Euripus), except, perhaps, in the almost uniform tendency from monarchy to aristocracy in the earliest times. At first sight there appears to be a similar inversion in the last step of the Platonic succession; for tyranny, instead of being the natural end of democracy, in early Greek history appears rather as a stage leading to democracy; the reign of Peisistratus and his sons is an episode which comes between the legislation of Solon and the constitution of Cleisthenes; and some secret cause common to them all seems to have led the greater part of Hellas at her first appearance in the dawn of history, e.g. Athens, Argos, Corinth, Sicyon, and nearly every State with the exception of Sparta, through a similar stage of tyranny which ended either in oligarchy or democracy. But then we must remember that Plato is describing rather the contemporary governments of the Sicilian States, which alternated between democracy and tyranny, than the ancient history of Athens or Corinth.

The portrait of the tyrant himself is just such as the later Greek delighted to draw of Phalaris and Dionysius, in which, as in the lives of mediaeval saints or mythic heroes, the conduct and actions of one were attributed to another in order to fill up the outline. There was no enormity which the Greek was not today to believe of them; the tyrant was the negation of government and law; his assassination was glorious; there was no crime, however unnatural, which might not with probability be attributed to him. In this, Plato was only following the common thought of his countrymen, which he embellished and exaggerated with all the power of his genius. There is no need to suppose that he drew from life; or that his knowledge of tyrants is derived from a personal acquaintance with Dionysius. The manner in which he speaks of them would rather tend to render doubtful his ever having 'consorted' with them, or entertained the schemes, which are attributed to him in the Epistles, of regenerating Sicily by their help.

Plato in a hyperbolical and serio-comic vein exaggerates the follies of democracy which he also sees reflected in social life. To him democracy is a state of individualism or dissolution; in which every one is doing what is right in his own eyes. Of a people animated by a common spirit of liberty, rising as one man to repel the Persian host, which is the leading idea of democracy in Herodotus and Thucydides, he never seems to think. But if he is not a believer in liberty, still less is he a lover of tyranny. His deeper and more serious condemnation is reserved for the tyrant, who is the ideal of wickedness and also of weakness, and who in his utter helplessness and suspiciousness is leading an almost impossible existence, without that remnant of good which, in Plato's opinion, was required to give power to evil (Book I). This ideal of wickedness living in helpless misery, is the reverse of that other portrait of perfect injustice ruling in happiness and splendour, which first of all Thrasymachus, and afterwards the sons of Ariston had drawn, and is also the reverse of the king whose rule of life is the good of his subjects.

Each of these governments and individuals has a corresponding ethical gradation: the ideal State is under the rule of reason, not extinguishing but harmonizing the passions, and training them in virtue; in the timocracy and the timocratic man the constitution, whether of the State or of the individual, is based, first, upon courage, and secondly, upon the love of honour; this latter virtue, which is hardly to be esteemed a virtue, has superseded all the rest. In the second stage of decline the virtues have altogether disappeared, and the love of gain has succeeded to them; in the third stage, or democracy, the various passions are allowed to have free play, and the virtues and vices are impartially cultivated. But this freedom, which leads to many curious extravagances of character, is in reality only a state of weakness and dissipation. At last, one monster passion takes possession of the whole nature of man – this is tyranny. In all of them excess – the excess first of wealth and then of freedom, is the element of decay.

The eighth book of the Republic abounds in pictures of life and fanciful allusions; the use of metaphorical language is carried to a greater extent than anywhere else in Plato. We may remark,

(1), the description of the two nations in one, which become more and more divided in the Greek Republics, as in feudal times, and perhaps also in our own;

(2), the notion of democracy expressed in a sort of Pythagorean formula as equality among unequals;

(3), the free and easy ways of men and animals, which are characteristic of liberty, as foreign mercenaries and universal mistrust are of the tyrant;

(4), the proposal that mere debts should not be recoverable by law is a speculation which has often been entertained by reformers of the law in modern times, and is in harmony with the tendencies of modern legislation. Debt and land were the two great difficulties of the ancient lawgiver: in modern times we may be said to have almost, if not quite, solved the first of these difficulties, but hardly the second.

Still more remarkable are the corresponding portraits of individuals: there is the family picture of the father and mother and the old servant of the timocratical man, and the outward respectability and inherent meanness of the oligarchical; the uncontrolled licence and freedom of the democrat, in which the young Alcibiades seems to be depicted, doing right or wrong as he pleases, and who at last, like the prodigal, goes into a far country (note here the play of language by which the democratic man is himself represented under the image of a State having a citadel and receiving embassies); and there is the wild-beast nature, which breaks loose in his successor. The hit about the tyrant being a parricide; the representation of the tyrant's life as an obscene dream; the rhetorical surprise of a more miserable than the most miserable of men in Book IX; the hint to the poets that if they are the friends of tyrants there is no place for them in a constitutional State, and that they are too clever not to see the propriety of their own expulsion; the continuous image of the drones who are of two kinds, swelling at last into the monster drone having wings (Book IX), – are among Plato's happiest touches.

There remains to be considered the great difficulty of this book of the Republic, the so-called number of the State. This is a puzzle almost as great as the Number of the Beast in the Book of Revelation, and though apparently known to Aristotle, is referred to by Cicero as a proverb of obscurity (Ep. ad Att.). And some have imagined that there is no answer to the puzzle, and that Plato has been practising upon his readers. But such a deception as this is inconsistent with the manner in which Aristotle speaks of the number (Pol.), and would have been ridiculous to any reader of the Republic who was acquainted with Greek mathematics. As little reason is there for supposing that Plato intentionally used obscure expressions; the obscurity arises from our want of familiarity with the subject. On the other hand, Plato himself indicates that he is not altogether serious, and in describing his number as a solemn jest of the Muses, he appears to imply some degree of satire on the symbolical use of number. (Compare Cratylus; Protag.)

Our hope of understanding the passage depends principally on an accurate study of the words themselves; on which a faint light is thrown by the parallel passage in the ninth book. Another help is the allusion in Aristotle, who makes the important remark that the latter part of the passage (Greek) describes a solid figure. (Pol. – 'He only says that nothing is abiding, but that all things change in a certain cycle; and that the origin of the change is a base of numbers which are in the ratio of 4:3; and this when combined with a figure of five gives two harmonies; he means when the number of this figure becomes solid.') Some further clue may be gathered from the appearance of the Pythagorean triangle, which is denoted by the numbers 3, 4, 5, and in which, as in every right-angled triangle, the squares of the two lesser sides equal the square of the hypotenuse (9 + 16 = 25).

Plato begins by speaking of a perfect or cyclical number (Tim.), i.e. a number in which the sum of the divisors equals the whole; this is the divine or perfect number in which all lesser cycles or revolutions are complete. He also speaks of a human or imperfect number, having four terms and three intervals of numbers which are related to one another in certain proportions; these he converts into figures, and finds in them when they have been raised to the third power certain elements of number, which give two 'harmonies,' the one square, the other oblong; but he does not say that the square number answers to the divine, or the oblong number to the human cycle; nor is any intimation given that the first or divine number represents the period of the world, the second the period of the state, or of the human race as Zeller supposes; nor is the divine number afterwards mentioned (Arist.). The second is the number of generations or births, and presides over them in the same mysterious manner in which the stars preside over them, or in which, according to the Pythagoreans, opportunity, justice, marriage, are represented by some number or figure. This is probably the number 216.

The explanation given in the text supposes the two harmonies to make up the number 8000. This explanation derives a certain plausibility from the circumstance that 8000 is the ancient number of the Spartan citizens (Herod.), and would be what Plato might have called 'a number which nearly concerns the population of a city'; the mysterious disappearance of the Spartan population may possibly have suggested to him the first cause of his decline of States. The lesser or square 'harmony,' of 400, might be a symbol of the guardians, – the larger or oblong 'harmony,' of the people, and the numbers 3, 4, 5 might refer respectively to the three orders in the State or parts of the soul, the four virtues, the five forms of government. The harmony of the musical scale, which is elsewhere used as a symbol of the harmony of the state, is also indicated. For the numbers 3, 4, 5, which represent the sides of the Pythagorean triangle, also denote the intervals of the scale.

The terms used in the statement of the problem may be explained as follows. A perfect number (Greek), as already stated, is one which is equal to the sum of its divisors. Thus 6, which is the first perfect or cyclical number, = 1 + 2 + 3. The words (Greek), 'terms' or 'notes,' and (Greek), 'intervals,' are applicable to music as well as to number and figure. (Greek) is the 'base' on which the whole calculation depends, or the 'lowest term' from which it can be worked out. The words (Greek) have been variously translated – 'squared and cubed' (Donaldson), 'equalling and equalled in power' (Weber), 'by involution and evolution,' i.e. by raising the power and extracting the root (as in the translation). Numbers are called 'like and unlike' (Greek) when the factors or the sides of the planes and cubes which they represent are or are not in the same ratio: e.g. 8 and 27 = 2 cubed and 3 cubed; and conversely. 'Waxing' (Greek) numbers, called also 'increasing' (Greek), are those which are exceeded by the sum of their divisors: e.g. 12 and 18 are less than 16 and 21. 'Waning' (Greek) numbers, called also 'decreasing' (Greek) are those which succeed the sum of their divisors: e.g. 8 and 27 exceed 7 and 13. The words translated 'commensurable and agreeable to one another' (Greek) seem to be different ways of describing the same relation, with more or less precision. They are equivalent to 'expressible in terms having the same relation to one another,' like the series 8, 12, 18, 27, each of which numbers is in the relation of (1 and 1/2) to the preceding. The 'base,' or 'fundamental number, which has 1/3 added to it' (1 and 1/3) = 4/3 or a musical fourth. (Greek) is a 'proportion' of numbers as of musical notes, applied either to the parts or factors of a single number or to the relation of one number to another. The first harmony is a 'square' number (Greek); the second harmony is an 'oblong' number (Greek), i.e. a number representing a figure of which the opposite sides only are equal. (Greek) = 'numbers squared from' or 'upon diameters'; (Greek) = 'rational,' i.e. omitting fractions, (Greek), 'irrational,' i.e. including fractions; e.g. 49 is a square of the rational diameter of a figure the side of which = 5: 50, of an irrational diameter of the same. For several of the explanations here given and for a good deal besides I am indebted to an excellent article on the Platonic Number by Dr. Donaldson (Proc. of the Philol. Society).

The conclusions which he draws from these data are summed up by him as follows. Having assumed that the number of the perfect or divine cycle is the number of the world, and the number of the imperfect cycle the number of the state, he proceeds: 'The period of the world is defined by the perfect number 6, that of the state by the cube of that number or 216, which is the product of the last pair of terms in the Platonic Tetractys (a series of seven terms, 1, 2, 3, 4, 9, 8, 27); and if we take this as the basis of our computation, we shall have two cube numbers (Greek), viz. 8 and 27;

and the mean proportionals between these, viz. 12 and 18, will furnish three intervals and four terms, and these terms and intervals stand related to one another in the sesqui-altera ratio, i.e. each term is to the preceding as 3/2. Now if we remember that the number 216 = 8 x 27 = 3 cubed + 4 cubed + 5 cubed, and 3 squared + 4 squared = 5 squared, we must admit that this number implies the numbers 3, 4, 5, to which musicians attach so much importance. And if we combine the ratio 4/3 with the number 5, or multiply the ratios of the sides by the hypotenuse, we shall by first squaring and then cubing obtain two expressions, which denote the ratio of the two last pairs of terms in the Platonic Tetractys, the former multiplied by the square, the latter by the cube of the number 10, the sum of the first four digits which constitute the Platonic Tetractys.' The two (Greek) he elsewhere explains as follows: 'The first (Greek) is (Greek), in other words (4/3 x 5) all squared = 100 x 2 squared over 3 squared. The second (Greek), a cube of the same root, is described as 100 multiplied (alpha) by the rational diameter of 5 diminished by unity, i.e., as shown above, 48: (beta) by two incommensurable diameters, i.e. the two first irrationals, or 2 and 3: and (gamma) by the cube of 3, or 27. Thus we have (48 + 5 + 27) 100 = 1000 x 2 cubed. This second harmony is to be the cube of the number of which the former harmony is the square, and therefore must be divided by the cube of 3. In other words, the whole expression will be: (1), for the first harmony, 400/9: (2), for the second harmony, 8000/27.'

The reasons which have inclined me to agree with Dr. Donaldson and also with Schleiermacher in supposing that 216 is the Platonic number of births are: (1) that it coincides with the description of the number given in the first part of the passage (Greek...): (2) that the number 216 with its permutations would have been familiar to a Greek mathematician, though unfamiliar to us: (3) that 216 is the cube of 6, and also the sum of 3 cubed, 4 cubed, 5 cubed, the numbers 3, 4, 5 representing the Pythagorean triangle, of which the sides when squared equal the square of the hypotenuse (9 + 16 = 25): (4) that it is also the period of the Pythagorean Metempsychosis: (5) the three ultimate terms or bases (3, 4, 5) of which 216 is composed answer to the third, fourth, fifth in the musical scale: (6) that the number 216 is the product of the cubes of 2 and 3, which are the two last terms in the Platonic Tetractys: (7) that the Pythagorean triangle is said by Plutarch (de Is. et Osir.), Proclus (super prima Eucl.), and Quintilian (de Musica) to be contained in this passage, so that the tradition of the school seems to point in the same direction: (8) that the Pythagorean triangle is called also the figure of marriage (Greek).

But though agreeing with Dr. Donaldson thus far, I see no reason for supposing, as he does, that the first or perfect number is the world, the human or imperfect number the state; nor has he given any proof that the second harmony is a cube. Nor do I think that (Greek) can mean 'two incommensurables,' which he arbitrarily assumes to be 2 and 3, but rather, as the preceding clause implies, (Greek), i.e. two square numbers based upon irrational diameters of a figure the side of which is 5 = 50 x 2.

The greatest objection to the translation is the sense given to the words (Greek), 'a base of three with a third added to it, multiplied by 5.' In this somewhat forced manner Plato introduces once more the numbers of the Pythagorean triangle. But the coincidences in the numbers which follow are in favour of the explanation. The first harmony of 400, as has been already remarked, probably represents the rulers; the second and oblong harmony of 7600, the people.

And here we take leave of the difficulty. The discovery of the riddle would be useless, and would throw no light on ancient mathematics. The point of interest is that Plato should have used such a symbol, and that so much of the Pythagorean spirit should have prevailed in him. His general meaning is that divine creation is perfect, and is represented or presided over by a perfect or cyclical number; human generation is imperfect, and represented or presided over by an imperfect number or series of numbers. The number 5040, which is the number of the citizens in the Laws, is expressly based by him on utilitarian grounds, namely, the convenience of the number for division; it is also made up of the first seven digits multiplied by one another. The contrast of the perfect and imperfect number may have been easily suggested by the corrections of the cycle, which were made first by Meton and secondly by Callippus; (the latter is said to have been a pupil of Plato). Of the degree of importance or of exactness to be attributed to the problem, the number of the tyrant in Book IX (729 = 365 x 2), and the slight correction of the error in the number 5040/12 (Laws), may furnish a criterion. There is nothing surprising in the circumstance that those who were seeking for order in nature and had found order in number, should have imagined one to give law to the other. Plato believes in a power of number far beyond what he could see realized in the world around him, and he knows the great influence which 'the little matter of 1, 2, 3' exercises upon education. He may even be thought to have a prophetic anticipation of the discoveries of Quetelet and others, that numbers depend upon numbers; e.g. – in population, the numbers of births and the respective numbers of children born of either sex, on the respective ages of parents, i.e. on other numbers.

BOOK IX.

Last of all comes the tyrannical man, about whom we have to enquire, Whence is he, and how does he live – in happiness or in misery? There is, however, a previous question of the nature and number of the appetites, which I should like to consider first. Some of them are unlawful, and yet admit of being chastened and weakened in various degrees by the power of reason and law. 'What appetites do you mean?' I mean those which are awake when the reasoning powers are asleep, which get up and walk about naked without any self-respect or shame; and there is no conceivable folly or crime, however cruel or unnatural, of which, in imagination, they may not be guilty. 'True,' he said; 'very true.' But when a man's pulse beats temperately; and he has supped on a feast of reason and come to a knowledge of himself before going to rest, and has satisfied his desires just enough to prevent their perturbing his reason, which remains clear and luminous, and when he is free from quarrel and heat, – the visions which he has on his bed are least irregular and abnormal. Even in good men there is such an irregular wild-beast nature, which peers out in sleep.

To return: – You remember what was said of the democrat; that he was the son of a miserly father, who encouraged the saving desires and repressed the ornamental and expensive ones; presently the youth got into fine company, and began to entertain a dislike to his father's narrow ways; and being a better man than the corrupters of his youth, he came to a mean, and led a life, not of lawless or slavish passion, but of regular and successive indulgence. Now imagine that the youth has become a father, and has a son who is exposed to the same temptations, and has companions who lead him into every sort of iniquity, and parents and friends who try to keep him right. The counsellors of evil find that their only chance of retaining him is to implant in his soul a monster drone, or love; while other desires buzz around him and mystify him with sweet sounds and scents, this monster love takes possession of him, and puts an end to every true or modest thought or wish. Love, like drunkenness and madness, is a tyranny; and the tyrannical man, whether made by nature or habit, is just a drinking, lusting, furious sort of animal.

And how does such an one live? 'Nay, that you must tell me.' Well then, I fancy that he will live amid revelries and harlotries, and love will be the lord and master of the house. Many desires require much money, and so he spends all that he has and borrows more; and when he has nothing the young ravens are still in the nest in which they were hatched, crying for food. Love urges them on; and they must be gratified by force or fraud, or if not, they become painful and troublesome; and as the new pleasures succeed the old ones, so will the son take possession of the goods of his parents; if they show signs of refusing, he will defraud and deceive them; and if they openly resist, what then? 'I can only say, that I should not much like to be in their place.' But, O heavens, Adeimantus, to think that for some new-fangled and unnecessary love he will give up his old father and mother, best and dearest of friends, or enslave them to the fancies of the hour! Truly a tyrannical son is a blessing to his father and mother! When there is no more to be got out of them, he turns burglar or pickpocket, or robs a temple. Love overmasters the thoughts of his youth, and he becomes in sober reality the monster that he was sometimes in sleep. He waxes strong in all violence and lawlessness; and is ready for any deed of daring that will supply the wants of his rabble-rout. In a well-ordered State there are only a few such, and these in time of war go out and become the mercenaries of a tyrant. But in time of peace they stay at home and do mischief; they are the thieves, footpads, cut-purses, man-stealers of the community; or if they are able to speak, they turn false-witnesses and informers. 'No small catalogue of crimes truly, even if the perpetrators are few.' Yes, I said; but small and great are relative terms, and no crimes which are committed by them approach those of the tyrant, whom this class, growing strong and numerous, create out of themselves. If the people yield, well and good, but, if they resist, then, as before he beat his father and mother, so now he beats his fatherland and motherland, and places his mercenaries over them. Such men in their early days live with flatterers, and they themselves flatter others, in order to gain their ends; but they soon discard their followers when they have no longer any need of them; they are always either masters or servants, – the joys of friendship are unknown to them. And they are utterly treacherous and unjust, if the nature of justice be at all understood by us. They realize our dream; and he who is the most of a tyrant by nature, and leads the life of a tyrant for the longest time, will be the worst of them, and being the worst of them, will also be the most miserable.

Like man, like State, – the tyrannical man will answer to tyranny, which is the extreme opposite of the royal State; for one is the best and the other the worst. But which is the happier? Great and terrible as the tyrant may appear enthroned amid his satellites, let us not be afraid to go in and ask; and the answer is, that the monarchical is the happiest, and the tyrannical the most miserable of States. And may we not ask the same question about the men themselves, requesting some one to look into them who is able to penetrate the inner nature of man, and will not be panic-struck by the vain pomp of tyranny? I will suppose that he is one who has lived with him, and has seen him in family life, or perhaps in the hour of trouble and danger.

Assuming that we ourselves are the impartial judge for whom we seek, let us begin by comparing the individual and State, and ask first of all, whether the State is likely to be free or enslaved – Will there not be a little freedom and a great deal of slavery? And the freedom is of the bad, and the slavery of the good; and this applies to the man as well as to the State; for his soul is full of meanness and slavery, and the better part is enslaved to the worse. He cannot do what he would, and his mind is full of confusion; he is the very reverse of a freeman. The State will be poor and full of misery and sorrow; and the man's soul will also be poor and full of sorrows, and he will be the most miserable of men. No, not the most miserable, for there is yet a more miserable. 'Who is that?' The tyrannical man who has the misfortune also to become a public tyrant. 'There I suspect that you are right.' Say rather, 'I am sure;' conjecture is out of place in an enquiry of this nature. He is like a wealthy owner of slaves, only he has more of them than any private individual. You will say, 'The owners of slaves are not generally in any fear of them.' But why? Because the whole city is in a league which protects the individual. Suppose however that one of these owners and his household is carried off by a god into a wilderness, where there are no freemen to help him – will he not be in an agony of terror? – will he not be compelled to flatter his slaves and to promise them many things sore against his will? And suppose the same god who carried him off were to surround him with neighbours who declare that no man ought to have slaves, and that the owners of them should be punished with death. 'Still worse and worse! He will be in the midst of his enemies.' And is not our tyrant such a captive soul, who is tormented by a swarm of passions which he cannot indulge; living indoors always like a woman, and jealous of those who can go out and see the world?

Having so many evils, will not the most miserable of men be still more miserable in a public station? Master of others when he is not master of himself; like a sick man who is compelled to be an athlete; the meanest of slaves and the most abject of flatterers; wanting all things, and never able to satisfy his desires; always in fear and distraction, like the State of which he is the representative. His jealous, hateful, faithless temper grows worse with command; he is more and more faithless, envious, unrighteous, – the most wretched of men, a misery to himself and to others. And so let us have a final trial and proclamation; need we hire a herald, or shall I proclaim the result? 'Made the proclamation yourself.' The son of Ariston (the best) is of opinion that the best and justest of men is also the happiest, and that this is he who is the most royal master of himself; and that the unjust man is he who is the greatest tyrant of himself and of his State. And I add further − 'seen or unseen by gods or men.'

This is our first proof. The second is derived from the three kinds of pleasure, which answer to the three elements of the soul − reason, passion, desire; under which last is comprehended avarice as well as sensual appetite, while passion includes ambition, party-feeling, love of reputation. Reason, again, is solely directed to the attainment of truth, and careless of money and reputation. In accordance with the difference of men's natures, one of these three principles is in the ascendant, and they have their several pleasures corresponding to them. Interrogate now the three natures, and each one will be found praising his own pleasures and depreciating those of others. The money-maker will contrast the vanity of knowledge with the solid advantages of wealth. The ambitious man will despise knowledge which brings no honour; whereas the philosopher will regard only the fruition of truth, and will call other pleasures necessary rather than good. Now, how shall we decide between them? Is there any better criterion than experience and knowledge? And which of the three has the truest knowledge and the widest experience? The experience of youth makes the philosopher acquainted with the two kinds of desire, but the avaricious and the ambitious man never taste the pleasures of truth and wisdom. Honour he has equally with them; they are 'judged of him,' but he is 'not judged of them,' for they never attain to the knowledge of true being. And his instrument is reason, whereas their standard is only wealth and honour; and if by reason we are to judge, his good will be the truest. And so we arrive at the result that the pleasure of the rational part of the soul, and a life passed in such pleasure is the pleasantest. He who has a right to judge judges thus. Next comes the life of ambition, and, in the third place, that of money-making.

Twice has the just man overthrown the unjust − once more, as in an Olympian contest, first offering up a prayer to the saviour Zeus, let him try a fall. A wise man whispers to me that the pleasures of the wise are true and pure; all others are a shadow only. Let us examine this: Is not pleasure opposed to pain, and is there not a mean state which is neither? When a man is sick, nothing is more pleasant to him than health. But this he never found out while he was well. In pain he desires only to cease from pain; on the other hand, when he is in an ecstasy of pleasure, rest is painful to him. Thus rest or cessation is both pleasure and pain. But can that which is neither become both? Again, pleasure and pain are motions, and the absence of them is rest; but if so, how can the absence of either of them be the other? Thus we are led to infer that the contradiction is an appearance only, and witchery of the senses. And these are not the only pleasures, for there are others which have no preceding pains. Pure pleasure then is not the absence of pain, nor pure pain the absence of pleasure; although most of the pleasures which reach the mind through the body are reliefs of pain, and have not only their reactions when they depart, but their anticipations before they come. They can be best described in a simile. There is in nature an upper, lower, and middle region, and he who passes from the lower to the middle imagines that he is going up and is already in the upper world; and if he were taken back again would think, and truly think, that he was descending. All this arises out of his ignorance of the true upper, middle, and lower regions. And a like confusion happens with pleasure and pain, and with many other things. The man who compares grey with black, calls grey white; and the man who compares absence of pain with pain, calls the absence of pain pleasure. Again, hunger and thirst are inanitions of the body, ignorance and folly of the soul; and food is the satisfaction of the one, knowledge of the other. Now which is the purer satisfaction – that of eating and drinking, or that of knowledge? Consider the matter thus: The satisfaction of that which has more existence is truer than of that which has less. The invariable and immortal has a more real existence than the variable and mortal, and has a corresponding measure of knowledge and truth. The soul, again, has more existence and truth and knowledge than the body, and is therefore more really satisfied and has a more natural pleasure. Those who feast only on earthly food, are always going at random up to the middle and down again; but they never pass into the true upper world, or have a taste of true pleasure. They are like fatted beasts, full of gluttony and sensuality, and ready to kill one another by reason of their insatiable lust; for they are not filled with true being, and their vessel is leaky (Gorgias). Their pleasures are mere shadows of pleasure, mixed with pain, coloured and intensified by contrast, and therefore intensely desired; and men go fighting about them, as Stesichorus says that the Greeks fought about the shadow of Helen at Troy, because they know not the truth.

The same may be said of the passionate element: – the desires of the ambitious soul, as well as of the covetous, have an inferior satisfaction. Only when under the guidance of reason do either of the other principles do their own business or attain the pleasure which is natural to them.

When not attaining, they compel the other parts of the soul to pursue a shadow of pleasure which is not theirs. And the more distant they are from philosophy and reason, the more distant they will be from law and order, and the more illusive will be their pleasures. The desires of love and tyranny are the farthest from law, and those of the king are nearest to it. There is one genuine pleasure, and two spurious ones: the tyrant goes beyond even the latter; he has run away altogether from law and reason. Nor can the measure of his inferiority be told, except in a figure. The tyrant is the third removed from the oligarch, and has therefore, not a shadow of his pleasure, but the shadow of a shadow only. The oligarch, again, is thrice removed from the king, and thus we get the formula 3 x 3, which is the number of a surface, representing the shadow which is the tyrant's pleasure, and if you like to cube this 'number of the beast,' you will find that the measure of the difference amounts to 729; the king is 729 times more happy than the tyrant. And this extraordinary number is NEARLY equal to the number of days and nights in a year (365 x 2 = 730); and is therefore concerned with human life. This is the interval between a good and bad man in happiness only: what must be the difference between them in comeliness of life and virtue!

Perhaps you may remember some one saying at the beginning of our discussion that the unjust man was profited if he had the reputation of justice. Now that we know the nature of justice and injustice, let us make an image of the soul, which will personify his words. First of all, fashion a multitudinous beast, having a ring of heads of all manner of animals, tame and wild, and able to produce and change them at pleasure. Suppose now another form of a lion, and another of a man; the second smaller than the first, the third than the second; join them together and cover them with a human skin, in which they are completely concealed. When this has been done, let us tell the supporter of injustice that he is feeding up the beasts and starving the man. The maintainer of justice, on the other hand, is trying to strengthen the man; he is nourishing the gentle principle within him, and making an alliance with the lion heart, in order that he may be able to keep down the many-headed hydra, and bring all into unity with each other and with themselves. Thus in every point of view, whether in relation to pleasure, honour, or advantage, the just man is right, and the unjust wrong.

But now, let us reason with the unjust, who is not intentionally in error. Is not the noble that which subjects the beast to the man, or rather to the God in man; the ignoble, that which subjects the man to the beast? And if so, who would receive gold on condition that he was to degrade the noblest part of himself under the worst? – who would sell his son or daughter into the hands of brutal and evil men, for any amount of money? And will he sell his own fairer and diviner part without any compunction to the most godless and foul? Would he not be worse than Eriphyle, who sold her husband's life for a necklace? And intemperance is the letting loose of the multiform monster, and pride and sullenness are the growth and increase of the lion and serpent element, while luxury and effeminacy are caused by a too great relaxation of spirit. Flattery and meanness again arise when the spirited element is subjected to avarice, and the lion is habituated to become a monkey. The real disgrace of handicraft arts is, that those who are engaged in them have to flatter, instead of mastering their desires; therefore we say that they should be placed under the control of the better principle in another because they have none in themselves; not, as Thrasymachus imagined, to the injury of the subjects, but for their good. And our intention in educating the young, is to give them self-control; the law desires to nurse up in them a higher principle, and when they have acquired this, they may go their ways.

'What, then, shall a man profit, if he gain the whole world' and become more and more wicked? Or what shall he profit by escaping discovery, if the concealment of evil prevents the cure? If he had been punished, the brute within him would have been silenced, and the gentler element liberated; and he would have united temperance, justice, and wisdom in his soul – a union better far than any combination of bodily gifts. The man of understanding will honour knowledge above all; in the next place he will keep under his body, not only for the sake of health and strength, but in order to attain the most perfect harmony of body and soul. In the acquisition of riches, too, he will aim at order and harmony; he will not desire to heap up wealth without measure, but he will fear that the increase of wealth will disturb the constitution of his own soul. For the same reason he will only accept such honours as will make him a better man; any others he will decline. 'In that case,' said he, 'he will never be a politician.' Yes, but he will, in his own city; though probably not in his native country, unless by some divine accident. 'You mean that he will be a citizen of the ideal city, which has no place upon earth.' But in heaven, I replied, there is a pattern of such a city, and he who wishes may order his life after that image. Whether such a state is or ever will be matters not; he will act according to that pattern and no other...

The most noticeable points in the 9th Book of the Republic are: – (1) the account of pleasure; (2) the number of the interval which divides the king from the tyrant; (3) the pattern which is in heaven.

1. Plato's account of pleasure is remarkable for moderation, and in this respect contrasts with the later Platonists and the views which are attributed to them by Aristotle. He is not, like the Cynics, opposed to all pleasure, but rather desires that the several parts of the soul shall have their natural satisfaction; he even agrees with the Epicureans in describing pleasure as something more than the absence of pain. This is proved by the circumstance that there are pleasures which have no antecedent pains (as he also remarks in the Philebus), such as the pleasures of smell, and also the pleasures of hope and anticipation. In the previous book he had made the distinction between necessary and unnecessary pleasure, which is repeated by Aristotle, and he now observes that there are a further class of 'wild beast' pleasures, corresponding to Aristotle's (Greek). He dwells upon the relative and unreal character of sensual pleasures and the illusion which arises out of the contrast of pleasure and pain, pointing out the superiority of the pleasures of reason, which are at rest, over the fleeting pleasures of sense and emotion. The pre-eminence of royal pleasure is shown by the fact that reason is able to form a judgment of the lower pleasures, while the two lower parts of the soul are incapable of judging the pleasures of reason. Thus, in his treatment of pleasure, as in many other subjects, the philosophy of Plato is 'sawn up into quantities' by Aristotle; the analysis which was originally made by him became in the next generation the foundation of further technical distinctions. Both in Plato and Aristotle we note the illusion under which the ancients fell of regarding the transience of pleasure as a proof of its unreality, and of confounding the permanence of the intellectual pleasures with the unchangeableness of the knowledge from which they are derived. Neither do we like to admit that the pleasures of knowledge, though more elevating, are not more lasting than other pleasures, and are almost equally dependent on the accidents of our bodily state (Introduction to Philebus).

2. The number of the interval which separates the king from the tyrant, and royal from tyrannical pleasures, is 729, the cube of 9. Which Plato characteristically designates as a number concerned with human life, because NEARLY equivalent to the number of days and nights in the year. He is desirous of proclaiming that the interval between them is immeasurable, and invents a formula to give expression to his idea. Those who spoke of justice as a cube, of virtue as an art of measuring (Prot.), saw

no inappropriateness in conceiving the soul under the figure of a line, or the pleasure of the tyrant as separated from the pleasure of the king by the numerical interval of 729. And in modern times we sometimes use metaphorically what Plato employed as a philosophical formula. 'It is not easy to estimate the loss of the tyrant, except perhaps in this way,' says Plato. So we might say, that although the life of a good man is not to be compared to that of a bad man, yet you may measure the difference between them by valuing one minute of the one at an hour of the other ('One day in thy courts is better than a thousand'), or you might say that 'there is an infinite difference.' But this is not so much as saying, in homely phrase, 'They are a thousand miles asunder.' And accordingly Plato finds the natural vehicle of his thoughts in a progression of numbers; this arithmetical formula he draws out with the utmost seriousness, and both here and in the number of generation seems to find an additional proof of the truth of his speculation in forming the number into a geometrical figure; just as persons in our own day are apt to fancy that a statement is verified when it has been only thrown into an abstract form. In speaking of the number 729 as proper to human life, he probably intended to intimate that one year of the tyrannical = 12 hours of the royal life.

The simple observation that the comparison of two similar solids is effected by the comparison of the cubes of their sides, is the mathematical groundwork of this fanciful expression. There is some difficulty in explaining the steps by which the number 729 is obtained; the oligarch is removed in the third degree from the royal and aristocratical, and the tyrant in the third degree from the oligarchical; but we have to arrange the terms as the sides of a square and to count the oligarch twice over, thus reckoning them not as = 5 but as = 9. The square of 9 is passed lightly over as only a step towards the cube.

3. Towards the close of the Republic, Plato seems to be more and more convinced of the ideal character of his own speculations. At the end of the 9th Book the pattern which is in heaven takes the place of the city of philosophers on earth. The vision which has received form and substance at his hands, is now discovered to be at a distance. And yet this distant kingdom is also the rule of man's life. ('Say not lo! here, or lo! there, for the kingdom of God is within you.') Thus a note is struck which prepares for the revelation of a future life in the following Book. But the future life is present still; the ideal of politics is to be realized in the individual.

BOOK X.

Many things pleased me in the order of our State, but there was nothing which I liked better than the regulation about poetry. The division of the soul throws a new light on our exclusion of imitation. I do not mind telling you in confidence that all poetry is an outrage on the understanding, unless the hearers have that balm of knowledge which heals error. I have loved Homer ever since I was a boy, and even now he appears to me to be the great master of tragic poetry. But much as I love the man, I love truth more, and therefore I must speak out: and first of all, will you explain what is imitation, for really I do not understand? 'How likely then that I should understand!' That might very well be, for the duller often sees better than the keener eye. 'True, but in your presence I can hardly venture to say what I think.' Then suppose that we begin in our old fashion, with the doctrine of universals. Let us assume the existence of beds and tables. There is one idea of a bed, or of a table, which the maker of each had in his mind when making them; he did not make the ideas of beds and tables, but he made beds and tables according to the ideas. And is there not a maker of the works of all workmen, who makes not only vessels but plants and animals, himself, the earth and heaven, and things in heaven and under the earth? He makes the Gods also. 'He must be a wizard indeed!' But do you not see that there is a sense in which you could do the same? You have only to take a mirror, and catch the reflection of the sun, and the earth, or anything else – there now you have made them. 'Yes, but only in appearance.' Exactly so; and the painter is such a creator as you are with the mirror, and he is even more unreal than the carpenter; although neither the carpenter nor any other artist can be supposed to make the absolute bed. 'Not if philosophers may be believed.' Nor need we wonder that his bed has but an imperfect relation to the truth. Reflect: – Here are three beds; one in nature, which is made by God; another, which is made by the carpenter; and the third, by the painter. God only made one, nor could he have made more than one; for if there had been two, there would always have been a third – more absolute and abstract than either, under which they would have been included. We may therefore conceive God to be the natural maker of the bed, and in a lower sense the carpenter is also the maker; but the painter is rather the imitator of what the other two make; he has to do with a creation which is thrice removed from reality. And the tragic poet is an imitator, and, like every other imitator, is thrice removed from the king and from the truth. The painter imitates not the original bed, but the bed made by the carpenter. And this, without being really different, appears to be different, and has many points of view, of which only one is caught by the painter, who represents everything because he represents a piece of everything, and that piece an image. And he can paint any other artist, although he knows nothing of their arts; and this with sufficient skill to deceive children or simple people. Suppose now that somebody came to us and told us, how he had met a man who knew all that everybody knows, and better than anybody: − should we not infer him to be a simpleton who, having no discernment of truth and falsehood, had met with a wizard or enchanter, whom he fancied to be all-wise? And when we hear persons saying that Homer and the tragedians know all the arts and all the virtues, must we not infer that they are under a similar delusion? they do not see that the poets are imitators, and that their creations are only imitations. 'Very true.' But if a person could create as well as imitate, he would rather leave some permanent work and not an imitation only; he would rather be the receiver than the giver of praise? 'Yes, for then he would have more honour and advantage.'

Let us now interrogate Homer and the poets. Friend Homer, say I to him, I am not going to ask you about medicine, or any art to which your poems incidentally refer, but about their main subjects − war, military tactics, politics. If you are only twice and not thrice removed from the truth − not an imitator or an image-maker, please to inform us what good you have ever done to mankind? Is there any city which professes to have received laws from you, as Sicily and Italy have from Charondas, Sparta from Lycurgus, Athens from Solon? Or was any war ever carried on by your counsels? or is any invention attributed to you, as there is to Thales and Anacharsis? Or is there any Homeric way of life, such as the Pythagorean was, in which you instructed men, and which is called after you? 'No, indeed; and Creophylus (Flesh-child) was even more unfortunate in his breeding than he was in his name, if, as tradition says, Homer in his lifetime was allowed by him and his other friends to starve.' Yes, but could this ever have happened if Homer had really been the educator of Hellas? Would he not have had many devoted followers? If Protagoras and Prodicus can persuade their contemporaries that no one can manage house or State without them, is it likely that Homer and Hesiod would have been allowed to go about as beggars − I mean if they had really been able to do the world any good? − would not men have compelled them to stay where they were, or have followed them about in order to get education? But they did not; and therefore we may infer that Homer and all the poets are only imitators, who do but imitate the appearances of things. For as a painter by a knowledge of figure and colour can paint a cobbler without any practice in cobbling, so the poet can delineate any art in the colours of language, and give harmony and rhythm to the cobbler and also to the general; and you know how mere narration, when deprived of the ornaments of metre, is like a face which has lost the beauty of youth and never had any other. Once more, the imitator has no knowledge of reality, but only of appearance. The painter paints, and the artificer makes a bridle and reins, but neither understands the use of them – the knowledge of this is confined to the horseman; and so of other things. Thus we have three arts: one of use, another of invention, a third of imitation; and the user furnishes the rule to the two others. The flute-player will know the good and bad flute, and the maker will put faith in him; but the imitator will neither know nor have faith – neither science nor true opinion can be ascribed to him. Imitation, then, is devoid of knowledge, being only a kind of play or sport, and the tragic and epic poets are imitators in the highest degree.

And now let us enquire, what is the faculty in man which answers to imitation. Allow me to explain my meaning: Objects are differently seen when in the water and when out of the water, when near and when at a distance; and the painter or juggler makes use of this variation to impose upon us. And the art of measuring and weighing and calculating comes in to save our bewildered minds from the power of appearance; for, as we were saying, two contrary opinions of the same about the same and at the same time, cannot both of them be true. But which of them is true is determined by the art of calculation; and this is allied to the better faculty in the soul, as the arts of imitation are to the worse. And the same holds of the ear as well as of the eye, of poetry as well as painting. The imitation is of actions voluntary or involuntary, in which there is an expectation of a good or bad result, and present experience of pleasure and pain. But is a man in harmony with himself when he is the subject of these conflicting influences? Is there not rather a contradiction in him? Let me further ask, whether he is more likely to control sorrow when he is alone or when he is in company. 'In the latter case.' Feeling would lead him to indulge his sorrow, but reason and law control him and enjoin patience; since he cannot know whether his affliction is good or evil, and no human thing is of any great consequence, while sorrow is certainly a hindrance to good counsel. For when we stumble, we should not, like children, make an uproar; we should take the measures which reason prescribes, not raising a lament, but finding a cure. And the better part of us is ready to follow reason, while the irrational principle is full of sorrow and distraction at the recollection of our troubles. Unfortunately, however, this latter furnishes the chief materials of the imitative arts. Whereas reason is ever in repose and cannot easily be displayed, especially to a mixed multitude who have no experience of her. Thus the poet is like the painter in two ways: first he paints an inferior degree of truth, and secondly, he is concerned with an inferior part of the soul. He indulges the feelings, while he enfeebles the reason; and we refuse to allow him to have authority over the mind of man; for he has no measure of greater and less, and is a maker of images and very far gone from truth.

But we have not yet mentioned the heaviest count in the indictment – the power which poetry has of injuriously exciting the feelings. When we hear some passage in which a hero laments his sufferings at tedious length, you know that we sympathize with him and praise the poet; and yet in our own sorrows such an exhibition of feeling is regarded as effeminate and unmanly (Ion). Now, ought a man to feel pleasure in seeing another do what he hates and abominates in himself? Is he not giving way to a sentiment which in his own case he would control? – he is off his guard because the sorrow is another's; and he thinks that he may indulge his feelings without disgrace, and will be the gainer by the pleasure. But the inevitable consequence is that he who begins by weeping at the sorrows of others, will end by weeping at his own. The same is true of comedy, – you may often laugh at buffoonery which you would be ashamed to utter, and the love of coarse merriment on the stage will at last turn you into a buffoon at home. Poetry feeds and waters the passions and desires; she lets them rule instead of ruling them. And therefore, when we hear the encomiasts of Homer affirming that he is the educator of Hellas, and that all life should be regulated by his precepts, we may allow the excellence of their intentions, and agree with them in thinking Homer a great poet and tragedian. But we shall continue to prohibit all poetry which goes beyond hymns to the Gods and praises of famous men. Not pleasure and pain, but law and reason shall rule in our State.

These are our grounds for expelling poetry; but lest she should charge us with discourtesy, let us also make an apology to her. We will remind her that there is an ancient quarrel between poetry and philosophy, of which there are many traces in the writings of the poets, such as the saying of 'the she-dog, yelping at her mistress,' and 'the philosophers who are ready to circumvent Zeus,' and 'the philosophers who are paupers.' Nevertheless we bear her no ill-will, and will gladly allow her to return upon condition that she makes a defence of herself in verse; and her supporters who are not poets may speak in prose. We confess her charms; but if she cannot show

THE REPUBLIC

that she is useful as well as delightful, like rational lovers, we must renounce our love, though endeared to us by early associations. Having come to years of discretion, we know that poetry is not truth, and that a man should be careful how he introduces her to that state or constitution which he himself is; for there is a mighty issue at stake – no less than the good or evil of a human soul. And it is not worth while to forsake justice and virtue for the attractions of poetry, any more than for the sake of honour or wealth. 'I agree with you.'

And yet the rewards of virtue are greater far than I have described. 'And can we conceive things greater still?' Not, perhaps, in this brief span of life: but should an immortal being care about anything short of eternity? 'I do not understand what you mean?' Do you not know that the soul is immortal? 'Surely you are not prepared to prove that?' Indeed I am. 'Then let me hear this argument, of which you make so light.'

You would admit that everything has an element of good and of evil. In all things there is an inherent corruption; and if this cannot destroy them, nothing else will. The soul too has her own corrupting principles, which are injustice, intemperance, cowardice, and the like. But none of these destroy the soul in the same sense that disease destroys the body. The soul may be full of all iniquities, but is not, by reason of them, brought any nearer to death. Nothing which was not destroyed from within ever perished by external affection of evil. The body, which is one thing, cannot be destroyed by food, which is another, unless the badness of the food is communicated to the body. Neither can the soul, which is one thing, be corrupted by the body, which is another, unless she herself is infected. And as no bodily evil can infect the soul, neither can any bodily evil, whether disease or violence, or any other destroy the soul, unless it can be shown to render her unholy and unjust. But no one will ever prove that the souls of men become more unjust when they die. If a person has the audacity to say the contrary, the answer is – Then why do criminals require the hand of the executioner, and not die of themselves? 'Truly,' he said, 'injustice would not be very terrible if it brought a cessation of evil; but I rather believe that the injustice which murders others may tend to quicken and stimulate the life of the unjust.' You are quite right. If sin which is her own natural and inherent evil cannot destroy the soul, hardly will anything else destroy her. But the soul which cannot be destroyed either by internal or external evil must be immortal and everlasting. And if this be true, souls will always exist in the same number. They cannot diminish, because they cannot be destroyed; nor yet increase, for the increase of the immortal must come from something mortal, and so all would end in immortality. Neither is the soul variable and diverse; for that which is immortal must be of the fairest and simplest composition. If we would conceive her truly, and so behold justice and injustice in their own nature, she must be viewed by the light of reason pure as at birth, or as she is reflected in philosophy when holding converse with the divine and immortal and eternal. In her present condition we see her only like the sea-god Glaucus, bruised and maimed in the sea which is the world, and covered with shells and stones which are incrusted upon her from the entertainments of earth.

Thus far, as the argument required, we have said nothing of the rewards and honours which the poets attribute to justice; we have contented ourselves with showing that justice in herself is best for the soul in herself, even if a man should put on a Gyges' ring and have the helmet of Hades too. And now you shall repay me what you borrowed; and I will enumerate the rewards of justice in life and after death. I granted, for the sake of argument, as you will remember, that evil might perhaps escape the knowledge of Gods and men, although this was really impossible. And since I have shown that justice has reality, you must grant me also that she has the palm of appearance. In the first place, the just man is known to the Gods, and he is therefore the friend of the Gods, and he will receive at their hands every good, always excepting such evil as is the necessary consequence of former sins. All things end in good to him, either in life or after death, even what appears to be evil; for the Gods have a care of him who desires to be in their likeness. And what shall we say of men? Is not honesty the best policy? The clever rogue makes a great start at first, but breaks down before he reaches the goal, and slinks away in dishonour; whereas the true runner perseveres to the end, and receives the prize. And you must allow me to repeat all the blessings which you attributed to the fortunate unjust – they bear rule in the city, they marry and give in marriage to whom they will; and the evils which you attributed to the unfortunate just, do really fall in the end on the unjust, although, as you implied, their sufferings are better veiled in silence.

But all the blessings of this present life are as nothing when compared with those which await good men after death. 'I should like to hear about them.' Come, then, and I will tell you the story of Er, the son of Armenius, a valiant man. He was supposed to have died in battle, but ten days afterwards his body was found untouched by corruption and sent home for burial. On the twelfth day he was placed on the funeral pyre and there he came to life again, and told what he had seen in the world below. He said that his soul went with a great company to a place, in which there were two chasms near together in the earth beneath, and two corresponding chasms in the heaven above. And there were judges sitting in the intermediate space, bidding the just ascend by the heavenly way on the right hand, having the seal of their judgment set upon them before, while the unjust, having the seal behind, were bidden to descend by the way on the left hand. Him they told to look and listen, as he was to be their messenger to men from the world below. And he beheld and saw the souls departing after judgment at either chasm; some who came from earth, were worn and travel-stained; others, who came from heaven, were clean and bright. They seemed glad to meet and rest awhile in the meadow; here they discoursed with one another of what they had seen in the other world. Those who came from earth wept at the remembrance of their sorrows, but the spirits from above spoke of glorious sights and heavenly bliss. He said that for every evil deed they were punished tenfold – now the journey was of a thousand years' duration, because the life of man was reckoned as a hundred years – and the rewards of virtue were in the same proportion. He added something hardly worth repeating about infants dying almost as soon as they were born. Of parricides and other murderers he had tortures still more terrible to narrate. He was present when one of the spirits asked – Where is Ardiaeus the Great? (This Ardiaeus was a cruel tyrant, who had murdered his father, and his elder brother, a thousand years before.) Another spirit answered, 'He comes not hither, and will never come. And I myself,' he added, 'actually saw this terrible sight. At the entrance of the chasm, as we were about to reascend, Ardiaeus appeared, and some other sinners – most of whom had been tyrants, but not all – and just as they fancied that they were returning to life, the chasm gave a roar, and then wild, fiery-looking men who knew the meaning of the sound, seized him and several others, and bound them hand and foot and threw them down, and dragged them along at the side of the road, lacerating them and carding them like wool, and explaining to the passers-by, that they were going to be cast into hell.' The greatest terror of the pilgrims ascending was lest they should hear the voice, and when there was silence one by one they passed up with joy. To these sufferings there were corresponding delights.

On the eighth day the souls of the pilgrims resumed their journey, and in four days came to a spot whence they looked down upon a line of light, in colour like a rainbow, only brighter and clearer. One day more brought them to the place, and they saw that this was the column of light which binds together the whole universe. The ends of the column were fastened to heaven, and from them hung the distaff of Necessity, on which all the heavenly bodies turned – the hook and spindle were of adamant, and the whorl of a mixed substance. The whorl was in form like a number of boxes fitting into one another with their edges turned upwards, making together a single whorl which was pierced by the spindle. The outermost had the rim broadest, and the inner whorls were smaller and smaller, and had their rims narrower. The largest (the fixed stars) was spangled – the seventh (the sun) was brightest – the eighth (the moon) shone by the light of the seventh – the second and fifth (Saturn and Mercury) were most like one another and yellower than the eighth – the third (Jupiter) had the whitest light – the fourth (Mars) was red – the sixth (Venus) was in whiteness second. The whole had one motion, but while this was revolving in one direction the seven inner circles were moving in the opposite, with various degrees of swiftness and slowness. The spindle turned on the knees of Necessity, and a Siren stood hymning upon each circle, while Lachesis, Clotho, and Atropos, the daughters of Necessity, sat on thrones at equal intervals, singing of past, present, and future, responsive to the music of the Sirens; Clotho from time to time guiding the outer circle with a touch of her right hand; Atropos with her left hand touching and guiding the inner circles; Lachesis in turn putting forth her hand from time to time to guide both of them. On their arrival the pilgrims went to Lachesis, and there was an interpreter who arranged them, and taking from her knees lots, and samples of lives, got up into a pulpit and said: 'Mortal souls, hear the words of Lachesis, the daughter of Necessity. A new period of mortal life has begun, and you may choose what divinity you please; the responsibility of choosing is with you – God is blameless.' After speaking thus, he cast the lots among them and each one took up the lot which fell near him. He then placed on the ground before them the samples of lives, many more than the souls present; and there were all sorts of lives, of men and of animals. There were tyrannies ending in misery and exile, and lives of men and women famous for their different qualities; and also mixed lives, made up of wealth and poverty, sickness and health. Here, Glaucon, is the great risk of human life, and therefore the whole of education should be directed to the acquisition of such a knowledge as will teach a man to refuse the evil and choose the good. He should know all the combinations which occur in life – of beauty with poverty or with wealth, – of knowledge with external goods, – and at last choose with reference to the nature of the soul, regarding that only as the better life which makes men better, and leaving the rest. And a man must take with him an iron sense of truth and right into the world below, that there too he may remain undazzled by wealth or the allurements of evil, and be determined to avoid the extremes and choose the mean. For this, as the messenger reported the interpreter to have said, is the true happiness of man; and any one, as he proclaimed, may, if he choose with understanding, have a good lot, even though he come last. 'Let not the first be careless in his choice, nor the last despair.' He spoke; and when he had spoken, he who had drawn the first lot chose a tyranny: he did not see that he was fated to devour his own children – and when he discovered his mistake, he wept and beat his breast, blaming chance and the Gods and anybody rather than himself. He was one of those who had come from heaven, and in his previous life had been a citizen of a well-ordered State, but he had only habit and no philosophy. Like many another, he made a bad choice, because he had no experience of life; whereas those who came from earth and had seen trouble were not in such a hurry to choose. But if a man had followed philosophy while upon earth, and had been moderately fortunate in his lot, he might not only be happy here, but his pilgrimage both from and to this world would be smooth and heavenly. Nothing was more curious than the spectacle of the choice, at once sad and laughable and wonderful; most of the souls only seeking to avoid their own condition in a previous life. He saw the soul of Orpheus changing into a swan because he would not be born of a woman; there was Thamyras becoming a nightingale; musical birds, like the swan, choosing to be men; the twentieth soul, which was that of Ajax, preferring the life of a lion to that of a man, in remembrance of the injustice which was done to him in the judgment of the arms; and Agamemnon, from a like enmity to human nature, passing into an eagle. About the middle was the soul of Atalanta choosing the honours of an athlete, and next to her Epeus taking the nature of a workwoman; among the last was Thersites, who was changing himself into a monkey. Thither, the last of all, came Odysseus, and sought the lot of a private man, which lay neglected and despised, and when he found it he went away rejoicing, and said that if he had been first instead of last, his choice would have been the same. Men, too, were seen passing into animals, and wild and tame animals changing into one another.

When all the souls had chosen they went to Lachesis, who sent with each of them their genius or attendant to fulfil their lot. He first of all brought them under the hand of Clotho, and drew them within the revolution of the spindle impelled by her hand; from her they were carried to Atropos, who made the threads irreversible; whence, without turning round, they passed beneath the throne of Necessity; and when they had all passed, they moved on in scorching heat to the plain of Forgetfulness and rested at evening by the river Unmindful, whose water could not be retained in any vessel; of this they had all to drink a certain quantity – some of them drank more than was required, and he who drank forgot all things. Er himself was prevented from drinking. When they had gone to rest, about the middle of the night there were thunderstorms and earthquakes, and suddenly they were all driven divers ways, shooting like stars to their birth. Concerning his return to the body, he only knew that awaking suddenly in the morning he found himself lying on the pyre.

Thus, Glaucon, the tale has been saved, and will be our salvation, if we believe that the soul is immortal, and hold fast to the heavenly way of Justice and Knowledge. So shall we pass undefiled over the river of Forgetfulness, and be dear to ourselves and to the Gods, and have a crown of reward and happiness both in this world and also in the millennial pilgrimage of the other.

The Tenth Book of the Republic of Plato falls into two divisions: first, resuming an old thread which has been interrupted, Socrates assails the poets, who, now that the nature of the soul has been analyzed, are seen to be very far gone from the truth; and secondly, having shown the reality of the happiness of the just, he demands that appearance shall be restored to him, and then proceeds to prove the immortality of the soul. The argument, as in the Phaedo and Gorgias, is supplemented by the vision of a future life.

Why Plato, who was himself a poet, and whose dialogues are poems and dramas, should have been hostile to the poets as a class, and especially to the dramatic poets; why he should not have seen that truth may be embodied in verse as well as in prose, and that there are some indefinable lights and shadows of human life which can only be expressed in poetry – some elements of imagination which always entwine with reason; why he should have supposed epic verse to be inseparably associated with the impurities of the old Hellenic mythology; why he should try Homer and Hesiod by the unfair and prosaic test of utility, – are questions which have always been debated amongst students of Plato. Though unable to give a complete answer to them, we may show – first, that his views arose naturally out of the circumstances of his age; and secondly, we may elicit the truth as well as the error which is contained in them.

He is the enemy of the poets because poetry was declining in his own lifetime, and a theatrocracy, as he says in the Laws, had taken the place of an intellectual aristocracy. Euripides exhibited the last phase of the tragic drama, and in him Plato saw the friend and apologist of tyrants, and the

Sophist of tragedy. The old comedy was almost extinct; the new had not yet arisen. Dramatic and lyric poetry, like every other branch of Greek literature, was falling under the power of rhetoric. There was no 'second or third' to Aeschylus and Sophocles in the generation which followed them. Aristophanes, in one of his later comedies (Frogs), speaks of 'thousands of tragedy-making prattlers,' whose attempts at poetry he compares to the chirping of swallows; 'their garrulity went far beyond Euripides,' – 'they appeared once upon the stage, and there was an end of them.' To a man of genius who had a real appreciation of the godlike Aeschylus and the noble and gentle Sophocles, though disagreeing with some parts of their 'theology' (Rep.), these 'minor poets' must have been contemptible and intolerable. There is no feeling stronger in the dialogues of Plato than a sense of the decline and decay both in literature and in politics which marked his own age. Nor can he have been expected to look with favour on the licence of Aristophanes, now at the end of his career, who had begun by satirizing Socrates in the Clouds, and in a similar spirit forty years afterwards had satirized the founders of ideal commonwealths in his Eccleziazusae, or Female Parliament (Laws).

There were other reasons for the antagonism of Plato to poetry. The profession of an actor was regarded by him as a degradation of human nature, for 'one man in his life' cannot 'play many parts;' the characters which the actor performs seem to destroy his own character, and to leave nothing which can be truly called himself. Neither can any man live his life and act it. The actor is the slave of his art, not the master of it. Taking this view Plato is more decided in his expulsion of the dramatic than of the epic poets, though he must have known that the Greek tragedians afforded noble lessons and examples of virtue and patriotism, to which nothing in Homer can be compared. But great dramatic or even great rhetorical power is hardly consistent with firmness or strength of mind, and dramatic talent is often incidentally associated with a weak or dissolute character.

In the Tenth Book Plato introduces a new series of objections. First, he says that the poet or painter is an imitator, and in the third degree removed from the truth. His creations are not tested by rule and measure; they are only appearances. In modern times we should say that art is not merely imitation, but rather the expression of the ideal in forms of sense. Even adopting the humble image of Plato, from which his argument derives a colour, we should maintain that the artist may ennoble the bed which he paints by the folds of the drapery, or by the feeling of home which he introduces; and there have been modern painters who have imparted such an ideal interest to a blacksmith's or a carpenter's shop. The eye or mind which feels as well as sees can give dignity and pathos to a ruined mill, or a straw-built shed (Rembrandt), to the hull of a vessel 'going to its last home' (Turner). Still more would this apply to the greatest works of art, which seem to be the visible embodiment of the divine. Had Plato been asked whether the Zeus or Athene of Pheidias was the imitation of an imitation only, would he not have been compelled to admit that something more was to be found in them than in the form of any mortal; and that the rule of proportion to which they conformed was 'higher far than any geometry or arithmetic could express?' (Statesman.)

Again, Plato objects to the imitative arts that they express the emotional rather than the rational part of human nature. He does not admit Aristotle's theory, that tragedy or other serious imitations are a purgation of the passions by pity and fear; to him they appear only to afford the opportunity of indulging them. Yet we must acknowledge that we may sometimes cure disordered emotions by giving expression to them; and that they often gain strength when pent up within our own breast. It is not every indulgence of the feelings which is to be condemned. For there may be a gratification of the higher as well as of the lower – thoughts which are too deep or too sad to be expressed by ourselves, may find an utterance in the words of poets. Every one would acknowledge that there have been times when they were consoled and elevated by beautiful music or by the sublimity of architecture or by the peacefulness of nature. Plato has himself admitted, in the earlier part of the Republic, that the arts might have the effect of harmonizing as well as of enervating the mind; but in the Tenth Book he regards them through a Stoic or Puritan medium. He asks only 'What good have they done?' and is not satisfied with the reply, that 'They have given innocent pleasure to mankind.'

He tells us that he rejoices in the banishment of the poets, since he has found by the analysis of the soul that they are concerned with the inferior faculties. He means to say that the higher faculties have to do with universals, the lower with particulars of sense. The poets are on a level with their own age, but not on a level with Socrates and Plato; and he was well aware that Homer and Hesiod could not be made a rule of life by any process of legitimate interpretation; his ironical use of them is in fact a denial of their authority; he saw, too, that the poets were not critics – as he says in the Apology, 'Any one was a better interpreter of their writings than they were themselves. He himself ceased to be a poet when he became a disciple of Socrates; though, as he tells us of Solon, 'he might have been one of the greatest of them, if he had not been deterred by other pursuits' (Tim.) Thus from many points of view there is an antagonism between Plato and the poets, which was foreshadowed to him in the old quarrel between philosophy and poetry. The poets, as he says in the Protagoras, were the Sophists of their day; and his dislike of the one class is reflected on the other. He regards them both as the enemies of reasoning and abstraction, though in the case of Euripides more with reference to his immoral sentiments about tyrants and the like. For Plato is the prophet who 'came into the world to convince men' – first of the fallibility of sense and opinion, and secondly of the reality of abstract ideas. Whatever strangeness there may be in modern times in opposing philosophy to poetry, which to us seem to have so many elements in common, the strangeness will disappear if we conceive of poetry as allied to sense, and of philosophy as equivalent to thought and abstraction. Unfortunately the very word 'idea,' which to Plato is expressive of the most real of all things, is associated in our minds with an element of subjectiveness and unreality. We may note also how he differs from Aristotle who declares poetry to be truer than history, for the opposite reason, because it is concerned with universals, not like history, with particulars (Poet).

The things which are seen are opposed in Scripture to the things which are unseen – they are equally opposed in Plato to universals and ideas. To him all particulars appear to be floating about in a world of sense; they have a taint of error or even of evil. There is no difficulty in seeing that this is an illusion; for there is no more error or variation in an individual man, horse, bed, etc., than in the class man, horse, bed, etc.; nor is the truth which is displayed in individual instances less certain than that which is conveyed through the medium of ideas. But Plato, who is deeply impressed with the real importance of universals as instruments of thought, attributes to them an essential truth which is imaginary and unreal; for universals may be often false and particulars true. Had he attained to any clear conception of the individual, which is the synthesis of the universal and the particular; or had he been able to distinguish between opinion and sensation, which the ambiguity of the words (Greek) and the like, tended to confuse, he would not have denied truth to the particulars of sense.

But the poets are also the representatives of falsehood and feigning in all departments of life and knowledge, like the sophists and rhetoricians of the Gorgias and Phaedrus; they are the false priests, false prophets, lying spirits, enchanters of the world. There is another count put into the indictment against them by Plato, that they are the friends of the tyrant, and bask in the sunshine of his patronage. Despotism in all ages has had an apparatus of false ideas and false teachers at its service – in the history of Modern Europe as well as of Greece and Rome. For no government of men depends solely upon force; without some corruption of literature and morals – some appeal to the imagination of the masses – some pretence to the favour of heaven – some element of good giving power to evil, tyranny, even for a short time, cannot be maintained. The Greek tyrants were not insensible to the importance of awakening in their cause a Pseudo-Hellenic feeling; they were proud of successes at the Olympic games; they were not devoid of the love of literature and art. Plato is thinking in the first instance of Greek poets who had graced the courts of Dionysius or Archelaus: and the old spirit of freedom is roused within him at their prostitution of the Tragic Muse in the praises of tyranny. But his prophetic eye extends beyond them to the false teachers of other ages who are the creatures of the government under which they live. He compares the corruption of his contemporaries with the idea of a perfect society, and gathers up into one mass of evil the evils and errors of mankind; to him they are personified in the rhetoricians, sophists, poets, rulers who deceive and govern the world.

A further objection which Plato makes to poetry and the imitative arts is that they excite the emotions. Here the modern reader will be disposed to introduce a distinction which appears to have escaped him. For the emotions are neither bad nor good in themselves, and are not most likely to be controlled by the attempt to eradicate them, but by the moderate indulgence of them. And the vocation of art is to present thought in the form of feeling, to enlist the feelings on the side of reason, to inspire even for a moment courage or resignation; perhaps to suggest a sense of infinity and eternity in a way which mere language is incapable of attaining. True, the same power which in the purer age of art embodies gods and heroes only, may be made to express the voluptuous image of a Corinthian courtezan. But this only shows that art, like other outward things, may be turned to good and also to evil, and is not more closely connected with the higher than with the lower part of the soul. All imitative art is subject to certain limitations, and therefore necessarily partakes of the nature of a compromise. Something of ideal truth is sacrificed for the sake of the representation, and something in the exactness of the representation is sacrificed to the ideal. Still, works of art have a permanent element; they idealize and detain the passing thought, and are the intermediates between sense and ideas.

In the present stage of the human mind, poetry and other forms of fiction may certainly be regarded as a good. But we can also imagine the existence of an age in which a severer conception of truth has either banished or transformed them. At any rate we must admit that they hold a different place at different periods of the world's history. In the infancy of mankind, poetry, with the exception of proverbs, is the whole of literature, and the only instrument of intellectual culture; in modern times she is the shadow or echo of her former self, and appears to have a precarious existence. Milton in his day doubted whether an epic poem was any longer possible. At the same time we must remember, that what Plato would have called the charms of poetry have been partly transferred to prose; he himself (Statesman) admits rhetoric to be the handmaiden of Politics, and proposes to find in the strain of law (Laws) a substitute for the old poets. Among ourselves the creative power seems often to be growing weaker, and scientific fact to be more engrossing and overpowering to the mind than formerly. The illusion of the feelings commonly called love, has hitherto been the inspiring influence of modern poetry and romance, and has exercised a humanizing if not a strengthening influence on the world. But may not the stimulus which love has given to fancy be some day exhausted? The modern English novel which is the most popular of all forms of reading is not more than a century or two old: will the tale of love a hundred years hence, after so many thousand variations of the same theme, be still received with unabated interest?

Art cannot claim to be on a level with philosophy or religion, and may often corrupt them. It is possible to conceive a mental state in which all artistic representations are regarded as a false and imperfect expression, either of the religious ideal or of the philosophical ideal. The fairest forms may be revolting in certain moods of mind, as is proved by the fact that the Mahometans, and many sects of Christians, have renounced the use of pictures and images. The beginning of a great religion, whether Christian or Gentile, has not been 'wood or stone,' but a spirit moving in the hearts of men. The disciples have met in a large upper room or in 'holes and caves of the earth'; in the second or third generation, they have had mosques, temples, churches, monasteries. And the revival or reform of religions, like the first revelation of them, has come from within and has generally disregarded external ceremonies and accompaniments.

But poetry and art may also be the expression of the highest truth and the purest sentiment. Plato himself seems to waver between two opposite views – when, as in the third Book, he insists that youth should be brought up amid wholesome imagery; and again in Book X, when he banishes the poets from his Republic. Admitting that the arts, which some of us almost deify, have fallen short of their higher aim, we must admit on the other hand that to banish imagination wholly would be suicidal as well as impossible. For nature too is a form of art; and a breath of the fresh air or a single glance at the varying landscape would in an instant revive and reillumine the extinguished spark of poetry in the human breast. In the lower stages of civilization imagination more than reason distinguishes man from the animals; and to banish art would be to banish thought, to banish language, to banish the expression of all truth. No religion is wholly devoid of external forms; even the Mahometan who renounces the use of pictures and images has a temple in which he worships the Most High, as solemn and beautiful as any Greek or Christian building. Feeling too and thought are not really opposed; for he who thinks must feel before he can execute. And the highest thoughts, when they become familiarized to us, are always tending to pass into the form of feeling.

Plato does not seriously intend to expel poets from life and society. But he feels strongly the unreality of their writings; he is protesting against the degeneracy of poetry in his own day as we might protest against the want of serious purpose in modern fiction, against the unseemliness or extravagance of some of our poets or novelists, against the time-serving of preachers or public writers, against the regardlessness of truth which to the eye of the philosopher seems to characterize the greater part of the world. For we too have reason to complain that our poets and novelists 'paint inferior truth' and 'are concerned with the inferior part of the soul'; that the readers of them become what they read and are injuriously affected by them. And we look in vain for that healthy atmosphere of which Plato speaks, – 'the beauty which meets the sense like a breeze and imperceptibly draws the soul, even in childhood, into harmony with the beauty of reason.'

For there might be a poetry which would be the hymn of divine perfection, the harmony of goodness and truth among men: a strain which should renew the youth of the world, and bring back the ages in which the poet was man's only teacher and best friend, – which would find materials in the living present as well as in the romance of the past, and might subdue to the fairest forms of speech and verse the intractable materials of modern civilisation, – which might elicit the simple principles, or, as Plato would have called them, the essential forms, of truth and justice out of the variety of opinion and the complexity of modern society, – which would preserve all the good of each generation and leave the bad unsung, – which should be based not on vain longings or faint imaginings, but on a clear insight into the nature of man. Then the tale of love might begin again in poetry or prose, two in one, united in the pursuit of knowledge, or the service of God and man; and feelings of love might still be the incentive to great thoughts and heroic deeds as in the days of Dante or Petrarch; and many types of manly and womanly beauty might appear among us, rising above the ordinary level of humanity, and many lives which were like poems (Laws), be not only written, but lived by us. A few such strains have been heard among men in the tragedies of Aeschylus and Sophocles, whom Plato quotes, not, as Homer is quoted by him, in irony, but with deep and serious approval, – in the poetry of Milton and Wordsworth, and in passages of other English poets, – first and above all in the Hebrew prophets and psalmists. Shakespeare has taught us how great men should speak and act; he has drawn characters of a wonderful purity and depth; he has ennobled the human mind, but, like Homer (Rep.), he 'has left no way of life.' The next greatest poet of modern times, Goethe, is concerned with 'a lower degree of truth'; he paints the world as a stage on which 'all the men and women are merely players'; he cultivates life as an art, but he furnishes no ideals of truth and action. The poet may rebel against any attempt to set limits to his fancy; and he may argue truly that moralizing in verse is not poetry. Possibly, like Mephistopheles in Faust, he may retaliate on his adversaries. But the philosopher will still be justified in asking, 'How may the heavenly gift of poesy be devoted to the good of mankind?'

Returning to Plato, we may observe that a similar mixture of truth and error appears in other parts of the argument. He is aware of the absurdity of mankind framing their whole lives according to Homer; just as in the Phaedrus he intimates the absurdity of interpreting mythology upon rational principles; both these were the modern tendencies of his own age, which he deservedly ridicules. On the other hand, his argument that Homer, if he had been able to teach mankind anything worth knowing, would not have been allowed by them to go about begging as a rhapsodist, is both false and contrary to the spirit of Plato (Rep.). It may be compared with those other paradoxes of the Gorgias, that 'No statesman was ever unjustly put to death by the city of which he was the head'; and that 'No Sophist was ever defrauded by his pupils' (Gorg.)...

The argument for immortality seems to rest on the absolute dualism of soul and body. Admitting the existence of the soul, we know of no force which is able to put an end to her. Vice is her own proper evil; and if she cannot be destroyed by that, she cannot be destroyed by any other. Yet

Plato has acknowledged that the soul may be so overgrown by the incrustations of earth as to lose her original form; and in the Timaeus he recognizes more strongly than in the Republic the influence which the body has over the mind, denying even the voluntariness of human actions, on the ground that they proceed from physical states (Tim.). In the Republic, as elsewhere, he wavers between the original soul which has to be restored, and the character which is developed by training and education...

The vision of another world is ascribed to Er, the son of Armenius, who is said by Clement of Alexandria to have been Zoroaster. The tale has certainly an oriental character, and may be compared with the pilgrimages of the soul in the Zend Avesta (Haug, Avesta). But no trace of acquaintance with Zoroaster is found elsewhere in Plato's writings, and there is no reason for giving him the name of Er the Pamphylian. The philosophy of Heracleitus cannot be shown to be borrowed from Zoroaster, and still less the myths of Plato.

The local arrangement of the vision is less distinct than that of the Phaedrus and Phaedo. Astronomy is mingled with symbolism and mythology; the great sphere of heaven is represented under the symbol of a cylinder or box, containing the seven orbits of the planets and the fixed stars; this is suspended from an axis or spindle which turns on the knees of Necessity; the revolutions of the seven orbits contained in the cylinder are guided by the fates, and their harmonious motion produces the music of the spheres. Through the innermost or eighth of these, which is the moon, is passed the spindle; but it is doubtful whether this is the continuation of the column of light, from which the pilgrims contemplate the heavens; the words of Plato imply that they are connected, but not the same. The column itself is clearly not of adamant. The spindle (which is of adamant) is fastened to the ends of the chains which extend to the middle of the column of light – this column is said to hold together the heaven; but whether it hangs from the spindle, or is at right angles to it, is not explained. The cylinder containing the orbits of the stars is almost as much a symbol as the figure of Necessity turning the spindle; – for the outermost rim is the sphere of the fixed stars, and nothing is said about the intervals of space which divide the paths of the stars in the heavens. The description is both a picture and an orrery, and therefore is necessarily inconsistent with itself. The column of light is not the Milky Way – which is neither straight, nor like a rainbow – but the imaginary axis of the earth. This is compared to the rainbow in respect not of form but of colour, and not to the undergirders of a trireme, but to the straight rope running from prow to stern in which the undergirders meet.

The orrery or picture of the heavens given in the Republic differs in its mode of representation from the circles of the same and of the other in the Timaeus. In both the fixed stars are distinguished from the planets, and they move in orbits without them, although in an opposite direction: in the Republic as in the Timaeus they are all moving round the axis of the world. But we are not certain that in the former they are moving round the earth. No distinct mention is made in the Republic of the circles of the same and other; although both in the Timaeus and in the Republic the motion of the fixed stars is supposed to coincide with the motion of the whole. The relative thickness of the rims is perhaps designed to express the relative distances of the planets. Plato probably intended to represent the earth, from which Er and his companions are viewing the heavens, as stationary in place; but whether or not herself revolving, unless this is implied in the revolution of the axis, is uncertain (Timaeus). The spectator may be supposed to look at the heavenly bodies, either from above or below. The earth is a sort of earth and heaven in one, like the heaven of the Phaedrus, on the back of which the spectator goes out to take a peep at the stars and is borne round in the revolution. There is no distinction between the equator and the ecliptic. But Plato is no doubt led to imagine that the planets have an opposite motion to that of the fixed stars, in order to account for their appearances in the heavens. In the description of the meadow, and the retribution of the good and evil after death, there are traces of Homer.

The description of the axis as a spindle, and of the heavenly bodies as forming a whole, partly arises out of the attempt to connect the motions of the heavenly bodies with the mythological image of the web, or weaving of the Fates. The giving of the lots, the weaving of them, and the making of them irreversible, which are ascribed to the three Fates – Lachesis, Clotho, Atropos, are obviously derived from their names. The element of chance in human life is indicated by the order of the lots. But chance, however adverse, may be overcome by the wisdom of man, if he knows how to choose aright; there is a worse enemy to man than chance; this enemy is himself. He who was moderately fortunate in the number of the lot – even the very last comer – might have a good life if he chose with wisdom. And as Plato does not like to make an assertion which is unproven, he more than confirms this statement a few sentences afterwards by the example of Odysseus, who chose last. But the virtue which is founded on habit is not sufficient to enable a man to choose; he must add to virtue knowledge, if he is to act rightly when placed in new circumstances. The routine of good actions and good habits is an inferior sort of goodness; and, as Coleridge says, 'Common sense is intolerable which is not based on metaphysics,' so Plato would have said, 'Habit is worthless which is not based upon philosophy.'

The freedom of the will to refuse the evil and to choose the good is distinctly asserted. 'Virtue is free, and as a man honours or dishonours her he will have more or less of her.' The life of man is 'rounded' by necessity; there are circumstances prior to birth which affect him (Pol.). But within the walls of necessity there is an open space in which he is his own master, and can study for himself the effects which the variously compounded gifts of nature or fortune have upon the soul, and act accordingly. All men cannot have the first choice in everything. But the lot of all men is good enough, if they choose wisely and will live diligently.

The verisimilitude which is given to the pilgrimage of a thousand years, by the intimation that Ardiaeus had lived a thousand years before; the coincidence of Er coming to life on the twelfth day after he was supposed to have been dead with the seven days which the pilgrims passed in the meadow, and the four days during which they journeyed to the column of light; the precision with which the soul is mentioned who chose the twentieth lot; the passing remarks that there was no definite character among the souls, and that the souls which had chosen ill blamed any one rather than themselves; or that some of the souls drank more than was necessary of the waters of Forgetfulness, while Er himself was hindered from drinking; the desire of Odysseus to rest at last, unlike the conception of him in Dante and Tennyson; the feigned ignorance of how Er returned to the body, when the other souls went shooting like stars to their birth, – add greatly to the probability of the narrative. They are such touches of nature as the art of Defoe might have introduced when he wished to win credibility for marvels and apparitions.

*****

There still remain to be considered some points which have been intentionally reserved to the end: (1) the Janus-like character of the Republic, which presents two faces – one an Hellenic state, the other a kingdom of philosophers. Connected with the latter of the two aspects are (2) the paradoxes of the Republic, as they have been termed by Morgenstern: (a) the community of property; (b) of families; (c) the rule of philosophers; (d) the analogy of the individual and the State, which, like some other analogies in the Republic, is carried too far. We may then proceed to consider (3) the subject of education as conceived by Plato, bringing together in a general view the education of youth and the education of after-life; (4) we may note further some essential differences between ancient and modern politics which are suggested by the Republic; (5) we may compare the Politicus and the Laws; (6) we may observe the influence exercised by Plato on his imitators; and (7) take occasion to consider the nature and value of political, and (8) of religious ideals.

1. Plato expressly says that he is intending to found an Hellenic State (Book V). Many of his regulations are characteristically Spartan; such as the prohibition of gold and silver, the common meals of the men, the military training of the youth, the gymnastic exercises of the women. The life of Sparta was the life of a camp (Laws), enforced even more rigidly in time of peace than in war; the citizens of Sparta, like Plato's, were forbidden to trade – they were to be soldiers and not shopkeepers. Nowhere else in Greece was the individual so completely subjected to the State; the time when he was to marry, the education of his children, the clothes which he was to wear, the food which he was to eat, were all prescribed by law. Some of the best enactments in the Republic, such as the reverence to be paid to parents and elders, and some of the worst, such as the exposure of deformed children, are borrowed from the practice of Sparta. The encouragement of friendships between men and youths, or of men with one another, as affording incentives to bravery, is also Spartan; in Sparta too a nearer approach was made than in any other Greek State to equality of the sexes, and to community of property; and while there was probably less of licentiousness in the sense of immorality, the tie of marriage was regarded more lightly than in the rest of Greece. The 'suprema lex' was the preservation of the family, and the interest of the State. The coarse strength of a military government was not favourable to purity and refinement; and the excessive strictness of some regulations seems to have produced a reaction. Of all Hellenes the Spartans were most accessible to bribery; several of the greatest of them might be described in the words of Plato as having a 'fierce secret longing after gold and silver.' Though not in the strict sense communists, the principle of communism was maintained among them in their division of lands, in their common meals, in their slaves, and in the free use of one another's goods. Marriage was a public institution: and the women were educated by the State, and sang and danced in public with the men.

Many traditions were preserved at Sparta of the severity with which the magistrates had maintained the primitive rule of music and poetry; as in the Republic of Plato, the new-fangled poet was to be expelled. Hymns to the Gods, which are the only kind of music admitted into the ideal State, were the only kind which was permitted at Sparta. The Spartans, though an unpoetical race, were nevertheless lovers of poetry; they had been stirred by the Elegiac strains of Tyrtaeus, they had crowded around Hippias to hear his recitals of Homer; but in this they resembled the citizens of the timocratic rather than of the ideal State. The council of elder men also corresponds to the Spartan gerousia; and the freedom with which they are permitted to judge about matters of detail agrees with what we are told of that institution. Once more, the military rule of not spoiling the dead or offering arms at the temples; the moderation in the pursuit of enemies; the importance attached to the physical well-being of the citizens; the use of warfare for the sake of defence rather than of aggression – are features probably suggested by the spirit and practice of Sparta.

To the Spartan type the ideal State reverts in the first decline; and the character of the individual timocrat is borrowed from the Spartan citizen. The love of Lacedaemon not only affected Plato and Xenophon, but was shared by many undistinguished Athenians; there they seemed to find a principle which was wanting in their own democracy. The (Greek) of the Spartans attracted them, that is to say, not the goodness of their laws, but the spirit of order and loyalty which prevailed. Fascinated by the idea, citizens of Athens would imitate the Lacedaemonians in their dress and manners; they were known to the contemporaries of Plato as 'the persons who had their ears bruised,' like the Roundheads of the Commonwealth. The love of another church or country when seen at a distance only, the longing for an imaginary simplicity in civilized times, the fond desire of a past which never has been, or of a future which never will be, – these are aspirations of the human mind which are often felt among ourselves. Such feelings meet with a response in the Republic of Plato.

But there are other features of the Platonic Republic, as, for example, the literary and philosophical education, and the grace and beauty of life, which are the reverse of Spartan. Plato wishes to give his citizens a taste of Athenian freedom as well as of Lacedaemonian discipline. His individual genius is purely Athenian, although in theory he is a lover of Sparta; and he is something more than either – he has also a true Hellenic feeling. He is desirous of humanizing the wars of Hellenes against one another; he acknowledges that the Delphian God is the grand hereditary interpreter of all Hellas. The spirit of harmony and the Dorian mode are to prevail, and the whole State is to have an external beauty which is the reflex of the harmony within. But he has not yet found out the truth which he afterwards enunciated in the Laws – that he was a better legislator who made men to be of one mind, than he who trained them for war. The citizens, as in other Hellenic States, democratic as well as aristocratic, are really an upper class; for, although no mention is made of slaves, the lower classes are allowed to fade away into the distance, and are represented in the individual by the passions. Plato has no idea either of a social State in which all classes are harmonized, or of a federation of Hellas or the world in which different nations or States have a place. His city is equipped for war rather than for peace, and this would seem to be justified by the ordinary condition of Hellenic States. The myth of the earth-born men is an embodiment of the orthodox tradition of Hellas, and the allusion to the four ages of the world is also sanctioned by the authority of Hesiod and the poets. Thus we see that the Republic is partly founded on the ideal of the old Greek polis, partly on the actual circumstances of Hellas in that age. Plato, like the old painters, retains the traditional form, and like them he has also a vision of a city in the clouds.

There is yet another thread which is interwoven in the texture of the work; for the Republic is not only a Dorian State, but a Pythagorean league. The 'way of life' which was connected with the name of Pythagoras, like the Catholic monastic orders, showed the power which the mind of an individual might exercise over his contemporaries, and may have naturally suggested to Plato the possibility of reviving such 'mediaeval institutions.' The Pythagoreans, like Plato, enforced a rule of life and a moral and intellectual training. The influence ascribed to music, which to us seems exaggerated, is also a Pythagorean feature; it is not to be regarded as representing the real influence of music in the Greek world. More nearly than any other government of Hellas, the Pythagorean league of three hundred was an aristocracy of virtue. For once in the history of mankind the philosophy of order or (Greek), expressing and consequently enlisting on its side the combined endeavours of the better part of the people, obtained the management of public affairs and held possession of it for a considerable time (until about B.C. 500). Probably only in States prepared by Dorian institutions would such a league have been possible. The rulers, like Plato's (Greek), were required to submit to a severe training in order to prepare the way for the education of the other members of the community. Long after the dissolution of the Order, eminent Pythagoreans, such as Archytas of Tarentum, retained their political influence over the cities of

Magna Graecia. There was much here that was suggestive to the kindred spirit of Plato, who had doubtless meditated deeply on the 'way of life of Pythagoras' (Rep.) and his followers. Slight traces of Pythagoreanism are to be found in the mystical number of the State, in the number which expresses the interval between the king and the tyrant, in the doctrine of transmigration, in the music of the spheres, as well as in the great though secondary importance ascribed to mathematics in education.

 But as in his philosophy, so also in the form of his State, he goes far beyond the old Pythagoreans. He attempts a task really impossible, which is to unite the past of Greek history with the future of philosophy, analogous to that other impossibility, which has often been the dream of Christendom, the attempt to unite the past history of Europe with the kingdom of Christ. Nothing actually existing in the world at all resembles Plato's ideal State; nor does he himself imagine that such a State is possible. This he repeats again and again; e.g. in the Republic, or in the Laws where, casting a glance back on the Republic, he admits that the perfect state of communism and philosophy was impossible in his own age, though still to be retained as a pattern. The same doubt is implied in the earnestness with which he argues in the Republic that ideals are none the worse because they cannot be realized in fact, and in the chorus of laughter, which like a breaking wave will, as he anticipates, greet the mention of his proposals; though like other writers of fiction, he uses all his art to give reality to his inventions. When asked how the ideal polity can come into being, he answers ironically, 'When one son of a king becomes a philosopher'; he designates the fiction of the earth-born men as 'a noble lie'; and when the structure is finally complete, he fairly tells you that his Republic is a vision only, which in some sense may have reality, but not in the vulgar one of a reign of philosophers upon earth. It has been said that Plato flies as well as walks, but this falls short of the truth; for he flies and walks at the same time, and is in the air and on firm ground in successive instants.

 Niebuhr has asked a trifling question, which may be briefly noticed in this place – Was Plato a good citizen? If by this is meant, Was he loyal to Athenian institutions? – he can hardly be said to be the friend of democracy: but neither is he the friend of any other existing form of government; all of them he regarded as 'states of faction' (Laws); none attained to his ideal of a voluntary rule over voluntary subjects, which seems indeed more nearly to describe democracy than any other; and the worst of them is tyranny. The truth is, that the question has hardly any meaning when applied to a great philosopher whose writings are not meant for a particular age and country, but for all time and all mankind. The decline of Athenian politics was probably the motive which led Plato to frame an ideal State, and the Republic may be regarded as reflecting the departing glory of Hellas. As well might we complain of St. Augustine, whose great work 'The City of God' originated in a similar motive, for not being loyal to the Roman Empire. Even a nearer parallel might be afforded by the first Christians, who cannot fairly be charged with being bad citizens because, though 'subject to the higher powers,' they were looking forward to a city which is in heaven.

2. The idea of the perfect State is full of paradox when judged of according to the ordinary notions of mankind. The paradoxes of one age have been said to become the commonplaces of the next; but the paradoxes of Plato are at least as paradoxical to us as they were to his contemporaries. The modern world has either sneered at them as absurd, or denounced them as unnatural and immoral; men have been pleased to find in Aristotle's criticisms of them the anticipation of their own good sense. The wealthy and cultivated classes have disliked and also dreaded them; they have pointed with satisfaction to the failure of efforts to realize them in practice. Yet since they are the thoughts of one of the greatest of human intelligences, and of one who had done most to elevate morality and religion, they seem to deserve a better treatment at our hands. We may have to address the public, as Plato does poetry, and assure them that we mean no harm to existing institutions. There are serious errors which have a side of truth and which therefore may fairly demand a careful consideration: there are truths mixed with error of which we may indeed say, 'The half is better than the whole.' Yet 'the half' may be an important contribution to the study of human nature.

(a) The first paradox is the community of goods, which is mentioned slightly at the end of the third Book, and seemingly, as Aristotle observes, is confined to the guardians; at least no mention is made of the other classes. But the omission is not of any real significance, and probably arises out of the plan of the work, which prevents the writer from entering into details.

Aristotle censures the community of property much in the spirit of modern political economy, as tending to repress industry, and as doing away with the spirit of benevolence. Modern writers almost refuse to consider the subject, which is supposed to have been long ago settled by the common opinion of mankind. But it must be remembered that the sacredness of property is a notion far more fixed in modern than in ancient times. The world has grown older, and is therefore more conservative. Primitive society offered many examples of land held in common, either by a tribe or by a township, and such may probably have been the original form of landed tenure. Ancient legislators had invented various modes of dividing and preserving the divisions of land among the citizens; according to Aristotle there were nations who held the land in common and divided the produce, and there were others who divided the land and stored the produce in common. The evils of debt and the inequality of property were far greater in ancient than in modern times, and the accidents to which property was subject from war, or revolution, or taxation, or other legislative interference, were also greater. All these circumstances gave property a less fixed and sacred character. The early Christians are believed to have held their property in common, and the principle is sanctioned by the words of Christ himself, and has been maintained as a counsel of perfection in almost all ages of the Church. Nor have there been wanting instances of modern enthusiasts who have made a religion of communism; in every age of religious excitement notions like Wycliffe's 'inheritance of grace' have tended to prevail. A like spirit, but fiercer and more violent, has appeared in politics. 'The preparation of the Gospel of peace' soon becomes the red flag of Republicanism.

We can hardly judge what effect Plato's views would have upon his own contemporaries; they would perhaps have seemed to them only an exaggeration of the Spartan commonwealth. Even modern writers would acknowledge that the right of private property is based on expediency, and may be interfered with in a variety of ways for the public good. Any other mode of vesting property which was found to be more advantageous, would in time acquire the same basis of right; 'the most useful,' in Plato's words, 'would be the most sacred.' The lawyers and ecclesiastics of former ages would have spoken of property as a sacred institution. But they only meant by such language to oppose the greatest amount of resistance to any invasion of the rights of individuals and of the Church.

When we consider the question, without any fear of immediate application to practice, in the spirit of Plato's Republic, are we quite sure that the received notions of property are the best? Is the distribution of wealth which is customary in civilized countries the most favourable that can be conceived for the education and development of the mass of mankind? Can 'the spectator of all time and all existence' be quite convinced that one or two thousand years hence, great changes will not have taken place in the rights of property, or even that the very notion of property, beyond what is necessary for personal maintenance, may not have disappeared? This was a distinction familiar to Aristotle, though likely to be laughed at among ourselves. Such a change would not be greater than some other changes through which the world has passed in the transition from ancient to modern society, for example, the emancipation of the serfs in Russia, or the abolition of slavery in America and the West Indies; and not so great as the difference which separates the Eastern village community from the Western world. To accomplish such a revolution in the course of a few centuries, would imply a rate of progress not more rapid than has actually taken place during the last fifty or sixty years. The kingdom of Japan underwent more change in five or six years than Europe in five or six hundred. Many opinions and beliefs which have been cherished among ourselves quite as strongly as the sacredness of property have passed away; and the most untenable propositions respecting the right of bequests or entail have been maintained with as much fervour as the most moderate. Some one will be heard to ask whether a state of society can be final in which the interests of thousands are perilled on the life or character of a single person. And many will indulge the hope that our present condition may, after all, be only transitional, and may conduct to a higher, in which property, besides ministering to the enjoyment of the few, may also furnish the means of the highest culture to all, and will be a greater benefit to the public generally, and also more under the control of public authority. There may come a time when the saying, 'Have I not a right to do what I will with my own?' will appear to be a barbarous relic of individualism; – when the possession of a part may be a greater blessing to each and all than the possession of the whole is now to any one.

Such reflections appear visionary to the eye of the practical statesman, but they are within the range of possibility to the philosopher. He can imagine that in some distant age or clime, and through the influence of some individual, the notion of common property may or might have sunk as deep into the heart of a race, and have become as fixed to them, as private property is to ourselves. He knows that this latter institution is not more than four or five thousand years old: may not the end revert to the beginning? In our own age even Utopias affect the spirit of legislation, and an abstract idea may exercise a great influence on practical politics.

The objections that would be generally urged against Plato's community of property, are the old ones of Aristotle, that motives for exertion would be taken away, and that disputes would arise when each was dependent upon all. Every man would produce as little and consume as much as he liked. The experience of civilized nations has hitherto been adverse to Socialism. The effort is too great for human nature; men try to live in common, but the personal feeling is always breaking in. On the other hand it may be doubted whether our present notions of property are not conventional, for they differ in different countries and in different states of society. We boast of an individualism which is not freedom, but rather an artificial result of the industrial state of modern Europe. The individual is nominally free, but he is also powerless in a world bound hand and foot in the chains of economic necessity. Even if we cannot expect the mass of mankind to become disinterested, at any rate we observe in them a power of organization which fifty years ago would never have been suspected. The same forces which have revolutionized the political system of Europe, may effect a similar change in the social and industrial relations of mankind. And if we suppose the influence of some good as well as neutral motives working in the community, there will be no absurdity in expecting that the mass of mankind having power, and becoming enlightened about the higher possibilities of human life, when they learn how much more is attainable for all than is at present the possession of a favoured few, may pursue the common interest with an intelligence and persistency which mankind have hitherto never seen.

Now that the world has once been set in motion, and is no longer held fast under the tyranny of custom and ignorance; now that criticism has pierced the veil of tradition and the past no longer overpowers the present, – the progress of civilization may be expected to be far greater and swifter than heretofore. Even at our present rate of speed the point at which we may arrive in two or three generations is beyond the power of imagination to foresee. There are forces in the world which work, not in an arithmetical, but in a geometrical ratio of increase. Education, to use the expression of Plato, moves like a wheel with an ever-multiplying rapidity. Nor can we say how great may be its influence, when it becomes universal, – when it has been inherited by many generations, – when it is freed from the trammels of superstition and rightly adapted to the wants and capacities of different classes of men and women. Neither do we know how much more the co-operation of minds or of hands may be capable of accomplishing, whether in labour or in study. The resources of the natural sciences are not half-developed as yet; the soil of the earth, instead of growing more barren, may become many times more fertile than hitherto; the uses of machinery far greater, and also more minute than at present. New secrets of physiology may be revealed, deeply affecting human nature in its innermost recesses.

The standard of health may be raised and the lives of men prolonged by sanitary and medical knowledge. There may be peace, there may be leisure, there may be innocent refreshments of many kinds. The ever-increasing power of locomotion may join the extremes of earth. There may be mysterious workings of the human mind, such as occur only at great crises of history. The East and the West may meet together, and all nations may contribute their thoughts and their experience to the common stock of humanity. Many other elements enter into a speculation of this kind. But it is better to make an end of them. For such reflections appear to the majority far-fetched, and to men of science, commonplace.

(b) Neither to the mind of Plato nor of Aristotle did the doctrine of community of property present at all the same difficulty, or appear to be the same violation of the common Hellenic sentiment, as the community of wives and children. This paradox he prefaces by another proposal, that the occupations of men and women shall be the same, and that to this end they shall have a common training and education. Male and female animals have the same pursuits – why not also the two sexes of man?

But have we not here fallen into a contradiction? for we were saying that different natures should have different pursuits. How then can men and women have the same? And is not the proposal inconsistent with our notion of the division of labour? – These objections are no sooner raised than answered; for, according to Plato, there is no organic difference between men and women, but only the accidental one that men beget and women bear children. Following the analogy of the other animals, he contends that all natural gifts are scattered about indifferently among both sexes, though there may be a superiority of degree on the part of the men. The objection on the score of decency to their taking part in the same gymnastic exercises, is met by Plato's assertion that the existing feeling is a matter of habit.

That Plato should have emancipated himself from the ideas of his own country and from the example of the East, shows a wonderful independence of mind. He is conscious that women are half the human race, in some respects the more important half (Laws); and for the sake both of men and women he desires to raise the woman to a higher level of existence. He brings, not sentiment, but philosophy to bear upon a question which both in ancient and modern times has been chiefly regarded in the light of custom or feeling. The Greeks had noble conceptions of womanhood in the goddesses Athene and Artemis, and in the heroines Antigone and Andromache. But these ideals had no counterpart in actual life. The Athenian woman was in no way the equal of her husband; she was not the entertainer of his guests or the mistress of his house, but only his housekeeper and the mother of his children. She took no part in military or political matters; nor is there any instance in the later ages of Greece of a woman becoming famous in literature. 'Hers is the greatest glory who has the least renown among men,' is the historian's conception of feminine excellence. A very different ideal of womanhood is held up by Plato to the world; she is to be the companion of the man, and to share with him in the toils of war and in the cares of government. She is to be similarly trained both in bodily and mental exercises. She is to lose as far as possible the incidents of maternity and the characteristics of the female sex.

The modern antagonist of the equality of the sexes would argue that the differences between men and women are not confined to the single point urged by Plato; that sensibility, gentleness, grace, are the qualities of women, while energy, strength, higher intelligence, are to be looked for in men. And the criticism is just: the differences affect the whole nature, and are not, as Plato supposes, confined to a single point. But neither can we say how far these differences are due to education and the opinions of mankind, or physically inherited from the habits and opinions of former generations. Women have been always taught, not exactly that they are slaves, but that they are in an inferior position, which is also supposed to have compensating advantages; and to this position they have conformed. It is also true that the physical form may easily change in the course of generations through the mode of life; and the weakness or delicacy, which was once a matter of opinion, may become a physical fact. The characteristics of sex vary greatly in different countries and ranks of society, and at different ages in the same individuals. Plato may have been right in denying that there was any ultimate difference in the sexes of man other than that which exists in animals, because all other differences may be conceived to disappear in other states of society, or under different circumstances of life and training.

The first wave having been passed, we proceed to the second – community of wives and children. 'Is it possible? Is it desirable?' For as Glaucon intimates, and as we far more strongly insist, 'Great doubts may be entertained about both these points.' Any free discussion of the question is impossible, and mankind are perhaps right in not allowing the ultimate bases of social life to be examined. Few of us can safely enquire into the things which nature hides, any more than we can dissect our own bodies. Still, the manner in which Plato arrived at his conclusions should be considered. For here, as Mr. Grote has remarked, is a wonderful thing, that one of the wisest and best of men should have entertained ideas of morality which are wholly at variance with our own. And if we would do Plato justice, we must examine carefully the character of his proposals. First, we may observe that the relations of the sexes supposed by him are the reverse of licentious: he seems rather to aim at an impossible strictness. Secondly, he conceives the family to be the natural enemy of the state; and he entertains the serious hope that an universal brotherhood may take the place of private interests – an aspiration which, although not justified by experience, has possessed many noble minds. On the other hand, there is no sentiment or imagination in the connections which men and women are supposed by him to form; human beings return to the level of the animals, neither exalting to heaven, nor yet abusing the natural instincts. All that world of poetry and fancy which the passion of love has called forth in modern literature and romance would have been banished by Plato. The arrangements of marriage in the Republic are directed to one object – the improvement of the race. In successive generations a great development both of bodily and mental qualities might be possible. The analogy of animals tends to show that mankind can within certain limits receive a change of nature. And as in animals we should commonly choose the best for breeding, and destroy the others, so there must be a selection made of the human beings whose lives are worthy to be preserved.

We start back horrified from this Platonic ideal, in the belief, first, that the higher feelings of humanity are far too strong to be crushed out; secondly, that if the plan could be carried into execution we should be poorly recompensed by improvements in the breed for the loss of the best things in life. The greatest regard for the weakest and meanest of human beings – the infant, the criminal, the insane, the idiot, truly seems to us one of the noblest results of Christianity. We have learned, though as yet imperfectly, that the individual man has an endless value in the sight of God, and that we honour Him when we honour the darkened and disfigured image of Him (Laws). This is the lesson which Christ taught in a parable when He said, 'Their angels do always behold the face of My Father which is in heaven.' Such lessons are only partially realized in any age; they were foreign to the age of Plato, as they have very different degrees of strength in different countries or ages of the Christian world. To the Greek the family was a religious and customary institution binding the members together by a tie inferior in strength to that of friendship, and having a less solemn and sacred sound than that of country. The relationship which existed on the lower level of custom, Plato imagined that he was raising to the higher level of nature and reason; while from the modern and Christian point of view we regard him as sanctioning murder and destroying the first principles of morality.

The great error in these and similar speculations is that the difference between man and the animals is forgotten in them. The human being is regarded with the eye of a dog- or bird-fancier, or at best of a slave-owner; the higher or human qualities are left out. The breeder of animals aims chiefly at size or speed or strength; in a few cases at courage or temper; most often the fitness of the animal for food is the great desideratum. But mankind are not bred to be eaten, nor yet for their superiority in fighting or in running or in drawing carts. Neither does the improvement of the human race consist merely in the increase of the bones and flesh, but in the growth and enlightenment of the mind. Hence there must be 'a marriage of true minds' as well as of bodies, of imagination and reason as well as of lusts and instincts. Men and women without feeling or imagination are justly called brutes; yet Plato takes away these qualities and puts nothing in their place, not even the desire of a noble offspring, since parents are not to know their own children. The most important transaction of social life, he who is the idealist philosopher converts into the most brutal. For the pair are to have no relation to one another, except at the hymeneal festival; their children are not theirs, but the state's; nor is any tie of affection to unite them. Yet here the analogy of the animals might have saved Plato from a gigantic error, if he had 'not lost sight of his own illustration.' For the 'nobler sort of birds and beasts' nourish and protect their offspring and are faithful to one another.

An eminent physiologist thinks it worth while 'to try and place life on a physical basis.' But should not life rest on the moral rather than upon the physical? The higher comes first, then the lower, first the human and rational, afterwards the animal. Yet they are not absolutely divided; and in times of sickness or moments of self-indulgence they seem to be only different aspects of a common human nature which includes them both. Neither is the moral the limit of the physical, but the expansion and enlargement of it, – the highest form which the physical is capable of receiving. As Plato would say, the body does not take care of the body, and still less of the mind, but the mind takes care of both. In all human action not that which is common to man and the animals is the characteristic element, but that which distinguishes him from them. Even if we admit the physical basis, and resolve all virtue into health of body 'la facon que notre sang circule,' still on merely physical grounds we must come back to ideas. Mind and reason and duty and conscience, under these or other names, are always reappearing. There cannot be health of body without health of mind; nor health of mind without the sense of duty and the love of truth (Charm).

That the greatest of ancient philosophers should in his regulations about marriage have fallen into the error of separating body and mind, does indeed appear surprising. Yet the wonder is not so much that Plato should have entertained ideas of morality which to our own age are revolting, but that he should have contradicted himself to an extent which is hardly credible, falling in an instant from the heaven of idealism into the crudest animalism. Rejoicing in the newly found gift of reflection, he appears to have thought out a subject about which he had better have followed the enlightened feeling of his own age. The general sentiment of Hellas was opposed to his monstrous fancy. The old poets, and in later time the tragedians, showed no want of respect for the family, on which much of their religion was based. But the example of Sparta, and perhaps in some degree the tendency to defy public opinion, seems to have misled him. He will make one family out of all the families of the state. He will select the finest specimens of men and women and breed from these only.

Yet because the illusion is always returning (for the animal part of human nature will from time to time assert itself in the disguise of philosophy as well as of poetry), and also because any departure from established morality, even where this is not intended, is apt to be unsettling, it may be worth while to draw out a little more at length the objections to the Platonic marriage. In the first place, history shows that wherever polygamy has been largely allowed the race has deteriorated. One man to one woman is the law of God and nature. Nearly all the civilized peoples of the world at some period before the age of written records, have become monogamists; and the step when once taken has never been retraced. The exceptions occurring among Brahmins or Mahometans or the ancient Persians, are of that sort which may be said to prove the rule. The connexions formed between superior and inferior races hardly ever produce a noble offspring, because they are licentious; and because the children in such cases usually despise the mother and are neglected by the father who is ashamed of them. Barbarous nations when they are introduced by Europeans to vice die out; polygamist peoples either import and adopt children from other countries, or dwindle in numbers, or both. Dynasties and aristocracies which have disregarded the laws of nature have decreased in numbers and degenerated in stature; 'mariages de convenance' leave their enfeebling stamp on the offspring of them (King Lear). The marriage of near relations, or the marrying in and in of the same family tends constantly to weakness or idiocy in the children, sometimes assuming the form as they grow older of passionate licentiousness. The common prostitute rarely has any offspring. By such unmistakable evidence is the authority of morality asserted in the relations of the sexes: and so many more elements enter into this 'mystery' than are dreamed of by Plato and some other philosophers.

 Recent enquirers have indeed arrived at the conclusion that among primitive tribes there existed a community of wives as of property, and that the captive taken by the spear was the only wife or slave whom any man was permitted to call his own. The partial existence of such customs among some of the lower races of man, and the survival of peculiar ceremonies in the marriages of some civilized nations, are thought to furnish a proof of similar institutions having been once universal. There can be no question that the study of anthropology has considerably changed our views respecting the first appearance of man upon the earth. We know more about the aborigines of the world than formerly, but our increasing knowledge shows above all things how little we know. With all the helps which written monuments afford, we do but faintly realize the condition of man two thousand or three thousand years ago. Of what his condition was when removed to a distance 200,000 or 300,000 years, when the majority of mankind were lower and nearer the animals than any tribe now existing upon the earth, we cannot even entertain conjecture. Plato (Laws) and Aristotle (Metaph.) may have been more right than we imagine in supposing that some forms of civilisation were discovered and lost several times over. If we cannot argue that all barbarism is a degraded civilization, neither can we set any limits to the depth of degradation to which the human race may sink through war, disease, or isolation. And if we are to draw inferences about the origin of marriage from the practice of barbarous nations, we should also consider the remoter analogy of the animals. Many birds and animals, especially the carnivorous, have only one mate, and the love and care of offspring which seems to be natural is inconsistent with the primitive theory of marriage. If we go back to an imaginary state in which men were almost animals and the companions of them, we have as much right to argue from what is animal to what is human as from the barbarous to the civilized man. The record of animal life on the globe is fragmentary, – the connecting links are wanting and cannot be supplied; the record of social life is still more fragmentary and precarious. Even if we admit that our first ancestors had no such institution as marriage, still the stages by which men passed from outer barbarism to the comparative civilization of China, Assyria, and Greece, or even of the ancient Germans, are wholly unknown to us.

Such speculations are apt to be unsettling, because they seem to show that an institution which was thought to be a revelation from heaven, is only the growth of history and experience. We ask what is the origin of marriage, and we are told that like the right of property, after many wars and contests, it has gradually arisen out of the selfishness of barbarians. We stand face to face with human nature in its primitive nakedness. We are compelled to accept, not the highest, but the lowest account of the origin of human society. But on the other hand we may truly say that every step in human progress has been in the same direction, and that in the course of ages the idea of marriage and of the family has been more and more defined and consecrated. The civilized East is immeasurably in advance of any savage tribes; the Greeks and Romans have improved upon the East; the Christian nations have been stricter in their views of the marriage relation than any of the ancients. In this as in so many other things, instead of looking back with regret to the past, we should look forward with hope to the future. We must consecrate that which we believe to be the most holy, and that 'which is the most holy will be the most useful.' There is more reason for maintaining the sacredness of the marriage tie, when we see the benefit of it, than when we only felt a vague religious horror about the violation of it. But in all times of transition, when established beliefs are being undermined, there is a danger that in the passage from the old to the new we may insensibly let go the moral principle, finding an excuse for listening to the voice of passion in the uncertainty of knowledge, or the fluctuations of opinion. And there are many persons in our own day who, enlightened by the study of anthropology, and fascinated by what is new and strange, some using the language of fear, others of hope, are inclined to believe that a time will come when through the self-assertion of women, or the rebellious spirit of children, by the analysis of human relations, or by the force of outward circumstances, the ties of family life may be broken or greatly relaxed. They point to societies in America and elsewhere which tend to show that the destruction of the family need not necessarily involve the overthrow of all morality. Wherever we may think of such speculations, we can hardly deny that they have been more rife in this generation than in any other; and whither they are tending, who can predict?

To the doubts and queries raised by these 'social reformers' respecting the relation of the sexes and the moral nature of man, there is a sufficient answer, if any is needed. The difference about them and us is really one of fact. They are speaking of man as they wish or fancy him to be, but we are speaking of him as he is. They isolate the animal part of his nature; we regard him as a creature having many sides, or aspects, moving between good and evil, striving to rise above himself and to become 'a little lower than the angels.' We also, to use a Platonic formula, are not ignorant of the dissatisfactions and incompatibilities of family life, of the meannesses of trade, of the flatteries of one class of society by another, of the impediments which the family throws in the way of lofty aims and aspirations. But we are conscious that there are evils and dangers in the background greater still, which are not appreciated, because they are either concealed or suppressed. What a condition of man would that be, in which human passions were controlled by no authority, divine or human, in which there was no shame or decency, no higher affection overcoming or sanctifying the natural instincts, but simply a rule of health! Is it for this that we are asked to throw away the civilization which is the growth of ages?

For strength and health are not the only qualities to be desired; there are the more important considerations of mind and character and soul. We know how human nature may be degraded; we do not know how by artificial means any improvement in the breed can be effected. The problem is a complex one, for if we go back only four steps (and these at least enter into the composition of a child), there are commonly thirty progenitors to be taken into account. Many curious facts, rarely admitting of proof, are told us respecting the inheritance of disease or character from a remote ancestor. We can trace the physical resemblances of parents and children in the same family –

'Sic oculos, sic ille manus, sic ora ferebat';

but scarcely less often the differences which distinguish children both from their parents and from one another. We are told of similar mental peculiarities running in families, and again of a tendency, as in the animals, to revert to a common or original stock. But we have a difficulty in distinguishing what is a true inheritance of genius or other qualities, and what is mere imitation or the result of similar circumstances. Great men and great women have rarely had great fathers and mothers. Nothing that we know of in the circumstances of their birth or lineage will explain their appearance. Of the English poets of the last and two preceding centuries scarcely a descendant remains, – none have ever been distinguished. So deeply has nature hidden her secret, and so ridiculous is the fancy which has been entertained by some that we might in time by suitable marriage arrangements or, as Plato would have said, 'by an ingenious system of lots,' produce a Shakespeare or a Milton. Even supposing that we could breed men having the tenacity of bulldogs, or, like the Spartans, 'lacking the wit to run away in battle,' would the world be any the better? Many of the noblest specimens of the human race have been among the weakest physically. Tyrtaeus or Aesop, or our own Newton, would have been exposed at Sparta; and some of the fairest and strongest men and women have been among the wickedest and worst. Not by the Platonic device of uniting the strong and fair with the strong and fair, regardless of sentiment and morality, nor yet by his other device of combining dissimilar natures (Statesman), have mankind gradually passed from the brutality and licentiousness of primitive marriage to marriage Christian and civilized.

Few persons would deny that we bring into the world an inheritance of mental and physical qualities derived first from our parents, or through them from some remoter ancestor, secondly from our race, thirdly from the general condition of mankind into which we are born. Nothing is commoner than the remark, that 'So and so is like his father or his uncle'; and an aged person may not unfrequently note a resemblance in a youth to a long-forgotten ancestor, observing that 'Nature sometimes skips a generation.' It may be true also, that if we knew more about our ancestors, these similarities would be even more striking to us. Admitting the facts which are thus described in a popular way, we may however remark that there is no method of difference by which they can be defined or estimated, and that they constitute only a small part of each individual. The doctrine of heredity may seem to take out of our hands the conduct of our own lives, but it is the idea, not the fact, which is really terrible to us. For what we have received from our ancestors is only a fraction of what we are, or may become. The knowledge that drunkenness or insanity has been prevalent in a family may be the best safeguard against their recurrence in a future generation. The parent will be most awake to the vices or diseases in his child of which he is most sensible within himself. The whole of life may be directed to their prevention or cure. The traces of consumption may become fainter, or be wholly effaced: the inherent tendency to vice or crime may be eradicated. And so heredity, from being a curse, may become a blessing. We acknowledge that in the matter of our birth, as in our nature generally, there are previous circumstances which affect us. But upon this platform of circumstances or within this wall of necessity, we have still the power of creating a life for ourselves by the informing energy of the human will.

There is another aspect of the marriage question to which Plato is a stranger. All the children born in his state are foundlings. It never occurred to him that the greater part of them, according to universal experience, would have perished. For children can only be brought up in families. There is a subtle sympathy between the mother and the child which cannot be supplied by other mothers, or by 'strong nurses one or more' (Laws). If Plato's 'pen' was as fatal as the Creches of Paris, or the foundling hospital of Dublin, more than nine-tenths of his children would have perished. There would have been no need to expose or put out of the way the weaklier children, for they would have died of themselves. So emphatically does nature protest against the destruction of the family.

What Plato had heard or seen of Sparta was applied by him in a mistaken way to his ideal commonwealth. He probably observed that both the Spartan men and women were superior in form and strength to the other Greeks; and this superiority he was disposed to attribute to the laws and customs relating to marriage. He did not consider that the desire of a noble offspring was a passion among the Spartans, or that their physical superiority was to be attributed chiefly, not to their marriage customs, but to their temperance and training. He did not reflect that Sparta was great, not in consequence of the relaxation of morality, but in spite of it, by virtue of a political principle stronger far than existed in any other Grecian state. Least of all did he observe that Sparta did not really produce the finest specimens of the Greek race. The genius, the political inspiration of Athens, the love of liberty – all that has made Greece famous with posterity, were wanting among the Spartans. They had no Themistocles, or Pericles, or Aeschylus, or Sophocles, or Socrates, or Plato. The individual was not allowed to appear above the state; the laws were fixed, and he had no business to alter or reform them. Yet whence has the progress of cities and nations arisen, if not from remarkable individuals, coming into the world we know not how, and from causes over which we have no control? Something too much may have been said in modern times of the value of individuality. But we can hardly condemn too strongly a system which, instead of fostering the scattered seeds or sparks of genius and character, tends to smother and extinguish them.

Still, while condemning Plato, we must acknowledge that neither Christianity, nor any other form of religion and society, has hitherto been able to cope with this most difficult of social problems, and that the side from which Plato regarded it is that from which we turn away. Population is the most untameable force in the political and social world. Do we not find, especially in large cities, that the greatest hindrance to the amelioration of the poor is their improvidence in marriage? – a small fault truly, if not involving endless consequences. There are whole countries too, such as India, or, nearer home, Ireland, in which a right solution of the marriage question seems to lie at the foundation of the happiness of the community. There are too many people on a given space, or they marry too early and bring into the world a sickly and half-developed offspring; or owing to the very conditions of their existence, they become emaciated and hand on a similar life to their descendants. But who can oppose the voice of prudence to the 'mightiest passions of mankind' (Laws), especially when they have been licensed by custom and religion? In addition to the influences of education, we seem to require some new principles of right and wrong in these matters, some force of opinion, which may indeed be already heard whispering in private, but has never affected the moral sentiments of mankind in general. We unavoidably lose sight of the principle of utility, just in that action of our lives in which we have the most need of it. The influences which we can bring to bear upon this question are chiefly indirect. In a generation or two, education, emigration, improvements in agriculture and manufactures, may have provided the solution. The state physician hardly likes to probe the wound: it is beyond his art; a matter which he cannot safely let alone, but which he dare not touch:

'We do but skin and film the ulcerous place.'

When again in private life we see a whole family one by one dropping into the grave under the Ate of some inherited malady, and the parents perhaps surviving them, do our minds ever go back silently to that day twenty-five or thirty years before on which under the fairest auspices, amid the rejoicings of friends and acquaintances, a bride and bridegroom joined hands with one another? In making such a reflection we are not opposing physical considerations to moral, but moral to physical; we are seeking to make the voice of reason heard, which drives us back from the extravagance of sentimentalism on common sense. The late Dr. Combe is said by his biographer to have resisted the temptation to marriage, because he knew that he was subject to hereditary consumption. One who deserved to be called a man of genius, a friend of my youth, was in the habit of wearing a black ribbon on his wrist, in order to remind him that, being liable to outbreaks of insanity, he must not give way to the natural impulses of affection: he died unmarried in a lunatic asylum. These two little facts suggest the reflection that a very few persons have done from a sense of duty what the rest of mankind ought to have done under like circumstances, if they had allowed themselves to think of all the misery which they were about to bring into the world. If we could prevent such marriages without any violation of feeling or propriety, we clearly ought; and the prohibition in the course of time would be protected by a 'horror naturalis' similar to that which, in all civilized ages and countries, has prevented the marriage of near relations by blood. Mankind would have been the happier, if some things which are now allowed had from the beginning been denied to them; if the sanction of religion could have prohibited practices inimical to health; if sanitary principles could in early ages have been invested with a superstitious awe. But, living as we do far on in the world's history, we are no longer able to stamp at once with the impress of religion a new prohibition. A free agent cannot have his fancies regulated by law; and the execution of the law would be rendered impossible, owing to the uncertainty of the cases in which marriage was to be forbidden. Who can weigh virtue, or even fortune against health, or moral and mental qualities against bodily? Who can measure probabilities against certainties? There has been some good as well as evil in the discipline of suffering; and there are diseases, such as consumption, which have exercised a refining and softening influence on the character. Youth is too inexperienced to balance such nice considerations; parents do not often think of them, or think of them too late. They are at a distance and may probably be averted; change of place, a new state of life, the interests of a home may be the cure of them. So persons vainly reason when their minds are already made up and their fortunes irrevocably linked together. Nor is there any ground for supposing that marriages are to any great extent influenced by reflections of this sort, which seem unable to make any head against the irresistible impulse of individual attachment.

Lastly, no one can have observed the first rising flood of the passions in youth, the difficulty of regulating them, and the effects on the whole mind and nature which follow from them, the stimulus which is given to them by the imagination, without feeling that there is something unsatisfactory in our method of treating them. That the most important influence on human life should be wholly left to chance or shrouded in mystery, and instead of being disciplined or understood, should be required to conform only to an external standard of propriety – cannot be regarded by the philosopher as a safe or satisfactory condition of human things. And still those who have the charge of youth may find a way by watchfulness, by affection, by the manliness and innocence of their own lives, by occasional hints, by general admonitions which every one can apply for himself, to mitigate this terrible evil which eats out the heart of individuals and corrupts the moral sentiments of nations. In no duty towards others is there more need of reticence and self-restraint. So great is the danger lest he who would be the counsellor of another should reveal the secret prematurely, lest he should get another too much into his power; or fix the passing impression of evil by demanding the confession of it.

Nor is Plato wrong in asserting that family attachments may interfere with higher aims. If there have been some who 'to party gave up what was meant for mankind,' there have certainly been others who to family gave up what was meant for mankind or for their country. The cares of children, the necessity of procuring money for their support, the flatteries of the rich by the poor, the exclusiveness of caste, the pride of birth or wealth, the tendency of family life to divert men from the pursuit of the ideal or the heroic, are as lowering in our own age as in that of Plato. And if we prefer to look at the gentle influences of home, the development of the affections, the amenities of society, the devotion of one member of a family for the good of the others, which form one side of the picture, we must not quarrel with him, or perhaps ought rather to be grateful to him, for having presented to us the reverse. Without attempting to defend Plato on grounds of morality, we may allow that there is an aspect of the world which has not unnaturally led him into error.

We hardly appreciate the power which the idea of the State, like all other abstract ideas, exercised over the mind of Plato. To us the State seems to be built up out of the family, or sometimes to be the framework in which family and social life is contained. But to Plato in his present mood of mind the family is only a disturbing influence which, instead of filling up, tends to disarrange the higher unity of the State. No organization is needed except a political, which, regarded from another point of view, is a military one. The State is all-sufficing for the wants of man, and, like the idea of the Church in later ages, absorbs all other desires and affections. In time of war the thousand citizens are to stand like a rampart impregnable against the world or the Persian host; in time of peace the preparation for war and their duties to the State, which are also their duties to one another, take up their whole life and time. The only other interest which is allowed to them besides that of war, is the interest of philosophy. When they are too old to be soldiers they are to retire from active life and to have a second novitiate of study and contemplation. There is an element of monasticism even in Plato's communism. If he could have done without children, he might have converted his Republic into a religious order. Neither in the Laws, when the daylight of common sense breaks in upon him, does he retract his error. In the state of which he would be the founder, there is no marrying or giving in marriage: but because of the infirmity of mankind, he condescends to allow the law of nature to prevail.

(c) But Plato has an equal, or, in his own estimation, even greater paradox in reserve, which is summed up in the famous text, 'Until kings are philosophers or philosophers are kings, cities will never cease from ill.' And by philosophers he explains himself to mean those who are capable of apprehending ideas, especially the idea of good. To the attainment of this higher knowledge the second education is directed. Through a process of training which has already made them good citizens they are now to be made good legislators. We find with some surprise (not unlike the feeling which Aristotle in a well-known passage describes the hearers of Plato's lectures as experiencing, when they went to a discourse on the idea of good, expecting to be instructed in moral truths, and received instead of them arithmetical and mathematical formulae) that Plato does not propose for his future legislators any study of finance or law or military tactics, but only of abstract mathematics, as a preparation for the still more abstract conception of good. We ask, with Aristotle, What is the use of a man knowing the idea of good, if he does not know what is good for this individual, this state, this condition of society? We cannot understand how Plato's legislators or guardians are to be fitted for their work of statesmen by the study of the five mathematical sciences. We vainly search in Plato's own writings for any explanation of this seeming absurdity.

The discovery of a great metaphysical conception seems to ravish the mind with a prophetic consciousness which takes away the power of estimating its value. No metaphysical enquirer has ever fairly criticised his own speculations; in his own judgment they have been above criticism; nor has he understood that what to him seemed to be absolute truth may reappear in the next generation as a form of logic or an instrument of thought. And posterity have also sometimes equally misapprehended the real value of his speculations. They appear to them to have contributed nothing to the stock of human knowledge. The IDEA of good is apt to be regarded by the modern thinker as an unmeaning abstraction; but he forgets that this abstraction is waiting ready for use, and will hereafter be filled up by the divisions of knowledge. When mankind do not as yet know that the world is subject to law, the introduction of the mere conception of law or design or final cause, and the far-off anticipation of the harmony of knowledge, are great steps onward. Even the crude generalization of the unity of all things leads men to view the world with different eyes, and may easily affect their conception of human life and of politics, and also their own conduct and character (Tim). We can imagine how a great mind like that of Pericles might derive elevation from his intercourse with Anaxagoras (Phaedr.). To be struggling towards a higher but unattainable conception is a more favourable intellectual condition than to rest satisfied in a narrow portion of ascertained fact. And the earlier, which have sometimes been the greater ideas of science, are often lost sight of at a later period. How rarely can we say of any modern enquirer in the magnificent language of Plato, that 'He is the spectator of all time and of all existence!'

Nor is there anything unnatural in the hasty application of these vast metaphysical conceptions to practical and political life. In the first enthusiasm of ideas men are apt to see them everywhere, and to apply them in the most remote sphere. They do not understand that the experience of ages is required to enable them to fill up 'the intermediate axioms.' Plato himself seems to have imagined that the truths of psychology, like those of astronomy and harmonics, would be arrived at by a process of deduction, and that the method which he has pursued in the Fourth Book, of inferring them from experience and the use of language, was imperfect and only provisional. But when, after having arrived at the idea of good, which is the end of the science of dialectic, he is asked, What is the nature, and what are the divisions of the science? He refuses to answer, as if intending by the refusal to intimate that the state of knowledge which then existed was not such as would allow the philosopher to enter into his final rest. The previous sciences must first be studied, and will, we may add, continue to be studied tell the end of time, although in a sense different from any which Plato could have conceived. But we may observe, that while he is aware of the vacancy of his own ideal, he is full of enthusiasm in the contemplation of it. Looking into the orb of light, he sees nothing, but he is warmed and elevated. The Hebrew prophet believed that faith in God would enable him to govern the world; the Greek philosopher imagined that contemplation of the good would make a legislator. There is as much to be filled up in the one case as in the other, and the one mode of conception is to the Israelite what the other is to the Greek. Both find a repose in a divine perfection, which, whether in a more personal or impersonal form, exists without them and independently of them, as well as within them.

There is no mention of the idea of good in the Timaeus, nor of the divine Creator of the world in the Republic; and we are naturally led to ask in what relation they stand to one another. Is God above or below the idea of good? Or is the Idea of Good another mode of conceiving God? The latter appears to be the truer answer. To the Greek philosopher the perfection and unity of God was a far higher conception than his personality, which he hardly found a word to express, and which to him would have seemed to be borrowed from mythology. To the Christian, on the other hand, or to the modern thinker in general, it is difficult, if not impossible, to attach reality to what he terms mere abstraction; while to Plato this very abstraction is the truest and most real of all things. Hence, from a difference in forms of thought, Plato appears to be resting on a creation of his own mind only. But if we may be allowed to paraphrase the idea of good by the words 'intelligent principle of law and order in the universe, embracing equally man and nature,' we begin to find a meeting-point between him and ourselves.

The question whether the ruler or statesman should be a philosopher is one that has not lost interest in modern times. In most countries of Europe and Asia there has been some one in the course of ages who has truly united the power of command with the power of thought and reflection, as there have been also many false combinations of these qualities. Some kind of speculative power is necessary both in practical and political life; like the rhetorician in the Phaedrus, men require to have a conception of the varieties of human character, and to be raised on great occasions above the commonplaces of ordinary life. Yet the idea of the philosopher-statesman has never been popular with the mass of mankind; partly because he cannot take the world into his confidence or make them understand the motives from which he acts; and also because they are jealous of a power which they do not understand. The revolution which human nature desires to effect step by step in many ages is likely to be precipitated by him in a single year or life. They are afraid that in the pursuit of his greater aims he may disregard the common feelings of humanity, he is too apt to be looking into the distant future or back into the remote past, and unable to see actions or events which, to use an expression of Plato's 'are tumbling out at his feet.' Besides, as Plato would say, there are other corruptions of these philosophical statesmen. Either 'the native hue of resolution is sicklied o'er with the pale cast of thought,' and at the moment when action above all things is required he is undecided, or general principles are enunciated by him in order to cover some change of policy; or his ignorance of the world has made him more easily fall a prey to the arts of others; or in some cases he has been converted into a courtier, who enjoys the luxury of holding liberal opinions, but was never known to perform a liberal action. No wonder that mankind have been in the habit of calling statesmen of this class pedants, sophisters, doctrinaires, visionaries. For, as we may be allowed to say, a little parodying the words of Plato, 'they have seen bad imitations of the philosopher-statesman.' But a man in whom the power of thought and action are perfectly balanced, equal to the present, reaching forward to the future, 'such a one,' ruling in a constitutional state, 'they have never seen.'

But as the philosopher is apt to fail in the routine of political life, so the ordinary statesman is also apt to fail in extraordinary crises. When the face of the world is beginning to alter, and thunder is heard in the distance, he is still guided by his old maxims, and is the slave of his inveterate party prejudices; he cannot perceive the signs of the times; instead of looking forward he looks back; he learns nothing and forgets nothing; with 'wise saws and modern instances' he would stem the rising tide of revolution. He lives more and more within the circle of his own party, as the world without him becomes stronger. This seems to be the reason why the old order of things makes so poor a figure when confronted with the new, why churches can never reform, why most political changes are made blindly and convulsively. The great crises in the history of nations have often been met by an ecclesiastical positiveness, and a more obstinate reassertion of principles which have lost their hold upon a nation. The fixed ideas of a reactionary statesman may be compared to madness; they grow upon him, and he becomes possessed by them; no judgement of others is ever admitted by him to be weighed in the balance against his own.

(d) Plato, labouring under what, to modern readers, appears to have been a confusion of ideas, assimilates the state to the individual, and fails to distinguish Ethics from Politics. He thinks that to be most of a state which is most like one man, and in which the citizens have the greatest uniformity of character. He does not see that the analogy is partly fallacious, and that the will or character of a state or nation is really the balance or rather the surplus of individual wills, which are limited by the condition of having to act in common. The movement of a body of men can never have the pliancy or facility of a single man; the freedom of the individual, which is always limited, becomes still more straitened when transferred to a nation. The powers of action and feeling are necessarily weaker and more balanced when they are diffused through a community; whence arises the often discussed question, 'Can a nation, like an individual, have a conscience?'

We hesitate to say that the characters of nations are nothing more than the sum of the characters of the individuals who compose them; because there may be tendencies in individuals which react upon one another. A whole nation may be wiser than any one man in it; or may be animated by some common opinion or feeling which could not equally have affected the mind of a single person, or may have been inspired by a leader of genius to perform acts more than human. Plato does not appear to have analysed the complications which arise out of the collective action of mankind. Neither is he capable of seeing that analogies, though specious as arguments, may often have no foundation in fact, or of distinguishing between what is intelligible or vividly present to the mind, and what is true. In this respect he is far below Aristotle, who is comparatively seldom imposed upon by false analogies. He cannot disentangle the arts from the virtues – at least he is always arguing from one to the other. His notion of music is transferred from harmony of sounds to harmony of life: in this he is assisted by the ambiguities of language as well as by the prevalence of Pythagorean notions. And having once assimilated the state to the individual, he imagines that he will find the succession of states paralleled in the lives of individuals.

Still, through this fallacious medium, a real enlargement of ideas is attained. When the virtues as yet presented no distinct conception to the mind, a great advance was made by the comparison of them with the arts; for virtue is partly art, and has an outward form as well as an inward principle. The harmony of music affords a lively image of the harmonies of the world and of human life, and may be regarded as a splendid illustration which was naturally mistaken for a real analogy. In the same way the identification of ethics with politics has a tendency to give definiteness to ethics, and also to elevate and ennoble men's notions of the aims of government and of the duties of citizens; for ethics from one point of view may be conceived as an idealized law and politics; and politics, as ethics reduced to the conditions of human society. There have been evils which have arisen out of the attempt to identify them, and this has led to the separation or antagonism of them, which has been introduced by modern political writers. But we may likewise feel that something has been lost in their separation, and that the ancient philosophers who estimated the moral and intellectual wellbeing of mankind first, and the wealth of nations and individuals second, may have a salutary influence on the speculations of modern times. Many political maxims originate in a reaction against an opposite error; and when the errors against which they were directed have passed away, they in turn become errors.

3. Plato's views of education are in several respects remarkable; like the rest of the Republic they are partly Greek and partly ideal, beginning with the ordinary curriculum of the Greek youth, and extending to after-life. Plato is the first writer who distinctly says that education is to comprehend the whole of life, and to be a preparation for another in which education begins again. This is the continuous thread which runs through the Republic, and which more than any other of his ideas admits of an application to modern life.

He has long given up the notion that virtue cannot be taught; and he is disposed to modify the thesis of the Protagoras, that the virtues are one and not many. He is not unwilling to admit the sensible world into his scheme of truth. Nor does he assert in the Republic the involuntariness of vice, which is maintained by him in the Timaeus, Sophist, and Laws (Protag., Apol., Gorg.). Nor do the so-called Platonic ideas recovered from a former state of existence affect his theory of mental improvement. Still we observe in him the remains of the old Socratic doctrine, that true knowledge must be elicited from within, and is to be sought for in ideas, not in particulars of sense. Education, as he says, will implant a principle of intelligence which is better than ten thousand eyes. The paradox that the virtues are one, and the kindred notion that all virtue is knowledge, are not entirely renounced; the first is seen in the supremacy given to justice over the rest; the second in the tendency to absorb the moral virtues in the intellectual, and to centre all goodness in the contemplation of the idea of good. The world of sense is still depreciated and identified with opinion, though admitted to be a shadow of the true. In the Republic he is evidently impressed with the conviction that vice arises chiefly from ignorance and may be cured by education; the multitude are hardly to be deemed responsible for what they do. A faint allusion to the doctrine of reminiscence occurs in the Tenth Book; but Plato's views of education have no more real connection with a previous state of existence than our own; he only proposes to elicit from the mind that which is there already. Education is represented by him, not as the filling of a vessel, but as the turning the eye of the soul towards the light.

He treats first of music or literature, which he divides into true and false, and then goes on to gymnastics; of infancy in the Republic he takes no notice, though in the Laws he gives sage counsels about the nursing of children and the management of the mothers, and would have an education which is even prior to birth. But in the Republic he begins with the age at which the child is capable of receiving ideas, and boldly asserts, in language which sounds paradoxical to modern ears, that he must be taught the false before he can learn the true. The modern and ancient philosophical world are not agreed about truth and falsehood; the one identifies truth almost exclusively with fact, the other with ideas. This is the difference between ourselves and Plato, which is, however, partly a difference of words. For we too should admit that a child must receive many lessons which he imperfectly understands; he must be taught some things in a figure only, some too which he can hardly be expected to believe when he grows older; but we should limit the use of fiction by the necessity of the case. Plato would draw the line differently; according to him the aim of early education is not truth as a matter of fact, but truth as a matter of principle; the child is to be taught first simple religious truths, and then simple moral truths, and insensibly to learn the lesson of good manners and good taste. He would make an entire reformation of the old mythology; like Xenophanes and Heracleitus he is sensible of the deep chasm which separates his own age from Homer and Hesiod, whom he quotes and invests with an imaginary authority, but only for his own purposes. The lusts and treacheries of the gods are to be banished; the terrors of the world below are to be dispelled; the misbehaviour of the Homeric heroes is not to be a model for youth. But there is another strain heard in Homer which may teach our youth endurance; and something may be learnt in medicine from the simple practice of the Homeric age. The principles on which religion is to be based are two only: first, that God is true; secondly, that he is good. Modern and Christian writers have often fallen short of these; they can hardly be said to have gone beyond them.

The young are to be brought up in happy surroundings, out of the way of sights or sounds which may hurt the character or vitiate the taste. They are to live in an atmosphere of health; the breeze is always to be wafting to them the impressions of truth and goodness. Could such an education be realized, or if our modern religious education could be bound up with truth and virtue and good manners and good taste, that would be the best hope of human improvement. Plato, like ourselves, is looking forward to changes in the moral and religious world, and is preparing for them. He recognizes the danger of unsettling young men's minds by sudden changes of laws and principles, by destroying the sacredness of one set of ideas when there is nothing else to take their place. He is afraid too of the influence of the drama, on the ground that it encourages false sentiment, and therefore he would not have his children taken to the theatre; he thinks that the effect on the spectators is bad, and on the actors still worse. His idea of education is that of harmonious growth, in which are insensibly learnt the lessons of temperance and endurance, and the body and mind develope in equal proportions. The first principle which runs through all art and nature is simplicity; this also is to be the rule of human life.

The second stage of education is gymnastic, which answers to the period of muscular growth and development. The simplicity which is enforced in music is extended to gymnastic; Plato is aware that the training of the body may be inconsistent with the training of the mind, and that bodily exercise may be easily overdone. Excessive training of the body is apt to give men a headache or to render them sleepy at a lecture on philosophy, and this they attribute not to the true cause, but to the nature of the subject. Two points are noticeable in Plato's treatment of gymnastic: – First, that the time of training is entirely separated from the time of literary education. He seems to have thought that two things of an opposite and different nature could not be learnt at the same time. Here we can hardly agree with him; and, if we may judge by experience, the effect of spending three years between the ages of fourteen and seventeen in mere bodily exercise would be far from improving to the intellect. Secondly, he affirms that music and gymnastic are not, as common opinion is apt to imagine, intended, the one for the cultivation of the mind and the other of the body, but that they are both equally designed for the improvement of the mind. The body, in his view, is the servant of the mind; the subjection of the lower to the higher is for the advantage of both. And doubtless the mind may exercise a very great and paramount influence over the body, if exerted not at particular moments and by fits and starts, but continuously, in making preparation for the whole of life. Other Greek writers saw the mischievous tendency of Spartan discipline (Arist. Pol; Thuc.). But only Plato recognized the fundamental error on which the practice was based.

The subject of gymnastic leads Plato to the sister subject of medicine, which he further illustrates by the parallel of law. The modern disbelief in medicine has led in this, as in some other departments of knowledge, to a demand for greater simplicity; physicians are becoming aware that they often make diseases 'greater and more complicated' by their treatment of them (Rep.). In two thousand years their art has made but slender progress; what they have gained in the analysis of the parts is in a great degree lost by their feebler conception of the human frame as a whole. They have attended more to the cure of diseases than to the conditions of health; and the improvements in medicine have been more than counterbalanced by the disuse of regular training. Until lately they have hardly thought of air and water, the importance of which was well understood by the ancients; as

Aristotle remarks, 'Air and water, being the elements which we most use, have the greatest effect upon health' (Polit.). For ages physicians have been under the dominion of prejudices which have only recently given way; and now there are as many opinions in medicine as in theology, and an equal degree of scepticism and some want of toleration about both. Plato has several good notions about medicine; according to him, 'the eye cannot be cured without the rest of the body, nor the body without the mind' (Charm.). No man of sense, he says in the Timaeus, would take physic; and we heartily sympathize with him in the Laws when he declares that 'the limbs of the rustic worn with toil will derive more benefit from warm baths than from the prescriptions of a not over wise doctor.' But we can hardly praise him when, in obedience to the authority of Homer, he depreciates diet, or approve of the inhuman spirit in which he would get rid of invalid and useless lives by leaving them to die. He does not seem to have considered that the 'bridle of Theages' might be accompanied by qualities which were of far more value to the State than the health or strength of the citizens; or that the duty of taking care of the helpless might be an important element of education in a State. The physician himself (this is a delicate and subtle observation) should not be a man in robust health; he should have, in modern phraseology, a nervous temperament; he should have experience of disease in his own person, in order that his powers of observation may be quickened in the case of others.

The perplexity of medicine is paralleled by the perplexity of law; in which, again, Plato would have men follow the golden rule of simplicity. Greater matters are to be determined by the legislator or by the oracle of Delphi, lesser matters are to be left to the temporary regulation of the citizens themselves. Plato is aware that laissez faire is an important element of government. The diseases of a State are like the heads of a hydra; they multiply when they are cut off. The true remedy for them is not extirpation but prevention. And the way to prevent them is to take care of education, and education will take care of all the rest. So in modern times men have often felt that the only political measure worth having – the only one which would produce any certain or lasting effect, was a measure of national education. And in our own more than in any previous age the necessity has been recognized of restoring the ever-increasing confusion of law to simplicity and common sense.

When the training in music and gymnastic is completed, there follows the first stage of active and public life. But soon education is to begin again from a new point of view. In the interval between the Fourth and Seventh

Books we have discussed the nature of knowledge, and have thence been led to form a higher conception of what was required of us. For true knowledge, according to Plato, is of abstractions, and has to do, not with particulars or individuals, but with universals only; not with the beauties of poetry, but with the ideas of philosophy. And the great aim of education is the cultivation of the habit of abstraction. This is to be acquired through the study of the mathematical sciences. They alone are capable of giving ideas of relation, and of arousing the dormant energies of thought.

Mathematics in the age of Plato comprehended a very small part of that which is now included in them; but they bore a much larger proportion to the sum of human knowledge. They were the only organon of thought which the human mind at that time possessed, and the only measure by which the chaos of particulars could be reduced to rule and order. The faculty which they trained was naturally at war with the poetical or imaginative; and hence to Plato, who is everywhere seeking for abstractions and trying to get rid of the illusions of sense, nearly the whole of education is contained in them. They seemed to have an inexhaustible application, partly because their true limits were not yet understood. These Plato himself is beginning to investigate; though not aware that number and figure are mere abstractions of sense, he recognizes that the forms used by geometry are borrowed from the sensible world. He seeks to find the ultimate ground of mathematical ideas in the idea of good, though he does not satisfactorily explain the connexion between them; and in his conception of the relation of ideas to numbers, he falls very far short of the definiteness attributed to him by Aristotle (Met.). But if he fails to recognize the true limits of mathematics, he also reaches a point beyond them; in his view, ideas of number become secondary to a higher conception of knowledge. The dialectician is as much above the mathematician as the mathematician is above the ordinary man. The one, the self-proving, the good which is the higher sphere of dialectic, is the perfect truth to which all things ascend, and in which they finally repose.

This self-proving unity or idea of good is a mere vision of which no distinct explanation can be given, relative only to a particular stage in Greek philosophy. It is an abstraction under which no individuals are comprehended, a whole which has no parts (Arist., Nic. Eth.). The vacancy of such a form was perceived by Aristotle, but not by Plato. Nor did he recognize that in the dialectical process are included two or more methods of investigation which are at variance with each other. He did not see that whether he took the longer or the shorter road, no advance could be made in this way. And yet such visions often have an immense effect; for although the method of science cannot anticipate science, the idea of science, not as it is, but as it will be in the future, is a great and inspiring principle. In the pursuit of knowledge we are always pressing forward to something beyond us; and as a false conception of knowledge, for example the scholastic philosophy, may lead men astray during many ages, so the true ideal, though vacant, may draw all their thoughts in a right direction. It makes a great difference whether the general expectation of knowledge, as this indefinite feeling may be termed, is based upon a sound judgment. For mankind may often entertain a true conception of what knowledge ought to be when they have but a slender experience of facts. The correlation of the sciences, the consciousness of the unity of nature, the idea of classification, the sense of proportion, the unwillingness to stop short of certainty or to confound probability with truth, are important principles of the higher education. Although Plato could tell us nothing, and perhaps knew that he could tell us nothing, of the absolute truth, he has exercised an influence on the human mind which even at the present day is not exhausted; and political and social questions may yet arise in which the thoughts of Plato may be read anew and receive a fresh meaning.

The Idea of good is so called only in the Republic, but there are traces of it in other dialogues of Plato. It is a cause as well as an idea, and from this point of view may be compared with the creator of the Timaeus, who out of his goodness created all things. It corresponds to a certain extent with the modern conception of a law of nature, or of a final cause, or of both in one, and in this regard may be connected with the measure and symmetry of the Philebus. It is represented in the Symposium under the aspect of beauty, and is supposed to be attained there by stages of initiation, as here by regular gradations of knowledge. Viewed subjectively, it is the process or science of dialectic. This is the science which, according to the Phaedrus, is the true basis of rhetoric, which alone is able to distinguish the natures and classes of men and things; which divides a whole into the natural parts, and reunites the scattered parts into a natural or organized whole; which defines the abstract essences or universal ideas of all things, and connects them; which pierces the veil of hypotheses and reaches the final cause or first principle of all; which regards the sciences in relation to the idea of good. This ideal science is the highest process of thought, and may be described as the soul conversing with herself or holding communion with eternal truth and beauty, and in another form is the everlasting question and answer – the ceaseless interrogative of Socrates. The dialogues of Plato are themselves examples of the nature and method of dialectic. Viewed objectively, the idea of good is a power or cause which makes the world without us correspond with the world within. Yet this world without us is still a world of ideas. With Plato the investigation of nature is another department of knowledge, and in this he seeks to attain only probable conclusions (Timaeus).

If we ask whether this science of dialectic which Plato only half explains to us is more akin to logic or to metaphysics, the answer is that in his mind the two sciences are not as yet distinguished, any more than the subjective and objective aspects of the world and of man, which German philosophy has revealed to us. Nor has he determined whether his science of dialectic is at rest or in motion, concerned with the contemplation of absolute being, or with a process of development and evolution. Modern metaphysics may be described as the science of abstractions, or as the science of the evolution of thought; modern logic, when passing beyond the bounds of mere Aristotelian forms, may be defined as the science of method. The germ of both of them is contained in the Platonic dialectic; all metaphysicians have something in common with the ideas of Plato; all logicians have derived something from the method of Plato. The nearest approach in modern philosophy to the universal science of Plato, is to be found in the Hegelian 'succession of moments in the unity of the idea.' Plato and Hegel alike seem to have conceived the world as the correlation of abstractions; and not impossibly they would have understood one another better than any of their commentators understand them (Swift's Voyage to Laputa. 'Having a desire to see those ancients who were most renowned for wit and learning, I set apart one day on purpose. I proposed that Homer and Aristotle might appear at the head of all their commentators; but these were so numerous that some hundreds were forced to attend in the court and outward rooms of the palace. I knew, and could distinguish these two heroes, at first sight, not only from the crowd, but from each other. Homer was the taller and comelier person of the two, walked very erect for one of his age, and his eyes were the most quick and piercing I ever beheld. Aristotle stooped much, and made use of a staff. His visage was meagre, his hair lank and thin, and his voice hollow. I soon discovered that both of them were perfect strangers to the rest of the company, and had never seen or heard of them before. And I had a whisper from a ghost, who shall be nameless, "That these commentators always kept in the most distant quarters from their principals, in the lower world, through a consciousness of shame and guilt, because they had so horribly misrepresented the meaning of these authors to posterity." I introduced Didymus and Eustathius to Homer, and prevailed on him to treat them better than perhaps they deserved, for he soon found they wanted a genius to enter into the spirit of a poet. But Aristotle was out of all patience with the account I gave him of Scotus and Ramus, as I presented them to him; and he asked them "whether the rest of the tribe were as great dunces as themselves?"'). There is, however, a difference between them: for whereas Hegel is thinking of all the minds of men as one mind, which developes the stages of the idea in different countries or at different times in the same country, with Plato these gradations are regarded only as an order of thought or ideas; the history of the human mind had not yet dawned upon him.

Many criticisms may be made on Plato's theory of education. While in some respects he unavoidably falls short of modern thinkers, in others he is in advance of them. He is opposed to the modes of education which prevailed in his own time; but he can hardly be said to have discovered new ones. He does not see that education is relative to the characters of individuals; he only desires to impress the same form of the state on the minds of all. He has no sufficient idea of the effect of literature on the formation of the mind, and greatly exaggerates that of mathematics. His aim is above all things to train the reasoning faculties; to implant in the mind the spirit and power of abstraction; to explain and define general notions, and, if possible, to connect them. No wonder that in the vacancy of actual knowledge his followers, and at times even he himself, should have fallen away from the doctrine of ideas, and have returned to that branch of knowledge in which alone the relation of the one and many can be truly seen – the science of number. In his views both of teaching and training he might be styled, in modern language, a doctrinaire; after the Spartan fashion he would have his citizens cast in one mould; he does not seem to consider that some degree of freedom, 'a little wholesome neglect,' is necessary to strengthen and develope the character and to give play to the individual nature. His citizens would not have acquired that knowledge which in the vision of Er is supposed to be gained by the pilgrims from their experience of evil.

On the other hand, Plato is far in advance of modern philosophers and theologians when he teaches that education is to be continued through life and will begin again in another. He would never allow education of some kind to cease; although he was aware that the proverbial saying of Solon, 'I grow old learning many things,' cannot be applied literally. Himself ravished with the contemplation of the idea of good, and delighting in solid geometry (Rep.), he has no difficulty in imagining that a lifetime might be passed happily in such pursuits. We who know how many more men of business there are in the world than real students or thinkers, are not equally sanguine. The education which he proposes for his citizens is really the ideal life of the philosopher or man of genius, interrupted, but only for a time, by practical duties, – a life not for the many, but for the few.

Yet the thought of Plato may not be wholly incapable of application to our own times. Even if regarded as an ideal which can never be realized, it may have a great effect in elevating the characters of mankind, and raising them above the routine of their ordinary occupation or profession. It is the best form under which we can conceive the whole of life. Nevertheless the idea of Plato is not easily put into practice. For the education of after life is necessarily the education which each one gives himself. Men and women cannot be brought together in schools or colleges at forty or fifty years of age; and if they could the result would be disappointing. The destination of most men is what Plato would call 'the Den' for the whole of life, and with that they are content. Neither have they teachers or advisers with whom they can take counsel in riper years. There is no 'schoolmaster abroad' who will tell them of their faults, or inspire them with the higher sense of duty, or with the ambition of a true success in life; no Socrates who will convict them of ignorance; no Christ, or follower of Christ, who will reprove them of sin. Hence they have a difficulty in receiving the first element of improvement, which is self-knowledge. The hopes of youth no longer stir them; they rather wish to rest than to pursue high objects. A few only who have come across great men and women, or eminent teachers of religion and morality, have received a second life from them, and have lighted a candle from the fire of their genius.

The want of energy is one of the main reasons why so few persons continue to improve in later years. They have not the will, and do not know the way. They 'never try an experiment,' or look up a point of interest for themselves; they make no sacrifices for the sake of knowledge; their minds, like their bodies, at a certain age become fixed. Genius has been defined as 'the power of taking pains'; but hardly any one keeps up his interest in knowledge throughout a whole life. The troubles of a family, the business of making money, the demands of a profession destroy the elasticity of the mind. The waxen tablet of the memory which was once capable of receiving 'true thoughts and clear impressions' becomes hard and crowded; there is not room for the accumulations of a long life (Theaet.). The student, as years advance, rather makes an exchange of knowledge than adds to his stores. There is no pressing necessity to learn; the stock of Classics or

History or Natural Science which was enough for a man at twenty-five is enough for him at fifty. Neither is it easy to give a definite answer to any one who asks how he is to improve. For self-education consists in a thousand things, commonplace in themselves, – in adding to what we are by nature something of what we are not; in learning to see ourselves as others see us; in judging, not by opinion, but by the evidence of facts; in seeking out the society of superior minds; in a study of lives and writings of great men; in observation of the world and character; in receiving kindly the natural influence of different times of life; in any act or thought which is raised above the practice or opinions of mankind; in the pursuit of some new or original enquiry; in any effort of mind which calls forth some latent power.

If any one is desirous of carrying out in detail the Platonic education of after-life, some such counsels as the following may be offered to him: – That he shall choose the branch of knowledge to which his own mind most distinctly inclines, and in which he takes the greatest delight, either one which seems to connect with his own daily employment, or, perhaps, furnishes the greatest contrast to it. He may study from the speculative side the profession or business in which he is practically engaged. He may make Homer, Dante, Shakespeare, Plato, Bacon the friends and companions of his life. He may find opportunities of hearing the living voice of a great teacher. He may select for enquiry some point of history or some unexplained phenomenon of nature. An hour a day passed in such scientific or literary pursuits will furnish as many facts as the memory can retain, and will give him 'a pleasure not to be repented of' (Timaeus). Only let him beware of being the slave of crotchets, or of running after a Will o' the Wisp in his ignorance, or in his vanity of attributing to himself the gifts of a poet or assuming the air of a philosopher. He should know the limits of his own powers. Better to build up the mind by slow additions, to creep on quietly from one thing to another, to gain insensibly new powers and new interests in knowledge, than to form vast schemes which are never destined to be realized. But perhaps, as Plato would say, 'This is part of another subject' (Tim.); though we may also defend our digression by his example (Theaet.).

4. We remark with surprise that the progress of nations or the natural growth of institutions which fill modern treatises on political philosophy seem hardly ever to have attracted the attention of Plato and Aristotle. The ancients were familiar with the mutability of human affairs; they could moralize over the ruins of cities and the fall of empires (Plato, Statesman,

and Sulpicius' Letter to Cicero); by them fate and chance were deemed to be real powers, almost persons, and to have had a great share in political events. The wiser of them like Thucydides believed that 'what had been would be again,' and that a tolerable idea of the future could be gathered from the past. Also they had dreams of a Golden Age which existed once upon a time and might still exist in some unknown land, or might return again in the remote future. But the regular growth of a state enlightened by experience, progressing in knowledge, improving in the arts, of which the citizens were educated by the fulfilment of political duties, appears never to have come within the range of their hopes and aspirations. Such a state had never been seen, and therefore could not be conceived by them. Their experience (Aristot. Metaph.; Plato, Laws) led them to conclude that there had been cycles of civilization in which the arts had been discovered and lost many times over, and cities had been overthrown and rebuilt again and again, and deluges and volcanoes and other natural convulsions had altered the face of the earth. Tradition told them of many destructions of mankind and of the preservation of a remnant. The world began again after a deluge and was reconstructed out of the fragments of itself. Also they were acquainted with empires of unknown antiquity, like the Egyptian or Assyrian; but they had never seen them grow, and could not imagine, any more than we can, the state of man which preceded them. They were puzzled and awestricken by the Egyptian monuments, of which the forms, as Plato says, not in a figure, but literally, were ten thousand years old (Laws), and they contrasted the antiquity of Egypt with their own short memories.

The early legends of Hellas have no real connection with the later history: they are at a distance, and the intermediate region is concealed from view; there is no road or path which leads from one to the other. At the beginning of Greek history, in the vestibule of the temple, is seen standing first of all the figure of the legislator, himself the interpreter and servant of the God. The fundamental laws which he gives are not supposed to change with time and circumstances. The salvation of the state is held rather to depend on the inviolable maintenance of them. They were sanctioned by the authority of heaven, and it was deemed impiety to alter them. The desire to maintain them unaltered seems to be the origin of what at first sight is very surprising to us – the intolerant zeal of Plato against innovators in religion or politics (Laws); although with a happy inconsistency he is also willing that the laws of other countries should be studied and improvements in legislation privately communicated to the Nocturnal Council (Laws). The additions which were made to them in later ages in order to meet the increasing complexity of affairs were still ascribed by a fiction to the original legislator; and the words of such enactments at Athens were disputed over as if they had been the words of Solon himself. Plato hopes to preserve in a later generation the mind of the legislator; he would have his citizens remain within the lines which he has laid down for them. He would not harass them with minute regulations, he would have allowed some changes in the laws: but not changes which would affect the fundamental institutions of the state, such for example as would convert an aristocracy into a timocracy, or a timocracy into a popular form of government.

Passing from speculations to facts, we observe that progress has been the exception rather than the law of human history. And therefore we are not surprised to find that the idea of progress is of modern rather than of ancient date; and, like the idea of a philosophy of history, is not more than a century or two old. It seems to have arisen out of the impression left on the human mind by the growth of the Roman Empire and of the Christian Church, and to be due to the political and social improvements which they introduced into the world; and still more in our own century to the idealism of the first French Revolution and the triumph of American Independence; and in a yet greater degree to the vast material prosperity and growth of population in England and her colonies and in America. It is also to be ascribed in a measure to the greater study of the philosophy of history. The optimist temperament of some great writers has assisted the creation of it, while the opposite character has led a few to regard the future of the world as dark. The 'spectator of all time and of all existence' sees more of 'the increasing purpose which through the ages ran' than formerly: but to the inhabitant of a small state of Hellas the vision was necessarily limited like the valley in which he dwelt. There was no remote past on which his eye could rest, nor any future from which the veil was partly lifted up by the analogy of history. The narrowness of view, which to ourselves appears so singular, was to him natural, if not unavoidable.

5. For the relation of the Republic to the Statesman and the Laws, and the two other works of Plato which directly treat of politics, see the Introductions to the two latter; a few general points of comparison may be touched upon in this place.

And first of the Laws.

(1) The Republic, though probably written at intervals, yet speaking generally and judging by the indications of thought and style, may be

reasonably ascribed to the middle period of Plato's life: the Laws are certainly the work of his declining years, and some portions of them at any rate seem to have been written in extreme old age.

(2) The Republic is full of hope and aspiration: the Laws bear the stamp of failure and disappointment. The one is a finished work which received the last touches of the author: the other is imperfectly executed, and apparently unfinished. The one has the grace and beauty of youth: the other has lost the poetical form, but has more of the severity and knowledge of life which is characteristic of old age.

(3) The most conspicuous defect of the Laws is the failure of dramatic power, whereas the Republic is full of striking contrasts of ideas and oppositions of character.

(4) The Laws may be said to have more the nature of a sermon, the Republic of a poem; the one is more religious, the other more intellectual.

(5) Many theories of Plato, such as the doctrine of ideas, the government of the world by philosophers, are not found in the Laws; the immortality of the soul is first mentioned in xii; the person of Socrates has altogether disappeared. The community of women and children is renounced; the institution of common or public meals for women (Laws) is for the first time introduced (Ar. Pol.).

(6) There remains in the Laws the old enmity to the poets, who are ironically saluted in high-flown terms, and, at the same time, are peremptorily ordered out of the city, if they are not willing to submit their poems to the censorship of the magistrates (Rep.).

(7) Though the work is in most respects inferior, there are a few passages in the Laws, such as the honour due to the soul, the evils of licentious or unnatural love, the whole of Book x. (religion), the dishonesty of retail trade, and bequests, which come more home to us, and contain more of what may be termed the modern element in Plato than almost anything in the Republic.

The relation of the two works to one another is very well given:

(1) by Aristotle in the Politics from the side of the Laws: –

'The same, or nearly the same, objections apply to Plato's later work, the Laws, and therefore we had better examine briefly the constitution which is therein described. In the Republic, Socrates has definitely settled in all a few questions only; such as the community of women and children, the community of property, and the constitution of the state. The population is divided into two classes – one of husbandmen, and the other of warriors; from this latter is taken a third class of counsellors and rulers of the state. But Socrates has not determined whether the husbandmen and artists are to have a share in the government, and whether they too are to carry arms and share in military service or not. He certainly thinks that the women ought to share in the education of the guardians, and to fight by their side. The remainder of the work is filled up with digressions foreign to the main subject, and with discussions about the education of the guardians. In the Laws there is hardly anything but laws; not much is said about the constitution. This, which he had intended to make more of the ordinary type, he gradually brings round to the other or ideal form. For with the exception of the community of women and property, he supposes everything to be the same in both states; there is to be the same education; the citizens of both are to live free from servile occupations, and there are to be common meals in both. The only difference is that in the Laws the common meals are extended to women, and the warriors number about 5000, but in the Republic only 1000.'

(2) by Plato in the Laws (Book v.), from the side of the Republic: –

'The first and highest form of the state and of the government and of the law is that in which there prevails most widely the ancient saying that "Friends have all things in common." Whether there is now, or ever will be, this communion of women and children and of property, in which the private and individual is altogether banished from life, and things which are by nature private, such as eyes and ears and hands, have become common, and all men express praise and blame, and feel joy and sorrow, on the same occasions, and the laws unite the city to the utmost, – whether all this is possible or not, I say that no man, acting upon any other principle, will ever constitute a state more exalted in virtue, or truer or better than this. Such a state, whether inhabited by Gods or sons of Gods, will make them blessed who dwell therein; and therefore to this we are to look for the pattern of the state, and to cling to this, and, as far as possible, to seek for one which is like this. The state which we have now in hand, when created, will be nearest to immortality and unity in the next degree; and after that, by the grace of God, we will complete the third one. And we will begin by speaking of the nature and origin of the second.'

The comparatively short work called the Statesman or Politicus in its style and manner is more akin to the Laws, while in its idealism it rather resembles the Republic. As far as we can judge by various indications of language and thought, it must be later than the one and of course earlier than the other. In both the Republic and Statesman a close connection is maintained between Politics and Dialectic. In the Statesman, enquiries into the principles of Method are interspersed with discussions about Politics. The comparative advantages of the rule of law and of a person are considered, and the decision given in favour of a person (Arist. Pol.). But much may be said on the other side, nor is the opposition necessary; for a person may rule by law, and law may be so applied as to be the living voice of the legislator. As in the Republic, there is a myth, describing, however, not a future, but a former existence of mankind. The question is asked, 'Whether the state of innocence which is described in the myth, or a state like our own which possesses art and science and distinguishes good from evil, is the preferable condition of man.' To this question of the comparative happiness of civilized and primitive life, which was so often discussed in the last century and in our own, no answer is given. The Statesman, though less perfect in style than the Republic and of far less range, may justly be regarded as one of the greatest of Plato's dialogues.

6. Others as well as Plato have chosen an ideal Republic to be the vehicle of thoughts which they could not definitely express, or which went beyond their own age. The classical writing which approaches most nearly to the Republic of Plato is the 'De Republica' of Cicero; but neither in this nor in any other of his dialogues does he rival the art of Plato. The manners are clumsy and inferior; the hand of the rhetorician is apparent at every turn. Yet noble sentiments are constantly recurring: the true note of Roman patriotism – 'We Romans are a great people' – resounds through the whole work. Like Socrates, Cicero turns away from the phenomena of the heavens to civil and political life. He would rather not discuss the 'two Suns' of which all Rome was talking, when he can converse about 'the two nations in one' which had divided Rome ever since the days of the Gracchi. Like Socrates again, speaking in the person of Scipio, he is afraid lest he should assume too much the character of a teacher, rather than of an equal who is discussing among friends the two sides of a question. He would confine the terms King or State to the rule of reason and justice, and he will not concede that title either to a democracy or to a monarchy. But under the rule of reason and justice he is willing to include the natural superior ruling over the natural inferior, which he compares to the soul ruling over the body. He prefers a mixture of forms of government to any single one. The

two portraits of the just and the unjust, which occur in the second book of the Republic, are transferred to the state – Philus, one of the interlocutors, maintaining against his will the necessity of injustice as a principle of government, while the other, Laelius, supports the opposite thesis. His views of language and number are derived from Plato; like him he denounces the drama. He also declares that if his life were to be twice as long he would have no time to read the lyric poets. The picture of democracy is translated by him word for word, though he had hardly shown himself able to 'carry the jest' of Plato. He converts into a stately sentence the humorous fancy about the animals, who 'are so imbued with the spirit of democracy that they make the passers-by get out of their way.' His description of the tyrant is imitated from Plato, but is far inferior. The second book is historical, and claims for the Roman constitution (which is to him the ideal) a foundation of fact such as Plato probably intended to have given to the Republic in the Critias. His most remarkable imitation of Plato is the adaptation of the vision of Er, which is converted by Cicero into the 'Somnium Scipionis'; he has 'romanized' the myth of the Republic, adding an argument for the immortality of the soul taken from the Phaedrus, and some other touches derived from the Phaedo and the Timaeus. Though a beautiful tale and containing splendid passages, the 'Somnium Scipionis; is very inferior to the vision of Er; it is only a dream, and hardly allows the reader to suppose that the writer believes in his own creation. Whether his dialogues were framed on the model of the lost dialogues of Aristotle, as he himself tells us, or of Plato, to which they bear many superficial resemblances, he is still the Roman orator; he is not conversing, but making speeches, and is never able to mould the intractable Latin to the grace and ease of the Greek Platonic dialogue. But if he is defective in form, much more is he inferior to the Greek in matter; he nowhere in his philosophical writings leaves upon our minds the impression of an original thinker.

Plato's Republic has been said to be a church and not a state; and such an ideal of a city in the heavens has always hovered over the Christian world, and is embodied in St. Augustine's 'De Civitate Dei,' which is suggested by the decay and fall of the Roman Empire, much in the same manner in which we may imagine the Republic of Plato to have been influenced by the decline of Greek politics in the writer's own age. The difference is that in the time of Plato the degeneracy, though certain, was gradual and insensible: whereas the taking of Rome by the Goths stirred like an earthquake the age of St. Augustine. Men were inclined to believe that the overthrow of the city was to be ascribed to the anger felt by the old Roman deities at the neglect of their worship. St. Augustine maintains the opposite thesis; he argues that the destruction of the Roman Empire is due, not to the rise of Christianity, but to the vices of Paganism. He wanders over Roman history, and over Greek philosophy and mythology, and finds everywhere crime, impiety and falsehood. He compares the worst parts of the Gentile religions with the best elements of the faith of Christ. He shows nothing of the spirit which led others of the early Christian Fathers to recognize in the writings of the Greek philosophers the power of the divine truth. He traces the parallel of the kingdom of God, that is, the history of the Jews, contained in their scriptures, and of the kingdoms of the world, which are found in gentile writers, and pursues them both into an ideal future. It need hardly be remarked that his use both of Greek and of Roman historians and of the sacred writings of the Jews is wholly uncritical. The heathen mythology, the Sybilline oracles, the myths of Plato, the dreams of Neo-Platonists are equally regarded by him as matter of fact. He must be acknowledged to be a strictly polemical or controversial writer who makes the best of everything on one side and the worst of everything on the other. He has no sympathy with the old Roman life as Plato has with Greek life, nor has he any idea of the ecclesiastical kingdom which was to arise out of the ruins of the Roman empire. He is not blind to the defects of the Christian Church, and looks forward to a time when Christian and Pagan shall be alike brought before the judgment-seat, and the true City of God shall appear...The work of St. Augustine is a curious repertory of antiquarian learning and quotations, deeply penetrated with Christian ethics, but showing little power of reasoning, and a slender knowledge of the Greek literature and language. He was a great genius, and a noble character, yet hardly capable of feeling or understanding anything external to his own theology. Of all the ancient philosophers he is most attracted by Plato, though he is very slightly acquainted with his writings. He is inclined to believe that the idea of creation in the Timaeus is derived from the narrative in Genesis; and he is strangely taken with the coincidence (?) of Plato's saying that 'the philosopher is the lover of God,' and the words of the Book of Exodus in which God reveals himself to Moses (Exod.) He dwells at length on miracles performed in his own day, of which the evidence is regarded by him as irresistible. He speaks in a very interesting manner of the beauty and utility of nature and of the human frame, which he conceives to afford a foretaste of the heavenly state and of the resurrection of the body. The book is not really what to most persons the title of it would imply, and belongs to an age which has passed away. But it contains many fine passages and thoughts which are for all time.

The short treatise de Monarchia of Dante is by far the most remarkable of mediaeval ideals, and bears the impress of the great genius in whom Italy and the Middle Ages are so vividly reflected. It is the vision of an Universal Empire, which is supposed to be the natural and necessary government of the world, having a divine authority distinct from the Papacy, yet coextensive with it. It is not 'the ghost of the dead Roman Empire sitting crowned upon the grave thereof,' but the legitimate heir and successor of it, justified by the ancient virtues of the Romans and the beneficence of their rule. Their right to be the governors of the world is also confirmed by the testimony of miracles, and acknowledged by St. Paul when he appealed to Caesar, and even more emphatically by Christ Himself, Who could not have made atonement for the sins of men if He had not been condemned by a divinely authorized tribunal. The necessity for the establishment of an Universal Empire is proved partly by a priori arguments such as the unity of God and the unity of the family or nation; partly by perversions of Scripture and history, by false analogies of nature, by misapplied quotations from the classics, and by odd scraps and commonplaces of logic, showing a familiar but by no means exact knowledge of Aristotle (of Plato there is none). But a more convincing argument still is the miserable state of the world, which he touchingly describes. He sees no hope of happiness or peace for mankind until all nations of the earth are comprehended in a single empire. The whole treatise shows how deeply the idea of the Roman Empire was fixed in the minds of his contemporaries. Not much argument was needed to maintain the truth of a theory which to his own contemporaries seemed so natural and congenial. He speaks, or rather preaches, from the point of view, not of the ecclesiastic, but of the layman, although, as a good Catholic, he is willing to acknowledge that in certain respects the Empire must submit to the Church. The beginning and end of all his noble reflections and of his arguments, good and bad, is the aspiration 'that in this little plot of earth belonging to mortal man life may pass in freedom and peace.' So inextricably is his vision of the future bound up with the beliefs and circumstances of his own age.

The 'Utopia' of Sir Thomas More is a surprising monument of his genius, and shows a reach of thought far beyond his contemporaries. The book was written by him at the age of about 34 or 35, and is full of the generous sentiments of youth. He brings the light of Plato to bear upon the miserable state of his own country. Living not long after the Wars of the Roses, and in the dregs of the Catholic Church in England, he is indignant at the corruption of the clergy, at the luxury of the nobility and gentry, at the sufferings of the poor, at the calamities caused by war. To the eye of More the whole world was in dissolution and decay; and side by side with the misery and oppression which he has described in the First Book of the Utopia, he places in the Second Book the ideal state which by the help of Plato he had constructed. The times were full of stir and intellectual interest. The distant murmur of the Reformation was beginning to be heard. To minds like More's, Greek literature was a revelation: there had arisen an art of interpretation, and the New Testament was beginning to be understood as it had never been before, and has not often been since, in its natural sense. The life there depicted appeared to him wholly unlike that of Christian commonwealths, in which 'he saw nothing but a certain conspiracy of rich men procuring their own commodities under the name and title of the Commonwealth.' He thought that Christ, like Plato, 'instituted all things common,' for which reason, he tells us, the citizens of Utopia were the more willing to receive his doctrines ('Howbeit, I think this was no small help and furtherance in the matter, that they heard us say that Christ instituted among his, all things common, and that the same community doth yet remain in the rightest Christian communities' (Utopia).). The community of property is a fixed idea with him, though he is aware of the arguments which may be urged on the other side ('These things (I say), when I consider with myself, I hold well with Plato, and do nothing marvel that he would make no laws for them that refused those laws, whereby all men should have and enjoy equal portions of riches and commodities. For the wise men did easily foresee this to be the one and only way to the wealth of a community, if equality of all things should be brought in and established' (Utopia).). We wonder how in the reign of Henry VIII, though veiled in another language and published in a foreign country, such speculations could have been endured.

He is gifted with far greater dramatic invention than any one who succeeded him, with the exception of Swift. In the art of feigning he is a worthy disciple of Plato. Like him, starting from a small portion of fact, he founds his tale with admirable skill on a few lines in the Latin narrative of the voyages of Amerigo Vespucci. He is very precise about dates and facts, and has the power of making us believe that the narrator of the tale must have been an eyewitness. We are fairly puzzled by his manner of mixing up real and imaginary persons; his boy John Clement and Peter Giles, citizen of Antwerp, with whom he disputes about the precise words which are supposed to have been used by the (imaginary) Portuguese traveller, Raphael Hythloday. 'I have the more cause,' says Hythloday, 'to fear that my words shall not be believed, for that I know how difficultly and hardly I myself would have believed another man telling the same, if I had not myself seen it with mine own eyes.' Or again: 'If you had been with me in Utopia, and had presently seen their fashions and laws as I did which lived there five years and more, and would never have come thence, but only to make the new land known here,' etc. More greatly regrets that he forgot to ask Hythloday in what part of the world Utopia is situated; he 'would have spent no small sum of money rather than it should have escaped him,' and he begs Peter Giles to see Hythloday or write to him and obtain an answer to the question. After this we are not surprised to hear that a Professor of Divinity (perhaps 'a late famous vicar of Croydon in Surrey,' as the translator thinks) is desirous of being sent thither as a missionary by the High Bishop, 'yea, and that he may himself be made Bishop of Utopia, nothing doubting that he must obtain this Bishopric with suit; and he counteth that a godly suit which proceedeth not of the desire of honour or lucre, but only of a godly zeal.' The design may have failed through the disappearance of Hythloday, concerning whom we have 'very uncertain news' after his departure. There is no doubt, however, that he had told More and Giles the exact situation of the island, but unfortunately at the same moment More's attention, as he is reminded in a letter from Giles, was drawn off by a servant, and one of the company from a cold caught on shipboard coughed so loud as to prevent Giles from hearing. And 'the secret has perished' with him; to this day the place of Utopia remains unknown.

 The words of Phaedrus, 'O Socrates, you can easily invent Egyptians or anything,' are recalled to our mind as we read this lifelike fiction. Yet the greater merit of the work is not the admirable art, but the originality of thought. More is as free as Plato from the prejudices of his age, and far more tolerant. The Utopians do not allow him who believes not in the immortality of the soul to share in the administration of the state (Laws), 'howbeit they put him to no punishment, because they be persuaded that it is in no man's power to believe what he list'; and 'no man is to be blamed for reasoning in support of his own religion ('One of our company in my presence was sharply punished. He, as soon as he was baptised, began, against our wills, with more earnest affection than wisdom, to reason of Christ's religion, and began to wax so hot in his matter, that he did not only prefer our religion before all other, but also did despise and condemn all other, calling them profane, and the followers of them wicked and devilish, and the children of everlasting damnation. When he had thus long reasoned the matter, they laid hold on him, accused him, and condemned him into exile, not as a despiser of religion, but as a seditious person and a raiser up of dissension among the people').' In the public services 'no prayers be used, but such as every man may boldly pronounce without giving offence to any sect.' He says significantly, 'There be that give worship to a man that was once of excellent virtue or of famous glory, not only as God, but also the chiefest and highest God. But the most and the wisest part, rejecting all these, believe that there is a certain godly power unknown, far above the capacity and reach of man's wit, dispersed throughout all the world, not in bigness, but in virtue and power. Him they call the Father of all. To Him alone they attribute the beginnings, the increasings, the proceedings, the changes, and the ends of all things. Neither give they any divine honours to any other than him.' So far was More from sharing the popular beliefs of his time. Yet at the end he reminds us that he does not in all respects agree with the customs and opinions of the Utopians which he describes. And we should let him have the benefit of this saving clause, and not rudely withdraw the veil behind which he has been pleased to conceal himself.

Nor is he less in advance of popular opinion in his political and moral speculations. He would like to bring military glory into contempt; he would set all sorts of idle people to profitable occupation, including in the same class, priests, women, noblemen, gentlemen, and 'sturdy and valiant beggars,' that the labour of all may be reduced to six hours a day. His dislike of capital punishment, and plans for the reformation of offenders; his detestation of priests and lawyers (Compare his satirical observation: 'They (the Utopians) have priests of exceeding holiness, and therefore very few.); his remark that 'although every one may hear of ravenous dogs and wolves and cruel man-eaters, it is not easy to find states that are well and wisely governed,' are curiously at variance with the notions of his age and indeed with his own life. There are many points in which he shows a modern feeling and a prophetic insight like Plato. He is a sanitary reformer; he maintains that civilized states have a right to the soil of waste countries; he is inclined to the opinion which places happiness in virtuous pleasures, but herein, as he thinks, not disagreeing from those other philosophers who define virtue to be a life according to nature. He extends the idea of happiness so as to include the happiness of others; and he argues ingeniously, 'All men agree that we ought to make others happy; but if others, how much more ourselves!' And still he thinks that there may be a more excellent way, but to this no man's reason can attain unless heaven should inspire him with a higher truth. His ceremonies before marriage; his humane proposal that war should be carried on by assassinating the leaders of the enemy, may be compared to some of the paradoxes of Plato. He has a charming fancy, like the affinities of Greeks and barbarians in the

Timaeus, that the Utopians learnt the language of the Greeks with the more readiness because they were originally of the same race with them. He is penetrated with the spirit of Plato, and quotes or adapts many thoughts both from the Republic and from the Timaeus. He prefers public duties to private, and is somewhat impatient of the importunity of relations. His citizens have no silver or gold of their own, but are ready enough to pay them to their mercenaries. There is nothing of which he is more contemptuous than the love of money. Gold is used for fetters of criminals, and diamonds and pearls for children's necklaces (When the ambassadors came arrayed in gold and peacocks' feathers 'to the eyes of all the Utopians except very few, which had been in other countries for some reasonable cause, all that gorgeousness of apparel seemed shameful and reproachful. In so much that they most reverently saluted the vilest and most abject of them for lords – passing over the ambassadors themselves without any honour, judging them by their wearing of golden chains to be bondmen. You should have seen children also, that had cast away their pearls and precious stones, when they saw the like sticking upon the ambassadors' caps, dig and push their mothers under the sides, saying thus to them – "Look, though he were a little child still." But the mother; yea and that also in good earnest: "Peace, son," saith she, "I think he be some of the ambassadors' fools."')

   Like Plato he is full of satirical reflections on governments and princes; on the state of the world and of knowledge. The hero of his discourse (Hythloday) is very unwilling to become a minister of state, considering that he would lose his independence and his advice would never be heeded (Compare an exquisite passage, of which the conclusion is as follows: 'And verily it is naturally given...suppressed and ended.') He ridicules the new logic of his time; the Utopians could never be made to understand the doctrine of Second Intentions ('For they have not devised one of all those rules of restrictions, amplifications, and suppositions, very wittily invented in the small Logicals, which here our children in every place do learn. Furthermore, they were never yet able to find out the second intentions; insomuch that none of them all could ever see man himself in common, as they call him, though he be (as you know) bigger than was ever any giant, yea, and pointed to of us even with our finger.') He is very severe on the sports of the gentry; the Utopians count 'hunting the lowest, the vilest, and the most abject part of butchery.' He quotes the words of the Republic in which the philosopher is described 'standing out of the way under a wall until the driving storm of sleet and rain be overpast,' which admit of a singular application to More's own fate; although, writing twenty years before (about the year 1514), he can hardly be supposed to have foreseen this. There is no touch of satire which strikes deeper than his quiet remark that the greater part of the precepts of Christ are more at variance with the lives of ordinary Christians than the discourse of Utopia ('And yet the most part of them is more dissident from the manners of the world now a days, than my communication was. But preachers, sly and wily men, following your counsel (as I suppose) because they saw men evil-willing to frame their manners to Christ's rule, they have wrested and wried his doctrine, and, like a rule of lead, have applied it to men's manners, that by some means at the least way, they might agree together.')

The 'New Atlantis' is only a fragment, and far inferior in merit to the 'Utopia.' The work is full of ingenuity, but wanting in creative fancy, and by no means impresses the reader with a sense of credibility. In some places Lord Bacon is characteristically different from Sir Thomas More, as, for example, in the external state which he attributes to the governor of Solomon's House, whose dress he minutely describes, while to Sir Thomas More such trappings appear simple ridiculous. Yet, after this programme of dress, Bacon adds the beautiful trait, 'that he had a look as though he pitied men.' Several things are borrowed by him from the Timaeus; but he has injured the unity of style by adding thoughts and passages which are taken from the Hebrew Scriptures.

The 'City of the Sun' written by Campanella (1568-1639), a Dominican friar, several years after the 'New Atlantis' of Bacon, has many resemblances to the Republic of Plato. The citizens have wives and children in common; their marriages are of the same temporary sort, and are arranged by the magistrates from time to time. They do not, however, adopt his system of lots, but bring together the best natures, male and female, 'according to philosophical rules.' The infants until two years of age are brought up by their mothers in public temples; and since individuals for the most part educate their children badly, at the beginning of their third year they are committed to the care of the State, and are taught at first, not out of books, but from paintings of all kinds, which are emblazoned on the walls of the city. The city has six interior circuits of walls, and an outer wall which is the seventh. On this outer wall are painted the figures of legislators and philosophers, and on each of the interior walls the symbols or forms of some one of the sciences are delineated. The women are, for the most part, trained, like the men, in warlike and other exercises; but they have two special occupations of their own. After a battle, they and the boys soothe and relieve the wounded warriors; also they encourage them with embraces and pleasant words. Some elements of the Christian or Catholic religion are preserved among them. The life of the Apostles is greatly admired by this people because they had all things in common; and the short prayer which Jesus Christ taught men is used in their worship. It is a duty of the chief magistrates to pardon sins, and therefore the whole people make secret confession of them to the magistrates, and they to their chief, who is a sort of Rector Metaphysicus; and by this means he is well informed of all that is going on in the minds of men. After confession, absolution is granted to the citizens collectively, but no one is mentioned by name. There also exists among them a practice of perpetual prayer, performed by a succession of priests, who change every hour. Their religion is a worship of God in Trinity, that is of Wisdom, Love and Power, but without any distinction of persons. They behold in the sun the reflection of His glory; mere graven images they reject, refusing to fall under the 'tyranny' of idolatry.

Many details are given about their customs of eating and drinking, about their mode of dressing, their employments, their wars. Campanella looks forward to a new mode of education, which is to be a study of nature, and not of Aristotle. He would not have his citizens waste their time in the consideration of what he calls 'the dead signs of things.' He remarks that he who knows one science only, does not really know that one any more than the rest, and insists strongly on the necessity of a variety of knowledge. More scholars are turned out in the City of the Sun in one year than by contemporary methods in ten or fifteen. He evidently believes, like Bacon, that henceforward natural science will play a great part in education, a hope which seems hardly to have been realized, either in our own or in any former age; at any rate the fulfilment of it has been long deferred.

There is a good deal of ingenuity and even originality in this work, and a most enlightened spirit pervades it. But it has little or no charm of style, and falls very far short of the 'New Atlantis' of Bacon, and still more of the 'Utopia' of Sir Thomas More. It is full of inconsistencies, and though borrowed from Plato, shows but a superficial acquaintance with his writings. It is a work such as one might expect to have been written by a philosopher and man of genius who was also a friar, and who had spent twenty-seven years of his life in a prison of the Inquisition. The most interesting feature of the book, common to Plato and Sir Thomas More, is the deep feeling which is shown by the writer, of the misery and ignorance prevailing among the lower classes in his own time. Campanella takes note of Aristotle's answer to Plato's community of property, that in a society where all things are common, no individual would have any motive to work (Arist. Pol.): he replies, that his citizens being happy and contented in themselves (they are required to work only four hours a day), will have greater regard for their fellows than exists among men at present. He thinks, like Plato, that if he abolishes private feelings and interests, a great public feeling will take their place.

Other writings on ideal states, such as the 'Oceana' of Harrington, in which the Lord Archon, meaning Cromwell, is described, not as he was, but as he ought to have been; or the 'Argenis' of Barclay, which is an historical allegory of his own time, are too unlike Plato to be worth mentioning. More interesting than either of these, and far more Platonic in style and thought, is Sir John Eliot's 'Monarchy of Man,' in which the prisoner of the Tower, no longer able 'to be a politician in the land of his birth,' turns away from politics to view 'that other city which is within him,' and finds on the very threshold of the grave that the secret of human happiness is the mastery of self. The change of government in the time of the English Commonwealth set men thinking about first principles, and gave rise to many works of this class...The great original genius of Swift owes nothing to Plato; nor is there any trace in the conversation or in the works of Dr. Johnson of any acquaintance with his writings. He probably would have refuted Plato without reading him, in the same fashion in which he supposed himself to have refuted Bishop Berkeley's theory of the non-existence of matter. If we except the so-called English Platonists, or rather Neo-Platonists, who never understood their master, and the writings of Coleridge, who was to some extent a kindred spirit, Plato has left no permanent impression on English literature.

7. Human life and conduct are affected by ideals in the same way that they are affected by the examples of eminent men. Neither the one nor the other are immediately applicable to practice, but there is a virtue flowing from them which tends to raise individuals above the common routine of society or trade, and to elevate States above the mere interests of commerce or the necessities of self-defence. Like the ideals of art they are partly framed by the omission of particulars; they require to be viewed at a certain distance, and are apt to fade away if we attempt to approach them. They gain an imaginary distinctness when embodied in a State or in a system of philosophy, but they still remain the visions of 'a world unrealized.' More striking and obvious to the ordinary mind are the examples of great men, who have served their own generation and are remembered in another. Even in our own family circle there may have been some one, a woman, or

even a child, in whose face has shone forth a goodness more than human. The ideal then approaches nearer to us, and we fondly cling to it. The ideal of the past, whether of our own past lives or of former states of society, has a singular fascination for the minds of many. Too late we learn that such ideals cannot be recalled, though the recollection of them may have a humanizing influence on other times. But the abstractions of philosophy are to most persons cold and vacant; they give light without warmth; they are like the full moon in the heavens when there are no stars appearing. Men cannot live by thought alone; the world of sense is always breaking in upon them. They are for the most part confined to a corner of earth, and see but a little way beyond their own home or place of abode; they 'do not lift up their eyes to the hills'; they are not awake when the dawn appears. But in Plato we have reached a height from which a man may look into the distance and behold the future of the world and of philosophy. The ideal of the State and of the life of the philosopher; the ideal of an education continuing through life and extending equally to both sexes; the ideal of the unity and correlation of knowledge; the faith in good and immortality – are the vacant forms of light on which Plato is seeking to fix the eye of mankind.

8. Two other ideals, which never appeared above the horizon in Greek Philosophy, float before the minds of men in our own day: one seen more clearly than formerly, as though each year and each generation brought us nearer to some great change; the other almost in the same degree retiring from view behind the laws of nature, as if oppressed by them, but still remaining a silent hope of we know not what hidden in the heart of man. The first ideal is the future of the human race in this world; the second the future of the individual in another. The first is the more perfect realization of our own present life; the second, the abnegation of it: the one, limited by experience, the other, transcending it. Both of them have been and are powerful motives of action; there are a few in whom they have taken the place of all earthly interests. The hope of a future for the human race at first sight seems to be the more disinterested, the hope of individual existence the more egotistical, of the two motives. But when men have learned to resolve their hope of a future either for themselves or for the world into the will of God – 'not my will but Thine,' the difference between them falls away; and they may be allowed to make either of them the basis of their lives, according to their own individual character or temperament. There is as much faith in the willingness to work for an unseen future in this world as in another. Neither is it inconceivable that some rare nature may feel his duty to another generation, or to another century, almost as

strongly as to his own, or that living always in the presence of God, he may realize another world as vividly as he does this.

The greatest of all ideals may, or rather must be conceived by us under similitudes derived from human qualities; although sometimes, like the Jewish prophets, we may dash away these figures of speech and describe the nature of God only in negatives. These again by degrees acquire a positive meaning. It would be well, if when meditating on the higher truths either of philosophy or religion, we sometimes substituted one form of expression for another, lest through the necessities of language we should become the slaves of mere words.

There is a third ideal, not the same, but akin to these, which has a place in the home and heart of every believer in the religion of Christ, and in which men seem to find a nearer and more familiar truth, the Divine man, the Son of Man, the Saviour of mankind, Who is the first-born and head of the whole family in heaven and earth, in Whom the Divine and human, that which is without and that which is within the range of our earthly faculties, are indissolubly united. Neither is this divine form of goodness wholly separable from the ideal of the Christian Church, which is said in the New Testament to be 'His body,' or at variance with those other images of good which Plato sets before us. We see Him in a figure only, and of figures of speech we select but a few, and those the simplest, to be the expression of Him. We behold Him in a picture, but He is not there. We gather up the fragments of His discourses, but neither do they represent Him as He truly was. His dwelling is neither in heaven nor earth, but in the heart of man. This is that image which Plato saw dimly in the distance, which, when existing among men, he called, in the language of Homer, 'the likeness of God,' the likeness of a nature which in all ages men have felt to be greater and better than themselves, and which in endless forms, whether derived from Scripture or nature, from the witness of history or from the human heart, regarded as a person or not as a person, with or without parts or passions, existing in space or not in space, is and will always continue to be to mankind the Idea of Good.

THE REPUBLIC.

PERSONS OF THE DIALOGUE.

Socrates, who is the narrator.

Glaucon.

Adeimantus.

Polemarchus.

Cephalus.

Thrasymachus.

Cleitophon.

And others who are mute auditors.

The scene is laid in the house of Cephalus at the Piraeus; and the whole dialogue is narrated by Socrates the day after it actually took place to Timaeus, Hermocrates, Critias, and a nameless person, who are introduced in the Timaeus.

BOOK I.

I went down yesterday to the Piraeus with Glaucon the son of Ariston, that I might offer up my prayers to the goddess (Bendis, the Thracian Artemis.); and also because I wanted to see in what manner they would celebrate the festival, which was a new thing. I was delighted with the procession of the inhabitants; but that of the Thracians was equally, if not more, beautiful. When we had finished our prayers and viewed the spectacle, we turned in the direction of the city; and at that instant Polemarchus the son of Cephalus chanced to catch sight of us from a distance as we were starting on our way home, and told his servant to run and bid us wait for him. The servant took hold of me by the cloak behind, and said: Polemarchus desires you to wait.

I turned round, and asked him where his master was.

There he is, said the youth, coming after you, if you will only wait.

Certainly we will, said Glaucon; and in a few minutes Polemarchus appeared, and with him Adeimantus, Glaucon's brother, Niceratus the son of Nicias, and several others who had been at the procession.

Polemarchus said to me: I perceive, Socrates, that you and your companion are already on your way to the city.

You are not far wrong, I said.

But do you see, he rejoined, how many we are?

Of course.

And are you stronger than all these? for if not, you will have to remain where you are.

May there not be the alternative, I said, that we may persuade you to let us go?

But can you persuade us, if we refuse to listen to you? he said.

Certainly not, replied Glaucon.

Then we are not going to listen; of that you may be assured.

Adeimantus added: Has no one told you of the torch-race on horseback in honour of the goddess which will take place in the evening?

With horses! I replied: That is a novelty. Will horsemen carry torches and pass them one to another during the race?

Yes, said Polemarchus, and not only so, but a festival will be celebrated at night, which you certainly ought to see. Let us rise soon after supper and see this festival; there will be a gathering of young men, and we will have a good talk. Stay then, and do not be perverse.

Glaucon said: I suppose, since you insist, that we must.

Very good, I replied.

Accordingly we went with Polemarchus to his house; and there we found his brothers Lysias and Euthydemus, and with them Thrasymachus the Chalcedonian, Charmantides the Paeanian, and Cleitophon the son of Aristonymus. There too was Cephalus the father of Polemarchus, whom I had not seen for a long time, and I thought him very much aged. He was seated on a cushioned chair, and had a garland on his head, for he had been sacrificing in the court; and there were some other chairs in the room arranged in a semicircle, upon which we sat down by him. He saluted me eagerly, and then he said: –

You don't come to see me, Socrates, as often as you ought: If I were still able to go and see you I would not ask you to come to me. But at my age I can hardly get to the city, and therefore you should come oftener to the Piraeus. For let me tell you, that the more the pleasures of the body fade away, the greater to me is the pleasure and charm of conversation. Do not then deny my request, but make our house your resort and keep company with these young men; we are old friends, and you will be quite at home with us.

I replied: There is nothing which for my part I like better, Cephalus, than conversing with aged men; for I regard them as travellers who have gone a journey which I too may have to go, and of whom I ought to enquire, whether the way is smooth and easy, or rugged and difficult. And this is a question which I should like to ask of you who have arrived at that time which the poets call the 'threshold of old age' – Is life harder towards the end, or what report do you give of it?

I will tell you, Socrates, he said, what my own feeling is. Men of my age flock together; we are birds of a feather, as the old proverb says; and at our meetings the tale of my acquaintance commonly is – I cannot eat, I cannot drink; the pleasures of youth and love are fled away: there was a good time once, but now that is gone, and life is no longer life. Some complain of the slights which are put upon them by relations, and they will tell you sadly of how many evils their old age is the cause. But to me, Socrates, these complainers seem to blame that which is not really in fault. For if old age were the cause, I too being old, and every other old man, would have felt as they do. But this is not my own experience, nor that of others whom I have known. How well I remember the aged poet Sophocles, when in answer to the question, How does love suit with age, Sophocles, – are you still the man you were? Peace, he replied; most gladly have I escaped the thing of which you speak; I feel as if I had escaped from a mad and furious master. His words have often occurred to my mind since, and they seem as good to me now as at the time when he uttered them. For certainly old age has a great sense of calm and freedom; when the passions relax their hold, then, as Sophocles says, we are freed from the grasp not of one mad master only, but of many. The truth is, Socrates, that these regrets, and also the complaints about relations, are to be attributed to the same cause, which is not old age, but men's characters and tempers; for he who is of a calm and happy nature will hardly feel the pressure of age, but to him who is of an opposite disposition youth and age are equally a burden.

I listened in admiration, and wanting to draw him out, that he might go on – Yes, Cephalus, I said: but I rather suspect that people in general are not convinced by you when you speak thus; they think that old age sits lightly upon you, not because of your happy disposition, but because you are rich, and wealth is well known to be a great comforter.

You are right, he replied; they are not convinced: and there is something in what they say; not, however, so much as they imagine. I might answer them as Themistocles answered the Seriphian who was abusing him and saying that he was famous, not for his own merits but because he was an Athenian: 'If you had been a native of my country or I of yours, neither of us would have been famous.' And to those who are not rich and are impatient of old age, the same reply may be made; for to the good poor man old age cannot be a light burden, nor can a bad rich man ever have peace with himself.

May I ask, Cephalus, whether your fortune was for the most part inherited or acquired by you?

Acquired! Socrates; do you want to know how much I acquired? In the art of making money I have been midway between my father and grandfather: for my grandfather, whose name I bear, doubled and trebled the value of his patrimony, that which he inherited being much what I possess now; but my father Lysanias reduced the property below what it is at present: and I shall be satisfied if I leave to these my sons not less but a little more than I received.

That was why I asked you the question, I replied, because I see that you are indifferent about money, which is a characteristic rather of those who have inherited their fortunes than of those who have acquired them; the makers of fortunes have a second love of money as a creation of their own, resembling the affection of authors for their own poems, or of parents for their children, besides that natural love of it for the sake of use and profit which is common to them and all men. And hence they are very bad company, for they can talk about nothing but the praises of wealth.

That is true, he said.

Yes, that is very true, but may I ask another question? – What do you consider to be the greatest blessing which you have reaped from your wealth?

One, he said, of which I could not expect easily to convince others. For let me tell you, Socrates, that when a man thinks himself to be near death, fears and cares enter into his mind which he never had before; the tales of a world below and the punishment which is exacted there of deeds done here were once a laughing matter to him, but now he is tormented with the thought that they may be true: either from the weakness of age, or because he is now drawing nearer to that other place, he has a clearer view of these things; suspicions and alarms crowd thickly upon him, and he begins to reflect and consider what wrongs he has done to others. And when he finds that the sum of his transgressions is great he will many a time like a child start up in his sleep for fear, and he is filled with dark forebodings. But to him who is conscious of no sin, sweet hope, as Pindar charmingly says, is the kind nurse of his age:

'Hope,' he says, 'cherishes the soul of him who lives in justice and holiness, and is the nurse of his age and the companion of his journey; – hope which is mightiest to sway the restless soul of man.'

How admirable are his words! And the great blessing of riches, I do not say to every man, but to a good man, is, that he has had no occasion to deceive or to defraud others, either intentionally or unintentionally; and when he departs to the world below he is not in any apprehension about offerings due to the gods or debts which he owes to men. Now to this peace of mind the possession of wealth greatly contributes; and therefore I say, that, setting one thing against another, of the many advantages which wealth has to give, to a man of sense this is in my opinion the greatest.

Well said, Cephalus, I replied; but as concerning justice, what is it? – to speak the truth and to pay your debts – no more than this? And even to this are there not exceptions? Suppose that a friend when in his right mind has deposited arms with me and he asks for them when he is not in his right mind, ought I to give them back to him? No one would say that I ought or that I should be right in doing so, any more than they would say that I ought always to speak the truth to one who is in his condition.

You are quite right, he replied.

But then, I said, speaking the truth and paying your debts is not a correct definition of justice.

Quite correct, Socrates, if Simonides is to be believed, said Polemarchus interposing.

I fear, said Cephalus, that I must go now, for I have to look after the sacrifices, and I hand over the argument to Polemarchus and the company.

Is not Polemarchus your heir? I said.

To be sure, he answered, and went away laughing to the sacrifices.

Tell me then, O thou heir of the argument, what did Simonides say, and according to you truly say, about justice?

He said that the repayment of a debt is just, and in saying so he appears to me to be right.

I should be sorry to doubt the word of such a wise and inspired man, but his meaning, though probably clear to you, is the reverse of clear to me. For he certainly does not mean, as we were just now saying, that I ought to return a deposit of arms or of anything else to one who asks for it when he is not in his right senses; and yet a deposit cannot be denied to be a debt.

True.

Then when the person who asks me is not in his right mind I am by no means to make the return?

Certainly not.

When Simonides said that the repayment of a debt was justice, he did not mean to include that case?

Certainly not; for he thinks that a friend ought always to do good to a friend and never evil.

You mean that the return of a deposit of gold which is to the injury of the receiver, if the two parties are friends, is not the repayment of a debt, – that is what you would imagine him to say?

Yes.

And are enemies also to receive what we owe to them?

To be sure, he said, they are to receive what we owe them, and an enemy, as I take it, owes to an enemy that which is due or proper to him – that is to say, evil.

Simonides, then, after the manner of poets, would seem to have spoken darkly of the nature of justice; for he really meant to say that justice is the giving to each man what is proper to him, and this he termed a debt.

That must have been his meaning, he said.

By heaven! I replied; and if we asked him what due or proper thing is given by medicine, and to whom, what answer do you think that he would make to us?

He would surely reply that medicine gives drugs and meat and drink to human bodies.

And what due or proper thing is given by cookery, and to what?

Seasoning to food.

And what is that which justice gives, and to whom?

If, Socrates, we are to be guided at all by the analogy of the preceding instances, then justice is the art which gives good to friends and evil to enemies.

That is his meaning then?

I think so.

And who is best able to do good to his friends and evil to his enemies in time of sickness?

The physician.

Or when they are on a voyage, amid the perils of the sea?

The pilot.

And in what sort of actions or with a view to what result is the just man most able to do harm to his enemy and good to his friend?

In going to war against the one and in making alliances with the other.

But when a man is well, my dear Polemarchus, there is no need of a physician?

No.

And he who is not on a voyage has no need of a pilot?

No.

Then in time of peace justice will be of no use?

I am very far from thinking so.

You think that justice may be of use in peace as well as in war?

Yes.

Like husbandry for the acquisition of corn?

Yes.

Or like shoemaking for the acquisition of shoes, – that is what you mean?

Yes.

And what similar use or power of acquisition has justice in time of peace?

In contracts, Socrates, justice is of use.

And by contracts you mean partnerships?

Exactly.

But is the just man or the skilful player a more useful and better partner at a game of draughts?

The skilful player.

And in the laying of bricks and stones is the just man a more useful or better partner than the builder?

Quite the reverse.

Then in what sort of partnership is the just man a better partner than the harp-player, as in playing the harp the harp-player is certainly a better partner than the just man?

In a money partnership.

Yes, Polemarchus, but surely not in the use of money; for you do not want a just man to be your counsellor in the purchase or sale of a horse; a man who is knowing about horses would be better for that, would he not?

Certainly.

And when you want to buy a ship, the shipwright or the pilot would be better?

True.

Then what is that joint use of silver or gold in which the just man is to be preferred?

When you want a deposit to be kept safely.

You mean when money is not wanted, but allowed to lie?

Precisely.

That is to say, justice is useful when money is useless?

That is the inference.

And when you want to keep a pruning-hook safe, then justice is useful to the individual and to the state; but when you want to use it, then the art of the vine-dresser?

Clearly.

And when you want to keep a shield or a lyre, and not to use them, you would say that justice is useful; but when you want to use them, then the art of the soldier or of the musician?

Certainly.

And so of all other things; – justice is useful when they are useless, and useless when they are useful?

That is the inference.

Then justice is not good for much. But let us consider this further point: Is not he who can best strike a blow in a boxing match or in any kind of fighting best able to ward off a blow?

Certainly.

And he who is most skilful in preventing or escaping from a disease is best able to create one?

True.

And he is the best guard of a camp who is best able to steal a march upon the enemy?

Certainly.

Then he who is a good keeper of anything is also a good thief?

That, I suppose, is to be inferred.

Then if the just man is good at keeping money, he is good at stealing it.

That is implied in the argument.

Then after all the just man has turned out to be a thief. And this is a lesson which I suspect you must have learnt out of Homer; for he, speaking of Autolycus, the maternal grandfather of Odysseus, who is a favourite of his, affirms that

'He was excellent above all men in theft and perjury.'

And so, you and Homer and Simonides are agreed that justice is an art of theft; to be practised however 'for the good of friends and for the harm of enemies,' – that was what you were saying?

No, certainly not that, though I do not now know what I did say; but I still stand by the latter words.

Well, there is another question: By friends and enemies do we mean those who are so really, or only in seeming?

Surely, he said, a man may be expected to love those whom he thinks good, and to hate those whom he thinks evil.

Yes, but do not persons often err about good and evil: many who are not good seem to be so, and conversely?

That is true.

Then to them the good will be enemies and the evil will be their friends? True.

And in that case they will be right in doing good to the evil and evil to the good?

Clearly.

But the good are just and would not do an injustice?

True.

Then according to your argument it is just to injure those who do no wrong?

Nay, Socrates; the doctrine is immoral.

Then I suppose that we ought to do good to the just and harm to the unjust?

I like that better.

But see the consequence: – Many a man who is ignorant of human nature has friends who are bad friends, and in that case he ought to do harm to them; and he has good enemies whom he ought to benefit; but, if so, we shall be saying the very opposite of that which we affirmed to be the meaning of Simonides.

Very true, he said: and I think that we had better correct an error into which we seem to have fallen in the use of the words 'friend' and 'enemy.'

What was the error, Polemarchus? I asked.

We assumed that he is a friend who seems to be or who is thought good.

And how is the error to be corrected?

We should rather say that he is a friend who is, as well as seems, good; and that he who seems only, and is not good, only seems to be and is not a friend; and of an enemy the same may be said.

You would argue that the good are our friends and the bad our enemies?

Yes.

And instead of saying simply as we did at first, that it is just to do good to our friends and harm to our enemies, we should further say: It is just to do good to our friends when they are good and harm to our enemies when they are evil?

Yes, that appears to me to be the truth.

But ought the just to injure any one at all?

Undoubtedly he ought to injure those who are both wicked and his enemies.

When horses are injured, are they improved or deteriorated?

The latter.

Deteriorated, that is to say, in the good qualities of horses, not of dogs?

Yes, of horses.

And dogs are deteriorated in the good qualities of dogs, and not of horses?

Of course.

And will not men who are injured be deteriorated in that which is the proper virtue of man?

Certainly.

And that human virtue is justice?

To be sure.

Then men who are injured are of necessity made unjust?

That is the result.

But can the musician by his art make men unmusical?

Certainly not.

Or the horseman by his art make them bad horsemen?

Impossible.

And can the just by justice make men unjust, or speaking generally, can the good by virtue make them bad?

Assuredly not.

Any more than heat can produce cold?

It cannot.

Or drought moisture?

Clearly not.

Nor can the good harm any one?

Impossible.

And the just is the good?

Certainly.

Then to injure a friend or any one else is not the act of a just man, but of the opposite, who is the unjust?

I think that what you say is quite true, Socrates.

Then if a man says that justice consists in the repayment of debts, and that good is the debt which a just man owes to his friends, and evil the debt which he owes to his enemies, – to say this is not wise; for it is not true, if, as has been clearly shown, the injuring of another can be in no case just.

I agree with you, said Polemarchus.

Then you and I are prepared to take up arms against any one who attributes such a saying to Simonides or Bias or Pittacus, or any other wise man or seer?

I am quite ready to do battle at your side, he said.

Shall I tell you whose I believe the saying to be?

Whose?

I believe that Periander or Perdiccas or Xerxes or Ismenias the Theban, or some other rich and mighty man, who had a great opinion of his own power, was the first to say that justice is 'doing good to your friends and harm to your enemies.'

Most true, he said.

Yes, I said; but if this definition of justice also breaks down, what other can be offered?

Several times in the course of the discussion Thrasymachus had made an attempt to get the argument into his own hands, and had been put down by the rest of the company, who wanted to hear the end. But when Polemarchus and I had done speaking and there was a pause, he could no longer hold his peace; and, gathering himself up, he came at us like a wild beast, seeking to devour us. We were quite panic-stricken at the sight of him.

He roared out to the whole company: What folly, Socrates, has taken possession of you all? And why, sillybillies, do you knock under to one another? I say that if you want really to know what justice is, you should not only ask but answer, and you should not seek honour to yourself from the refutation of an opponent, but have your own answer; for there is many a one who can ask and cannot answer. And now I will not have you say that justice is duty or advantage or profit or gain or interest, for this sort of nonsense will not do for me; I must have clearness and accuracy.

I was panic-stricken at his words, and could not look at him without trembling. Indeed I believe that if I had not fixed my eye upon him, I should have been struck dumb: but when I saw his fury rising, I looked at him first, and was therefore able to reply to him.

Thrasymachus, I said, with a quiver, don't be hard upon us. Polemarchus and I may have been guilty of a little mistake in the argument, but I can assure you that the error was not intentional. If we were seeking for a piece of gold, you would not imagine that we were 'knocking under to one another,' and so losing our chance of finding it. And why, when we are seeking for justice, a thing more precious than many pieces of gold, do you say that we are weakly yielding to one another and not doing our utmost to get at the truth? Nay, my good friend, we are most willing and anxious to do so, but the fact is that we cannot. And if so, you people who know all things should pity us and not be angry with us.

How characteristic of Socrates! he replied, with a bitter laugh; – that's your ironical style! Did I not foresee – have I not already told you, that whatever he was asked he would refuse to answer, and try irony or any other shuffle, in order that he might avoid answering?

You are a philosopher, Thrasymachus, I replied, and well know that if you ask a person what numbers make up twelve, taking care to prohibit him whom you ask from answering twice six, or three times four, or six times two, or four times three, 'for this sort of nonsense will not do for me,' – then obviously, if that is your way of putting the question, no one can answer you. But suppose that he were to retort, 'Thrasymachus, what do you mean? If one of these numbers which you interdict be the true answer to the question, am I falsely to say some other number which is not the right one? – is that your meaning?' – How would you answer him?

Just as if the two cases were at all alike! he said.

Why should they not be? I replied; and even if they are not, but only appear to be so to the person who is asked, ought he not to say what he thinks, whether you and I forbid him or not?

I presume then that you are going to make one of the interdicted answers?

I dare say that I may, notwithstanding the danger, if upon reflection I approve of any of them.

But what if I give you an answer about justice other and better, he said, than any of these? What do you deserve to have done to you?

Done to me! – as becomes the ignorant, I must learn from the wise – that is what I deserve to have done to me.

What, and no payment! a pleasant notion!

I will pay when I have the money, I replied.

But you have, Socrates, said Glaucon: and you, Thrasymachus, need be under no anxiety about money, for we will all make a contribution for Socrates.

Yes, he replied, and then Socrates will do as he always does – refuse to answer himself, but take and pull to pieces the answer of some one else.

Why, my good friend, I said, how can any one answer who knows, and says that he knows, just nothing; and who, even if he has some faint notions of his own, is told by a man of authority not to utter them? The natural thing is, that the speaker should be some one like yourself who professes to know and can tell what he knows. Will you then kindly answer, for the edification of the company and of myself?

Glaucon and the rest of the company joined in my request, and Thrasymachus, as any one might see, was in reality eager to speak; for he thought that he had an excellent answer, and would distinguish himself. But at first he affected to insist on my answering; at length he consented to begin. Behold, he said, the wisdom of Socrates; he refuses to teach himself, and goes about learning of others, to whom he never even says Thank you.

That I learn of others, I replied, is quite true; but that I am ungrateful I wholly deny. Money I have none, and therefore I pay in praise, which is all I have; and how ready I am to praise any one who appears to me to speak well you will very soon find out when you answer; for I expect that you will answer well.

Listen, then, he said; I proclaim that justice is nothing else than the interest of the stronger. And now why do you not praise me? But of course you won't.

Let me first understand you, I replied. Justice, as you say, is the interest of the stronger. What, Thrasymachus, is the meaning of this? You cannot mean to say that because Polydamas, the pancratiast, is stronger than we are, and finds the eating of beef conducive to his bodily strength, that to eat beef is therefore equally for our good who are weaker than he is, and right and just for us?

That's abominable of you, Socrates; you take the words in the sense which is most damaging to the argument.

Not at all, my good sir, I said; I am trying to understand them; and I wish that you would be a little clearer.

Well, he said, have you never heard that forms of government differ; there are tyrannies, and there are democracies, and there are aristocracies?

Yes, I know.

And the government is the ruling power in each state?

Certainly.

And the different forms of government make laws democratical, aristocratical, tyrannical, with a view to their several interests; and these laws, which are made by them for their own interests, are the justice which they deliver to their subjects, and him who transgresses them they punish as a breaker of the law, and unjust. And that is what I mean when I say that in all states there is the same principle of justice, which is the interest of the government; and as the government must be supposed to have power, the only reasonable conclusion is, that everywhere there is one principle of justice, which is the interest of the stronger.

Now I understand you, I said; and whether you are right or not I will try to discover. But let me remark, that in defining justice you have yourself used the word 'interest' which you forbade me to use. It is true, however, that in your definition the words 'of the stronger' are added.

A small addition, you must allow, he said.

Great or small, never mind about that: we must first enquire whether what you are saying is the truth. Now we are both agreed that justice is interest of some sort, but you go on to say 'of the stronger'; about this addition I am not so sure, and must therefore consider further.

Proceed.

I will; and first tell me, Do you admit that it is just for subjects to obey their rulers?

I do.

But are the rulers of states absolutely infallible, or are they sometimes liable to err?

To be sure, he replied, they are liable to err.

Then in making their laws they may sometimes make them rightly, and sometimes not?

True.

When they make them rightly, they make them agreeably to their interest; when they are mistaken, contrary to their interest; you admit that?

Yes.

And the laws which they make must be obeyed by their subjects, – and that is what you call justice?

Doubtless.

Then justice, according to your argument, is not only obedience to the interest of the stronger but the reverse?

What is that you are saying? he asked.

I am only repeating what you are saying, I believe. But let us consider: Have we not admitted that the rulers may be mistaken about their own interest in what they command, and also that to obey them is justice? Has not that been admitted?

Yes.

Then you must also have acknowledged justice not to be for the interest of the stronger, when the rulers unintentionally command things to be done which are to their own injury. For if, as you say, justice is the obedience which the subject renders to their commands, in that case, O wisest of men, is there any escape from the conclusion that the weaker are commanded to do, not what is for the interest, but what is for the injury of the stronger?

Nothing can be clearer, Socrates, said Polemarchus.

Yes, said Cleitophon, interposing, if you are allowed to be his witness.

But there is no need of any witness, said Polemarchus, for Thrasymachus himself acknowledges that rulers may sometimes command what is not for their own interest, and that for subjects to obey them is justice.

Yes, Polemarchus, – Thrasymachus said that for subjects to do what was commanded by their rulers is just.

Yes, Cleitophon, but he also said that justice is the interest of the stronger, and, while admitting both these propositions, he further acknowledged that the stronger may command the weaker who are his subjects to do what is not for his own interest; whence follows that justice is the injury quite as much as the interest of the stronger.

But, said Cleitophon, he meant by the interest of the stronger what the stronger thought to be his interest, – this was what the weaker had to do; and this was affirmed by him to be justice.

Those were not his words, rejoined Polemarchus.

Never mind, I replied, if he now says that they are, let us accept his statement. Tell me, Thrasymachus, I said, did you mean by justice what the stronger thought to be his interest, whether really so or not?

Certainly not, he said. Do you suppose that I call him who is mistaken the stronger at the time when he is mistaken?

Yes, I said, my impression was that you did so, when you admitted that the ruler was not infallible but might be sometimes mistaken.

You argue like an informer, Socrates. Do you mean, for example, that he who is mistaken about the sick is a physician in that he is mistaken? or that he who errs in arithmetic or grammar is an arithmetician or grammarian at the time when he is making the mistake, in respect of the mistake? True, we say that the physician or arithmetician or grammarian has made a mistake, but this is only a way of speaking; for the fact is that neither the grammarian nor any other person of skill ever makes a mistake in so far as he is what his name implies; they none of them err unless their skill fails them, and then they cease to be skilled artists. No artist or sage or ruler errs at the time when he is what his name implies; though he is commonly said to err, and I adopted the common mode of speaking. But to be perfectly accurate, since you are such a lover of accuracy, we should say that the ruler, in so far as he is a ruler, is unerring, and, being unerring, always commands that which is for his own interest; and the subject is required to execute his commands; and therefore, as I said at first and now repeat, justice is the interest of the stronger.

Indeed, Thrasymachus, and do I really appear to you to argue like an informer?

Certainly, he replied.

And do you suppose that I ask these questions with any design of injuring you in the argument?

Nay, he replied, 'suppose' is not the word – I know it; but you will be found out, and by sheer force of argument you will never prevail.

I shall not make the attempt, my dear man; but to avoid any misunderstanding occurring between us in future, let me ask, in what sense do you speak of a ruler or stronger whose interest, as you were saying, he being the superior, it is just that the inferior should execute – is he a ruler in the popular or in the strict sense of the term?

In the strictest of all senses, he said. And now cheat and play the informer if you can; I ask no quarter at your hands. But you never will be able, never.

And do you imagine, I said, that I am such a madman as to try and cheat, Thrasymachus? I might as well shave a lion.

Why, he said, you made the attempt a minute ago, and you failed.

Enough, I said, of these civilities. It will be better that I should ask you a question: Is the physician, taken in that strict sense of which you are speaking, a healer of the sick or a maker of money? And remember that I am now speaking of the true physician.

A healer of the sick, he replied.

And the pilot – that is to say, the true pilot – is he a captain of sailors or a mere sailor?

A captain of sailors.

The circumstance that he sails in the ship is not to be taken into account; neither is he to be called a sailor; the name pilot by which he is distinguished has nothing to do with sailing, but is significant of his skill and of his authority over the sailors.

Very true, he said.

Now, I said, every art has an interest?

Certainly.

For which the art has to consider and provide?

Yes, that is the aim of art.

And the interest of any art is the perfection of it – this and nothing else?

What do you mean?

I mean what I may illustrate negatively by the example of the body. Suppose you were to ask me whether the body is self-sufficing or has wants, I should reply: Certainly the body has wants; for the body may be ill and require to be cured, and has therefore interests to which the art of medicine ministers; and this is the origin and intention of medicine, as you will acknowledge. Am I not right?

Quite right, he replied.

But is the art of medicine or any other art faulty or deficient in any quality in the same way that the eye may be deficient in sight or the ear fail of hearing, and therefore requires another art to provide for the interests of seeing and hearing – has art in itself, I say, any similar liability to fault or defect, and does every art require another supplementary art to provide for its interests, and that another and another without end? Or have the arts to look only after their own interests? Or have they no need either of themselves or of another? – having no faults or defects, they have no need to correct them, either by the exercise of their own art or of any other; they have only to consider the interest of their subject-matter. For every art remains pure and faultless while remaining true – that is to say, while perfect and unimpaired. Take the words in your precise sense, and tell me whether I am not right.

Yes, clearly.

Then medicine does not consider the interest of medicine, but the interest of the body?

True, he said.

Nor does the art of horsemanship consider the interests of the art of horsemanship, but the interests of the horse; neither do any other arts care for themselves, for they have no needs; they care only for that which is the subject of their art?

True, he said.

But surely, Thrasymachus, the arts are the superiors and rulers of their own subjects?

To this he assented with a good deal of reluctance.

Then, I said, no science or art considers or enjoins the interest of the stronger or superior, but only the interest of the subject and weaker?

He made an attempt to contest this proposition also, but finally acquiesced.

Then, I continued, no physician, in so far as he is a physician, considers his own good in what he prescribes, but the good of his patient; for the true physician is also a ruler having the human body as a subject, and is not a mere money-maker; that has been admitted?

Yes.

And the pilot likewise, in the strict sense of the term, is a ruler of sailors and not a mere sailor?

That has been admitted.

And such a pilot and ruler will provide and prescribe for the interest of the sailor who is under him, and not for his own or the ruler's interest?

He gave a reluctant 'Yes.'

Then, I said, Thrasymachus, there is no one in any rule who, in so far as he is a ruler, considers or enjoins what is for his own interest, but always what is for the interest of his subject or suitable to his art; to that he looks, and that alone he considers in everything which he says and does.

When we had got to this point in the argument, and every one saw that the definition of justice had been completely upset, Thrasymachus, instead of replying to me, said: Tell me, Socrates, have you got a nurse?

Why do you ask such a question, I said, when you ought rather to be answering?

Because she leaves you to snivel, and never wipes your nose: she has not even taught you to know the shepherd from the sheep.

What makes you say that? I replied.

Because you fancy that the shepherd or neatherd fattens or tends the sheep or oxen with a view to their own good and not to the good of himself or his master; and you further imagine that the rulers of states, if they are true rulers, never think of their subjects as sheep, and that they are not studying their own advantage day and night. Oh, no; and so entirely astray are you in your ideas about the just and unjust as not even to know that justice and the just are in reality another's good; that is to say, the interest of the ruler and stronger, and the loss of the subject and servant; and injustice the opposite; for the unjust is lord over the truly simple and just: he is the stronger, and his subjects do what is for his interest, and minister to his happiness, which is very far from being their own. Consider further, most foolish Socrates, that the just is always a loser in comparison with the unjust. First of all, in private contracts: wherever the unjust is the partner of the just you will find that, when the partnership is dissolved, the unjust man has always more and the just less. Secondly, in their dealings with the State: when there is an income-tax, the just man will pay more and the unjust less on the same amount of income; and when there is anything to be received the one gains nothing and the other much. Observe also what happens when they take an office; there is the just man neglecting his affairs and perhaps suffering other losses, and getting nothing out of the public, because he is just; moreover he is hated by his friends and acquaintance for refusing to serve them in unlawful ways. But all this is reversed in the case of the unjust man. I am speaking, as before, of injustice on a large scale in which the advantage of the unjust is most apparent; and my meaning will be most clearly seen if we turn to that highest form of injustice in which the criminal is the happiest of men, and the sufferers or those who refuse to do injustice are the most miserable – that is to say tyranny, which by fraud and force takes away the property of others, not little by little but wholesale; comprehending in one, things sacred as well as profane, private and public; for which acts of wrong, if he were detected perpetrating any one of them singly, he would be punished and incur great disgrace – they who do such wrong in particular cases are called robbers of temples, and man-stealers and burglars and swindlers and thieves. But when a man besides taking away the money of the citizens has made slaves of them, then, instead of these names of reproach, he is termed happy and blessed, not only by the citizens but by all who hear of his having achieved the consummation of injustice. For mankind censure injustice, fearing that they may be the victims of it and not because they shrink from committing it. And thus, as I have shown, Socrates, injustice, when on a sufficient scale, has more strength and freedom and mastery than justice; and, as I said at first, justice is the interest of the stronger, whereas injustice is a man's own profit and interest.

Thrasymachus, when he had thus spoken, having, like a bath-man, deluged our ears with his words, had a mind to go away. But the company would not let him; they insisted that he should remain and defend his position; and I myself added my own humble request that he would not leave us. Thrasymachus, I said to him, excellent man, how suggestive are your remarks! And are you going to run away before you have fairly taught or learned whether they are true or not? Is the attempt to determine the way of man's life so small a matter in your eyes – to determine how life may be passed by each one of us to the greatest advantage?

And do I differ from you, he said, as to the importance of the enquiry?

You appear rather, I replied, to have no care or thought about us, Thrasymachus – whether we live better or worse from not knowing what you say you know, is to you a matter of indifference. Prithee, friend, do not keep your knowledge to yourself; we are a large party; and any benefit which you confer upon us will be amply rewarded. For my own part I openly declare that I am not convinced, and that I do not believe injustice to be more gainful than justice, even if uncontrolled and allowed to have free play. For, granting that there may be an unjust man who is able to commit injustice either by fraud or force, still this does not convince me of the superior advantage of injustice, and there may be others who are in the same predicament with myself. Perhaps we may be wrong; if so, you in your wisdom should convince us that we are mistaken in preferring justice to injustice.

And how am I to convince you, he said, if you are not already convinced by what I have just said; what more can I do for you? Would you have me put the proof bodily into your souls?

Heaven forbid! I said; I would only ask you to be consistent; or, if you change, change openly and let there be no deception. For I must remark, Thrasymachus, if you will recall what was previously said, that although you began by defining the true physician in an exact sense, you did not observe a like exactness when speaking of the shepherd; you thought that the shepherd as a shepherd tends the sheep not with a view to their own good, but like a mere diner or banquetter with a view to the pleasures of the table; or, again, as a trader for sale in the market, and not as a shepherd. Yet surely the art of the shepherd is concerned only with the good of his subjects; he has only to provide the best for them, since the perfection of the art is already ensured whenever all the requirements of it are satisfied. And that was what I was saying just now about the ruler. I conceived that the art of the ruler, considered as ruler, whether in a state or in private life, could only regard the good of his flock or subjects; whereas you seem to think that the rulers in states, that is to say, the true rulers, like being in authority.

Think! Nay, I am sure of it.

Then why in the case of lesser offices do men never take them willingly without payment, unless under the idea that they govern for the advantage not of themselves but of others? Let me ask you a question: Are not the several arts different, by reason of their each having a separate function?

And, my dear illustrious friend, do say what you think, that we may make a little progress.

Yes, that is the difference, he replied.

And each art gives us a particular good and not merely a general one – medicine, for example, gives us health; navigation, safety at sea, and so on?

Yes, he said.

And the art of payment has the special function of giving pay: but we do not confuse this with other arts, any more than the art of the pilot is to be confused with the art of medicine, because the health of the pilot may be improved by a sea voyage. You would not be inclined to say, would you, that navigation is the art of medicine, at least if we are to adopt your exact use of language?

Certainly not.

Or because a man is in good health when he receives pay you would not say that the art of payment is medicine?

I should not.

Nor would you say that medicine is the art of receiving pay because a man takes fees when he is engaged in healing?

Certainly not.

And we have admitted, I said, that the good of each art is specially confined to the art?

Yes.

Then, if there be any good which all artists have in common, that is to be attributed to something of which they all have the common use?

True, he replied.

And when the artist is benefited by receiving pay the advantage is gained by an additional use of the art of pay, which is not the art professed by him?

He gave a reluctant assent to this.

Then the pay is not derived by the several artists from their respective arts. But the truth is, that while the art of medicine gives health, and the art of the builder builds a house, another art attends them which is the art of pay. The various arts may be doing their own business and benefiting that over which they preside, but would the artist receive any benefit from his art unless he were paid as well?

I suppose not.

But does he therefore confer no benefit when he works for nothing?

Certainly, he confers a benefit.

Then now, Thrasymachus, there is no longer any doubt that neither arts nor governments provide for their own interests; but, as we were before saying, they rule and provide for the interests of their subjects who are the weaker and not the stronger – to their good they attend and not to the good of the superior. And this is the reason, my dear Thrasymachus, why, as I was just now saying, no one is willing to govern; because no one likes to take in hand the reformation of evils which are not his concern without remuneration. For, in the execution of his work, and in giving his orders to another, the true artist does not regard his own interest, but always that of his subjects; and therefore in order that rulers may be willing to rule, they must be paid in one of three modes of payment, money, or honour, or a penalty for refusing.

What do you mean, Socrates? said Glaucon. The first two modes of payment are intelligible enough, but what the penalty is I do not understand, or how a penalty can be a payment.

You mean that you do not understand the nature of this payment which to the best men is the great inducement to rule? Of course you know that ambition and avarice are held to be, as indeed they are, a disgrace?

Very true.

And for this reason, I said, money and honour have no attraction for them; good men do not wish to be openly demanding payment for governing and so to get the name of hirelings, nor by secretly helping themselves out of the public revenues to get the name of thieves. And not being ambitious they do not care about honour. Wherefore necessity must be laid upon them, and they must be induced to serve from the fear of punishment. And this, as I imagine, is the reason why the forwardness to take office, instead of waiting to be compelled, has been deemed dishonourable. Now the worst part of the punishment is that he who refuses to rule is liable to be ruled by one who is worse than himself. And the fear of this, as I conceive, induces the good to take office, not because they would, but because they cannot help – not under the idea that they are going to have any benefit or enjoyment themselves, but as a necessity, and because they are not able to commit the task of ruling to any one who is better than themselves, or indeed as good. For there is reason to think that if a city were composed entirely of good men, then to avoid office would be as much an object of contention as to obtain office is at present; then we should have plain proof that the true ruler is not meant by nature to regard his own interest, but that of his subjects; and every one who knew this would choose rather to receive a benefit from another than to have the trouble of conferring one. So far am I from agreeing with Thrasymachus that justice is the interest of the stronger. This latter question need not be further discussed at present; but when Thrasymachus says that the life of the unjust is more advantageous than that of the just, his new statement appears to me to be of a far more serious character. Which of us has spoken truly? And which sort of life, Glaucon, do you prefer?

I for my part deem the life of the just to be the more advantageous, he answered.

Did you hear all the advantages of the unjust which Thrasymachus was rehearsing?

Yes, I heard him, he replied, but he has not convinced me.

Then shall we try to find some way of convincing him, if we can, that he is saying what is not true?

Most certainly, he replied.

If, I said, he makes a set speech and we make another recounting all the advantages of being just, and he answers and we rejoin, there must be a numbering and measuring of the goods which are claimed on either side, and in the end we shall want judges to decide; but if we proceed in our enquiry as we lately did, by making admissions to one another, we shall unite the offices of judge and advocate in our own persons.

Very good, he said.

And which method do I understand you to prefer? I said.

That which you propose.

Well, then, Thrasymachus, I said, suppose you begin at the beginning and answer me. You say that perfect injustice is more gainful than perfect justice?

Yes, that is what I say, and I have given you my reasons.

And what is your view about them? Would you call one of them virtue and the other vice?

Certainly.

I suppose that you would call justice virtue and injustice vice?

What a charming notion! So likely too, seeing that I affirm injustice to be profitable and justice not.

What else then would you say?

The opposite, he replied.

And would you call justice vice?

No, I would rather say sublime simplicity.

Then would you call injustice malignity?

No; I would rather say discretion.

And do the unjust appear to you to be wise and good?

Yes, he said; at any rate those of them who are able to be perfectly unjust, and who have the power of subduing states and nations; but perhaps you imagine me to be talking of cutpurses. Even this profession if undetected has advantages, though they are not to be compared with those of which I was just now speaking.

I do not think that I misapprehend your meaning, Thrasymachus, I replied; but still I cannot hear without amazement that you class injustice with wisdom and virtue, and justice with the opposite.

Certainly I do so class them.

Now, I said, you are on more substantial and almost unanswerable ground; for if the injustice which you were maintaining to be profitable had been admitted by you as by others to be vice and deformity, an answer might have been given to you on received principles; but now I perceive that you will call injustice honourable and strong, and to the unjust you will attribute all the qualities which were attributed by us before to the just, seeing that you do not hesitate to rank injustice with wisdom and virtue.

You have guessed most infallibly, he replied.

Then I certainly ought not to shrink from going through with the argument so long as I have reason to think that you, Thrasymachus, are speaking your real mind; for I do believe that you are now in earnest and are not amusing yourself at our expense.

I may be in earnest or not, but what is that to you? – to refute the argument is your business.

Very true, I said; that is what I have to do: But will you be so good as answer yet one more question? Does the just man try to gain any advantage over the just?

Far otherwise; if he did he would not be the simple amusing creature which he is.

And would he try to go beyond just action?

He would not.

And how would he regard the attempt to gain an advantage over the unjust; would that be considered by him as just or unjust?

He would think it just, and would try to gain the advantage; but he would not be able.

Whether he would or would not be able, I said, is not to the point. My question is only whether the just man, while refusing to have more than another just man, would wish and claim to have more than the unjust?

Yes, he would.

And what of the unjust – does he claim to have more than the just man and to do more than is just?

Of course, he said, for he claims to have more than all men.

And the unjust man will strive and struggle to obtain more than the unjust man or action, in order that he may have more than all?

True.

We may put the matter thus, I said – the just does not desire more than his like but more than his unlike, whereas the unjust desires more than both his like and his unlike?

Nothing, he said, can be better than that statement.

And the unjust is good and wise, and the just is neither?

Good again, he said.

And is not the unjust like the wise and good and the just unlike them?

Of course, he said, he who is of a certain nature, is like those who are of a certain nature; he who is not, not.

Each of them, I said, is such as his like is?

Certainly, he replied.

Very good, Thrasymachus, I said; and now to take the case of the arts: you would admit that one man is a musician and another not a musician?

Yes.

And which is wise and which is foolish?

Clearly the musician is wise, and he who is not a musician is foolish.

And he is good in as far as he is wise, and bad in as far as he is foolish?

Yes.

And you would say the same sort of thing of the physician?

Yes.

And do you think, my excellent friend, that a musician when he adjusts the lyre would desire or claim to exceed or go beyond a musician in the tightening and loosening the strings?

I do not think that he would.

But he would claim to exceed the non-musician?

Of course.

And what would you say of the physician? In prescribing meats and drinks would he wish to go beyond another physician or beyond the practice of medicine?

He would not.

But he would wish to go beyond the non-physician?

Yes.

And about knowledge and ignorance in general; see whether you think that any man who has knowledge ever would wish to have the choice of saying or doing more than another man who has knowledge. Would he not rather say or do the same as his like in the same case?

That, I suppose, can hardly be denied.

And what of the ignorant? would he not desire to have more than either the knowing or the ignorant?

I dare say.

And the knowing is wise?

Yes.

And the wise is good?

True.

Then the wise and good will not desire to gain more than his like, but more than his unlike and opposite?

I suppose so.

Whereas the bad and ignorant will desire to gain more than both?

Yes.

But did we not say, Thrasymachus, that the unjust goes beyond both his like and unlike? Were not these your words?

They were.

And you also said that the just will not go beyond his like but his unlike?

Yes.

Then the just is like the wise and good, and the unjust like the evil and ignorant?

That is the inference.

And each of them is such as his like is?

That was admitted.

Then the just has turned out to be wise and good and the unjust evil and ignorant.

Thrasymachus made all these admissions, not fluently, as I repeat them, but with extreme reluctance; it was a hot summer's day, and the perspiration poured from him in torrents; and then I saw what I had never seen before, Thrasymachus blushing. As we were now agreed that justice was virtue and wisdom, and injustice vice and ignorance, I proceeded to another point:

Well, I said, Thrasymachus, that matter is now settled; but were we not also saying that injustice had strength; do you remember?

Yes, I remember, he said, but do not suppose that I approve of what you are saying or have no answer; if however I were to answer, you would be quite certain to accuse me of haranguing; therefore either permit me to have my say out, or if you would rather ask, do so, and I will answer 'Very good,' as they say to story-telling old women, and will nod 'Yes' and 'No.'

Certainly not, I said, if contrary to your real opinion.

Yes, he said, I will, to please you, since you will not let me speak. What else would you have?

Nothing in the world, I said; and if you are so disposed I will ask and you shall answer.

Proceed.

Then I will repeat the question which I asked before, in order that our examination of the relative nature of justice and injustice may be carried on regularly. A statement was made that injustice is stronger and more powerful than justice, but now justice, having been identified with wisdom and virtue, is easily shown to be stronger than injustice, if injustice is ignorance; this can no longer be questioned by any one. But I want to view the matter, Thrasymachus, in a different way: You would not deny that a state may be unjust and may be unjustly attempting to enslave other states, or may have already enslaved them, and may be holding many of them in subjection?

True, he replied; and I will add that the best and most perfectly unjust state will be most likely to do so.

I know, I said, that such was your position; but what I would further consider is, whether this power which is possessed by the superior state can exist or be exercised without justice or only with justice.

If you are right in your view, and justice is wisdom, then only with justice; but if I am right, then without justice.

I am delighted, Thrasymachus, to see you not only nodding assent and dissent, but making answers which are quite excellent.

That is out of civility to you, he replied.

You are very kind, I said; and would you have the goodness also to inform me, whether you think that a state, or an army, or a band of robbers and thieves, or any other gang of evil-doers could act at all if they injured one another?

No indeed, he said, they could not.

But if they abstained from injuring one another, then they might act together better?

And this is because injustice creates divisions and hatreds and fighting, and justice imparts harmony and friendship; is not that true, Thrasymachus?

I agree, he said, because I do not wish to quarrel with you.

How good of you, I said; but I should like to know also whether injustice, having this tendency to arouse hatred, wherever existing, among slaves or among freemen, will not make them hate one another and set them at variance and render them incapable of common action?

Certainly.

And even if injustice be found in two only, will they not quarrel and fight, and become enemies to one another and to the just?

They will.

And suppose injustice abiding in a single person, would your wisdom say that she loses or that she retains her natural power?

Let us assume that she retains her power.

Yet is not the power which injustice exercises of such a nature that wherever she takes up her abode, whether in a city, in an army, in a family, or in any other body, that body is, to begin with, rendered incapable of united action by reason of sedition and distraction; and does it not become its own enemy and at variance with all that opposes it, and with the just? Is not this the case?

Yes, certainly.

And is not injustice equally fatal when existing in a single person; in the first place rendering him incapable of action because he is not at unity with himself, and in the second place making him an enemy to himself and the just? Is not that true, Thrasymachus?

Yes.

And O my friend, I said, surely the gods are just?

Granted that they are.

240 | P a g e

But if so, the unjust will be the enemy of the gods, and the just will be their friend?

Feast away in triumph, and take your fill of the argument; I will not oppose you, lest I should displease the company.

Well then, proceed with your answers, and let me have the remainder of my repast. For we have already shown that the just are clearly wiser and better and abler than the unjust, and that the unjust are incapable of common action; nay more, that to speak as we did of men who are evil acting at any time vigorously together, is not strictly true, for if they had been perfectly evil, they would have laid hands upon one another; but it is evident that there must have been some remnant of justice in them, which enabled them to combine; if there had not been they would have injured one another as well as their victims; they were but half-villains in their enterprises; for had they been whole villains, and utterly unjust, they would have been utterly incapable of action. That, as I believe, is the truth of the matter, and not what you said at first. But whether the just have a better and happier life than the unjust is a further question which we also proposed to consider. I think that they have, and for the reasons which I have given; but still I should like to examine further, for no light matter is at stake, nothing less than the rule of human life.

Proceed.

I will proceed by asking a question: Would you not say that a horse has some end?

I should.

And the end or use of a horse or of anything would be that which could not be accomplished, or not so well accomplished, by any other thing?

I do not understand, he said.

Let me explain: Can you see, except with the eye?

Certainly not.

Or hear, except with the ear?

No.

These then may be truly said to be the ends of these organs?

They may.

But you can cut off a vine-branch with a dagger or with a chisel, and in many other ways?

Of course.

And yet not so well as with a pruning-hook made for the purpose?

True.

May we not say that this is the end of a pruning-hook?

We may.

Then now I think you will have no difficulty in understanding my meaning when I asked the question whether the end of anything would be that which could not be accomplished, or not so well accomplished, by any other thing?

I understand your meaning, he said, and assent.

And that to which an end is appointed has also an excellence? Need I ask again whether the eye has an end?

It has.

And has not the eye an excellence?

Yes.

And the ear has an end and an excellence also?

True.

And the same is true of all other things; they have each of them an end and a special excellence?

That is so.

Well, and can the eyes fulfil their end if they are wanting in their own proper excellence and have a defect instead?

How can they, he said, if they are blind and cannot see?

You mean to say, if they have lost their proper excellence, which is sight; but I have not arrived at that point yet. I would rather ask the question more generally, and only enquire whether the things which fulfil their ends fulfil them by their own proper excellence, and fail of fulfilling them by their own defect?

Certainly, he replied.

I might say the same of the ears; when deprived of their own proper excellence they cannot fulfil their end?

True.

And the same observation will apply to all other things?

I agree.

Well; and has not the soul an end which nothing else can fulfil? for example, to superintend and command and deliberate and the like. Are not these functions proper to the soul, and can they rightly be assigned to any other?

To no other.

And is not life to be reckoned among the ends of the soul?

Assuredly, he said.

And has not the soul an excellence also?

Yes.

And can she or can she not fulfil her own ends when deprived of that excellence?

She cannot.

Then an evil soul must necessarily be an evil ruler and superintendent, and the good soul a good ruler?

Yes, necessarily.

And we have admitted that justice is the excellence of the soul, and injustice the defect of the soul?

That has been admitted.

Then the just soul and the just man will live well, and the unjust man will live ill?

That is what your argument proves.

And he who lives well is blessed and happy, and he who lives ill the reverse of happy?

Certainly.

Then the just is happy, and the unjust miserable?

So be it.

But happiness and not misery is profitable.

Of course.

Then, my blessed Thrasymachus, injustice can never be more profitable than justice.

Let this, Socrates, he said, be your entertainment at the Bendidea.

For which I am indebted to you, I said, now that you have grown gentle towards me and have left off scolding. Nevertheless, I have not been well entertained; but that was my own fault and not yours. As an epicure snatches a taste of every dish which is successively brought to table, he not having allowed himself time to enjoy the one before, so have I gone from one subject to another without having discovered what I sought at first, the nature of justice. I left that enquiry and turned away to consider whether justice is virtue and wisdom or evil and folly; and when there arose a further question about the comparative advantages of justice and injustice, I could not refrain from passing on to that. And the result of the whole discussion has been that I know nothing at all. For I know not what justice is, and therefore I am not likely to know whether it is or is not a virtue, nor can I say whether the just man is happy or unhappy.

BOOK II.

With these words I was thinking that I had made an end of the discussion; but the end, in truth, proved to be only a beginning. For Glaucon, who is always the most pugnacious of men, was dissatisfied at Thrasymachus' retirement; he wanted to have the battle out. So he said to me: Socrates, do you wish really to persuade us, or only to seem to have persuaded us, that to be just is always better than to be unjust?

I should wish really to persuade you, I replied, if I could.

Then you certainly have not succeeded. Let me ask you now: – How would you arrange goods – are there not some which we welcome for their own sakes, and independently of their consequences, as, for example, harmless pleasures and enjoyments, which delight us at the time, although nothing follows from them?

I agree in thinking that there is such a class, I replied.

Is there not also a second class of goods, such as knowledge, sight, health, which are desirable not only in themselves, but also for their results?

Certainly, I said.

And would you not recognize a third class, such as gymnastic, and the care of the sick, and the physician's art; also the various ways of money-making – these do us good but we regard them as disagreeable; and no one would choose them for their own sakes, but only for the sake of some reward or result which flows from them?

There is, I said, this third class also. But why do you ask?

Because I want to know in which of the three classes you would place justice?

In the highest class, I replied, – among those goods which he who would be happy desires both for their own sake and for the sake of their results.

Then the many are of another mind; they think that justice is to be reckoned in the troublesome class, among goods which are to be pursued for the sake of rewards and of reputation, but in themselves are disagreeable and rather to be avoided.

I know, I said, that this is their manner of thinking, and that this was the thesis which Thrasymachus was maintaining just now, when he censured justice and praised injustice. But I am too stupid to be convinced by him.

I wish, he said, that you would hear me as well as him, and then I shall see whether you and I agree. For Thrasymachus seems to me, like a snake, to have been charmed by your voice sooner than he ought to have been; but to my mind the nature of justice and injustice have not yet been made clear. Setting aside their rewards and results, I want to know what they are in themselves, and how they inwardly work in the soul. If you, please, then, I will revive the argument of Thrasymachus. And first I will speak of the nature and origin of justice according to the common view of them. Secondly, I will show that all men who practise justice do so against their will, of necessity, but not as a good. And thirdly, I will argue that there is reason in this view, for the life of the unjust is after all better far than the life of the just – if what they say is true, Socrates, since I myself am not of their opinion. But still I acknowledge that I am perplexed when I hear the voices of Thrasymachus and myriads of others dinning in my ears; and, on the other hand, I have never yet heard the superiority of justice to injustice maintained by any one in a satisfactory way. I want to hear justice praised in respect of itself; then I shall be satisfied, and you are the person from whom I think that I am most likely to hear this; and therefore I will praise the unjust life to the utmost of my power, and my manner of speaking will indicate the manner in which I desire to hear you too praising justice and censuring injustice. Will you say whether you approve of my proposal?

Indeed I do; nor can I imagine any theme about which a man of sense would oftener wish to converse.

I am delighted, he replied, to hear you say so, and shall begin by speaking, as I proposed, of the nature and origin of justice.

They say that to do injustice is, by nature, good; to suffer injustice, evil; but that the evil is greater than the good. And so when men have both done and suffered injustice and have had experience of both, not being able to avoid the one and obtain the other, they think that they had better agree among themselves to have neither; hence there arise laws and mutual covenants; and that which is ordained by law is termed by them lawful and just. This they affirm to be the origin and nature of justice; – it is a mean or compromise, between the best of all, which is to do injustice and not be punished, and the worst of all, which is to suffer injustice without the power of retaliation; and justice, being at a middle point between the two, is tolerated not as a good, but as the lesser evil, and honoured by reason of the inability of men to do injustice. For no man who is worthy to be called a man would ever submit to such an agreement if he were able to resist; he would be mad if he did. Such is the received account, Socrates, of the nature and origin of justice.

Now that those who practise justice do so involuntarily and because they have not the power to be unjust will best appear if we imagine something of this kind: having given both to the just and the unjust power to do what they will, let us watch and see whither desire will lead them; then we shall discover in the very act the just and unjust man to be proceeding along the same road, following their interest, which all natures deem to be their good, and are only diverted into the path of justice by the force of law. The liberty which we are supposing may be most completely given to them in the form of such a power as is said to have been possessed by Gyges, the ancestor of Croesus the Lydian. According to the tradition, Gyges was a shepherd in the service of the king of Lydia; there was a great storm, and an earthquake made an opening in the earth at the place where he was feeding his flock. Amazed at the sight, he descended into the opening, where, among other marvels, he beheld a hollow brazen horse, having doors, at which he stooping and looking in saw a dead body of stature, as appeared to him, more than human, and having nothing on but a gold ring; this he took from the finger of the dead and reascended. Now the shepherds met together, according to custom, that they might send their monthly report about the flocks to the king; into their assembly he came having the ring on his finger, and as he was sitting among them he chanced to turn the collet of the ring inside his hand, when instantly he became invisible to the rest of the company and they began to speak of him as if he were no longer present. He was astonished at this, and again touching the ring he turned the collet outwards and reappeared; he made several trials of the ring, and always with the same result – when he turned the collet inwards he became invisible, when outwards he reappeared. Whereupon he contrived to be chosen one of the messengers who were sent to the court; whereas soon as he arrived he seduced the queen, and with her help conspired against the king and slew him, and took the kingdom. Suppose now that there were two such magic rings, and the just put on one of them and the unjust the other; no man can be imagined to be of such an iron nature that he would stand fast in justice. No man would keep his hands off what was not his own when he could safely take what he liked out of the market, or go into houses and lie with any one at his pleasure, or kill or release from prison whom he would, and in all respects be like a God among men. Then the actions of the just would be as the actions of the unjust; they would both come at last to the same point. And this we may truly affirm to be a great proof that a man is just, not willingly or because he thinks that justice is any good to him individually, but of necessity, for wherever any one thinks that he can safely be unjust, there he is unjust. For all men believe in their hearts that injustice is far more profitable to the individual than justice, and he who argues as I have been supposing, will say that they are right. If you could imagine any one obtaining this power of becoming invisible, and never doing any wrong or touching what was another's, he would be thought by the lookers-on to be a most wretched idiot, although they would praise him to one another's faces, and keep up appearances with one another from a fear that they too might suffer injustice. Enough of this.

Now, if we are to form a real judgment of the life of the just and unjust, we must isolate them; there is no other way; and how is the isolation to be effected? I answer: Let the unjust man be entirely unjust, and the just man entirely just; nothing is to be taken away from either of them, and both are to be perfectly furnished for the work of their respective lives. First, let the unjust be like other distinguished masters of craft; like the skilful pilot or physician, who knows intuitively his own powers and keeps within their limits, and who, if he fails at any point, is able to recover himself. So let the unjust make his unjust attempts in the right way, and lie hidden if he means to be great in his injustice: (he who is found out is nobody:) for the highest reach of injustice is, to be deemed just when you are not. Therefore I say that in the perfectly unjust man we must assume the most perfect injustice; there is to be no deduction, but we must allow him, while doing the most unjust acts, to have acquired the greatest reputation for justice. If he have taken a false step he must be able to recover himself; he must be one who can speak with effect, if any of his deeds come to light, and who can force his way where force is required by his courage and strength, and command of money and friends. And at his side let us place the just man in his nobleness and simplicity, wishing, as Aeschylus says, to be and not to seem good. There must be no seeming, for if he seem to be just he will be honoured and rewarded, and then we shall not know whether he is just for the sake of justice or for the sake of honours and rewards; therefore, let him be clothed in justice only, and have no other covering; and he must be imagined in a state of life the opposite of the former. Let him be the best of men, and let him be thought the worst; then he will have been put to the proof; and we shall see whether he will be affected by the fear of infamy and its consequences. And let him continue thus to the hour of death; being just and seeming to be unjust. When both have reached the uttermost extreme, the one of justice and the other of injustice, let judgment be given which of them is the happier of the two.

Heavens! my dear Glaucon, I said, how energetically you polish them up for the decision, first one and then the other, as if they were two statues.

I do my best, he said. And now that we know what they are like there is no difficulty in tracing out the sort of life which awaits either of them. This I will proceed to describe; but as you may think the description a little too coarse, I ask you to suppose, Socrates, that the words which follow are not mine. – Let me put them into the mouths of the eulogists of injustice: They will tell you that the just man who is thought unjust will be scourged, racked, bound – will have his eyes burnt out; and, at last, after suffering every kind of evil, he will be impaled: Then he will understand that he ought to seem only, and not to be, just; the words of Aeschylus may be more truly spoken of the unjust than of the just. For the unjust is pursuing a reality; he does not live with a view to appearances – he wants to be really unjust and not to seem only: –

'His mind has a soil deep and fertile, Out of which spring his prudent counsels.'

In the first place, he is thought just, and therefore bears rule in the city; he can marry whom he will, and give in marriage to whom he will; also he can trade and deal where he likes, and always to his own advantage, because he has no misgivings about injustice; and at every contest, whether in public or private, he gets the better of his antagonists, and gains at their expense, and is rich, and out of his gains he can benefit his friends, and harm his enemies; moreover, he can offer sacrifices, and dedicate gifts to the gods abundantly and magnificently, and can honour the gods or any man whom he wants to honour in a far better style than the just, and therefore he is likely to be dearer than they are to the gods. And thus, Socrates, gods and men are said to unite in making the life of the unjust better than the life of the just.

I was going to say something in answer to Glaucon, when Adeimantus, his brother, interposed: Socrates, he said, you do not suppose that there is nothing more to be urged?

Why, what else is there? I answered.

The strongest point of all has not been even mentioned, he replied.

Well, then, according to the proverb, 'Let brother help brother' – if he fails in any part do you assist him; although I must confess that Glaucon has already said quite enough to lay me in the dust, and take from me the power of helping justice.

Nonsense, he replied. But let me add something more: There is another side to Glaucon's argument about the praise and censure of justice and injustice, which is equally required in order to bring out what I believe to be his meaning. Parents and tutors are always telling their sons and their wards that they are to be just; but why? not for the sake of justice, but for the sake of character and reputation; in the hope of obtaining for him who is reputed just some of those offices, marriages, and the like which Glaucon has enumerated among the advantages accruing to the unjust from the reputation of justice. More, however, is made of appearances by this class of persons than by the others; for they throw in the good opinion of the gods, and will tell you of a shower of benefits which the heavens, as they say, rain upon the pious; and this accords with the testimony of the noble Hesiod and Homer, the first of whom says, that the gods make the oaks of the just –

'To bear acorns at their summit, and bees in the middle; And the sheep are bowed down with the weight of their fleeces,'

and many other blessings of a like kind are provided for them. And Homer has a very similar strain; for he speaks of one whose fame is –

'As the fame of some blameless king who, like a god, Maintains justice; to whom the black earth brings forth Wheat and barley, whose trees are bowed with fruit, And his sheep never fail to bear, and the sea gives him fish.'

Still grander are the gifts of heaven which Musaeus and his son vouchsafe to the just; they take them down into the world below, where they have the saints lying on couches at a feast, everlastingly drunk, crowned with garlands; their idea seems to be that an immortality of drunkenness is the highest meed of virtue. Some extend their rewards yet further; the posterity, as they say, of the faithful and just shall survive to the third and fourth generation. This is the style in which they praise justice. But about the wicked there is another strain; they bury them in a slough in Hades, and make them carry water in a sieve; also while they are yet living they bring them to infamy, and inflict upon them the punishments which Glaucon described as the portion of the just who are reputed to be unjust; nothing else does their invention supply. Such is their manner of praising the one and censuring the other.

Once more, Socrates, I will ask you to consider another way of speaking about justice and injustice, which is not confined to the poets, but is found in prose writers. The universal voice of mankind is always declaring that justice and virtue are honourable, but grievous and toilsome; and that the pleasures of vice and injustice are easy of attainment, and are only censured by law and opinion. They say also that honesty is for the most part less profitable than dishonesty; and they are quite ready to call wicked men happy, and to honour them both in public and private when they are rich or in any other way influential, while they despise and overlook those who may be weak and poor, even though acknowledging them to be better than the others. But most extraordinary of all is their mode of speaking about virtue and the gods: they say that the gods apportion calamity and misery to many good men, and good and happiness to the wicked. And mendicant prophets go to rich men's doors and persuade them that they have a power committed to them by the gods of making an atonement for a man's own or his ancestor's sins by sacrifices or charms, with rejoicings and feasts; and they promise to harm an enemy, whether just or unjust, at a small cost; with magic arts and incantations binding heaven, as they say, to execute their will. And the poets are the authorities to whom they appeal, now smoothing the path of vice with the words of Hesiod; –

'Vice may be had in abundance without trouble; the way is smooth and her dwelling-place is near. But before virtue the gods have set toil,'

and a tedious and uphill road: then citing Homer as a witness that the gods may be influenced by men; for he also says: –

'The gods, too, may be turned from their purpose; and men pray to them and avert their wrath by sacrifices and soothing entreaties, and by libations and the odour of fat, when they have sinned and transgressed.'

And they produce a host of books written by Musaeus and Orpheus, who were children of the Moon and the Muses – that is what they say – according to which they perform their ritual, and persuade not only individuals, but whole cities, that expiations and atonements for sin may be made by sacrifices and amusements which fill a vacant hour, and are equally at the service of the living and the dead; the latter sort they call

THE REPUBLIC

mysteries, and they redeem us from the pains of hell, but if we neglect them no one knows what awaits us.

He proceeded: And now when the young hear all this said about virtue and vice, and the way in which gods and men regard them, how are their minds likely to be affected, my dear Socrates, – those of them, I mean, who are quickwitted, and, like bees on the wing, light on every flower, and from all that they hear are prone to draw conclusions as to what manner of persons they should be and in what way they should walk if they would make the best of life? Probably the youth will say to himself in the words of Pindar –

'Can I by justice or by crooked ways of deceit ascend a loftier tower which may be a fortress to me all my days?'

For what men say is that, if I am really just and am not also thought just profit there is none, but the pain and loss on the other hand are unmistakeable. But if, though unjust, I acquire the reputation of justice, a heavenly life is promised to me. Since then, as philosophers prove, appearance tyrannizes over truth and is lord of happiness, to appearance I must devote myself. I will describe around me a picture and shadow of virtue to be the vestibule and exterior of my house; behind I will trail the subtle and crafty fox, as Archilochus, greatest of sages, recommends. But I hear some one exclaiming that the concealment of wickedness is often difficult; to which I answer, Nothing great is easy. Nevertheless, the argument indicates this, if we would be happy, to be the path along which we should proceed. With a view to concealment we will establish secret brotherhoods and political clubs. And there are professors of rhetoric who teach the art of persuading courts and assemblies; and so, partly by persuasion and partly by force, I shall make unlawful gains and not be punished. Still I hear a voice saying that the gods cannot be deceived, neither can they be compelled. But what if there are no gods? or, suppose them to have no care of human things – why in either case should we mind about concealment? And even if there are gods, and they do care about us, yet we know of them only from tradition and the genealogies of the poets; and these are the very persons who say that they may be influenced and turned by 'sacrifices and soothing entreaties and by offerings.' Let us be consistent then, and believe both or neither. If the poets speak truly, why then we had better be unjust, and offer of the fruits of injustice; for if we are just, although we may escape the vengeance of heaven, we shall lose the gains of injustice; but, if we are unjust, we shall keep the gains, and by our sinning and praying, and praying and sinning, the gods will be propitiated, and we shall not be punished. 'But there is a world below in which either we or our posterity will suffer for our unjust deeds.' Yes, my friend, will be the reflection, but there are mysteries and atoning deities, and these have great power. That is what mighty cities declare; and the children of the gods, who were their poets and prophets, bear a like testimony.

On what principle, then, shall we any longer choose justice rather than the worst injustice? when, if we only unite the latter with a deceitful regard to appearances, we shall fare to our mind both with gods and men, in life and after death, as the most numerous and the highest authorities tell us. Knowing all this, Socrates, how can a man who has any superiority of mind or person or rank or wealth, be willing to honour justice; or indeed to refrain from laughing when he hears justice praised? And even if there should be some one who is able to disprove the truth of my words, and who is satisfied that justice is best, still he is not angry with the unjust, but is very ready to forgive them, because he also knows that men are not just of their own free will; unless, peradventure, there be some one whom the divinity within him may have inspired with a hatred of injustice, or who has attained knowledge of the truth – but no other man. He only blames injustice who, owing to cowardice or age or some weakness, has not the power of being unjust. And this is proved by the fact that when he obtains the power, he immediately becomes unjust as far as he can be.

The cause of all this, Socrates, was indicated by us at the beginning of the argument, when my brother and I told you how astonished we were to find that of all the professing panegyrists of justice – beginning with the ancient heroes of whom any memorial has been preserved to us, and ending with the men of our own time – no one has ever blamed injustice or praised justice except with a view to the glories, honours, and benefits which flow from them. No one has ever adequately described either in verse or prose the true essential nature of either of them abiding in the soul, and invisible to any human or divine eye; or shown that of all the things of a man's soul which he has within him, justice is the greatest good, and injustice the greatest evil. Had this been the universal strain, had you sought to persuade us of this from our youth upwards, we should not have been on the watch to keep one another from doing wrong, but every one would have been his own watchman, because afraid, if he did wrong, of harbouring in himself the greatest of evils. I dare say that Thrasymachus and others would seriously hold the language which I have been merely repeating, and words even stronger than these about justice and injustice, grossly, as I conceive, perverting their true nature. But I speak in this vehement manner, as I must frankly confess to you, because I want to hear from you the opposite side; and I would ask you to show not only the superiority which justice has over injustice, but what effect they have on the possessor of them which makes the one to be a good and the other an evil to him. And please, as Glaucon requested of you, to exclude reputations; for unless you take away from each of them his true reputation and add on the false, we shall say that you do not praise justice, but the appearance of it; we shall think that you are only exhorting us to keep injustice dark, and that you really agree with Thrasymachus in thinking that justice is another's good and the interest of the stronger, and that injustice is a man's own profit and interest, though injurious to the weaker. Now as you have admitted that justice is one of that highest class of goods which are desired indeed for their results, but in a far greater degree for their own sakes – like sight or hearing or knowledge or health, or any other real and natural and not merely conventional good – I would ask you in your praise of justice to regard one point only: I mean the essential good and evil which justice and injustice work in the possessors of them. Let others praise justice and censure injustice, magnifying the rewards and honours of the one and abusing the other; that is a manner of arguing which, coming from them, I am ready to tolerate, but from you who have spent your whole life in the consideration of this question, unless I hear the contrary from your own lips, I expect something better. And therefore, I say, not only prove to us that justice is better than injustice, but show what they either of them do to the possessor of them, which makes the one to be a good and the other an evil, whether seen or unseen by gods and men.

I had always admired the genius of Glaucon and Adeimantus, but on hearing these words I was quite delighted, and said: Sons of an illustrious father, that was not a bad beginning of the Elegiac verses which the admirer of Glaucon made in honour of you after you had distinguished yourselves at the battle of Megara: –

'Sons of Ariston,' he sang, 'divine offspring of an illustrious hero.'

The epithet is very appropriate, for there is something truly divine in being able to argue as you have done for the superiority of injustice, and remaining unconvinced by your own arguments. And I do believe that you are not convinced – this I infer from your general character, for had I judged only from your speeches I should have mistrusted you. But now, the greater my confidence in you, the greater is my difficulty in knowing what to say. For I am in a strait between two; on the one hand I feel that I am unequal to the task; and my inability is brought home to me by the fact that you were not satisfied with the answer which I made to Thrasymachus, proving, as I thought, the superiority which justice has over injustice. And yet I cannot refuse to help, while breath and speech remain to me; I am afraid that there would be an impiety in being present when justice is evil spoken of and not lifting up a hand in her defence. And therefore I had best give such help as I can.

Glaucon and the rest entreated me by all means not to let the question drop, but to proceed in the investigation. They wanted to arrive at the truth, first, about the nature of justice and injustice, and secondly, about their relative advantages. I told them, what I really thought, that the enquiry would be of a serious nature, and would require very good eyes. Seeing then, I said, that we are no great wits, I think that we had better adopt a method which I may illustrate thus; suppose that a short-sighted person had been asked by some one to read small letters from a distance; and it occurred to some one else that they might be found in another place which was larger and in which the letters were larger – if they were the same and he could read the larger letters first, and then proceed to the lesser – this would have been thought a rare piece of good fortune.

Very true, said Adeimantus; but how does the illustration apply to our enquiry?

I will tell you, I replied; justice, which is the subject of our enquiry, is, as you know, sometimes spoken of as the virtue of an individual, and sometimes as the virtue of a State.

True, he replied.

And is not a State larger than an individual?

It is.

Then in the larger the quantity of justice is likely to be larger and more easily discernible. I propose therefore that we enquire into the nature of justice and injustice, first as they appear in the State, and secondly in the individual, proceeding from the greater to the lesser and comparing them.

That, he said, is an excellent proposal.

And if we imagine the State in process of creation, we shall see the justice and injustice of the State in process of creation also.

I dare say.

When the State is completed there may be a hope that the object of our search will be more easily discovered.

Yes, far more easily.

But ought we to attempt to construct one? I said; for to do so, as I am inclined to think, will be a very serious task. Reflect therefore.

I have reflected, said Adeimantus, and am anxious that you should proceed.

A State, I said, arises, as I conceive, out of the needs of mankind; no one is self-sufficing, but all of us have many wants. Can any other origin of a State be imagined?

There can be no other.

Then, as we have many wants, and many persons are needed to supply them, one takes a helper for one purpose and another for another; and when these partners and helpers are gathered together in one habitation the body of inhabitants is termed a State.

True, he said.

And they exchange with one another, and one gives, and another receives, under the idea that the exchange will be for their good.

Very true.

Then, I said, let us begin and create in idea a State; and yet the true creator is necessity, who is the mother of our invention.

Of course, he replied.

Now the first and greatest of necessities is food, which is the condition of life and existence.

Certainly.

The second is a dwelling, and the third clothing and the like.

True.

And now let us see how our city will be able to supply this great demand: We may suppose that one man is a husbandman, another a builder, some one else a weaver – shall we add to them a shoemaker, or perhaps some other purveyor to our bodily wants?

Quite right.

The barest notion of a State must include four or five men.

Clearly.

And how will they proceed? Will each bring the result of his labours into a common stock? – the individual husbandman, for example, producing for four, and labouring four times as long and as much as he need in the provision of food with which he supplies others as well as himself; or will he have nothing to do with others and not be at the trouble of producing for them, but provide for himself alone a fourth of the food in a fourth of the time, and in the remaining three fourths of his time be employed in making a house or a coat or a pair of shoes, having no partnership with others, but supplying himself all his own wants?

Adeimantus thought that he should aim at producing food only and not at producing everything.

Probably, I replied, that would be the better way; and when I hear you say this, I am myself reminded that we are not all alike; there are diversities of natures among us which are adapted to different occupations.

Very true.

And will you have a work better done when the workman has many occupations, or when he has only one?

When he has only one.

Further, there can be no doubt that a work is spoilt when not done at the right time?

No doubt.

For business is not disposed to wait until the doer of the business is at leisure; but the doer must follow up what he is doing, and make the business his first object.

He must.

And if so, we must infer that all things are produced more plentifully and easily and of a better quality when one man does one thing which is natural to him and does it at the right time, and leaves other things.

Undoubtedly.

Then more than four citizens will be required; for the husbandman will not make his own plough or mattock, or other implements of agriculture, if they are to be good for anything. Neither will the builder make his tools – and he too needs many; and in like manner the weaver and shoemaker.

True.

Then carpenters, and smiths, and many other artisans, will be sharers in our little State, which is already beginning to grow?

True.

Yet even if we add neatherds, shepherds, and other herdsmen, in order that our husbandmen may have oxen to plough with, and builders as well as husbandmen may have draught cattle, and curriers and weavers fleeces and hides, – still our State will not be very large.

That is true; yet neither will it be a very small State which contains all these.

Then, again, there is the situation of the city – to find a place where nothing need be imported is wellnigh impossible.

Impossible.

Then there must be another class of citizens who will bring the required supply from another city?

There must.

But if the trader goes empty-handed, having nothing which they require who would supply his need, he will come back empty-handed.

That is certain.

And therefore what they produce at home must be not only enough for themselves, but such both in quantity and quality as to accommodate those from whom their wants are supplied.

Very true.

Then more husbandmen and more artisans will be required?

They will.

Not to mention the importers and exporters, who are called merchants?

Yes.

Then we shall want merchants?

We shall.

And if merchandise is to be carried over the sea, skilful sailors will also be needed, and in considerable numbers?

Yes, in considerable numbers.

Then, again, within the city, how will they exchange their productions? To secure such an exchange was, as you will remember, one of our principal objects when we formed them into a society and constituted a State.

Clearly they will buy and sell.

Then they will need a market-place, and a money-token for purposes of exchange.

Certainly.

Suppose now that a husbandman, or an artisan, brings some production to market, and he comes at a time when there is no one to exchange with him, – is he to leave his calling and sit idle in the market-place?

Not at all; he will find people there who, seeing the want, undertake the office of salesmen. In well-ordered states they are commonly those who are the weakest in bodily strength, and therefore of little use for any other purpose; their duty is to be in the market, and to give money in exchange for goods to those who desire to sell and to take money from those who desire to buy.

This want, then, creates a class of retail-traders in our State. Is not 'retailer' the term which is applied to those who sit in the market-place engaged in buying and selling, while those who wander from one city to another are called merchants?

Yes, he said.

And there is another class of servants, who are intellectually hardly on the level of companionship; still they have plenty of bodily strength for labour, which accordingly they sell, and are called, if I do not mistake, hirelings, hire being the name which is given to the price of their labour.

True.

Then hirelings will help to make up our population?

Yes.

And now, Adeimantus, is our State matured and perfected?

I think so.

Where, then, is justice, and where is injustice, and in what part of the State did they spring up?

Probably in the dealings of these citizens with one another. I cannot imagine that they are more likely to be found any where else.

I dare say that you are right in your suggestion, I said; we had better think the matter out, and not shrink from the enquiry.

Let us then consider, first of all, what will be their way of life, now that we have thus established them. Will they not produce corn, and wine, and clothes, and shoes, and build houses for themselves? And when they are housed, they will work, in summer, commonly, stripped and barefoot, but in winter substantially clothed and shod. They will feed on barley-meal and flour of wheat, baking and kneading them, making noble cakes and loaves; these they will serve up on a mat of reeds or on clean leaves, themselves reclining the while upon beds strewn with yew or myrtle. And they and their children will feast, drinking of the wine which they have made, wearing garlands on their heads, and hymning the praises of the gods, in happy converse with one another. And they will take care that their families do not exceed their means; having an eye to poverty or war.

But, said Glaucon, interposing, you have not given them a relish to their meal.

True, I replied, I had forgotten; of course they must have a relish – salt, and olives, and cheese, and they will boil roots and herbs such as country people prepare; for a dessert we shall give them figs, and peas, and beans; and they will roast myrtle-berries and acorns at the fire, drinking in moderation. And with such a diet they may be expected to live in peace and health to a good old age, and bequeath a similar life to their children after them.

Yes, Socrates, he said, and if you were providing for a city of pigs, how else would you feed the beasts?

But what would you have, Glaucon? I replied.

Why, he said, you should give them the ordinary conveniences of life. People who are to be comfortable are accustomed to lie on sofas, and dine off tables, and they should have sauces and sweets in the modern style.

Yes, I said, now I understand: the question which you would have me consider is, not only how a State, but how a luxurious State is created; and possibly there is no harm in this, for in such a State we shall be more likely to see how justice and injustice originate. In my opinion the true and healthy constitution of the State is the one which I have described. But if you wish also to see a State at fever-heat, I have no objection. For I suspect that many will not be satisfied with the simpler way of life. They will be for adding sofas, and tables, and other furniture; also dainties, and perfumes, and incense, and courtesans, and cakes, all these not of one sort only, but in every variety; we must go beyond the necessaries of which I was at first speaking, such as houses, and clothes, and shoes: the arts of the painter and the embroiderer will have to be set in motion, and gold and ivory and all sorts of materials must be procured.

True, he said.

Then we must enlarge our borders; for the original healthy State is no longer sufficient. Now will the city have to fill and swell with a multitude of callings which are not required by any natural want; such as the whole tribe of hunters and actors, of whom one large class have to do with forms and colours; another will be the votaries of music – poets and their attendant train of rhapsodists, players, dancers, contractors; also makers of divers kinds of articles, including women's dresses. And we shall want more servants. Will not tutors be also in request, and nurses wet and dry, tirewomen and barbers, as well as confectioners and cooks; and swineherds, too, who were not needed and therefore had no place in the former edition of our State, but are needed now? They must not be forgotten: and there will be animals of many other kinds, if people eat them.

Certainly.

And living in this way we shall have much greater need of physicians than before?

Much greater.

And the country which was enough to support the original inhabitants will be too small now, and not enough?

Quite true.

Then a slice of our neighbours' land will be wanted by us for pasture and tillage, and they will want a slice of ours, if, like ourselves, they exceed the limit of necessity, and give themselves up to the unlimited accumulation of wealth?

That, Socrates, will be inevitable.

And so we shall go to war, Glaucon. Shall we not?

Most certainly, he replied.

Then without determining as yet whether war does good or harm, thus much we may affirm, that now we have discovered war to be derived from causes which are also the causes of almost all the evils in States, private as well as public.

Undoubtedly.

And our State must once more enlarge; and this time the enlargement will be nothing short of a whole army, which will have to go out and fight with the invaders for all that we have, as well as for the things and persons whom we were describing above.

Why? he said; are they not capable of defending themselves?

No, I said; not if we were right in the principle which was acknowledged by all of us when we were framing the State: the principle, as you will remember, was that one man cannot practise many arts with success.

Very true, he said.

But is not war an art?

Certainly.

And an art requiring as much attention as shoemaking?

Quite true.

And the shoemaker was not allowed by us to be a husbandman, or a weaver, or a builder – in order that we might have our shoes well made; but to him and to every other worker was assigned one work for which he was by nature fitted, and at that he was to continue working all his life long and at no other; he was not to let opportunities slip, and then he would become a good workman. Now nothing can be more important than that the work of a soldier should be well done. But is war an art so easily acquired that a man may be a warrior who is also a husbandman, or shoemaker, or other artisan; although no one in the world would be a good dice or draught player who merely took up the game as a recreation, and had not from his earliest years devoted himself to this and nothing else? No tools will make a man a skilled workman, or master of defence, nor be of any use to him who has not learned how to handle them, and has never bestowed any attention upon them. How then will he who takes up a shield or other implement of war become a good fighter all in a day, whether with heavy-armed or any other kind of troops?

Yes, he said, the tools which would teach men their own use would be beyond price.

And the higher the duties of the guardian, I said, the more time, and skill, and art, and application will be needed by him?

No doubt, he replied.

Will he not also require natural aptitude for his calling?

Certainly.

Then it will be our duty to select, if we can, natures which are fitted for the task of guarding the city?

It will.

And the selection will be no easy matter, I said; but we must be brave and do our best.

We must.

Is not the noble youth very like a well-bred dog in respect of guarding and watching?

What do you mean?

I mean that both of them ought to be quick to see, and swift to overtake the enemy when they see him; and strong too if, when they have caught him, they have to fight with him.

All these qualities, he replied, will certainly be required by them.

Well, and your guardian must be brave if he is to fight well?

Certainly.

And is he likely to be brave who has no spirit, whether horse or dog or any other animal? Have you never observed how invincible and unconquerable is spirit and how the presence of it makes the soul of any creature to be absolutely fearless and indomitable?

I have.

Then now we have a clear notion of the bodily qualities which are required in the guardian.

True.

And also of the mental ones; his soul is to be full of spirit?

Yes.

But are not these spirited natures apt to be savage with one another, and with everybody else?

A difficulty by no means easy to overcome, he replied.

Whereas, I said, they ought to be dangerous to their enemies, and gentle to their friends; if not, they will destroy themselves without waiting for their enemies to destroy them.

True, he said.

What is to be done then? I said; how shall we find a gentle nature which has also a great spirit, for the one is the contradiction of the other?

True.

He will not be a good guardian who is wanting in either of these two qualities; and yet the combination of them appears to be impossible; and hence we must infer that to be a good guardian is impossible.

I am afraid that what you say is true, he replied.

Here feeling perplexed I began to think over what had preceded. – My friend, I said, no wonder that we are in a perplexity; for we have lost sight of the image which we had before us.

What do you mean? he said.

I mean to say that there do exist natures gifted with those opposite qualities.

And where do you find them?

Many animals, I replied, furnish examples of them; our friend the dog is a very good one: you know that well-bred dogs are perfectly gentle to their familiars and acquaintances, and the reverse to strangers.

Yes, I know.

Then there is nothing impossible or out of the order of nature in our finding a guardian who has a similar combination of qualities?

Certainly not.

Would not he who is fitted to be a guardian, besides the spirited nature, need to have the qualities of a philosopher?

I do not apprehend your meaning.

The trait of which I am speaking, I replied, may be also seen in the dog, and is remarkable in the animal.

What trait?

Why, a dog, whenever he sees a stranger, is angry; when an acquaintance, he welcomes him, although the one has never done him any harm, nor the other any good. Did this never strike you as curious?

The matter never struck me before; but I quite recognise the truth of your remark.

And surely this instinct of the dog is very charming; – your dog is a true philosopher.

Why?

Why, because he distinguishes the face of a friend and of an enemy only by the criterion of knowing and not knowing. And must not an animal be a lover of learning who determines what he likes and dislikes by the test of knowledge and ignorance?

Most assuredly.

And is not the love of learning the love of wisdom, which is philosophy?

They are the same, he replied.

And may we not say confidently of man also, that he who is likely to be gentle to his friends and acquaintances, must by nature be a lover of wisdom and knowledge?

That we may safely affirm.

Then he who is to be a really good and noble guardian of the State will require to unite in himself philosophy and spirit and swiftness and strength?

Undoubtedly.

Then we have found the desired natures; and now that we have found them, how are they to be reared and educated? Is not this an enquiry which may be expected to throw light on the greater enquiry which is our final end – How do justice and injustice grow up in States? for we do not want either to omit what is to the point or to draw out the argument to an inconvenient length.

Adeimantus thought that the enquiry would be of great service to us.

Then, I said, my dear friend, the task must not be given up, even if somewhat long.

Certainly not.

Come then, and let us pass a leisure hour in story-telling, and our story shall be the education of our heroes.

By all means.

And what shall be their education? Can we find a better than the traditional sort? – and this has two divisions, gymnastic for the body, and music for the soul.

True.

Shall we begin education with music, and go on to gymnastic afterwards?

By all means.

And when you speak of music, do you include literature or not?

I do.

And literature may be either true or false?

Yes.

And the young should be trained in both kinds, and we begin with the false?

I do not understand your meaning, he said.

You know, I said, that we begin by telling children stories which, though not wholly destitute of truth, are in the main fictitious; and these stories are told them when they are not of an age to learn gymnastics.

Very true.

That was my meaning when I said that we must teach music before gymnastics.

Quite right, he said.

You know also that the beginning is the most important part of any work, especially in the case of a young and tender thing; for that is the time at which the character is being formed and the desired impression is more readily taken.

Quite true.

And shall we just carelessly allow children to hear any casual tales which may be devised by casual persons, and to receive into their minds ideas for the most part the very opposite of those which we should wish them to have when they are grown up?

We cannot.

Then the first thing will be to establish a censorship of the writers of fiction, and let the censors receive any tale of fiction which is good, and reject the bad; and we will desire mothers and nurses to tell their children the authorised ones only. Let them fashion the mind with such tales, even more fondly than they mould the body with their hands; but most of those which are now in use must be discarded.

Of what tales are you speaking? he said.

You may find a model of the lesser in the greater, I said; for they are necessarily of the same type, and there is the same spirit in both of them.

Very likely, he replied; but I do not as yet know what you would term the greater.

Those, I said, which are narrated by Homer and Hesiod, and the rest of the poets, who have ever been the great story-tellers of mankind.

But which stories do you mean, he said; and what fault do you find with them?

A fault which is most serious, I said; the fault of telling a lie, and, what is more, a bad lie.

But when is this fault committed?

Whenever an erroneous representation is made of the nature of gods and heroes, – as when a painter paints a portrait not having the shadow of a likeness to the original.

Yes, he said, that sort of thing is certainly very blameable; but what are the stories which you mean?

First of all, I said, there was that greatest of all lies in high places, which the poet told about Uranus, and which was a bad lie too, – I mean what Hesiod says that Uranus did, and how Cronus retaliated on him. The doings of Cronus, and the sufferings which in turn his son inflicted upon him, even if they were true, ought certainly not to be lightly told to young and thoughtless persons; if possible, they had better be buried in silence. But if there is an absolute necessity for their mention, a chosen few might hear them in a mystery, and they should sacrifice not a common (Eleusinian) pig, but some huge and unprocurable victim; and then the number of the hearers will be very few indeed.

Why, yes, said he, those stories are extremely objectionable.

Yes, Adeimantus, they are stories not to be repeated in our State; the young man should not be told that in committing the worst of crimes he is far from doing anything outrageous; and that even if he chastises his father when he does wrong, in whatever manner, he will only be following the example of the first and greatest among the gods.

I entirely agree with you, he said; in my opinion those stories are quite unfit to be repeated.

Neither, if we mean our future guardians to regard the habit of quarrelling among themselves as of all things the basest, should any word be said to them of the wars in heaven, and of the plots and fightings of the gods against one another, for they are not true. No, we shall never mention the battles of the giants, or let them be embroidered on garments; and we shall be silent about the innumerable other quarrels of gods and heroes with their friends and relatives. If they would only believe us we would tell them that quarrelling is unholy, and that never up to this time has there been any quarrel between citizens; this is what old men and old women should begin by telling children; and when they grow up, the poets also should be told to compose for them in a similar spirit. But the narrative of Hephaestus binding Here his mother, or how on another occasion Zeus sent him flying for taking her part when she was being beaten, and all the battles of the gods in Homer – these tales must not be admitted into our State, whether they are supposed to have an allegorical meaning or not. For a young person cannot judge what is allegorical and what is literal; anything that he receives into his mind at that age is likely to become indelible and unalterable; and therefore it is most important that the tales which the young first hear should be models of virtuous thoughts.

There you are right, he replied; but if any one asks where are such models to be found and of what tales are you speaking – how shall we answer him?

I said to him, You and I, Adeimantus, at this moment are not poets, but founders of a State: now the founders of a State ought to know the general forms in which poets should cast their tales, and the limits which must be observed by them, but to make the tales is not their business.

Very true, he said; but what are these forms of theology which you mean?

Something of this kind, I replied: – God is always to be represented as he truly is, whatever be the sort of poetry, epic, lyric or tragic, in which the representation is given.

Right.

And is he not truly good? and must he not be represented as such?

Certainly.

And no good thing is hurtful?

No, indeed.

And that which is not hurtful hurts not?

Certainly not.

And that which hurts not does no evil?

No.

And can that which does no evil be a cause of evil?

Impossible.

And the good is advantageous?

Yes.

And therefore the cause of well-being?

Yes.

It follows therefore that the good is not the cause of all things, but of the good only?

Assuredly.

Then God, if he be good, is not the author of all things, as the many assert, but he is the cause of a few things only, and not of most things that occur to men. For few are the goods of human life, and many are the evils, and the good is to be attributed to God alone; of the evils the causes are to be sought elsewhere, and not in him.

That appears to me to be most true, he said.

Then we must not listen to Homer or to any other poet who is guilty of the folly of saying that two casks

'Lie at the threshold of Zeus, full of lots, one of good, the other of evil lots,'

and that he to whom Zeus gives a mixture of the two

'Sometimes meets with evil fortune, at other times with good;'

but that he to whom is given the cup of unmingled ill,

'Him wild hunger drives o'er the beauteous earth.'

And again –

'Zeus, who is the dispenser of good and evil to us.'

And if any one asserts that the violation of oaths and treaties, which was really the work of Pandarus, was brought about by Athene and Zeus, or that the strife and contention of the gods was instigated by Themis and Zeus, he shall not have our approval; neither will we allow our young men to hear the words of Aeschylus, that

'God plants guilt among men when he desires utterly to destroy a house.'

And if a poet writes of the sufferings of Niobe – the subject of the tragedy in which these iambic verses occur – or of the house of Pelops, or of the Trojan war or on any similar theme, either we must not permit him to say that these are the works of God, or if they are of God, he must devise some explanation of them such as we are seeking; he must say that God did what was just and right, and they were the better for being punished; but that those who are punished are miserable, and that God is the author of their misery – the poet is not to be permitted to say; though he may say that the wicked are miserable because they require to be punished, and are benefited by receiving punishment from God; but that God being good is the author of evil to any one is to be strenuously denied, and not to be said or sung or heard in verse or prose by any one whether old or young in any well-ordered commonwealth. Such a fiction is suicidal, ruinous, impious.

I agree with you, he replied, and am ready to give my assent to the law.

Let this then be one of our rules and principles concerning the gods, to which our poets and reciters will be expected to conform, – that God is not the author of all things, but of good only.

That will do, he said.

And what do you think of a second principle? Shall I ask you whether God is a magician, and of a nature to appear insidiously now in one shape, and now in another – sometimes himself changing and passing into many forms, sometimes deceiving us with the semblance of such transformations; or is he one and the same immutably fixed in his own proper image?

I cannot answer you, he said, without more thought.

Well, I said; but if we suppose a change in anything, that change must be effected either by the thing itself, or by some other thing?

Most certainly.

And things which are at their best are also least liable to be altered or discomposed; for example, when healthiest and strongest, the human frame is least liable to be affected by meats and drinks, and the plant which is in the fullest vigour also suffers least from winds or the heat of the sun or any similar causes.

Of course.

And will not the bravest and wisest soul be least confused or deranged by any external influence?

True.

And the same principle, as I should suppose, applies to all composite things – furniture, houses, garments: when good and well made, they are least altered by time and circumstances.

Very true.

Then everything which is good, whether made by art or nature, or both, is least liable to suffer change from without?

True.

But surely God and the things of God are in every way perfect?

Of course they are.

Then he can hardly be compelled by external influence to take many shapes?

He cannot.

But may he not change and transform himself?

Clearly, he said, that must be the case if he is changed at all.

And will he then change himself for the better and fairer, or for the worse and more unsightly?

If he change at all he can only change for the worse, for we cannot suppose him to be deficient either in virtue or beauty.

Very true, Adeimantus; but then, would any one, whether God or man, desire to make himself worse?

Impossible.

Then it is impossible that God should ever be willing to change; being, as is supposed, the fairest and best that is conceivable, every God remains absolutely and for ever in his own form.

That necessarily follows, he said, in my judgment.

Then, I said, my dear friend, let none of the poets tell us that

'The gods, taking the disguise of strangers from other lands, walk up and down cities in all sorts of forms;'

and let no one slander Proteus and Thetis, neither let any one, either in tragedy or in any other kind of poetry, introduce Here disguised in the likeness of a priestess asking an alms

'For the life-giving daughters of Inachus the river of Argos;'

– let us have no more lies of that sort. Neither must we have mothers under the influence of the poets scaring their children with a bad version of these myths – telling how certain gods, as they say, 'Go about by night in the likeness of so many strangers and in divers forms;' but let them take heed lest they make cowards of their children, and at the same time speak blasphemy against the gods.

Heaven forbid, he said.

But although the gods are themselves unchangeable, still by witchcraft and deception they may make us think that they appear in various forms?

Perhaps, he replied.

Well, but can you imagine that God will be willing to lie, whether in word or deed, or to put forth a phantom of himself?

I cannot say, he replied.

Do you not know, I said, that the true lie, if such an expression may be allowed, is hated of gods and men?

What do you mean? he said.

I mean that no one is willingly deceived in that which is the truest and highest part of himself, or about the truest and highest matters; there, above all, he is most afraid of a lie having possession of him.

Still, he said, I do not comprehend you.

The reason is, I replied, that you attribute some profound meaning to my words; but I am only saying that deception, or being deceived or uninformed about the highest realities in the highest part of themselves, which is the soul, and in that part of them to have and to hold the lie, is what mankind least like; – that, I say, is what they utterly detest.

There is nothing more hateful to them.

And, as I was just now remarking, this ignorance in the soul of him who is deceived may be called the true lie; for the lie in words is only a kind of imitation and shadowy image of a previous affection of the soul, not pure unadulterated falsehood. Am I not right?

Perfectly right.

The true lie is hated not only by the gods, but also by men?

Yes.

Whereas the lie in words is in certain cases useful and not hateful; in dealing with enemies – that would be an instance; or again, when those whom we call our friends in a fit of madness or illusion are going to do some harm, then it is useful and is a sort of medicine or preventive; also in the tales of mythology, of which we were just now speaking – because we do not know the truth about ancient times, we make falsehood as much like truth as we can, and so turn it to account.

Very true, he said.

But can any of these reasons apply to God? Can we suppose that he is ignorant of antiquity, and therefore has recourse to invention?

That would be ridiculous, he said.

Then the lying poet has no place in our idea of God?

I should say not.

Or perhaps he may tell a lie because he is afraid of enemies?

That is inconceivable.

But he may have friends who are senseless or mad?

But no mad or senseless person can be a friend of God.

Then no motive can be imagined why God should lie?

None whatever.

Then the superhuman and divine is absolutely incapable of falsehood?

Yes.

Then is God perfectly simple and true both in word and deed; he changes not; he deceives not, either by sign or word, by dream or waking vision.

Your thoughts, he said, are the reflection of my own.

You agree with me then, I said, that this is the second type or form in which we should write and speak about divine things. The gods are not magicians who transform themselves, neither do they deceive mankind in any way.

I grant that.

Then, although we are admirers of Homer, we do not admire the lying dream which Zeus sends to Agamemnon; neither will we praise the verses of Aeschylus in which Thetis says that Apollo at her nuptials

'Was celebrating in song her fair progeny whose days were to be long, and to know no sickness. And when he had spoken of my lot as in all things blessed of heaven he raised a note of triumph and cheered my soul. And I thought that the word of Phoebus, being divine and full of prophecy, would not fail. And now he himself who uttered the strain, he who was present at the banquet, and who said this – he it is who has slain my son.'

These are the kind of sentiments about the gods which will arouse our anger; and he who utters them shall be refused a chorus; neither shall we allow teachers to make use of them in the instruction of the young, meaning, as we do, that our guardians, as far as men can be, should be true worshippers of the gods and like them.

I entirely agree, he said, in these principles, and promise to make them my laws.

BOOK III.

Such then, I said, are our principles of theology – some tales are to be told, and others are not to be told to our disciples from their youth upwards, if we mean them to honour the gods and their parents, and to value friendship with one another.

Yes; and I think that our principles are right, he said.

But if they are to be courageous, must they not learn other lessons besides these, and lessons of such a kind as will take away the fear of death? Can any man be courageous who has the fear of death in him?

Certainly not, he said.

And can he be fearless of death, or will he choose death in battle rather than defeat and slavery, who believes the world below to be real and terrible?

Impossible.

Then we must assume a control over the narrators of this class of tales as well as over the others, and beg them not simply to revile but rather to commend the world below, intimating to them that their descriptions are untrue, and will do harm to our future warriors.

That will be our duty, he said.

Then, I said, we shall have to obliterate many obnoxious passages, beginning with the verses,

'I would rather be a serf on the land of a poor and portionless man than rule over all the dead who have come to nought.'

We must also expunge the verse, which tells us how Pluto feared,

'Lest the mansions grim and squalid which the gods abhor should be seen both of mortals and immortals.'

And again: –

'O heavens! verily in the house of Hades there is soul and ghostly form but no mind at all!'

Again of Tiresias: –

'(To him even after death did Persephone grant mind,) that he alone should be wise; but the other souls are flitting shades.'

Again: –

'The soul flying from the limbs had gone to Hades, lamenting her fate, leaving manhood and youth.'

Again: –

'And the soul, with shrilling cry, passed like smoke beneath the earth.'

And, –

'As bats in hollow of mystic cavern, whenever any of them has dropped out of the string and falls from the rock, fly shrilling and cling to one another, so did they with shrilling cry hold together as they moved.'

And we must beg Homer and the other poets not to be angry if we strike out these and similar passages, not because they are unpoetical, or unattractive to the popular ear, but because the greater the poetical charm of them, the less are they meet for the ears of boys and men who are meant to be free, and who should fear slavery more than death.

Undoubtedly.

Also we shall have to reject all the terrible and appalling names which describe the world below – Cocytus and Styx, ghosts under the earth, and sapless shades, and any similar words of which the very mention causes a shudder to pass through the inmost soul of him who hears them. I do not say that these horrible stories may not have a use of some kind; but there is a danger that the nerves of our guardians may be rendered too excitable and effeminate by them.

There is a real danger, he said.

Then we must have no more of them.

True.

Another and a nobler strain must be composed and sung by us.

Clearly.

And shall we proceed to get rid of the weepings and wailings of famous men?

They will go with the rest.

But shall we be right in getting rid of them? Reflect: our principle is that the good man will not consider death terrible to any other good man who is his comrade.

Yes; that is our principle.

And therefore he will not sorrow for his departed friend as though he had suffered anything terrible?

He will not.

Such an one, as we further maintain, is sufficient for himself and his own happiness, and therefore is least in need of other men.

True, he said.

And for this reason the loss of a son or brother, or the deprivation of fortune, is to him of all men least terrible.

Assuredly.

And therefore he will be least likely to lament, and will bear with the greatest equanimity any misfortune of this sort which may befall him.

Yes, he will feel such a misfortune far less than another.

Then we shall be right in getting rid of the lamentations of famous men, and making them over to women (and not even to women who are good for anything), or to men of a baser sort, that those who are being educated by us to be the defenders of their country may scorn to do the like.

That will be very right.

Then we will once more entreat Homer and the other poets not to depict Achilles, who is the son of a goddess, first lying on his side, then on his back, and then on his face; then starting up and sailing in a frenzy along the shores of the barren sea; now taking the sooty ashes in both his hands and pouring them over his head, or weeping and wailing in the various modes which Homer has delineated. Nor should he describe Priam the kinsman of the gods as praying and beseeching,

'Rolling in the dirt, calling each man loudly by his name.'

Still more earnestly will we beg of him at all events not to introduce the gods lamenting and saying,

'Alas! my misery! Alas! that I bore the bravest to my sorrow.'

But if he must introduce the gods, at any rate let him not dare so completely to misrepresent the greatest of the gods, as to make him say –

'O heavens! with my eyes verily I behold a dear friend of mine chased round and round the city, and my heart is sorrowful.'

Or again: –

Woe is me that I am fated to have Sarpedon, dearest of men to me, subdued at the hands of Patroclus the son of Menoetius.'

For if, my sweet Adeimantus, our youth seriously listen to such unworthy representations of the gods, instead of laughing at them as they ought, hardly will any of them deem that he himself, being but a man, can be dishonoured by similar actions; neither will he rebuke any inclination which may arise in his mind to say and do the like. And instead of having any shame or self-control, he will be always whining and lamenting on slight occasions.

Yes, he said, that is most true.

Yes, I replied; but that surely is what ought not to be, as the argument has just proved to us; and by that proof we must abide until it is disproved by a better.

It ought not to be.

Neither ought our guardians to be given to laughter. For a fit of laughter which has been indulged to excess almost always produces a violent reaction.

So I believe.

Then persons of worth, even if only mortal men, must not be represented as overcome by laughter, and still less must such a representation of the gods be allowed.

Still less of the gods, as you say, he replied.

Then we shall not suffer such an expression to be used about the gods as that of Homer when he describes how

'Inextinguishable laughter arose among the blessed gods, when they saw Hephaestus bustling about the mansion.'

On your views, we must not admit them.

On my views, if you like to father them on me; that we must not admit them is certain.

Again, truth should be highly valued; if, as we were saying, a lie is useless to the gods, and useful only as a medicine to men, then the use of such medicines should be restricted to physicians; private individuals have no business with them.

Clearly not, he said.

Then if any one at all is to have the privilege of lying, the rulers of the State should be the persons; and they, in their dealings either with enemies or with their own citizens, may be allowed to lie for the public good. But nobody else should meddle with anything of the kind; and although the rulers have this privilege, for a private man to lie to them in return is to be deemed a more heinous fault than for the patient or the pupil of a gymnasium not to speak the truth about his own bodily illnesses to the physician or to the trainer, or for a sailor not to tell the captain what is happening about the ship and the rest of the crew, and how things are going with himself or his fellow sailors.

Most true, he said.

If, then, the ruler catches anybody beside himself lying in the State,

'Any of the craftsmen, whether he be priest or physician or carpenter,' he will punish him for introducing a practice which is equally subversive and destructive of ship or State.

Most certainly, he said, if our idea of the State is ever carried out.

In the next place our youth must be temperate?

Certainly.

Are not the chief elements of temperance, speaking generally, obedience to commanders and self-control in sensual pleasures?

True.

Then we shall approve such language as that of Diomede in Homer,

'Friend, sit still and obey my word,'

and the verses which follow,

'The Greeks marched breathing prowess, ...in silent awe of their leaders,'

and other sentiments of the same kind.

We shall.

What of this line,

'O heavy with wine, who hast the eyes of a dog and the heart of a stag,'

and of the words which follow? Would you say that these, or any similar impertinences which private individuals are supposed to address to their rulers, whether in verse or prose, are well or ill spoken?

They are ill spoken.

They may very possibly afford some amusement, but they do not conduce to temperance. And therefore they are likely to do harm to our young men – you would agree with me there?

Yes.

And then, again, to make the wisest of men say that nothing in his opinion is more glorious than

'When the tables are full of bread and meat, and the cup-bearer carries round wine which he draws from the bowl and pours into the cups,'

is it fit or conducive to temperance for a young man to hear such words? Or the verse

'The saddest of fates is to die and meet destiny from hunger?'

What would you say again to the tale of Zeus, who, while other gods and men were asleep and he the only person awake, lay devising plans, but forgot them all in a moment through his lust, and was so completely overcome at the sight of Here that he would not even go into the hut, but wanted to lie with her on the ground, declaring that he had never been in such a state of rapture before, even when they first met one another

'Without the knowledge of their parents;'

or that other tale of how Hephaestus, because of similar goings on, cast a chain around Ares and Aphrodite?

Indeed, he said, I am strongly of opinion that they ought not to hear that sort of thing.

But any deeds of endurance which are done or told by famous men, these they ought to see and hear; as, for example, what is said in the verses,

'He smote his breast, and thus reproached his heart, Endure, my heart; far worse hast thou endured!'

Certainly, he said.

In the next place, we must not let them be receivers of gifts or lovers of money.

Certainly not.

Neither must we sing to them of

'Gifts persuading gods, and persuading reverend kings.'

Neither is Phoenix, the tutor of Achilles, to be approved or deemed to have given his pupil good counsel when he told him that he should take the gifts of the Greeks and assist them; but that without a gift he should not lay aside his anger. Neither will we believe or acknowledge Achilles himself to have been such a lover of money that he took Agamemnon's gifts, or that when he had received payment he restored the dead body of Hector, but that without payment he was unwilling to do so.

Undoubtedly, he said, these are not sentiments which can be approved.

Loving Homer as I do, I hardly like to say that in attributing these feelings to Achilles, or in believing that they are truly attributed to him, he is guilty of downright impiety. As little can I believe the narrative of his insolence to Apollo, where he says,

'Thou hast wronged me, O far-darter, most abominable of deities. Verily I would be even with thee, if I had only the power;'

or his insubordination to the river-god, on whose divinity he is ready to lay hands; or his offering to the dead Patroclus of his own hair, which had been previously dedicated to the other river-god Spercheius, and that he actually performed this vow; or that he dragged Hector round the tomb of Patroclus, and slaughtered the captives at the pyre; of all this I cannot believe that he was guilty, any more than I can allow our citizens to believe that he, the wise Cheiron's pupil, the son of a goddess and of Peleus who was the gentlest of men and third in descent from Zeus, was so disordered in his wits as to be at one time the slave of two seemingly inconsistent passions, meanness, not untainted by avarice, combined with overweening contempt of gods and men.

You are quite right, he replied.

And let us equally refuse to believe, or allow to be repeated, the tale of Theseus son of Poseidon, or of Peirithous son of Zeus, going forth as they did to perpetrate a horrid rape; or of any other hero or son of a god daring to do such impious and dreadful things as they falsely ascribe to them in our day: and let us further compel the poets to declare either that these acts were not done by them, or that they were not the sons of gods; – both in the same breath they shall not be permitted to affirm. We will not have them trying to persuade our youth that the gods are the authors of evil, and that heroes are no better than men – sentiments which, as we were saying, are neither pious nor true, for we have already proved that evil cannot come from the gods.

Assuredly not.

And further they are likely to have a bad effect on those who hear them; for everybody will begin to excuse his own vices when he is convinced that similar wickednesses are always being perpetrated by –

'The kindred of the gods, the relatives of Zeus, whose ancestral altar, the altar of Zeus, is aloft in air on the peak of Ida,'

and who have

'the blood of deities yet flowing in their veins.'

And therefore let us put an end to such tales, lest they engender laxity of morals among the young.

By all means, he replied.

But now that we are determining what classes of subjects are or are not to be spoken of, let us see whether any have been omitted by us. The manner in which gods and demigods and heroes and the world below should be treated has been already laid down.

Very true.

And what shall we say about men? That is clearly the remaining portion of our subject.

Clearly so.

But we are not in a condition to answer this question at present, my friend.

Why not?

Because, if I am not mistaken, we shall have to say that about men poets and story-tellers are guilty of making the gravest misstatements when they tell us that wicked men are often happy, and the good miserable; and that injustice is profitable when undetected, but that justice is a man's own loss and another's gain – these things we shall forbid them to utter, and command them to sing and say the opposite.

To be sure we shall, he replied.

But if you admit that I am right in this, then I shall maintain that you have implied the principle for which we have been all along contending.

I grant the truth of your inference.

That such things are or are not to be said about men is a question which we cannot determine until we have discovered what justice is, and how naturally advantageous to the possessor, whether he seem to be just or not.

Most true, he said.

Enough of the subjects of poetry: let us now speak of the style; and when this has been considered, both matter and manner will have been completely treated.

I do not understand what you mean, said Adeimantus.

Then I must make you understand; and perhaps I may be more intelligible if I put the matter in this way. You are aware, I suppose, that all mythology and poetry is a narration of events, either past, present, or to come?

Certainly, he replied.

And narration may be either simple narration, or imitation, or a union of the two?

That again, he said, I do not quite understand.

I fear that I must be a ridiculous teacher when I have so much difficulty in making myself apprehended. Like a bad speaker, therefore, I will not take the whole of the subject, but will break a piece off in illustration of my meaning. You know the first lines of the Iliad, in which the poet says that Chryses prayed Agamemnon to release his daughter, and that Agamemnon flew into a passion with him; whereupon Chryses, failing of his object, invoked the anger of the God against the Achaeans. Now as far as these lines,

'And he prayed all the Greeks, but especially the two sons of Atreus, the chiefs of the people,'

the poet is speaking in his own person; he never leads us to suppose that he is any one else. But in what follows he takes the person of Chryses, and then he does all that he can to make us believe that the speaker is not Homer, but the aged priest himself. And in this double form he has cast the entire narrative of the events which occurred at Troy and in Ithaca and throughout the Odyssey.

Yes.

And a narrative it remains both in the speeches which the poet recites from time to time and in the intermediate passages?

Quite true.

But when the poet speaks in the person of another, may we not say that he assimilates his style to that of the person who, as he informs you, is going to speak?

Certainly.

And this assimilation of himself to another, either by the use of voice or gesture, is the imitation of the person whose character he assumes?

Of course.

Then in this case the narrative of the poet may be said to proceed by way of imitation?

Very true.

Or, if the poet everywhere appears and never conceals himself, then again the imitation is dropped, and his poetry becomes simple narration. However, in order that I may make my meaning quite clear, and that you may no more say, 'I don't understand,' I will show how the change might be effected. If Homer had said, 'The priest came, having his daughter's ransom in his hands, supplicating the Achaeans, and above all the kings;' and then if, instead of speaking in the person of Chryses, he had continued in his own person, the words would have been, not imitation, but simple narration. The passage would have run as follows (I am no poet, and therefore I drop the metre), 'The priest came and prayed the gods on behalf of the Greeks that they might capture Troy and return safely home, but begged that they would give him back his daughter, and take the ransom which he brought, and respect the God. Thus he spoke, and the other Greeks revered the priest and assented. But Agamemnon was wroth, and bade him depart and not come again, lest the staff and chaplets of the God should be of no avail to him – the daughter of Chryses should not be released, he said – she should grow old with him in Argos. And then he told him to go away and not to provoke him, if he intended to get home unscathed. And the old man went away in fear and silence, and, when he had left the camp, he called upon Apollo by his many names, reminding him of everything which he had done pleasing to him, whether in building his temples, or in offering sacrifice, and praying that his good deeds might be returned to him, and that the Achaeans might expiate his tears by the arrows of the god,' – and so on. In this way the whole becomes simple narrative.

I understand, he said.

Or you may suppose the opposite case – that the intermediate passages are omitted, and the dialogue only left.

That also, he said, I understand; you mean, for example, as in tragedy.

You have conceived my meaning perfectly; and if I mistake not, what you failed to apprehend before is now made clear to you, that poetry and mythology are, in some cases, wholly imitative – instances of this are supplied by tragedy and comedy; there is likewise the opposite style, in which the poet is the only speaker – of this the dithyramb affords the best example; and the combination of both is found in epic, and in several other styles of poetry. Do I take you with me?

Yes, he said; I see now what you meant.

I will ask you to remember also what I began by saying, that we had done with the subject and might proceed to the style.

Yes, I remember.

In saying this, I intended to imply that we must come to an understanding about the mimetic art, – whether the poets, in narrating their stories, are to be allowed by us to imitate, and if so, whether in whole or in part, and if the latter, in what parts; or should all imitation be prohibited?

You mean, I suspect, to ask whether tragedy and comedy shall be admitted into our State?

Yes, I said; but there may be more than this in question: I really do not know as yet, but whither the argument may blow, thither we go.

And go we will, he said.

Then, Adeimantus, let me ask you whether our guardians ought to be imitators; or rather, has not this question been decided by the rule already laid down that one man can only do one thing well, and not many; and that if he attempt many, he will altogether fail of gaining much reputation in any?

Certainly.

And this is equally true of imitation; no one man can imitate many things as well as he would imitate a single one?

He cannot.

Then the same person will hardly be able to play a serious part in life, and at the same time to be an imitator and imitate many other parts as well; for even when two species of imitation are nearly allied, the same persons cannot succeed in both, as, for example, the writers of tragedy and comedy – did you not just now call them imitations?

Yes, I did; and you are right in thinking that the same persons cannot succeed in both.

Any more than they can be rhapsodists and actors at once?

True.

Neither are comic and tragic actors the same; yet all these things are but imitations.

They are so.

And human nature, Adeimantus, appears to have been coined into yet smaller pieces, and to be as incapable of imitating many things well, as of performing well the actions of which the imitations are copies.

Quite true, he replied.

If then we adhere to our original notion and bear in mind that our guardians, setting aside every other business, are to dedicate themselves wholly to the maintenance of freedom in the State, making this their craft, and engaging in no work which does not bear on this end, they ought not to practise or imitate anything else; if they imitate at all, they should imitate from youth upward only those characters which are suitable to their profession – the courageous, temperate, holy, free, and the like; but they should not depict or be skilful at imitating any kind of illiberality or baseness, lest from imitation they should come to be what they imitate. Did you never observe how imitations, beginning in early youth and continuing far into life, at length grow into habits and become a second nature, affecting body, voice, and mind?

Yes, certainly, he said.

Then, I said, we will not allow those for whom we profess a care and of whom we say that they ought to be good men, to imitate a woman, whether young or old, quarrelling with her husband, or striving and vaunting against the gods in conceit of her happiness, or when she is in affliction, or sorrow, or weeping; and certainly not one who is in sickness, love, or labour.

Very right, he said.

Neither must they represent slaves, male or female, performing the offices of slaves?

They must not.

And surely not bad men, whether cowards or any others, who do the reverse of what we have just been prescribing, who scold or mock or revile one another in drink or out of drink, or who in any other manner sin against themselves and their neighbours in word or deed, as the manner of such is. Neither should they be trained to imitate the action or speech of men or women who are mad or bad; for madness, like vice, is to be known but not to be practised or imitated.

Very true, he replied.

Neither may they imitate smiths or other artificers, or oarsmen, or boatswains, or the like?

How can they, he said, when they are not allowed to apply their minds to the callings of any of these?

Nor may they imitate the neighing of horses, the bellowing of bulls, the murmur of rivers and roll of the ocean, thunder, and all that sort of thing?

Nay, he said, if madness be forbidden, neither may they copy the behaviour of madmen.

You mean, I said, if I understand you aright, that there is one sort of narrative style which may be employed by a truly good man when he has anything to say, and that another sort will be used by a man of an opposite character and education.

And which are these two sorts? he asked.

Suppose, I answered, that a just and good man in the course of a narration comes on some saying or action of another good man, – I should imagine that he will like to personate him, and will not be ashamed of this sort of imitation: he will be most ready to play the part of the good man when he is acting firmly and wisely; in a less degree when he is overtaken by illness or love or drink, or has met with any other disaster. But when he comes to a character which is unworthy of him, he will not make a study of that; he will disdain such a person, and will assume his likeness, if at all, for a moment only when he is performing some good action; at other times he will be ashamed to play a part which he has never practised, nor will he like to fashion and frame himself after the baser models; he feels the employment of such an art, unless in jest, to be beneath him, and his mind revolts at it.

So I should expect, he replied.

Then he will adopt a mode of narration such as we have illustrated out of Homer, that is to say, his style will be both imitative and narrative; but there will be very little of the former, and a great deal of the latter. Do you agree?

Certainly, he said; that is the model which such a speaker must necessarily take.

But there is another sort of character who will narrate anything, and, the worse he is, the more unscrupulous he will be; nothing will be too bad for him: and he will be ready to imitate anything, not as a joke, but in right good earnest, and before a large company. As I was just now saying, he will attempt to represent the roll of thunder, the noise of wind and hail, or the creaking of wheels, and pulleys, and the various sounds of flutes, pipes, trumpets, and all sorts of instruments: he will bark like a dog, bleat like a sheep, or crow like a cock; his entire art will consist in imitation of voice and gesture, and there will be very little narration.

That, he said, will be his mode of speaking.

These, then, are the two kinds of style?

Yes.

And you would agree with me in saying that one of them is simple and has but slight changes; and if the harmony and rhythm are also chosen for their simplicity, the result is that the speaker, if he speaks correctly, is always pretty much the same in style, and he will keep within the limits of a single harmony (for the changes are not great), and in like manner he will make use of nearly the same rhythm?

That is quite true, he said.

Whereas the other requires all sorts of harmonies and all sorts of rhythms, if the music and the style are to correspond, because the style has all sorts of changes.

That is also perfectly true, he replied.

And do not the two styles, or the mixture of the two, comprehend all poetry, and every form of expression in words? No one can say anything except in one or other of them or in both together.

They include all, he said.

And shall we receive into our State all the three styles, or one only of the two unmixed styles? or would you include the mixed?

I should prefer only to admit the pure imitator of virtue.

Yes, I said, Adeimantus, but the mixed style is also very charming: and indeed the pantomimic, which is the opposite of the one chosen by you, is the most popular style with children and their attendants, and with the world in general.

I do not deny it.

But I suppose you would argue that such a style is unsuitable to our State, in which human nature is not twofold or manifold, for one man plays one part only?

Yes; quite unsuitable.

And this is the reason why in our State, and in our State only, we shall find a shoemaker to be a shoemaker and not a pilot also, and a husbandman to be a husbandman and not a dicast also, and a soldier a soldier and not a trader also, and the same throughout?

True, he said.

And therefore when any one of these pantomimic gentlemen, who are so clever that they can imitate anything, comes to us, and makes a proposal to exhibit himself and his poetry, we will fall down and worship him as a sweet and holy and wonderful being; but we must also inform him that in our State such as he are not permitted to exist; the law will not allow them. And so when we have anointed him with myrrh, and set a garland of wool upon his head, we shall send him away to another city. For we mean to employ for our souls' health the rougher and severer poet or story-teller, who will imitate the style of the virtuous only, and will follow those models which we prescribed at first when we began the education of our soldiers.

We certainly will, he said, if we have the power.

Then now, my friend, I said, that part of music or literary education which relates to the story or myth may be considered to be finished; for the matter and manner have both been discussed.

I think so too, he said.

Next in order will follow melody and song.

That is obvious.

Every one can see already what we ought to say about them, if we are to be consistent with ourselves.

I fear, said Glaucon, laughing, that the word 'every one' hardly includes me, for I cannot at the moment say what they should be; though I may guess.

At any rate you can tell that a song or ode has three parts – the words, the melody, and the rhythm; that degree of knowledge I may presuppose?

Yes, he said; so much as that you may.

And as for the words, there will surely be no difference between words which are and which are not set to music; both will conform to the same laws, and these have been already determined by us?

Yes.

And the melody and rhythm will depend upon the words?

Certainly.

We were saying, when we spoke of the subject-matter, that we had no need of lamentation and strains of sorrow?

True.

And which are the harmonies expressive of sorrow? You are musical, and can tell me.

The harmonies which you mean are the mixed or tenor Lydian, and the full-toned or bass Lydian, and such like.

These then, I said, must be banished; even to women who have a character to maintain they are of no use, and much less to men.

Certainly.

In the next place, drunkenness and softness and indolence are utterly unbecoming the character of our guardians.

Utterly unbecoming.

And which are the soft or drinking harmonies?

The Ionian, he replied, and the Lydian; they are termed 'relaxed.'

Well, and are these of any military use?

Quite the reverse, he replied; and if so the Dorian and the Phrygian are the only ones which you have left.

I answered: Of the harmonies I know nothing, but I want to have one warlike, to sound the note or accent which a brave man utters in the hour of danger and stern resolve, or when his cause is failing, and he is going to wounds or death or is overtaken by some other evil, and at every such crisis meets the blows of fortune with firm step and a determination to endure; and another to be used by him in times of peace and freedom of action, when there is no pressure of necessity, and he is seeking to persuade God by prayer, or man by instruction and admonition, or on the other hand, when he is expressing his willingness to yield to persuasion or entreaty or admonition, and which represents him when by prudent conduct he has attained his end, not carried away by his success, but acting moderately and wisely under the circumstances, and acquiescing in the event. These two harmonies I ask you to leave; the strain of necessity and the strain of freedom, the strain of the unfortunate and the strain of the fortunate, the strain of courage, and the strain of temperance; these, I say, leave.

And these, he replied, are the Dorian and Phrygian harmonies of which I was just now speaking.

Then, I said, if these and these only are to be used in our songs and melodies, we shall not want multiplicity of notes or a panharmonic scale?

I suppose not.

Then we shall not maintain the artificers of lyres with three corners and complex scales, or the makers of any other many-stringed curiously-harmonised instruments?

Certainly not.

But what do you say to flute-makers and flute-players? Would you admit them into our State when you reflect that in this composite use of harmony the flute is worse than all the stringed instruments put together; even the panharmonic music is only an imitation of the flute?

Clearly not.

There remain then only the lyre and the harp for use in the city, and the shepherds may have a pipe in the country.

That is surely the conclusion to be drawn from the argument.

The preferring of Apollo and his instruments to Marsyas and his instruments is not at all strange, I said.

Not at all, he replied.

And so, by the dog of Egypt, we have been unconsciously purging the State, which not long ago we termed luxurious.

And we have done wisely, he replied.

Then let us now finish the purgation, I said. Next in order to harmonies, rhythms will naturally follow, and they should be subject to the same rules, for we ought not to seek out complex systems of metre, or metres of every kind, but rather to discover what rhythms are the expressions of a courageous and harmonious life; and when we have found them, we shall adapt the foot and the melody to words having a like spirit, not the words to the foot and melody. To say what these rhythms are will be your duty – you must teach me them, as you have already taught me the harmonies.

But, indeed, he replied, I cannot tell you. I only know that there are some three principles of rhythm out of which metrical systems are framed, just as in sounds there are four notes (i.e. the four notes of the tetrachord.) out of which all the harmonies are composed; that is an observation which I have made. But of what sort of lives they are severally the imitations I am unable to say.

Then, I said, we must take Damon into our counsels; and he will tell us what rhythms are expressive of meanness, or insolence, or fury, or other unworthiness, and what are to be reserved for the expression of opposite feelings. And I think that I have an indistinct recollection of his mentioning a complex Cretic rhythm; also a dactylic or heroic, and he arranged them in some manner which I do not quite understand, making the rhythms equal in the rise and fall of the foot, long and short alternating; and, unless I am mistaken, he spoke of an iambic as well as of a trochaic rhythm, and assigned to them short and long quantities. Also in some cases he appeared to praise or censure the movement of the foot quite as much as the rhythm; or perhaps a combination of the two; for I am not certain what he meant. These matters, however, as I was saying, had better be referred to Damon himself, for the analysis of the subject would be difficult, you know? (Socrates expresses himself carelessly in accordance with his assumed ignorance of the details of the subject. In the first part of the sentence he appears to be speaking of paeonic rhythms which are in the ratio of 3/2; in the second part, of dactylic and anapaestic rhythms, which are in the ratio of 1/1; in the last clause, of iambic and trochaic rhythms, which are in the ratio of 1/2 or 2/1.)

Rather so, I should say.

But there is no difficulty in seeing that grace or the absence of grace is an effect of good or bad rhythm.

None at all.

And also that good and bad rhythm naturally assimilate to a good and bad style; and that harmony and discord in like manner follow style; for our principle is that rhythm and harmony are regulated by the words, and not the words by them.

Just so, he said, they should follow the words.

And will not the words and the character of the style depend on the temper of the soul?

Yes.

And everything else on the style?

Yes.

Then beauty of style and harmony and grace and good rhythm depend on simplicity, – I mean the true simplicity of a rightly and nobly ordered mind and character, not that other simplicity which is only an euphemism for folly?

Very true, he replied.

And if our youth are to do their work in life, must they not make these graces and harmonies their perpetual aim?

They must.

And surely the art of the painter and every other creative and constructive art are full of them, – weaving, embroidery, architecture, and every kind of manufacture; also nature, animal and vegetable, – in all of them there is grace or the absence of grace. And ugliness and discord and inharmonious motion are nearly allied to ill words and ill nature, as grace and harmony are the twin sisters of goodness and virtue and bear their likeness.

That is quite true, he said.

But shall our superintendence go no further, and are the poets only to be required by us to express the image of the good in their works, on pain, if they do anything else, of expulsion from our State? Or is the same control to be extended to other artists, and are they also to be prohibited from exhibiting the opposite forms of vice and intemperance and meanness and indecency in sculpture and building and the other creative arts; and is he who cannot conform to this rule of ours to be prevented from practising his art in our State, lest the taste of our citizens be corrupted by him? We would not have our guardians grow up amid images of moral deformity, as in some noxious pasture, and there browse and feed upon many a baneful herb and flower day by day, little by little, until they silently gather a festering mass of corruption in their own soul. Let our artists rather be those who are gifted to discern the true nature of the beautiful and graceful; then will our youth dwell in a land of health, amid fair sights and sounds, and receive the good in everything; and beauty, the effluence of fair works, shall flow into the eye and ear, like a health-giving breeze from a purer region, and insensibly draw the soul from earliest years into likeness and sympathy with the beauty of reason.

There can be no nobler training than that, he replied.

And therefore, I said, Glaucon, musical training is a more potent instrument than any other, because rhythm and harmony find their way into the inward places of the soul, on which they mightily fasten, imparting grace, and making the soul of him who is rightly educated graceful, or of him who is ill-educated ungraceful; and also because he who has received this true education of the inner being will most shrewdly perceive omissions or faults in art and nature, and with a true taste, while he praises and rejoices over and receives into his soul the good, and becomes noble and good, he will justly blame and hate the bad, now in the days of his youth, even before he is able to know the reason why; and when reason comes he will recognise and salute the friend with whom his education has made him long familiar.

Yes, he said, I quite agree with you in thinking that our youth should be trained in music and on the grounds which you mention.

Just as in learning to read, I said, we were satisfied when we knew the letters of the alphabet, which are very few, in all their recurring sizes and combinations; not slighting them as unimportant whether they occupy a space large or small, but everywhere eager to make them out; and not thinking ourselves perfect in the art of reading until we recognise them wherever they are found:

True –

Or, as we recognise the reflection of letters in the water, or in a mirror, only when we know the letters themselves; the same art and study giving us the knowledge of both:

Exactly –

Even so, as I maintain, neither we nor our guardians, whom we have to educate, can ever become musical until we and they know the essential forms of temperance, courage, liberality, magnificence, and their kindred, as well as the contrary forms, in all their combinations, and can recognise them and their images wherever they are found, not slighting them either in small things or great, but believing them all to be within the sphere of one art and study.

Most assuredly.

And when a beautiful soul harmonizes with a beautiful form, and the two are cast in one mould, that will be the fairest of sights to him who has an eye to see it?

The fairest indeed.

And the fairest is also the loveliest?

That may be assumed.

And the man who has the spirit of harmony will be most in love with the loveliest; but he will not love him who is of an inharmonious soul?

That is true, he replied, if the deficiency be in his soul; but if there be any merely bodily defect in another he will be patient of it, and will love all the same.

I perceive, I said, that you have or have had experiences of this sort, and I agree. But let me ask you another question: Has excess of pleasure any affinity to temperance?

How can that be? he replied; pleasure deprives a man of the use of his faculties quite as much as pain.

Or any affinity to virtue in general?

None whatever.

Any affinity to wantonness and intemperance?

Yes, the greatest.

And is there any greater or keener pleasure than that of sensual love?

No, nor a madder.

Whereas true love is a love of beauty and order – temperate and harmonious?

Quite true, he said.

Then no intemperance or madness should be allowed to approach true love?

Certainly not.

Then mad or intemperate pleasure must never be allowed to come near the lover and his beloved; neither of them can have any part in it if their love is of the right sort?

No, indeed, Socrates, it must never come near them.

Then I suppose that in the city which we are founding you would make a law to the effect that a friend should use no other familiarity to his love than a father would use to his son, and then only for a noble purpose, and he must first have the other's consent; and this rule is to limit him in all his intercourse, and he is never to be seen going further, or, if he exceeds, he is to be deemed guilty of coarseness and bad taste.

I quite agree, he said.

Thus much of music, which makes a fair ending; for what should be the end of music if not the love of beauty?

I agree, he said.

After music comes gymnastic, in which our youth are next to be trained.

Certainly.

THE REPUBLIC

Gymnastic as well as music should begin in early years; the training in it should be careful and should continue through life. Now my belief is, – and this is a matter upon which I should like to have your opinion in confirmation of my own, but my own belief is, – not that the good body by any bodily excellence improves the soul, but, on the contrary, that the good soul, by her own excellence, improves the body as far as this may be possible. What do you say?

Yes, I agree.

Then, to the mind when adequately trained, we shall be right in handing over the more particular care of the body; and in order to avoid prolixity we will now only give the general outlines of the subject.

Very good.

That they must abstain from intoxication has been already remarked by us; for of all persons a guardian should be the last to get drunk and not know where in the world he is.

Yes, he said; that a guardian should require another guardian to take care of him is ridiculous indeed.

But next, what shall we say of their food; for the men are in training for the great contest of all – are they not?

Yes, he said.

And will the habit of body of our ordinary athletes be suited to them?

Why not?

I am afraid, I said, that a habit of body such as they have is but a sleepy sort of thing, and rather perilous to health. Do you not observe that these athletes sleep away their lives, and are liable to most dangerous illnesses if they depart, in ever so slight a degree, from their customary regimen?

Yes, I do.

Then, I said, a finer sort of training will be required for our warrior athletes, who are to be like wakeful dogs, and to see and hear with the utmost keenness; amid the many changes of water and also of food, of summer heat and winter cold, which they will have to endure when on a campaign, they must not be liable to break down in health.

That is my view.

The really excellent gymnastic is twin sister of that simple music which we were just now describing.

How so?

Why, I conceive that there is a gymnastic which, like our music, is simple and good; and especially the military gymnastic.

What do you mean?

My meaning may be learned from Homer; he, you know, feeds his heroes at their feasts, when they are campaigning, on soldiers' fare; they have no fish, although they are on the shores of the Hellespont, and they are not allowed boiled meats but only roast, which is the food most convenient for soldiers, requiring only that they should light a fire, and not involving the trouble of carrying about pots and pans.

True.

And I can hardly be mistaken in saying that sweet sauces are nowhere mentioned in Homer. In proscribing them, however, he is not singular; all professional athletes are well aware that a man who is to be in good condition should take nothing of the kind.

Yes, he said; and knowing this, they are quite right in not taking them.

Then you would not approve of Syracusan dinners, and the refinements of Sicilian cookery?

I think not.

Nor, if a man is to be in condition, would you allow him to have a Corinthian girl as his fair friend?

Certainly not.

Neither would you approve of the delicacies, as they are thought, of Athenian confectionary?

Certainly not.

All such feeding and living may be rightly compared by us to melody and song composed in the panharmonic style, and in all the rhythms.

Exactly.

There complexity engendered licence, and here disease; whereas simplicity in music was the parent of temperance in the soul; and simplicity in gymnastic of health in the body.

Most true, he said.

But when intemperance and diseases multiply in a State, halls of justice and medicine are always being opened; and the arts of the doctor and the lawyer give themselves airs, finding how keen is the interest which not only the slaves but the freemen of a city take about them.

Of course.

And yet what greater proof can there be of a bad and disgraceful state of education than this, that not only artisans and the meaner sort of people need the skill of first-rate physicians and judges, but also those who would profess to have had a liberal education? Is it not disgraceful, and a great sign of want of good-breeding, that a man should have to go abroad for his law and physic because he has none of his own at home, and must therefore surrender himself into the hands of other men whom he makes lords and judges over him?

Of all things, he said, the most disgraceful.

Would you say 'most,' I replied, when you consider that there is a further stage of the evil in which a man is not only a life-long litigant, passing all his days in the courts, either as plaintiff or defendant, but is actually led by his bad taste to pride himself on his litigiousness; he imagines that he is a master in dishonesty; able to take every crooked turn, and wriggle into and out of every hole, bending like a withy and getting out of the way of justice: and all for what? – in order to gain small points not worth mentioning, he not knowing that so to order his life as to be able to do without a napping judge is a far higher and nobler sort of thing. Is not that still more disgraceful?

Yes, he said, that is still more disgraceful.

Well, I said, and to require the help of medicine, not when a wound has to be cured, or on occasion of an epidemic, but just because, by indolence and a habit of life such as we have been describing, men fill themselves with waters and winds, as if their bodies were a marsh, compelling the ingenious sons of Asclepius to find more names for diseases, such as flatulence and catarrh; is not this, too, a disgrace?

Yes, he said, they do certainly give very strange and newfangled names to diseases.

Yes, I said, and I do not believe that there were any such diseases in the days of Asclepius; and this I infer from the circumstance that the hero Eurypylus, after he has been wounded in Homer, drinks a posset of Pramnian wine well besprinkled with barley-meal and grated cheese, which are certainly inflammatory, and yet the sons of Asclepius who were at the Trojan war do not blame the damsel who gives him the drink, or rebuke Patroclus, who is treating his case.

Well, he said, that was surely an extraordinary drink to be given to a person in his condition.

Not so extraordinary, I replied, if you bear in mind that in former days, as is commonly said, before the time of Herodicus, the guild of Asclepius did not practise our present system of medicine, which may be said to educate diseases. But Herodicus, being a trainer, and himself of a sickly constitution, by a combination of training and doctoring found out a way of torturing first and chiefly himself, and secondly the rest of the world.

How was that? he said.

By the invention of lingering death; for he had a mortal disease which he perpetually tended, and as recovery was out of the question, he passed his entire life as a valetudinarian; he could do nothing but attend upon himself, and he was in constant torment whenever he departed in anything from his usual regimen, and so dying hard, by the help of science he struggled on to old age.

A rare reward of his skill!

Yes, I said; a reward which a man might fairly expect who never understood that, if Asclepius did not instruct his descendants in valetudinarian arts, the omission arose, not from ignorance or inexperience of such a branch of medicine, but because he knew that in all well-ordered states every individual has an occupation to which he must attend, and has therefore no leisure to spend in continually being ill. This we remark in the case of the artisan, but, ludicrously enough, do not apply the same rule to people of the richer sort.

How do you mean? he said.

I mean this: When a carpenter is ill he asks the physician for a rough and ready cure; an emetic or a purge or a cautery or the knife, – these are his remedies. And if some one prescribes for him a course of dietetics, and tells him that he must swathe and swaddle his head, and all that sort of thing, he replies at once that he has no time to be ill, and that he sees no good in a life which is spent in nursing his disease to the neglect of his customary employment; and therefore bidding good-bye to this sort of physician, he resumes his ordinary habits, and either gets well and lives and does his business, or, if his constitution fails, he dies and has no more trouble.

Yes, he said, and a man in his condition of life ought to use the art of medicine thus far only.

Has he not, I said, an occupation; and what profit would there be in his life if he were deprived of his occupation?

Quite true, he said.

But with the rich man this is otherwise; of him we do not say that he has any specially appointed work which he must perform, if he would live.

He is generally supposed to have nothing to do.

Then you never heard of the saying of Phocylides, that as soon as a man has a livelihood he should practise virtue?

Nay, he said, I think that he had better begin somewhat sooner.

Let us not have a dispute with him about this, I said; but rather ask ourselves: Is the practice of virtue obligatory on the rich man, or can he live without it? And if obligatory on him, then let us raise a further question, whether this dieting of disorders, which is an impediment to the application of the mind in carpentering and the mechanical arts, does not equally stand in the way of the sentiment of Phocylides?

Of that, he replied, there can be no doubt; such excessive care of the body, when carried beyond the rules of gymnastic, is most inimical to the practice of virtue.

Yes, indeed, I replied, and equally incompatible with the management of a house, an army, or an office of state; and, what is most important of all, irreconcileable with any kind of study or thought or self-reflection – there is a constant suspicion that headache and giddiness are to be ascribed to philosophy, and hence all practising or making trial of virtue in the higher sense is absolutely stopped; for a man is always fancying that he is being made ill, and is in constant anxiety about the state of his body.

Yes, likely enough.

And therefore our politic Asclepius may be supposed to have exhibited the power of his art only to persons who, being generally of healthy constitution and habits of life, had a definite ailment; such as these he cured by purges and operations, and bade them live as usual, herein consulting the interests of the State; but bodies which disease had penetrated through and through he would not have attempted to cure by gradual processes of evacuation and infusion: he did not want to lengthen out good-for-nothing lives, or to have weak fathers begetting weaker sons; – if a man was not able to live in the ordinary way he had no business to cure him; for such a cure would have been of no use either to himself, or to the State.

Then, he said, you regard Asclepius as a statesman.

Clearly; and his character is further illustrated by his sons. Note that they were heroes in the days of old and practised the medicines of which I am speaking at the siege of Troy: You will remember how, when Pandarus wounded Menelaus, they

'Sucked the blood out of the wound, and sprinkled soothing remedies,'

but they never prescribed what the patient was afterwards to eat or drink in the case of Menelaus, any more than in the case of Eurypylus; the remedies, as they conceived, were enough to heal any man who before he was wounded was healthy and regular in his habits; and even though he did happen to drink a posset of Pramnian wine, he might get well all the same. But they would have nothing to do with unhealthy and intemperate subjects, whose lives were of no use either to themselves or others; the art of medicine was not designed for their good, and though they were as rich as Midas, the sons of Asclepius would have declined to attend them.

They were very acute persons, those sons of Asclepius.

Naturally so, I replied. Nevertheless, the tragedians and Pindar disobeying our behests, although they acknowledge that Asclepius was the son of Apollo, say also that he was bribed into healing a rich man who was at the point of death, and for this reason he was struck by lightning. But we, in accordance with the principle already affirmed by us, will not believe them when they tell us both; – if he was the son of a god, we maintain that he was not avaricious; or, if he was avaricious, he was not the son of a god.

All that, Socrates, is excellent; but I should like to put a question to you: Ought there not to be good physicians in a State, and are not the best those who have treated the greatest number of constitutions good and bad? and are not the best judges in like manner those who are acquainted with all sorts of moral natures?

Yes, I said, I too would have good judges and good physicians. But do you know whom I think good?

Will you tell me?

I will, if I can. Let me however note that in the same question you join two things which are not the same.

How so? he asked.

Why, I said, you join physicians and judges. Now the most skilful physicians are those who, from their youth upwards, have combined with the knowledge of their art the greatest experience of disease; they had better not be robust in health, and should have had all manner of diseases in their own persons. For the body, as I conceive, is not the instrument with which they cure the body; in that case we could not allow them ever to be or to have been sickly; but they cure the body with the mind, and the mind which has become and is sick can cure nothing.

That is very true, he said.

But with the judge it is otherwise; since he governs mind by mind; he ought not therefore to have been trained among vicious minds, and to have associated with them from youth upwards, and to have gone through the whole calendar of crime, only in order that he may quickly infer the crimes of others as he might their bodily diseases from his own self-consciousness; the honourable mind which is to form a healthy judgment should have had no experience or contamination of evil habits when young. And this is the reason why in youth good men often appear to be simple, and are easily practised upon by the dishonest, because they have no examples of what evil is in their own souls.

Yes, he said, they are far too apt to be deceived.

Therefore, I said, the judge should not be young; he should have learned to know evil, not from his own soul, but from late and long observation of the nature of evil in others: knowledge should be his guide, not personal experience.

Yes, he said, that is the ideal of a judge.

Yes, I replied, and he will be a good man (which is my answer to your question); for he is good who has a good soul. But the cunning and suspicious nature of which we spoke, – he who has committed many crimes, and fancies himself to be a master in wickedness, when he is amongst his fellows, is wonderful in the precautions which he takes, because he judges of them by himself: but when he gets into the company of men of virtue, who have the experience of age, he appears to be a fool again, owing to his unseasonable suspicions; he cannot recognise an honest man, because he has no pattern of honesty in himself; at the same time, as the bad are more numerous than the good, and he meets with them oftener, he thinks himself, and is by others thought to be, rather wise than foolish.

Most true, he said.

Then the good and wise judge whom we are seeking is not this man, but the other; for vice cannot know virtue too, but a virtuous nature, educated by time, will acquire a knowledge both of virtue and vice: the virtuous, and not the vicious, man has wisdom – in my opinion.

And in mine also.

This is the sort of medicine, and this is the sort of law, which you will sanction in your state. They will minister to better natures, giving health both of soul and of body; but those who are diseased in their bodies they will leave to die, and the corrupt and incurable souls they will put an end to themselves.

That is clearly the best thing both for the patients and for the State.

And thus our youth, having been educated only in that simple music which, as we said, inspires temperance, will be reluctant to go to law.

Clearly.

And the musician, who, keeping to the same track, is content to practise the simple gymnastic, will have nothing to do with medicine unless in some extreme case.

That I quite believe.

The very exercises and tolls which he undergoes are intended to stimulate the spirited element of his nature, and not to increase his strength; he will not, like common athletes, use exercise and regimen to develope his muscles.

Very right, he said.

Neither are the two arts of music and gymnastic really designed, as is often supposed, the one for the training of the soul, the other for the training of the body.

What then is the real object of them?

I believe, I said, that the teachers of both have in view chiefly the improvement of the soul.

How can that be? he asked.

Did you never observe, I said, the effect on the mind itself of exclusive devotion to gymnastic, or the opposite effect of an exclusive devotion to music?

In what way shown? he said.

The one producing a temper of hardness and ferocity, the other of softness and effeminacy, I replied.

Yes, he said, I am quite aware that the mere athlete becomes too much of a savage, and that the mere musician is melted and softened beyond what is good for him.

Yet surely, I said, this ferocity only comes from spirit, which, if rightly educated, would give courage, but, if too much intensified, is liable to become hard and brutal.

That I quite think.

On the other hand the philosopher will have the quality of gentleness. And this also, when too much indulged, will turn to softness, but, if educated rightly, will be gentle and moderate.

True.

And in our opinion the guardians ought to have both these qualities?

Assuredly.

And both should be in harmony?

Beyond question.

And the harmonious soul is both temperate and courageous?

Yes.

And the inharmonious is cowardly and boorish?

Very true.

And, when a man allows music to play upon him and to pour into his soul through the funnel of his ears those sweet and soft and melancholy airs of which we were just now speaking, and his whole life is passed in warbling and the delights of song; in the first stage of the process the passion or spirit which is in him is tempered like iron, and made useful, instead of brittle and useless. But, if he carries on the softening and soothing process, in the next stage he begins to melt and waste, until he has wasted away his spirit and cut out the sinews of his soul; and he becomes a feeble warrior.

Very true.

If the element of spirit is naturally weak in him the change is speedily accomplished, but if he have a good deal, then the power of music weakening the spirit renders him excitable; – on the least provocation he flames up at once, and is speedily extinguished; instead of having spirit he grows irritable and passionate and is quite impracticable.

Exactly.

And so in gymnastics, if a man takes violent exercise and is a great feeder, and the reverse of a great student of music and philosophy, at first the high condition of his body fills him with pride and spirit, and he becomes twice the man that he was.

Certainly.

And what happens? if he do nothing else, and holds no converse with the Muses, does not even that intelligence which there may be in him, having no taste of any sort of learning or enquiry or thought or culture, grow feeble and dull and blind, his mind never waking up or receiving nourishment, and his senses not being purged of their mists?

True, he said.

And he ends by becoming a hater of philosophy, uncivilized, never using the weapon of persuasion, – he is like a wild beast, all violence and fierceness, and knows no other way of dealing; and he lives in all ignorance and evil conditions, and has no sense of propriety and grace.

That is quite true, he said.

And as there are two principles of human nature, one the spirited and the other the philosophical, some God, as I should say, has given mankind two arts answering to them (and only indirectly to the soul and body), in order that these two principles (like the strings of an instrument) may be relaxed or drawn tighter until they are duly harmonized.

That appears to be the intention.

And he who mingles music with gymnastic in the fairest proportions, and best attempers them to the soul, may be rightly called the true musician and harmonist in a far higher sense than the tuner of the strings.

You are quite right, Socrates.

And such a presiding genius will be always required in our State if the government is to last.

Yes, he will be absolutely necessary.

Such, then, are our principles of nurture and education: Where would be the use of going into further details about the dances of our citizens, or about their hunting and coursing, their gymnastic and equestrian contests? For these all follow the general principle, and having found that, we shall have no difficulty in discovering them.

I dare say that there will be no difficulty.

Very good, I said; then what is the next question? Must we not ask who are to be rulers and who subjects?

Certainly.

There can be no doubt that the elder must rule the younger.

Clearly.

And that the best of these must rule.

That is also clear.

Now, are not the best husbandmen those who are most devoted to husbandry?

Yes.

And as we are to have the best of guardians for our city, must they not be those who have most the character of guardians?

Yes.

And to this end they ought to be wise and efficient, and to have a special care of the State?

True.

And a man will be most likely to care about that which he loves?

To be sure.

And he will be most likely to love that which he regards as having the same interests with himself, and that of which the good or evil fortune is supposed by him at any time most to affect his own?

Very true, he replied.

Then there must be a selection. Let us note among the guardians those who in their whole life show the greatest eagerness to do what is for the good of their country, and the greatest repugnance to do what is against her interests.

Those are the right men.

And they will have to be watched at every age, in order that we may see whether they preserve their resolution, and never, under the influence either of force or enchantment, forget or cast off their sense of duty to the State.

How cast off? he said.

I will explain to you, I replied. A resolution may go out of a man's mind either with his will or against his will; with his will when he gets rid of a falsehood and learns better, against his will whenever he is deprived of a truth.

I understand, he said, the willing loss of a resolution; the meaning of the unwilling I have yet to learn.

Why, I said, do you not see that men are unwillingly deprived of good, and willingly of evil? Is not to have lost the truth an evil, and to possess the truth a good? and you would agree that to conceive things as they are is to possess the truth?

Yes, he replied; I agree with you in thinking that mankind are deprived of truth against their will.

And is not this involuntary deprivation caused either by theft, or force, or enchantment?

Still, he replied, I do not understand you.

I fear that I must have been talking darkly, like the tragedians. I only mean that some men are changed by persuasion and that others forget; argument steals away the hearts of one class, and time of the other; and this I call theft. Now you understand me?

Yes.

Those again who are forced, are those whom the violence of some pain or grief compels to change their opinion.

I understand, he said, and you are quite right.

And you would also acknowledge that the enchanted are those who change their minds either under the softer influence of pleasure, or the sterner influence of fear?

Yes, he said; everything that deceives may be said to enchant.

Therefore, as I was just now saying, we must enquire who are the best guardians of their own conviction that what they think the interest of the State is to be the rule of their lives. We must watch them from their youth upwards, and make them perform actions in which they are most likely to forget or to be deceived, and he who remembers and is not deceived is to be selected, and he who fails in the trial is to be rejected. That will be the way?

Yes.

And there should also be toils and pains and conflicts prescribed for them, in which they will be made to give further proof of the same qualities.

Very right, he replied.

And then, I said, we must try them with enchantments – that is the third sort of test – and see what will be their behaviour: like those who take colts amid noise and tumult to see if they are of a timid nature, so must we take our youth amid terrors of some kind, and again pass them into pleasures, and prove them more thoroughly than gold is proved in the furnace, that we may discover whether they are armed against all enchantments, and of a noble bearing always, good guardians of themselves and of the music which they have learned, and retaining under all circumstances a rhythmical and harmonious nature, such as will be most serviceable to the individual and to the State. And he who at every age, as boy and youth and in mature life, has come out of the trial victorious and pure, shall be appointed a ruler and guardian of the State; he shall be honoured in life and death, and shall receive sepulture and other memorials of honour, the greatest that we have to give. But him who fails, we must reject. I am inclined to think that this is the sort of way in which our rulers and guardians should be chosen and appointed. I speak generally, and not with any pretension to exactness.

And, speaking generally, I agree with you, he said.

And perhaps the word 'guardian' in the fullest sense ought to be applied to this higher class only who preserve us against foreign enemies and maintain peace among our citizens at home, that the one may not have the will, or the others the power, to harm us. The young men whom we before called guardians may be more properly designated auxiliaries and supporters of the principles of the rulers.

I agree with you, he said.

How then may we devise one of those needful falsehoods of which we lately spoke – just one royal lie which may deceive the rulers, if that be possible, and at any rate the rest of the city?

What sort of lie? he said.

Nothing new, I replied; only an old Phoenician tale (Laws) of what has often occurred before now in other places, (as the poets say, and have made the world believe,) though not in our time, and I do not know whether such an event could ever happen again, or could now even be made probable, if it did.

How your words seem to hesitate on your lips!

You will not wonder, I replied, at my hesitation when you have heard.

Speak, he said, and fear not.

Well then, I will speak, although I really know not how to look you in the face, or in what words to utter the audacious fiction, which I propose to communicate gradually, first to the rulers, then to the soldiers, and lastly to the people. They are to be told that their youth was a dream, and the education and training which they received from us, an appearance only; in reality during all that time they were being formed and fed in the womb of the earth, where they themselves and their arms and appurtenances were manufactured; when they were completed, the earth, their mother, sent them up; and so, their country being their mother and also their nurse, they are bound to advise for her good, and to defend her against attacks, and her citizens they are to regard as children of the earth and their own brothers.

You had good reason, he said, to be ashamed of the lie which you were going to tell.

True, I replied, but there is more coming; I have only told you half. Citizens, we shall say to them in our tale, you are brothers, yet God has framed you differently. Some of you have the power of command, and in the composition of these he has mingled gold, wherefore also they have the greatest honour; others he has made of silver, to be auxiliaries; others again who are to be husbandmen and craftsmen he has composed of brass and iron; and the species will generally be preserved in the children. But as all are of the same original stock, a golden parent will sometimes have a silver son, or a silver parent a golden son. And God proclaims as a first principle to the rulers, and above all else, that there is nothing which they should so anxiously guard, or of which they are to be such good guardians, as of the purity of the race. They should observe what elements mingle in their offspring; for if the son of a golden or silver parent has an admixture of brass and iron, then nature orders a transposition of ranks, and the eye of the ruler must not be pitiful towards the child because he has to descend in the scale and become a husbandman or artisan, just as there may be sons of artisans who having an admixture of gold or silver in them are raised to honour, and become guardians or auxiliaries. For an oracle says that when a man of brass or iron guards the State, it will be destroyed. Such is the tale; is there any possibility of making our citizens believe in it?

Not in the present generation, he replied; there is no way of accomplishing this; but their sons may be made to believe in the tale, and their sons' sons, and posterity after them.

I see the difficulty, I replied; yet the fostering of such a belief will make them care more for the city and for one another. Enough, however, of the fiction, which may now fly abroad upon the wings of rumour, while we arm our earth-born heroes, and lead them forth under the command of their rulers. Let them look round and select a spot whence they can best suppress insurrection, if any prove refractory within, and also defend themselves against enemies, who like wolves may come down on the fold from without; there let them encamp, and when they have encamped, let them sacrifice to the proper Gods and prepare their dwellings.

Just so, he said.

And their dwellings must be such as will shield them against the cold of winter and the heat of summer.

I suppose that you mean houses, he replied.

Yes, I said; but they must be the houses of soldiers, and not of shop-keepers.

What is the difference? he said.

That I will endeavour to explain, I replied. To keep watch-dogs, who, from want of discipline or hunger, or some evil habit or other, would turn upon the sheep and worry them, and behave not like dogs but wolves, would be a foul and monstrous thing in a shepherd?

Truly monstrous, he said.

And therefore every care must be taken that our auxiliaries, being stronger than our citizens, may not grow to be too much for them and become savage tyrants instead of friends and allies?

Yes, great care should be taken.

And would not a really good education furnish the best safeguard?

But they are well-educated already, he replied.

I cannot be so confident, my dear Glaucon, I said; I am much more certain that they ought to be, and that true education, whatever that may be, will have the greatest tendency to civilize and humanize them in their relations to one another, and to those who are under their protection.

Very true, he replied.

And not only their education, but their habitations, and all that belongs to them, should be such as will neither impair their virtue as guardians, nor tempt them to prey upon the other citizens. Any man of sense must acknowledge that.

He must.

Then now let us consider what will be their way of life, if they are to realize our idea of them. In the first place, none of them should have any property of his own beyond what is absolutely necessary; neither should they have a private house or store closed against any one who has a mind to enter; their provisions should be only such as are required by trained warriors, who are men of temperance and courage; they should agree to receive from the citizens a fixed rate of pay, enough to meet the expenses of the year and no more; and they will go to mess and live together like soldiers in a camp. Gold and silver we will tell them that they have from God; the diviner metal is within them, and they have therefore no need of the dross which is current among men, and ought not to pollute the divine by any such earthly admixture; for that commoner metal has been the source of many unholy deeds, but their own is undefiled. And they alone of all the citizens may not touch or handle silver or gold, or be under the same roof with them, or wear them, or drink from them. And this will be their salvation, and they will be the saviours of the State. But should they ever acquire homes or lands or moneys of their own, they will become housekeepers and husbandmen instead of guardians, enemies and tyrants instead of allies of the other citizens; hating and being hated, plotting and being plotted against, they will pass their whole life in much greater terror of internal than of external enemies, and the hour of ruin, both to themselves and to the rest of the State, will be at hand. For all which reasons may we not say that thus shall our State be ordered, and that these shall be the regulations appointed by us for guardians concerning their houses and all other matters?

Yes, said Glaucon.

BOOK IV.

Here Adeimantus interposed a question: How would you answer, Socrates, said he, if a person were to say that you are making these people miserable, and that they are the cause of their own unhappiness; the city in fact belongs to them, but they are none the better for it; whereas other men acquire lands, and build large and handsome houses, and have everything handsome about them, offering sacrifices to the gods on their own account, and practising hospitality; moreover, as you were saying just now, they have gold and silver, and all that is usual among the favourites of fortune; but our poor citizens are no better than mercenaries who are quartered in the city and are always mounting guard?

Yes, I said; and you may add that they are only fed, and not paid in addition to their food, like other men; and therefore they cannot, if they would, take a journey of pleasure; they have no money to spend on a mistress or any other luxurious fancy, which, as the world goes, is thought to be happiness; and many other accusations of the same nature might be added.

But, said he, let us suppose all this to be included in the charge.

You mean to ask, I said, what will be our answer?

Yes.

If we proceed along the old path, my belief, I said, is that we shall find the answer. And our answer will be that, even as they are, our guardians may very likely be the happiest of men; but that our aim in founding the State was not the disproportionate happiness of any one class, but the greatest happiness of the whole; we thought that in a State which is ordered with a view to the good of the whole we should be most likely to find justice, and in the ill-ordered State injustice: and, having found them, we might then decide which of the two is the happier. At present, I take it, we are fashioning the happy State, not piecemeal, or with a view of making a few happy citizens, but as a whole; and by-and-by we will proceed to view the opposite kind of State. Suppose that we were painting a statue, and some one came up to us and said, Why do you not put the most beautiful colours on the most beautiful parts of the body – the eyes ought to be purple, but you have made them black – to him we might fairly answer, Sir, you would not surely have us beautify the eyes to such a degree that they are no longer eyes; consider rather whether, by giving this and the other features their due proportion, we make the whole beautiful. And so I say to you, do not compel us to assign to the guardians a sort of happiness which will make them anything but guardians; for we too can clothe our husbandmen in royal apparel, and set crowns of gold on their heads, and bid them till the ground as much as they like, and no more. Our potters also might be allowed to repose on couches, and feast by the fireside, passing round the winecup, while their wheel is conveniently at hand, and working at pottery only as much as they like; in this way we might make every class happy – and then, as you imagine, the whole State would be happy. But do not put this idea into our heads; for, if we listen to you, the husbandman will be no longer a husbandman, the potter will cease to be a potter, and no one will have the character of any distinct class in the State. Now this is not of much consequence where the corruption of society, and pretension to be what you are not, is confined to cobblers; but when the guardians of the laws and of the government are only seeming and not real guardians, then see how they turn the State upside down; and on the other hand they alone have the power of giving order and happiness to the State. We mean our guardians to be true saviours and not the destroyers of the State, whereas our opponent is thinking of peasants at a festival, who are enjoying a life of revelry, not of citizens who are doing their duty to the State. But, if so, we mean different things, and he is speaking of something which is not a State. And therefore we must consider whether in appointing our guardians we would look to their greatest happiness individually, or whether this principle of happiness does not rather reside in the State as a whole. But if the latter be the truth, then the guardians and auxiliaries, and all others equally with them, must be compelled or induced to do their own work in the best way. And thus the whole State will grow up in a noble order, and the several classes will receive the proportion of happiness which nature assigns to them.

I think that you are quite right.

I wonder whether you will agree with another remark which occurs to me.

What may that be?

There seem to be two causes of the deterioration of the arts.

What are they?

Wealth, I said, and poverty.

How do they act?

The process is as follows: When a potter becomes rich, will he, think you, any longer take the same pains with his art?

Certainly not.

He will grow more and more indolent and careless?

Very true.

And the result will be that he becomes a worse potter?

Yes; he greatly deteriorates.

But, on the other hand, if he has no money, and cannot provide himself with tools or instruments, he will not work equally well himself, nor will he teach his sons or apprentices to work equally well.

Certainly not.

Then, under the influence either of poverty or of wealth, workmen and their work are equally liable to degenerate?

That is evident.

Here, then, is a discovery of new evils, I said, against which the guardians will have to watch, or they will creep into the city unobserved.

What evils?

Wealth, I said, and poverty; the one is the parent of luxury and indolence, and the other of meanness and viciousness, and both of discontent.

That is very true, he replied; but still I should like to know, Socrates, how our city will be able to go to war, especially against an enemy who is rich and powerful, if deprived of the sinews of war.

There would certainly be a difficulty, I replied, in going to war with one such enemy; but there is no difficulty where there are two of them.

How so? he asked.

In the first place, I said, if we have to fight, our side will be trained warriors fighting against an army of rich men.

That is true, he said.

And do you not suppose, Adeimantus, that a single boxer who was perfect in his art would easily be a match for two stout and well-to-do gentlemen who were not boxers?

Hardly, if they came upon him at once.

What, now, I said, if he were able to run away and then turn and strike at the one who first came up? And supposing he were to do this several times under the heat of a scorching sun, might he not, being an expert, overturn more than one stout personage?

Certainly, he said, there would be nothing wonderful in that.

And yet rich men probably have a greater superiority in the science and practise of boxing than they have in military qualities.

Likely enough.

Then we may assume that our athletes will be able to fight with two or three times their own number?

I agree with you, for I think you right.

And suppose that, before engaging, our citizens send an embassy to one of the two cities, telling them what is the truth: Silver and gold we neither have nor are permitted to have, but you may; do you therefore come and help us in war, and take the spoils of the other city: Who, on hearing these words, would choose to fight against lean wiry dogs, rather than, with the dogs on their side, against fat and tender sheep?

That is not likely; and yet there might be a danger to the poor State if the wealth of many States were to be gathered into one.

But how simple of you to use the term State at all of any but our own!

Why so?

You ought to speak of other States in the plural number; not one of them is a city, but many cities, as they say in the game. For indeed any city, however small, is in fact divided into two, one the city of the poor, the other of the rich; these are at war with one another; and in either there are many smaller divisions, and you would be altogether beside the mark if you treated them all as a single State. But if you deal with them as many, and give the wealth or power or persons of the one to the others, you will always have a great many friends and not many enemies. And your State, while the wise order which has now been prescribed continues to prevail in her, will be the greatest of States, I do not mean to say in reputation or appearance, but in deed and truth, though she number not more than a thousand defenders. A single State which is her equal you will hardly find, either among Hellenes or barbarians, though many that appear to be as great and many times greater.

That is most true, he said.

And what, I said, will be the best limit for our rulers to fix when they are considering the size of the State and the amount of territory which they are to include, and beyond which they will not go?

What limit would you propose?

I would allow the State to increase so far as is consistent with unity; that, I think, is the proper limit.

Very good, he said.

Here then, I said, is another order which will have to be conveyed to our guardians: Let our city be accounted neither large nor small, but one and self-sufficing.

And surely, said he, this is not a very severe order which we impose upon them.

And the other, said I, of which we were speaking before is lighter still, – I mean the duty of degrading the offspring of the guardians when inferior, and of elevating into the rank of guardians the offspring of the lower classes, when naturally superior. The intention was, that, in the case of the citizens generally, each individual should be put to the use for which nature intended him, one to one work, and then every man would do his own business, and be one and not many; and so the whole city would be one and not many.

Yes, he said; that is not so difficult.

The regulations which we are prescribing, my good Adeimantus, are not, as might be supposed, a number of great principles, but trifles all, if care be taken, as the saying is, of the one great thing, – a thing, however, which I would rather call, not great, but sufficient for our purpose.

What may that be? he asked.

Education, I said, and nurture: If our citizens are well educated, and grow into sensible men, they will easily see their way through all these, as well as other matters which I omit; such, for example, as marriage, the possession of women and the procreation of children, which will all follow the general principle that friends have all things in common, as the proverb says.

That will be the best way of settling them.

Also, I said, the State, if once started well, moves with accumulating force like a wheel. For good nurture and education implant good constitutions, and these good constitutions taking root in a good education improve more and more, and this improvement affects the breed in man as in other animals.

Very possibly, he said.

Then to sum up: This is the point to which, above all, the attention of our rulers should be directed, – that music and gymnastic be preserved in their original form, and no innovation made. They must do their utmost to maintain them intact. And when any one says that mankind most regard

'The newest song which the singers have,'

they will be afraid that he may be praising, not new songs, but a new kind of song; and this ought not to be praised, or conceived to be the meaning of the poet; for any musical innovation is full of danger to the whole State, and ought to be prohibited. So Damon tells me, and I can quite believe him; – he says that when modes of music change, the fundamental laws of the State always change with them.

Yes, said Adeimantus; and you may add my suffrage to Damon's and your own.

Then, I said, our guardians must lay the foundations of their fortress in music?

Yes, he said; the lawlessness of which you speak too easily steals in.

Yes, I replied, in the form of amusement; and at first sight it appears harmless.

Why, yes, he said, and there is no harm; were it not that little by little this spirit of licence, finding a home, imperceptibly penetrates into manners and customs; whence, issuing with greater force, it invades contracts between man and man, and from contracts goes on to laws and constitutions, in utter recklessness, ending at last, Socrates, by an overthrow of all rights, private as well as public.

Is that true? I said.

That is my belief, he replied.

Then, as I was saying, our youth should be trained from the first in a stricter system, for if amusements become lawless, and the youths themselves become lawless, they can never grow up into well-conducted and virtuous citizens.

Very true, he said.

And when they have made a good beginning in play, and by the help of music have gained the habit of good order, then this habit of order, in a manner how unlike the lawless play of the others! will accompany them in all their actions and be a principle of growth to them, and if there be any fallen places in the State will raise them up again.

Very true, he said.

Thus educated, they will invent for themselves any lesser rules which their predecessors have altogether neglected.

What do you mean?

I mean such things as these: – when the young are to be silent before their elders; how they are to show respect to them by standing and making them sit; what honour is due to parents; what garments or shoes are to be worn; the mode of dressing the hair; deportment and manners in general. You would agree with me?

Yes.

But there is, I think, small wisdom in legislating about such matters, – I doubt if it is ever done; nor are any precise written enactments about them likely to be lasting.

Impossible.

It would seem, Adeimantus, that the direction in which education starts a man, will determine his future life. Does not like always attract like?

To be sure.

Until some one rare and grand result is reached which may be good, and may be the reverse of good?

That is not to be denied.

And for this reason, I said, I shall not attempt to legislate further about them.

Naturally enough, he replied.

Well, and about the business of the agora, and the ordinary dealings between man and man, or again about agreements with artisans; about insult and injury, or the commencement of actions, and the appointment of juries, what would you say? there may also arise questions about any impositions and exactions of market and harbour dues which may be required, and in general about the regulations of markets, police, harbours, and the like. But, oh heavens! shall we condescend to legislate on any of these particulars?

I think, he said, that there is no need to impose laws about them on good men; what regulations are necessary they will find out soon enough for themselves.

Yes, I said, my friend, if God will only preserve to them the laws which we have given them.

And without divine help, said Adeimantus, they will go on for ever making and mending their laws and their lives in the hope of attaining perfection.

You would compare them, I said, to those invalids who, having no self-restraint, will not leave off their habits of intemperance?

Exactly.

Yes, I said; and what a delightful life they lead! they are always doctoring and increasing and complicating their disorders, and always fancying that they will be cured by any nostrum which anybody advises them to try.

Such cases are very common, he said, with invalids of this sort.

Yes, I replied; and the charming thing is that they deem him their worst enemy who tells them the truth, which is simply that, unless they give up eating and drinking and wenching and idling, neither drug nor cautery nor spell nor amulet nor any other remedy will avail.

Charming! he replied. I see nothing charming in going into a passion with a man who tells you what is right.

These gentlemen, I said, do not seem to be in your good graces.

Assuredly not.

Nor would you praise the behaviour of States which act like the men whom I was just now describing. For are there not ill-ordered States in which the citizens are forbidden under pain of death to alter the constitution; and yet he who most sweetly courts those who live under this regime and indulges them and fawns upon them and is skilful in anticipating and gratifying their humours is held to be a great and good statesman – do not these States resemble the persons whom I was describing?

Yes, he said; the States are as bad as the men; and I am very far from praising them.

But do you not admire, I said, the coolness and dexterity of these ready ministers of political corruption?

Yes, he said, I do; but not of all of them, for there are some whom the applause of the multitude has deluded into the belief that they are really statesmen, and these are not much to be admired.

What do you mean? I said; you should have more feeling for them. When a man cannot measure, and a great many others who cannot measure declare that he is four cubits high, can he help believing what they say?

Nay, he said, certainly not in that case.

Well, then, do not be angry with them; for are they not as good as a play, trying their hand at paltry reforms such as I was describing; they are always fancying that by legislation they will make an end of frauds in contracts, and the other rascalities which I was mentioning, not knowing that they are in reality cutting off the heads of a hydra?

Yes, he said; that is just what they are doing.

I conceive, I said, that the true legislator will not trouble himself with this class of enactments whether concerning laws or the constitution either in an ill-ordered or in a well-ordered State; for in the former they are quite useless, and in the latter there will be no difficulty in devising them; and many of them will naturally flow out of our previous regulations.

What, then, he said, is still remaining to us of the work of legislation?

Nothing to us, I replied; but to Apollo, the God of Delphi, there remains the ordering of the greatest and noblest and chiefest things of all.

Which are they? he said.

The institution of temples and sacrifices, and the entire service of gods, demigods, and heroes; also the ordering of the repositories of the dead, and the rites which have to be observed by him who would propitiate the inhabitants of the world below. These are matters of which we are ignorant ourselves, and as founders of a city we should be unwise in trusting them to any interpreter but our ancestral deity. He is the god who sits in the centre, on the navel of the earth, and he is the interpreter of religion to all mankind.

You are right, and we will do as you propose.

But where, amid all this, is justice? son of Ariston, tell me where. Now that our city has been made habitable, light a candle and search, and get your brother and Polemarchus and the rest of our friends to help, and let us see where in it we can discover justice and where injustice, and in what they differ from one another, and which of them the man who would be happy should have for his portion, whether seen or unseen by gods and men.

Nonsense, said Glaucon: did you not promise to search yourself, saying that for you not to help justice in her need would be an impiety?

I do not deny that I said so, and as you remind me, I will be as good as my word; but you must join.

We will, he replied.

Well, then, I hope to make the discovery in this way: I mean to begin with the assumption that our State, if rightly ordered, is perfect.

That is most certain.

And being perfect, is therefore wise and valiant and temperate and just.

That is likewise clear.

And whichever of these qualities we find in the State, the one which is not found will be the residue?

Very good.

If there were four things, and we were searching for one of them, wherever it might be, the one sought for might be known to us from the first, and there would be no further trouble; or we might know the other three first, and then the fourth would clearly be the one left.

Very true, he said.

And is not a similar method to be pursued about the virtues, which are also four in number?

Clearly.

First among the virtues found in the State, wisdom comes into view, and in this I detect a certain peculiarity.

What is that?

The State which we have been describing is said to be wise as being good in counsel?

Very true.

And good counsel is clearly a kind of knowledge, for not by ignorance, but by knowledge, do men counsel well?

Clearly.

And the kinds of knowledge in a State are many and diverse?

Of course.

There is the knowledge of the carpenter; but is that the sort of knowledge which gives a city the title of wise and good in counsel?

Certainly not; that would only give a city the reputation of skill in carpentering.

Then a city is not to be called wise because possessing a knowledge which counsels for the best about wooden implements?

Certainly not.

Nor by reason of a knowledge which advises about brazen pots, I said, nor as possessing any other similar knowledge?

Not by reason of any of them, he said.

Nor yet by reason of a knowledge which cultivates the earth; that would give the city the name of agricultural?

Yes.

Well, I said, and is there any knowledge in our recently-founded State among any of the citizens which advises, not about any particular thing in the State, but about the whole, and considers how a State can best deal with itself and with other States?

There certainly is.

And what is this knowledge, and among whom is it found? I asked.

It is the knowledge of the guardians, he replied, and is found among those whom we were just now describing as perfect guardians.

And what is the name which the city derives from the possession of this sort of knowledge?

The name of good in counsel and truly wise.

And will there be in our city more of these true guardians or more smiths?

The smiths, he replied, will be far more numerous.

Will not the guardians be the smallest of all the classes who receive a name from the profession of some kind of knowledge?

Much the smallest.

And so by reason of the smallest part or class, and of the knowledge which resides in this presiding and ruling part of itself, the whole State, being thus constituted according to nature, will be wise; and this, which has the only knowledge worthy to be called wisdom, has been ordained by nature to be of all classes the least.

Most true.

Thus, then, I said, the nature and place in the State of one of the four virtues has somehow or other been discovered.

And, in my humble opinion, very satisfactorily discovered, he replied.

Again, I said, there is no difficulty in seeing the nature of courage, and in what part that quality resides which gives the name of courageous to the State.

How do you mean?

Why, I said, every one who calls any State courageous or cowardly, will be thinking of the part which fights and goes out to war on the State's behalf.

No one, he replied, would ever think of any other.

The rest of the citizens may be courageous or may be cowardly, but their courage or cowardice will not, as I conceive, have the effect of making the city either the one or the other.

Certainly not.

The city will be courageous in virtue of a portion of herself which preserves under all circumstances that opinion about the nature of things to be feared and not to be feared in which our legislator educated them; and this is what you term courage.

I should like to hear what you are saying once more, for I do not think that I perfectly understand you.

I mean that courage is a kind of salvation.

Salvation of what?

Of the opinion respecting things to be feared, what they are and of what nature, which the law implants through education; and I mean by the words 'under all circumstances' to intimate that in pleasure or in pain, or under the influence of desire or fear, a man preserves, and does not lose this opinion. Shall I give you an illustration?

If you please.

You know, I said, that dyers, when they want to dye wool for making the true sea-purple, begin by selecting their white colour first; this they prepare and dress with much care and pains, in order that the white ground may take the purple hue in full perfection. The dyeing then proceeds; and whatever is dyed in this manner becomes a fast colour, and no washing either with lyes or without them can take away the bloom. But, when the ground has not been duly prepared, you will have noticed how poor is the look either of purple or of any other colour.

Yes, he said; I know that they have a washed-out and ridiculous appearance.

Then now, I said, you will understand what our object was in selecting our soldiers, and educating them in music and gymnastic; we were contriving influences which would prepare them to take the dye of the laws in perfection, and the colour of their opinion about dangers and of every other opinion was to be indelibly fixed by their nurture and training, not to be washed away by such potent lyes as pleasure – mightier agent far in washing the soul than any soda or lye; or by sorrow, fear, and desire, the mightiest of all other solvents. And this sort of universal saving power of true opinion in conformity with law about real and false dangers I call and maintain to be courage, unless you disagree.

But I agree, he replied; for I suppose that you mean to exclude mere uninstructed courage, such as that of a wild beast or of a slave – this, in your opinion, is not the courage which the law ordains, and ought to have another name.

Most certainly.

Then I may infer courage to be such as you describe?

Why, yes, said I, you may, and if you add the words 'of a citizen,' you will not be far wrong; – hereafter, if you like, we will carry the examination further, but at present we are seeking not for courage but justice; and for the purpose of our enquiry we have said enough.

You are right, he replied.

Two virtues remain to be discovered in the State – first, temperance, and then justice which is the end of our search.

Very true.

Now, can we find justice without troubling ourselves about temperance?

I do not know how that can be accomplished, he said, nor do I desire that justice should be brought to light and temperance lost sight of; and therefore I wish that you would do me the favour of considering temperance first.

Certainly, I replied, I should not be justified in refusing your request.

Then consider, he said.

Yes, I replied; I will; and as far as I can at present see, the virtue of temperance has more of the nature of harmony and symphony than the preceding.

How so? he asked.

Temperance, I replied, is the ordering or controlling of certain pleasures and desires; this is curiously enough implied in the saying of 'a man being his own master;' and other traces of the same notion may be found in language.

No doubt, he said.

There is something ridiculous in the expression 'master of himself;' for the master is also the servant and the servant the master; and in all these modes of speaking the same person is denoted.

Certainly.

The meaning is, I believe, that in the human soul there is a better and also a worse principle; and when the better has the worse under control, then a man is said to be master of himself; and this is a term of praise: but when, owing to evil education or association, the better principle, which is also the smaller, is overwhelmed by the greater mass of the worse – in this case he is blamed and is called the slave of self and unprincipled.

Yes, there is reason in that.

And now, I said, look at our newly-created State, and there you will find one of these two conditions realized; for the State, as you will acknowledge, may be justly called master of itself, if the words 'temperance' and 'self-mastery' truly express the rule of the better part over the worse.

Yes, he said, I see that what you say is true.

Let me further note that the manifold and complex pleasures and desires and pains are generally found in children and women and servants, and in the freemen so called who are of the lowest and more numerous class.

Certainly, he said.

Whereas the simple and moderate desires which follow reason, and are under the guidance of mind and true opinion, are to be found only in a few, and those the best born and best educated.

Very true.

These two, as you may perceive, have a place in our State; and the meaner desires of the many are held down by the virtuous desires and wisdom of the few.

That I perceive, he said.

Then if there be any city which may be described as master of its own pleasures and desires, and master of itself, ours may claim such a designation?

Certainly, he replied.

It may also be called temperate, and for the same reasons?

Yes.

And if there be any State in which rulers and subjects will be agreed as to the question who are to rule, that again will be our State?

Undoubtedly.

And the citizens being thus agreed among themselves, in which class will temperance be found – in the rulers or in the subjects?

In both, as I should imagine, he replied.

Do you observe that we were not far wrong in our guess that temperance was a sort of harmony?

Why so?

Why, because temperance is unlike courage and wisdom, each of which resides in a part only, the one making the State wise and the other valiant; not so temperance, which extends to the whole, and runs through all the notes of the scale, and produces a harmony of the weaker and the stronger and the middle class, whether you suppose them to be stronger or weaker in wisdom or power or numbers or wealth, or anything else. Most truly then may we deem temperance to be the agreement of the naturally superior and inferior, as to the right to rule of either, both in states and individuals.

I entirely agree with you.

And so, I said, we may consider three out of the four virtues to have been discovered in our State. The last of those qualities which make a state virtuous must be justice, if we only knew what that was.

The inference is obvious.

The time then has arrived, Glaucon, when, like huntsmen, we should surround the cover, and look sharp that justice does not steal away, and pass out of sight and escape us; for beyond a doubt she is somewhere in this country: watch therefore and strive to catch a sight of her, and if you see her first, let me know.

Would that I could! but you should regard me rather as a follower who has just eyes enough to see what you show him – that is about as much as I am good for.

Offer up a prayer with me and follow.

I will, but you must show me the way.

Here is no path, I said, and the wood is dark and perplexing; still we must push on.

Let us push on.

Here I saw something: Halloo! I said, I begin to perceive a track, and I believe that the quarry will not escape.

Good news, he said.

Truly, I said, we are stupid fellows.

Why so?

Why, my good sir, at the beginning of our enquiry, ages ago, there was justice tumbling out at our feet, and we never saw her; nothing could be more ridiculous. Like people who go about looking for what they have in their hands – that was the way with us – we looked not at what we were seeking, but at what was far off in the distance; and therefore, I suppose, we missed her.

What do you mean?

I mean to say that in reality for a long time past we have been talking of justice, and have failed to recognise her.

I grow impatient at the length of your exordium.

Well then, tell me, I said, whether I am right or not: You remember the original principle which we were always laying down at the foundation of the State, that one man should practise one thing only, the thing to which his nature was best adapted; – now justice is this principle or a part of it.

Yes, we often said that one man should do one thing only.

Further, we affirmed that justice was doing one's own business, and not being a busybody; we said so again and again, and many others have said the same to us.

Yes, we said so.

Then to do one's own business in a certain way may be assumed to be justice. Can you tell me whence I derive this inference?

I cannot, but I should like to be told.

Because I think that this is the only virtue which remains in the State when the other virtues of temperance and courage and wisdom are abstracted; and, that this is the ultimate cause and condition of the existence of all of them, and while remaining in them is also their preservative; and we were saying that if the three were discovered by us, justice would be the fourth or remaining one.

That follows of necessity.

If we are asked to determine which of these four qualities by its presence contributes most to the excellence of the State, whether the agreement of rulers and subjects, or the preservation in the soldiers of the opinion which the law ordains about the true nature of dangers, or wisdom and watchfulness in the rulers, or whether this other which I am mentioning, and which is found in children and women, slave and freeman, artisan, ruler, subject, – the quality, I mean, of every one doing his own work, and not being a busybody, would claim the palm – the question is not so easily answered.

Certainly, he replied, there would be a difficulty in saying which.

Then the power of each individual in the State to do his own work appears to compete with the other political virtues, wisdom, temperance, courage.

Yes, he said.

And the virtue which enters into this competition is justice?

Exactly.

Let us look at the question from another point of view: Are not the rulers in a State those to whom you would entrust the office of determining suits at law?

Certainly.

And are suits decided on any other ground but that a man may neither take what is another's, nor be deprived of what is his own?

Yes; that is their principle.

Which is a just principle?

Yes.

Then on this view also justice will be admitted to be the having and doing what is a man's own, and belongs to him?

Very true.

Think, now, and say whether you agree with me or not. Suppose a carpenter to be doing the business of a cobbler, or a cobbler of a carpenter; and suppose them to exchange their implements or their duties, or the same person to be doing the work of both, or whatever be the change; do you think that any great harm would result to the State?

Not much.

But when the cobbler or any other man whom nature designed to be a trader, having his heart lifted up by wealth or strength or the number of his followers, or any like advantage, attempts to force his way into the class of warriors, or a warrior into that of legislators and guardians, for which he is unfitted, and either to take the implements or the duties of the other; or when one man is trader, legislator, and warrior all in one, then I think you will agree with me in saying that this interchange and this meddling of one with another is the ruin of the State.

Most true.

Seeing then, I said, that there are three distinct classes, any meddling of one with another, or the change of one into another, is the greatest harm to the State, and may be most justly termed evil-doing?

Precisely.

And the greatest degree of evil-doing to one's own city would be termed by you injustice?

Certainly.

This then is injustice; and on the other hand when the trader, the auxiliary, and the guardian each do their own business, that is justice, and will make the city just.

I agree with you.

We will not, I said, be over-positive as yet; but if, on trial, this conception of justice be verified in the individual as well as in the State, there will be no longer any room for doubt; if it be not verified, we must have a fresh enquiry. First let us complete the old investigation, which we began, as you remember, under the impression that, if we could previously examine justice on the larger scale, there would be less difficulty in discerning her in the individual. That larger example appeared to be the State, and accordingly we constructed as good a one as we could, knowing well that in the good State justice would be found. Let the discovery which we made be now applied to the individual – if they agree, we shall be satisfied; or, if there be a difference in the individual, we will come back to the State and have another trial of the theory. The friction of the two when rubbed together may possibly strike a light in which justice will shine forth, and the vision which is then revealed we will fix in our souls.

That will be in regular course; let us do as you say.

I proceeded to ask: When two things, a greater and less, are called by the same name, are they like or unlike in so far as they are called the same?

Like, he replied.

The just man then, if we regard the idea of justice only, will be like the just State?

He will.

And a State was thought by us to be just when the three classes in the State severally did their own business; and also thought to be temperate and valiant and wise by reason of certain other affections and qualities of these same classes?

True, he said.

And so of the individual; we may assume that he has the same three principles in his own soul which are found in the State; and he may be rightly described in the same terms, because he is affected in the same manner?

Certainly, he said.

Once more then, O my friend, we have alighted upon an easy question – whether the soul has these three principles or not?

An easy question! Nay, rather, Socrates, the proverb holds that hard is the good.

Very true, I said; and I do not think that the method which we are employing is at all adequate to the accurate solution of this question; the true method is another and a longer one. Still we may arrive at a solution not below the level of the previous enquiry.

May we not be satisfied with that? he said; – under the circumstances, I am quite content.

I too, I replied, shall be extremely well satisfied.

Then faint not in pursuing the speculation, he said.

Must we not acknowledge, I said, that in each of us there are the same principles and habits which there are in the State; and that from the individual they pass into the State? – how else can they come there? Take the quality of passion or spirit; – it would be ridiculous to imagine that this quality, when found in States, is not derived from the individuals who are supposed to possess it, e.g. the Thracians, Scythians, and in general the northern nations; and the same may be said of the love of knowledge, which is the special characteristic of our part of the world, or of the love of money, which may, with equal truth, be attributed to the Phoenicians and Egyptians.

Exactly so, he said.

There is no difficulty in understanding this.

None whatever.

But the question is not quite so easy when we proceed to ask whether these principles are three or one; whether, that is to say, we learn with one part of our nature, are angry with another, and with a third part desire the satisfaction of our natural appetites; or whether the whole soul comes into play in each sort of action – to determine that is the difficulty.

Yes, he said; there lies the difficulty.

Then let us now try and determine whether they are the same or different.

How can we? he asked.

I replied as follows: The same thing clearly cannot act or be acted upon in the same part or in relation to the same thing at the same time, in contrary ways; and therefore whenever this contradiction occurs in things apparently the same, we know that they are really not the same, but different.

Good.

For example, I said, can the same thing be at rest and in motion at the same time in the same part?

Impossible.

Still, I said, let us have a more precise statement of terms, lest we should hereafter fall out by the way. Imagine the case of a man who is standing and also moving his hands and his head, and suppose a person to say that one and the same person is in motion and at rest at the same moment – to such a mode of speech we should object, and should rather say that one part of him is in motion while another is at rest.

Very true.

And suppose the objector to refine still further, and to draw the nice distinction that not only parts of tops, but whole tops, when they spin round with their pegs fixed on the spot, are at rest and in motion at the same time (and he may say the same of anything which revolves in the same spot), his objection would not be admitted by us, because in such cases things are not at rest and in motion in the same parts of themselves; we should rather say that they have both an axis and a circumference, and that the axis stands still, for there is no deviation from the perpendicular; and that the circumference goes round. But if, while revolving, the axis inclines either to the right or left, forwards or backwards, then in no point of view can they be at rest.

That is the correct mode of describing them, he replied.

Then none of these objections will confuse us, or incline us to believe that the same thing at the same time, in the same part or in relation to the same thing, can act or be acted upon in contrary ways.

Certainly not, according to my way of thinking.

Yet, I said, that we may not be compelled to examine all such objections, and prove at length that they are untrue, let us assume their absurdity, and go forward on the understanding that hereafter, if this assumption turn out to be untrue, all the consequences which follow shall be withdrawn.

Yes, he said, that will be the best way.

Well, I said, would you not allow that assent and dissent, desire and aversion, attraction and repulsion, are all of them opposites, whether they are regarded as active or passive (for that makes no difference in the fact of their opposition)?

Yes, he said, they are opposites.

Well, I said, and hunger and thirst, and the desires in general, and again willing and wishing, – all these you would refer to the classes already mentioned. You would say – would you not? – that the soul of him who desires is seeking after the object of his desire; or that he is drawing to himself the thing which he wishes to possess: or again, when a person wants anything to be given him, his mind, longing for the realization of his desire, intimates his wish to have it by a nod of assent, as if he had been asked a question?

Very true.

And what would you say of unwillingness and dislike and the absence of desire; should not these be referred to the opposite class of repulsion and rejection?

Certainly.

Admitting this to be true of desire generally, let us suppose a particular class of desires, and out of these we will select hunger and thirst, as they are termed, which are the most obvious of them?

Let us take that class, he said.

The object of one is food, and of the other drink?

Yes.

And here comes the point: is not thirst the desire which the soul has of drink, and of drink only; not of drink qualified by anything else; for example, warm or cold, or much or little, or, in a word, drink of any particular sort: but if the thirst be accompanied by heat, then the desire is of cold drink; or, if accompanied by cold, then of warm drink; or, if the thirst be excessive, then the drink which is desired will be excessive; or, if not great, the quantity of drink will also be small: but thirst pure and simple will desire drink pure and simple, which is the natural satisfaction of thirst, as food is of hunger?

Yes, he said; the simple desire is, as you say, in every case of the simple object, and the qualified desire of the qualified object.

But here a confusion may arise; and I should wish to guard against an opponent starting up and saying that no man desires drink only, but good drink, or food only, but good food; for good is the universal object of desire, and thirst being a desire, will necessarily be thirst after good drink; and the same is true of every other desire.

Yes, he replied, the opponent might have something to say.

Nevertheless I should still maintain, that of relatives some have a quality attached to either term of the relation; others are simple and have their correlatives simple.

I do not know what you mean.

Well, you know of course that the greater is relative to the less?

Certainly.

And the much greater to the much less?

Yes.

And the sometime greater to the sometime less, and the greater that is to be to the less that is to be?

Certainly, he said.

And so of more and less, and of other correlative terms, such as the double and the half, or again, the heavier and the lighter, the swifter and the slower; and of hot and cold, and of any other relatives; – is not this true of all of them?

Yes.

And does not the same principle hold in the sciences? The object of science is knowledge (assuming that to be the true definition), but the object of a particular science is a particular kind of knowledge; I mean, for example, that the science of house-building is a kind of knowledge which is defined and distinguished from other kinds and is therefore termed architecture.

Certainly.

Because it has a particular quality which no other has?

Yes.

And it has this particular quality because it has an object of a particular kind; and this is true of the other arts and sciences?

Yes.

Now, then, if I have made myself clear, you will understand my original meaning in what I said about relatives. My meaning was, that if one term of a relation is taken alone, the other is taken alone; if one term is qualified, the other is also qualified. I do not mean to say that relatives may not be disparate, or that the science of health is healthy, or of disease necessarily diseased, or that the sciences of good and evil are therefore good and evil; but only that, when the term science is no longer used absolutely, but has a qualified object which in this case is the nature of health and disease, it becomes defined, and is hence called not merely science, but the science of medicine.

I quite understand, and I think as you do.

Would you not say that thirst is one of these essentially relative terms, having clearly a relation –

Yes, thirst is relative to drink.

And a certain kind of thirst is relative to a certain kind of drink; but thirst taken alone is neither of much nor little, nor of good nor bad, nor of any particular kind of drink, but of drink only?

Certainly.

Then the soul of the thirsty one, in so far as he is thirsty, desires only drink; for this he yearns and tries to obtain it?

That is plain.

And if you suppose something which pulls a thirsty soul away from drink, that must be different from the thirsty principle which draws him like a beast to drink; for, as we were saying, the same thing cannot at the same time with the same part of itself act in contrary ways about the same.

Impossible.

No more than you can say that the hands of the archer push and pull the bow at the same time, but what you say is that one hand pushes and the other pulls.

Exactly so, he replied.

And might a man be thirsty, and yet unwilling to drink?

Yes, he said, it constantly happens.

And in such a case what is one to say? Would you not say that there was something in the soul bidding a man to drink, and something else forbidding him, which is other and stronger than the principle which bids him?

I should say so.

And the forbidding principle is derived from reason, and that which bids and attracts proceeds from passion and disease?

Clearly.

Then we may fairly assume that they are two, and that they differ from one another; the one with which a man reasons, we may call the rational principle of the soul, the other, with which he loves and hungers and thirsts and feels the flutterings of any other desire, may be termed the irrational or appetitive, the ally of sundry pleasures and satisfactions?

Yes, he said, we may fairly assume them to be different.

Then let us finally determine that there are two principles existing in the soul. And what of passion, or spirit? Is it a third, or akin to one of the preceding?

I should be inclined to say – akin to desire.

Well, I said, there is a story which I remember to have heard, and in which I put faith. The story is, that Leontius, the son of Aglaion, coming up one day from the Piraeus, under the north wall on the outside, observed some dead bodies lying on the ground at the place of execution. He felt a desire to see them, and also a dread and abhorrence of them; for a time he struggled and covered his eyes, but at length the desire got the better of him; and forcing them open, he ran up to the dead bodies, saying, Look, ye wretches, take your fill of the fair sight.

I have heard the story myself, he said.

The moral of the tale is, that anger at times goes to war with desire, as though they were two distinct things.

Yes; that is the meaning, he said.

And are there not many other cases in which we observe that when a man's desires violently prevail over his reason, he reviles himself, and is angry at the violence within him, and that in this struggle, which is like the struggle of factions in a State, his spirit is on the side of his reason; – but for the passionate or spirited element to take part with the desires when reason decides that she should not be opposed, is a sort of thing which I believe that you never observed occurring in yourself, nor, as I should imagine, in any one else?

Certainly not.

Suppose that a man thinks he has done a wrong to another, the nobler he is the less able is he to feel indignant at any suffering, such as hunger, or cold, or any other pain which the injured person may inflict upon him – these he deems to be just, and, as I say, his anger refuses to be excited by them.

True, he said.

But when he thinks that he is the sufferer of the wrong, then he boils and chafes, and is on the side of what he believes to be justice; and because he suffers hunger or cold or other pain he is only the more determined to persevere and conquer. His noble spirit will not be quelled until he either slays or is slain; or until he hears the voice of the shepherd, that is, reason, bidding his dog bark no more.

The illustration is perfect, he replied; and in our State, as we were saying, the auxiliaries were to be dogs, and to hear the voice of the rulers, who are their shepherds.

I perceive, I said, that you quite understand me; there is, however, a further point which I wish you to consider.

What point?

You remember that passion or spirit appeared at first sight to be a kind of desire, but now we should say quite the contrary; for in the conflict of the soul spirit is arrayed on the side of the rational principle.

Most assuredly.

But a further question arises: Is passion different from reason also, or only a kind of reason; in which latter case, instead of three principles in the soul, there will only be two, the rational and the concupiscent; or rather, as the State was composed of three classes, traders, auxiliaries, counsellors, so may there not be in the individual soul a third element which is passion or spirit, and when not corrupted by bad education is the natural auxiliary of reason?

Yes, he said, there must be a third.

Yes, I replied, if passion, which has already been shown to be different from desire, turn out also to be different from reason.

But that is easily proved: – We may observe even in young children that they are full of spirit almost as soon as they are born, whereas some of them never seem to attain to the use of reason, and most of them late enough.

Excellent, I said, and you may see passion equally in brute animals, which is a further proof of the truth of what you are saying. And we may once more appeal to the words of Homer, which have been already quoted by us,

'He smote his breast, and thus rebuked his soul,'

for in this verse Homer has clearly supposed the power which reasons about the better and worse to be different from the unreasoning anger which is rebuked by it.

Very true, he said.

And so, after much tossing, we have reached land, and are fairly agreed that the same principles which exist in the State exist also in the individual, and that they are three in number.

Exactly.

Must we not then infer that the individual is wise in the same way, and in virtue of the same quality which makes the State wise?

Certainly.

Also that the same quality which constitutes courage in the State constitutes courage in the individual, and that both the State and the individual bear the same relation to all the other virtues?

Assuredly.

And the individual will be acknowledged by us to be just in the same way in which the State is just?

That follows, of course.

We cannot but remember that the justice of the State consisted in each of the three classes doing the work of its own class?

We are not very likely to have forgotten, he said.

We must recollect that the individual in whom the several qualities of his nature do their own work will be just, and will do his own work?

Yes, he said, we must remember that too.

And ought not the rational principle, which is wise, and has the care of the whole soul, to rule, and the passionate or spirited principle to be the subject and ally?

Certainly.

And, as we were saying, the united influence of music and gymnastic will bring them into accord, nerving and sustaining the reason with noble words and lessons, and moderating and soothing and civilizing the wildness of passion by harmony and rhythm?

Quite true, he said.

And these two, thus nurtured and educated, and having learned truly to know their own functions, will rule over the concupiscent, which in each of us is the largest part of the soul and by nature most insatiable of gain; over this they will keep guard, lest, waxing great and strong with the fulness of bodily pleasures, as they are termed, the concupiscent soul, no longer confined to her own sphere, should attempt to enslave and rule those who are not her natural-born subjects, and overturn the whole life of man?

Very true, he said.

Both together will they not be the best defenders of the whole soul and the whole body against attacks from without; the one counselling, and the other fighting under his leader, and courageously executing his commands and counsels?

True.

And he is to be deemed courageous whose spirit retains in pleasure and in pain the commands of reason about what he ought or ought not to fear?

Right, he replied.

And him we call wise who has in him that little part which rules, and which proclaims these commands; that part too being supposed to have a knowledge of what is for the interest of each of the three parts and of the whole?

Assuredly.

And would you not say that he is temperate who has these same elements in friendly harmony, in whom the one ruling principle of reason, and the two subject ones of spirit and desire are equally agreed that reason ought to rule, and do not rebel?

Certainly, he said, that is the true account of temperance whether in the State or individual.

And surely, I said, we have explained again and again how and by virtue of what quality a man will be just.

That is very certain.

And is justice dimmer in the individual, and is her form different, or is she the same which we found her to be in the State?

There is no difference in my opinion, he said.

Because, if any doubt is still lingering in our minds, a few commonplace instances will satisfy us of the truth of what I am saying.

What sort of instances do you mean?

If the case is put to us, must we not admit that the just State, or the man who is trained in the principles of such a State, will be less likely than the unjust to make away with a deposit of gold or silver? Would any one deny this?

No one, he replied.

Will the just man or citizen ever be guilty of sacrilege or theft, or treachery either to his friends or to his country?

Never.

Neither will he ever break faith where there have been oaths or agreements?

Impossible.

No one will be less likely to commit adultery, or to dishonour his father and mother, or to fail in his religious duties?

No one.

And the reason is that each part of him is doing its own business, whether in ruling or being ruled?

Exactly so.

Are you satisfied then that the quality which makes such men and such states is justice, or do you hope to discover some other?

Not I, indeed.

Then our dream has been realized; and the suspicion which we entertained at the beginning of our work of construction, that some divine power must have conducted us to a primary form of justice, has now been verified?

Yes, certainly.

And the division of labour which required the carpenter and the shoemaker and the rest of the citizens to be doing each his own business, and not another's, was a shadow of justice, and for that reason it was of use?

Clearly.

But in reality justice was such as we were describing, being concerned however, not with the outward man, but with the inward, which is the true self and concernment of man: for the just man does not permit the several elements within him to interfere with one another, or any of them to do the work of others, – he sets in order his own inner life, and is his own master and his own law, and at peace with himself; and when he has bound together the three principles within him, which may be compared to the higher, lower, and middle notes of the scale, and the intermediate intervals – when he has bound all these together, and is no longer many, but has become one entirely temperate and perfectly adjusted nature, then he proceeds to act, if he has to act, whether in a matter of property, or in the treatment of the body, or in some affair of politics or private business; always thinking and calling that which preserves and co-operates with this harmonious condition, just and good action, and the knowledge which presides over it, wisdom, and that which at any time impairs this condition, he will call unjust action, and the opinion which presides over it ignorance.

You have said the exact truth, Socrates.

Very good; and if we were to affirm that we had discovered the just man and the just State, and the nature of justice in each of them, we should not be telling a falsehood?

Most certainly not.

May we say so, then?

Let us say so.

And now, I said, injustice has to be considered.

Clearly.

Must not injustice be a strife which arises among the three principles – a meddlesomeness, and interference, and rising up of a part of the soul against the whole, an assertion of unlawful authority, which is made by a rebellious subject against a true prince, of whom he is the natural vassal, – what is all this confusion and delusion but injustice, and intemperance and cowardice and ignorance, and every form of vice?

Exactly so.

And if the nature of justice and injustice be known, then the meaning of acting unjustly and being unjust, or, again, of acting justly, will also be perfectly clear?

What do you mean? he said.

Why, I said, they are like disease and health; being in the soul just what disease and health are in the body.

How so? he said.

Why, I said, that which is healthy causes health, and that which is unhealthy causes disease.

Yes.

And just actions cause justice, and unjust actions cause injustice?

That is certain.

And the creation of health is the institution of a natural order and government of one by another in the parts of the body; and the creation of disease is the production of a state of things at variance with this natural order?

True.

And is not the creation of justice the institution of a natural order and government of one by another in the parts of the soul, and the creation of injustice the production of a state of things at variance with the natural order?

Exactly so, he said.

Then virtue is the health and beauty and well-being of the soul, and vice the disease and weakness and deformity of the same?

True.

And do not good practices lead to virtue, and evil practices to vice?

Assuredly.

Still our old question of the comparative advantage of justice and injustice has not been answered: Which is the more profitable, to be just and act justly and practise virtue, whether seen or unseen of gods and men, or to be unjust and act unjustly, if only unpunished and unreformed?

In my judgment, Socrates, the question has now become ridiculous. We know that, when the bodily constitution is gone, life is no longer endurable, though pampered with all kinds of meats and drinks, and having all wealth and all power; and shall we be told that when the very essence of the vital principle is undermined and corrupted, life is still worth having to a man, if only he be allowed to do whatever he likes with the single exception that he is not to acquire justice and virtue, or to escape from injustice and vice; assuming them both to be such as we have described?

Yes, I said, the question is, as you say, ridiculous. Still, as we are near the spot at which we may see the truth in the clearest manner with our own eyes, let us not faint by the way.

Certainly not, he replied.

Come up hither, I said, and behold the various forms of vice, those of them, I mean, which are worth looking at.

I am following you, he replied: proceed.

I said, The argument seems to have reached a height from which, as from some tower of speculation, a man may look down and see that virtue is one, but that the forms of vice are innumerable; there being four special ones which are deserving of note.

What do you mean? he said.

I mean, I replied, that there appear to be as many forms of the soul as there are distinct forms of the State.

How many?

There are five of the State, and five of the soul, I said.

What are they?

The first, I said, is that which we have been describing, and which may be said to have two names, monarchy and aristocracy, accordingly as rule is exercised by one distinguished man or by many.

True, he replied.

But I regard the two names as describing one form only; for whether the government is in the hands of one or many, if the governors have been trained in the manner which we have supposed, the fundamental laws of the State will be maintained.

That is true, he replied.

BOOK V.

Such is the good and true City or State, and the good and true man is of the same pattern; and if this is right every other is wrong; and the evil is one which affects not only the ordering of the State, but also the regulation of the individual soul, and is exhibited in four forms.

What are they? he said.

I was proceeding to tell the order in which the four evil forms appeared to me to succeed one another, when Polemarchus, who was sitting a little way off, just beyond Adeimantus, began to whisper to him: stretching forth his hand, he took hold of the upper part of his coat by the shoulder, and drew him towards him, leaning forward himself so as to be quite close and saying something in his ear, of which I only caught the words, 'Shall we let him off, or what shall we do?'

Certainly not, said Adeimantus, raising his voice.

Who is it, I said, whom you are refusing to let off?

You, he said.

I repeated, Why am I especially not to be let off?

Why, he said, we think that you are lazy, and mean to cheat us out of a whole chapter which is a very important part of the story; and you fancy that we shall not notice your airy way of proceeding; as if it were self-evident to everybody, that in the matter of women and children 'friends have all things in common.'

And was I not right, Adeimantus?

Yes, he said; but what is right in this particular case, like everything else, requires to be explained; for community may be of many kinds. Please, therefore, to say what sort of community you mean. We have been long expecting that you would tell us something about the family life of your citizens – how they will bring children into the world, and rear them when they have arrived, and, in general, what is the nature of this community of women and children – for we are of opinion that the right or wrong management of such matters will have a great and paramount influence on the State for good or for evil. And now, since the question is still undetermined, and you are taking in hand another State, we have resolved, as you heard, not to let you go until you give an account of all this.

To that resolution, said Glaucon, you may regard me as saying Agreed.

And without more ado, said Thrasymachus, you may consider us all to be equally agreed.

I said, You know not what you are doing in thus assailing me: What an argument are you raising about the State! Just as I thought that I had finished, and was only too glad that I had laid this question to sleep, and was reflecting how fortunate I was in your acceptance of what I then said, you ask me to begin again at the very foundation, ignorant of what a hornet's nest of words you are stirring. Now I foresaw this gathering trouble, and avoided it.

For what purpose do you conceive that we have come here, said Thrasymachus, – to look for gold, or to hear discourse?

Yes, but discourse should have a limit.

Yes, Socrates, said Glaucon, and the whole of life is the only limit which wise men assign to the hearing of such discourses. But never mind about us; take heart yourself and answer the question in your own way: What sort of community of women and children is this which is to prevail among our guardians? and how shall we manage the period between birth and education, which seems to require the greatest care? Tell us how these things will be.

Yes, my simple friend, but the answer is the reverse of easy; many more doubts arise about this than about our previous conclusions. For the practicability of what is said may be doubted; and looked at in another point of view, whether the scheme, if ever so practicable, would be for the best, is also doubtful. Hence I feel a reluctance to approach the subject, lest our aspiration, my dear friend, should turn out to be a dream only.

Fear not, he replied, for your audience will not be hard upon you; they are not sceptical or hostile.

I said: My good friend, I suppose that you mean to encourage me by these words.

Yes, he said.

Then let me tell you that you are doing just the reverse; the encouragement which you offer would have been all very well had I myself believed that I knew what I was talking about: to declare the truth about matters of high interest which a man honours and loves among wise men who love him need occasion no fear or faltering in his mind; but to carry on an argument when you are yourself only a hesitating enquirer, which is my condition, is a dangerous and slippery thing; and the danger is not that I shall be laughed at (of which the fear would be childish), but that I shall miss the truth where I have most need to be sure of my footing, and drag my friends after me in my fall. And I pray Nemesis not to visit upon me the words which I am going to utter. For I do indeed believe that to be an involuntary homicide is a less crime than to be a deceiver about beauty or goodness or justice in the matter of laws. And that is a risk which I would rather run among enemies than among friends, and therefore you do well to encourage me.

Glaucon laughed and said: Well then, Socrates, in case you and your argument do us any serious injury you shall be acquitted beforehand of the homicide, and shall not be held to be a deceiver; take courage then and speak.

Well, I said, the law says that when a man is acquitted he is free from guilt, and what holds at law may hold in argument.

Then why should you mind?

Well, I replied, I suppose that I must retrace my steps and say what I perhaps ought to have said before in the proper place. The part of the men has been played out, and now properly enough comes the turn of the women. Of them I will proceed to speak, and the more readily since I am invited by you.

For men born and educated like our citizens, the only way, in my opinion, of arriving at a right conclusion about the possession and use of women and children is to follow the path on which we originally started, when we said that the men were to be the guardians and watchdogs of the herd.

True.

Let us further suppose the birth and education of our women to be subject to similar or nearly similar regulations; then we shall see whether the result accords with our design.

What do you mean?

What I mean may be put into the form of a question, I said: Are dogs divided into hes and shes, or do they both share equally in hunting and in keeping watch and in the other duties of dogs? or do we entrust to the males the entire and exclusive care of the flocks, while we leave the females at home, under the idea that the bearing and suckling their puppies is labour enough for them?

No, he said, they share alike; the only difference between them is that the males are stronger and the females weaker.

But can you use different animals for the same purpose, unless they are bred and fed in the same way?

You cannot.

Then, if women are to have the same duties as men, they must have the same nurture and education?

Yes.

The education which was assigned to the men was music and gymnastic.

Yes.

Then women must be taught music and gymnastic and also the art of war, which they must practise like the men?

That is the inference, I suppose.

I should rather expect, I said, that several of our proposals, if they are carried out, being unusual, may appear ridiculous.

No doubt of it.

Yes, and the most ridiculous thing of all will be the sight of women naked in the palaestra, exercising with the men, especially when they are no longer young; they certainly will not be a vision of beauty, any more than the enthusiastic old men who in spite of wrinkles and ugliness continue to frequent the gymnasia.

Yes, indeed, he said: according to present notions the proposal would be thought ridiculous.

But then, I said, as we have determined to speak our minds, we must not fear the jests of the wits which will be directed against this sort of innovation; how they will talk of women's attainments both in music and gymnastic, and above all about their wearing armour and riding upon horseback!

Very true, he replied.

Yet having begun we must go forward to the rough places of the law; at the same time begging of these gentlemen for once in their life to be serious. Not long ago, as we shall remind them, the Hellenes were of the opinion, which is still generally received among the barbarians, that the sight of a naked man was ridiculous and improper; and when first the Cretans and then the Lacedaemonians introduced the custom, the wits of that day might equally have ridiculed the innovation.

No doubt.

But when experience showed that to let all things be uncovered was far better than to cover them up, and the ludicrous effect to the outward eye vanished before the better principle which reason asserted, then the man was perceived to be a fool who directs the shafts of his ridicule at any other sight but that of folly and vice, or seriously inclines to weigh the beautiful by any other standard but that of the good.

Very true, he replied.

First, then, whether the question is to be put in jest or in earnest, let us come to an understanding about the nature of woman: Is she capable of sharing either wholly or partially in the actions of men, or not at all? And is the art of war one of those arts in which she can or can not share? That will be the best way of commencing the enquiry, and will probably lead to the fairest conclusion.

That will be much the best way.

Shall we take the other side first and begin by arguing against ourselves; in this manner the adversary's position will not be undefended.

Why not? he said.

Then let us put a speech into the mouths of our opponents. They will say: 'Socrates and Glaucon, no adversary need convict you, for you yourselves, at the first foundation of the State, admitted the principle that everybody was to do the one work suited to his own nature.' And certainly, if I am not mistaken, such an admission was made by us. 'And do not the natures of men and women differ very much indeed?' And we shall reply: Of course they do. Then we shall be asked, 'Whether the tasks assigned to men and to women should not be different, and such as are agreeable to their different natures?' Certainly they should. 'But if so, have you not fallen into a serious inconsistency in saying that men and women, whose natures are so entirely different, ought to perform the same actions?' – What defence will you make for us, my good Sir, against any one who offers these objections?

That is not an easy question to answer when asked suddenly; and I shall and I do beg of you to draw out the case on our side.

These are the objections, Glaucon, and there are many others of a like kind, which I foresaw long ago; they made me afraid and reluctant to take in hand any law about the possession and nurture of women and children.

By Zeus, he said, the problem to be solved is anything but easy.

Why yes, I said, but the fact is that when a man is out of his depth, whether he has fallen into a little swimming bath or into mid ocean, he has to swim all the same.

Very true.

And must not we swim and try to reach the shore: we will hope that Arion's dolphin or some other miraculous help may save us?

I suppose so, he said.

Well then, let us see if any way of escape can be found. We acknowledged – did we not? that different natures ought to have different pursuits, and that men's and women's natures are different. And now what are we saying? – that different natures ought to have the same pursuits, – this is the inconsistency which is charged upon us.

Precisely.

Verily, Glaucon, I said, glorious is the power of the art of contradiction!

Why do you say so?

Because I think that many a man falls into the practice against his will. When he thinks that he is reasoning he is really disputing, just because he cannot define and divide, and so know that of which he is speaking; and he will pursue a merely verbal opposition in the spirit of contention and not of fair discussion.

Yes, he replied, such is very often the case; but what has that to do with us and our argument?

A great deal; for there is certainly a danger of our getting unintentionally into a verbal opposition.

In what way?

Why we valiantly and pugnaciously insist upon the verbal truth, that different natures ought to have different pursuits, but we never considered at all what was the meaning of sameness or difference of nature, or why we distinguished them when we assigned different pursuits to different natures and the same to the same natures.

Why, no, he said, that was never considered by us.

I said: Suppose that by way of illustration we were to ask the question whether there is not an opposition in nature between bald men and hairy men; and if this is admitted by us, then, if bald men are cobblers, we should forbid the hairy men to be cobblers, and conversely?

That would be a jest, he said.

Yes, I said, a jest; and why? because we never meant when we constructed the State, that the opposition of natures should extend to every difference, but only to those differences which affected the pursuit in which the individual is engaged; we should have argued, for example, that a physician and one who is in mind a physician may be said to have the same nature.

True.

Whereas the physician and the carpenter have different natures?

Certainly.

And if, I said, the male and female sex appear to differ in their fitness for any art or pursuit, we should say that such pursuit or art ought to be assigned to one or the other of them; but if the difference consists only in women bearing and men begetting children, this does not amount to a proof that a woman differs from a man in respect of the sort of education she should receive; and we shall therefore continue to maintain that our guardians and their wives ought to have the same pursuits.

Very true, he said.

Next, we shall ask our opponent how, in reference to any of the pursuits or arts of civic life, the nature of a woman differs from that of a man?

That will be quite fair.

And perhaps he, like yourself, will reply that to give a sufficient answer on the instant is not easy; but after a little reflection there is no difficulty.

Yes, perhaps.

Suppose then that we invite him to accompany us in the argument, and then we may hope to show him that there is nothing peculiar in the constitution of women which would affect them in the administration of the State.

By all means.

Let us say to him: Come now, and we will ask you a question: – when you spoke of a nature gifted or not gifted in any respect, did you mean to say that one man will acquire a thing easily, another with difficulty; a little learning will lead the one to discover a great deal; whereas the other, after much study and application, no sooner learns than he forgets; or again, did you mean, that the one has a body which is a good servant to his mind, while the body of the other is a hindrance to him? – would not these be the sort of differences which distinguish the man gifted by nature from the one who is ungifted?

No one will deny that.

And can you mention any pursuit of mankind in which the male sex has not all these gifts and qualities in a higher degree than the female? Need I waste time in speaking of the art of weaving, and the management of pancakes and preserves, in which womankind does really appear to be great, and in which for her to be beaten by a man is of all things the most absurd?

You are quite right, he replied, in maintaining the general inferiority of the female sex: although many women are in many things superior to many men, yet on the whole what you say is true.

And if so, my friend, I said, there is no special faculty of administration in a state which a woman has because she is a woman, or which a man has by virtue of his sex, but the gifts of nature are alike diffused in both; all the pursuits of men are the pursuits of women also, but in all of them a woman is inferior to a man.

Very true.

Then are we to impose all our enactments on men and none of them on women?

That will never do.

One woman has a gift of healing, another not; one is a musician, and another has no music in her nature?

Very true.

And one woman has a turn for gymnastic and military exercises, and another is unwarlike and hates gymnastics?

Certainly.

And one woman is a philosopher, and another is an enemy of philosophy; one has spirit, and another is without spirit?

That is also true.

Then one woman will have the temper of a guardian, and another not. Was not the selection of the male guardians determined by differences of this sort?

Yes.

Men and women alike possess the qualities which make a guardian; they differ only in their comparative strength or weakness.

Obviously.

And those women who have such qualities are to be selected as the companions and colleagues of men who have similar qualities and whom they resemble in capacity and in character?

Very true.

And ought not the same natures to have the same pursuits?

They ought.

Then, as we were saying before, there is nothing unnatural in assigning music and gymnastic to the wives of the guardians – to that point we come round again.

Certainly not.

The law which we then enacted was agreeable to nature, and therefore not an impossibility or mere aspiration; and the contrary practice, which prevails at present, is in reality a violation of nature.

That appears to be true.

We had to consider, first, whether our proposals were possible, and secondly whether they were the most beneficial?

Yes.

And the possibility has been acknowledged?

Yes.

The very great benefit has next to be established?

Quite so.

You will admit that the same education which makes a man a good guardian will make a woman a good guardian; for their original nature is the same?

Yes.

I should like to ask you a question.

What is it?

Would you say that all men are equal in excellence, or is one man better than another?

The latter.

And in the commonwealth which we were founding do you conceive the guardians who have been brought up on our model system to be more perfect men, or the cobblers whose education has been cobbling?

What a ridiculous question!

You have answered me, I replied: Well, and may we not further say that our guardians are the best of our citizens?

By far the best.

And will not their wives be the best women?

Yes, by far the best.

And can there be anything better for the interests of the State than that the men and women of a State should be as good as possible?

There can be nothing better.

And this is what the arts of music and gymnastic, when present in such manner as we have described, will accomplish?

Certainly.

Then we have made an enactment not only possible but in the highest degree beneficial to the State?

True.

Then let the wives of our guardians strip, for their virtue will be their robe, and let them share in the toils of war and the defence of their country; only in the distribution of labours the lighter are to be assigned to the women, who are the weaker natures, but in other respects their duties are to be the same. And as for the man who laughs at naked women exercising their bodies from the best of motives, in his laughter he is plucking

'A fruit of unripe wisdom,'

and he himself is ignorant of what he is laughing at, or what he is about; – for that is, and ever will be, the best of sayings, That the useful is the noble and the hurtful is the base.

Very true.

Here, then, is one difficulty in our law about women, which we may say that we have now escaped; the wave has not swallowed us up alive for enacting that the guardians of either sex should have all their pursuits in common; to the utility and also to the possibility of this arrangement the consistency of the argument with itself bears witness.

Yes, that was a mighty wave which you have escaped.

Yes, I said, but a greater is coming; you will not think much of this when you see the next.

Go on; let me see.

The law, I said, which is the sequel of this and of all that has preceded, is to the following effect, – 'that the wives of our guardians are to be common, and their children are to be common, and no parent is to know his own child, nor any child his parent.'

Yes, he said, that is a much greater wave than the other; and the possibility as well as the utility of such a law are far more questionable.

I do not think, I said, that there can be any dispute about the very great utility of having wives and children in common; the possibility is quite another matter, and will be very much disputed.

I think that a good many doubts may be raised about both.

You imply that the two questions must be combined, I replied. Now I meant that you should admit the utility; and in this way, as I thought, I should escape from one of them, and then there would remain only the possibility.

But that little attempt is detected, and therefore you will please to give a defence of both.

Well, I said, I submit to my fate. Yet grant me a little favour: let me feast my mind with the dream as day dreamers are in the habit of feasting themselves when they are walking alone; for before they have discovered any means of effecting their wishes – that is a matter which never troubles them – they would rather not tire themselves by thinking about possibilities; but assuming that what they desire is already granted to them, they proceed with their plan, and delight in detailing what they mean to do when their wish has come true – that is a way which they have of not doing much good to a capacity which was never good for much. Now I myself am beginning to lose heart, and I should like, with your permission, to pass over the question of possibility at present. Assuming therefore the possibility of the proposal, I shall now proceed to enquire how the rulers will carry out these arrangements, and I shall demonstrate that our plan, if executed, will be of the greatest benefit to the State and to the guardians. First of all, then, if you have no objection, I will endeavour with your help to consider the advantages of the measure; and hereafter the question of possibility.

I have no objection; proceed.

First, I think that if our rulers and their auxiliaries are to be worthy of the name which they bear, there must be willingness to obey in the one and the power of command in the other; the guardians must themselves obey the laws, and they must also imitate the spirit of them in any details which are entrusted to their care.

That is right, he said.

You, I said, who are their legislator, having selected the men, will now select the women and give them to them; – they must be as far as possible of like natures with them; and they must live in common houses and meet at common meals. None of them will have anything specially his or her own; they will be together, and will be brought up together, and will associate at gymnastic exercises. And so they will be drawn by a necessity of their natures to have intercourse with each other – necessity is not too strong a word, I think?

Yes, he said; – necessity, not geometrical, but another sort of necessity which lovers know, and which is far more convincing and constraining to the mass of mankind.

True, I said; and this, Glaucon, like all the rest, must proceed after an orderly fashion; in a city of the blessed, licentiousness is an unholy thing which the rulers will forbid.

Yes, he said, and it ought not to be permitted.

Then clearly the next thing will be to make matrimony sacred in the highest degree, and what is most beneficial will be deemed sacred?

Exactly.

And how can marriages be made most beneficial? – that is a question which I put to you, because I see in your house dogs for hunting, and of the nobler sort of birds not a few. Now, I beseech you, do tell me, have you ever attended to their pairing and breeding?

In what particulars?

Why, in the first place, although they are all of a good sort, are not some better than others?

True.

And do you breed from them all indifferently, or do you take care to breed from the best only?

From the best.

And do you take the oldest or the youngest, or only those of ripe age?

I choose only those of ripe age.

And if care was not taken in the breeding, your dogs and birds would greatly deteriorate?

Certainly.

And the same of horses and animals in general?

Undoubtedly.

Good heavens! my dear friend, I said, what consummate skill will our rulers need if the same principle holds of the human species!

Certainly, the same principle holds; but why does this involve any particular skill?

Because, I said, our rulers will often have to practise upon the body corporate with medicines. Now you know that when patients do not require medicines, but have only to be put under a regimen, the inferior sort of practitioner is deemed to be good enough; but when medicine has to be given, then the doctor should be more of a man.

That is quite true, he said; but to what are you alluding?

I mean, I replied, that our rulers will find a considerable dose of falsehood and deceit necessary for the good of their subjects: we were saying that the use of all these things regarded as medicines might be of advantage.

And we were very right.

And this lawful use of them seems likely to be often needed in the regulations of marriages and births.

How so?

Why, I said, the principle has been already laid down that the best of either sex should be united with the best as often, and the inferior with the inferior, as seldom as possible; and that they should rear the offspring of the one sort of union, but not of the other, if the flock is to be maintained in first-rate condition. Now these goings on must be a secret which the rulers only know, or there will be a further danger of our herd, as the guardians may be termed, breaking out into rebellion.

Very true.

Had we not better appoint certain festivals at which we will bring together the brides and bridegrooms, and sacrifices will be offered and suitable hymeneal songs composed by our poets: the number of weddings is a matter which must be left to the discretion of the rulers, whose aim will be to preserve the average of population? There are many other things which they will have to consider, such as the effects of wars and diseases and any similar agencies, in order as far as this is possible to prevent the State from becoming either too large or too small.

Certainly, he replied.

We shall have to invent some ingenious kind of lots which the less worthy may draw on each occasion of our bringing them together, and then they will accuse their own ill-luck and not the rulers.

To be sure, he said.

And I think that our braver and better youth, besides their other honours and rewards, might have greater facilities of intercourse with women given them; their bravery will be a reason, and such fathers ought to have as many sons as possible.

True.

And the proper officers, whether male or female or both, for offices are to be held by women as well as by men –

Yes –

The proper officers will take the offspring of the good parents to the pen or fold, and there they will deposit them with certain nurses who dwell in a separate quarter; but the offspring of the inferior, or of the better when they chance to be deformed, will be put away in some mysterious, unknown place, as they should be.

Yes, he said, that must be done if the breed of the guardians is to be kept pure.

They will provide for their nurture, and will bring the mothers to the fold when they are full of milk, taking the greatest possible care that no mother recognises her own child; and other wet-nurses may be engaged if more are required. Care will also be taken that the process of suckling shall not be protracted too long; and the mothers will have no getting up at night or other trouble, but will hand over all this sort of thing to the nurses and attendants.

You suppose the wives of our guardians to have a fine easy time of it when they are having children.

Why, said I, and so they ought. Let us, however, proceed with our scheme. We were saying that the parents should be in the prime of life?

Very true.

And what is the prime of life? May it not be defined as a period of about twenty years in a woman's life, and thirty in a man's?

Which years do you mean to include?

A woman, I said, at twenty years of age may begin to bear children to the State, and continue to bear them until forty; a man may begin at five-and-twenty, when he has passed the point at which the pulse of life beats quickest, and continue to beget children until he be fifty-five.

Certainly, he said, both in men and women those years are the prime of physical as well as of intellectual vigour.

Any one above or below the prescribed ages who takes part in the public hymeneals shall be said to have done an unholy and unrighteous thing; the child of which he is the father, if it steals into life, will have been conceived under auspices very unlike the sacrifices and prayers, which at each hymeneal priestesses and priest and the whole city will offer, that the new generation may be better and more useful than their good and useful parents, whereas his child will be the offspring of darkness and strange lust.

Very true, he replied.

And the same law will apply to any one of those within the prescribed age who forms a connection with any woman in the prime of life without the sanction of the rulers; for we shall say that he is raising up a bastard to the State, uncertified and unconsecrated.

Very true, he replied.

This applies, however, only to those who are within the specified age: after that we allow them to range at will, except that a man may not marry his daughter or his daughter's daughter, or his mother or his mother's mother; and women, on the other hand, are prohibited from marrying their sons or fathers, or son's son or father's father, and so on in either direction. And we grant all this, accompanying the permission with strict orders to prevent any embryo which may come into being from seeing the light; and if any force a way to the birth, the parents must understand that the offspring of such an union cannot be maintained, and arrange accordingly.

That also, he said, is a reasonable proposition. But how will they know who are fathers and daughters, and so on?

They will never know. The way will be this: – dating from the day of the hymeneal, the bridegroom who was then married will call all the male children who are born in the seventh and tenth month afterwards his sons, and the female children his daughters, and they will call him father, and he will call their children his grandchildren, and they will call the elder generation grandfathers and grandmothers. All who were begotten at the time when their fathers and mothers came together will be called their brothers and sisters, and these, as I was saying, will be forbidden to inter-marry. This, however, is not to be understood as an absolute prohibition of the marriage of brothers and sisters; if the lot favours them, and they receive the sanction of the Pythian oracle, the law will allow them.

Quite right, he replied.

Such is the scheme, Glaucon, according to which the guardians of our State are to have their wives and families in common. And now you would have the argument show that this community is consistent with the rest of our polity, and also that nothing can be better – would you not?

Yes, certainly.

Shall we try to find a common basis by asking of ourselves what ought to be the chief aim of the legislator in making laws and in the organization of a State, – what is the greatest good, and what is the greatest evil, and then consider whether our previous description has the stamp of the good or of the evil?

By all means.

Can there be any greater evil than discord and distraction and plurality where unity ought to reign? or any greater good than the bond of unity?

There cannot.

And there is unity where there is community of pleasures and pains – where all the citizens are glad or grieved on the same occasions of joy and sorrow?

No doubt.

Yes; and where there is no common but only private feeling a State is disorganized – when you have one half of the world triumphing and the other plunged in grief at the same events happening to the city or the citizens?

Certainly.

Such differences commonly originate in a disagreement about the use of the terms 'mine' and 'not mine,' 'his' and 'not his.'

Exactly so.

And is not that the best-ordered State in which the greatest number of persons apply the terms 'mine' and 'not mine' in the same way to the same thing?

Quite true.

Or that again which most nearly approaches to the condition of the individual – as in the body, when but a finger of one of us is hurt, the whole frame, drawn towards the soul as a centre and forming one kingdom under the ruling power therein, feels the hurt and sympathizes all together with the part affected, and we say that the man has a pain in his finger; and the same expression is used about any other part of the body, which has a sensation of pain at suffering or of pleasure at the alleviation of suffering.

Very true, he replied; and I agree with you that in the best-ordered State there is the nearest approach to this common feeling which you describe.

Then when any one of the citizens experiences any good or evil, the whole State will make his case their own, and will either rejoice or sorrow with him?

Yes, he said, that is what will happen in a well-ordered State.

It will now be time, I said, for us to return to our State and see whether this or some other form is most in accordance with these fundamental principles.

Very good.

Our State like every other has rulers and subjects?

True.

All of whom will call one another citizens?

Of course.

But is there not another name which people give to their rulers in other States?

Generally they call them masters, but in democratic States they simply call them rulers.

And in our State what other name besides that of citizens do the people give the rulers?

They are called saviours and helpers, he replied.

And what do the rulers call the people?

Their maintainers and foster-fathers.

And what do they call them in other States?

Slaves.

And what do the rulers call one another in other States?

Fellow-rulers.

And what in ours?

Fellow-guardians.

Did you ever know an example in any other State of a ruler who would speak of one of his colleagues as his friend and of another as not being his friend?

Yes, very often.

And the friend he regards and describes as one in whom he has an interest, and the other as a stranger in whom he has no interest?

Exactly.

But would any of your guardians think or speak of any other guardian as a stranger?

Certainly he would not; for every one whom they meet will be regarded by them either as a brother or sister, or father or mother, or son or daughter, or as the child or parent of those who are thus connected with him.

Capital, I said; but let me ask you once more: Shall they be a family in name only; or shall they in all their actions be true to the name? For example, in the use of the word 'father,' would the care of a father be implied and the filial reverence and duty and obedience to him which the law commands; and is the violator of these duties to be regarded as an impious and unrighteous person who is not likely to receive much good either at the hands of God or of man? Are these to be or not to be the strains which the children will hear repeated in their ears by all the citizens about those who are intimated to them to be their parents and the rest of their kinsfolk?

These, he said, and none other; for what can be more ridiculous than for them to utter the names of family ties with the lips only and not to act in the spirit of them?

Then in our city the language of harmony and concord will be more often heard than in any other. As I was describing before, when any one is well or ill, the universal word will be 'with me it is well' or 'it is ill.'

Most true.

And agreeably to this mode of thinking and speaking, were we not saying that they will have their pleasures and pains in common?

Yes, and so they will.

And they will have a common interest in the same thing which they will alike call 'my own,' and having this common interest they will have a common feeling of pleasure and pain?

Yes, far more so than in other States.

And the reason of this, over and above the general constitution of the State, will be that the guardians will have a community of women and children?

That will be the chief reason.

And this unity of feeling we admitted to be the greatest good, as was implied in our own comparison of a well-ordered State to the relation of the body and the members, when affected by pleasure or pain?

That we acknowledged, and very rightly.

Then the community of wives and children among our citizens is clearly the source of the greatest good to the State?

Certainly.

And this agrees with the other principle which we were affirming, – that the guardians were not to have houses or lands or any other property; their pay was to be their food, which they were to receive from the other citizens, and they were to have no private expenses; for we intended them to preserve their true character of guardians.

Right, he replied.

Both the community of property and the community of families, as I am saying, tend to make them more truly guardians; they will not tear the city in pieces by differing about 'mine' and 'not mine;' each man dragging any acquisition which he has made into a separate house of his own, where he has a separate wife and children and private pleasures and pains; but all will be affected as far as may be by the same pleasures and pains because they are all of one opinion about what is near and dear to them, and therefore they all tend towards a common end.

Certainly, he replied.

And as they have nothing but their persons which they can call their own, suits and complaints will have no existence among them; they will be delivered from all those quarrels of which money or children or relations are the occasion.

Of course they will.

Neither will trials for assault or insult ever be likely to occur among them. For that equals should defend themselves against equals we shall maintain to be honourable and right; we shall make the protection of the person a matter of necessity.

That is good, he said.

Yes; and there is a further good in the law; viz. that if a man has a quarrel with another he will satisfy his resentment then and there, and not proceed to more dangerous lengths.

Certainly.

To the elder shall be assigned the duty of ruling and chastising the younger.

Clearly.

Nor can there be a doubt that the younger will not strike or do any other violence to an elder, unless the magistrates command him; nor will he slight him in any way. For there are two guardians, shame and fear, mighty to prevent him: shame, which makes men refrain from laying hands on those who are to them in the relation of parents; fear, that the injured one will be succoured by the others who are his brothers, sons, fathers.

That is true, he replied.

Then in every way the laws will help the citizens to keep the peace with one another?

Yes, there will be no want of peace.

And as the guardians will never quarrel among themselves there will be no danger of the rest of the city being divided either against them or against one another.

None whatever.

I hardly like even to mention the little meannesses of which they will be rid, for they are beneath notice: such, for example, as the flattery of the rich by the poor, and all the pains and pangs which men experience in bringing up a family, and in finding money to buy necessaries for their household, borrowing and then repudiating, getting how they can, and giving the money into the hands of women and slaves to keep – the many evils of so many kinds which people suffer in this way are mean enough and obvious enough, and not worth speaking of.

Yes, he said, a man has no need of eyes in order to perceive that.

And from all these evils they will be delivered, and their life will be blessed as the life of Olympic victors and yet more blessed.

How so?

The Olympic victor, I said, is deemed happy in receiving a part only of the blessedness which is secured to our citizens, who have won a more glorious victory and have a more complete maintenance at the public cost. For the victory which they have won is the salvation of the whole State; and the crown with which they and their children are crowned is the fulness of all that life needs; they receive rewards from the hands of their country while living, and after death have an honourable burial.

Yes, he said, and glorious rewards they are.

Do you remember, I said, how in the course of the previous discussion some one who shall be nameless accused us of making our guardians unhappy – they had nothing and might have possessed all things – to whom we replied that, if an occasion offered, we might perhaps hereafter consider this question, but that, as at present advised, we would make our guardians truly guardians, and that we were fashioning the State with a view to the greatest happiness, not of any particular class, but of the whole?

Yes, I remember.

And what do you say, now that the life of our protectors is made out to be far better and nobler than that of Olympic victors – is the life of shoemakers, or any other artisans, or of husbandmen, to be compared with it?

Certainly not.

At the same time I ought here to repeat what I have said elsewhere, that if any of our guardians shall try to be happy in such a manner that he will cease to be a guardian, and is not content with this safe and harmonious life, which, in our judgment, is of all lives the best, but infatuated by some youthful conceit of happiness which gets up into his head shall seek to appropriate the whole state to himself, then he will have to learn how wisely Hesiod spoke, when he said, 'half is more than the whole.'

If he were to consult me, I should say to him: Stay where you are, when you have the offer of such a life.

You agree then, I said, that men and women are to have a common way of life such as we have described – common education, common children; and they are to watch over the citizens in common whether abiding in the city or going out to war; they are to keep watch together, and to hunt together like dogs; and always and in all things, as far as they are able, women are to share with the men? And in so doing they will do what is best, and will not violate, but preserve the natural relation of the sexes.

I agree with you, he replied.

The enquiry, I said, has yet to be made, whether such a community be found possible – as among other animals, so also among men – and if possible, in what way possible?

You have anticipated the question which I was about to suggest.

There is no difficulty, I said, in seeing how war will be carried on by them.

How?

Why, of course they will go on expeditions together; and will take with them any of their children who are strong enough, that, after the manner of the artisan's child, they may look on at the work which they will have to do when they are grown up; and besides looking on they will have to help and be of use in war, and to wait upon their fathers and mothers. Did you never observe in the arts how the potters' boys look on and help, long before they touch the wheel?

Yes, I have.

And shall potters be more careful in educating their children and in giving them the opportunity of seeing and practising their duties than our guardians will be?

The idea is ridiculous, he said.

There is also the effect on the parents, with whom, as with other animals, the presence of their young ones will be the greatest incentive to valour.

That is quite true, Socrates; and yet if they are defeated, which may often happen in war, how great the danger is! the children will be lost as well as their parents, and the State will never recover.

True, I said; but would you never allow them to run any risk?

I am far from saying that.

Well, but if they are ever to run a risk should they not do so on some occasion when, if they escape disaster, they will be the better for it?

Clearly.

Whether the future soldiers do or do not see war in the days of their youth is a very important matter, for the sake of which some risk may fairly be incurred.

Yes, very important.

This then must be our first step, – to make our children spectators of war; but we must also contrive that they shall be secured against danger; then all will be well.

True.

Their parents may be supposed not to be blind to the risks of war, but to know, as far as human foresight can, what expeditions are safe and what dangerous?

That may be assumed.

And they will take them on the safe expeditions and be cautious about the dangerous ones?

True.

And they will place them under the command of experienced veterans who will be their leaders and teachers?

Very properly.

Still, the dangers of war cannot be always foreseen; there is a good deal of chance about them?

True.

Then against such chances the children must be at once furnished with wings, in order that in the hour of need they may fly away and escape.

What do you mean? he said.

I mean that we must mount them on horses in their earliest youth, and when they have learnt to ride, take them on horseback to see war: the horses must not be spirited and warlike, but the most tractable and yet the swiftest that can be had. In this way they will get an excellent view of what is hereafter to be their own business; and if there is danger they have only to follow their elder leaders and escape.

I believe that you are right, he said.

Next, as to war; what are to be the relations of your soldiers to one another and to their enemies? I should be inclined to propose that the soldier who leaves his rank or throws away his arms, or is guilty of any other act of cowardice, should be degraded into the rank of a husbandman or artisan. What do you think?

By all means, I should say.

And he who allows himself to be taken prisoner may as well be made a present of to his enemies; he is their lawful prey, and let them do what they like with him.

Certainly.

But the hero who has distinguished himself, what shall be done to him? In the first place, he shall receive honour in the army from his youthful comrades; every one of them in succession shall crown him. What do you say?

I approve.

And what do you say to his receiving the right hand of fellowship?

To that too, I agree.

But you will hardly agree to my next proposal.

What is your proposal?

That he should kiss and be kissed by them.

Most certainly, and I should be disposed to go further, and say: Let no one whom he has a mind to kiss refuse to be kissed by him while the expedition lasts. So that if there be a lover in the army, whether his love be youth or maiden, he may be more eager to win the prize of valour.

Capital, I said. That the brave man is to have more wives than others has been already determined: and he is to have first choices in such matters more than others, in order that he may have as many children as possible?

Agreed.

Again, there is another manner in which, according to Homer, brave youths should be honoured; for he tells how Ajax, after he had distinguished himself in battle, was rewarded with long chines, which seems to be a compliment appropriate to a hero in the flower of his age, being not only a tribute of honour but also a very strengthening thing.

Most true, he said.

Then in this, I said, Homer shall be our teacher; and we too, at sacrifices and on the like occasions, will honour the brave according to the measure of their valour, whether men or women, with hymns and those other distinctions which we were mentioning; also with

'seats of precedence, and meats and full cups;'

and in honouring them, we shall be at the same time training them.

That, he replied, is excellent.

Yes, I said; and when a man dies gloriously in war shall we not say, in the first place, that he is of the golden race?

To be sure.

Nay, have we not the authority of Hesiod for affirming that when they are dead

'They are holy angels upon the earth, authors of good, averters of evil, the guardians of speech-gifted men'?

Yes; and we accept his authority.

We must learn of the god how we are to order the sepulture of divine and heroic personages, and what is to be their special distinction; and we must do as he bids?

By all means.

And in ages to come we will reverence them and kneel before their sepulchres as at the graves of heroes. And not only they but any who are deemed pre-eminently good, whether they die from age, or in any other way, shall be admitted to the same honours.

That is very right, he said.

Next, how shall our soldiers treat their enemies? What about this?

In what respect do you mean?

First of all, in regard to slavery? Do you think it right that Hellenes should enslave Hellenic States, or allow others to enslave them, if they can help? Should not their custom be to spare them, considering the danger which there is that the whole race may one day fall under the yoke of the barbarians?

To spare them is infinitely better.

Then no Hellene should be owned by them as a slave; that is a rule which they will observe and advise the other Hellenes to observe.

Certainly, he said; they will in this way be united against the barbarians and will keep their hands off one another.

Next as to the slain; ought the conquerors, I said, to take anything but their armour? Does not the practice of despoiling an enemy afford an excuse for not facing the battle? Cowards skulk about the dead, pretending that they are fulfilling a duty, and many an army before now has been lost from this love of plunder.

Very true.

And is there not illiberality and avarice in robbing a corpse, and also a degree of meanness and womanishness in making an enemy of the dead body when the real enemy has flown away and left only his fighting gear behind him, – is not this rather like a dog who cannot get at his assailant, quarrelling with the stones which strike him instead?

Very like a dog, he said.

Then we must abstain from spoiling the dead or hindering their burial?

Yes, he replied, we most certainly must.

Neither shall we offer up arms at the temples of the gods, least of all the arms of Hellenes, if we care to maintain good feeling with other Hellenes; and, indeed, we have reason to fear that the offering of spoils taken from kinsmen may be a pollution unless commanded by the god himself?

Very true.

Again, as to the devastation of Hellenic territory or the burning of houses, what is to be the practice?

May I have the pleasure, he said, of hearing your opinion?

Both should be forbidden, in my judgment; I would take the annual produce and no more. Shall I tell you why?

Pray do.

Why, you see, there is a difference in the names 'discord' and 'war,' and I imagine that there is also a difference in their natures; the one is expressive of what is internal and domestic, the other of what is external and foreign; and the first of the two is termed discord, and only the second, war.

That is a very proper distinction, he replied.

And may I not observe with equal propriety that the Hellenic race is all united together by ties of blood and friendship, and alien and strange to the barbarians?

Very good, he said.

And therefore when Hellenes fight with barbarians and barbarians with Hellenes, they will be described by us as being at war when they fight, and by nature enemies, and this kind of antagonism should be called war; but when Hellenes fight with one another we shall say that Hellas is then in a state of disorder and discord, they being by nature friends; and such enmity is to be called discord.

I agree.

Consider then, I said, when that which we have acknowledged to be discord occurs, and a city is divided, if both parties destroy the lands and burn the houses of one another, how wicked does the strife appear! No true lover of his country would bring himself to tear in pieces his own nurse and mother: There might be reason in the conqueror depriving the conquered of their harvest, but still they would have the idea of peace in their hearts and would not mean to go on fighting for ever.

Yes, he said, that is a better temper than the other.

And will not the city, which you are founding, be an Hellenic city?

It ought to be, he replied.

Then will not the citizens be good and civilized?

Yes, very civilized.

And will they not be lovers of Hellas, and think of Hellas as their own land, and share in the common temples?

Most certainly.

And any difference which arises among them will be regarded by them as discord only – a quarrel among friends, which is not to be called a war?

Certainly not.

Then they will quarrel as those who intend some day to be reconciled?

Certainly.

They will use friendly correction, but will not enslave or destroy their opponents; they will be correctors, not enemies?

Just so.

And as they are Hellenes themselves they will not devastate Hellas, nor will they burn houses, nor ever suppose that the whole population of a city – men, women, and children – are equally their enemies, for they know that the guilt of war is always confined to a few persons and that the many are their friends. And for all these reasons they will be unwilling to waste their lands and rase their houses; their enmity to them will only last until the many innocent sufferers have compelled the guilty few to give satisfaction?

I agree, he said, that our citizens should thus deal with their Hellenic enemies; and with barbarians as the Hellenes now deal with one another.

Then let us enact this law also for our guardians: – that they are neither to devastate the lands of Hellenes nor to burn their houses.

Agreed; and we may agree also in thinking that these, like all our previous enactments, are very good.

But still I must say, Socrates, that if you are allowed to go on in this way you will entirely forget the other question which at the commencement of this discussion you thrust aside: – Is such an order of things possible, and how, if at all? For I am quite ready to acknowledge that the plan which you propose, if only feasible, would do all sorts of good to the State. I will add, what you have omitted, that your citizens will be the bravest of warriors, and will never leave their ranks, for they will all know one another, and each will call the other father, brother, son; and if you suppose the women to join their armies, whether in the same rank or in the rear, either as a terror to the enemy, or as auxiliaries in case of need, I know that they will then be absolutely invincible; and there are many domestic advantages which might also be mentioned and which I also fully acknowledge: but, as I admit all these advantages and as many more as you please, if only this State of yours were to come into existence, we need say no more about them; assuming then the existence of the State, let us now turn to the question of possibility and ways and means – the rest may be left.

If I loiter for a moment, you instantly make a raid upon me, I said, and have no mercy; I have hardly escaped the first and second waves, and you seem not to be aware that you are now bringing upon me the third, which is the greatest and heaviest. When you have seen and heard the third wave, I think you will be more considerate and will acknowledge that some fear and hesitation was natural respecting a proposal so extraordinary as that which I have now to state and investigate.

The more appeals of this sort which you make, he said, the more determined are we that you shall tell us how such a State is possible: speak out and at once.

Let me begin by reminding you that we found our way hither in the search after justice and injustice.

True, he replied; but what of that?

I was only going to ask whether, if we have discovered them, we are to require that the just man should in nothing fail of absolute justice; or may we be satisfied with an approximation, and the attainment in him of a higher degree of justice than is to be found in other men?

The approximation will be enough.

We were enquiring into the nature of absolute justice and into the character of the perfectly just, and into injustice and the perfectly unjust, that we might have an ideal. We were to look at these in order that we might judge of our own happiness and unhappiness according to the standard which they exhibited and the degree in which we resembled them, but not with any view of showing that they could exist in fact.

True, he said.

Would a painter be any the worse because, after having delineated with consummate art an ideal of a perfectly beautiful man, he was unable to show that any such man could ever have existed?

He would be none the worse.

Well, and were we not creating an ideal of a perfect State?

To be sure.

And is our theory a worse theory because we are unable to prove the possibility of a city being ordered in the manner described?

Surely not, he replied.

That is the truth, I said. But if, at your request, I am to try and show how and under what conditions the possibility is highest, I must ask you, having this in view, to repeat your former admissions.

What admissions?

I want to know whether ideals are ever fully realized in language? Does not the word express more than the fact, and must not the actual, whatever a man may think, always, in the nature of things, fall short of the truth? What do you say?

I agree.

Then you must not insist on my proving that the actual State will in every respect coincide with the ideal: if we are only able to discover how a city may be governed nearly as we proposed, you will admit that we have discovered the possibility which you demand; and will be contented. I am sure that I should be contented – will not you?

Yes, I will.

Let me next endeavour to show what is that fault in States which is the cause of their present maladministration, and what is the least change which will enable a State to pass into the truer form; and let the change, if possible, be of one thing only, or, if not, of two; at any rate, let the changes be as few and slight as possible.

Certainly, he replied.

I think, I said, that there might be a reform of the State if only one change were made, which is not a slight or easy though still a possible one.

What is it? he said.

Now then, I said, I go to meet that which I liken to the greatest of the waves; yet shall the word be spoken, even though the wave break and drown me in laughter and dishonour; and do you mark my words.

Proceed.

I said: 'Until philosophers are kings, or the kings and princes of this world have the spirit and power of philosophy, and political greatness and wisdom meet in one, and those commoner natures who pursue either to the exclusion of the other are compelled to stand aside, cities will never have rest from their evils, – nor the human race, as I believe, – and then only will this our State have a possibility of life and behold the light of day.' Such was the thought, my dear Glaucon, which I would fain have uttered if it had not seemed too extravagant; for to be convinced that in no other State can there be happiness private or public is indeed a hard thing.

Socrates, what do you mean? I would have you consider that the word which you have uttered is one at which numerous persons, and very respectable persons too, in a figure pulling off their coats all in a moment, and seizing any weapon that comes to hand, will run at you might and main, before you know where you are, intending to do heaven knows what; and if you don't prepare an answer, and put yourself in motion, you will be 'pared by their fine wits,' and no mistake.

You got me into the scrape, I said.

And I was quite right; however, I will do all I can to get you out of it; but I can only give you good-will and good advice, and, perhaps, I may be able to fit answers to your questions better than another – that is all. And now, having such an auxiliary, you must do your best to show the unbelievers that you are right.

I ought to try, I said, since you offer me such invaluable assistance. And I think that, if there is to be a chance of our escaping, we must explain to them whom we mean when we say that philosophers are to rule in the State; then we shall be able to defend ourselves: There will be discovered to be some natures who ought to study philosophy and to be leaders in the State; and others who are not born to be philosophers, and are meant to be followers rather than leaders.

Then now for a definition, he said.

Follow me, I said, and I hope that I may in some way or other be able to give you a satisfactory explanation.

Proceed.

I dare say that you remember, and therefore I need not remind you, that a lover, if he is worthy of the name, ought to show his love, not to some one part of that which he loves, but to the whole.

I really do not understand, and therefore beg of you to assist my memory.

Another person, I said, might fairly reply as you do; but a man of pleasure like yourself ought to know that all who are in the flower of youth do somehow or other raise a pang or emotion in a lover's breast, and are thought by him to be worthy of his affectionate regards. Is not this a way which you have with the fair: one has a snub nose, and you praise his charming face; the hook-nose of another has, you say, a royal look; while he who is neither snub nor hooked has the grace of regularity: the dark visage is manly, the fair are children of the gods; and as to the sweet 'honey pale,' as they are called, what is the very name but the invention of a lover who talks in diminutives, and is not averse to paleness if appearing on the cheek of youth? In a word, there is no excuse which you will not make, and nothing which you will not say, in order not to lose a single flower that blooms in the spring-time of youth.

If you make me an authority in matters of love, for the sake of the argument, I assent.

And what do you say of lovers of wine? Do you not see them doing the same? They are glad of any pretext of drinking any wine.

Very good.

And the same is true of ambitious men; if they cannot command an army, they are willing to command a file; and if they cannot be honoured by really great and important persons, they are glad to be honoured by lesser and meaner people, – but honour of some kind they must have.

Exactly.

Once more let me ask: Does he who desires any class of goods, desire the whole class or a part only?

The whole.

And may we not say of the philosopher that he is a lover, not of a part of wisdom only, but of the whole?

Yes, of the whole.

And he who dislikes learning, especially in youth, when he has no power of judging what is good and what is not, such an one we maintain not to be a philosopher or a lover of knowledge, just as he who refuses his food is not hungry, and may be said to have a bad appetite and not a good one?

Very true, he said.

Whereas he who has a taste for every sort of knowledge and who is curious to learn and is never satisfied, may be justly termed a philosopher? Am I not right?

Glaucon said: If curiosity makes a philosopher, you will find many a strange being will have a title to the name. All the lovers of sights have a delight in learning, and must therefore be included. Musical amateurs, too, are a folk strangely out of place among philosophers, for they are the last persons in the world who would come to anything like a philosophical discussion, if they could help, while they run about at the Dionysiac festivals as if they had let out their ears to hear every chorus; whether the performance is in town or country – that makes no difference – they are there. Now are we to maintain that all these and any who have similar tastes, as well as the professors of quite minor arts, are philosophers?

Certainly not, I replied; they are only an imitation.

He said: Who then are the true philosophers?

Those, I said, who are lovers of the vision of truth.

That is also good, he said; but I should like to know what you mean?

To another, I replied, I might have a difficulty in explaining; but I am sure that you will admit a proposition which I am about to make.

What is the proposition?

That since beauty is the opposite of ugliness, they are two?

Certainly.

And inasmuch as they are two, each of them is one?

True again.

And of just and unjust, good and evil, and of every other class, the same remark holds: taken singly, each of them is one; but from the various combinations of them with actions and things and with one another, they are seen in all sorts of lights and appear many?

Very true.

And this is the distinction which I draw between the sight-loving, art-loving, practical class and those of whom I am speaking, and who are alone worthy of the name of philosophers.

How do you distinguish them? he said.

The lovers of sounds and sights, I replied, are, as I conceive, fond of fine tones and colours and forms and all the artificial products that are made out of them, but their mind is incapable of seeing or loving absolute beauty.

True, he replied.

Few are they who are able to attain to the sight of this.

Very true.

And he who, having a sense of beautiful things has no sense of absolute beauty, or who, if another lead him to a knowledge of that beauty is unable to follow – of such an one I ask, Is he awake or in a dream only? Reflect: is not the dreamer, sleeping or waking, one who likens dissimilar things, who puts the copy in the place of the real object?

I should certainly say that such an one was dreaming.

But take the case of the other, who recognises the existence of absolute beauty and is able to distinguish the idea from the objects which participate in the idea, neither putting the objects in the place of the idea nor the idea in the place of the objects – is he a dreamer, or is he awake?

He is wide awake.

And may we not say that the mind of the one who knows has knowledge, and that the mind of the other, who opines only, has opinion?

Certainly.

But suppose that the latter should quarrel with us and dispute our statement, can we administer any soothing cordial or advice to him, without revealing to him that there is sad disorder in his wits?

We must certainly offer him some good advice, he replied.

Come, then, and let us think of something to say to him. Shall we begin by assuring him that he is welcome to any knowledge which he may have, and that we are rejoiced at his having it? But we should like to ask him a question: Does he who has knowledge know something or nothing? (You must answer for him.)

I answer that he knows something.

Something that is or is not?

Something that is; for how can that which is not ever be known?

And are we assured, after looking at the matter from many points of view, that absolute being is or may be absolutely known, but that the utterly non-existent is utterly unknown?

Nothing can be more certain.

Good. But if there be anything which is of such a nature as to be and not to be, that will have a place intermediate between pure being and the absolute negation of being?

Yes, between them.

And, as knowledge corresponded to being and ignorance of necessity to not-being, for that intermediate between being and not-being there has to be discovered a corresponding intermediate between ignorance and knowledge, if there be such?

Certainly.

Do we admit the existence of opinion?

Undoubtedly.

As being the same with knowledge, or another faculty?

Another faculty.

Then opinion and knowledge have to do with different kinds of matter corresponding to this difference of faculties?

Yes.

And knowledge is relative to being and knows being. But before I proceed further I will make a division.

What division?

I will begin by placing faculties in a class by themselves: they are powers in us, and in all other things, by which we do as we do. Sight and hearing, for example, I should call faculties. Have I clearly explained the class which I mean?

Yes, I quite understand.

Then let me tell you my view about them. I do not see them, and therefore the distinctions of figure, colour, and the like, which enable me to discern the differences of some things, do not apply to them. In speaking of a faculty I think only of its sphere and its result; and that which has the same sphere and the same result I call the same faculty, but that which has another sphere and another result I call different. Would that be your way of speaking?

Yes.

And will you be so very good as to answer one more question? Would you say that knowledge is a faculty, or in what class would you place it?

Certainly knowledge is a faculty, and the mightiest of all faculties.

And is opinion also a faculty?

Certainly, he said; for opinion is that with which we are able to form an opinion.

And yet you were acknowledging a little while ago that knowledge is not the same as opinion?

Why, yes, he said: how can any reasonable being ever identify that which is infallible with that which errs?

An excellent answer, proving, I said, that we are quite conscious of a distinction between them.

Yes.

Then knowledge and opinion having distinct powers have also distinct spheres or subject-matters?

That is certain.

Being is the sphere or subject-matter of knowledge, and knowledge is to know the nature of being?

Yes.

And opinion is to have an opinion?

Yes.

And do we know what we opine? or is the subject-matter of opinion the same as the subject-matter of knowledge?

Nay, he replied, that has been already disproven; if difference in faculty implies difference in the sphere or subject-matter, and if, as we were saying, opinion and knowledge are distinct faculties, then the sphere of knowledge and of opinion cannot be the same.

Then if being is the subject-matter of knowledge, something else must be the subject-matter of opinion?

Yes, something else.

Well then, is not-being the subject-matter of opinion? or, rather, how can there be an opinion at all about not-being? Reflect: when a man has an opinion, has he not an opinion about something? Can he have an opinion which is an opinion about nothing?

Impossible.

He who has an opinion has an opinion about some one thing?

Yes.

And not-being is not one thing but, properly speaking, nothing?

True.

Of not-being, ignorance was assumed to be the necessary correlative; of being, knowledge?

True, he said.

Then opinion is not concerned either with being or with not-being?

Not with either.

And can therefore neither be ignorance nor knowledge?

That seems to be true.

But is opinion to be sought without and beyond either of them, in a greater clearness than knowledge, or in a greater darkness than ignorance?

In neither.

Then I suppose that opinion appears to you to be darker than knowledge, but lighter than ignorance?

Both; and in no small degree.

And also to be within and between them?

Yes.

Then you would infer that opinion is intermediate?

No question.

But were we not saying before, that if anything appeared to be of a sort which is and is not at the same time, that sort of thing would appear also to lie in the interval between pure being and absolute not-being; and that the corresponding faculty is neither knowledge nor ignorance, but will be found in the interval between them?

True.

And in that interval there has now been discovered something which we call opinion?

There has.

Then what remains to be discovered is the object which partakes equally of the nature of being and not-being, and cannot rightly be termed either, pure and simple; this unknown term, when discovered, we may truly call the subject of opinion, and assign each to their proper faculty, – the extremes to the faculties of the extremes and the mean to the faculty of the mean.

True.

This being premised, I would ask the gentleman who is of opinion that there is no absolute or unchangeable idea of beauty – in whose opinion the beautiful is the manifold – he, I say, your lover of beautiful sights, who cannot bear to be told that the beautiful is one, and the just is one, or that anything is one – to him I would appeal, saying, Will you be so very kind, sir, as to tell us whether, of all these beautiful things, there is one which will not be found ugly; or of the just, which will not be found unjust; or of the holy, which will not also be unholy?

No, he replied; the beautiful will in some point of view be found ugly; and the same is true of the rest.

And may not the many which are doubles be also halves? – doubles, that is, of one thing, and halves of another?

Quite true.

And things great and small, heavy and light, as they are termed, will not be denoted by these any more than by the opposite names?

True; both these and the opposite names will always attach to all of them.

And can any one of those many things which are called by particular names be said to be this rather than not to be this?

He replied: They are like the punning riddles which are asked at feasts or the children's puzzle about the eunuch aiming at the bat, with what he hit him, as they say in the puzzle, and upon what the bat was sitting. The individual objects of which I am speaking are also a riddle, and have a double sense: nor can you fix them in your mind, either as being or not-being, or both, or neither.

Then what will you do with them? I said. Can they have a better place than between being and not-being? For they are clearly not in greater darkness or negation than not-being, or more full of light and existence than being.

That is quite true, he said.

Thus then we seem to have discovered that the many ideas which the multitude entertain about the beautiful and about all other things are tossing about in some region which is half-way between pure being and pure not-being?

We have.

Yes; and we had before agreed that anything of this kind which we might find was to be described as matter of opinion, and not as matter of knowledge; being the intermediate flux which is caught and detained by the intermediate faculty.

Quite true.

Then those who see the many beautiful, and who yet neither see absolute beauty, nor can follow any guide who points the way thither; who see the many just, and not absolute justice, and the like, – such persons may be said to have opinion but not knowledge?

That is certain.

But those who see the absolute and eternal and immutable may be said to know, and not to have opinion only?

Neither can that be denied.

The one love and embrace the subjects of knowledge, the other those of opinion? The latter are the same, as I dare say you will remember, who listened to sweet sounds and gazed upon fair colours, but would not tolerate the existence of absolute beauty.

Yes, I remember.

Shall we then be guilty of any impropriety in calling them lovers of opinion rather than lovers of wisdom, and will they be very angry with us for thus describing them?

I shall tell them not to be angry; no man should be angry at what is true.

But those who love the truth in each thing are to be called lovers of wisdom and not lovers of opinion.

Assuredly.

BOOK VI.

And thus, Glaucon, after the argument has gone a weary way, the true and the false philosophers have at length appeared in view.

I do not think, he said, that the way could have been shortened.

I suppose not, I said; and yet I believe that we might have had a better view of both of them if the discussion could have been confined to this one subject and if there were not many other questions awaiting us, which he who desires to see in what respect the life of the just differs from that of the unjust must consider.

And what is the next question? he asked.

Surely, I said, the one which follows next in order. Inasmuch as philosophers only are able to grasp the eternal and unchangeable, and those who wander in the region of the many and variable are not philosophers, I must ask you which of the two classes should be the rulers of our State?

And how can we rightly answer that question?

Whichever of the two are best able to guard the laws and institutions of our State – let them be our guardians.

Very good.

Neither, I said, can there be any question that the guardian who is to keep anything should have eyes rather than no eyes?

There can be no question of that.

And are not those who are verily and indeed wanting in the knowledge of the true being of each thing, and who have in their souls no clear pattern, and are unable as with a painter's eye to look at the absolute truth and to that original to repair, and having perfect vision of the other world to order the laws about beauty, goodness, justice in this, if not already ordered, and to guard and preserve the order of them – are not such persons, I ask, simply blind?

Truly, he replied, they are much in that condition.

And shall they be our guardians when there are others who, besides being their equals in experience and falling short of them in no particular of virtue, also know the very truth of each thing?

There can be no reason, he said, for rejecting those who have this greatest of all great qualities; they must always have the first place unless they fail in some other respect.

Suppose then, I said, that we determine how far they can unite this and the other excellences.

By all means.

In the first place, as we began by observing, the nature of the philosopher has to be ascertained. We must come to an understanding about him, and, when we have done so, then, if I am not mistaken, we shall also acknowledge that such an union of qualities is possible, and that those in whom they are united, and those only, should be rulers in the State.

What do you mean?

Let us suppose that philosophical minds always love knowledge of a sort which shows them the eternal nature not varying from generation and corruption.

Agreed.

And further, I said, let us agree that they are lovers of all true being; there is no part whether greater or less, or more or less honourable, which they are willing to renounce; as we said before of the lover and the man of ambition.

True.

And if they are to be what we were describing, is there not another quality which they should also possess?

What quality?

Truthfulness: they will never intentionally receive into their mind falsehood, which is their detestation, and they will love the truth.

Yes, that may be safely affirmed of them.

'May be,' my friend, I replied, is not the word; say rather 'must be affirmed:' for he whose nature is amorous of anything cannot help loving all that belongs or is akin to the object of his affections.

Right, he said.

And is there anything more akin to wisdom than truth?

How can there be?

Can the same nature be a lover of wisdom and a lover of falsehood?

Never.

The true lover of learning then must from his earliest youth, as far as in him lies, desire all truth?

Assuredly.

But then again, as we know by experience, he whose desires are strong in one direction will have them weaker in others; they will be like a stream which has been drawn off into another channel.

True.

He whose desires are drawn towards knowledge in every form will be absorbed in the pleasures of the soul, and will hardly feel bodily pleasure – I mean, if he be a true philosopher and not a sham one.

That is most certain.

Such an one is sure to be temperate and the reverse of covetous; for the motives which make another man desirous of having and spending, have no place in his character.

Very true.

Another criterion of the philosophical nature has also to be considered.

What is that?

There should be no secret corner of illiberality; nothing can be more antagonistic than meanness to a soul which is ever longing after the whole of things both divine and human.

Most true, he replied.

Then how can he who has magnificence of mind and is the spectator of all time and all existence, think much of human life?

He cannot.

Or can such an one account death fearful?

No indeed.

Then the cowardly and mean nature has no part in true philosophy?

Certainly not.

Or again: can he who is harmoniously constituted, who is not covetous or mean, or a boaster, or a coward – can he, I say, ever be unjust or hard in his dealings?

Impossible.

Then you will soon observe whether a man is just and gentle, or rude and unsociable; these are the signs which distinguish even in youth the philosophical nature from the unphilosophical.

True.

There is another point which should be remarked.

What point?

Whether he has or has not a pleasure in learning; for no one will love that which gives him pain, and in which after much toil he makes little progress.

Certainly not.

And again, if he is forgetful and retains nothing of what he learns, will he not be an empty vessel?

That is certain.

Labouring in vain, he must end in hating himself and his fruitless occupation? Yes.

Then a soul which forgets cannot be ranked among genuine philosophic natures; we must insist that the philosopher should have a good memory?

Certainly.

And once more, the inharmonious and unseemly nature can only tend to disproportion?

Undoubtedly.

And do you consider truth to be akin to proportion or to disproportion?

To proportion.

Then, besides other qualities, we must try to find a naturally well-proportioned and gracious mind, which will move spontaneously towards the true being of everything.

Certainly.

Well, and do not all these qualities, which we have been enumerating, go together, and are they not, in a manner, necessary to a soul, which is to have a full and perfect participation of being?

They are absolutely necessary, he replied.

And must not that be a blameless study which he only can pursue who has the gift of a good memory, and is quick to learn, – noble, gracious, the friend of truth, justice, courage, temperance, who are his kindred?

The god of jealousy himself, he said, could find no fault with such a study.

And to men like him, I said, when perfected by years and education, and to these only you will entrust the State.

Here Adeimantus interposed and said: To these statements, Socrates, no one can offer a reply; but when you talk in this way, a strange feeling passes over the minds of your hearers: They fancy that they are led astray a little at each step in the argument, owing to their own want of skill in asking and answering questions; these littles accumulate, and at the end of the discussion they are found to have sustained a mighty overthrow and all their former notions appear to be turned upside down. And as unskilful players of draughts are at last shut up by their more skilful adversaries and have no piece to move, so they too find themselves shut up at last; for they have nothing to say in this new game of which words are the counters; and yet all the time they are in the right. The observation is suggested to me by what is now occurring. For any one of us might say, that although in words he is not able to meet you at each step of the argument, he sees as a fact that the votaries of philosophy, when they carry on the study, not only in youth as a part of education, but as the pursuit of their maturer years, most of them become strange monsters, not to say utter rogues, and that those who may be considered the best of them are made useless to the world by the very study which you extol.

Well, and do you think that those who say so are wrong?

I cannot tell, he replied; but I should like to know what is your opinion.

Hear my answer; I am of opinion that they are quite right.

Then how can you be justified in saying that cities will not cease from evil until philosophers rule in them, when philosophers are acknowledged by us to be of no use to them?

You ask a question, I said, to which a reply can only be given in a parable.

Yes, Socrates; and that is a way of speaking to which you are not at all accustomed, I suppose.

I perceive, I said, that you are vastly amused at having plunged me into such a hopeless discussion; but now hear the parable, and then you will be still more amused at the meagreness of my imagination: for the manner in which the best men are treated in their own States is so grievous that no single thing on earth is comparable to it; and therefore, if I am to plead their cause, I must have recourse to fiction, and put together a figure made up of many things, like the fabulous unions of goats and stags which are found in pictures. Imagine then a fleet or a ship in which there is a captain who is taller and stronger than any of the crew, but he is a little deaf and has a similar infirmity in sight, and his knowledge of navigation is not much better. The sailors are quarrelling with one another about the steering – every one is of opinion that he has a right to steer, though he has never learned the art of navigation and cannot tell who taught him or when he learned, and will further assert that it cannot be taught, and they are ready to cut in pieces any one who says the contrary. They throng about the captain, begging and praying him to commit the helm to them; and if at any time they do not prevail, but others are preferred to them, they kill the others or throw them overboard, and having first chained up the noble captain's senses with drink or some narcotic drug, they mutiny and take possession of the ship and make free with the stores; thus, eating and drinking, they proceed on their voyage in such manner as might be expected of them. Him who is their partisan and cleverly aids them in their plot for getting the ship out of the captain's hands into their own whether by force or persuasion, they compliment with the name of sailor, pilot, able seaman, and abuse the other sort of man, whom they call a good-for-nothing; but that the true pilot must pay attention to the year and seasons and sky and stars and winds, and whatever else belongs to his art, if he intends to be really qualified for the command of a ship, and that he must and will be the steerer, whether other people like or not – the possibility of this union of authority with the steerer's art has never seriously entered into their thoughts or been made part of their calling. Now in vessels which are in a state of mutiny and by sailors who are mutineers, how will the true pilot be regarded? Will he not be called by them a prater, a star-gazer, a good-for-nothing?

Of course, said Adeimantus.

Then you will hardly need, I said, to hear the interpretation of the figure, which describes the true philosopher in his relation to the State; for you understand already.

Certainly.

Then suppose you now take this parable to the gentleman who is surprised at finding that philosophers have no honour in their cities; explain it to him and try to convince him that their having honour would be far more extraordinary.

I will.

Say to him, that, in deeming the best votaries of philosophy to be useless to the rest of the world, he is right; but also tell him to attribute their uselessness to the fault of those who will not use them, and not to themselves. The pilot should not humbly beg the sailors to be commanded by him – that is not the order of nature; neither are 'the wise to go to the doors of the rich' – the ingenious author of this saying told a lie – but the truth is, that, when a man is ill, whether he be rich or poor, to the physician he must go, and he who wants to be governed, to him who is able to govern.

The ruler who is good for anything ought not to beg his subjects to be ruled by him; although the present governors of mankind are of a different stamp; they may be justly compared to the mutinous sailors, and the true helmsmen to those who are called by them good-for-nothings and star-gazers.

Precisely so, he said.

For these reasons, and among men like these, philosophy, the noblest pursuit of all, is not likely to be much esteemed by those of the opposite faction; not that the greatest and most lasting injury is done to her by her opponents, but by her own professing followers, the same of whom you suppose the accuser to say, that the greater number of them are arrant rogues, and the best are useless; in which opinion I agreed.

Yes.

And the reason why the good are useless has now been explained?

True.

Then shall we proceed to show that the corruption of the majority is also unavoidable, and that this is not to be laid to the charge of philosophy any more than the other?

By all means.

And let us ask and answer in turn, first going back to the description of the gentle and noble nature. Truth, as you will remember, was his leader, whom he followed always and in all things; failing in this, he was an impostor, and had no part or lot in true philosophy.

Yes, that was said.

Well, and is not this one quality, to mention no others, greatly at variance with present notions of him?

Certainly, he said.

And have we not a right to say in his defence, that the true lover of knowledge is always striving after being – that is his nature; he will not rest in the multiplicity of individuals which is an appearance only, but will go on – the keen edge will not be blunted, nor the force of his desire abate until he have attained the knowledge of the true nature of every essence by a sympathetic and kindred power in the soul, and by that power drawing near and mingling and becoming incorporate with very being, having begotten mind and truth, he will have knowledge and will live and grow truly, and then, and not till then, will he cease from his travail.

Nothing, he said, can be more just than such a description of him.

And will the love of a lie be any part of a philosopher's nature? Will he not utterly hate a lie?

He will.

And when truth is the captain, we cannot suspect any evil of the band which he leads?

Impossible.

Justice and health of mind will be of the company, and temperance will follow after?

True, he replied.

Neither is there any reason why I should again set in array the philosopher's virtues, as you will doubtless remember that courage, magnificence, apprehension, memory, were his natural gifts. And you objected that, although no one could deny what I then said, still, if you leave words and look at facts, the persons who are thus described are some of them manifestly useless, and the greater number utterly depraved; we were then led to enquire into the grounds of these accusations, and have now arrived at the point of asking why are the majority bad, which question of necessity brought us back to the examination and definition of the true philosopher.

Exactly.

And we have next to consider the corruptions of the philosophic nature, why so many are spoiled and so few escape spoiling – I am speaking of those who were said to be useless but not wicked – and, when we have done with them, we will speak of the imitators of philosophy, what manner of men are they who aspire after a profession which is above them and of which they are unworthy, and then, by their manifold inconsistencies, bring upon philosophy, and upon all philosophers, that universal reprobation of which we speak.

What are these corruptions? he said.

I will see if I can explain them to you. Every one will admit that a nature having in perfection all the qualities which we required in a philosopher, is a rare plant which is seldom seen among men.

Rare indeed.

And what numberless and powerful causes tend to destroy these rare natures!

What causes?

In the first place there are their own virtues, their courage, temperance, and the rest of them, every one of which praiseworthy qualities (and this is a most singular circumstance) destroys and distracts from philosophy the soul which is the possessor of them.

That is very singular, he replied.

Then there are all the ordinary goods of life – beauty, wealth, strength, rank, and great connections in the State – you understand the sort of things – these also have a corrupting and distracting effect.

I understand; but I should like to know more precisely what you mean about them.

Grasp the truth as a whole, I said, and in the right way; you will then have no difficulty in apprehending the preceding remarks, and they will no longer appear strange to you.

And how am I to do so? he asked.

Why, I said, we know that all germs or seeds, whether vegetable or animal, when they fail to meet with proper nutriment or climate or soil, in proportion to their vigour, are all the more sensitive to the want of a suitable environment, for evil is a greater enemy to what is good than to what is not.

Very true.

There is reason in supposing that the finest natures, when under alien conditions, receive more injury than the inferior, because the contrast is greater.

Certainly.

And may we not say, Adeimantus, that the most gifted minds, when they are ill-educated, become pre-eminently bad? Do not great crimes and the spirit of pure evil spring out of a fulness of nature ruined by education rather than from any inferiority, whereas weak natures are scarcely capable of any very great good or very great evil?

There I think that you are right.

And our philosopher follows the same analogy – he is like a plant which, having proper nurture, must necessarily grow and mature into all virtue, but, if sown and planted in an alien soil, becomes the most noxious of all weeds, unless he be preserved by some divine power. Do you really think, as people so often say, that our youth are corrupted by Sophists, or that private teachers of the art corrupt them in any degree worth speaking of? Are not the public who say these things the greatest of all Sophists? And do they not educate to perfection young and old, men and women alike, and fashion them after their own hearts?

When is this accomplished? he said.

When they meet together, and the world sits down at an assembly, or in a court of law, or a theatre, or a camp, or in any other popular resort, and there is a great uproar, and they praise some things which are being said or done, and blame other things, equally exaggerating both, shouting and clapping their hands, and the echo of the rocks and the place in which they are assembled redoubles the sound of the praise or blame – at such a time will not a young man's heart, as they say, leap within him? Will any private training enable him to stand firm against the overwhelming flood of popular opinion? or will he be carried away by the stream? Will he not have the notions of good and evil which the public in general have – he will do as they do, and as they are, such will he be?

Yes, Socrates; necessity will compel him.

And yet, I said, there is a still greater necessity, which has not been mentioned.

What is that?

The gentle force of attainder or confiscation or death, which, as you are aware, these new Sophists and educators, who are the public, apply when their words are powerless.

Indeed they do; and in right good earnest.

Now what opinion of any other Sophist, or of any private person, can be expected to overcome in such an unequal contest?

None, he replied.

No, indeed, I said, even to make the attempt is a great piece of folly; there neither is, nor has been, nor is ever likely to be, any different type of character which has had no other training in virtue but that which is supplied by public opinion – I speak, my friend, of human virtue only; what is more than human, as the proverb says, is not included: for I would not have you ignorant that, in the present evil state of governments, whatever is saved and comes to good is saved by the power of God, as we may truly say.

I quite assent, he replied.

Then let me crave your assent also to a further observation.

What are you going to say?

Why, that all those mercenary individuals, whom the many call Sophists and whom they deem to be their adversaries, do, in fact, teach nothing but the opinion of the many, that is to say, the opinions of their assemblies; and this is their wisdom. I might compare them to a man who should study the tempers and desires of a mighty strong beast who is fed by him – he would learn how to approach and handle him, also at what times and from what causes he is dangerous or the reverse, and what is the meaning of his several cries, and by what sounds, when another utters them, he is soothed or infuriated; and you may suppose further, that when, by continually attending upon him, he has become perfect in all this, he calls his knowledge wisdom, and makes of it a system or art, which he proceeds to teach, although he has no real notion of what he means by the principles or passions of which he is speaking, but calls this honourable and that dishonourable, or good or evil, or just or unjust, all in accordance with the tastes and tempers of the great brute. Good he pronounces to be that in which the beast delights and evil to be that which he dislikes; and he can give no other account of them except that the just and noble are the necessary, having never himself seen, and having no power of explaining to others the nature of either, or the difference between them, which is immense. By heaven, would not such an one be a rare educator?

Indeed he would.

And in what way does he who thinks that wisdom is the discernment of the tempers and tastes of the motley multitude, whether in painting or music, or, finally, in politics, differ from him whom I have been describing? For when a man consorts with the many, and exhibits to them his poem or other work of art or the service which he has done the State, making them his judges when he is not obliged, the so-called necessity of Diomede will oblige him to produce whatever they praise. And yet the reasons are utterly ludicrous which they give in confirmation of their own notions about the honourable and good. Did you ever hear any of them which were not?

No, nor am I likely to hear.

You recognise the truth of what I have been saying? Then let me ask you to consider further whether the world will ever be induced to believe in the existence of absolute beauty rather than of the many beautiful, or of the absolute in each kind rather than of the many in each kind?

Certainly not.

Then the world cannot possibly be a philosopher?

Impossible.

And therefore philosophers must inevitably fall under the censure of the world?

They must.

And of individuals who consort with the mob and seek to please them?

That is evident.

Then, do you see any way in which the philosopher can be preserved in his calling to the end? and remember what we were saying of him, that he was to have quickness and memory and courage and magnificence – these were admitted by us to be the true philosopher's gifts.

Yes.

Will not such an one from his early childhood be in all things first among all, especially if his bodily endowments are like his mental ones?

Certainly, he said.

And his friends and fellow-citizens will want to use him as he gets older for their own purposes?

No question.

Falling at his feet, they will make requests to him and do him honour and flatter him, because they want to get into their hands now, the power which he will one day possess.

That often happens, he said.

And what will a man such as he is be likely to do under such circumstances, especially if he be a citizen of a great city, rich and noble, and a tall proper youth? Will he not be full of boundless aspirations, and fancy himself able to manage the affairs of Hellenes and of barbarians, and having got such notions into his head will he not dilate and elevate himself in the fulness of vain pomp and senseless pride?

To be sure he will.

Now, when he is in this state of mind, if some one gently comes to him and tells him that he is a fool and must get understanding, which can only be got by slaving for it, do you think that, under such adverse circumstances, he will be easily induced to listen?

Far otherwise.

And even if there be some one who through inherent goodness or natural reasonableness has had his eyes opened a little and is humbled and taken captive by philosophy, how will his friends behave when they think that they are likely to lose the advantage which they were hoping to reap from his companionship? Will they not do and say anything to prevent him from yielding to his better nature and to render his teacher powerless, using to this end private intrigues as well as public prosecutions?

There can be no doubt of it.

And how can one who is thus circumstanced ever become a philosopher?

Impossible.

Then were we not right in saying that even the very qualities which make a man a philosopher may, if he be ill-educated, divert him from philosophy, no less than riches and their accompaniments and the other so-called goods of life?

We were quite right.

Thus, my excellent friend, is brought about all that ruin and failure which I have been describing of the natures best adapted to the best of all pursuits; they are natures which we maintain to be rare at any time; this being the class out of which come the men who are the authors of the greatest evil to States and individuals; and also of the greatest good when the tide carries them in that direction; but a small man never was the doer of any great thing either to individuals or to States.

That is most true, he said.

And so philosophy is left desolate, with her marriage rite incomplete: for her own have fallen away and forsaken her, and while they are leading a false and unbecoming life, other unworthy persons, seeing that she has no kinsmen to be her protectors, enter in and dishonour her; and fasten upon her the reproaches which, as you say, her reprovers utter, who affirm of her votaries that some are good for nothing, and that the greater number deserve the severest punishment.

That is certainly what people say.

Yes; and what else would you expect, I said, when you think of the puny creatures who, seeing this land open to them – a land well stocked with fair names and showy titles – like prisoners running out of prison into a sanctuary, take a leap out of their trades into philosophy; those who do so being probably the cleverest hands at their own miserable crafts? For, although philosophy be in this evil case, still there remains a dignity about her which is not to be found in the arts. And many are thus attracted by her whose natures are imperfect and whose souls are maimed and disfigured by their meannesses, as their bodies are by their trades and crafts. Is not this unavoidable?

Yes.

Are they not exactly like a bald little tinker who has just got out of durance and come into a fortune; he takes a bath and puts on a new coat, and is decked out as a bridegroom going to marry his master's daughter, who is left poor and desolate?

A most exact parallel.

What will be the issue of such marriages? Will they not be vile and bastard?

There can be no question of it.

And when persons who are unworthy of education approach philosophy and make an alliance with her who is in a rank above them what sort of ideas and opinions are likely to be generated? Will they not be sophisms captivating to the ear, having nothing in them genuine, or worthy of or akin to true wisdom?

No doubt, he said.

Then, Adeimantus, I said, the worthy disciples of philosophy will be but a small remnant: perchance some noble and well-educated person, detained by exile in her service, who in the absence of corrupting influences remains devoted to her; or some lofty soul born in a mean city, the politics of which he contemns and neglects; and there may be a gifted few who leave the arts, which they justly despise, and come to her; – or peradventure there are some who are restrained by our friend Theages' bridle; for everything in the life of Theages conspired to divert him from philosophy; but ill-health kept him away from politics. My own case of the internal sign is hardly worth mentioning, for rarely, if ever, has such a monitor been given to any other man. Those who belong to this small class have tasted how sweet and blessed a possession philosophy is, and have also seen enough of the madness of the multitude; and they know that no politician is honest, nor is there any champion of justice at whose side they may fight and be saved. Such an one may be compared to a man who has fallen among wild beasts – he will not join in the wickedness of his fellows, but neither is he able singly to resist all their fierce natures, and therefore seeing that he would be of no use to the State or to his friends, and reflecting that he would have to throw away his life without doing any good either to himself or others, he holds his peace, and goes his own way. He is like one who, in the storm of dust and sleet which the driving wind hurries along, retires under the shelter of a wall; and seeing the rest of mankind full of wickedness, he is content, if only he can live his own life and be pure from evil or unrighteousness, and depart in peace and good-will, with bright hopes.

Yes, he said, and he will have done a great work before he departs.

A great work – yes; but not the greatest, unless he find a State suitable to him; for in a State which is suitable to him, he will have a larger growth and be the saviour of his country, as well as of himself.

The causes why philosophy is in such an evil name have now been sufficiently explained: the injustice of the charges against her has been shown – is there anything more which you wish to say?

Nothing more on that subject, he replied; but I should like to know which of the governments now existing is in your opinion the one adapted to her.

Not any of them, I said; and that is precisely the accusation which I bring against them – not one of them is worthy of the philosophic nature, and hence that nature is warped and estranged; – as the exotic seed which is sown in a foreign land becomes denaturalized, and is wont to be overpowered and to lose itself in the new soil, even so this growth of philosophy, instead of persisting, degenerates and receives another character. But if philosophy ever finds in the State that perfection which she herself is, then will be seen that she is in truth divine, and that all other things, whether natures of men or institutions, are but human; – and now, I know, that you are going to ask, What that State is:

No, he said; there you are wrong, for I was going to ask another question – whether it is the State of which we are the founders and inventors, or some other?

Yes, I replied, ours in most respects; but you may remember my saying before, that some living authority would always be required in the State having the same idea of the constitution which guided you when as legislator you were laying down the laws.

That was said, he replied.

Yes, but not in a satisfactory manner; you frightened us by interposing objections, which certainly showed that the discussion would be long and difficult; and what still remains is the reverse of easy.

What is there remaining?

The question how the study of philosophy may be so ordered as not to be the ruin of the State: All great attempts are attended with risk; 'hard is the good,' as men say.

Still, he said, let the point be cleared up, and the enquiry will then be complete.

I shall not be hindered, I said, by any want of will, but, if at all, by a want of power: my zeal you may see for yourselves; and please to remark in what I am about to say how boldly and unhesitatingly I declare that States should pursue philosophy, not as they do now, but in a different spirit.

In what manner?

At present, I said, the students of philosophy are quite young; beginning when they are hardly past childhood, they devote only the time saved from moneymaking and housekeeping to such pursuits; and even those of them who are reputed to have most of the philosophic spirit, when they come within sight of the great difficulty of the subject, I mean dialectic, take themselves off. In after life when invited by some one else, they may, perhaps, go and hear a lecture, and about this they make much ado, for philosophy is not considered by them to be their proper business: at last, when they grow old, in most cases they are extinguished more truly than Heracleitus' sun, inasmuch as they never light up again. (Heraclitus said that the sun was extinguished every evening and relighted every morning.)

But what ought to be their course?

Just the opposite. In childhood and youth their study, and what philosophy they learn, should be suited to their tender years: during this period while they are growing up towards manhood, the chief and special care should be given to their bodies that they may have them to use in the service of philosophy; as life advances and the intellect begins to mature, let them increase the gymnastics of the soul; but when the strength of our citizens fails and is past civil and military duties, then let them range at will and engage in no serious labour, as we intend them to live happily here, and to crown this life with a similar happiness in another.

How truly in earnest you are, Socrates! he said; I am sure of that; and yet most of your hearers, if I am not mistaken, are likely to be still more earnest in their opposition to you, and will never be convinced; Thrasymachus least of all.

Do not make a quarrel, I said, between Thrasymachus and me, who have recently become friends, although, indeed, we were never enemies; for I shall go on striving to the utmost until I either convert him and other men, or do something which may profit them against the day when they live again, and hold the like discourse in another state of existence.

You are speaking of a time which is not very near.

Rather, I replied, of a time which is as nothing in comparison with eternity. Nevertheless, I do not wonder that the many refuse to believe; for they have never seen that of which we are now speaking realized; they have seen only a conventional imitation of philosophy, consisting of words artificially brought together, not like these of ours having a natural unity. But a human being who in word and work is perfectly moulded, as far as he can be, into the proportion and likeness of virtue – such a man ruling in a city which bears the same image, they have never yet seen, neither one nor many of them – do you think that they ever did?

No indeed.

No, my friend, and they have seldom, if ever, heard free and noble sentiments; such as men utter when they are earnestly and by every means in their power seeking after truth for the sake of knowledge, while they look coldly on the subtleties of controversy, of which the end is opinion and strife, whether they meet with them in the courts of law or in society.

They are strangers, he said, to the words of which you speak.

And this was what we foresaw, and this was the reason why truth forced us to admit, not without fear and hesitation, that neither cities nor States nor individuals will ever attain perfection until the small class of philosophers whom we termed useless but not corrupt are providentially compelled, whether they will or not, to take care of the State, and until a like necessity be laid on the State to obey them; or until kings, or if not kings, the sons of kings or princes, are divinely inspired with a true love of true philosophy. That either or both of these alternatives are impossible, I see no reason to affirm: if they were so, we might indeed be justly ridiculed as dreamers and visionaries. Am I not right?

Quite right.

If then, in the countless ages of the past, or at the present hour in some foreign clime which is far away and beyond our ken, the perfected philosopher is or has been or hereafter shall be compelled by a superior power to have the charge of the State, we are ready to assert to the death, that this our constitution has been, and is – yea, and will be whenever the Muse of Philosophy is queen. There is no impossibility in all this; that there is a difficulty, we acknowledge ourselves.

My opinion agrees with yours, he said.

But do you mean to say that this is not the opinion of the multitude?

I should imagine not, he replied.

O my friend, I said, do not attack the multitude: they will change their minds, if, not in an aggressive spirit, but gently and with the view of soothing them and removing their dislike of over-education, you show them your philosophers as they really are and describe as you were just now doing their character and profession, and then mankind will see that he of whom you are speaking is not such as they supposed – if they view him in this new light, they will surely change their notion of him, and answer in another strain. Who can be at enmity with one who loves them, who that is himself gentle and free from envy will be jealous of one in whom there is no jealousy? Nay, let me answer for you, that in a few this harsh temper may be found but not in the majority of mankind.

I quite agree with you, he said.

And do you not also think, as I do, that the harsh feeling which the many entertain towards philosophy originates in the pretenders, who rush in uninvited, and are always abusing them, and finding fault with them, who make persons instead of things the theme of their conversation? and nothing can be more unbecoming in philosophers than this.

It is most unbecoming.

For he, Adeimantus, whose mind is fixed upon true being, has surely no time to look down upon the affairs of earth, or to be filled with malice and envy, contending against men; his eye is ever directed towards things fixed and immutable, which he sees neither injuring nor injured by one another, but all in order moving according to reason; these he imitates, and to these he will, as far as he can, conform himself. Can a man help imitating that with which he holds reverential converse?

Impossible.

And the philosopher holding converse with the divine order, becomes orderly and divine, as far as the nature of man allows; but like every one else, he will suffer from detraction.

Of course.

And if a necessity be laid upon him of fashioning, not only himself, but human nature generally, whether in States or individuals, into that which he beholds elsewhere, will he, think you, be an unskilful artificer of justice, temperance, and every civil virtue?

Anything but unskilful.

And if the world perceives that what we are saying about him is the truth, will they be angry with philosophy? Will they disbelieve us, when we tell them that no State can be happy which is not designed by artists who imitate the heavenly pattern?

They will not be angry if they understand, he said. But how will they draw out the plan of which you are speaking?

They will begin by taking the State and the manners of men, from which, as from a tablet, they will rub out the picture, and leave a clean surface. This is no easy task. But whether easy or not, herein will lie the difference between them and every other legislator, – they will have nothing to do either with individual or State, and will inscribe no laws, until they have either found, or themselves made, a clean surface.

They will be very right, he said.

Having effected this, they will proceed to trace an outline of the constitution?

No doubt.

And when they are filling in the work, as I conceive, they will often turn their eyes upwards and downwards: I mean that they will first look at absolute justice and beauty and temperance, and again at the human copy; and will mingle and temper the various elements of life into the image of a man; and this they will conceive according to that other image, which, when existing among men, Homer calls the form and likeness of God.

Very true, he said.

And one feature they will erase, and another they will put in, until they have made the ways of men, as far as possible, agreeable to the ways of God?

Indeed, he said, in no way could they make a fairer picture.

And now, I said, are we beginning to persuade those whom you described as rushing at us with might and main, that the painter of constitutions is such an one as we are praising; at whom they were so very indignant because to his hands we committed the State; and are they growing a little calmer at what they have just heard?

Much calmer, if there is any sense in them.

Why, where can they still find any ground for objection? Will they doubt that the philosopher is a lover of truth and being?

They would not be so unreasonable.

Or that his nature, being such as we have delineated, is akin to the highest good?

Neither can they doubt this.

But again, will they tell us that such a nature, placed under favourable circumstances, will not be perfectly good and wise if any ever was? Or will they prefer those whom we have rejected?

Surely not.

Then will they still be angry at our saying, that, until philosophers bear rule, States and individuals will have no rest from evil, nor will this our imaginary State ever be realized?

I think that they will be less angry.

Shall we assume that they are not only less angry but quite gentle, and that they have been converted and for very shame, if for no other reason, cannot refuse to come to terms?

By all means, he said.

Then let us suppose that the reconciliation has been effected. Will any one deny the other point, that there may be sons of kings or princes who are by nature philosophers?

Surely no man, he said.

And when they have come into being will any one say that they must of necessity be destroyed; that they can hardly be saved is not denied even by us; but that in the whole course of ages no single one of them can escape – who will venture to affirm this?

Who indeed!

But, said I, one is enough; let there be one man who has a city obedient to his will, and he might bring into existence the ideal polity about which the world is so incredulous.

Yes, one is enough.

The ruler may impose the laws and institutions which we have been describing, and the citizens may possibly be willing to obey them?

Certainly.

And that others should approve, of what we approve, is no miracle or impossibility?

I think not.

But we have sufficiently shown, in what has preceded, that all this, if only possible, is assuredly for the best.

We have.

And now we say not only that our laws, if they could be enacted, would be for the best, but also that the enactment of them, though difficult, is not impossible.

Very good.

And so with pain and toil we have reached the end of one subject, but more remains to be discussed; – how and by what studies and pursuits will the saviours of the constitution be created, and at what ages are they to apply themselves to their several studies?

Certainly.

I omitted the troublesome business of the possession of women, and the procreation of children, and the appointment of the rulers, because I knew that the perfect State would be eyed with jealousy and was difficult of attainment; but that piece of cleverness was not of much service to me, for I had to discuss them all the same. The women and children are now disposed of, but the other question of the rulers must be investigated from the very beginning. We were saying, as you will remember, that they were to be lovers of their country, tried by the test of pleasures and pains, and neither in hardships, nor in dangers, nor at any other critical moment were to lose their patriotism – he was to be rejected who failed, but he who always came forth pure, like gold tried in the refiner's fire, was to be made a ruler, and to receive honours and rewards in life and after death. This was the sort of thing which was being said, and then the argument turned aside and veiled her face; not liking to stir the question which has now arisen.

I perfectly remember, he said.

Yes, my friend, I said, and I then shrank from hazarding the bold word; but now let me dare to say – that the perfect guardian must be a philosopher.

Yes, he said, let that be affirmed.

And do not suppose that there will be many of them; for the gifts which were deemed by us to be essential rarely grow together; they are mostly found in shreds and patches.

What do you mean? he said.

You are aware, I replied, that quick intelligence, memory, sagacity, cleverness, and similar qualities, do not often grow together, and that persons who possess them and are at the same time high-spirited and magnanimous are not so constituted by nature as to live orderly and in a peaceful and settled manner; they are driven any way by their impulses, and all solid principle goes out of them.

Very true, he said.

On the other hand, those steadfast natures which can better be depended upon, which in a battle are impregnable to fear and immovable, are equally immovable when there is anything to be learned; they are always in a torpid state, and are apt to yawn and go to sleep over any intellectual toil.

Quite true.

And yet we were saying that both qualities were necessary in those to whom the higher education is to be imparted, and who are to share in any office or command.

Certainly, he said.

And will they be a class which is rarely found?

Yes, indeed.

Then the aspirant must not only be tested in those labours and dangers and pleasures which we mentioned before, but there is another kind of probation which we did not mention – he must be exercised also in many kinds of knowledge, to see whether the soul will be able to endure the highest of all, or will faint under them, as in any other studies and exercises.

Yes, he said, you are quite right in testing him. But what do you mean by the highest of all knowledge?

You may remember, I said, that we divided the soul into three parts; and distinguished the several natures of justice, temperance, courage, and wisdom?

Indeed, he said, if I had forgotten, I should not deserve to hear more.

And do you remember the word of caution which preceded the discussion of them?

To what do you refer?

We were saying, if I am not mistaken, that he who wanted to see them in their perfect beauty must take a longer and more circuitous way, at the end of which they would appear; but that we could add on a popular exposition of them on a level with the discussion which had preceded. And you replied that such an exposition would be enough for you, and so the enquiry was continued in what to me seemed to be a very inaccurate manner; whether you were satisfied or not, it is for you to say.

Yes, he said, I thought and the others thought that you gave us a fair measure of truth.

But, my friend, I said, a measure of such things which in any degree falls short of the whole truth is not fair measure; for nothing imperfect is the measure of anything, although persons are too apt to be contented and think that they need search no further.

Not an uncommon case when people are indolent.

Yes, I said; and there cannot be any worse fault in a guardian of the State and of the laws.

True.

The guardian then, I said, must be required to take the longer circuit, and toil at learning as well as at gymnastics, or he will never reach the highest knowledge of all which, as we were just now saying, is his proper calling.

What, he said, is there a knowledge still higher than this – higher than justice and the other virtues?

Yes, I said, there is. And of the virtues too we must behold not the outline merely, as at present – nothing short of the most finished picture should satisfy us. When little things are elaborated with an infinity of pains, in order that they may appear in their full beauty and utmost clearness, how ridiculous that we should not think the highest truths worthy of attaining the highest accuracy!

A right noble thought; but do you suppose that we shall refrain from asking you what is this highest knowledge?

Nay, I said, ask if you will; but I am certain that you have heard the answer many times, and now you either do not understand me or, as I rather think, you are disposed to be troublesome; for you have often been told that the idea of good is the highest knowledge, and that all other things become useful and advantageous only by their use of this. You can hardly be ignorant that of this I was about to speak, concerning which, as you have often heard me say, we know so little; and, without which, any other knowledge or possession of any kind will profit us nothing. Do you think that the possession of all other things is of any value if we do not possess the good? or the knowledge of all other things if we have no knowledge of beauty and goodness?

Assuredly not.

You are further aware that most people affirm pleasure to be the good, but the finer sort of wits say it is knowledge?

Yes.

And you are aware too that the latter cannot explain what they mean by knowledge, but are obliged after all to say knowledge of the good?

How ridiculous!

Yes, I said, that they should begin by reproaching us with our ignorance of the good, and then presume our knowledge of it – for the good they define to be knowledge of the good, just as if we understood them when they use the term 'good' – this is of course ridiculous.

Most true, he said.

And those who make pleasure their good are in equal perplexity; for they are compelled to admit that there are bad pleasures as well as good.

Certainly.

And therefore to acknowledge that bad and good are the same?

True.

There can be no doubt about the numerous difficulties in which this question is involved.

There can be none.

Further, do we not see that many are willing to do or to have or to seem to be what is just and honourable without the reality; but no one is satisfied with the appearance of good – the reality is what they seek; in the case of the good, appearance is despised by every one.

Very true, he said.

Of this then, which every soul of man pursues and makes the end of all his actions, having a presentiment that there is such an end, and yet hesitating because neither knowing the nature nor having the same assurance of this as of other things, and therefore losing whatever good there is in other things, – of a principle such and so great as this ought the best men in our State, to whom everything is entrusted, to be in the darkness of ignorance?

Certainly not, he said.

I am sure, I said, that he who does not know how the beautiful and the just are likewise good will be but a sorry guardian of them; and I suspect that no one who is ignorant of the good will have a true knowledge of them.

That, he said, is a shrewd suspicion of yours.

And if we only have a guardian who has this knowledge our State will be perfectly ordered?

Of course, he replied; but I wish that you would tell me whether you conceive this supreme principle of the good to be knowledge or pleasure, or different from either?

Aye, I said, I knew all along that a fastidious gentleman like you would not be contented with the thoughts of other people about these matters.

True, Socrates; but I must say that one who like you has passed a lifetime in the study of philosophy should not be always repeating the opinions of others, and never telling his own.

Well, but has any one a right to say positively what he does not know?

Not, he said, with the assurance of positive certainty; he has no right to do that: but he may say what he thinks, as a matter of opinion.

And do you not know, I said, that all mere opinions are bad, and the best of them blind? You would not deny that those who have any true notion without intelligence are only like blind men who feel their way along the road?

Very true.

And do you wish to behold what is blind and crooked and base, when others will tell you of brightness and beauty?

Still, I must implore you, Socrates, said Glaucon, not to turn away just as you are reaching the goal; if you will only give such an explanation of the good as you have already given of justice and temperance and the other virtues, we shall be satisfied.

Yes, my friend, and I shall be at least equally satisfied, but I cannot help fearing that I shall fail, and that my indiscreet zeal will bring ridicule upon me. No, sweet sirs, let us not at present ask what is the actual nature of the good, for to reach what is now in my thoughts would be an effort too great for me. But of the child of the good who is likest him, I would fain speak, if I could be sure that you wished to hear – otherwise, not.

By all means, he said, tell us about the child, and you shall remain in our debt for the account of the parent.

I do indeed wish, I replied, that I could pay, and you receive, the account of the parent, and not, as now, of the offspring only; take, however, this latter by way of interest, and at the same time have a care that I do not render a false account, although I have no intention of deceiving you.

Yes, we will take all the care that we can: proceed.

Yes, I said, but I must first come to an understanding with you, and remind you of what I have mentioned in the course of this discussion, and at many other times.

What?

The old story, that there is a many beautiful and a many good, and so of other things which we describe and define; to all of them the term 'many' is applied.

True, he said.

And there is an absolute beauty and an absolute good, and of other things to which the term 'many' is applied there is an absolute; for they may be brought under a single idea, which is called the essence of each.

Very true.

The many, as we say, are seen but not known, and the ideas are known but not seen.

Exactly.

And what is the organ with which we see the visible things?

The sight, he said.

And with the hearing, I said, we hear, and with the other senses perceive the other objects of sense?

True.

But have you remarked that sight is by far the most costly and complex piece of workmanship which the artificer of the senses ever contrived?

No, I never have, he said.

Then reflect; has the ear or voice need of any third or additional nature in order that the one may be able to hear and the other to be heard?

Nothing of the sort.

No, indeed, I replied; and the same is true of most, if not all, the other senses – you would not say that any of them requires such an addition?

Certainly not.

But you see that without the addition of some other nature there is no seeing or being seen?

How do you mean?

Sight being, as I conceive, in the eyes, and he who has eyes wanting to see; colour being also present in them, still unless there be a third nature specially adapted to the purpose, the owner of the eyes will see nothing and the colours will be invisible.

Of what nature are you speaking?

Of that which you term light, I replied.

True, he said.

Noble, then, is the bond which links together sight and visibility, and great beyond other bonds by no small difference of nature; for light is their bond, and light is no ignoble thing?

Nay, he said, the reverse of ignoble.

And which, I said, of the gods in heaven would you say was the lord of this element? Whose is that light which makes the eye to see perfectly and the visible to appear?

You mean the sun, as you and all mankind say.

May not the relation of sight to this deity be described as follows?

How?

Neither sight nor the eye in which sight resides is the sun?

No.

Yet of all the organs of sense the eye is the most like the sun?

By far the most like.

And the power which the eye possesses is a sort of effluence which is dispensed from the sun?

Exactly.

Then the sun is not sight, but the author of sight who is recognised by sight?

True, he said.

And this is he whom I call the child of the good, whom the good begat in his own likeness, to be in the visible world, in relation to sight and the things of sight, what the good is in the intellectual world in relation to mind and the things of mind:

Will you be a little more explicit? he said.

Why, you know, I said, that the eyes, when a person directs them towards objects on which the light of day is no longer shining, but the moon and stars only, see dimly, and are nearly blind; they seem to have no clearness of vision in them?

Very true.

But when they are directed towards objects on which the sun shines, they see clearly and there is sight in them?

Certainly.

And the soul is like the eye: when resting upon that on which truth and being shine, the soul perceives and understands, and is radiant with intelligence; but when turned towards the twilight of becoming and perishing, then she has opinion only, and goes blinking about, and is first of one opinion and then of another, and seems to have no intelligence?

Just so.

Now, that which imparts truth to the known and the power of knowing to the knower is what I would have you term the idea of good, and this you will deem to be the cause of science, and of truth in so far as the latter becomes the subject of knowledge; beautiful too, as are both truth and knowledge, you will be right in esteeming this other nature as more beautiful than either; and, as in the previous instance, light and sight may be truly said to be like the sun, and yet not to be the sun, so in this other sphere, science and truth may be deemed to be like the good, but not the good; the good has a place of honour yet higher.

What a wonder of beauty that must be, he said, which is the author of science and truth, and yet surpasses them in beauty; for you surely cannot mean to say that pleasure is the good?

God forbid, I replied; but may I ask you to consider the image in another point of view?

In what point of view?

You would say, would you not, that the sun is not only the author of visibility in all visible things, but of generation and nourishment and growth, though he himself is not generation?

Certainly.

In like manner the good may be said to be not only the author of knowledge to all things known, but of their being and essence, and yet the good is not essence, but far exceeds essence in dignity and power.

Glaucon said, with a ludicrous earnestness: By the light of heaven, how amazing!

Yes, I said, and the exaggeration may be set down to you; for you made me utter my fancies.

And pray continue to utter them; at any rate let us hear if there is anything more to be said about the similitude of the sun.

Yes, I said, there is a great deal more.

Then omit nothing, however slight.

I will do my best, I said; but I should think that a great deal will have to be omitted.

I hope not, he said.

You have to imagine, then, that there are two ruling powers, and that one of them is set over the intellectual world, the other over the visible. I do not say heaven, lest you should fancy that I am playing upon the name ('ourhanoz, orhatoz'). May I suppose that you have this distinction of the visible and intelligible fixed in your mind?

I have.

Now take a line which has been cut into two unequal parts, and divide each of them again in the same proportion, and suppose the two main divisions to answer, one to the visible and the other to the intelligible, and then compare the subdivisions in respect of their clearness and want of clearness, and you will find that the first section in the sphere of the visible consists of images. And by images I mean, in the first place, shadows, and in the second place, reflections in water and in solid, smooth and polished bodies and the like: Do you understand?

Yes, I understand.

Imagine, now, the other section, of which this is only the resemblance, to include the animals which we see, and everything that grows or is made.

Very good.

Would you not admit that both the sections of this division have different degrees of truth, and that the copy is to the original as the sphere of opinion is to the sphere of knowledge?

Most undoubtedly.

Next proceed to consider the manner in which the sphere of the intellectual is to be divided.

In what manner?

Thus: – There are two subdivisions, in the lower of which the soul uses the figures given by the former division as images; the enquiry can only be hypothetical, and instead of going upwards to a principle descends to the other end; in the higher of the two, the soul passes out of hypotheses, and goes up to a principle which is above hypotheses, making no use of images as in the former case, but proceeding only in and through the ideas themselves.

I do not quite understand your meaning, he said.

Then I will try again; you will understand me better when I have made some preliminary remarks. You are aware that students of geometry, arithmetic, and the kindred sciences assume the odd and the even and the figures and three kinds of angles and the like in their several branches of science; these are their hypotheses, which they and every body are supposed to know, and therefore they do not deign to give any account of them either to themselves or others; but they begin with them, and go on until they arrive at last, and in a consistent manner, at their conclusion?

Yes, he said, I know.

And do you not know also that although they make use of the visible forms and reason about them, they are thinking not of these, but of the ideals which they resemble; not of the figures which they draw, but of the absolute square and the absolute diameter, and so on – the forms which they draw or make, and which have shadows and reflections in water of their own, are converted by them into images, but they are really seeking to behold the things themselves, which can only be seen with the eye of the mind?

That is true.

And of this kind I spoke as the intelligible, although in the search after it the soul is compelled to use hypotheses; not ascending to a first principle, because she is unable to rise above the region of hypothesis, but employing the objects of which the shadows below are resemblances in their turn as images, they having in relation to the shadows and reflections of them a greater distinctness, and therefore a higher value.

I understand, he said, that you are speaking of the province of geometry and the sister arts.

And when I speak of the other division of the intelligible, you will understand me to speak of that other sort of knowledge which reason herself attains by the power of dialectic, using the hypotheses not as first principles, but only as hypotheses – that is to say, as steps and points of departure into a world which is above hypotheses, in order that she may soar beyond them to the first principle of the whole; and clinging to this and then to that which depends on this, by successive steps she descends again without the aid of any sensible object, from ideas, through ideas, and in ideas she ends.

I understand you, he replied; not perfectly, for you seem to me to be describing a task which is really tremendous; but, at any rate, I understand you to say that knowledge and being, which the science of dialectic contemplates, are clearer than the notions of the arts, as they are termed, which proceed from hypotheses only: these are also contemplated by the understanding, and not by the senses: yet, because they start from hypotheses and do not ascend to a principle, those who contemplate them appear to you not to exercise the higher reason upon them, although when a first principle is added to them they are cognizable by the higher reason.

And the habit which is concerned with geometry and the cognate sciences I suppose that you would term understanding and not reason, as being intermediate between opinion and reason.

You have quite conceived my meaning, I said; and now, corresponding to these four divisions, let there be four faculties in the soul – reason answering to the highest, understanding to the second, faith (or conviction) to the third, and perception of shadows to the last – and let there be a scale of them, and let us suppose that the several faculties have clearness in the same degree that their objects have truth.

I understand, he replied, and give my assent, and accept your arrangement.

BOOK VII.

And now, I said, let me show in a figure how far our nature is enlightened or unenlightened: – Behold! human beings living in a underground den, which has a mouth open towards the light and reaching all along the den; here they have been from their childhood, and have their legs and necks chained so that they cannot move, and can only see before them, being prevented by the chains from turning round their heads. Above and behind them a fire is blazing at a distance, and between the fire and the prisoners there is a raised way; and you will see, if you look, a low wall built along the way, like the screen which marionette players have in front of them, over which they show the puppets.

I see.

And do you see, I said, men passing along the wall carrying all sorts of vessels, and statues and figures of animals made of wood and stone and various materials, which appear over the wall? Some of them are talking, others silent.

You have shown me a strange image, and they are strange prisoners.

Like ourselves, I replied; and they see only their own shadows, or the shadows of one another, which the fire throws on the opposite wall of the cave?

True, he said; how could they see anything but the shadows if they were never allowed to move their heads?

And of the objects which are being carried in like manner they would only see the shadows?

Yes, he said.

And if they were able to converse with one another, would they not suppose that they were naming what was actually before them?

Very true.

And suppose further that the prison had an echo which came from the other side, would they not be sure to fancy when one of the passers-by spoke that the voice which they heard came from the passing shadow?

No question, he replied.

To them, I said, the truth would be literally nothing but the shadows of the images.

That is certain.

And now look again, and see what will naturally follow if the prisoners are released and disabused of their error. At first, when any of them is liberated and compelled suddenly to stand up and turn his neck round and walk and look towards the light, he will suffer sharp pains; the glare will distress him, and he will be unable to see the realities of which in his former state he had seen the shadows; and then conceive some one saying to him, that what he saw before was an illusion, but that now, when he is approaching nearer to being and his eye is turned towards more real existence, he has a clearer vision, – what will be his reply? And you may further imagine that his instructor is pointing to the objects as they pass and requiring him to name them, – will he not be perplexed? Will he not fancy that the shadows which he formerly saw are truer than the objects which are now shown to him?

Far truer.

And if he is compelled to look straight at the light, will he not have a pain in his eyes which will make him turn away to take refuge in the objects of vision which he can see, and which he will conceive to be in reality clearer than the things which are now being shown to him?

True, he said.

And suppose once more, that he is reluctantly dragged up a steep and rugged ascent, and held fast until he is forced into the presence of the sun himself, is he not likely to be pained and irritated? When he approaches the light his eyes will be dazzled, and he will not be able to see anything at all of what are now called realities.

Not all in a moment, he said.

He will require to grow accustomed to the sight of the upper world. And first he will see the shadows best, next the reflections of men and other objects in the water, and then the objects themselves; then he will gaze upon the light of the moon and the stars and the spangled heaven; and he will see the sky and the stars by night better than the sun or the light of the sun by day?

Certainly.

Last of all he will be able to see the sun, and not mere reflections of him in the water, but he will see him in his own proper place, and not in another; and he will contemplate him as he is.

Certainly.

He will then proceed to argue that this is he who gives the season and the years, and is the guardian of all that is in the visible world, and in a certain way the cause of all things which he and his fellows have been accustomed to behold?

Clearly, he said, he would first see the sun and then reason about him.

And when he remembered his old habitation, and the wisdom of the den and his fellow-prisoners, do you not suppose that he would felicitate himself on the change, and pity them?

Certainly, he would.

And if they were in the habit of conferring honours among themselves on those who were quickest to observe the passing shadows and to remark which of them went before, and which followed after, and which were together; and who were therefore best able to draw conclusions as to the future, do you think that he would care for such honours and glories, or envy the possessors of them? Would he not say with Homer,

'Better to be the poor servant of a poor master,'

and to endure anything, rather than think as they do and live after their manner?

Yes, he said, I think that he would rather suffer anything than entertain these false notions and live in this miserable manner.

Imagine once more, I said, such an one coming suddenly out of the sun to be replaced in his old situation; would he not be certain to have his eyes full of darkness?

To be sure, he said.

And if there were a contest, and he had to compete in measuring the shadows with the prisoners who had never moved out of the den, while his sight was still weak, and before his eyes had become steady (and the time which would be needed to acquire this new habit of sight might be very considerable), would he not be ridiculous? Men would say of him that up he went and down he came without his eyes; and that it was better not even to think of ascending; and if any one tried to loose another and lead him up to the light, let them only catch the offender, and they would put him to death.

No question, he said.

This entire allegory, I said, you may now append, dear Glaucon, to the previous argument; the prison-house is the world of sight, the light of the fire is the sun, and you will not misapprehend me if you interpret the journey upwards to be the ascent of the soul into the intellectual world according to my poor belief, which, at your desire, I have expressed – whether rightly or wrongly God knows. But, whether true or false, my opinion is that in the world of knowledge the idea of good appears last of all, and is seen only with an effort; and, when seen, is also inferred to be the universal author of all things beautiful and right, parent of light and of the lord of light in this visible world, and the immediate source of reason and truth in the intellectual; and that this is the power upon which he who would act rationally either in public or private life must have his eye fixed.

I agree, he said, as far as I am able to understand you.

Moreover, I said, you must not wonder that those who attain to this beatific vision are unwilling to descend to human affairs; for their souls are ever hastening into the upper world where they desire to dwell; which desire of theirs is very natural, if our allegory may be trusted.

Yes, very natural.

And is there anything surprising in one who passes from divine contemplations to the evil state of man, misbehaving himself in a ridiculous manner; if, while his eyes are blinking and before he has become accustomed to the surrounding darkness, he is compelled to fight in courts of law, or in other places, about the images or the shadows of images of justice, and is endeavouring to meet the conceptions of those who have never yet seen absolute justice?

Anything but surprising, he replied.

Any one who has common sense will remember that the bewilderments of the eyes are of two kinds, and arise from two causes, either from coming out of the light or from going into the light, which is true of the mind's eye, quite as much as of the bodily eye; and he who remembers this when he sees any one whose vision is perplexed and weak, will not be too ready to laugh; he will first ask whether that soul of man has come out of the brighter life, and is unable to see because unaccustomed to the dark, or having turned from darkness to the day is dazzled by excess of light. And he will count the one happy in his condition and state of being, and he will pity the other; or, if he have a mind to laugh at the soul which comes from below into the light, there will be more reason in this than in the laugh which greets him who returns from above out of the light into the den.

That, he said, is a very just distinction.

But then, if I am right, certain professors of education must be wrong when they say that they can put a knowledge into the soul which was not there before, like sight into blind eyes.

They undoubtedly say this, he replied.

Whereas, our argument shows that the power and capacity of learning exists in the soul already; and that just as the eye was unable to turn from darkness to light without the whole body, so too the instrument of knowledge can only by the movement of the whole soul be turned from the world of becoming into that of being, and learn by degrees to endure the sight of being, and of the brightest and best of being, or in other words, of the good.

Very true.

And must there not be some art which will effect conversion in the easiest and quickest manner; not implanting the faculty of sight, for that exists already, but has been turned in the wrong direction, and is looking away from the truth?

Yes, he said, such an art may be presumed.

And whereas the other so-called virtues of the soul seem to be akin to bodily qualities, for even when they are not originally innate they can be implanted later by habit and exercise, the virtue of wisdom more than anything else contains a divine element which always remains, and by this conversion is rendered useful and profitable; or, on the other hand, hurtful and useless. Did you never observe the narrow intelligence flashing from the keen eye of a clever rogue – how eager he is, how clearly his paltry soul sees the way to his end; he is the reverse of blind, but his keen eye-sight is forced into the service of evil, and he is mischievous in proportion to his cleverness?

Very true, he said.

But what if there had been a circumcision of such natures in the days of their youth; and they had been severed from those sensual pleasures, such as eating and drinking, which, like leaden weights, were attached to them at their birth, and which drag them down and turn the vision of their souls upon the things that are below – if, I say, they had been released from these impediments and turned in the opposite direction, the very same faculty in them would have seen the truth as keenly as they see what their eyes are turned to now.

Very likely.

Yes, I said; and there is another thing which is likely, or rather a necessary inference from what has preceded, that neither the uneducated and uninformed of the truth, nor yet those who never make an end of their education, will be able ministers of State; not the former, because they have no single aim of duty which is the rule of all their actions, private as well as public; nor the latter, because they will not act at all except upon compulsion, fancying that they are already dwelling apart in the islands of the blest.

Very true, he replied.

Then, I said, the business of us who are the founders of the State will be to compel the best minds to attain that knowledge which we have already shown to be the greatest of all – they must continue to ascend until they arrive at the good; but when they have ascended and seen enough we must not allow them to do as they do now.

What do you mean?

441 | P a g e

I mean that they remain in the upper world: but this must not be allowed; they must be made to descend again among the prisoners in the den, and partake of their labours and honours, whether they are worth having or not.

But is not this unjust? he said; ought we to give them a worse life, when they might have a better?

You have again forgotten, my friend, I said, the intention of the legislator, who did not aim at making any one class in the State happy above the rest; the happiness was to be in the whole State, and he held the citizens together by persuasion and necessity, making them benefactors of the State, and therefore benefactors of one another; to this end he created them, not to please themselves, but to be his instruments in binding up the State.

True, he said, I had forgotten.

Observe, Glaucon, that there will be no injustice in compelling our philosophers to have a care and providence of others; we shall explain to them that in other States, men of their class are not obliged to share in the toils of politics: and this is reasonable, for they grow up at their own sweet will, and the government would rather not have them. Being self-taught, they cannot be expected to show any gratitude for a culture which they have never received. But we have brought you into the world to be rulers of the hive, kings of yourselves and of the other citizens, and have educated you far better and more perfectly than they have been educated, and you are better able to share in the double duty. Wherefore each of you, when his turn comes, must go down to the general underground abode, and get the habit of seeing in the dark. When you have acquired the habit, you will see ten thousand times better than the inhabitants of the den, and you will know what the several images are, and what they represent, because you have seen the beautiful and just and good in their truth. And thus our State, which is also yours, will be a reality, and not a dream only, and will be administered in a spirit unlike that of other States, in which men fight with one another about shadows only and are distracted in the struggle for power, which in their eyes is a great good. Whereas the truth is that the State in which the rulers are most reluctant to govern is always the best and most quietly governed, and the State in which they are most eager, the worst.

Quite true, he replied.

And will our pupils, when they hear this, refuse to take their turn at the toils of State, when they are allowed to spend the greater part of their time with one another in the heavenly light?

Impossible, he answered; for they are just men, and the commands which we impose upon them are just; there can be no doubt that every one of them will take office as a stern necessity, and not after the fashion of our present rulers of State.

Yes, my friend, I said; and there lies the point. You must contrive for your future rulers another and a better life than that of a ruler, and then you may have a well-ordered State; for only in the State which offers this, will they rule who are truly rich, not in silver and gold, but in virtue and wisdom, which are the true blessings of life. Whereas if they go to the administration of public affairs, poor and hungering after their own private advantage, thinking that hence they are to snatch the chief good, order there can never be; for they will be fighting about office, and the civil and domestic broils which thus arise will be the ruin of the rulers themselves and of the whole State.

Most true, he replied.

And the only life which looks down upon the life of political ambition is that of true philosophy. Do you know of any other?

Indeed, I do not, he said.

And those who govern ought not to be lovers of the task? For, if they are, there will be rival lovers, and they will fight.

No question.

Who then are those whom we shall compel to be guardians? Surely they will be the men who are wisest about affairs of State, and by whom the State is best administered, and who at the same time have other honours and another and a better life than that of politics?

They are the men, and I will choose them, he replied.

And now shall we consider in what way such guardians will be produced, and how they are to be brought from darkness to light, – as some are said to have ascended from the world below to the gods?

By all means, he replied.

The process, I said, is not the turning over of an oyster-shell (In allusion to a game in which two parties fled or pursued according as an oyster-shell which was thrown into the air fell with the dark or light side uppermost.), but the turning round of a soul passing from a day which is little better than night to the true day of being, that is, the ascent from below, which we affirm to be true philosophy?

Quite so.

And should we not enquire what sort of knowledge has the power of effecting such a change?

Certainly.

What sort of knowledge is there which would draw the soul from becoming to being? And another consideration has just occurred to me: You will remember that our young men are to be warrior athletes?

Yes, that was said.

Then this new kind of knowledge must have an additional quality?

What quality?

Usefulness in war.

Yes, if possible.

There were two parts in our former scheme of education, were there not?

Just so.

There was gymnastic which presided over the growth and decay of the body, and may therefore be regarded as having to do with generation and corruption?

True.

Then that is not the knowledge which we are seeking to discover?

No.

But what do you say of music, which also entered to a certain extent into our former scheme?

Music, he said, as you will remember, was the counterpart of gymnastic, and trained the guardians by the influences of habit, by harmony making them harmonious, by rhythm rhythmical, but not giving them science; and the words, whether fabulous or possibly true, had kindred elements of rhythm and harmony in them. But in music there was nothing which tended to that good which you are now seeking.

You are most accurate, I said, in your recollection; in music there certainly was nothing of the kind. But what branch of knowledge is there, my dear Glaucon, which is of the desired nature; since all the useful arts were reckoned mean by us?

Undoubtedly; and yet if music and gymnastic are excluded, and the arts are also excluded, what remains?

Well, I said, there may be nothing left of our special subjects; and then we shall have to take something which is not special, but of universal application.

What may that be?

A something which all arts and sciences and intelligences use in common, and which every one first has to learn among the elements of education.

What is that?

The little matter of distinguishing one, two, and three – in a word, number and calculation: – do not all arts and sciences necessarily partake of them?

Yes.

Then the art of war partakes of them?

To be sure.

Then Palamedes, whenever he appears in tragedy, proves Agamemnon ridiculously unfit to be a general. Did you never remark how he declares that he had invented number, and had numbered the ships and set in array the ranks of the army at Troy; which implies that they had never been numbered before, and Agamemnon must be supposed literally to have been incapable of counting his own feet – how could he if he was ignorant of number? And if that is true, what sort of general must he have been?

I should say a very strange one, if this was as you say.

Can we deny that a warrior should have a knowledge of arithmetic?

Certainly he should, if he is to have the smallest understanding of military tactics, or indeed, I should rather say, if he is to be a man at all.

I should like to know whether you have the same notion which I have of this study?

What is your notion?

It appears to me to be a study of the kind which we are seeking, and which leads naturally to reflection, but never to have been rightly used; for the true use of it is simply to draw the soul towards being.

Will you explain your meaning? he said.

I will try, I said; and I wish you would share the enquiry with me, and say 'yes' or 'no' when I attempt to distinguish in my own mind what branches of knowledge have this attracting power, in order that we may have clearer proof that arithmetic is, as I suspect, one of them.

Explain, he said.

I mean to say that objects of sense are of two kinds; some of them do not invite thought because the sense is an adequate judge of them; while in the case of other objects sense is so untrustworthy that further enquiry is imperatively demanded.

You are clearly referring, he said, to the manner in which the senses are imposed upon by distance, and by painting in light and shade.

No, I said, that is not at all my meaning.

Then what is your meaning?

When speaking of uninviting objects, I mean those which do not pass from one sensation to the opposite; inviting objects are those which do; in this latter case the sense coming upon the object, whether at a distance or near, gives no more vivid idea of anything in particular than of its opposite. An illustration will make my meaning clearer: – here are three fingers – a little finger, a second finger, and a middle finger.

Very good.

You may suppose that they are seen quite close: And here comes the point.

What is it?

Each of them equally appears a finger, whether seen in the middle or at the extremity, whether white or black, or thick or thin – it makes no difference; a finger is a finger all the same. In these cases a man is not compelled to ask of thought the question what is a finger? for the sight never intimates to the mind that a finger is other than a finger.

True.

And therefore, I said, as we might expect, there is nothing here which invites or excites intelligence.

There is not, he said.

But is this equally true of the greatness and smallness of the fingers? Can sight adequately perceive them? and is no difference made by the circumstance that one of the fingers is in the middle and another at the extremity? And in like manner does the touch adequately perceive the qualities of thickness or thinness, of softness or hardness? And so of the other senses; do they give perfect intimations of such matters? Is not their mode of operation on this wise – the sense which is concerned with the quality of hardness is necessarily concerned also with the quality of softness, and only intimates to the soul that the same thing is felt to be both hard and soft?

You are quite right, he said.

And must not the soul be perplexed at this intimation which the sense gives of a hard which is also soft? What, again, is the meaning of light and heavy, if that which is light is also heavy, and that which is heavy, light?

Yes, he said, these intimations which the soul receives are very curious and require to be explained.

Yes, I said, and in these perplexities the soul naturally summons to her aid calculation and intelligence, that she may see whether the several objects announced to her are one or two.

True.

And if they turn out to be two, is not each of them one and different?

Certainly.

And if each is one, and both are two, she will conceive the two as in a state of division, for if there were undivided they could only be conceived of as one?

True.

The eye certainly did see both small and great, but only in a confused manner; they were not distinguished.

Yes.

Whereas the thinking mind, intending to light up the chaos, was compelled to reverse the process, and look at small and great as separate and not confused.

Very true.

Was not this the beginning of the enquiry 'What is great?' and 'What is small?'

Exactly so.

And thus arose the distinction of the visible and the intelligible.

Most true.

This was what I meant when I spoke of impressions which invited the intellect, or the reverse – those which are simultaneous with opposite impressions, invite thought; those which are not simultaneous do not.

I understand, he said, and agree with you.

And to which class do unity and number belong?

I do not know, he replied.

Think a little and you will see that what has preceded will supply the answer; for if simple unity could be adequately perceived by the sight or by any other sense, then, as we were saying in the case of the finger, there would be nothing to attract towards being; but when there is some contradiction always present, and one is the reverse of one and involves the conception of plurality, then thought begins to be aroused within us, and the soul perplexed and wanting to arrive at a decision asks 'What is absolute unity?' This is the way in which the study of the one has a power of drawing and converting the mind to the contemplation of true being.

And surely, he said, this occurs notably in the case of one; for we see the same thing to be both one and infinite in multitude?

Yes, I said; and this being true of one must be equally true of all number?

Certainly.

And all arithmetic and calculation have to do with number?

Yes.

And they appear to lead the mind towards truth?

Yes, in a very remarkable manner.

Then this is knowledge of the kind for which we are seeking, having a double use, military and philosophical; for the man of war must learn the art of number or he will not know how to array his troops, and the philosopher also, because he has to rise out of the sea of change and lay hold of true being, and therefore he must be an arithmetician.

That is true.

And our guardian is both warrior and philosopher?

Certainly.

Then this is a kind of knowledge which legislation may fitly prescribe; and we must endeavour to persuade those who are to be the principal men of our State to go and learn arithmetic, not as amateurs, but they must carry on the study until they see the nature of numbers with the mind only; nor again, like merchants or retail-traders, with a view to buying or selling, but for the sake of their military use, and of the soul herself; and because this will be the easiest way for her to pass from becoming to truth and being.

That is excellent, he said.

Yes, I said, and now having spoken of it, I must add how charming the science is! and in how many ways it conduces to our desired end, if pursued in the spirit of a philosopher, and not of a shopkeeper!

How do you mean?

I mean, as I was saying, that arithmetic has a very great and elevating effect, compelling the soul to reason about abstract number, and rebelling against the introduction of visible or tangible objects into the argument. You know how steadily the masters of the art repel and ridicule any one who attempts to divide absolute unity when he is calculating, and if you divide, they multiply (Meaning either (1) that they integrate the number because they deny the possibility of fractions; or (2) that division is regarded by them as a process of multiplication, for the fractions of one continue to be units.), taking care that one shall continue one and not become lost in fractions.

That is very true.

Now, suppose a person were to say to them: O my friends, what are these wonderful numbers about which you are reasoning, in which, as you say, there is a unity such as you demand, and each unit is equal, invariable, indivisible, – what would they answer?

They would answer, as I should conceive, that they were speaking of those numbers which can only be realized in thought.

Then you see that this knowledge may be truly called necessary, necessitating as it clearly does the use of the pure intelligence in the attainment of pure truth?

Yes; that is a marked characteristic of it.

And have you further observed, that those who have a natural talent for calculation are generally quick at every other kind of knowledge; and even the dull, if they have had an arithmetical training, although they may derive no other advantage from it, always become much quicker than they would otherwise have been.

Very true, he said.

And indeed, you will not easily find a more difficult study, and not many as difficult.

You will not.

And, for all these reasons, arithmetic is a kind of knowledge in which the best natures should be trained, and which must not be given up.

I agree.

Let this then be made one of our subjects of education. And next, shall we enquire whether the kindred science also concerns us?

You mean geometry?

Exactly so.

Clearly, he said, we are concerned with that part of geometry which relates to war; for in pitching a camp, or taking up a position, or closing or extending the lines of an army, or any other military manoeuvre, whether in actual battle or on a march, it will make all the difference whether a general is or is not a geometrician.

Yes, I said, but for that purpose a very little of either geometry or calculation will be enough; the question relates rather to the greater and more advanced part of geometry – whether that tends in any degree to make more easy the vision of the idea of good; and thither, as I was saying, all things tend which compel the soul to turn her gaze towards that place, where is the full perfection of being, which she ought, by all means, to behold.

True, he said.

Then if geometry compels us to view being, it concerns us; if becoming only, it does not concern us?

Yes, that is what we assert.

Yet anybody who has the least acquaintance with geometry will not deny that such a conception of the science is in flat contradiction to the ordinary language of geometricians.

How so?

They have in view practice only, and are always speaking, in a narrow and ridiculous manner, of squaring and extending and applying and the like – they confuse the necessities of geometry with those of daily life; whereas knowledge is the real object of the whole science.

Certainly, he said.

Then must not a further admission be made?

What admission?

That the knowledge at which geometry aims is knowledge of the eternal, and not of aught perishing and transient.

That, he replied, may be readily allowed, and is true.

Then, my noble friend, geometry will draw the soul towards truth, and create the spirit of philosophy, and raise up that which is now unhappily allowed to fall down.

Nothing will be more likely to have such an effect.

Then nothing should be more sternly laid down than that the inhabitants of your fair city should by all means learn geometry. Moreover the science has indirect effects, which are not small.

Of what kind? he said.

There are the military advantages of which you spoke, I said; and in all departments of knowledge, as experience proves, any one who has studied geometry is infinitely quicker of apprehension than one who has not.

Yes indeed, he said, there is an infinite difference between them.

Then shall we propose this as a second branch of knowledge which our youth will study?

Let us do so, he replied.

And suppose we make astronomy the third – what do you say?

I am strongly inclined to it, he said; the observation of the seasons and of months and years is as essential to the general as it is to the farmer or sailor.

I am amused, I said, at your fear of the world, which makes you guard against the appearance of insisting upon useless studies; and I quite admit the difficulty of believing that in every man there is an eye of the soul which, when by other pursuits lost and dimmed, is by these purified and re-illumined; and is more precious far than ten thousand bodily eyes, for by it alone is truth seen. Now there are two classes of persons: one class of those who will agree with you and will take your words as a revelation; another class to whom they will be utterly unmeaning, and who will naturally deem them to be idle tales, for they see no sort of profit which is to be obtained from them. And therefore you had better decide at once with which of the two you are proposing to argue. You will very likely say with neither, and that your chief aim in carrying on the argument is your own improvement; at the same time you do not grudge to others any benefit which they may receive.

I think that I should prefer to carry on the argument mainly on my own behalf.

Then take a step backward, for we have gone wrong in the order of the sciences.

What was the mistake? he said.

After plane geometry, I said, we proceeded at once to solids in revolution, instead of taking solids in themselves; whereas after the second dimension the third, which is concerned with cubes and dimensions of depth, ought to have followed.

That is true, Socrates; but so little seems to be known as yet about these subjects.

Why, yes, I said, and for two reasons: – in the first place, no government patronises them; this leads to a want of energy in the pursuit of them, and they are difficult; in the second place, students cannot learn them unless they have a director. But then a director can hardly be found, and even if he could, as matters now stand, the students, who are very conceited, would not attend to him. That, however, would be otherwise if the whole State became the director of these studies and gave honour to them; then disciples would want to come, and there would be continuous and earnest search, and discoveries would be made; since even now, disregarded as they are by the world, and maimed of their fair proportions, and although none of their votaries can tell the use of them, still these studies force their way by their natural charm, and very likely, if they had the help of the State, they would some day emerge into light.

Yes, he said, there is a remarkable charm in them. But I do not clearly understand the change in the order. First you began with a geometry of plane surfaces?

Yes, I said.

And you placed astronomy next, and then you made a step backward?

Yes, and I have delayed you by my hurry; the ludicrous state of solid geometry, which, in natural order, should have followed, made me pass over this branch and go on to astronomy, or motion of solids.

True, he said.

Then assuming that the science now omitted would come into existence if encouraged by the State, let us go on to astronomy, which will be fourth.

The right order, he replied. And now, Socrates, as you rebuked the vulgar manner in which I praised astronomy before, my praise shall be given in your own spirit. For every one, as I think, must see that astronomy compels the soul to look upwards and leads us from this world to another.

Every one but myself, I said; to every one else this may be clear, but not to me.

And what then would you say?

I should rather say that those who elevate astronomy into philosophy appear to me to make us look downwards and not upwards.

What do you mean? he asked.

You, I replied, have in your mind a truly sublime conception of our knowledge of the things above. And I dare say that if a person were to throw his head back and study the fretted ceiling, you would still think that his mind was the percipient, and not his eyes. And you are very likely right, and I may be a simpleton: but, in my opinion, that knowledge only which is of being and of the unseen can make the soul look upwards, and whether a man gapes at the heavens or blinks on the ground, seeking to learn some particular of sense, I would deny that he can learn, for nothing of that sort is matter of science; his soul is looking downwards, not upwards, whether his way to knowledge is by water or by land, whether he floats, or only lies on his back.

I acknowledge, he said, the justice of your rebuke. Still, I should like to ascertain how astronomy can be learned in any manner more conducive to that knowledge of which we are speaking?

I will tell you, I said: The starry heaven which we behold is wrought upon a visible ground, and therefore, although the fairest and most perfect of visible things, must necessarily be deemed inferior far to the true motions of absolute swiftness and absolute slowness, which are relative to each other, and carry with them that which is contained in them, in the true number and in every true figure. Now, these are to be apprehended by reason and intelligence, but not by sight.

True, he replied.

The spangled heavens should be used as a pattern and with a view to that higher knowledge; their beauty is like the beauty of figures or pictures excellently wrought by the hand of Daedalus, or some other great artist, which we may chance to behold; any geometrician who saw them would appreciate the exquisiteness of their workmanship, but he would never dream of thinking that in them he could find the true equal or the true double, or the truth of any other proportion.

No, he replied, such an idea would be ridiculous.

And will not a true astronomer have the same feeling when he looks at the movements of the stars? Will he not think that heaven and the things in heaven are framed by the Creator of them in the most perfect manner? But he will never imagine that the proportions of night and day, or of both to the month, or of the month to the year, or of the stars to these and to one another, and any other things that are material and visible can also be eternal and subject to no deviation – that would be absurd; and it is equally absurd to take so much pains in investigating their exact truth.

I quite agree, though I never thought of this before.

Then, I said, in astronomy, as in geometry, we should employ problems, and let the heavens alone if we would approach the subject in the right way and so make the natural gift of reason to be of any real use.

That, he said, is a work infinitely beyond our present astronomers.

Yes, I said; and there are many other things which must also have a similar extension given to them, if our legislation is to be of any value. But can you tell me of any other suitable study?

No, he said, not without thinking.

Motion, I said, has many forms, and not one only; two of them are obvious enough even to wits no better than ours; and there are others, as I imagine, which may be left to wiser persons.

But where are the two?

There is a second, I said, which is the counterpart of the one already named.

And what may that be?

The second, I said, would seem relatively to the ears to be what the first is to the eyes; for I conceive that as the eyes are designed to look up at the stars, so are the ears to hear harmonious motions; and these are sister sciences – as the Pythagoreans say, and we, Glaucon, agree with them?

Yes, he replied.

But this, I said, is a laborious study, and therefore we had better go and learn of them; and they will tell us whether there are any other applications of these sciences. At the same time, we must not lose sight of our own higher object.

What is that?

There is a perfection which all knowledge ought to reach, and which our pupils ought also to attain, and not to fall short of, as I was saying that they did in astronomy. For in the science of harmony, as you probably know, the same thing happens. The teachers of harmony compare the sounds and consonances which are heard only, and their labour, like that of the astronomers, is in vain.

Yes, by heaven! he said; and 'tis as good as a play to hear them talking about their condensed notes, as they call them; they put their ears close alongside of the strings like persons catching a sound from their neighbour's wall – one set of them declaring that they distinguish an intermediate note and have found the least interval which should be the unit of measurement; the others insisting that the two sounds have passed into the same – either party setting their ears before their understanding.

You mean, I said, those gentlemen who tease and torture the strings and rack them on the pegs of the instrument: I might carry on the metaphor and speak after their manner of the blows which the plectrum gives, and make accusations against the strings, both of backwardness and forwardness to sound; but this would be tedious, and therefore I will only say that these are not the men, and that I am referring to the Pythagoreans, of whom I was just now proposing to enquire about harmony. For they too are in error, like the astronomers; they investigate the numbers of the harmonies which are heard, but they never attain to problems – that is to say, they never reach the natural harmonies of number, or reflect why some numbers are harmonious and others not.

That, he said, is a thing of more than mortal knowledge.

A thing, I replied, which I would rather call useful; that is, if sought after with a view to the beautiful and good; but if pursued in any other spirit, useless.

Very true, he said.

Now, when all these studies reach the point of inter-communion and connection with one another, and come to be considered in their mutual affinities, then, I think, but not till then, will the pursuit of them have a value for our objects; otherwise there is no profit in them.

I suspect so; but you are speaking, Socrates, of a vast work.

What do you mean? I said; the prelude or what? Do you not know that all this is but the prelude to the actual strain which we have to learn? For you surely would not regard the skilled mathematician as a dialectician?

Assuredly not, he said; I have hardly ever known a mathematician who was capable of reasoning.

But do you imagine that men who are unable to give and take a reason will have the knowledge which we require of them?

Neither can this be supposed.

And so, Glaucon, I said, we have at last arrived at the hymn of dialectic. This is that strain which is of the intellect only, but which the faculty of sight will nevertheless be found to imitate; for sight, as you may remember, was imagined by us after a while to behold the real animals and stars, and last of all the sun himself. And so with dialectic; when a person starts on the discovery of the absolute by the light of reason only, and without any assistance of sense, and perseveres until by pure intelligence he arrives at the perception of the absolute good, he at last finds himself at the end of the intellectual world, as in the case of sight at the end of the visible.

Exactly, he said.

Then this is the progress which you call dialectic?

True.

But the release of the prisoners from chains, and their translation from the shadows to the images and to the light, and the ascent from the underground den to the sun, while in his presence they are vainly trying to look on animals and plants and the light of the sun, but are able to perceive even with their weak eyes the images in the water (which are divine), and are the shadows of true existence (not shadows of images cast by a light of fire, which compared with the sun is only an image) – this power of elevating the highest principle in the soul to the contemplation of that which is best in existence, with which we may compare the raising of that faculty which is the very light of the body to the sight of that which is brightest in the material and visible world – this power is given, as I was saying, by all that study and pursuit of the arts which has been described.

I agree in what you are saying, he replied, which may be hard to believe, yet, from another point of view, is harder still to deny. This, however, is not a theme to be treated of in passing only, but will have to be discussed again and again. And so, whether our conclusion be true or false, let us assume all this, and proceed at once from the prelude or preamble to the chief strain (A play upon the Greek word, which means both 'law' and 'strain.'), and describe that in like manner. Say, then, what is the nature and what are the divisions of dialectic, and what are the paths which lead thither; for these paths will also lead to our final rest.

Dear Glaucon, I said, you will not be able to follow me here, though I would do my best, and you should behold not an image only but the absolute truth, according to my notion. Whether what I told you would or would not have been a reality I cannot venture to say; but you would have seen something like reality; of that I am confident.

Doubtless, he replied.

But I must also remind you, that the power of dialectic alone can reveal this, and only to one who is a disciple of the previous sciences.

Of that assertion you may be as confident as of the last.

And assuredly no one will argue that there is any other method of comprehending by any regular process all true existence or of ascertaining what each thing is in its own nature; for the arts in general are concerned with the desires or opinions of men, or are cultivated with a view to production and construction, or for the preservation of such productions and constructions; and as to the mathematical sciences which, as we were saying, have some apprehension of true being – geometry and the like – they only dream about being, but never can they behold the waking reality so long as they leave the hypotheses which they use unexamined, and are unable to give an account of them. For when a man knows not his own first principle, and when the conclusion and intermediate steps are also constructed out of he knows not what, how can he imagine that such a fabric of convention can ever become science?

Impossible, he said.

Then dialectic, and dialectic alone, goes directly to the first principle and is the only science which does away with hypotheses in order to make her ground secure; the eye of the soul, which is literally buried in an outlandish slough, is by her gentle aid lifted upwards; and she uses as handmaids and helpers in the work of conversion, the sciences which we have been discussing. Custom terms them sciences, but they ought to have some other name, implying greater clearness than opinion and less clearness than science: and this, in our previous sketch, was called understanding. But why should we dispute about names when we have realities of such importance to consider?

Why indeed, he said, when any name will do which expresses the thought of the mind with clearness?

At any rate, we are satisfied, as before, to have four divisions; two for intellect and two for opinion, and to call the first division science, the second understanding, the third belief, and the fourth perception of shadows, opinion being concerned with becoming, and intellect with being; and so to make a proportion: –

As being is to becoming, so is pure intellect to opinion. And as intellect is to opinion, so is science to belief, and understanding to the perception of shadows.

But let us defer the further correlation and subdivision of the subjects of opinion and of intellect, for it will be a long enquiry, many times longer than this has been.

As far as I understand, he said, I agree.

And do you also agree, I said, in describing the dialectician as one who attains a conception of the essence of each thing? And he who does not possess and is therefore unable to impart this conception, in whatever degree he fails, may in that degree also be said to fail in intelligence? Will you admit so much?

Yes, he said; how can I deny it?

And you would say the same of the conception of the good? Until the person is able to abstract and define rationally the idea of good, and unless he can run the gauntlet of all objections, and is ready to disprove them, not by appeals to opinion, but to absolute truth, never faltering at any step of the argument – unless he can do all this, you would say that he knows neither the idea of good nor any other good; he apprehends only a shadow, if anything at all, which is given by opinion and not by science; – dreaming and slumbering in this life, before he is well awake here, he arrives at the world below, and has his final quietus.

In all that I should most certainly agree with you.

And surely you would not have the children of your ideal State, whom you are nurturing and educating – if the ideal ever becomes a reality – you would not allow the future rulers to be like posts (Literally 'lines,' probably the starting-point of a race-course.), having no reason in them, and yet to be set in authority over the highest matters?

Certainly not.

Then you will make a law that they shall have such an education as will enable them to attain the greatest skill in asking and answering questions?

Yes, he said, you and I together will make it.

Dialectic, then, as you will agree, is the coping-stone of the sciences, and is set over them; no other science can be placed higher – the nature of knowledge can no further go?

I agree, he said.

But to whom we are to assign these studies, and in what way they are to be assigned, are questions which remain to be considered.

Yes, clearly.

You remember, I said, how the rulers were chosen before?

Certainly, he said.

The same natures must still be chosen, and the preference again given to the surest and the bravest, and, if possible, to the fairest; and, having noble and generous tempers, they should also have the natural gifts which will facilitate their education.

And what are these?

Such gifts as keenness and ready powers of acquisition; for the mind more often faints from the severity of study than from the severity of gymnastics: the toil is more entirely the mind's own, and is not shared with the body.

Very true, he replied.

Further, he of whom we are in search should have a good memory, and be an unwearied solid man who is a lover of labour in any line; or he will never be able to endure the great amount of bodily exercise and to go through all the intellectual discipline and study which we require of him.

Certainly, he said; he must have natural gifts.

The mistake at present is, that those who study philosophy have no vocation, and this, as I was before saying, is the reason why she has fallen into disrepute: her true sons should take her by the hand and not bastards.

What do you mean?

In the first place, her votary should not have a lame or halting industry – I mean, that he should not be half industrious and half idle: as, for example, when a man is a lover of gymnastic and hunting, and all other bodily exercises, but a hater rather than a lover of the labour of learning or listening or enquiring. Or the occupation to which he devotes himself may be of an opposite kind, and he may have the other sort of lameness.

Certainly, he said.

And as to truth, I said, is not a soul equally to be deemed halt and lame which hates voluntary falsehood and is extremely indignant at herself and others when they tell lies, but is patient of involuntary falsehood, and does not mind wallowing like a swinish beast in the mire of ignorance, and has no shame at being detected?

To be sure.

And, again, in respect of temperance, courage, magnificence, and every other virtue, should we not carefully distinguish between the true son and the bastard? for where there is no discernment of such qualities states and individuals unconsciously err; and the state makes a ruler, and the individual a friend, of one who, being defective in some part of virtue, is in a figure lame or a bastard.

That is very true, he said.

All these things, then, will have to be carefully considered by us; and if only those whom we introduce to this vast system of education and training are sound in body and mind, justice herself will have nothing to say against us, and we shall be the saviours of the constitution and of the State; but, if our pupils are men of another stamp, the reverse will happen, and we shall pour a still greater flood of ridicule on philosophy than she has to endure at present.

That would not be creditable.

Certainly not, I said; and yet perhaps, in thus turning jest into earnest I am equally ridiculous.

In what respect?

I had forgotten, I said, that we were not serious, and spoke with too much excitement. For when I saw philosophy so undeservedly trampled under foot of men I could not help feeling a sort of indignation at the authors of her disgrace: and my anger made me too vehement.

Indeed! I was listening, and did not think so.

But I, who am the speaker, felt that I was. And now let me remind you that, although in our former selection we chose old men, we must not do so in this. Solon was under a delusion when he said that a man when he grows old may learn many things – for he can no more learn much than he can run much; youth is the time for any extraordinary toil.

Of course.

And, therefore, calculation and geometry and all the other elements of instruction, which are a preparation for dialectic, should be presented to the mind in childhood; not, however, under any notion of forcing our system of education.

Why not?

Because a freeman ought not to be a slave in the acquisition of knowledge of any kind. Bodily exercise, when compulsory, does no harm to the body; but knowledge which is acquired under compulsion obtains no hold on the mind.

Very true.

Then, my good friend, I said, do not use compulsion, but let early education be a sort of amusement; you will then be better able to find out the natural bent.

That is a very rational notion, he said.

Do you remember that the children, too, were to be taken to see the battle on horseback; and that if there were no danger they were to be brought close up and, like young hounds, have a taste of blood given them?

Yes, I remember.

The same practice may be followed, I said, in all these things – labours, lessons, dangers – and he who is most at home in all of them ought to be enrolled in a select number.

At what age?

At the age when the necessary gymnastics are over: the period whether of two or three years which passes in this sort of training is useless for any other purpose; for sleep and exercise are unpropitious to learning; and the trial of who is first in gymnastic exercises is one of the most important tests to which our youth are subjected.

Certainly, he replied.

After that time those who are selected from the class of twenty years old will be promoted to higher honour, and the sciences which they learned without any order in their early education will now be brought together, and they will be able to see the natural relationship of them to one another and to true being.

Yes, he said, that is the only kind of knowledge which takes lasting root.

Yes, I said; and the capacity for such knowledge is the great criterion of dialectical talent: the comprehensive mind is always the dialectical.

I agree with you, he said.

These, I said, are the points which you must consider; and those who have most of this comprehension, and who are most steadfast in their learning, and in their military and other appointed duties, when they have arrived at the age of thirty have to be chosen by you out of the select class, and elevated to higher honour; and you will have to prove them by the help of dialectic, in order to learn which of them is able to give up the use of sight and the other senses, and in company with truth to attain absolute being: And here, my friend, great caution is required.

Why great caution?

Do you not remark, I said, how great is the evil which dialectic has introduced?

What evil? he said.

The students of the art are filled with lawlessness.

Quite true, he said.

Do you think that there is anything so very unnatural or inexcusable in their case? or will you make allowance for them?

In what way make allowance?

I want you, I said, by way of parallel, to imagine a supposititious son who is brought up in great wealth; he is one of a great and numerous family, and has many flatterers. When he grows up to manhood, he learns that his alleged are not his real parents; but who the real are he is unable to discover. Can you guess how he will be likely to behave towards his flatterers and his supposed parents, first of all during the period when he is ignorant of the false relation, and then again when he knows? Or shall I guess for you?

If you please.

Then I should say, that while he is ignorant of the truth he will be likely to honour his father and his mother and his supposed relations more than the flatterers; he will be less inclined to neglect them when in need, or to do or say anything against them; and he will be less willing to disobey them in any important matter.

He will.

But when he has made the discovery, I should imagine that he would diminish his honour and regard for them, and would become more devoted to the flatterers; their influence over him would greatly increase; he would now live after their ways, and openly associate with them, and, unless he were of an unusually good disposition, he would trouble himself no more about his supposed parents or other relations.

Well, all that is very probable. But how is the image applicable to the disciples of philosophy?

In this way: you know that there are certain principles about justice and honour, which were taught us in childhood, and under their parental authority we have been brought up, obeying and honouring them.

That is true.

There are also opposite maxims and habits of pleasure which flatter and attract the soul, but do not influence those of us who have any sense of right, and they continue to obey and honour the maxims of their fathers.

True.

Now, when a man is in this state, and the questioning spirit asks what is fair or honourable, and he answers as the legislator has taught him, and then arguments many and diverse refute his words, until he is driven into believing that nothing is honourable any more than dishonourable, or just and good any more than the reverse, and so of all the notions which he most valued, do you think that he will still honour and obey them as before?

Impossible.

And when he ceases to think them honourable and natural as heretofore, and he fails to discover the true, can he be expected to pursue any life other than that which flatters his desires?

He cannot.

And from being a keeper of the law he is converted into a breaker of it?

Unquestionably.

Now all this is very natural in students of philosophy such as I have described, and also, as I was just now saying, most excusable.

Yes, he said; and, I may add, pitiable.

Therefore, that your feelings may not be moved to pity about our citizens who are now thirty years of age, every care must be taken in introducing them to dialectic.

Certainly.

There is a danger lest they should taste the dear delight too early; for youngsters, as you may have observed, when they first get the taste in their mouths, argue for amusement, and are always contradicting and refuting others in imitation of those who refute them; like puppy-dogs, they rejoice in pulling and tearing at all who come near them.

Yes, he said, there is nothing which they like better.

And when they have made many conquests and received defeats at the hands of many, they violently and speedily get into a way of not believing anything which they believed before, and hence, not only they, but philosophy and all that relates to it is apt to have a bad name with the rest of the world.

Too true, he said.

But when a man begins to get older, he will no longer be guilty of such insanity; he will imitate the dialectician who is seeking for truth, and not the eristic, who is contradicting for the sake of amusement; and the greater moderation of his character will increase instead of diminishing the honour of the pursuit.

Very true, he said.

And did we not make special provision for this, when we said that the disciples of philosophy were to be orderly and steadfast, not, as now, any chance aspirant or intruder?

Very true.

Suppose, I said, the study of philosophy to take the place of gymnastics and to be continued diligently and earnestly and exclusively for twice the number of years which were passed in bodily exercise – will that be enough?

Would you say six or four years? he asked.

Say five years, I replied; at the end of the time they must be sent down again into the den and compelled to hold any military or other office which young men are qualified to hold: in this way they will get their experience of life, and there will be an opportunity of trying whether, when they are drawn all manner of ways by temptation, they will stand firm or flinch.

And how long is this stage of their lives to last?

Fifteen years, I answered; and when they have reached fifty years of age, then let those who still survive and have distinguished themselves in every action of their lives and in every branch of knowledge come at last to their consummation: the time has now arrived at which they must raise the eye of the soul to the universal light which lightens all things, and behold the absolute good; for that is the pattern according to which they are to order the State and the lives of individuals, and the remainder of their own lives also; making philosophy their chief pursuit, but, when their turn comes, toiling also at politics and ruling for the public good, not as though they were performing some heroic action, but simply as a matter of duty; and when they have brought up in each generation others like themselves and left them in their place to be governors of the State, then they will depart to the Islands of the Blest and dwell there; and the city will give them public memorials and sacrifices and honour them, if the Pythian oracle consent, as demigods, but if not, as in any case blessed and divine.

You are a sculptor, Socrates, and have made statues of our governors faultless in beauty.

Yes, I said, Glaucon, and of our governesses too; for you must not suppose that what I have been saying applies to men only and not to women as far as their natures can go.

There you are right, he said, since we have made them to share in all things like the men.

Well, I said, and you would agree (would you not?) that what has been said about the State and the government is not a mere dream, and although difficult not impossible, but only possible in the way which has been supposed; that is to say, when the true philosopher kings are born in a State, one or more of them, despising the honours of this present world which they deem mean and worthless, esteeming above all things right and the honour that springs from right, and regarding justice as the greatest and most necessary of all things, whose ministers they are, and whose principles will be exalted by them when they set in order their own city?

How will they proceed?

They will begin by sending out into the country all the inhabitants of the city who are more than ten years old, and will take possession of their children, who will be unaffected by the habits of their parents; these they will train in their own habits and laws, I mean in the laws which we have given them: and in this way the State and constitution of which we were speaking will soonest and most easily attain happiness, and the nation which has such a constitution will gain most.

Yes, that will be the best way. And I think, Socrates, that you have very well described how, if ever, such a constitution might come into being.

Enough then of the perfect State, and of the man who bears its image – there is no difficulty in seeing how we shall describe him.

There is no difficulty, he replied; and I agree with you in thinking that nothing more need be said.

BOOK VIII.

And so, Glaucon, we have arrived at the conclusion that in the perfect State wives and children are to be in common; and that all education and the pursuits of war and peace are also to be common, and the best philosophers and the bravest warriors are to be their kings?

That, replied Glaucon, has been acknowledged.

Yes, I said; and we have further acknowledged that the governors, when appointed themselves, will take their soldiers and place them in houses such as we were describing, which are common to all, and contain nothing private, or individual; and about their property, you remember what we agreed?

Yes, I remember that no one was to have any of the ordinary possessions of mankind; they were to be warrior athletes and guardians, receiving from the other citizens, in lieu of annual payment, only their maintenance, and they were to take care of themselves and of the whole State.

True, I said; and now that this division of our task is concluded, let us find the point at which we digressed, that we may return into the old path.

There is no difficulty in returning; you implied, then as now, that you had finished the description of the State: you said that such a State was good, and that the man was good who answered to it, although, as now appears, you had more excellent things to relate both of State and man. And you said further, that if this was the true form, then the others were false; and of the false forms, you said, as I remember, that there were four principal ones, and that their defects, and the defects of the individuals corresponding to them, were worth examining. When we had seen all the individuals, and finally agreed as to who was the best and who was the worst of them, we were to consider whether the best was not also the happiest, and the worst the most miserable. I asked you what were the four forms of government of which you spoke, and then Polemarchus and Adeimantus put in their word; and you began again, and have found your way to the point at which we have now arrived.

Your recollection, I said, is most exact.

Then, like a wrestler, he replied, you must put yourself again in the same position; and let me ask the same questions, and do you give me the same answer which you were about to give me then.

Yes, if I can, I will, I said.

I shall particularly wish to hear what were the four constitutions of which you were speaking.

That question, I said, is easily answered: the four governments of which I spoke, so far as they have distinct names, are, first, those of Crete and Sparta, which are generally applauded; what is termed oligarchy comes next; this is not equally approved, and is a form of government which teems with evils: thirdly, democracy, which naturally follows oligarchy, although very different: and lastly comes tyranny, great and famous, which differs from them all, and is the fourth and worst disorder of a State. I do not know, do you? of any other constitution which can be said to have a distinct character. There are lordships and principalities which are bought and sold, and some other intermediate forms of government. But these are nondescripts and may be found equally among Hellenes and among barbarians.

Yes, he replied, we certainly hear of many curious forms of government which exist among them.

Do you know, I said, that governments vary as the dispositions of men vary, and that there must be as many of the one as there are of the other? For we cannot suppose that States are made of 'oak and rock,' and not out of the human natures which are in them, and which in a figure turn the scale and draw other things after them?

Yes, he said, the States are as the men are; they grow out of human characters.

Then if the constitutions of States are five, the dispositions of individual minds will also be five?

Certainly.

Him who answers to aristocracy, and whom we rightly call just and good, we have already described.

We have.

Then let us now proceed to describe the inferior sort of natures, being the contentious and ambitious, who answer to the Spartan polity; also the oligarchical, democratical, and tyrannical. Let us place the most just by the side of the most unjust, and when we see them we shall be able to compare the relative happiness or unhappiness of him who leads a life of pure justice or pure injustice. The enquiry will then be completed. And we shall know whether we ought to pursue injustice, as Thrasymachus advises, or in accordance with the conclusions of the argument to prefer justice.

Certainly, he replied, we must do as you say.

Shall we follow our old plan, which we adopted with a view to clearness, of taking the State first and then proceeding to the individual, and begin with the government of honour? – I know of no name for such a government other than timocracy, or perhaps timarchy. We will compare with this the like character in the individual; and, after that, consider oligarchy and the oligarchical man; and then again we will turn our attention to democracy and the democratical man; and lastly, we will go and view the city of tyranny, and once more take a look into the tyrant's soul, and try to arrive at a satisfactory decision.

That way of viewing and judging of the matter will be very suitable.

First, then, I said, let us enquire how timocracy (the government of honour) arises out of aristocracy (the government of the best). Clearly, all political changes originate in divisions of the actual governing power; a government which is united, however small, cannot be moved.

Very true, he said.

In what way, then, will our city be moved, and in what manner will the two classes of auxiliaries and rulers disagree among themselves or with one another? Shall we, after the manner of Homer, pray the Muses to tell us 'how discord first arose'? Shall we imagine them in solemn mockery, to play and jest with us as if we were children, and to address us in a lofty tragic vein, making believe to be in earnest?

How would they address us?

After this manner: – A city which is thus constituted can hardly be shaken; but, seeing that everything which has a beginning has also an end, even a constitution such as yours will not last for ever, but will in time be dissolved. And this is the dissolution: – In plants that grow in the earth, as well as in animals that move on the earth's surface, fertility and sterility of soul and body occur when the circumferences of the circles of each are completed, which in short-lived existences pass over a short space, and in long-lived ones over a long space. But to the knowledge of human fecundity and sterility all the wisdom and education of your rulers will not attain; the laws which regulate them will not be discovered by an intelligence which is alloyed with sense, but will escape them, and they will bring children into the world when they ought not. Now that which is of divine birth has a period which is contained in a perfect number (i.e. a cyclical number, such as 6, which is equal to the sum of its divisors 1, 2, 3, so that when the circle or time represented by 6 is completed, the lesser times or rotations represented by 1, 2, 3 are also completed.), but the period of human birth is comprehended in a number in which first increments by involution and evolution (or squared and cubed) obtaining three intervals and four terms of like and unlike, waxing and waning numbers, make all the terms commensurable and agreeable to one another. (Probably the numbers 3, 4, 5, 6 of which the three first = the sides of the Pythagorean triangle. The terms will then be 3 cubed, 4 cubed, 5 cubed, which together = 6 cubed = 216.) The base of these (3) with a third added (4) when combined with five (20) and raised to the third power furnishes two harmonies; the first a square which is a hundred times as great (400 = 4 x 100) (Or the first a square which is 100 x 100 = 10,000. The whole number will then be 17,500 = a square of 100, and an oblong of 100 by 75.), and the other a figure having one side equal to the former, but oblong, consisting of a hundred numbers squared upon rational diameters of a square (i.e. omitting fractions), the side of which is five (7 x 7 = 49 x 100 = 4900), each of them being less by one (than the perfect square which includes the fractions, sc. 50) or less by (Or, 'consisting of two numbers squared upon irrational diameters,' etc. = 100. For other explanations of the passage see Introduction.) two perfect squares of irrational diameters (of a square the side of which is five = 50 + 50 = 100); and a hundred cubes of three (27 x 100 = 2700 + 4900 + 400 = 8000). Now this number represents a geometrical figure which has control over the good and evil of births. For when your guardians are ignorant of the law of births, and unite bride and bridegroom out of season, the children will not be goodly or fortunate. And though only the best of them will be appointed by their predecessors, still they will be unworthy to hold their fathers' places, and when they come into power as guardians, they will soon be found to fail in taking care of us, the Muses, first by under-valuing music; which neglect will soon extend to gymnastic; and hence the young men of your State will be less cultivated. In the succeeding generation rulers will be appointed who have lost the guardian power of testing the metal of your different races, which, like Hesiod's, are of gold and silver and brass and iron. And so iron will be mingled with silver, and brass with gold, and hence there will arise dissimilarity and inequality and irregularity, which always and in all places are causes of hatred and war. This the Muses affirm to be the stock from which discord has sprung, wherever arising; and this is their answer to us.

Yes, and we may assume that they answer truly.

Why, yes, I said, of course they answer truly; how can the Muses speak falsely?

And what do the Muses say next?

When discord arose, then the two races were drawn different ways: the iron and brass fell to acquiring money and land and houses and gold and silver; but the gold and silver races, not wanting money but having the true riches in their own nature, inclined towards virtue and the ancient order of things. There was a battle between them, and at last they agreed to distribute their land and houses among individual owners; and they enslaved their friends and maintainers, whom they had formerly protected in the condition of freemen, and made of them subjects and servants; and they themselves were engaged in war and in keeping a watch against them.

I believe that you have rightly conceived the origin of the change.

And the new government which thus arises will be of a form intermediate between oligarchy and aristocracy?

Very true.

Such will be the change, and after the change has been made, how will they proceed? Clearly, the new State, being in a mean between oligarchy and the perfect State, will partly follow one and partly the other, and will also have some peculiarities.

True, he said.

In the honour given to rulers, in the abstinence of the warrior class from agriculture, handicrafts, and trade in general, in the institution of common meals, and in the attention paid to gymnastics and military training – in all these respects this State will resemble the former.

True.

But in the fear of admitting philosophers to power, because they are no longer to be had simple and earnest, but are made up of mixed elements; and in turning from them to passionate and less complex characters, who are by nature fitted for war rather than peace; and in the value set by them upon military stratagems and contrivances, and in the waging of everlasting wars – this State will be for the most part peculiar.

Yes.

Yes, I said; and men of this stamp will be covetous of money, like those who live in oligarchies; they will have, a fierce secret longing after gold and silver, which they will hoard in dark places, having magazines and treasuries of their own for the deposit and concealment of them; also castles which are just nests for their eggs, and in which they will spend large sums on their wives, or on any others whom they please.

That is most true, he said.

And they are miserly because they have no means of openly acquiring the money which they prize; they will spend that which is another man's on the gratification of their desires, stealing their pleasures and running away like children from the law, their father: they have been schooled not by gentle influences but by force, for they have neglected her who is the true Muse, the companion of reason and philosophy, and have honoured gymnastic more than music.

Undoubtedly, he said, the form of government which you describe is a mixture of good and evil.

Why, there is a mixture, I said; but one thing, and one thing only, is predominantly seen, – the spirit of contention and ambition; and these are due to the prevalence of the passionate or spirited element.

Assuredly, he said.

Such is the origin and such the character of this State, which has been described in outline only; the more perfect execution was not required, for a sketch is enough to show the type of the most perfectly just and most perfectly unjust; and to go through all the States and all the characters of men, omitting none of them, would be an interminable labour.

Very true, he replied.

Now what man answers to this form of government-how did he come into being, and what is he like?

I think, said Adeimantus, that in the spirit of contention which characterises him, he is not unlike our friend Glaucon.

Perhaps, I said, he may be like him in that one point; but there are other respects in which he is very different.

In what respects?

He should have more of self-assertion and be less cultivated, and yet a friend of culture; and he should be a good listener, but no speaker. Such a person is apt to be rough with slaves, unlike the educated man, who is too proud for that; and he will also be courteous to freemen, and remarkably obedient to authority; he is a lover of power and a lover of honour; claiming to be a ruler, not because he is eloquent, or on any ground of that sort, but because he is a soldier and has performed feats of arms; he is also a lover of gymnastic exercises and of the chase.

Yes, that is the type of character which answers to timocracy.

Such an one will despise riches only when he is young; but as he gets older he will be more and more attracted to them, because he has a piece of the avaricious nature in him, and is not single-minded towards virtue, having lost his best guardian.

Who was that? said Adeimantus.

Philosophy, I said, tempered with music, who comes and takes up her abode in a man, and is the only saviour of his virtue throughout life.

Good, he said.

Such, I said, is the timocratical youth, and he is like the timocratical State.

Exactly.

His origin is as follows: – He is often the young son of a brave father, who dwells in an ill-governed city, of which he declines the honours and offices, and will not go to law, or exert himself in any way, but is ready to waive his rights in order that he may escape trouble.

And how does the son come into being?

The character of the son begins to develope when he hears his mother complaining that her husband has no place in the government, of which the consequence is that she has no precedence among other women. Further, when she sees her husband not very eager about money, and instead of battling and railing in the law courts or assembly, taking whatever happens to him quietly; and when she observes that his thoughts always centre in himself, while he treats her with very considerable indifference, she is annoyed, and says to her son that his father is only half a man and far too easy-going: adding all the other complaints about her own ill-treatment which women are so fond of rehearsing.

Yes, said Adeimantus, they give us plenty of them, and their complaints are so like themselves.

And you know, I said, that the old servants also, who are supposed to be attached to the family, from time to time talk privately in the same strain to the son; and if they see any one who owes money to his father, or is wronging him in any way, and he fails to prosecute them, they tell the youth that when he grows up he must retaliate upon people of this sort, and be more of a man than his father. He has only to walk abroad and he hears and sees the same sort of thing: those who do their own business in the city are called simpletons, and held in no esteem, while the busy-bodies are honoured and applauded. The result is that the young man, hearing and seeing all these things – hearing, too, the words of his father, and having a nearer view of his way of life, and making comparisons of him and others – is drawn opposite ways: while his father is watering and nourishing the rational principle in his soul, the others are encouraging the passionate and appetitive; and he being not originally of a bad nature, but having kept bad company, is at last brought by their joint influence to a middle point, and gives up the kingdom which is within him to the middle principle of contentiousness and passion, and becomes arrogant and ambitious.

You seem to me to have described his origin perfectly.

Then we have now, I said, the second form of government and the second type of character?

We have.

Next, let us look at another man who, as Aeschylus says,

'Is set over against another State;'

or rather, as our plan requires, begin with the State.

By all means.

I believe that oligarchy follows next in order.

And what manner of government do you term oligarchy?

A government resting on a valuation of property, in which the rich have power and the poor man is deprived of it.

I understand, he replied.

Ought I not to begin by describing how the change from timocracy to oligarchy arises?

Yes.

Well, I said, no eyes are required in order to see how the one passes into the other.

How?

The accumulation of gold in the treasury of private individuals is the ruin of timocracy; they invent illegal modes of expenditure; for what do they or their wives care about the law?

Yes, indeed.

And then one, seeing another grow rich, seeks to rival him, and thus the great mass of the citizens become lovers of money.

Likely enough.

And so they grow richer and richer, and the more they think of making a fortune the less they think of virtue; for when riches and virtue are placed together in the scales of the balance, the one always rises as the other falls.

True.

And in proportion as riches and rich men are honoured in the State, virtue and the virtuous are dishonoured.

Clearly.

And what is honoured is cultivated, and that which has no honour is neglected.

That is obvious.

And so at last, instead of loving contention and glory, men become lovers of trade and money; they honour and look up to the rich man, and make a ruler of him, and dishonour the poor man.

They do so.

They next proceed to make a law which fixes a sum of money as the qualification of citizenship; the sum is higher in one place and lower in another, as the oligarchy is more or less exclusive; and they allow no one whose property falls below the amount fixed to have any share in the government. These changes in the constitution they effect by force of arms, if intimidation has not already done their work.

Very true.

And this, speaking generally, is the way in which oligarchy is established.

Yes, he said; but what are the characteristics of this form of government, and what are the defects of which we were speaking?

First of all, I said, consider the nature of the qualification. Just think what would happen if pilots were to be chosen according to their property, and a poor man were refused permission to steer, even though he were a better pilot?

You mean that they would shipwreck?

Yes; and is not this true of the government of anything?

I should imagine so.

Except a city? – or would you include a city?

Nay, he said, the case of a city is the strongest of all, inasmuch as the rule of a city is the greatest and most difficult of all.

This, then, will be the first great defect of oligarchy?

Clearly.

And here is another defect which is quite as bad.

What defect?

The inevitable division: such a State is not one, but two States, the one of poor, the other of rich men; and they are living on the same spot and always conspiring against one another.

That, surely, is at least as bad.

Another discreditable feature is, that, for a like reason, they are incapable of carrying on any war. Either they arm the multitude, and then they are more afraid of them than of the enemy; or, if they do not call them out in the hour of battle, they are oligarchs indeed, few to fight as they are few to rule. And at the same time their fondness for money makes them unwilling to pay taxes.

How discreditable!

And, as we said before, under such a constitution the same persons have too many callings – they are husbandmen, tradesmen, warriors, all in one. Does that look well?

Anything but well.

There is another evil which is, perhaps, the greatest of all, and to which this State first begins to be liable.

What evil?

A man may sell all that he has, and another may acquire his property; yet after the sale he may dwell in the city of which he is no longer a part, being neither trader, nor artisan, nor horseman, nor hoplite, but only a poor, helpless creature.

Yes, that is an evil which also first begins in this State.

The evil is certainly not prevented there; for oligarchies have both the extremes of great wealth and utter poverty.

True.

But think again: In his wealthy days, while he was spending his money, was a man of this sort a whit more good to the State for the purposes of citizenship? Or did he only seem to be a member of the ruling body, although in truth he was neither ruler nor subject, but just a spendthrift?

As you say, he seemed to be a ruler, but was only a spendthrift.

May we not say that this is the drone in the house who is like the drone in the honeycomb, and that the one is the plague of the city as the other is of the hive?

Just so, Socrates.

And God has made the flying drones, Adeimantus, all without stings, whereas of the walking drones he has made some without stings but others have dreadful stings; of the stingless class are those who in their old age end as paupers; of the stingers come all the criminal class, as they are termed.

Most true, he said.

Clearly then, whenever you see paupers in a State, somewhere in that neighborhood there are hidden away thieves, and cut-purses and robbers of temples, and all sorts of malefactors.

Clearly.

Well, I said, and in oligarchical States do you not find paupers?

Yes, he said; nearly everybody is a pauper who is not a ruler.

And may we be so bold as to affirm that there are also many criminals to be found in them, rogues who have stings, and whom the authorities are careful to restrain by force?

Certainly, we may be so bold.

The existence of such persons is to be attributed to want of education, ill-training, and an evil constitution of the State?

True.

Such, then, is the form and such are the evils of oligarchy; and there may be many other evils.

Very likely.

Then oligarchy, or the form of government in which the rulers are elected for their wealth, may now be dismissed. Let us next proceed to consider the nature and origin of the individual who answers to this State.

By all means.

Does not the timocratical man change into the oligarchical on this wise?

How?

A time arrives when the representative of timocracy has a son: at first he begins by emulating his father and walking in his footsteps, but presently he sees him of a sudden foundering against the State as upon a sunken reef, and he and all that he has is lost; he may have been a general or some other high officer who is brought to trial under a prejudice raised by informers, and either put to death, or exiled, or deprived of the privileges of a citizen, and all his property taken from him.

Nothing more likely.

And the son has seen and known all this – he is a ruined man, and his fear has taught him to knock ambition and passion headforemost from his bosom's throne; humbled by poverty he takes to money-making and by mean and miserly savings and hard work gets a fortune together. Is not such an one likely to seat the concupiscent and covetous element on the vacant throne and to suffer it to play the great king within him, girt with tiara and chain and scimitar?

Most true, he replied.

And when he has made reason and spirit sit down on the ground obediently on either side of their sovereign, and taught them to know their place, he compels the one to think only of how lesser sums may be turned into larger ones, and will not allow the other to worship and admire anything but riches and rich men, or to be ambitious of anything so much as the acquisition of wealth and the means of acquiring it.

Of all changes, he said, there is none so speedy or so sure as the conversion of the ambitious youth into the avaricious one.

And the avaricious, I said, is the oligarchical youth?

Yes, he said; at any rate the individual out of whom he came is like the State out of which oligarchy came.

Let us then consider whether there is any likeness between them.

Very good.

First, then, they resemble one another in the value which they set upon wealth?

Certainly.

Also in their penurious, laborious character; the individual only satisfies his necessary appetites, and confines his expenditure to them; his other desires he subdues, under the idea that they are unprofitable.

True.

He is a shabby fellow, who saves something out of everything and makes a purse for himself; and this is the sort of man whom the vulgar applaud. Is he not a true image of the State which he represents?

He appears to me to be so; at any rate money is highly valued by him as well as by the State.

You see that he is not a man of cultivation, I said.

I imagine not, he said; had he been educated he would never have made a blind god director of his chorus, or given him chief honour.

Excellent! I said. Yet consider: Must we not further admit that owing to this want of cultivation there will be found in him dronelike desires as of pauper and rogue, which are forcibly kept down by his general habit of life?

True.

Do you know where you will have to look if you want to discover his rogueries?

Where must I look?

You should see him where he has some great opportunity of acting dishonestly, as in the guardianship of an orphan.

Aye.

It will be clear enough then that in his ordinary dealings which give him a reputation for honesty he coerces his bad passions by an enforced virtue; not making them see that they are wrong, or taming them by reason, but by necessity and fear constraining them, and because he trembles for his possessions.

To be sure.

Yes, indeed, my dear friend, but you will find that the natural desires of the drone commonly exist in him all the same whenever he has to spend what is not his own.

Yes, and they will be strong in him too.

The man, then, will be at war with himself; he will be two men, and not one; but, in general, his better desires will be found to prevail over his inferior ones.

True.

For these reasons such an one will be more respectable than most people; yet the true virtue of a unanimous and harmonious soul will flee far away and never come near him.

I should expect so.

And surely, the miser individually will be an ignoble competitor in a State for any prize of victory, or other object of honourable ambition; he will not spend his money in the contest for glory; so afraid is he of awakening his expensive appetites and inviting them to help and join in the struggle; in true oligarchical fashion he fights with a small part only of his resources, and the result commonly is that he loses the prize and saves his money.

Very true.

Can we any longer doubt, then, that the miser and money-maker answers to the oligarchical State?

There can be no doubt.

Next comes democracy; of this the origin and nature have still to be considered by us; and then we will enquire into the ways of the democratic man, and bring him up for judgment.

That, he said, is our method.

Well, I said, and how does the change from oligarchy into democracy arise? Is it not on this wise? – The good at which such a State aims is to become as rich as possible, a desire which is insatiable?

What then?

The rulers, being aware that their power rests upon their wealth, refuse to curtail by law the extravagance of the spendthrift youth because they gain by their ruin; they take interest from them and buy up their estates and thus increase their own wealth and importance?

To be sure.

There can be no doubt that the love of wealth and the spirit of moderation cannot exist together in citizens of the same state to any considerable extent; one or the other will be disregarded.

That is tolerably clear.

And in oligarchical States, from the general spread of carelessness and extravagance, men of good family have often been reduced to beggary?

Yes, often.

And still they remain in the city; there they are, ready to sting and fully armed, and some of them owe money, some have forfeited their

485 | P a g e

citizenship; a third class are in both predicaments; and they hate and conspire against those who have got their property, and against everybody else, and are eager for revolution.

That is true.

On the other hand, the men of business, stooping as they walk, and pretending not even to see those whom they have already ruined, insert their sting – that is, their money – into some one else who is not on his guard against them, and recover the parent sum many times over multiplied into a family of children: and so they make drone and pauper to abound in the State.

Yes, he said, there are plenty of them – that is certain.

The evil blazes up like a fire; and they will not extinguish it, either by restricting a man's use of his own property, or by another remedy:

What other?

One which is the next best, and has the advantage of compelling the citizens to look to their characters: – Let there be a general rule that every one shall enter into voluntary contracts at his own risk, and there will be less of this scandalous money-making, and the evils of which we were speaking will be greatly lessened in the State.

Yes, they will be greatly lessened.

At present the governors, induced by the motives which I have named, treat their subjects badly; while they and their adherents, especially the young men of the governing class, are habituated to lead a life of luxury and idleness both of body and mind; they do nothing, and are incapable of resisting either pleasure or pain.

Very true.

They themselves care only for making money, and are as indifferent as the pauper to the cultivation of virtue.

Yes, quite as indifferent.

Such is the state of affairs which prevails among them. And often rulers and their subjects may come in one another's way, whether on a journey or on some other occasion of meeting, on a pilgrimage or a march, as fellow-soldiers or fellow-sailors; aye and they may observe the behaviour of each other in the very moment of danger – for where danger is, there is no fear that the poor will be despised by the rich – and very likely the wiry sunburnt poor man may be placed in battle at the side of a wealthy one who has never spoilt his complexion and has plenty of superfluous flesh – when he sees such an one puffing and at his wits'-end, how can he avoid drawing the conclusion that men like him are only rich because no one has the courage to despoil them? And when they meet in private will not people be saying to one another 'Our warriors are not good for much'?

Yes, he said, I am quite aware that this is their way of talking.

And, as in a body which is diseased the addition of a touch from without may bring on illness, and sometimes even when there is no external provocation a commotion may arise within – in the same way wherever there is weakness in the State there is also likely to be illness, of which the occasion may be very slight, the one party introducing from without their oligarchical, the other their democratical allies, and then the State falls sick, and is at war with herself; and may be at times distracted, even when there is no external cause.

Yes, surely.

And then democracy comes into being after the poor have conquered their opponents, slaughtering some and banishing some, while to the remainder they give an equal share of freedom and power; and this is the form of government in which the magistrates are commonly elected by lot.

Yes, he said, that is the nature of democracy, whether the revolution has been effected by arms, or whether fear has caused the opposite party to withdraw.

And now what is their manner of life, and what sort of a government have they? for as the government is, such will be the man.

Clearly, he said.

In the first place, are they not free; and is not the city full of freedom and frankness – a man may say and do what he likes?

'Tis said so, he replied.

And where freedom is, the individual is clearly able to order for himself his own life as he pleases?

Clearly.

Then in this kind of State there will be the greatest variety of human natures?

There will.

This, then, seems likely to be the fairest of States, being like an embroidered robe which is spangled with every sort of flower. And just as women and children think a variety of colours to be of all things most charming, so there are many men to whom this State, which is spangled with the manners and characters of mankind, will appear to be the fairest of States.

Yes.

Yes, my good Sir, and there will be no better in which to look for a government.

Why?

Because of the liberty which reigns there – they have a complete assortment of constitutions; and he who has a mind to establish a State, as we have been doing, must go to a democracy as he would to a bazaar at which they sell them, and pick out the one that suits him; then, when he has made his choice, he may found his State.

He will be sure to have patterns enough.

And there being no necessity, I said, for you to govern in this State, even if you have the capacity, or to be governed, unless you like, or go to war when the rest go to war, or to be at peace when others are at peace, unless you are so disposed – there being no necessity also, because some law forbids you to hold office or be a dicast, that you should not hold office or be a dicast, if you have a fancy – is not this a way of life which for the moment is supremely delightful?

For the moment, yes.

And is not their humanity to the condemned in some cases quite charming? Have you not observed how, in a democracy, many persons, although they have been sentenced to death or exile, just stay where they are and walk about the world – the gentleman parades like a hero, and nobody sees or cares?

Yes, he replied, many and many a one.

See too, I said, the forgiving spirit of democracy, and the 'don't care' about trifles, and the disregard which she shows of all the fine principles which we solemnly laid down at the foundation of the city – as when we said that, except in the case of some rarely gifted nature, there never will be a good man who has not from his childhood been used to play amid things of beauty and make of them a joy and a study – how grandly does she trample all these fine notions of ours under her feet, never giving a thought to the pursuits which make a statesman, and promoting to honour any one who professes to be the people's friend.

Yes, she is of a noble spirit.

These and other kindred characteristics are proper to democracy, which is a charming form of government, full of variety and disorder, and dispensing a sort of equality to equals and unequals alike.

We know her well.

Consider now, I said, what manner of man the individual is, or rather consider, as in the case of the State, how he comes into being.

Very good, he said.

Is not this the way – he is the son of the miserly and oligarchical father who has trained him in his own habits?

Exactly.

And, like his father, he keeps under by force the pleasures which are of the spending and not of the getting sort, being those which are called unnecessary?

Obviously.

Would you like, for the sake of clearness, to distinguish which are the necessary and which are the unnecessary pleasures?

I should.

Are not necessary pleasures those of which we cannot get rid, and of which the satisfaction is a benefit to us? And they are rightly called so, because we are framed by nature to desire both what is beneficial and what is necessary, and cannot help it.

True.

We are not wrong therefore in calling them necessary?

We are not.

And the desires of which a man may get rid, if he takes pains from his youth upwards – of which the presence, moreover, does no good, and in some cases the reverse of good – shall we not be right in saying that all these are unnecessary?

Yes, certainly.

Suppose we select an example of either kind, in order that we may have a general notion of them?

Very good.

Will not the desire of eating, that is, of simple food and condiments, in so far as they are required for health and strength, be of the necessary class?

That is what I should suppose.

The pleasure of eating is necessary in two ways; it does us good and it is essential to the continuance of life?

Yes.

But the condiments are only necessary in so far as they are good for health?

Certainly.

And the desire which goes beyond this, of more delicate food, or other luxuries, which might generally be got rid of, if controlled and trained in youth, and is hurtful to the body, and hurtful to the soul in the pursuit of wisdom and virtue, may be rightly called unnecessary?

Very true.

May we not say that these desires spend, and that the others make money because they conduce to production?

Certainly.

And of the pleasures of love, and all other pleasures, the same holds good?

True.

And the drone of whom we spoke was he who was surfeited in pleasures and desires of this sort, and was the slave of the unnecessary desires, whereas he who was subject to the necessary only was miserly and oligarchical?

Very true.

Again, let us see how the democratical man grows out of the oligarchical: the following, as I suspect, is commonly the process.

What is the process?

When a young man who has been brought up as we were just now describing, in a vulgar and miserly way, has tasted drones' honey and has come to associate with fierce and crafty natures who are able to provide for him all sorts of refinements and varieties of pleasure – then, as you may imagine, the change will begin of the oligarchical principle within him into the democratical?

Inevitably.

And as in the city like was helping like, and the change was effected by an alliance from without assisting one division of the citizens, so too the young man is changed by a class of desires coming from without to assist the desires within him, that which is akin and alike again helping that which is akin and alike?

Certainly.

And if there be any ally which aids the oligarchical principle within him, whether the influence of a father or of kindred, advising or rebuking him, then there arises in his soul a faction and an opposite faction, and he goes to war with himself.

It must be so.

And there are times when the democratical principle gives way to the oligarchical, and some of his desires die, and others are banished; a spirit of reverence enters into the young man's soul and order is restored.

Yes, he said, that sometimes happens.

And then, again, after the old desires have been driven out, fresh ones spring up, which are akin to them, and because he their father does not know how to educate them, wax fierce and numerous.

Yes, he said, that is apt to be the way.

They draw him to his old associates, and holding secret intercourse with them, breed and multiply in him.

Very true.

At length they seize upon the citadel of the young man's soul, which they perceive to be void of all accomplishments and fair pursuits and true words, which make their abode in the minds of men who are dear to the gods, and are their best guardians and sentinels.

None better.

False and boastful conceits and phrases mount upwards and take their place.

They are certain to do so.

And so the young man returns into the country of the lotus-eaters, and takes up his dwelling there in the face of all men; and if any help be sent by his friends to the oligarchical part of him, the aforesaid vain conceits shut the gate of the king's fastness; and they will neither allow the embassy itself to enter, nor if private advisers offer the fatherly counsel of the aged will they listen to them or receive them. There is a battle and they gain the day, and then modesty, which they call silliness, is ignominiously thrust into exile by them, and temperance, which they nickname unmanliness, is trampled in the mire and cast forth; they persuade men that moderation and orderly expenditure are vulgarity and meanness, and so, by the help of a rabble of evil appetites, they drive them beyond the border.

Yes, with a will.

And when they have emptied and swept clean the soul of him who is now in their power and who is being initiated by them in great mysteries, the next thing is to bring back to their house insolence and anarchy and waste and impudence in bright array having garlands on their heads, and a great company with them, hymning their praises and calling them by sweet names; insolence they term breeding, and anarchy liberty, and waste magnificence, and impudence courage. And so the young man passes out of his original nature, which was trained in the school of necessity, into the freedom and libertinism of useless and unnecessary pleasures.

Yes, he said, the change in him is visible enough.

After this he lives on, spending his money and labour and time on unnecessary pleasures quite as much as on necessary ones; but if he be fortunate, and is not too much disordered in his wits, when years have elapsed, and the heyday of passion is over – supposing that he then re-admits into the city some part of the exiled virtues, and does not wholly give himself up to their successors – in that case he balances his pleasures and lives in a sort of equilibrium, putting the government of himself into the hands of the one which comes first and wins the turn; and when he has had enough of that, then into the hands of another; he despises none of them but encourages them all equally.

Very true, he said.

Neither does he receive or let pass into the fortress any true word of advice; if any one says to him that some pleasures are the satisfactions of good and noble desires, and others of evil desires, and that he ought to use and honour some and chastise and master the others – whenever this is repeated to him he shakes his head and says that they are all alike, and that one is as good as another.

Yes, he said; that is the way with him.

Yes, I said, he lives from day to day indulging the appetite of the hour; and sometimes he is lapped in drink and strains of the flute; then he becomes a water-drinker, and tries to get thin; then he takes a turn at gymnastics; sometimes idling and neglecting everything, then once more living the life of a philosopher; often he is busy with politics, and starts to his feet and says and does whatever comes into his head; and, if he is emulous of any one who is a warrior, off he is in that direction, or of men of business, once more in that. His life has neither law nor order; and this distracted existence he terms joy and bliss and freedom; and so he goes on.

Yes, he replied, he is all liberty and equality.

Yes, I said; his life is motley and manifold and an epitome of the lives of many; − he answers to the State which we described as fair and spangled. And many a man and many a woman will take him for their pattern, and many a constitution and many an example of manners is contained in him.

Just so.

Let him then be set over against democracy; he may truly be called the democratic man.

Let that be his place, he said.

Last of all comes the most beautiful of all, man and State alike, tyranny and the tyrant; these we have now to consider.

Quite true, he said.

Say then, my friend, In what manner does tyranny arise? − that it has a democratic origin is evident.

Clearly.

And does not tyranny spring from democracy in the same manner as democracy from oligarchy − I mean, after a sort?

How?

The good which oligarchy proposed to itself and the means by which it was maintained was excess of wealth − am I not right?

Yes.

THE REPUBLIC

And the insatiable desire of wealth and the neglect of all other things for the sake of money-getting was also the ruin of oligarchy?

True.

And democracy has her own good, of which the insatiable desire brings her to dissolution?

What good?

Freedom, I replied; which, as they tell you in a democracy, is the glory of the State – and that therefore in a democracy alone will the freeman of nature deign to dwell.

Yes; the saying is in every body's mouth.

I was going to observe, that the insatiable desire of this and the neglect of other things introduces the change in democracy, which occasions a demand for tyranny.

How so?

When a democracy which is thirsting for freedom has evil cup-bearers presiding over the feast, and has drunk too deeply of the strong wine of freedom, then, unless her rulers are very amenable and give a plentiful draught, she calls them to account and punishes them, and says that they are cursed oligarchs.

Yes, he replied, a very common occurrence.

Yes, I said; and loyal citizens are insultingly termed by her slaves who hug their chains and men of naught; she would have subjects who are like rulers, and rulers who are like subjects: these are men after her own heart, whom she praises and honours both in private and public. Now, in such a State, can liberty have any limit?

Certainly not.

By degrees the anarchy finds a way into private houses, and ends by getting among the animals and infecting them.

How do you mean?

I mean that the father grows accustomed to descend to the level of his sons and to fear them, and the son is on a level with his father, he having no respect or reverence for either of his parents; and this is his freedom, and the metic is equal with the citizen and the citizen with the metic, and the stranger is quite as good as either.

Yes, he said, that is the way.

And these are not the only evils, I said – there are several lesser ones: In such a state of society the master fears and flatters his scholars, and the scholars despise their masters and tutors; young and old are all alike; and the young man is on a level with the old, and is ready to compete with him in word or deed; and old men condescend to the young and are full of pleasantry and gaiety; they are loth to be thought morose and authoritative, and therefore they adopt the manners of the young.

Quite true, he said.

The last extreme of popular liberty is when the slave bought with money, whether male or female, is just as free as his or her purchaser; nor must I forget to tell of the liberty and equality of the two sexes in relation to each other.

Why not, as Aeschylus says, utter the word which rises to our lips?

That is what I am doing, I replied; and I must add that no one who does not know would believe, how much greater is the liberty which the animals who are under the dominion of man have in a democracy than in any other State: for truly, the she-dogs, as the proverb says, are as good as their she-mistresses, and the horses and asses have a way of marching along with all the rights and dignities of freemen; and they will run at any body who comes in their way if he does not leave the road clear for them: and all things are just ready to burst with liberty.

When I take a country walk, he said, I often experience what you describe. You and I have dreamed the same thing.

And above all, I said, and as the result of all, see how sensitive the citizens become; they chafe impatiently at the least touch of authority, and at length, as you know, they cease to care even for the laws, written or unwritten; they will have no one over them.

Yes, he said, I know it too well.

Such, my friend, I said, is the fair and glorious beginning out of which springs tyranny.

Glorious indeed, he said. But what is the next step?

The ruin of oligarchy is the ruin of democracy; the same disease magnified and intensified by liberty overmasters democracy – the truth being that the excessive increase of anything often causes a reaction in the opposite direction; and this is the case not only in the seasons and in vegetable and animal life, but above all in forms of government.

True.

The excess of liberty, whether in States or individuals, seems only to pass into excess of slavery.

Yes, the natural order.

And so tyranny naturally arises out of democracy, and the most aggravated form of tyranny and slavery out of the most extreme form of liberty?

As we might expect.

That, however, was not, as I believe, your question – you rather desired to know what is that disorder which is generated alike in oligarchy and democracy, and is the ruin of both?

Just so, he replied.

Well, I said, I meant to refer to the class of idle spendthrifts, of whom the more courageous are the leaders and the more timid the followers, the same whom we were comparing to drones, some stingless, and others having stings.

A very just comparison.

These two classes are the plagues of every city in which they are generated, being what phlegm and bile are to the body. And the good physician and lawgiver of the State ought, like the wise bee-master, to keep them at a distance and prevent, if possible, their ever coming in; and if they have anyhow found a way in, then he should have them and their cells cut out as speedily as possible.

Yes, by all means, he said.

Then, in order that we may see clearly what we are doing, let us imagine democracy to be divided, as indeed it is, into three classes; for in the first place freedom creates rather more drones in the democratic than there were in the oligarchical State.

That is true.

And in the democracy they are certainly more intensified.

How so?

Because in the oligarchical State they are disqualified and driven from office, and therefore they cannot train or gather strength; whereas in a democracy they are almost the entire ruling power, and while the keener sort speak and act, the rest keep buzzing about the bema and do not suffer a word to be said on the other side; hence in democracies almost everything is managed by the drones.

Very true, he said.

Then there is another class which is always being severed from the mass.

What is that?

They are the orderly class, which in a nation of traders is sure to be the richest.

Naturally so.

They are the most squeezable persons and yield the largest amount of honey to the drones.

Why, he said, there is little to be squeezed out of people who have little.

And this is called the wealthy class, and the drones feed upon them.

That is pretty much the case, he said.

The people are a third class, consisting of those who work with their own hands; they are not politicians, and have not much to live upon. This, when assembled, is the largest and most powerful class in a democracy.

True, he said; but then the multitude is seldom willing to congregate unless they get a little honey.

And do they not share? I said. Do not their leaders deprive the rich of their estates and distribute them among the people; at the same time taking care to reserve the larger part for themselves?

Why, yes, he said, to that extent the people do share.

And the persons whose property is taken from them are compelled to defend themselves before the people as they best can?

What else can they do?

And then, although they may have no desire of change, the others charge them with plotting against the people and being friends of oligarchy?

True.

And the end is that when they see the people, not of their own accord, but through ignorance, and because they are deceived by informers, seeking to do them wrong, then at last they are forced to become oligarchs in reality; they do not wish to be, but the sting of the drones torments them and breeds revolution in them.

That is exactly the truth.

Then come impeachments and judgments and trials of one another.

True.

The people have always some champion whom they set over them and nurse into greatness.

Yes, that is their way.

This and no other is the root from which a tyrant springs; when he first appears above ground he is a protector.

Yes, that is quite clear.

How then does a protector begin to change into a tyrant? Clearly when he does what the man is said to do in the tale of the Arcadian temple of Lycaean Zeus.

What tale?

The tale is that he who has tasted the entrails of a single human victim minced up with the entrails of other victims is destined to become a wolf. Did you never hear it?

Oh, yes.

And the protector of the people is like him; having a mob entirely at his disposal, he is not restrained from shedding the blood of kinsmen; by the favourite method of false accusation he brings them into court and murders them, making the life of man to disappear, and with unholy tongue and lips tasting the blood of his fellow citizens; some he kills and others he banishes, at the same time hinting at the abolition of debts and partition of lands: and after this, what will be his destiny? Must he not either perish at the hands of his enemies, or from being a man become a wolf – that is, a tyrant?

Inevitably.

This, I said, is he who begins to make a party against the rich?

The same.

After a while he is driven out, but comes back, in spite of his enemies, a tyrant full grown.

That is clear.

And if they are unable to expel him, or to get him condemned to death by a public accusation, they conspire to assassinate him.

Yes, he said, that is their usual way.

Then comes the famous request for a body-guard, which is the device of all those who have got thus far in their tyrannical career – 'Let not the people's friend,' as they say, 'be lost to them.'

Exactly.

The people readily assent; all their fears are for him – they have none for themselves.

Very true.

And when a man who is wealthy and is also accused of being an enemy of the people sees this, then, my friend, as the oracle said to Croesus,

'By pebbly Hermus' shore he flees and rests not, and is not ashamed to be a coward.'

And quite right too, said he, for if he were, he would never be ashamed again.

But if he is caught he dies.

Of course.

And he, the protector of whom we spoke, is to be seen, not 'larding the plain' with his bulk, but himself the overthrower of many, standing up in the chariot of State with the reins in his hand, no longer protector, but tyrant absolute.

No doubt, he said.

And now let us consider the happiness of the man, and also of the State in which a creature like him is generated.

Yes, he said, let us consider that.

At first, in the early days of his power, he is full of smiles, and he salutes every one whom he meets; – he to be called a tyrant, who is making promises in public and also in private! liberating debtors, and distributing land to the people and his followers, and wanting to be so kind and good to every one!

Of course, he said.

But when he has disposed of foreign enemies by conquest or treaty, and there is nothing to fear from them, then he is always stirring up some war or other, in order that the people may require a leader.

To be sure.

Has he not also another object, which is that they may be impoverished by payment of taxes, and thus compelled to devote themselves to their daily wants and therefore less likely to conspire against him?

Clearly.

And if any of them are suspected by him of having notions of freedom, and of resistance to his authority, he will have a good pretext for destroying them by placing them at the mercy of the enemy; and for all these reasons the tyrant must be always getting up a war.

He must.

Now he begins to grow unpopular.

A necessary result.

Then some of those who joined in setting him up, and who are in power, speak their minds to him and to one another, and the more courageous of them cast in his teeth what is being done.

Yes, that may be expected.

And the tyrant, if he means to rule, must get rid of them; he cannot stop while he has a friend or an enemy who is good for anything.

He cannot.

And therefore he must look about him and see who is valiant, who is high-minded, who is wise, who is wealthy; happy man, he is the enemy of them all, and must seek occasion against them whether he will or no, until he has made a purgation of the State.

Yes, he said, and a rare purgation.

Yes, I said, not the sort of purgation which the physicians make of the body; for they take away the worse and leave the better part, but he does the reverse.

If he is to rule, I suppose that he cannot help himself.

What a blessed alternative, I said: – to be compelled to dwell only with the many bad, and to be by them hated, or not to live at all!

Yes, that is the alternative.

And the more detestable his actions are to the citizens the more satellites and the greater devotion in them will he require?

Certainly.

And who are the devoted band, and where will he procure them?

They will flock to him, he said, of their own accord, if he pays them.

By the dog! I said, here are more drones, of every sort and from every land.

Yes, he said, there are.

But will he not desire to get them on the spot?

How do you mean?

He will rob the citizens of their slaves; he will then set them free and enrol them in his body-guard.

To be sure, he said; and he will be able to trust them best of all.

What a blessed creature, I said, must this tyrant be; he has put to death the others and has these for his trusted friends.

Yes, he said; they are quite of his sort.

Yes, I said, and these are the new citizens whom he has called into existence, who admire him and are his companions, while the good hate and avoid him.

Of course.

Verily, then, tragedy is a wise thing and Euripides a great tragedian.

Why so?

Why, because he is the author of the pregnant saying,

'Tyrants are wise by living with the wise;'

and he clearly meant to say that they are the wise whom the tyrant makes his companions.

Yes, he said, and he also praises tyranny as godlike; and many other things of the same kind are said by him and by the other poets.

And therefore, I said, the tragic poets being wise men will forgive us and any others who live after our manner if we do not receive them into our State, because they are the eulogists of tyranny.

Yes, he said, those who have the wit will doubtless forgive us.

But they will continue to go to other cities and attract mobs, and hire voices fair and loud and persuasive, and draw the cities over to tyrannies and democracies.

Very true.

Moreover, they are paid for this and receive honour – the greatest honour, as might be expected, from tyrants, and the next greatest from democracies; but the higher they ascend our constitution hill, the more their reputation fails, and seems unable from shortness of breath to proceed further.

True.

But we are wandering from the subject: Let us therefore return and enquire how the tyrant will maintain that fair and numerous and various and ever-changing army of his.

If, he said, there are sacred treasures in the city, he will confiscate and spend them; and in so far as the fortunes of attainted persons may suffice, he will be able to diminish the taxes which he would otherwise have to impose upon the people.

And when these fail?

Why, clearly, he said, then he and his boon companions, whether male or female, will be maintained out of his father's estate.

You mean to say that the people, from whom he has derived his being, will maintain him and his companions?

Yes, he said; they cannot help themselves.

But what if the people fly into a passion, and aver that a grown-up son ought not to be supported by his father, but that the father should be supported by the son? The father did not bring him into being, or settle him in life, in order that when his son became a man he should himself be the servant of his own servants and should support him and his rabble of slaves and companions; but that his son should protect him, and that by his help he might be emancipated from the government of the rich and aristocratic, as they are termed. And so he bids him and his companions depart, just as any other father might drive out of the house a riotous son and his undesirable associates.

By heaven, he said, then the parent will discover what a monster he has been fostering in his bosom; and, when he wants to drive him out, he will find that he is weak and his son strong.

Why, you do not mean to say that the tyrant will use violence? What! beat his father if he opposes him?

Yes, he will, having first disarmed him.

Then he is a parricide, and a cruel guardian of an aged parent; and this is real tyranny, about which there can be no longer a mistake: as the saying is, the people who would escape the smoke which is the slavery of freemen, has fallen into the fire which is the tyranny of slaves. Thus liberty, getting out of all order and reason, passes into the harshest and bitterest form of slavery.

True, he said.

Very well; and may we not rightly say that we have sufficiently discussed the nature of tyranny, and the manner of the transition from democracy to tyranny?

Yes, quite enough, he said.

BOOK IX.

Last of all comes the tyrannical man; about whom we have once more to ask, how is he formed out of the democratical? and how does he live, in happiness or in misery?

Yes, he said, he is the only one remaining.

There is, however, I said, a previous question which remains unanswered.

What question?

I do not think that we have adequately determined the nature and number of the appetites, and until this is accomplished the enquiry will always be confused.

Well, he said, it is not too late to supply the omission.

Very true, I said; and observe the point which I want to understand: Certain of the unnecessary pleasures and appetites I conceive to be unlawful; every one appears to have them, but in some persons they are controlled by the laws and by reason, and the better desires prevail over them – either they are wholly banished or they become few and weak; while in the case of others they are stronger, and there are more of them.

Which appetites do you mean?

I mean those which are awake when the reasoning and human and ruling power is asleep; then the wild beast within us, gorged with meat or drink, starts up and having shaken off sleep, goes forth to satisfy his desires; and there is no conceivable folly or crime – not excepting incest or any other unnatural union, or parricide, or the eating of forbidden food – which at such a time, when he has parted company with all shame and sense, a man may not be ready to commit.

Most true, he said.

But when a man's pulse is healthy and temperate, and when before going to sleep he has awakened his rational powers, and fed them on noble thoughts and enquiries, collecting himself in meditation; after having first indulged his appetites neither too much nor too little, but just enough to lay them to sleep, and prevent them and their enjoyments and pains from interfering with the higher principle – which he leaves in the solitude of pure abstraction, free to contemplate and aspire to the knowledge of the unknown, whether in past, present, or future: when again he has allayed the passionate element, if he has a quarrel against any one – I say, when, after pacifying the two irrational principles, he rouses up the third, which is reason, before he takes his rest, then, as you know, he attains truth most nearly, and is least likely to be the sport of fantastic and lawless visions.

I quite agree.

In saying this I have been running into a digression; but the point which I desire to note is that in all of us, even in good men, there is a lawless wild-beast nature, which peers out in sleep. Pray, consider whether I am right, and you agree with me.

Yes, I agree.

And now remember the character which we attributed to the democratic man. He was supposed from his youth upwards to have been trained under a miserly parent, who encouraged the saving appetites in him, but discountenanced the unnecessary, which aim only at amusement and ornament?

True.

And then he got into the company of a more refined, licentious sort of people, and taking to all their wanton ways rushed into the opposite extreme from an abhorrence of his father's meanness. At last, being a better man than his corruptors, he was drawn in both directions until he halted midway and led a life, not of vulgar and slavish passion, but of what he deemed moderate indulgence in various pleasures. After this manner the democrat was generated out of the oligarch?

Yes, he said; that was our view of him, and is so still.

And now, I said, years will have passed away, and you must conceive this man, such as he is, to have a son, who is brought up in his father's principles.

I can imagine him.

Then you must further imagine the same thing to happen to the son which has already happened to the father: – he is drawn into a perfectly lawless life, which by his seducers is termed perfect liberty; and his father and friends take part with his moderate desires, and the opposite party assist the opposite ones. As soon as these dire magicians and tyrant-makers find that they are losing their hold on him, they contrive to implant in him a master passion, to be lord over his idle and spendthrift lusts – a sort of monstrous winged drone – that is the only image which will adequately describe him.

Yes, he said, that is the only adequate image of him.

And when his other lusts, amid clouds of incense and perfumes and garlands and wines, and all the pleasures of a dissolute life, now let loose, come buzzing around him, nourishing to the utmost the sting of desire which they implant in his drone-like nature, then at last this lord of the soul, having Madness for the captain of his guard, breaks out into a frenzy: and if he finds in himself any good opinions or appetites in process of formation, and there is in him any sense of shame remaining, to these better principles he puts an end, and casts them forth until he has purged away temperance and brought in madness to the full.

Yes, he said, that is the way in which the tyrannical man is generated.

And is not this the reason why of old love has been called a tyrant?

I should not wonder.

Further, I said, has not a drunken man also the spirit of a tyrant?

He has.

And you know that a man who is deranged and not right in his mind, will fancy that he is able to rule, not only over men, but also over the gods?

That he will.

And the tyrannical man in the true sense of the word comes into being when, either under the influence of nature, or habit, or both, he becomes drunken, lustful, passionate? O my friend, is not that so?

Assuredly.

Such is the man and such is his origin. And next, how does he live?

Suppose, as people facetiously say, you were to tell me.

I imagine, I said, at the next step in his progress, that there will be feasts and carousals and revellings and courtezans, and all that sort of thing; Love is the lord of the house within him, and orders all the concerns of his soul.

That is certain.

Yes; and every day and every night desires grow up many and formidable, and their demands are many.

They are indeed, he said.

His revenues, if he has any, are soon spent.

True.

Then comes debt and the cutting down of his property.

Of course.

When he has nothing left, must not his desires, crowding in the nest like young ravens, be crying aloud for food; and he, goaded on by them, and especially by love himself, who is in a manner the captain of them, is in a frenzy, and would fain discover whom he can defraud or despoil of his property, in order that he may gratify them?

Yes, that is sure to be the case.

He must have money, no matter how, if he is to escape horrid pains and pangs.

He must.

And as in himself there was a succession of pleasures, and the new got the better of the old and took away their rights, so he being younger will claim to have more than his father and his mother, and if he has spent his own share of the property, he will take a slice of theirs.

No doubt he will.

And if his parents will not give way, then he will try first of all to cheat and deceive them.

Very true.

And if he fails, then he will use force and plunder them.

Yes, probably.

And if the old man and woman fight for their own, what then, my friend? Will the creature feel any compunction at tyrannizing over them?

Nay, he said, I should not feel at all comfortable about his parents.

But, O heavens! Adeimantus, on account of some new-fangled love of a harlot, who is anything but a necessary connection, can you believe that he would strike the mother who is his ancient friend and necessary to his very existence, and would place her under the authority of the other, when she is brought under the same roof with her; or that, under like circumstances, he would do the same to his withered old father, first and most indispensable of friends, for the sake of some newly-found blooming youth who is the reverse of indispensable?

Yes, indeed, he said; I believe that he would.

Truly, then, I said, a tyrannical son is a blessing to his father and mother.

He is indeed, he replied.

He first takes their property, and when that fails, and pleasures are beginning to swarm in the hive of his soul, then he breaks into a house, or steals the garments of some nightly wayfarer; next he proceeds to clear a temple. Meanwhile the old opinions which he had when a child, and which gave judgment about good and evil, are overthrown by those others which have just been emancipated, and are now the body-guard of love and share his empire. These in his democratic days, when he was still subject to the laws and to his father, were only let loose in the dreams of sleep. But now that he is under the dominion of love, he becomes always and in waking reality what he was then very rarely and in a dream only; he will commit the foulest murder, or eat forbidden food, or be guilty of any other horrid act. Love is his tyrant, and lives lordly in him and lawlessly, and being himself a king, leads him on, as a tyrant leads a State, to the performance of any reckless deed by which he can maintain himself and the rabble of his associates, whether those whom evil communications have brought in from without, or those whom he himself has allowed to break loose within him by reason of a similar evil nature in himself. Have we not here a picture of his way of life?

Yes, indeed, he said.

And if there are only a few of them in the State, and the rest of the people are well disposed, they go away and become the body-guard or mercenary soldiers of some other tyrant who may probably want them for a war; and if there is no war, they stay at home and do many little pieces of mischief in the city.

What sort of mischief?

For example, they are the thieves, burglars, cut-purses, foot-pads, robbers of temples, man-stealers of the community; or if they are able to speak they turn informers, and bear false witness, and take bribes.

A small catalogue of evils, even if the perpetrators of them are few in number.

Yes, I said; but small and great are comparative terms, and all these things, in the misery and evil which they inflict upon a State, do not come within a thousand miles of the tyrant; when this noxious class and their followers grow numerous and become conscious of their strength, assisted by the infatuation of the people, they choose from among themselves the one who has most of the tyrant in his own soul, and him they create their tyrant.

Yes, he said, and he will be the most fit to be a tyrant.

If the people yield, well and good; but if they resist him, as he began by beating his own father and mother, so now, if he has the power, he beats them, and will keep his dear old fatherland or motherland, as the Cretans say, in subjection to his young retainers whom he has introduced to be their rulers and masters. This is the end of his passions and desires.

Exactly.

When such men are only private individuals and before they get power, this is their character; they associate entirely with their own flatterers or ready tools; or if they want anything from anybody, they in their turn are equally ready to bow down before them: they profess every sort of affection for them; but when they have gained their point they know them no more.

Yes, truly.

They are always either the masters or servants and never the friends of anybody; the tyrant never tastes of true freedom or friendship.

Certainly not.

And may we not rightly call such men treacherous?

No question.

Also they are utterly unjust, if we were right in our notion of justice?

Yes, he said, and we were perfectly right.

Let us then sum up in a word, I said, the character of the worst man: he is the waking reality of what we dreamed.

Most true.

And this is he who being by nature most of a tyrant bears rule, and the longer he lives the more of a tyrant he becomes.

That is certain, said Glaucon, taking his turn to answer.

And will not he who has been shown to be the wickedest, be also the most miserable? and he who has tyrannized longest and most, most continually and truly miserable; although this may not be the opinion of men in general?

Yes, he said, inevitably.

And must not the tyrannical man be like the tyrannical State, and the democratical man like the democratical State; and the same of the others?

Certainly.

And as State is to State in virtue and happiness, so is man in relation to man?

To be sure.

Then comparing our original city, which was under a king, and the city which is under a tyrant, how do they stand as to virtue?

They are the opposite extremes, he said, for one is the very best and the other is the very worst.

There can be no mistake, I said, as to which is which, and therefore I will at once enquire whether you would arrive at a similar decision about their relative happiness and misery. And here we must not allow ourselves to be panic-stricken at the apparition of the tyrant, who is only a unit and may perhaps have a few retainers about him; but let us go as we ought into every corner of the city and look all about, and then we will give our opinion.

A fair invitation, he replied; and I see, as every one must, that a tyranny is the wretchedest form of government, and the rule of a king the happiest.

And in estimating the men too, may I not fairly make a like request, that I should have a judge whose mind can enter into and see through human nature? he must not be like a child who looks at the outside and is dazzled at the pompous aspect which the tyrannical nature assumes to the beholder, but let him be one who has a clear insight. May I suppose that the judgment is given in the hearing of us all by one who is able to judge, and has dwelt in the same place with him, and been present at his dally life and known him in his family relations, where he may be seen stripped of his tragedy attire, and again in the hour of public danger – he shall tell us about the happiness and misery of the tyrant when compared with other men?

That again, he said, is a very fair proposal.

Shall I assume that we ourselves are able and experienced judges and have before now met with such a person? We shall then have some one who will answer our enquiries.

By all means.

Let me ask you not to forget the parallel of the individual and the State; bearing this in mind, and glancing in turn from one to the other of them, will you tell me their respective conditions?

What do you mean? he asked.

Beginning with the State, I replied, would you say that a city which is governed by a tyrant is free or enslaved?

No city, he said, can be more completely enslaved.

And yet, as you see, there are freemen as well as masters in such a State?

Yes, he said, I see that there are – a few; but the people, speaking generally, and the best of them are miserably degraded and enslaved.

Then if the man is like the State, I said, must not the same rule prevail? his soul is full of meanness and vulgarity – the best elements in him are enslaved; and there is a small ruling part, which is also the worst and maddest.

Inevitably.

And would you say that the soul of such an one is the soul of a freeman, or of a slave?

He has the soul of a slave, in my opinion.

And the State which is enslaved under a tyrant is utterly incapable of acting voluntarily?

Utterly incapable.

And also the soul which is under a tyrant (I am speaking of the soul taken as a whole) is least capable of doing what she desires; there is a gadfly which goads her, and she is full of trouble and remorse?

Certainly.

And is the city which is under a tyrant rich or poor?

Poor.

And the tyrannical soul must be always poor and insatiable?

True.

And must not such a State and such a man be always full of fear?

Yes, indeed.

Is there any State in which you will find more of lamentation and sorrow and groaning and pain?

Certainly not.

And is there any man in whom you will find more of this sort of misery than in the tyrannical man, who is in a fury of passions and desires?

Impossible.

Reflecting upon these and similar evils, you held the tyrannical State to be the most miserable of States?

And I was right, he said.

Certainly, I said. And when you see the same evils in the tyrannical man, what do you say of him?

I say that he is by far the most miserable of all men.

There, I said, I think that you are beginning to go wrong.

What do you mean?

I do not think that he has as yet reached the utmost extreme of misery.

Then who is more miserable?

One of whom I am about to speak.

Who is that?

He who is of a tyrannical nature, and instead of leading a private life has been cursed with the further misfortune of being a public tyrant.

From what has been said, I gather that you are right.

Yes, I replied, but in this high argument you should be a little more certain, and should not conjecture only; for of all questions, this respecting good and evil is the greatest.

Very true, he said.

Let me then offer you an illustration, which may, I think, throw a light upon this subject.

What is your illustration?

The case of rich individuals in cities who possess many slaves: from them you may form an idea of the tyrant's condition, for they both have slaves; the only difference is that he has more slaves.

Yes, that is the difference.

You know that they live securely and have nothing to apprehend from their servants?

What should they fear?

Nothing. But do you observe the reason of this?

Yes; the reason is, that the whole city is leagued together for the protection of each individual.

Very true, I said. But imagine one of these owners, the master say of some fifty slaves, together with his family and property and slaves, carried off by a god into the wilderness, where there are no freemen to help him – will he not be in an agony of fear lest he and his wife and children should be put to death by his slaves?

Yes, he said, he will be in the utmost fear.

The time has arrived when he will be compelled to flatter divers of his slaves, and make many promises to them of freedom and other things, much against his will – he will have to cajole his own servants.

Yes, he said, that will be the only way of saving himself.

And suppose the same god, who carried him away, to surround him with neighbours who will not suffer one man to be the master of another, and who, if they could catch the offender, would take his life?

His case will be still worse, if you suppose him to be everywhere surrounded and watched by enemies.

And is not this the sort of prison in which the tyrant will be bound – he who being by nature such as we have described, is full of all sorts of fears and lusts? His soul is dainty and greedy, and yet alone, of all men in the city, he is never allowed to go on a journey, or to see the things which other freemen desire to see, but he lives in his hole like a woman hidden in the house, and is jealous of any other citizen who goes into foreign parts and sees anything of interest.

Very true, he said.

And amid evils such as these will not he who is ill-governed in his own person – the tyrannical man, I mean – whom you just now decided to be the most miserable of all – will not he be yet more miserable when, instead of leading a private life, he is constrained by fortune to be a public tyrant? He has to be master of others when he is not master of himself: he is like a diseased or paralytic man who is compelled to pass his life, not in retirement, but fighting and combating with other men.

Yes, he said, the similitude is most exact.

Is not his case utterly miserable? and does not the actual tyrant lead a worse life than he whose life you determined to be the worst?

Certainly.

He who is the real tyrant, whatever men may think, is the real slave, and is obliged to practise the greatest adulation and servility, and to be the flatterer of the vilest of mankind. He has desires which he is utterly unable to satisfy, and has more wants than any one, and is truly poor, if you know how to inspect the whole soul of him: all his life long he is beset with fear and is full of convulsions and distractions, even as the State which he resembles: and surely the resemblance holds?

Very true, he said.

Moreover, as we were saying before, he grows worse from having power: he becomes and is of necessity more jealous, more faithless, more unjust, more friendless, more impious, than he was at first; he is the purveyor and cherisher of every sort of vice, and the consequence is that he is supremely miserable, and that he makes everybody else as miserable as himself.

No man of any sense will dispute your words.

Come then, I said, and as the general umpire in theatrical contests proclaims the result, do you also decide who in your opinion is first in the scale of happiness, and who second, and in what order the others follow: there are five of them in all – they are the royal, timocratical, oligarchical, democratical, tyrannical.

The decision will be easily given, he replied; they shall be choruses coming on the stage, and I must judge them in the order in which they enter, by the criterion of virtue and vice, happiness and misery.

Need we hire a herald, or shall I announce, that the son of Ariston (the best) has decided that the best and justest is also the happiest, and that this is he who is the most royal man and king over himself; and that the worst and most unjust man is also the most miserable, and that this is he who being the greatest tyrant of himself is also the greatest tyrant of his State?

Make the proclamation yourself, he said.

And shall I add, 'whether seen or unseen by gods and men'?

Let the words be added.

Then this, I said, will be our first proof; and there is another, which may also have some weight.

What is that?

The second proof is derived from the nature of the soul: seeing that the individual soul, like the State, has been divided by us into three principles, the division may, I think, furnish a new demonstration.

Of what nature?

It seems to me that to these three principles three pleasures correspond; also three desires and governing powers.

How do you mean? he said.

There is one principle with which, as we were saying, a man learns, another with which he is angry; the third, having many forms, has no special name, but is denoted by the general term appetitive, from the extraordinary strength and vehemence of the desires of eating and drinking and the other sensual appetites which are the main elements of it; also money-loving, because such desires are generally satisfied by the help of money.

That is true, he said.

If we were to say that the loves and pleasures of this third part were concerned with gain, we should then be able to fall back on a single notion; and might truly and intelligibly describe this part of the soul as loving gain or money.

I agree with you.

Again, is not the passionate element wholly set on ruling and conquering and getting fame?

True.

Suppose we call it the contentious or ambitious – would the term be suitable?

Extremely suitable.

On the other hand, every one sees that the principle of knowledge is wholly directed to the truth, and cares less than either of the others for gain or fame.

Far less.

'Lover of wisdom,' 'lover of knowledge,' are titles which we may fitly apply to that part of the soul?

Certainly.

One principle prevails in the souls of one class of men, another in others, as may happen?

Yes.

Then we may begin by assuming that there are three classes of men – lovers of wisdom, lovers of honour, lovers of gain?

Exactly.

And there are three kinds of pleasure, which are their several objects?

Very true.

Now, if you examine the three classes of men, and ask of them in turn which of their lives is pleasantest, each will be found praising his own and depreciating that of others: the money-maker will contrast the vanity of honour or of learning if they bring no money with the solid advantages of gold and silver?

True, he said.

And the lover of honour – what will be his opinion? Will he not think that the pleasure of riches is vulgar, while the pleasure of learning, if it brings no distinction, is all smoke and nonsense to him?

Very true.

And are we to suppose, I said, that the philosopher sets any value on other pleasures in comparison with the pleasure of knowing the truth, and in that pursuit abiding, ever learning, not so far indeed from the heaven of pleasure? Does he not call the other pleasures necessary, under the idea that if there were no necessity for them, he would rather not have them?

There can be no doubt of that, he replied.

Since, then, the pleasures of each class and the life of each are in dispute, and the question is not which life is more or less honourable, or better or worse, but which is the more pleasant or painless – how shall we know who speaks truly?

I cannot myself tell, he said.

Well, but what ought to be the criterion? Is any better than experience and wisdom and reason?

There cannot be a better, he said.

Then, I said, reflect. Of the three individuals, which has the greatest experience of all the pleasures which we enumerated? Has the lover of gain, in learning the nature of essential truth, greater experience of the pleasure of knowledge than the philosopher has of the pleasure of gain?

The philosopher, he replied, has greatly the advantage; for he has of necessity always known the taste of the other pleasures from his childhood upwards: but the lover of gain in all his experience has not of necessity tasted – or, I should rather say, even had he desired, could hardly have tasted – the sweetness of learning and knowing truth.

Then the lover of wisdom has a great advantage over the lover of gain, for he has a double experience?

Yes, very great.

Again, has he greater experience of the pleasures of honour, or the lover of honour of the pleasures of wisdom?

Nay, he said, all three are honoured in proportion as they attain their object; for the rich man and the brave man and the wise man alike have their crowd of admirers, and as they all receive honour they all have experience of the pleasures of honour; but the delight which is to be found in the knowledge of true being is known to the philosopher only.

His experience, then, will enable him to judge better than any one?

Far better.

And he is the only one who has wisdom as well as experience?

Certainly.

Further, the very faculty which is the instrument of judgment is not possessed by the covetous or ambitious man, but only by the philosopher?

What faculty?

Reason, with whom, as we were saying, the decision ought to rest.

Yes.

And reasoning is peculiarly his instrument?

Certainly.

If wealth and gain were the criterion, then the praise or blame of the lover of gain would surely be the most trustworthy?

Assuredly.

Or if honour or victory or courage, in that case the judgment of the ambitious or pugnacious would be the truest?

Clearly.

But since experience and wisdom and reason are the judges –

The only inference possible, he replied, is that pleasures which are approved by the lover of wisdom and reason are the truest.

And so we arrive at the result, that the pleasure of the intelligent part of the soul is the pleasantest of the three, and that he of us in whom this is the ruling principle has the pleasantest life.

Unquestionably, he said, the wise man speaks with authority when he approves of his own life.

And what does the judge affirm to be the life which is next, and the pleasure which is next?

Clearly that of the soldier and lover of honour; who is nearer to himself than the money-maker.

Last comes the lover of gain?

Very true, he said.

Twice in succession, then, has the just man overthrown the unjust in this conflict; and now comes the third trial, which is dedicated to Olympian Zeus the saviour: a sage whispers in my ear that no pleasure except that of the wise is quite true and pure – all others are a shadow only; and surely this will prove the greatest and most decisive of falls?

Yes, the greatest; but will you explain yourself?

I will work out the subject and you shall answer my questions.

Proceed.

Say, then, is not pleasure opposed to pain?

True.

And there is a neutral state which is neither pleasure nor pain?

There is.

A state which is intermediate, and a sort of repose of the soul about either – that is what you mean?

Yes.

You remember what people say when they are sick?

What do they say?

That after all nothing is pleasanter than health. But then they never knew this to be the greatest of pleasures until they were ill.

Yes, I know, he said.

And when persons are suffering from acute pain, you must have heard them say that there is nothing pleasanter than to get rid of their pain?

I have.

And there are many other cases of suffering in which the mere rest and cessation of pain, and not any positive enjoyment, is extolled by them as the greatest pleasure?

Yes, he said; at the time they are pleased and well content to be at rest.

Again, when pleasure ceases, that sort of rest or cessation will be painful?

Doubtless, he said.

Then the intermediate state of rest will be pleasure and will also be pain?

So it would seem.

But can that which is neither become both?

I should say not.

And both pleasure and pain are motions of the soul, are they not?

Yes.

But that which is neither was just now shown to be rest and not motion, and in a mean between them?

Yes.

How, then, can we be right in supposing that the absence of pain is pleasure, or that the absence of pleasure is pain?

Impossible.

This then is an appearance only and not a reality; that is to say, the rest is pleasure at the moment and in comparison of what is painful, and painful in comparison of what is pleasant; but all these representations, when tried by the test of true pleasure, are not real but a sort of imposition?

That is the inference.

Look at the other class of pleasures which have no antecedent pains and you will no longer suppose, as you perhaps may at present, that pleasure is only the cessation of pain, or pain of pleasure.

What are they, he said, and where shall I find them?

There are many of them: take as an example the pleasures of smell, which are very great and have no antecedent pains; they come in a moment, and when they depart leave no pain behind them.

Most true, he said.

Let us not, then, be induced to believe that pure pleasure is the cessation of pain, or pain of pleasure.

No.

Still, the more numerous and violent pleasures which reach the soul through the body are generally of this sort – they are reliefs of pain.

That is true.

And the anticipations of future pleasures and pains are of a like nature?

Yes.

Shall I give you an illustration of them?

Let me hear.

You would allow, I said, that there is in nature an upper and lower and middle region?

I should.

And if a person were to go from the lower to the middle region, would he not imagine that he is going up; and he who is standing in the middle and sees whence he has come, would imagine that he is already in the upper region, if he has never seen the true upper world?

To be sure, he said; how can he think otherwise?

But if he were taken back again he would imagine, and truly imagine, that he was descending?

No doubt.

All that would arise out of his ignorance of the true upper and middle and lower regions?

Yes.

Then can you wonder that persons who are inexperienced in the truth, as they have wrong ideas about many other things, should also have wrong ideas about pleasure and pain and the intermediate state; so that when they are only being drawn towards the painful they feel pain and think the pain which they experience to be real, and in like manner, when drawn away from pain to the neutral or intermediate state, they firmly believe that they have reached the goal of satiety and pleasure; they, not knowing pleasure, err in contrasting pain with the absence of pain, which is like contrasting black with grey instead of white – can you wonder, I say, at this?

No, indeed; I should be much more disposed to wonder at the opposite.

Look at the matter thus: – Hunger, thirst, and the like, are inanitions of the bodily state?

Yes.

And ignorance and folly are inanitions of the soul?

True.

And food and wisdom are the corresponding satisfactions of either?

Certainly.

And is the satisfaction derived from that which has less or from that which has more existence the truer?

Clearly, from that which has more.

What classes of things have a greater share of pure existence in your judgment – those of which food and drink and condiments and all kinds of sustenance are examples, or the class which contains true opinion and knowledge and mind and all the different kinds of virtue? Put the question in this way: – Which has a more pure being – that which is concerned with the invariable, the immortal, and the true, and is of such a nature, and is found in such natures; or that which is concerned with and found in the variable and mortal, and is itself variable and mortal?

Far purer, he replied, is the being of that which is concerned with the invariable.

And does the essence of the invariable partake of knowledge in the same degree as of essence?

Yes, of knowledge in the same degree.

And of truth in the same degree?

Yes.

And, conversely, that which has less of truth will also have less of essence?

Necessarily.

Then, in general, those kinds of things which are in the service of the body have less of truth and essence than those which are in the service of the soul?

Far less.

And has not the body itself less of truth and essence than the soul?

Yes.

What is filled with more real existence, and actually has a more real existence, is more really filled than that which is filled with less real existence and is less real?

Of course.

And if there be a pleasure in being filled with that which is according to nature, that which is more really filled with more real being will more really and truly enjoy true pleasure; whereas that which participates in less real being will be less truly and surely satisfied, and will participate in an illusory and less real pleasure?

Unquestionably.

Those then who know not wisdom and virtue, and are always busy with gluttony and sensuality, go down and up again as far as the mean; and in this region they move at random throughout life, but they never pass into the true upper world; thither they neither look, nor do they ever find their way, neither are they truly filled with true being, nor do they taste of pure and abiding pleasure. Like cattle, with their eyes always looking down and their heads stooping to the earth, that is, to the dining-table, they fatten and feed and breed, and, in their excessive love of these delights, they kick and butt at one another with horns and hoofs which are made of iron; and they kill one another by reason of their insatiable lust. For they fill themselves with that which is not substantial, and the part of themselves which they fill is also unsubstantial and incontinent.

Verily, Socrates, said Glaucon, you describe the life of the many like an oracle.

Their pleasures are mixed with pains – how can they be otherwise? For they are mere shadows and pictures of the true, and are coloured by contrast, which exaggerates both light and shade, and so they implant in the minds of fools insane desires of themselves; and they are fought about as Stesichorus says that the Greeks fought about the shadow of Helen at Troy in ignorance of the truth.

Something of that sort must inevitably happen.

And must not the like happen with the spirited or passionate element of the soul? Will not the passionate man who carries his passion into action, be in the like case, whether he is envious and ambitious, or violent and contentious, or angry and discontented, if he be seeking to attain honour and victory and the satisfaction of his anger without reason or sense?

Yes, he said, the same will happen with the spirited element also.

Then may we not confidently assert that the lovers of money and honour, when they seek their pleasures under the guidance and in the company of reason and knowledge, and pursue after and win the pleasures which wisdom shows them, will also have the truest pleasures in the highest degree which is attainable to them, inasmuch as they follow truth; and they will have the pleasures which are natural to them, if that which is best for each one is also most natural to him?

Yes, certainly; the best is the most natural.

And when the whole soul follows the philosophical principle, and there is no division, the several parts are just, and do each of them their own business, and enjoy severally the best and truest pleasures of which they are capable?

Exactly.

But when either of the two other principles prevails, it fails in attaining its own pleasure, and compels the rest to pursue after a pleasure which is a shadow only and which is not their own?

True.

And the greater the interval which separates them from philosophy and reason, the more strange and illusive will be the pleasure?

Yes.

And is not that farthest from reason which is at the greatest distance from law and order?

Clearly.

And the lustful and tyrannical desires are, as we saw, at the greatest distance? Yes.

And the royal and orderly desires are nearest?

Yes.

Then the tyrant will live at the greatest distance from true or natural pleasure, and the king at the least?

Certainly.

But if so, the tyrant will live most unpleasantly, and the king most pleasantly?

Inevitably.

Would you know the measure of the interval which separates them?

Will you tell me?

There appear to be three pleasures, one genuine and two spurious: now the transgression of the tyrant reaches a point beyond the spurious; he has run away from the region of law and reason, and taken up his abode with certain slave pleasures which are his satellites, and the measure of his inferiority can only be expressed in a figure.

How do you mean?

I assume, I said, that the tyrant is in the third place from the oligarch; the democrat was in the middle?

Yes.

And if there is truth in what has preceded, he will be wedded to an image of pleasure which is thrice removed as to truth from the pleasure of the oligarch?

He will.

And the oligarch is third from the royal; since we count as one royal and aristocratical?

Yes, he is third.

Then the tyrant is removed from true pleasure by the space of a number which is three times three?

Manifestly.

The shadow then of tyrannical pleasure determined by the number of length will be a plane figure.

Certainly.

529 | P a g e

And if you raise the power and make the plane a solid, there is no difficulty in seeing how vast is the interval by which the tyrant is parted from the king.

Yes; the arithmetician will easily do the sum.

Or if some person begins at the other end and measures the interval by which the king is parted from the tyrant in truth of pleasure, he will find him, when the multiplication is completed, living 729 times more pleasantly, and the tyrant more painfully by this same interval.

What a wonderful calculation! And how enormous is the distance which separates the just from the unjust in regard to pleasure and pain!

Yet a true calculation, I said, and a number which nearly concerns human life, if human beings are concerned with days and nights and months and years. (729 NEARLY equals the number of days and nights in the year.)

Yes, he said, human life is certainly concerned with them.

Then if the good and just man be thus superior in pleasure to the evil and unjust, his superiority will be infinitely greater in propriety of life and in beauty and virtue?

Immeasurably greater.

Well, I said, and now having arrived at this stage of the argument, we may revert to the words which brought us hither: Was not some one saying that injustice was a gain to the perfectly unjust who was reputed to be just?

Yes, that was said.

Now then, having determined the power and quality of justice and injustice, let us have a little conversation with him.

What shall we say to him?

Let us make an image of the soul, that he may have his own words presented before his eyes.

Of what sort?

An ideal image of the soul, like the composite creations of ancient mythology, such as the Chimera or Scylla or Cerberus, and there are many others in which two or more different natures are said to grow into one.

There are said of have been such unions.

Then do you now model the form of a multitudinous, many-headed monster, having a ring of heads of all manner of beasts, tame and wild, which he is able to generate and metamorphose at will.

You suppose marvellous powers in the artist; but, as language is more pliable than wax or any similar substance, let there be such a model as you propose.

Suppose now that you make a second form as of a lion, and a third of a man, the second smaller than the first, and the third smaller than the second.

That, he said, is an easier task; and I have made them as you say.

And now join them, and let the three grow into one.

That has been accomplished.

Next fashion the outside of them into a single image, as of a man, so that he who is not able to look within, and sees only the outer hull, may believe the beast to be a single human creature.

I have done so, he said.

And now, to him who maintains that it is profitable for the human creature to be unjust, and unprofitable to be just, let us reply that, if he be right, it is profitable for this creature to feast the multitudinous monster and strengthen the lion and the lion-like qualities, but to starve and weaken the man, who is consequently liable to be dragged about at the mercy of either of the other two; and he is not to attempt to familiarize or harmonize them with one another – he ought rather to suffer them to fight and bite and devour one another.

Certainly, he said; that is what the approver of injustice says.

To him the supporter of justice makes answer that he should ever so speak and act as to give the man within him in some way or other the most complete mastery over the entire human creature. He should watch over the many-headed monster like a good husbandman, fostering and cultivating the gentle qualities, and preventing the wild ones from growing; he should be making the lion-heart his ally, and in common care of them all should be uniting the several parts with one another and with himself.

Yes, he said, that is quite what the maintainer of justice say.

And so from every point of view, whether of pleasure, honour, or advantage, the approver of justice is right and speaks the truth, and the disapprover is wrong and false and ignorant?

Yes, from every point of view.

Come, now, and let us gently reason with the unjust, who is not intentionally in error. 'Sweet Sir,' we will say to him, 'what think you of things esteemed noble and ignoble? Is not the noble that which subjects the beast to the man, or rather to the god in man; and the ignoble that which subjects the man to the beast?' He can hardly avoid saying Yes – can he now?

Not if he has any regard for my opinion.

But, if he agree so far, we may ask him to answer another question: 'Then how would a man profit if he received gold and silver on the condition that he was to enslave the noblest part of him to the worst? Who can imagine that a man who sold his son or daughter into slavery for money, especially if he sold them into the hands of fierce and evil men, would be the gainer, however large might be the sum which he received? And will any one say that he is not a miserable caitiff who remorselessly sells his own divine being to that which is most godless and detestable? Eriphyle took the necklace as the price of her husband's life, but he is taking a bribe in order to compass a worse ruin.'

Yes, said Glaucon, far worse – I will answer for him.

Has not the intemperate been censured of old, because in him the huge multiform monster is allowed to be too much at large?

Clearly.

And men are blamed for pride and bad temper when the lion and serpent element in them disproportionately grows and gains strength?

Yes.

And luxury and softness are blamed, because they relax and weaken this same creature, and make a coward of him?

Very true.

And is not a man reproached for flattery and meanness who subordinates the spirited animal to the unruly monster, and, for the sake of money, of which he can never have enough, habituates him in the days of his youth to be trampled in the mire, and from being a lion to become a monkey?

True, he said.

And why are mean employments and manual arts a reproach? Only because they imply a natural weakness of the higher principle; the individual is unable to control the creatures within him, but has to court them, and his great study is how to flatter them.

Such appears to be the reason.

And therefore, being desirous of placing him under a rule like that of the best, we say that he ought to be the servant of the best, in whom the Divine rules; not, as Thrasymachus supposed, to the injury of the servant, but because every one had better be ruled by divine wisdom dwelling within him; or, if this be impossible, then by an external authority, in order that we may be all, as far as possible, under the same government, friends and equals.

True, he said.

And this is clearly seen to be the intention of the law, which is the ally of the whole city; and is seen also in the authority which we exercise over children, and the refusal to let them be free until we have established in them a principle analogous to the constitution of a state, and by cultivation of this higher element have set up in their hearts a guardian and ruler like our own, and when this is done they may go their ways.

Yes, he said, the purpose of the law is manifest.

From what point of view, then, and on what ground can we say that a man is profited by injustice or intemperance or other baseness, which will make him a worse man, even though he acquire money or power by his wickedness?

From no point of view at all.

What shall he profit, if his injustice be undetected and unpunished? He who is undetected only gets worse, whereas he who is detected and punished has the brutal part of his nature silenced and humanized; the gentler element in him is liberated, and his whole soul is perfected and ennobled by the acquirement of justice and temperance and wisdom, more than the body ever is by receiving gifts of beauty, strength and health, in proportion as the soul is more honourable than the body.

Certainly, he said.

To this nobler purpose the man of understanding will devote the energies of his life. And in the first place, he will honour studies which impress these qualities on his soul and will disregard others?

Clearly, he said.

In the next place, he will regulate his bodily habit and training, and so far will he be from yielding to brutal and irrational pleasures, that he will regard even health as quite a secondary matter; his first object will be not that he may be fair or strong or well, unless he is likely thereby to gain temperance, but he will always desire so to attemper the body as to preserve the harmony of the soul?

Certainly he will, if he has true music in him.

And in the acquisition of wealth there is a principle of order and harmony which he will also observe; he will not allow himself to be dazzled by the foolish applause of the world, and heap up riches to his own infinite harm?

Certainly not, he said.

He will look at the city which is within him, and take heed that no disorder occur in it, such as might arise either from superfluity or from want; and upon this principle he will regulate his property and gain or spend according to his means.

Very true.

And, for the same reason, he will gladly accept and enjoy such honours as he deems likely to make him a better man; but those, whether private or public, which are likely to disorder his life, he will avoid?

Then, if that is his motive, he will not be a statesman.

By the dog of Egypt, he will! in the city which is his own he certainly will, though in the land of his birth perhaps not, unless he have a divine call.

I understand; you mean that he will be a ruler in the city of which we are the founders, and which exists in idea only; for I do not believe that there is such an one anywhere on earth?

In heaven, I replied, there is laid up a pattern of it, methinks, which he who desires may behold, and beholding, may set his own house in order. But whether such an one exists, or ever will exist in fact, is no matter; for he will live after the manner of that city, having nothing to do with any other.

I think so, he said.

BOOK X.

Of the many excellences which I perceive in the order of our State, there is none which upon reflection pleases me better than the rule about poetry.

To what do you refer?

To the rejection of imitative poetry, which certainly ought not to be received; as I see far more clearly now that the parts of the soul have been distinguished.

What do you mean?

Speaking in confidence, for I should not like to have my words repeated to the tragedians and the rest of the imitative tribe – but I do not mind saying to you, that all poetical imitations are ruinous to the understanding of the hearers, and that the knowledge of their true nature is the only antidote to them.

Explain the purport of your remark.

Well, I will tell you, although I have always from my earliest youth had an awe and love of Homer, which even now makes the words falter on my lips, for he is the great captain and teacher of the whole of that charming tragic company; but a man is not to be reverenced more than the truth, and therefore I will speak out.

Very good, he said.

Listen to me then, or rather, answer me.

Put your question.

Can you tell me what imitation is? for I really do not know.

A likely thing, then, that I should know.

Why not? for the duller eye may often see a thing sooner than the keener.

Very true, he said; but in your presence, even if I had any faint notion, I could not muster courage to utter it. Will you enquire yourself?

Well then, shall we begin the enquiry in our usual manner: Whenever a number of individuals have a common name, we assume them to have also a corresponding idea or form: – do you understand me?

I do.

Let us take any common instance; there are beds and tables in the world – plenty of them, are there not?

Yes.

But there are only two ideas or forms of them – one the idea of a bed, the other of a table.

True.

And the maker of either of them makes a bed or he makes a table for our use, in accordance with the idea – that is our way of speaking in this and similar instances – but no artificer makes the ideas themselves: how could he?

Impossible.

And there is another artist, – I should like to know what you would say of him.

Who is he?

One who is the maker of all the works of all other workmen.

What an extraordinary man!

Wait a little, and there will be more reason for your saying so. For this is he who is able to make not only vessels of every kind, but plants and animals, himself and all other things – the earth and heaven, and the things which are in heaven or under the earth; he makes the gods also.

He must be a wizard and no mistake.

Oh! you are incredulous, are you? Do you mean that there is no such maker or creator, or that in one sense there might be a maker of all these things but in another not? Do you see that there is a way in which you could make them all yourself?

What way?

An easy way enough; or rather, there are many ways in which the feat might be quickly and easily accomplished, none quicker than that of turning a mirror round and round – you would soon enough make the sun and the heavens, and the earth and yourself, and other animals and plants, and all the other things of which we were just now speaking, in the mirror.

Yes, he said; but they would be appearances only.

Very good, I said, you are coming to the point now. And the painter too is, as I conceive, just such another – a creator of appearances, is he not?

Of course.

But then I suppose you will say that what he creates is untrue. And yet there is a sense in which the painter also creates a bed?

Yes, he said, but not a real bed.

And what of the maker of the bed? were you not saying that he too makes, not the idea which, according to our view, is the essence of the bed, but only a particular bed?

Yes, I did.

Then if he does not make that which exists he cannot make true existence, but only some semblance of existence; and if any one were to say that the work of the maker of the bed, or of any other workman, has real existence, he could hardly be supposed to be speaking the truth.

At any rate, he replied, philosophers would say that he was not speaking the truth.

No wonder, then, that his work too is an indistinct expression of truth.

No wonder.

Suppose now that by the light of the examples just offered we enquire who this imitator is?

If you please.

Well then, here are three beds: one existing in nature, which is made by God, as I think that we may say – for no one else can be the maker?

No.

There is another which is the work of the carpenter?

Yes.

And the work of the painter is a third?

Yes.

Beds, then, are of three kinds, and there are three artists who superintend them: God, the maker of the bed, and the painter?

Yes, there are three of them.

God, whether from choice or from necessity, made one bed in nature and one only; two or more such ideal beds neither ever have been nor ever will be made by God.

Why is that?

Because even if He had made but two, a third would still appear behind them which both of them would have for their idea, and that would be the ideal bed and not the two others.

Very true, he said.

God knew this, and He desired to be the real maker of a real bed, not a particular maker of a particular bed, and therefore He created a bed which is essentially and by nature one only.

So we believe.

Shall we, then, speak of Him as the natural author or maker of the bed?

Yes, he replied; inasmuch as by the natural process of creation He is the author of this and of all other things.

And what shall we say of the carpenter – is not he also the maker of the bed?

Yes.

But would you call the painter a creator and maker?

Certainly not.

Yet if he is not the maker, what is he in relation to the bed?

I think, he said, that we may fairly designate him as the imitator of that which the others make.

Good, I said; then you call him who is third in the descent from nature an imitator?

Certainly, he said.

And the tragic poet is an imitator, and therefore, like all other imitators, he is thrice removed from the king and from the truth?

That appears to be so.

Then about the imitator we are agreed. And what about the painter? – I would like to know whether he may be thought to imitate that which originally exists in nature, or only the creations of artists?

The latter.

As they are or as they appear? you have still to determine this.

What do you mean?

I mean, that you may look at a bed from different points of view, obliquely or directly or from any other point of view, and the bed will appear different, but there is no difference in reality. And the same of all things.

Yes, he said, the difference is only apparent.

Now let me ask you another question: Which is the art of painting designed to be – an imitation of things as they are, or as they appear – of appearance or of reality?

Of appearance.

THE REPUBLIC

Then the imitator, I said, is a long way off the truth, and can do all things because he lightly touches on a small part of them, and that part an image. For example: A painter will paint a cobbler, carpenter, or any other artist, though he knows nothing of their arts; and, if he is a good artist, he may deceive children or simple persons, when he shows them his picture of a carpenter from a distance, and they will fancy that they are looking at a real carpenter.

Certainly.

And whenever any one informs us that he has found a man who knows all the arts, and all things else that anybody knows, and every single thing with a higher degree of accuracy than any other man – whoever tells us this, I think that we can only imagine him to be a simple creature who is likely to have been deceived by some wizard or actor whom he met, and whom he thought all-knowing, because he himself was unable to analyse the nature of knowledge and ignorance and imitation.

Most true.

And so, when we hear persons saying that the tragedians, and Homer, who is at their head, know all the arts and all things human, virtue as well as vice, and divine things too, for that the good poet cannot compose well unless he knows his subject, and that he who has not this knowledge can never be a poet, we ought to consider whether here also there may not be a similar illusion. Perhaps they may have come across imitators and been deceived by them; they may not have remembered when they saw their works that these were but imitations thrice removed from the truth, and could easily be made without any knowledge of the truth, because they are appearances only and not realities? Or, after all, they may be in the right, and poets do really know the things about which they seem to the many to speak so well?

The question, he said, should by all means be considered.

Now do you suppose that if a person were able to make the original as well as the image, he would seriously devote himself to the image-making branch? Would he allow imitation to be the ruling principle of his life, as if he had nothing higher in him?

I should say not.

The real artist, who knew what he was imitating, would be interested in realities and not in imitations; and would desire to leave as memorials of himself works many and fair; and, instead of being the author of encomiums, he would prefer to be the theme of them.

Yes, he said, that would be to him a source of much greater honour and profit.

Then, I said, we must put a question to Homer; not about medicine, or any of the arts to which his poems only incidentally refer: we are not going to ask him, or any other poet, whether he has cured patients like Asclepius, or left behind him a school of medicine such as the Asclepiads were, or whether he only talks about medicine and other arts at second-hand; but we have a right to know respecting military tactics, politics, education, which are the chiefest and noblest subjects of his poems, and we may fairly ask him about them. 'Friend Homer,' then we say to him, 'if you are only in the second remove from truth in what you say of virtue, and not in the third – not an image maker or imitator – and if you are able to discern what pursuits make men better or worse in private or public life, tell us what State was ever better governed by your help? The good order of Lacedaemon is due to Lycurgus, and many other cities great and small have been similarly benefited by others; but who says that you have been a good legislator to them and have done them any good? Italy and Sicily boast of Charondas, and there is Solon who is renowned among us; but what city has anything to say about you?' Is there any city which he might name?

I think not, said Glaucon; not even the Homerids themselves pretend that he was a legislator.

Well, but is there any war on record which was carried on successfully by him, or aided by his counsels, when he was alive?

There is not.

Or is there any invention of his, applicable to the arts or to human life, such as Thales the Milesian or Anacharsis the Scythian, and other ingenious men have conceived, which is attributed to him?

There is absolutely nothing of the kind.

But, if Homer never did any public service, was he privately a guide or teacher of any? Had he in his lifetime friends who loved to associate with him, and who handed down to posterity an Homeric way of life, such as was established by Pythagoras who was so greatly beloved for his wisdom, and whose followers are to this day quite celebrated for the order which was named after him?

Nothing of the kind is recorded of him. For surely, Socrates, Creophylus, the companion of Homer, that child of flesh, whose name always makes us laugh, might be more justly ridiculed for his stupidity, if, as is said, Homer was greatly neglected by him and others in his own day when he was alive?

Yes, I replied, that is the tradition. But can you imagine, Glaucon, that if Homer had really been able to educate and improve mankind – if he had possessed knowledge and not been a mere imitator – can you imagine, I say, that he would not have had many followers, and been honoured and loved by them? Protagoras of Abdera, and Prodicus of Ceos, and a host of others, have only to whisper to their contemporaries: 'You will never be able to manage either your own house or your own State until you appoint us to be your ministers of education' – and this ingenious device of theirs has such an effect in making men love them that their companions all but carry them about on their shoulders. And is it conceivable that the contemporaries of Homer, or again of Hesiod, would have allowed either of them to go about as rhapsodists, if they had really been able to make mankind virtuous? Would they not have been as unwilling to part with them as with gold, and have compelled them to stay at home with them? Or, if the master would not stay, then the disciples would have followed him about everywhere, until they had got education enough?

Yes, Socrates, that, I think, is quite true.

Then must we not infer that all these poetical individuals, beginning with Homer, are only imitators; they copy images of virtue and the like, but the truth they never reach? The poet is like a painter who, as we have already observed, will make a likeness of a cobbler though he understands nothing of cobbling; and his picture is good enough for those who know no more than he does, and judge only by colours and figures.

Quite so.

In like manner the poet with his words and phrases may be said to lay on the colours of the several arts, himself understanding their nature only enough to imitate them; and other people, who are as ignorant as he is, and judge only from his words, imagine that if he speaks of cobbling, or of military tactics, or of anything else, in metre and harmony and rhythm, he speaks very well – such is the sweet influence which melody and rhythm by nature have. And I think that you must have observed again and again what a poor appearance the tales of poets make when stripped of the colours which music puts upon them, and recited in simple prose.

Yes, he said.

They are like faces which were never really beautiful, but only blooming; and now the bloom of youth has passed away from them?

Exactly.

Here is another point: The imitator or maker of the image knows nothing of true existence; he knows appearances only. Am I not right?

Yes.

Then let us have a clear understanding, and not be satisfied with half an explanation.

Proceed.

Of the painter we say that he will paint reins, and he will paint a bit?

Yes.

And the worker in leather and brass will make them?

Certainly.

But does the painter know the right form of the bit and reins? Nay, hardly even the workers in brass and leather who make them; only the horseman who knows how to use them – he knows their right form.

Most true.

And may we not say the same of all things?

What?

That there are three arts which are concerned with all things: one which uses, another which makes, a third which imitates them?

Yes.

And the excellence or beauty or truth of every structure, animate or inanimate, and of every action of man, is relative to the use for which nature or the artist has intended them.

True.

Then the user of them must have the greatest experience of them, and he must indicate to the maker the good or bad qualities which develop themselves in use; for example, the flute-player will tell the flute-maker which of his flutes is satisfactory to the performer; he will tell him how he ought to make them, and the other will attend to his instructions?

Of course.

The one knows and therefore speaks with authority about the goodness and badness of flutes, while the other, confiding in him, will do what he is told by him?

True.

The instrument is the same, but about the excellence or badness of it the maker will only attain to a correct belief; and this he will gain from him who knows, by talking to him and being compelled to hear what he has to say, whereas the user will have knowledge?

True.

But will the imitator have either? Will he know from use whether or no his drawing is correct or beautiful? or will he have right opinion from being compelled to associate with another who knows and gives him instructions about what he should draw?

Neither.

Then he will no more have true opinion than he will have knowledge about the goodness or badness of his imitations?

I suppose not.

The imitative artist will be in a brilliant state of intelligence about his own creations?

Nay, very much the reverse.

And still he will go on imitating without knowing what makes a thing good or bad, and may be expected therefore to imitate only that which appears to be good to the ignorant multitude?

Just so.

Thus far then we are pretty well agreed that the imitator has no knowledge worth mentioning of what he imitates. Imitation is only a kind of play or sport, and the tragic poets, whether they write in Iambic or in Heroic verse, are imitators in the highest degree?

Very true.

And now tell me, I conjure you, has not imitation been shown by us to be concerned with that which is thrice removed from the truth?

Certainly.

And what is the faculty in man to which imitation is addressed?

What do you mean?

I will explain: The body which is large when seen near, appears small when seen at a distance?

True.

And the same object appears straight when looked at out of the water, and crooked when in the water; and the concave becomes convex, owing to the illusion about colours to which the sight is liable. Thus every sort of confusion is revealed within us; and this is that weakness of the human mind on which the art of conjuring and of deceiving by light and shadow and other ingenious devices imposes, having an effect upon us like magic.

True.

And the arts of measuring and numbering and weighing come to the rescue of the human understanding – there is the beauty of them – and the apparent greater or less, or more or heavier, no longer have the mastery over us, but give way before calculation and measure and weight?

Most true.

And this, surely, must be the work of the calculating and rational principle in the soul?

To be sure.

And when this principle measures and certifies that some things are equal, or that some are greater or less than others, there occurs an apparent contradiction?

True.

But were we not saying that such a contradiction is impossible – the same faculty cannot have contrary opinions at the same time about the same thing?

Very true.

Then that part of the soul which has an opinion contrary to measure is not the same with that which has an opinion in accordance with measure?

True.

And the better part of the soul is likely to be that which trusts to measure and calculation?

Certainly.

And that which is opposed to them is one of the inferior principles of the soul?

No doubt.

This was the conclusion at which I was seeking to arrive when I said that painting or drawing, and imitation in general, when doing their own proper work, are far removed from truth, and the companions and friends and associates of a principle within us which is equally removed from reason, and that they have no true or healthy aim.

Exactly.

The imitative art is an inferior who marries an inferior, and has inferior offspring.

Very true.

And is this confined to the sight only, or does it extend to the hearing also, relating in fact to what we term poetry?

Probably the same would be true of poetry.

Do not rely, I said, on a probability derived from the analogy of painting; but let us examine further and see whether the faculty with which poetical imitation is concerned is good or bad.

By all means.

We may state the question thus: – Imitation imitates the actions of men, whether voluntary or involuntary, on which, as they imagine, a good or bad result has ensued, and they rejoice or sorrow accordingly. Is there anything more?

No, there is nothing else.

But in all this variety of circumstances is the man at unity with himself – or rather, as in the instance of sight there was confusion and opposition in his opinions about the same things, so here also is there not strife and inconsistency in his life? Though I need hardly raise the question again, for I remember that all this has been already admitted; and the soul has been acknowledged by us to be full of these and ten thousand similar oppositions occurring at the same moment?

And we were right, he said.

Yes, I said, thus far we were right; but there was an omission which must now be supplied.

What was the omission?

Were we not saying that a good man, who has the misfortune to lose his son or anything else which is most dear to him, will bear the loss with more equanimity than another?

Yes.

But will he have no sorrow, or shall we say that although he cannot help sorrowing, he will moderate his sorrow?

The latter, he said, is the truer statement.

Tell me: will he be more likely to struggle and hold out against his sorrow when he is seen by his equals, or when he is alone?

It will make a great difference whether he is seen or not.

When he is by himself he will not mind saying or doing many things which he would be ashamed of any one hearing or seeing him do?

True.

There is a principle of law and reason in him which bids him resist, as well as a feeling of his misfortune which is forcing him to indulge his sorrow?

True.

But when a man is drawn in two opposite directions, to and from the same object, this, as we affirm, necessarily implies two distinct principles in him?

Certainly.

One of them is ready to follow the guidance of the law?

How do you mean?

The law would say that to be patient under suffering is best, and that we should not give way to impatience, as there is no knowing whether such things are good or evil; and nothing is gained by impatience; also, because no human thing is of serious importance, and grief stands in the way of that which at the moment is most required.

What is most required? he asked.

That we should take counsel about what has happened, and when the dice have been thrown order our affairs in the way which reason deems best; not, like children who have had a fall, keeping hold of the part struck and wasting time in setting up a howl, but always accustoming the soul forthwith to apply a remedy, raising up that which is sickly and fallen, banishing the cry of sorrow by the healing art.

Yes, he said, that is the true way of meeting the attacks of fortune.

Yes, I said; and the higher principle is ready to follow this suggestion of reason?

Clearly.

And the other principle, which inclines us to recollection of our troubles and to lamentation, and can never have enough of them, we may call irrational, useless, and cowardly?

Indeed, we may.

And does not the latter – I mean the rebellious principle – furnish a great variety of materials for imitation? Whereas the wise and calm temperament, being always nearly equable, is not easy to imitate or to appreciate when imitated, especially at a public festival when a promiscuous crowd is assembled in a theatre. For the feeling represented is one to which they are strangers.

Certainly.

Then the imitative poet who aims at being popular is not by nature made, nor is his art intended, to please or to affect the rational principle in the soul; but he will prefer the passionate and fitful temper, which is easily imitated?

Clearly.

And now we may fairly take him and place him by the side of the painter, for he is like him in two ways: first, inasmuch as his creations have an inferior degree of truth – in this, I say, he is like him; and he is also like him in being concerned with an inferior part of the soul; and therefore we shall be right in refusing to admit him into a well-ordered State, because he awakens and nourishes and strengthens the feelings and impairs the reason. As in a city when the evil are permitted to have authority and the good are put out of the way, so in the soul of man, as we maintain, the imitative poet implants an evil constitution, for he indulges the irrational nature which has no discernment of greater and less, but thinks the same thing at one time great and at another small – he is a manufacturer of images and is very far removed from the truth.

Exactly.

But we have not yet brought forward the heaviest count in our accusation: – the power which poetry has of harming even the good (and there are very few who are not harmed), is surely an awful thing?

Yes, certainly, if the effect is what you say.

Hear and judge: The best of us, as I conceive, when we listen to a passage of Homer, or one of the tragedians, in which he represents some pitiful hero who is drawling out his sorrows in a long oration, or weeping, and smiting his breast – the best of us, you know, delight in giving way to sympathy, and are in raptures at the excellence of the poet who stirs our feelings most.

Yes, of course I know.

But when any sorrow of our own happens to us, then you may observe that we pride ourselves on the opposite quality – we would fain be quiet and patient; this is the manly part, and the other which delighted us in the recitation is now deemed to be the part of a woman.

Very true, he said.

Now can we be right in praising and admiring another who is doing that which any one of us would abominate and be ashamed of in his own person?

No, he said, that is certainly not reasonable.

Nay, I said, quite reasonable from one point of view.

What point of view?

If you consider, I said, that when in misfortune we feel a natural hunger and desire to relieve our sorrow by weeping and lamentation, and that this feeling which is kept under control in our own calamities is satisfied and delighted by the poets; – the better nature in each of us, not having been sufficiently trained by reason or habit, allows the sympathetic element to break loose because the sorrow is another's; and the spectator fancies that there can be no disgrace to himself in praising and pitying any one who comes telling him what a good man he is, and making a fuss about his troubles; he thinks that the pleasure is a gain, and why should he be supercilious and lose this and the poem too? Few persons ever reflect, as I should imagine, that from the evil of other men something of evil is communicated to themselves. And so the feeling of sorrow which has gathered strength at the sight of the misfortunes of others is with difficulty repressed in our own.

How very true!

And does not the same hold also of the ridiculous? There are jests which you would be ashamed to make yourself, and yet on the comic stage, or indeed in private, when you hear them, you are greatly amused by them, and are not at all disgusted at their unseemliness; – the case of pity is repeated; – there is a principle in human nature which is disposed to raise a laugh, and this which you once restrained by reason, because you were afraid of being thought a buffoon, is now let out again; and having stimulated the risible faculty at the theatre, you are betrayed unconsciously to yourself into playing the comic poet at home.

Quite true, he said.

And the same may be said of lust and anger and all the other affections, of desire and pain and pleasure, which are held to be inseparable from every action – in all of them poetry feeds and waters the passions instead of drying them up; she lets them rule, although they ought to be controlled, if mankind are ever to increase in happiness and virtue.

I cannot deny it.

Therefore, Glaucon, I said, whenever you meet with any of the eulogists of Homer declaring that he has been the educator of Hellas, and that he is profitable for education and for the ordering of human things, and that you should take him up again and again and get to know him and regulate your whole life according to him, we may love and honour those who say these things – they are excellent people, as far as their lights extend; and we are ready to acknowledge that Homer is the greatest of poets and first of tragedy writers; but we must remain firm in our conviction that hymns to the gods and praises of famous men are the only poetry which ought to be admitted into our State. For if you go beyond this and allow the honeyed muse to enter, either in epic or lyric verse, not law and the reason of mankind, which by common consent have ever been deemed best, but pleasure and pain will be the rulers in our State.

That is most true, he said.

And now since we have reverted to the subject of poetry, let this our defence serve to show the reasonableness of our former judgment in sending away out of our State an art having the tendencies which we have described; for reason constrained us. But that she may not impute to us any harshness or want of politeness, let us tell her that there is an ancient quarrel between philosophy and poetry; of which there are many proofs, such as the saying of 'the yelping hound howling at her lord,' or of one 'mighty in the vain talk of fools,' and 'the mob of sages circumventing Zeus,' and the 'subtle thinkers who are beggars after all'; and there are innumerable other signs of ancient enmity between them. Notwithstanding this, let us assure our sweet friend and the sister arts of imitation, that if she will only prove her title to exist in a well-ordered State we shall be delighted to receive her – we are very conscious of her charms; but we may not on that account betray the truth. I dare say, Glaucon, that you are as much charmed by her as I am, especially when she appears in Homer?

Yes, indeed, I am greatly charmed.

Shall I propose, then, that she be allowed to return from exile, but upon this condition only – that she make a defence of herself in lyrical or some other metre?

Certainly.

And we may further grant to those of her defenders who are lovers of poetry and yet not poets the permission to speak in prose on her behalf: let them show not only that she is pleasant but also useful to States and to human life, and we will listen in a kindly spirit; for if this can be proved we shall surely be the gainers – I mean, if there is a use in poetry as well as a delight?

Certainly, he said, we shall be the gainers.

If her defence fails, then, my dear friend, like other persons who are enamoured of something, but put a restraint upon themselves when they think their desires are opposed to their interests, so too must we after the manner of lovers give her up, though not without a struggle. We too are inspired by that love of poetry which the education of noble States has implanted in us, and therefore we would have her appear at her best and truest; but so long as she is unable to make good her defence, this argument of ours shall be a charm to us, which we will repeat to ourselves while we listen to her strains; that we may not fall away into the childish love of her which captivates the many. At all events we are well aware that poetry being such as we have described is not to be regarded seriously as attaining to the truth; and he who listens to her, fearing for the safety of the city which is within him, should be on his guard against her seductions and make our words his law.

Yes, he said, I quite agree with you.

Yes, I said, my dear Glaucon, for great is the issue at stake, greater than appears, whether a man is to be good or bad. And what will any one be profited if under the influence of honour or money or power, aye, or under the excitement of poetry, he neglect justice and virtue?

Yes, he said; I have been convinced by the argument, as I believe that any one else would have been.

And yet no mention has been made of the greatest prizes and rewards which await virtue.

What, are there any greater still? If there are, they must be of an inconceivable greatness.

Why, I said, what was ever great in a short time? The whole period of three score years and ten is surely but a little thing in comparison with eternity?

Say rather 'nothing,' he replied.

And should an immortal being seriously think of this little space rather than of the whole?

Of the whole, certainly. But why do you ask?

Are you not aware, I said, that the soul of man is immortal and imperishable?

He looked at me in astonishment, and said: No, by heaven: And are you really prepared to maintain this?

Yes, I said, I ought to be, and you too – there is no difficulty in proving it.

I see a great difficulty; but I should like to hear you state this argument of which you make so light.

Listen then.

I am attending.

There is a thing which you call good and another which you call evil?

Yes, he replied.

Would you agree with me in thinking that the corrupting and destroying element is the evil, and the saving and improving element the good?

Yes.

And you admit that every thing has a good and also an evil; as ophthalmia is the evil of the eyes and disease of the whole body; as mildew is of corn, and rot of timber, or rust of copper and iron: in everything, or in almost everything, there is an inherent evil and disease?

Yes, he said.

And anything which is infected by any of these evils is made evil, and at last wholly dissolves and dies?

True.

The vice and evil which is inherent in each is the destruction of each; and if this does not destroy them there is nothing else that will; for good certainly will not destroy them, nor again, that which is neither good nor evil.

Certainly not.

If, then, we find any nature which having this inherent corruption cannot be dissolved or destroyed, we may be certain that of such a nature there is no destruction?

That may be assumed.

Well, I said, and is there no evil which corrupts the soul?

Yes, he said, there are all the evils which we were just now passing in review: unrighteousness, intemperance, cowardice, ignorance.

But does any of these dissolve or destroy her? – and here do not let us fall into the error of supposing that the unjust and foolish man, when he is detected, perishes through his own injustice, which is an evil of the soul. Take the analogy of the body: The evil of the body is a disease which wastes and reduces and annihilates the body; and all the things of which we were just now speaking come to annihilation through their own corruption attaching to them and inhering in them and so destroying them. Is not this true?

Yes.

Consider the soul in like manner. Does the injustice or other evil which exists in the soul waste and consume her? Do they by attaching to the soul and inhering in her at last bring her to death, and so separate her from the body?

Certainly not.

And yet, I said, it is unreasonable to suppose that anything can perish from without through affection of external evil which could not be destroyed from within by a corruption of its own?

It is, he replied.

Consider, I said, Glaucon, that even the badness of food, whether staleness, decomposition, or any other bad quality, when confined to the actual food, is not supposed to destroy the body; although, if the badness of food communicates corruption to the body, then we should say that the body has been destroyed by a corruption of itself, which is disease, brought on by this; but that the body, being one thing, can be destroyed by the badness of food, which is another, and which does not engender any natural infection – this we shall absolutely deny?

Very true.

And, on the same principle, unless some bodily evil can produce an evil of the soul, we must not suppose that the soul, which is one thing, can be dissolved by any merely external evil which belongs to another?

Yes, he said, there is reason in that.

Either, then, let us refute this conclusion, or, while it remains unrefuted, let us never say that fever, or any other disease, or the knife put to the throat, or even the cutting up of the whole body into the minutest pieces, can destroy the soul, until she herself is proved to become more unholy or unrighteous in consequence of these things being done to the body; but that the soul, or anything else if not destroyed by an internal evil, can be destroyed by an external one, is not to be affirmed by any man.

And surely, he replied, no one will ever prove that the souls of men become more unjust in consequence of death.

But if some one who would rather not admit the immortality of the soul boldly denies this, and says that the dying do really become more evil and unrighteous, then, if the speaker is right, I suppose that injustice, like disease, must be assumed to be fatal to the unjust, and that those who take this disorder die by the natural inherent power of destruction which evil has, and which kills them sooner or later, but in quite another way from that in which, at present, the wicked receive death at the hands of others as the penalty of their deeds?

Nay, he said, in that case injustice, if fatal to the unjust, will not be so very terrible to him, for he will be delivered from evil. But I rather suspect the opposite to be the truth, and that injustice which, if it have the power, will murder others, keeps the murderer alive – aye, and well awake too; so far removed is her dwelling-place from being a house of death.

True, I said; if the inherent natural vice or evil of the soul is unable to kill or destroy her, hardly will that which is appointed to be the destruction of some other body, destroy a soul or anything else except that of which it was appointed to be the destruction.

Yes, that can hardly be.

But the soul which cannot be destroyed by an evil, whether inherent or external, must exist for ever, and if existing for ever, must be immortal?

Certainly.

That is the conclusion, I said; and, if a true conclusion, then the souls must always be the same, for if none be destroyed they will not diminish in number. Neither will they increase, for the increase of the immortal natures must come from something mortal, and all things would thus end in immortality.

Very true.

But this we cannot believe – reason will not allow us – any more than we can believe the soul, in her truest nature, to be full of variety and difference and dissimilarity.

What do you mean? he said.

The soul, I said, being, as is now proven, immortal, must be the fairest of compositions and cannot be compounded of many elements?

Certainly not.

Her immortality is demonstrated by the previous argument, and there are many other proofs; but to see her as she really is, not as we now behold her, marred by communion with the body and other miseries, you must contemplate her with the eye of reason, in her original purity; and then her beauty will be revealed, and justice and injustice and all the things which we have described will be manifested more clearly. Thus far, we have spoken the truth concerning her as she appears at present, but we must remember also that we have seen her only in a condition which may be compared to that of the sea-god Glaucus, whose original image can hardly be discerned because his natural members are broken off and crushed and damaged by the waves in all sorts of ways, and incrustations have grown over them of seaweed and shells and stones, so that he is more like some monster than he is to his own natural form. And the soul which we behold is in a similar condition, disfigured by ten thousand ills. But not there, Glaucon, not there must we look.

Where then?

At her love of wisdom. Let us see whom she affects, and what society and converse she seeks in virtue of her near kindred with the immortal and eternal and divine; also how different she would become if wholly following this superior principle, and borne by a divine impulse out of the ocean in which she now is, and disengaged from the stones and shells and things of earth and rock which in wild variety spring up around her because she feeds upon earth, and is overgrown by the good things of this life as they are termed: then you would see her as she is, and know whether she have one shape only or many, or what her nature is. Of her affections and of the forms which she takes in this present life I think that we have now said enough.

True, he replied.

And thus, I said, we have fulfilled the conditions of the argument; we have not introduced the rewards and glories of justice, which, as you were saying, are to be found in Homer and Hesiod; but justice in her own nature has been shown to be best for the soul in her own nature. Let a man do what is just, whether he have the ring of Gyges or not, and even if in addition to the ring of Gyges he put on the helmet of Hades.

Very true.

And now, Glaucon, there will be no harm in further enumerating how many and how great are the rewards which justice and the other virtues procure to the soul from gods and men, both in life and after death.

Certainly not, he said.

Will you repay me, then, what you borrowed in the argument?

What did I borrow?

The assumption that the just man should appear unjust and the unjust just: for you were of opinion that even if the true state of the case could not possibly escape the eyes of gods and men, still this admission ought to be made for the sake of the argument, in order that pure justice might be weighed against pure injustice. Do you remember?

I should be much to blame if I had forgotten.

Then, as the cause is decided, I demand on behalf of justice that the estimation in which she is held by gods and men and which we acknowledge to be her due should now be restored to her by us; since she has been shown to confer reality, and not to deceive those who truly possess her, let what has been taken from her be given back, that so she may win that palm of appearance which is hers also, and which she gives to her own.

The demand, he said, is just.

In the first place, I said – and this is the first thing which you will have to give back – the nature both of the just and unjust is truly known to the gods.

Granted.

And if they are both known to them, one must be the friend and the other the enemy of the gods, as we admitted from the beginning?

True.

And the friend of the gods may be supposed to receive from them all things at their best, excepting only such evil as is the necessary consequence of former sins?

Certainly.

Then this must be our notion of the just man, that even when he is in poverty or sickness, or any other seeming misfortune, all things will in the end work together for good to him in life and death: for the gods have a care of any one whose desire is to become just and to be like God, as far as man can attain the divine likeness, by the pursuit of virtue?

Yes, he said; if he is like God he will surely not be neglected by him.

And of the unjust may not the opposite be supposed?

Certainly.

Such, then, are the palms of victory which the gods give the just?

That is my conviction.

And what do they receive of men? Look at things as they really are, and you will see that the clever unjust are in the case of runners, who run well from the starting-place to the goal but not back again from the goal: they go off at a great pace, but in the end only look foolish, slinking away with their ears draggling on their shoulders, and without a crown; but the true runner comes to the finish and receives the prize and is crowned. And this is the way with the just; he who endures to the end of every action and occasion of his entire life has a good report and carries off the prize which men have to bestow.

True.

And now you must allow me to repeat of the just the blessings which you were attributing to the fortunate unjust. I shall say of them, what you were saying of the others, that as they grow older, they become rulers in their own city if they care to be; they marry whom they like and give in marriage to whom they will; all that you said of the others I now say of these. And, on the other hand, of the unjust I say that the greater number, even though they escape in their youth, are found out at last and look foolish at the end of their course, and when they come to be old and miserable are flouted alike by stranger and citizen; they are beaten and then come those things unfit for ears polite, as you truly term them; they will be racked and have their eyes burned out, as you were saying. And you may suppose that I have repeated the remainder of your tale of horrors. But will you let me assume, without reciting them, that these things are true?

Certainly, he said, what you say is true.

These, then, are the prizes and rewards and gifts which are bestowed upon the just by gods and men in this present life, in addition to the other good things which justice of herself provides.

Yes, he said; and they are fair and lasting.

And yet, I said, all these are as nothing either in number or greatness in comparison with those other recompenses which await both just and unjust after death. And you ought to hear them, and then both just and unjust will have received from us a full payment of the debt which the argument owes to them.

Speak, he said; there are few things which I would more gladly hear.

Well, I said, I will tell you a tale; not one of the tales which Odysseus tells to the hero Alcinous, yet this too is a tale of a hero, Er the son of Armenius, a Pamphylian by birth. He was slain in battle, and ten days afterwards, when the bodies of the dead were taken up already in a state of corruption, his body was found unaffected by decay, and carried away home to be buried. And on the twelfth day, as he was lying on the funeral pile, he returned to life and told them what he had seen in the other world. He said that when his soul left the body he went on a journey with a great company, and that they came to a mysterious place at which there were two openings in the earth; they were near together, and over against them were two other openings in the heaven above. In the intermediate space there were judges seated, who commanded the just, after they had given judgment on them and had bound their sentences in front of them, to ascend by the heavenly way on the right hand; and in like manner the unjust were bidden by them to descend by the lower way on the left hand; these also bore the symbols of their deeds, but fastened on their backs. He drew near, and they told him that he was to be the messenger who would carry the report of the other world to men, and they bade him hear and see all that was to be heard and seen in that place. Then he beheld and saw on one side the souls departing at either opening of heaven and earth when sentence had been given on them; and at the two other openings other souls, some ascending out of the earth dusty and worn with travel, some descending out of heaven clean and bright. And arriving ever and anon they seemed to have come from a long journey, and they went forth with gladness into the meadow, where they encamped as at a festival; and those who knew one another embraced and conversed, the souls which came from earth curiously enquiring about the things above, and the souls which came from heaven about the things beneath. And they told one another of what had happened by the way, those from below weeping and sorrowing at the remembrance of the things which they had endured and seen in their journey beneath the earth (now the journey lasted a thousand years), while those from above were describing heavenly delights and visions of inconceivable beauty. The story, Glaucon, would take too long to tell; but the sum was this: – He said that for every wrong which they had done to any one they suffered tenfold; or once in a hundred years – such being reckoned to be the length of man's life, and the penalty being thus paid ten times in a thousand years. If, for example, there were any who had been the cause of many deaths, or had betrayed or enslaved cities or armies, or been guilty of any other evil behaviour, for each and all of their offences they received punishment ten times over, and the rewards of beneficence and justice and holiness were in the same proportion. I need hardly repeat what he said concerning young children dying almost as soon as they were born. Of piety and impiety to gods and parents, and of murderers, there were retributions other and greater far which he described. He mentioned that he was present when one of the spirits asked another, 'Where is Ardiaeus the Great?' (Now this Ardiaeus lived a thousand years before the time of Er: he had been the tyrant of some city of Pamphylia, and had murdered his aged father and his elder brother, and was said to have committed many other abominable crimes.) The answer of the other spirit was: 'He comes not hither and will never come. And this,' said he, 'was one of the dreadful sights which we ourselves witnessed. We were at the mouth of the cavern, and, having completed all our experiences, were about to reascend, when of a sudden Ardiaeus appeared and several others, most of whom were tyrants; and there were also besides the tyrants private individuals who had been great criminals: they were just, as they fancied, about to return into the upper world, but the mouth, instead of admitting them, gave a roar, whenever any of these incurable sinners or some one who had not been sufficiently punished tried to ascend; and then wild men of fiery aspect, who were standing by and heard the sound, seized and carried them off; and Ardiaeus and others they bound head and foot and hand, and threw them down and flayed them with scourges, and dragged them along the road at the side, carding them on thorns like wool, and declaring to the passers-by what were their crimes, and that they were being taken away to be cast into hell.' And of all the many terrors which they had endured, he said that there was none like the terror which each of them felt at that moment, lest they should hear the voice; and when there was silence, one by one they ascended with exceeding joy. These, said Er, were the penalties and retributions, and there were blessings as great.

Now when the spirits which were in the meadow had tarried seven days, on the eighth they were obliged to proceed on their journey, and, on the fourth day after, he said that they came to a place where they could see from above a line of light, straight as a column, extending right through the whole heaven and through the earth, in colour resembling the rainbow, only brighter and purer; another day's journey brought them to the place, and there, in the midst of the light, they saw the ends of the chains of heaven let down from above: for this light is the belt of heaven, and holds together the circle of the universe, like the under-girders of a trireme. From these ends is extended the spindle of Necessity, on which all the revolutions turn. The shaft and hook of this spindle are made of steel, and the whorl is made partly of steel and also partly of other materials. Now the whorl is in form like the whorl used on earth; and the description of it implied that there is one large hollow whorl which is quite scooped out, and into this is fitted another lesser one, and another, and another, and four others, making eight in all, like vessels which fit into one another; the whorls show their edges on the upper side, and on their lower side all together form one continuous whorl. This is pierced by the spindle, which is driven home through the centre of the eighth. The first and outermost whorl has the rim broadest, and the seven inner whorls are narrower, in the following proportions – the sixth is next to the first in size, the fourth next to the sixth; then comes the eighth; the seventh is fifth, the fifth is sixth, the third is seventh, last and eighth comes the second. The largest (or fixed stars) is spangled, and the seventh (or sun) is brightest; the eighth (or moon) coloured by the reflected light of the seventh; the second and fifth (Saturn and Mercury) are in colour like one another, and yellower than the preceding; the third (Venus) has the whitest light; the fourth (Mars) is reddish; the sixth (Jupiter) is in whiteness second. Now the whole spindle has the same motion; but, as the whole revolves in one direction, the seven inner circles move slowly in the other, and of these the swiftest is the eighth; next in swiftness are the seventh, sixth, and fifth, which move together; third in swiftness appeared to move according to the law of this reversed motion the fourth; the third appeared fourth and the second fifth.

The spindle turns on the knees of Necessity; and on the upper surface of each circle is a siren, who goes round with them, hymning a single tone or note. The eight together form one harmony; and round about, at equal intervals, there is another band, three in number, each sitting upon her throne: these are the Fates, daughters of Necessity, who are clothed in white robes and have chaplets upon their heads, Lachesis and Clotho and Atropos, who accompany with their voices the harmony of the sirens – Lachesis singing of the past, Clotho of the present, Atropos of the future; Clotho from time to time assisting with a touch of her right hand the revolution of the outer circle of the whorl or spindle, and Atropos with her left hand touching and guiding the inner ones, and Lachesis laying hold of either in turn, first with one hand and then with the other.

When Er and the spirits arrived, their duty was to go at once to Lachesis; but first of all there came a prophet who arranged them in order; then he took from the knees of Lachesis lots and samples of lives, and having mounted a high pulpit, spoke as follows: 'Hear the word of Lachesis, the daughter of Necessity. Mortal souls, behold a new cycle of life and mortality. Your genius will not be allotted to you, but you will choose your genius; and let him who draws the first lot have the first choice, and the life which he chooses shall be his destiny. Virtue is free, and as a man honours or dishonours her he will have more or less of her; the responsibility is with the chooser – God is justified.' When the Interpreter had thus spoken he scattered lots indifferently among them all, and each of them took up the lot which fell near him, all but Er himself (he was not allowed), and each as he took his lot perceived the number which he had obtained. Then the Interpreter placed on the ground before them the samples of lives; and there were many more lives than the souls present, and they were of all sorts. There were lives of every animal and of man in every condition. And there were tyrannies among them, some lasting out the tyrant's life, others which broke off in the middle and came to an end in poverty and exile and beggary; and there were lives of famous men, some who were famous for their form and beauty as well as for their strength and success in games, or, again, for their birth and the qualities of their ancestors; and some who were the reverse of famous for the opposite qualities. And of women likewise; there was not, however, any definite character in them, because the soul, when choosing a new life, must of necessity become different. But there was every other quality, and the all mingled with one another, and also with elements of wealth and poverty, and disease and health; and there were mean states also. And here, my dear Glaucon, is the supreme peril of our human state; and therefore the utmost care should be taken.

Let each one of us leave every other kind of knowledge and seek and follow one thing only, if peradventure he may be able to learn and may find some one who will make him able to learn and discern between good and evil, and so to choose always and everywhere the better life as he has opportunity. He should consider the bearing of all these things which have been mentioned severally and collectively upon virtue; he should know what the effect of beauty is when combined with poverty or wealth in a particular soul, and what are the good and evil consequences of noble and humble birth, of private and public station, of strength and weakness, of cleverness and dullness, and of all the natural and acquired gifts of the soul, and the operation of them when conjoined; he will then look at the nature of the soul, and from the consideration of all these qualities he will be able to determine which is the better and which is the worse; and so he will choose, giving the name of evil to the life which will make his soul more unjust, and good to the life which will make his soul more just; all else he will disregard. For we have seen and know that this is the best choice both in life and after death. A man must take with him into the world below an adamantine faith in truth and right, that there too he may be undazzled by the desire of wealth or the other allurements of evil, lest, coming upon tyrannies and similar villainies, he do irremediable wrongs to others and suffer yet worse himself; but let him know how to choose the mean and avoid the extremes on either side, as far as possible, not only in this life but in all that which is to come. For this is the way of happiness.

And according to the report of the messenger from the other world this was what the prophet said at the time: 'Even for the last comer, if he chooses wisely and will live diligently, there is appointed a happy and not undesirable existence. Let not him who chooses first be careless, and let not the last despair.' And when he had spoken, he who had the first choice came forward and in a moment chose the greatest tyranny; his mind having been darkened by folly and sensuality, he had not thought out the whole matter before he chose, and did not at first sight perceive that he was fated, among other evils, to devour his own children. But when he had time to reflect, and saw what was in the lot, he began to beat his breast and lament over his choice, forgetting the proclamation of the prophet; for, instead of throwing the blame of his misfortune on himself, he accused chance and the gods, and everything rather than himself. Now he was one of those who came from heaven, and in a former life had dwelt in a well-ordered State, but his virtue was a matter of habit only, and he had no philosophy. And it was true of others who were similarly overtaken, that the greater number of them came from heaven and therefore they had never been schooled by trial, whereas the pilgrims who came from earth having themselves suffered and seen others suffer, were not in a hurry to choose. And owing to this inexperience of theirs, and also because the lot was a chance, many of the souls exchanged a good destiny for an evil or an evil for a good. For if a man had always on his arrival in this world dedicated himself from the first to sound philosophy, and had been moderately fortunate in the number of the lot, he might, as the messenger reported, be happy here, and also his journey to another life and return to this, instead of being rough and underground, would be smooth and heavenly. Most curious, he said, was the spectacle – sad and laughable and strange; for the choice of the souls was in most cases based on their experience of a previous life. There he saw the soul which had once been Orpheus choosing the life of a swan out of enmity to the race of women, hating to be born of a woman because they had been his murderers; he beheld also the soul of Thamyras choosing the life of a nightingale; birds, on the other hand, like the swan and other musicians, wanting to be men. The soul which obtained the twentieth lot chose the life of a lion, and this was the soul of Ajax the son of Telamon, who would not be a man, remembering the injustice which was done him in the judgment about the arms. The next was Agamemnon, who took the life of an eagle, because, like Ajax, he hated human nature by reason of his sufferings. About the middle came the lot of Atalanta; she, seeing the great fame of an athlete, was unable to resist the temptation: and after her there followed the soul of Epeus the son of Panopeus passing into the nature of a woman cunning in the arts; and far away among the last who chose, the soul of the jester Thersites was putting on the form of a monkey. There came also the soul of Odysseus having yet to make a choice, and his lot happened to be the last of them all. Now the recollection of former toils had disenchanted him of ambition, and he went about for a considerable time in search of the life of a private man who had no cares; he had some difficulty in finding this, which was lying about and had been neglected by everybody else; and when he saw it, he said that he would have done the same had his lot been first instead of last, and that he was delighted to have it. And not only did men pass into animals, but I must also mention that there were animals tame and wild who changed into one another and into corresponding human natures – the good into the gentle and the evil into the savage, in all sorts of combinations.

 All the souls had now chosen their lives, and they went in the order of their choice to Lachesis, who sent with them the genius whom they had severally chosen, to be the guardian of their lives and the fulfiller of the choice: this genius led the souls first to Clotho, and drew them within the revolution of the spindle impelled by her hand, thus ratifying the destiny of each; and then, when they were fastened to this, carried them to Atropos, who spun the threads and made them irreversible, whence without turning round they passed beneath the throne of Necessity; and when they had all passed, they marched on in a scorching heat to the plain of Forgetfulness, which was a barren waste destitute of trees and verdure; and then towards evening they encamped by the river of Unmindfulness, whose water no vessel can hold; of this they were all obliged to drink a certain quantity, and those who were not saved by wisdom drank more than was necessary; and each one as he drank forgot all things. Now after they had gone to rest, about the middle of the night there was a thunderstorm and earthquake, and then in an instant they were driven upwards in all manner of ways to their birth, like stars shooting. He himself was hindered from drinking the water. But in what manner or by what means he returned to the body he could not say; only, in the morning, awaking suddenly, he found himself lying on the pyre.

And thus, Glaucon, the tale has been saved and has not perished, and will save us if we are obedient to the word spoken; and we shall pass safely over the river of Forgetfulness and our soul will not be defiled. Wherefore my counsel is, that we hold fast ever to the heavenly way and follow after justice and virtue always, considering that the soul is immortal and able to endure every sort of good and every sort of evil. Thus shall we live dear to one another and to the gods, both while remaining here and when, like conquerors in the games who go round to gather gifts, we receive our reward. And it shall be well with us both in this life and in the pilgrimage of a thousand years which we have been describing.